MARCH 4
1970

THE HONEYCOMB

by Adela Rogers St. Johns

THE HONEYCOMB

TELL NO MAN

FINAL VERDICT

Adela Rogers St. Johns

—◆—

THE HONEYCOMB

1969

DOUBLEDAY & COMPANY, INC., GARDEN CITY, NEW YORK

Grateful acknowledgment is made to the following for permission to reprint material copyrighted or controlled by them:

Chappell & Co., Inc., New York, and Chappell & Co., Ltd., London, for extracts from lyrics of *Camelot*, Copyright © 1960 by Alan J. Lerner and Frederick Lowe; and from lyrics of "Someday I'll Find You," by Noel Coward, Copyright © 1930 by Chappell & Co., Ltd., renewed.

Coward-McCann, Inc., and The Estate of Alice Duer Miller, for lines from "The White Cliffs of Dover" from *The White Cliffs*, by Alice Duer Miller. Copyright 1940 by Alice Duer Miller, renewed 1967 by Denning Miller.

Dodd, Mead & Company, for extracts from "The Old Vicarage, Grantchester" and "The Soldier," by Rupert Brooke, from *The Collected Poems of Rupert Brooke*.

Doubleday & Company, Inc., for poem "For the Birthday of a Middle-aged Child" by Aline Kilmer, from the book *Selected Poems* by Aline Kilmer, 1929.

Doubleday & Company, Inc., and Collins-Knowlton-Wing, Inc., for excerpt from *Advise and Consent* by Allen Drury. Copyright © 1959 by Allen Drury.

Norma Millay Ellis, for poem "Grown-up," by Edna St. Vincent Millay. From *Collected Poems*, by Edna St. Vincent Millay (Harper & Row). Copyright 1922, 1950 by Edna St. Vincent Millay.

Leo Feist, Inc., and Anne-Rachel Music Corporation, for lyrics from "Minnie the Mermaid." Words and music by Bud DeSylva. Copyright © 1923 by Leo Feist, Inc., New York, N.Y. Copyright renewed 1951. Published by Anne-Rachel Music Corporation, New York, N.Y., for the U.S. only. All rights for rest of world controlled by Leo Feist, Inc., International Copyright Reserved. All rights secured including the rights of public performance for profit.

Harcourt, Brace & World, Inc., for excerpts from *North to the Orient*, by Anne Morrow Lindbergh.

George G. Harrap & Company Limited, for excerpt from *These Our Children*, by Anthony Richardson.

New Directions Publishing Corporation, and Faber and Faber, Ltd., for excerpts from "Ballad of the Goodly Fere," by Ezra Pound, from *Personae*. Copyright 1926 by Ezra Pound.

The New Yorker, for excerpt from "The Metamorphosis of Philip Musica," by Robert Shaplen, and caption for a drawing by Lorenz.

Pantheon Books, a division of Random House, Inc., for excerpts from *Gift from the Sea*, by Anne Morrow Lindbergh.

Philip Morris, for television commercial lyrics. Copyright © by Philip Morris.

Photoplay magazine, for excerpt from "Our Adela," by Herbert Riley Howe.

Rand McNally & Company, for excerpt from *A Special Kind of Magic*, by Roy Newquist. Copyright 1967 by Rand McNally & Company.

PHOTO CREDITS

Cosmopolitan, 10
Twentieth Century-Fox Film Corporation, 14
Paramount Pictures, 17
M. Jaffe, 28
Engstead, 30

All photographs not credited are from the author's personal collection.

To Bill

ACKNOWLEDGMENTS

You have to have a stadium in which to play football. Likewise, some kind of cosmos must be created in which to write a book. Any book. People who want to write books, and who doesn't? it seems, say, "If I had *time.*" You will need *uninterrupted* time sometimes, also protection, silence, a place to put things, a room without windows, food, loving kindness, as little outside responsibility as possible, and much much understanding of the tribulations of *writing.* Behind any book that actually gets written are those who create this cosmos, whether in attic or library, office or suburban mansion, mountain fastness or beach sand. Without this even the best writers die young like Poe and Keats and Emily Brontë. And the worse write worser.

Therefore to those who over three years gave me a chance to write this book called *The Honeycomb,* I want to express inexpressible gratitude and the hope that I did my best for them.

My daughter *Elaine St. Johns,* working steadily, honestly, fearlessly and joyously, editing, cutting, judging, reminding, checking, fighting and cheering me on. Without this team effort it would have taken me another three years if at all. My son *Dick St. Johns,* who put aside his own work long enough to pay for it all. Without his financial care we would have had to spend the last year in an attic, and I am too old for that now. Wisely, diplomatically, he handled three fairly temperamental women—mother, sister, and wife Anna—who accepted this extra time-consumer with wit and a reassuring conviction that my book was important. Thus with inspired good will, good humor, and good sense he managed to keep roofs over our heads, clothes on our backs, bones in our cupboards, paid bills, and contented income tax collectors. (Three years is a long time.) *Margaret Cousins,* friend and editor (doesn't always follow), known to her authors as Maggie. On dark days when I had none left she supplied me with her confidence and as Red Schoendienst says about pitchers, What more can you give them? *Eddie Hubbell,* head of Metro-Goldwyn-Mayer's photo lab, whose sheer *genius* reproduced from old snapshots, newspaper photos, and even printed front pages the pictures used in this book. Without *him,* I'd have missed the faces of my grandfather and Mother Meyer, and the illustrations of me as an Unemployed Woman. *Dr. Robert Loveland,* on whom the St. Johns tribe relies, and who when I broke my best typewriting finger set it so that I never missed a day's typing at a crucial deadline moment, and *Dr. Fletcher Harding,* who added his prayers in the above and many other crises. My granddaughters: *Kris,* who drove, shopped, and accompanied me to luncheons while teaching at California Lutheran; *Kathy* and *Tracey,* who told me what teen-agers know and don't know and what they want to know and don't want to know as well as bringing me sunshine to grow by. My grandsons Bill St. Johns, whose Little League Canoga Park *Angels,* with my great-grandsons Billy and Mark, gave me my only recreation every Saturday afternoon and always reminded me of his father's Great Neck Swamp *Angels;* George, known in this book as Koko, who, as one of Bob Finch's team, did my political work for me. *Adele Schwartz,* her typing was flawless; more important, she convinced me she could hardly *wait* for my next batch of dirty copy; and *Charlotte Worth,* who pinch-hit when we needed her. *Dorothy Hertz,* who spent a lot of time for me in the Library of Congress, for I had never kept a single clipping in my newspaper days. None of us did. Dorothy came up with it all which I appreciated, for the Library of Congress is darkest Africa to me.

The *Beverly Wilshire Hotel.* My old friend and fellow Californian Hernando Courtright arranged that I should have care and, in spite of Warren Beatty as a next door neighbor, peace and quiet. Telephone operators who were like the private secretaries I never have; room waiters and room service which fed me even when I forgot to order; elevator operators who reminded me to take *walks;* Eloisa, Ruth, and Virginia, surrounding me with order without *ever* picking up a piece of paper from the floor.

To all newspapermen, past present and future everywhere. The Press— first of all freedoms on which all others depend. Especially Lee Ettelson, of San Francisco, Stu List of Chicago, Ed Murray of Phoenix, Herb Krauch and Agness Underwood of Los Angeles, Mary K. Murray, now public relations director of the Beverly Wilshire, and an altime Great, Irvin S. Cobb, who once in passing said, "A good story teller is a person who has a good memory and hopes no one else has."

BOOK ONE

BOOK ONE

CHAPTER 1

Once upon a time there was a girl who from eight to eighteen was lovingly called Nora by her father.

At eighteen, she got a *job* and became By Adela Rogers.

Then she got a *husband*. Not wishing to hurt his masculine pride, she became Adela Rogers St. Johns.

Later she had *children*.

And there I was, trying to drive three mules, which an old Irish proverb of my grandfather's declares no one can do. Ever.

At eighteen I must have been regarded as a woman, for I was one of the first woman reporters, maybe as an all-around, police beat, sports, sin, and society the first in the world.

I knew little enough about women, God wot. What I did know scared me out of my wits. I had been brought up exclusively by men in the offices of my father, Earl Rogers, leading criminal lawyer of *his* times and, judging by what I see around me today, of all time, and in the courtrooms where he tried his cases, from murder to the Queen of Chinatown. Though I had learned a little something about women by the time I stood up to debate the president of the *all-powerful* General Federation of Women's Clubs on the question *Is Modern Woman a Failure,* it nevertheless had to look like a rash young Quixote with a small lance rushing in where cherubim feared to tread. For here I am talking of Roaring Twenties and Fabulous Thirties when this experiment of the Modern Woman was still so new and all and we did not know whether we were to be *off* with the Old Woman before we were *on* with the New.

My dark ignorance about females and feminists was lighted by the wisdom of two women as far apart as the poles. My own mother had been a disaster to herself and me from first to last, poor soul. While I was so angry with God for a number of things I thought He had done unto me, I would not admit He had sent my Mrs. Valiant-for-Truth to fill that place, but I did know something good had arrived from somewhere. Many of us gave her the honorary title of Mother Meyer and she tried to explain to me that it wasn't the three mules I should worry and carry on about, but the emptiness so dangerous during a time of *growing pains.* The absence of good, she said, leaves a vacuum. If we were slothful, this could be filled by scum from the Slough of Despond and knickknacks from Vanity Fair.

What is present, Mother Meyer said, can be part of the uphill fight of our Progress. But there is a key to the Gate of the City, each must find it for herself, without it we can batter ourselves in pieces in our efforts to go through.

The other messenger who had carried warnings and knowledge to my youth was a good friend of my father's named Pearl Morton. She was the madame of a high-class sporting house in California, a woman of many virtues, though chastity was not among them. I learned about women from her as men saw them.

What *about* women? And what—good or bad—they always did to men?

What the hell is going on around here besides self-operating iceboxes and flying through the air and Carl Hubbell striking out Babe Ruth and Lou Gehrig and ole Double X Foxx in one inning? I said to myself along about that moment.

As my life has rocketed up and down and round and round all kinds of people keep asking me all kinds of questions. What philosophy comes from seeing and hearing and doing just about everything? *You* ought to write your autobiography, they say, you've covered—as you call it—everything from the Hauptmann Trial of the Century to the abdication of Edward VIII to the long-count Dempsey-Tunney fight in Chicago to the assassination of Huey Long. You've known everybody from Eleanor Roosevelt to Madame Chanel to Ma Barker to Jean Harlow. From Babe Ruth to Rudolph Valentino to Wyatt Earp to Bobby Kennedy. You've been from Hollywood to Baton Rouge to the Coliseum when they lit the Olympic torch to the behind-closed-doors testimony in the custody trial of little Gloria Vanderbilt. To these urgers I have continued to say that only those who have not contemplated the difficulty of telling the truth about anybody much less everybody and first and foremost yourself could suggest such a perilous undertaking. To do this at all, much less with integrity and that strange shibboleth called "good taste," happens about once a century.

For fifteen years, I have had a contract to tell this tale. Nobody but me will understand when I say I have finally decided to try to do it for the sake of the *men* of this country.

Now as I go back to the beginning of my three or four incarnations in *this* my life, the dangers of the last sixty years' Journey, since I was in my teens, loom above me like Mount Everest, for it is uphill all the way and it's longer because you slide *back* so often.

Any life that's been worth living has to be like that.

Yet now I am about to live it over again, it wasn't worth climbing in the first place unless I'm willing to tell about it.

The Manner of Her Setting Out.

This is the first page of Book II of *Pilgrim's Progress*—the Manner of Her Setting Out, the Woman Christiana and Her Children, Their Dangerous Journey and Safe Arrival in the Desired Country.

In my grandfather's church in Globe, Arizona, the bell in the tower was to sound the alarm for Indians as well as to call the pioneers to hear the Word of God and in those rugged days, he told me, if he had to have guidance in dealing with his neighbors, the ranchers, sheriffs, rangers, cowboys, gamblers, gunmen and dance hall girls, he turned to *Pilgrim's Progress* as the map made for him by a man who'd been that way before.

For the inspired Allegory of Christian, from the moment there is awakened in him the desire to reach the Delectable Mountain, faces every problem, every doubt of Everyman (and Everywoman), and, though in the distance he can see the Glory, he must climb the Hill of Difficulty, struggle through the Slough of Despond, find himself amid the glittering temptations of Vanity Fair, be imprisoned in Doubting Castle and tricked into the Cave of Despair. He must fall into the Ditch, and we have all said that ever since John Bunyan wrote of this pilgrimage in prison almost three hundred years ago.

When Christiana, his wife, with her children, starts out she must make the same Dangerous Journey and, while she forgets at the outset to take a Chart, such as the Bible, or to ask for a Conductor, she does accept Mercy as a traveling companion so that, though she meets the Monster and the Giant and My Lord Time-Server and Mrs. Two-Face, as all pilgrims do, she also finds Valiant-for-Truth and Great-Heart and Mr. Standfast to help her on her way.

Above all, for me, there was always Faithful, the best of them all, who walks beside the pilgrim and never forsakes him. Who never forsook me.

I knew *Pilgrim's Progress* by heart; my grandfather had taught it to me by the time I was seven.

Once on Virginia Graham's television show, *Girl Talk,* Virginia was speaking of our success in our chosen careers and Joan Crawford put her hand on mine and said, "You know what's remarkable about Adela and me? *We survived.*"

That Dangerous Journey.

It is violating all the rules, I know that, to tell you I have arrived in the Desired Country. With bleeding feet and shrinking soul and unforgettable suspense and loneliness and excitement I carried the Bundle of Doubt through hell and high water, through triumph and disaster. If Sir Edward Hillary hadn't reached the summit of Mount Everest we wouldn't care to read so much about his climb, nor dwell so long on his failures, slips, slides, dangers, death-defying hours going up *that* Hill of Difficulty.

He made it. He got to the top—we want to know how, we want to travel with him.

So many people nowadays write books about not getting anywhere at all. Solely about the defeats, despairs, collapses of character, and ultimate surrender.

I want to put the last sentence of this book first.

Look—*this is the Desired Country.*

I offer you this pilgrimage for your heart because I made it.

I have arrived safely at the Desired Country.

I must begin my story by leaping to a moment in my careening career that is by no means first chronologically, chronology is apt to be a bit of a bore anyhow, this leap will be no disadvantage to those who move in time and space with the ease of the young man on the flying trapeze. Up to the very day hour and minute when I faced Mrs. Alice Ames Winters I had been too busy swaggering around *living* to care much where I was going. *Hurry up please it's time—hurry up please—hurry up—*

On my feet facing this redoubtable opponent with the organic reluctance of a high school sophomore about to tackle Jimmy Brown, I began to think with my *stomach.* Many years before when I was only eight years old my father had taken me with him by night to the county jail to see a young man accused of shooting the Louisville Sport in a card game on Catalina Island. Leaning against Papa's knee, I had said, "He didn't do it, Papa. I know he couldn't do it." My stomach had told me that young Boyd *couldn't* shoot an unarmed man sitting down before him over a card game. Even the Associated Press learned in time to *respect* my stomach just as Papa had decided to do after it proved I was right about Boyd—who, as it happened, didn't do it.

I had never brought it into action regarding this major part of my journey. Now things came into some focus.

Enter Me.

Being dragged kicking and screaming onto the stage of a large theater jammed with Mrs. Alice Ames Winters, many clubwomen, *hostile,* four men judges of impressive rank, and three ladies ditto, *impartial.*

You can see for yourself! I mean the odds Las Vegas would have quoted.

2

Mr. Hearst—Mr. William Randolph Hearst—personally flung me into my famous debate with the national club leader Alice Ames Winters. Not

even Red Lewis could have bettered that name. Babbitt was *Babbitt,* and
Alice Ames Winters was *Alice Ames Winters*—the mere sight of it on this
paper forms ice cubes in my stomach. Yet as I have said it was on this
platform against probably the most formidable woman leader in America
that I crystallized my own three mules into an active personal influence—
or knew I was driving them.

The first I heard about a debate was a large black front page headline
in the Los Angeles *Evening Herald,* the biggest paper in the West.

IS MODERN WOMAN A FAILURE?
Herald Reporter St. Johns Challenges
Federation Club President to Debate.

Under this blockbuster type was a cockeyed, bareheaded newspaper
picture of me looking like one of Thurber's refugees from the flood, and
another of Mrs. Winters, who could well have been the original of Helen
Hokinson's *New Yorker* clubwomen. The two of us were a lovesome sight
betimes and I staggered across the city room to Campbell, sitting behind
the city desk, and said, "I didn't even *speak* to her. This woman could
run the Navy from the poop deck, what would I go challenging her to—or
for? *You* did this, you subhuman sadist."

In the silence that always fell on the city room if anybody bearded
Campbell, what I had intended as a dignified roar came out sounding
like somebody had stepped on my tail.

"Don't squeal at me," Campbell said.

"I am not squealing," I said.

What's more, I said to myself, I do not have to take any guff off you,
old Iron Mitten. Right there under my picture the caption says *"Nationally Known Writer."* Ha ha, I said to myself, if it's a big fat lie it's in your
Los Angeles *Evening Herald,* so you're stuck with it, baby.

By then I had covered, off and on, a good many stories for this Terrible Man.

The Rosebud Baby. Out of that Mabel Walker Willibrandt, later the
first woman Assistant Attorney General, got a special detail of cops to
prevent owners of nickelodeons from taking little girls who came to the
Saturday morning movies behind the silver screen and getting them with
babies, rosebud or otherwise. The press stood no nonsense then from
Jail Bait violators. They *went* to jail, we saw to that—nobody ever having
heard of Lolita.

The Clara Phillips murder case—a dilly, chiefly on account of Clara
was the best liar I ever saw on the witness stand. She almost got away
with it, too.

Back to Chicago for Leopold and Loeb, where I had to call Mr.

Hearst to say I thought Clarence Darrow had probably done it himself. At all times, as Damon Runyon warned me, I had trouble being an objective unprejudiced reporter, being born a rooter for or against something or somebody. Darrow still owed my father and me a lot of money for defending him from jury bribery. I couldn't be impartial about him—and here again the majority of the reporters there thought he'd had his hands on at least half a million bucks of the Leopold-Loeb fortunes. Up to his old tricks, though the press insisted that this time it was the judge he'd bribed, not the jury, to get the first two rich homosexual juvenile delinquents life sentences instead of the chair. It's at least interesting to note that the judge who tried it retired and has never been heard of from that day to this any more than Judge Crater.

Likewise, this period had included the Obenchain case, the Jack Morgan jewel robberies, and an old man accused of beating his wife to death. To my jumping jitters and incipient hysteria he had confessed all about it to me one day in the county jail. "You look like a real nice girl," he said reasonably. "Under all circumstances, she used to sit there all day in that chair and rock and rock and smile and smile. You can understand a man couldn't put up with that forever. So one day I got my ax and chopped that silly smile off her face. It was a great satisfaction to me."

Hollywood had grown up around me like the Emerald City of Oz.

Oh—I had learned about human nature under John B. T. Campbell.

Obviously at the time I got mixed up with *Madame President* I was back in the city room working on some special assignment.

I thought that Special Assignment, nationally known writer—*see if you can get St. Johns to come back and cover this one for us*—gave me a jump on Campbell. It didn't. A city editor is always a city editor.

Looking at the headline spread in front of him, Campbell said, "It was Mr. Hearst's idea."

"What's Mr. Hearst got to do with it?" I said.

"He read the story yesterday," Campbell said, that *real* carbolic acid oozing out of him. "He called and said, 'Why not challenge the lady?' He can always see something to keep a story alive—"

"Like giving my brains to a laboratory while I'm still alive," I said. "He doesn't *know*—I'm going to call him—"

"You do that," Campbell said.

In the old kitchen chair in front of *my* same recurring typewriter, I tried to think. Out of the corner of my eye I saw our club editor, Edna Lee Booker, sliding off into peripheral dimness and I said, "You come back here. I may need you."

This is what had happened.

As a favor to Bookie, I had gone the day before to Pasadena or Poker Flats or somewhere to speak to some Godforsaken woman's club *lunch-*

eon. They had asked Bookie to get a speaker. *What with those old biddies on the* Times *and the* Examiner, Bookie had said to me, *I have trouble getting any club news first, or exclusive. I'd like to do them this favor.* Bookie was then about twenty. So I said yes. True, once there, I had spoken half-assed about Is Modern Woman a Failure? I suppose I was having trouble with my own three mules whether I knew it or not, and my general assumption, based as usual on vague visceral reactions rather than thought process, was that sooner or later one of those mules was going to help kick in the Modern Woman's teeth. At that time, some forty years ago it was, it turned out pretty hot stuff.

Nobody had said it before and that makes anything hot stuff.

As I sat down to scattered applause, a full-bosomed lady with snow-white hair and the face of one born to command rose and said in ringing tone, "Ladies, may I have a word?"

Well, I knew instantly that they would no more deny her a word than they would deny a ham bone to a pursuing wolf.

That was the only hit I got in the next forty-eight times at bat.

The chairman rose to say that they were fortunate indeed, "We are honored, ladies, highly honored I may say, we have with us today as a most delightful surprise the President of Our Parent Organization. We shall be honored, Mrs. Winters, *highly* honored if I may say so—any word from you will be welcome—"

I thought of several, but at that time ladies only used those under anesthesia, and after that I passed into a better world where Parent Organizations went unheeded and unsung, nor did I emerge until Bookie brought the wheel chair. In the car she explained to me that Mrs. Winters had disagreed with everything I said. *Everything,* Bookie told me.

"She did, huh?" I said, as the miles back to town fled behind us. "Who cares? What's Hecuba to me Summer or Winter? It's all over now—all over now."

That's what I thought.

This is one of the unsinkable proofs that I am not and never was as good a newspaperman as William Randolph Hearst. Neither was anybody else.

Nothing was ever over as far as he was concerned. Unless we ran out of ink. Look at the way we carried on and *on* about Vivisection; in the end he made them clean it up. Or the Yellow Perils of Japan and China—I couldn't see that far ahead, I just knew that he always thought he was right and usually was.

The stab-in-the-back betrayal of my slight contretemps with Mrs. Winters hadn't come from Bookie. She wrote a good, dull, uninteresting routine story for her club department, page 24, where nobody but other clubwomen would ever see it unless they used it to line the garbage pail.

(This was pre-Garbage Disposal.) How was little Bookie to know—or should she?—that the Hound of the Baskervilles would be nosing around as usual and that he'd turn the one little paragraph about a courteous difference of opinion into a front page brawl—Campbell would put any argument, one between a wood louse and a boll weevil, on the front page. To give old John B. T. his due, he was among the first to recognize the news value of clubwomen and naturally as far as Sweet Alice Ames Ben Bolt was concerned he wept with delight to put her in headlines. He had looked up the GFWC, of which Mrs. AAW was pres.—it had millions of members all over the country and several hundred thousand of them were in our county. This had to mean circulation, and since we were not an endowed institution we wanted to publish what they wanted to read by somebody they wanted to read it BY. The General Federation of Women's Clubs has lost some of its steam now. I do assure you that under Alice Ames the Mail Order Gun Lobby would have been routed like the Gadarene Swine, and psychedelic drug pedlars on school grounds would have been handled gently but firmly with a meat cleaver. For a time after they got the vote, it looked like clubwomen might be the single greatest united force for GOOD and PEACE the world had ever known. Every city editor jumped at the crack of their whip.

For this reason, Campbell put my trivial flurry with the pres. on the front page where, as always on any front page of any newspaper, Hearst or otherwise in the U.S.A., the eagle eye of Mr. Hearst fell on it.

> Dear Mr. Ettelson (or Campbell or Howey): Don't you think what we really need is more *vigor* on our front pages? This one is as dead as it is dismal. Is everybody on vacation or just not paying attention? WRH

He was always paying attention to the Front Page, even when he went to Europe on a vacation.

I called him.

I said, "I am a reporter. I've never made but this one speech and *look* what I got myself into—"

"I know," the well-known, inimitable, always-imitated voice came wafting down most sympathetically from San Simeon. "However, I am sure you will acquit yourself with distinction."

"What do I know about debates?" I said frantically. "I never so much as heard one."

"The final arguments between your father and the district attorney in the courtroom," the voice said gently, "were in a measure debates, often with a man's life at stake."

"All right so I've seen Jack Barrymore act, but I can't do it," I said. "I'm not even sure what I *said*—or *she* said—"

"One reason I am anxious to proceed with this debate," Mr. Hearst said, "is that you are in my opinion on the right side. My mother fought hard to get the vote for women and as you know to encourage coeducation, both at the University of California and at the university in Palo Alto. My mother wished to give women every opportunity for bettering themselves and training their talents, but she was often disturbed at what would result if we went too fast. I have heard her say that this was the single most drastic move in history, that no one group, no single group had ever entered into so complete a change as the women of the twentieth century. We all know that change is not in itself necessarily progress. Unless we control this new freedom it may turn into license; women may lose their heads, and a nation is never any stronger than its women."

"Mr. Hearst," I said, trying to explain, "you have never *seen* Alice Ames Winters. She could replace the Statue of Liberty and nobody would notice."

"Your youth and fire will be more appealing to many," he said.

"*What* fire?" I said, but he ignored that and said, "Princess Pignatelli [then society editor of the Los Angeles *Examiner*] tells me that she's had a request from the Friday Morning Club; they would like to present this debate. The princess says this is the oldest and most respected of all clubs in the state and your grandmother was one of their first presidents."

"I wish to hell Grandma was here," I said. "Let her debate—"

"That," Mr. Hearst said, "is beyond my powers to arrange, but I thought that perhaps Marion and I would come down to support you—to root for you, in fact."

The idea of Mr. Hearst coming to hear me was dizzy enough. Marion Davies as part of an audience of clubwomen at a debate on Is Modern Woman a Failure? reached collapse proportions. Hope's last flicker died when, as I passed the desk on my way to what, for lack of a better word, we called the Ladies Room, Campbell said, "The president of the Friday Morning Club just called to say the demand for reservations is so great they've rented the Ambassador Theater."

I stopped. I said, "Jack, do me one favor? Don't *you* come."

"I couldn't stand to sit *here* and imagine it," John B. T. Campbell said.

Sure enough, when I mounted the stage at the Ambassador Theater there he was, J.B.T. himself, northern lights flashing in his eyes.

And Mr. Hearst with a bag of jelly beans.

And Marion in a decorous black suit.

According to an account in the opposition paper *a packed breathless audience of clubwomen and society leaders* was also present.

Further it alleges that *young Mrs. St. Johns made a rapid series of amazing statements,* though it does *not* mention that this took place only after she was flat on the floor for a count of nine.

For there can be no shadow of doubt that Mrs. Winters won the first round, no possible doubt whatever.

The stage was footlighted but I could still see over them. Square bang in the middle of the front row sat the jury of judges, selected by the California Federation of Women's Clubs. Mr. Hearst called them "sufficiently impressive." As far as I was concerned they would have shattered me if I hadn't already been in an advanced state of coma. For I recall totally my look at that row showing me Superior Judge Gordon Craig, Dr. Rufus von Kleinsmid, president of the University of Southern California, our senior citizen, Charles Loomis, Dr. Miriam van Waters, leading expert on Women's Prisons in the United States, Oda Falconer, best woman lawyer in California and our leading author, Gene Stratton Porter—just as well the faces in the second row were blurred momentarily.

Under Marquis of Queensberry rules for debate, I opened. I am aware that I wore a heather tweed suit which I thought proper for eleven in the morning, and my last conscious recollection as I got up from one of those folding chairs was that I'd forgotten to get it pressed and the skirt *bagged* —tweed does.

Halfway through whatever I was saying I saw that Mr. Hearst was eating jelly beans. *Thumbs down.* Like Louis B. Mayer if he rubbed his stomach while I was telling him a story. If they liked what you were doing neither of them did anything but listen.

Marion gave me a sort of dying swan wave of one white glove.

Some *coughing*. A few rustlings. Here and there a sidewise glance no better than a shrug. I spoke without notes, both Mr. Hearst and my father eschewed notes, this assumed however that you had something to say and knew what it was and could thus say or write it *without* notes.

I didn't.

Halfway through one look at the jury—I had been long trained to estimate juries—and I knew I was dead.

Mrs. Winters approached this matter from a less eccentric angle. With stately tread, she moved to the lectern in a gown of lavender and old lace, with pearls, with hair marcelled that morning. Moreover, she placed before her a typed manuscript of terror-striking size and neatness, opened it, passed a hand over it, put on gold-rimmed glasses and regarded it, took them off to show us she wasn't going to read it, it was just *there* to assure us she had done her homework; if facts, figures, statistics, weighty opinons were required they were at her fingertips. Surely it can't have been condescension to an already fallen foe that sparked her smile as she said, "Madame Chairman, Honored Judges, Ladies and Gentlemen and Fellow Members of the General Federation of Women's Clubs—"

And all the ships at sea, I thought, having forgotten all this mumbo-jumbo entirely. If I ever knew it. All Papa said was "Your Honor, Gentlemen of the Jury—"

I remember what she said. I prayed for the waters of Lethe to close over my head; nothing came of it. With that superiority that used to characterize Whitey Ford and other Yankee pitchers, Mrs. Winters set forth in intelligent arrangement of fact the *modern woman*. Like Columbus discovering America she claimed this New World for her sex. Entering fresh fields of endeavor, infiltrating new continents of learning, illumining new layers of Art and Culture, leavening the races, and by her gentle, firm, and inspired presence lifting even the market place to new heights of honor and honesty.

It was good.

With an accustomed bow to the uproar of applause she sat down and I figured that out of a possible eight votes she had eight and a half.

Then I was jolted by hearing the chairman, obviously repeating—half an hour now allowed for rebuttal—*Mrs. St. Johns*.

Rebuttal? What is this rebuttal? I hadn't butted in the first place, now I couldn't even lower a horn much less *re*butt. Nobody had told me anything about REbuttal. *Nil Nisi Bonum* was my motto.

Things coagulated to drive me into a sudden, unexpected rage of righteous indignation.

The jury! Well, I had seen juries changed before.

Faces in that smug audience rushed at me.

Estelle Lawton Lindsey, my friend, a newspaperwoman who'd gone into politics, been elected to the City Council, *her* eyes were closed as though she couldn't bear to see what was coming.

Like a frenzied fight manager watching his boy murdered, John B. T. Campbell's horror—HORROR—floated up to me, *nobody but me is allowed to put the whammy on my reporters*.

What detonated me was the self-satisfied smirk on the face of a lady who has been gathered to her reward for a good many years now. She belonged to the Wednesday Afternoon Musical, the Monday Night Republican, the Friday Morning, the Mothers for Liberty, the Betsy Ross Branch of the D.A.R., the Lady Elks, the female Eagles, the Committee for Campaigns to help Unmarried Mothers, the South Side Den Mothers as well as the P.T.A., and the League of Women Voters. The only thing she couldn't get into was the Gold Star Mothers. She also had a job playing the organ for weddings and graduations. I knew her well. I knew all about her husband, her house and her children, she lived on the same street as my Aunty Blanche.

I got my hair out of my eyes by nearly pulling it out by the roots, walked around in front of that dinky little soapbox on which Mrs. Winters' speech still reposed, and I can still hear—*yes I can*—the all-out shout, like Mike Quill or Aimee Semple McPherson, of my opening sentence.
I said:

> All right, all right, you asked for it. From where I stand, I can put my finger on five modern women. I know where their husbands were last night and they don't. From where I stand, I can tell one woman where her kid daughter was night before last; she was drunk on the floor at the Ship Cafe, a man entertainer went by and shoved her with his toe and said Charity Ass loud enough for everybody to hear and they all laughed. I can tell another woman I see from here that her husband is leading a double life and he likes his other family better—*that* other wife isn't modern a goddam bit. I see another well-known clubwoman and society leader on whom I can smell the white wash, if she's interested in anything besides being modern I can tell her why her secret bottle of whiskey gets empty so soon—her fifteen-year-old son drinks, too.

Well, boys and girls, by this time, as you can well imagine, the audience, composed of clubwomen and society leaders out front, was frozen in total, incredulous, non-coughing silence. No wiggling to ease the bored fanny. Nobody was looking at each other. They didn't dare.

> I don't just say STOP. No no no. I say Stop, Look, and Listen. I don't say you mustn't go forward into greater usefulness and help make a bigger better world. I just beg you on my bended knees to heed the big red sign, the waving red lanterns that say DANGER. DANGER AHEAD. *Road under Construction.*

> I don't care if my banker plays golf every afternoon. I don't care if I hear rumors that he's a bit of a gay fellow evenings. IF he is tending to his business, looking after my money. I never have much. I need it. His first duty is to take the care of my dough he agreed to when he became a banker.

> Your first duty is your children, your home, your husband, the sanity of your family.

> No nation can continue half slave and half free—I agree. Nor can it continue if the slave who has been emancipated only uses that freedom to get a little more dough to buy herself silk stockings, or to gather success for herself, or to roll in the same gutter with men. Throughout history, throughout all civilizations, a

nation has been as strong and as sound and as happy as the Family. The Family is the foundation of that happiness we seek, the safety we long for, the love and faith we have cherished. The First Unit. The man is the head of the house, but the foundation of the Family is the *character* and *joy* of the Mother.

IF the modern woman has tended to her own business—okay. If she hasn't then she must honestly, fearlessly figure out whether she wants to sip bootleg scotch and be Charity Ass—I know, it's vulgar, facts often are, and that's what you're called all too often —those very words—if you don't mind your husband's being a frequenter of Pearl Morton—now there's a woman who'd have no truck with this Modern Woman's freedom, Mrs. Morton has been a good friend of mine and she agrees with me that the Modern Woman is a failure. Mrs. Morton belongs to the oldest profession, one that has always been open to women, she once said to me No man who is happy at home has ever entered my house. They often, Mrs. Morton said to me, come to my house because there is nobody home at their own. They come because they are lonely, and that's the truth. Business, Mrs. Morton told me, has been very good, ever since the Modern Woman came into being.

I suppose I had been thinking partly of Dolly, who once had lived in Pearl Morton's house and who had been my father's mistress for a little while. I knew all too well how lonely my father had been.

By the time I finished with that, I was sweating.

I couldn't see the face of the woman who'd started me off on this any more; she was looking down.

Keep on the way you're going at the moment and in the coming generation you have "freed" we will need a new Diogenes to stalk the earth, searching for a happy woman.

That much of what I said I remember. The rest now is direct quotes from national newspaper coverage. Mrs. St. Johns said:

The women of today are miserable in their new so-called freedom. They know it's built on selfishness and indulgence. The entire object of existence—a right given us along with liberty by our own national declaration, has always been to find happiness. And happiness can only be obtained through success in living.

The girl of today has the opportunity of earning her own living and thereby becoming independent of men. As a result she now thinks she can refuse to take the marriage relationship seriously. She has been down for so many centuries under sometimes admittedly unfavorable conditions that now a path has been opened that leads to life and liberty and the pursuit of happiness she refuses to use any self-control and caution.

Not only is modern woman a failure but she must accept 90% of the blame for that failure. Woman is sacrificing the tremendous privilege of home, social and religious culture and the education of her children to run after false gods.

The way women are handling the gift of freedom at this minute has to lead directly to the destruction of a sane and normal civilization. We'd better get out of this sink of liberty-into-license and get back on the road.

Mrs. Winters had a rebuttal too.

Then there I was, waiting for another jury. I had spent so much of my life doing that. With Papa. I didn't dare look at anybody—I just sat as still as I could. Mrs. Winters was perfectly at ease, obviously it had never so much as occurred to her that she could lose this one.

But she did.

MODERN WOMAN FAILURE
JUDGES OF DEBATE DECIDE

That headline comes from a Chicago paper of the time.

One of the New York papers said:

MODERN WOMAN IS A FAILURE

This was the startling decision yesterday of three men and four women judges of a debate between Adela Rogers St. Johns, nationally known writer, and Mrs. Thomas G. Winters, prominent clubwoman and President of the National Federation, at the Ambassador Theater in Los Angeles.

The decision was read to an audience of clubwomen who made an unexpected and terrific uproar of applause over Mrs. St. Johns' victory and the words which condemned themselves.

They did—they actually stood up and broke into cheers.

Coming down into that wildly cheering throng at the Ambassador, I found Mr. Hearst pleased and Marion stuttering like Chinese New Year's with excitement. What really threw me was Campbell. Before he gave me a hug he wiped tears from his face. Tears! I'm sure they were of relief that one of his reporters had escaped a licking by such a healthy margin, but I was flabbergasted. I thought to myself, Is it possible that the Lord High Executioner is *human?*

3

From that preposterous victory, I went home to my so-called ranch in Whittier, California. This adored white elephant I had acquired when I developed an idiot earning power due to movies and magazine fiction. Like most of us in those early days, I regarded this as income. The ranch had twenty-two acres of walnut trees showing an amusing little deficit every year, a swimming pool when these were few, a championship tennis court, a stable with riding horses waited on by a groom in jodhpurs, and an eighteen-room stately home of Old England. I had paid extra for the weathered bricks and the whole thing was built on the quicksands of potential bankruptcy any time the bank refused to renew the second mortgage.

I loved it. The house, the orchards, the flower and vegetable gardens, the little stream, the eucalyptus groves, with a passion only those born under Taurus have for sticks and stones, and with the hunger of a child raised in the best hotels.

I sat down in the glowing redwood of my workroom-cum-library. A solemn hush fell upon me. Every candidate, I am sure, feels his ears grow long like the White Rabbit's as he listens to his voice committing him to lower taxes. I had just talked myself into a stand on the Modern Woman, of whom I had realized only as I was driving home *I* was a primary prototype, an incunabulum in swaddling clothes, not by my consent or choice or conviction, but by sheer accident of birth. The circumstances of being Earl Rogers' daughter for the first eighteen years of my life.

Far ahead of his time, my father had believed in careers for women.

He also believed that his daughter Nora should be a free soul, with an open mind for adventure, a heart rebellious against convention, prepared to learn from life, people, and the reading of all the books in the world—never mind about schools.

As a female member of the human race I was an involuntary pioneer. When I started my journey I had known nothing about the Modern Woman and since then had never had time to find out where I stood.

My equipment for this journey I now knew had been unorthodox.

I had learned about women from loving Pearl Morton and Dolly. From my mother, who disliked me so much that, fortunately for me, she had neglected to give me her version of what mothers are supposed to teach their daughters. Besides my daily lessons from my grandfather, who was a saint, I had learned about God, women must love God, and as a woman child I *had,* up to the moment when Grandpa died in agony. Then that love turned to hate for taking him from us when Papa and I needed him most. Finally, in the excitement of my father's law office, in the absorbing demands of my own life, I had come to ignore God entirely.

Now and then I learned from going to school. When I didn't, I had learned from pimps, professional prostitutes, gamblers, bank robbers, poets, newspapermen, jury bribers, millionaire dipsomaniacs, and murderers. Music came from my Aunty Blanche. Chess, baseball, embroidery, and some Greek—as well as what a *lady* is, can know, do, be, say, and how she should behave—came from my occasional contacts with my grandmother. Jack London, my godfather, showed me what the joy and pain of writing could be, and the woman to whom he was married gave me my second horror of how women can destroy men. A big, red-faced ham-handed detective named Bill Jory taught me how a *man* should die, that gratitude and loyalty are the chief virtues and the rarest, and that as he used to say, *You always gotta feel sorry for them poor lonesome bastards out there.*

Any modern psychologist would have said Nora was doomed.

I had one advantage.

The Manner of My Setting Out included a broken heart. I know I know I *know,* hearts do not break—that's old-fashioned folklore—but mine did, when at last I knew I couldn't save my father. It took a while for me to understand that I'd had an extraordinary childhood since I knew no other. It was filled with all kinds of things a child should not know nor see nor hear. None of this mattered. I had the one and only thing that is important to a child. My heart was always sure. Always. Papa loved me and he never sinned against that love. In spite of hell and Lucifer himself, I knew what love was—oh I did I did. Some people never find out, they will not accept it, but I knew love and I trusted it and it turned out to be the beam I followed toward the Desired Country.

When I went forth, the militant, often anarchistic march of the suffragettes had just begun. Women didn't yet have the *vote.* This was before the Model T, radio, television, airplanes, income tax, and traffic jams, when we only had one umpire and truly believed that we were too civilized ever to have another war. Almost immediately, I had become part of the suffrage movement. For thinking back I could still hear Mr. Hearst's high precise voice; he respected every word he spoke, nobody ever misunderstood an assignment from him. "Adela," he said, "I wish you would find a suffrage leader who takes better pictures. The ones we have are fine women but they are not photogenic. We are strongly behind votes for women, but these leaders will not make the battle for suffrage look attractive to the young. We must persuade young women to come to the front." *Page,* he really meant, so I found Inez Milholland Boissevain, in her twenties; in her puffed-sleeved shirtwaists and Merry Widow sailors she was beautiful enough even for the flashlight cameras of that day.

Young Adela Rogers still in pigtails trooped around from Texas to Montana with her to speak of this Sesame that was to open a brave new world for all. In spite of doctors' orders she made a speech one night in the rain and I kept my first death watch as she fought for her life against pneumonia. And lost.

When women had the vote, I had been led to believe, the streetcar named Utopia would be along any minute. In my quiet library years later, I could see Inez again as I'd last seen her, and I had to wonder whether hers—and mine—had been a Pyrrhic victory costing more than it has ever been worth.

While I was doing all this unexpected heavy thinking, Mother Meyer was upstairs in the guest suite I'd arranged for her. Though as my adopted mother—the best term I can think of for what she meant in my life—she was with me more and more, I hadn't taken her to the debate, I hadn't judged it to be all that important. I ought to want to talk it over with Mother but I didn't. We have, as of today, ceased to believe in a time to stop talking, everybody, everywhere, for a few minutes and let our own common sense, our inherited character, our *roots* take over. I knew as I resisted the first impulse to go babbling to Mother that silence *is* golden, it is our tube to more than we know ourselves. I said glumly to myself, You'll talk yourself out of it, you always do, you're such a liar, you invent bits and pieces to suit yourself, you give yourself the best of it even on a sleepless night, you make yourself believe it the way you arrange it, you practically never think before you speak. Talking got you into this, it is not going to get you out. Not even talking to Mother. Some things you have to get yourself.

Shut up, for once.

Think!

I lit a cigarette with care, my hands weren't quite steady, and tried to give myself a breather of tobacco. Then I summoned the poems, the music I loved best, always Mozart, to clear my head of the present hammering.

Be still, I said to myself, and *think*.

Thinking had never been my forte. Not quiet, constructive thinking a thing through, out or over. Feel—react—wait for inspiration, instinct, intuition, visceral response. Move into *imagination*, without that you are still in the cave—a cavewoman, no doubt. That is undoubtedly why, later, I clutched to my breast Picasso's line about trying to transcend the limitations his intelligence was trying to force upon him. On the other hand, some degree of intelligence might have resulted in limitations even Picasso would have been better not to have transcended.

As I heard my children and twenty-two little Mexican neighbors splashing in the pool, as the pat pat pat of the tennis balls told me my athletic second husband was enjoying a well-earned set at the end of *his* day, I confronted a situation I had placed on the front pages of America as of this very afternoon and tomorrow morning.

My winning warning that Modern Woman is a failure and in that future (where we all have to go, willy-nilly) would bring catastrophe would be quoted.

My fuse had been lit by Mrs. Winters. I had popped off.

What had I been up to? What did I believe? If I knew.

One person only I could communicate with *in silence.*

When something new comes your way, Papa had said to me in one of our last talks, *you'll know what I would have said about this or that. You know all my thoughts. I'll always be with you in your memory, and your love for me,* he had said, *which has survived so much worse things, will survive death and keep a channel open for us.* This memory, strong and vivid, was always mine, it was live green and bore new blossoms. We all have our memories, we shall get no other, but sometimes one is brighter than another, or we let some fade out and constantly tune in on others.

Popping off without knowing what I was talking about, without being willing to live up to it—Papa would despise this, I could hear him say so.

On that stage at the Ambassador Theater, I had brought Modern Woman to the bar of justice and gotten her convicted by a jury of her peers.

Her? *Me!* For I was not only prosecutor. I was also the Accused.

How was I going to answer my own charges?

Hell's bells, like a volcano erupting it had poured out of me, things I hadn't known I felt about myself or anybody else, things that could have germinated in my frenzied attempts to get my own three mules under control, which always left the tag end of a *husband*. As I bent my attention to remember what I'd said, bits and pieces, sentences out of context, amazing pronouncements began to come forth.

These must be faced.

All right.

Earl Rogers' daughter Nora, Adela Rogers St. Johns, reporter—you've been on the witness stand before, both of you.

Ask yourself the questions.

Do you use your freedom to get a little more dough to buy silk stockings your husband can't afford?

That's a badly framed question, however the answer is No. True, your husband's earnings cannot afford walnut groves and five servants, horses for Elaine and swimming pools for Billy and a Mary Poppins' nurse for

Dicky and schools for my kid brothers, Bryson and Thorny. That isn't for me, it's the best for my children, and if I can earn it, I should. Who's on first—my children!

Do you use careers-for-woman to make yourself a big shot instead of helping your husband?

No no. Newspaper work is the most exciting thing in the world to me, it's where I *live*. I would do it for nothing. I would do it forever without a By-Line. I love my work, not my career. If I do it as well as I can it looks like it has to make me a success and that means money and my name in headlines. But that is not why I do it. Ike—my husband Ike St. Johns—he had needed me to go to San Francisco with him on a key move in a big political campaign, he'd asked me to go. The mystery phone call that sent me to halt Ray Raymond's funeral and put Paul Kelly and Dorothy Mackaye on trial for murder had been where I went, however. When I had to choose a card! Ike had been one of those poor lonesome bastards out there I gotta be sorry for when he ended up that night at a place you pay for consolation; he always had to tell you all about everything. I had been kind about it; I hadn't taken it too seriously. He had taken my not taking it too seriously very seriously indeed.

Do you take the marriage relationship seriously?

You have to. If you want children there has to be a husband, doesn't there? That one out on the tennis court, you had better take him as seriously as he takes himself, or he'll try to make you. *He* won't end up at a place like Pearl Morton's or the amateur equivalent around nowadays. He wants to tell Knute Rockne how to coach a football game and anything I would say to halt his reckless project would be taken seriously as unwifely and belittling.

Do you think you can drive the three mules your grandfather's old Irish proverb said nobody can? Ever?

Why not? What's *ever*? Maybe many of those ladies listening to you today cannot drive three mules. That doesn't mean nobody can *ever*. I don't want to be uppity or bodacious or cock-a-doodle-doo about this, I said to myself, but overcoming an *ever* like that can be listed as progress. Two mules—your personal life and your work. Fair enough. Split your personal life two for one—your children, your husband. Be a mother—be a wife-housewife—is that three or four?

Who's on first, as Abbott and Costello say?

You have to run as fast as you can to stay in one place and then sprint to make progress. Like running the 440.

Do you sacrifice the tremendous privilege of religious culture to run after false gods of pleasure and material possessions?

I don't believe in religious culture. I do not run after gods, false or otherwise. Many great people are agnostic and they run after Ambition, Distraction, Uglification, and Derision. Those are not false gods.

There I stopped and lit my fourteenth cigarette. From within I heard a deep protest of confusion.

I had been pushed into this. I was being pushed too fast on all sides about everything. I loved it, in a way I loved the pace and tempo, but I jumped with confusion, too. My skin prickled with it. I had pushed out my first husband Ike almost without knowing it, come to *think* about it. I had let my second push into my life for all the wrong reasons. Not being a natural thinker in depth, I could do an incredible number of things without thinking about them at all. So could most women.

Nevertheless the things I'd said must have been there or I couldn't have said them, when that old lady's calm assumptions that the path she and her kind had set for the Modern Woman was safe and sane for all had pushed me into *rebuttal,* like a prancing goat.

You are not asking the right questions. Here's a key one.

If that lovable old cynic Diogenes shone his lantern on you would he find in you the honest woman who is making a success of living in this century and holding the reins over three mules with style and ease?

You have, I said to myself in answer, wonderful children, your own and some other people's. A good-looking husband no worse than average. A home you adore. A career in superlatives, to be honest about it. All this you are juggling with a degree of expertise that is spectacular to watch —at least.

Then why are you hearing seals bark where there are no seals?

I knew why I had said those things today but I couldn't connect it up. It didn't make sense. It didn't even make imagination. If Papa had been there to ask the questions—

A question was missing and I was shaking inside in terror because Papa wasn't there and never would be and I hadn't been able to save him, I hadn't been able to save the person who'd taught me what love was.

None of us, not even that fool woman sitting in the front row, not even cute old Alice Ames Winters, who wasn't going to live to see what came of all this, *she* could talk, had meant evil. Almost nobody ever does.

Nobody ever, for instance, ate toadstools on purpose.

It is unlikely that I will ever forget my first ambulance call as a police reporter, which no woman had been before me.

"All right, Swifty," the boys in the press room at the First Street Police Station had said kindly. "Get going."

I had taken the place for the *Herald* of a police reporter named Scotty. Against the law of the jungle that on a beat all news must be pooled, Scotty had scooped his brothers on a beautiful girl pickpocket. Scotty had a way with women. His wife once thought he'd had it with me and took a perfectly unjustified shot at me one night *in* the press room. Her aim was wild. This pool law was essential. No one could cover the whole beat, so a man from one paper took the Emergency Hospital, another the police courts, another any trial of magnitude going on, someone else covered the booking desk, a man stood by for the breaks and also on any running story. Everybody took turns at ambulance calls depending on who was in and not doing anything. When Scotty broke the faith Tex Talbot of the *Times,* later decorated as a marine in the Argonne, chased him through the Third Street Tunnel shooting at his feet—all police reporters carried guns, of course. J. B. T. Campbell's replacements had been ejected on sight. In desperation, he sent me. "You are Earl Rogers' offspring," he said gloomily. Also he felt they might not shoot at anyone in pigtails. They didn't. But when my turn came to go on an ambulance call they said, "All right, Swifty. Get going."

Breathless and shook from the ride behind screaming sirens, I followed the white-clad intern into a small flat on the outskirts of town where a family of five, father, mother, and three kids, lived. They were all dead when we got there. On the floor. Their faces were out of Dante's Inferno and the place reeked of their vomit, to which I instantly added mine.

They hadn't eaten toadstools, those poor sprawled corpses.

Whoever ate a toadstool?

They had eaten what they thought were mushrooms.

I have never eaten one since, I know they are all right and raised in cellars by cultures, etc., etc., but I cannot bring myself to take the chance.

This may not be learning philosophy in the gardens of Academe, but it is one way.

> . . . the way women are handling the gift of freedom at this minute has to lead directly to the destruction of a sane and normal civilization. We asked for this in the name of liberty but by using it as license we have turned it into a sink, we'd better get out of that and get back on the road.

This quote or something like it is from me—not Plato.

With a wave of apprehension more violent than any I have felt in my life until we dropped the bomb on Hiroshima, I knew that this much of what had exploded out of me in rebuttal I believed with my stomach—and my soul.

Papa would have known how to set up the questions so I'd know what was missing. He'd have built up to the last question I didn't know how or what to ask that would have brought it into focus.

I couldn't find it in the silence, I wasn't on the beam to the memory of it, that was why I felt suddenly so afraid and forlorn.

If I was off the road, off the ascent of a pilgrim's progress by whatever name, I must try to see where I'd gone off and where I was *now*. Me and my big mouth and my big shot. I needed to look at the map. The road map. The signposts.

So as I had used similitudes, as Hosea says, I came back to *Pilgrim's Progress*.

> This Book chalks all out before thine eyes
> The woman that seeks the everlasting Prize;
> It shows you whence she comes, whither she goes,
> What she has left undone, what she hath done;
> It also shows you how she runs and runs
> Till she unto the Gate of Glory comes.

The Gate of Glory was a high-sounding phrase. I had believed in my grandfather's *friend* Jesus Christ when he read to me about him, the same way I'd believed in Mowgli when Papa read him out loud to me from *The Jungle Book*. They had both become more or less fiction to me now, though they continued to crop up. At this point I certainly wasn't a Christian but no more were Christian and Christiana in the book. They had started up, that was all, and their doubts and fears were ever present. Running and running—and the journey was tough—and dangerous.

Whence she comes. Whither she goes.

Those words churned me on.

As that lovable old agnostic my forty-seventh cousin once removed Robert Green Ingersoll said in an optimistic moment, Every coffin asks whither and every cradle *whence*—what without asking?

In a nameless emptiness filled with the sound of my children playing and my career trumpeting and my home and husband surrounding me on all sides, I was haunted by my father not being there as he ought to have been, by my own terrible words of that morning clanking in my ears.

I had no idea *whither* I was going.

But I ought to be able to figure out *whence* I came.

CHAPTER 2

The bell captain, my contact, supporter, source of information, and long-time friend, who'd been at the Alexandria when my father and I lived there, wasn't around when I strolled into the lobby at my usual time around nine on that particular morning. As still the best hotel in town, the Alexandria was part of my beat, and since the most important man in any hotel is always the bell captain, I was glad Johnny was on my side.

Finding him mysteriously missing disturbed me. I had a special assignment which only happened when Brass came to town, a theater star like David Warfield or Maude Adams, Minnie Maddern Fiske, or somebody just back from Mexico or China with a tale to unfold. Otherwise I was just looking for a feature to brighten the paper. Brighten it brighten it brighten it, as Charles Dickens once posted on the bulletin board of *his* paper, the *Household Words*.

On this occasion we knew that the president of one of the biggest railroads in the country when railroads were the biggest thing in it—before oil or airplanes—was in residence.

"He'll be there all right, don't let them kid you," Jack Campbell, my city editor, had said to me, "but he's already sent word through his office here that he won't see any reporters before the big Harbor Conference this afternoon, and the meeting with the governor and the Railroad Commission tonight. Now listen carefully."

This gambit of Campbell's always exasperated me. But even then I realized that he could give an assignment, which many an editor and publisher cannot do. When Campbell got through telling you, you knew what you were going after, what was probably the best way to get it, and exactly what he wanted you to bring back alive.

"In Los Angeles," he said, "we have not got a natural harbor such as San Francisco Bay."

"This," I said, "reveals itself to my naked eye."

"The time has come," the city editor said, "we have to build us one. With a big harbor, Los Angeles, which the Spanish and the Franciscan fathers built inland, can grow into the biggest city in the state, maybe in the nation. We can't grow without a harbor to pick up our trade with the Orient and South America. This is big stuff, Southern California's future depends on it. We have to hook up our railroads with our shipping. As soon as possible so the harbor can take advantage of the opening of the Panama Canal next year.

"Now! Listen! Whether they'll construct it at Santa Monica or Long Beach or San Pedro—that's the question. Wherever, there will be a real estate boom. Roads'll have to be put in. All this is going to be settled *this* afternoon and tonight—too late for our last edition. The man who has the say-so is this railroad president who came in late last night in his private car and is, as I've told you, at the Alexandria not seeing reporters. Not even Sam Blythe, who's written railroad and political articles for *The Saturday Evening Post*. But it's on your beat, you've got things set up for yourself there, haven't you? What I want—where and when Los Angeles Harbor."

"Rah rah rah," I said.

Properly he ignored this. "If you could get a *hint* in time for the home or even the Green—you might as well have a shot at it. He can't do any more than throw you down the elevator shaft."

That's what he thought.

He had never met this free-wheeling president of this super-railroad and certainly he had never heard of the Collection of Opals he carried with him. Nor had I.

However if the tycoon had refused to see Sam Blythe, what chance had I, a seven-dollar-and-fifty-cent-a-week (paid in cash) rookie?

Unless Johnny my bell captain could finagle something to get me in.

Harbor construction and a real estate boom weren't exactly my forte, but I had caught some of Campbell's excitement, I could visualize exclusive headlines, it was what later would come to be called a *challenge*.

He can't do any more than throw you down the elevator shaft and a reporter's life is full of hazards and I *am* Miss Rogers of the *Herald*, I said to myself.

And right away I ran into major disaster. My pal the head bellman I couldn't find. If I'd known where he was, I'd have been twice as jittery. Try, Campbell had told me. I knew the desk clerks wouldn't dare play ball, all I'd get from them was He doesn't allow us to give out his room number. So I milled around the lobby and the mezzanine hoping to find a friend-in-need. Finally I saw an old bellboy whose brother Earl Rogers had once gotten off on a breaking-and-entering rap, and I asked him, Where is the railroad tycoon? He didn't give me a tumble, he looked right through me and kept on going. I barely caught the words he mumbled.

G on the fifth floor.

So I took the elevator to the fourth.

A on the fourth was the magnificent suite with its grand piano a girl named Dolly used to play when it had been home to Earl Rogers and the daughter he always called Nora. At fourteen, I had loved Dolly.

Probably the minister who'd made Papa throw her out on my account was right, but it was for me another black mark against ministers. I know now that she was kind of heart, whatever sins her body committed. I heard her heart for my father in her music. Already I had begun to treasure *kindness,* I had seen too much cruelty when Mama belittled my father and made him jealous on purpose. All her cat scratches left their mark on me, too. Cruelty as the mortal sin, nothing else shook me with cold terror. On my Dangerous Journey I ran from cruelty as from nothing else, so that I ran from the one man I probably should have married. I know now that Dolly had to leave us, but hers is one of the two suicides I shall weep over till I die. The other is his—Ray Helgesen's—the man I didn't marry. I couldn't have prevented Dolly's. But perhaps I made a mistake that day in Washington when I put my new hat on top of my head and walked out of the city room in the Washington *Herald* because I'd realized Helgesen's cold Swedish *intent* to hurt, an unkind thing done to me on purpose.

Well, as my brother Bogart, who'd been an ace in the Royal Flying Corps in the First World War, said on the day His Majesty's Government announced to me the death in action of my oldest son Bill—one thing Bogart had said, I pray of you, *don't* start shuffling that IF deck.

2

Now as a cub reporter I was walking past it on my way to the marble-and-iron staircase between floors where I could get to G on the fifth, where my railroad president was doubtless enjoying his first safe cup of coffee, he hoped. As I climbed steeply, the grand piano in A played for me once again our theme song, "Wait Till the Sun Shines, Nellie"—I could hear it as *plain.* On the last note a girl's voice chimed in and it said, "I think I ought to try for the Bar Exams next fall, don't you, Papa?"

The Bar Exams? Then what was I doing *here,* trying to find out where they were going to construct Los Angeles Harbor?

And I heard Papa's voice answering my question, "I'd rather see you dead," he had said.

That closed door into Suite A had led me back in memory more vivid than the real scene I was living in the now.

"I'd rather see you dead than a criminal lawyer," my father had said to me. I was stunned. Since I was eight, being a lawyer was what I'd set my heart on. I felt forlorn and bereft. It was his principle that a girl must know how to earn her living. At what? I couldn't play the piano well enough. A few weeks of summer stock in Salt Lake City and one part in Chicago had proved that the stage would lose nothing if I didn't become an actress.

Then my father said, "You know before he wrote *Pickwick Papers,*
Dickens was a reporter, and of course Kipling went to India for a newspaper."

I said, "Oh Papa, girls can't work on newspapers."

Papa said, "A few do. There is Winifred Black. And more will. Wait
till women get the vote."

"Do you think they will?" I said.

"Oh yes," my father said. "Nora, now I come to think of it, from the
time you were big enough to spank, you've had difficulty telling the difference between truth and your imagination. Can that be the mark of the
writer upon you? Of course on a newspaper where you come in contact
with human nature you would have to differentiate between fact and fiction most of the time—"

Before he finished, I knew. I said, "Oh Papa."

Papa introduced me to Mr. Hearst in his office at the San Francisco
Examiner. I was not quite eighteen and Mr. Hearst must have been a
few years older than Papa. I thought he was one of the handsomest men
I'd ever seen—oddly enough, he didn't scare me.

So I went to work on the San Francisco *Examiner* and a little later
when he was selecting a staff for the E. T. Earl paper he'd bought Mr.
Hearst sent me down to Los Angeles.

"I hope you won't mind," he said to me. "It has the advantage of being
an afternoon paper and that's better for a reporter."

Thus sometime in early 1913 I had reported to Jack Campbell, who
could have lived without me. He regarded a newspaper*woman* as a con-
tradiction in terms. The only editor who ever welcomed me was Walter
Howey, the greatest of all Hearst editors. Howey welcomed everything
new until he found out all about it. Then he used it or junked it.

The day I arrived in the *Herald* city room, however, John B. T. Campbell did not look friendly. His eyes went coldly over me from my pigtails
to my worn but polished brogues. He examined my well-cut tweed suit.
Eddie Schmidt was the tailor who became practically By Appointment to
Hollywood stars such as Clark Gable and Duke Wayne and to whom I
took Gary Cooper to get his first dinner jacket. Earl Rogers' daughter was
the only woman for whom he ever made a suit. My pigskin gloves, my
soft-brimmed Dobbs felt hat created no optimism about my future, or
Campbell's, with me in the city room. Moreover I was laboring under the
handicap that Mr. Hearst had hired me without consulting him. In tones
of frozen honey he said, "All right, Miss Rogers, you will start where
everyone starts—on the hotel beat."

The first time I met Leo Durocher after I became a sports writer I
thought that as a baseball manager he had the same qualities Campbell

had displayed as a city editor. I soon had to concede that Leo was kinder
to rookies. What Campbell was really like in my rookie days can be
sketchily indicated if I tell you about Gordon Seagrove, nicknamed Sad
by Campbell because of his rueful countenance. Sad Seagrove was then
our-man-on-the-courthouse-beat and one fine day he picked up a pair of
copy shears four feet long and chased Campbell into a telephone booth.
His intention, loudly proclaimed, was to cut Campbell's heart out if the
lily-livered son-of-a-bitch had one. I regret to tell you that no one in the
city room stirred hand or foot to rescue our gallant leader. All that saved
J.B.T. from the worms and Seagrove from the gallows was that the phone
booth was too small for the shears. I must also record that on another day
when he suggested I should take up streetwalking since obviously, he
said, I wasn't going to make it as a reporter, I threw his own desk telephone at him and hit him, what's more. As he was sitting in his *swivel*
chair this knocked him into the middle of the sports department but if
you think he let up on my leads or stories after this you are mistaken. *"A
Funny Thing Happened on the Way to the Divorce Court—"* "Don't *you*
tell *me* whether it's funny or not, wait until I laugh and then we'll know
whether it's funny or not—" *"A most pathetic thing took place yesterday
in Watts when four-year-old Charlie Smith on his scooter—"* "You see
tears streaming out of my eyes, that's the first time you'll know whether
it's pathetic or not—" But at least I heard no more about streetwalking,
though whether this was because he thought that skinny as I was I'd starve
to death or because he now saw a gleam of hope that I might make a reporter, deponent saith not.

Jack Campbell kept me on the hotel beat longer than most.

I was also supposed to keep an eye on my father's office. For news.

There wasn't much any more in what had once been the leading criminal
law office in the state and a *beat* as much as the D.A.'s headquarters.
I couldn't keep my eye on my father much, either. He'd asked me not to.
Promise me, Nora, don't sit up with the corpse. He was losing his fight
with John Barleycorn—up at the courthouse they said quietly, sadly, Earl
Rogers is trying to drink himself to death. I had known that—I'd known
I couldn't help him.

So I concentrated on the hotel beat.

Naturally I knew what a hotel was. Better than most.

And I soon learned what a beat was. Like a policeman, you were
responsible for whatever went on in that territory.

By the morning that the Los Angeles-shaking story about the harbor
broke, I had as Campbell said already set things up for myself in the
hotels including the Alexandria. Where the key figure, the railroad president, was in what we called hiding.

One contributing factor to what followed in what was the real opening gun of my career must be explained here. In appearance it is a coincidence, but I have now lived too long to believe in coincidences. A coincidence is a striking occurrence of two or more events at one time, apparently by chance. Nonsense. These things come about by some inner cross-circuiting of what you want, what you believe, what is necessary to you. Years later President Franklin D. Roosevelt told me that my story about the coincidences we would have to grant if we believed Hauptmann innocent was what convinced him that Hauptmann had murdered the Lindbergh baby.

What I was wearing that morning undoubtedly was part of what caused the railroad president to make the mistake he did. Before starting upstairs I had stopped in the ladies' room, as Papa had taught me, saying a first impression is invaluable and must be formed on what you give them to form it upon. Between my father and San Francisco I considered it unladylike, unchic, tawdry, and brash to appear on the street in the daytime in anything but a suit, preferably navy blue or tweed. Dresses were for indoors or after sundown under coats.

The girl I saw in the triple mirror was wearing a *dress* in a color we called American Beauty. I can *feel* again my chagrin when I saw also a frilled jabot. My hat was a soft rose-colored beaver and, this I can hardly believe but the image of that mirror is clear on my memory tape, curled down the back was a small ostrich plume in a lighter shade which I must call *pink*.

What the hell I was made up for in this at 9:30 A.M. I cannot tell. I only assume that I'd been out late on a date and had slept either in the city room (we did that too) or with my girl friend, Mabel Normand. Anyhow I hadn't had time to go home and change into daytime clothes and there I was all gussied up like a banana split.

3

G. A large mahogany door with a gold G on it.

To my resolute knock a strong, masculine voice said, "Come in," and in I went, my stomach churning. *He can't do any more than throw you down the elevator shaft* and girl reporters are expendable.

The man surprised me. He looked exactly like a railroad president, the one who made the Big Deal. Few people do—Dempsey and Jack Kennedy and Johnny Unitas and Ev Dirksen and John Glenn—but most not. This was why I stood smiling at him, probably giving him a wrong impression of a hard-working newspaperman covering a hotel beat.

I see that now.

As a matter of fact I saw it then, in about twenty minutes.

He was sitting at a room service table in the window, wearing a fine, dark woolen robe over pajamas that gave a glimpse of bright color. Around him the room was large, magnificently furnished in mahogany and plush, the wall-to-wall carpeting matched dark green drapes caught back by gold rope. Lace curtains had been drawn back, the morning sun and sky were bright enough to suit the Los Angeles Chamber of Commerce, and Sunny Southern California lay waiting for a nod from this lord of all he surveyed, including Santa Monica, San Pedro, and Long Beach just out of range.

My welcome was a lot warmer than I had expected.

He took a good look at me and said, "Well, well—good morning. Come on in."

I said, "Good morning to you. I am—"

He said, "I know—" which seemed odd. How could he? He said, "Had your breakfast?" and I said no—and of course I was always hungry. Moreover, I was trying to put on weight. Falsies had not yet been introduced, and I noted that all the girls at Pearl Morton's had bosoms. So when he picked up the phone for room service I said I'd like hot chocolate with whipped cream and some popovers with strawberry jam. Then I thought I'd better quit, it might take too long. I could see Jack Campbell's eyes peering at me from the end of a stick—the Home, the Street, the Green—all editions would be going, *Get it in here—it's no good to me on the fifth floor of the Alexandria.*

The president of the biggest railroad on earth opened his eyes wide at my order as it was, and I said, "I'm trying to put on a little weight," and he said, "You look all right to me," and I must say he had 'em trained. Food appeared as though by magic.

Panic set in.

My head spun, my heart had begun to sound to me as though I'd swallowed an alarm clock. Mr. Hearst had told me one day in a brief conversation that if the interviewee said *But you haven't interviewed me* you had done a fine job. But that was for the end and here we were, Mister Railroad and I—over the shining silver and napery provided by the Alexandria, me like an unstuck wreath of some kind and he distingué and self-possessed and we were only at the *beginning.* I had been beaten over the head by Campbell with the FACT that this successful Captain of Industry wouldn't tell ANYBODY where Los Angeles Harbor was going. Maybe he had to perform some flumdummery before he told the commission—I realized that he had a gleam in his eye, maybe if we came out first on street corners it would upset his coal car.

I was *in* to be sure—but why should he tell *me?*

Papa never came to me like the Ghost of Hamlet's father in the very armor he had worn, an approach we have allowed Shakespeare as valid for centuries, but I heard his voice as plainly as ever in our lives together. *You are not allowed to lead your witness; nonetheless, you must warm him up, put him at ease—and then lead him to water and make him drink.*

This man had to be an egotist. If this record is to contribute a mite to the sum of human understanding in which to understand all is to forgive all, I have to say here that all the successful men I have ever met, even Einstein, are in some measure egotists. Some emphasis upon and confidence in our ego is vital, otherwise mediocrity triumphs. I had to feel that this Casey Jones was as egotistical about railroads as Julius Caesar about the Roman legions.

"How did you happen to go into railroading, sir?" I asked.

Turned out this was the right leading question.

He told me, from the first stump he ever dug out of a right-of-way, through the first ties he ever laid and the first rails he ever stretched across the Rockies to expand this nation. This was the first railroad president I'd met, the first of those Big Industrialists who made America great I'd ever talked to. So while men are men, whether judges juries accused murderers or governors, the trade language and scenes and stories are different. This one had Daniel Boone elements which were just great. In those early days we were excessively *proud* of our country. We thought it was the greatest. We might have a family fight ourselves, but we never allowed anybody else to speak harshly of or to us.

So I did admire to hear this man tell of the hardships and victories of the men who moved along the steel Road West.

I don't recall exactly when or how we got to the opals.

Because it was then I began to have some idea, not of what was going on, but that something was.

I was naïve—that is true. You kept your virginity partly, I suppose, because without it you couldn't make a good marriage. Also, a good many of us had been brought up to be fastidious. We didn't roll much—either in gutters, back seats of cars, or even the hay. I had been kissed once—by a prize fighter named Stanley Ketchel and Papa had beaten me.

But I had been around though my experience had been academic. I had known McComas, who shot his mistress to death, the prosecution said because he was tired of her, *we* said in self-defense when she threw acid in his face. I remembered the Queen of Chinatown, who had started a tong war. I had never used any of this higher calculus in everyday life.

Now suddenly the Railroad King and Emperor stood before me with a black velvet tray on which lay a dozen gleaming unbelievably beautiful opals.

A jolt went through me.

Whatever its name was, it yanked me to my feet and I stood looking down at the opals—he did a sleight-of-hand and this time it was white velvet and only one, *black,* the devil himself might have worn it between his eyes.

How it happened I didn't yet know, but I was sure that this heavy-set, middle-aged brick-faced Man of La Mancha didn't have any *idea* that I was Miss Rogers of the *Herald.* Who he thought I was or why I'd walked in there I couldn't imagine, but I wished I hadn't eaten those last two popovers. They and the black hell-fire jewel and whatever it was I was trying not to suspect had landed on my jaw like Jack Johnson.

He was still telling me he was a collector, and collectors are collectors are collectors; opals were his birthstone. The opal was, he said, among the stones the ancients engraved, but it was not among the twelve stones which according to Mosaic law were on the breastplate of the high priest—those, he said, were:

Sardonyx Topaz Emerald
Carbuncle Sapphire Jasper
Ligure Agate Amethyst
Chrysolite Onyx Beryl

By that time between the strawberry jam and all it was coming out opalescently in my head as Sardonic Topaz the Green sports edition the Green the Santa Monica Bay the San Pedro Beryl and Long Beach Carbuncles—

Fortunately I knew from A on the fourth floor where the bathroom was and I got there just in time—*those* popovers were never going to help me gain any weight, that was for sure.

Now what?

—any worse than throw you down the elevator shaft—

Now at this time rape I knew was not a common practice. The cop on the beat wouldn't have allowed it, nice girls were chaperoned, they did not go out alone after dark, not girls with families, so the word was never printed, but the son of one of Papa's clients had been charged with it so I had looked it up in the dictionary. Papa was a great one for dictionaries. The one I'd used began the definition of Rape—A brassicaceous plant whose leaves are used for food for sheep—act of seizing and carrying off by force—then the crime of violating a woman forcibly—that had to be it, there was a girl in it, and Papa said that while she was legally underage she intended to use the rape charge for blackmail.

It could not be that any of these applied to my situation in G, and the point *driving* me was that *Campbell* wanted to know where the *harbor* was going. For the first time I was then solidly hit by the reportorial creative urge—my job, my beat, a story my people had a right to know about as soon as possible and I had a right to tell them and a duty to tell them first—

I would not leave this G on the fifth without my STORY.

I took a look at myself in the bathroom mirror. I pinched my cheeks and bit my lips (I had never heard of lipstick), and took off my hat. I remembered that my gentleman callers had spoken kindly of my ash-blond hair.

I began to think in terms of the eight questions Papa had once carefully planned out to ask Spreckels in the Calhoun case—*leading him.*

I can't just romp out and say, Look, friend, what I *really* came to find out is where—

In the first place he wouldn't tell me.

I had been on the right track with the railroads.

So I went back out smiling, and I meant it, and the color had come back to my face and I tossed my hat on the big table as though I meant to *stay*—and *be comfortable.*

My first question was, "Is it because it's your birthstone that you aren't afraid opals will bring you bad luck?"

He said, "Are you afraid of opals?"

I said, "I think I'd be afraid to wear one, I think it's terribly brave of you, but then—does anything scare you?" I don't remember saying you great big wonderful railroad president you, but whatever the black eye-lashes my Irish grandmothers had bequeathed to me could do in that line I did. I felt a fool, on the other hand it kind of settled my stomach. Of course the chocolate couldn't have made me fatter already, but I had a feeling of *being* fatter—almost as if at last I was growing bosoms.

"You know," I said, and I made it a question, "you can't imagine what it is like to hear a man like you telling of the things he has done. One of the greatest men in our country—because you are, I know that much."

He came toward me then, and I stood my ground.

He smelled of soap.

Sometimes you can see a man preening himself, it's the male peacock who has the tail feathers to preen and the lion has the ruff and the gentleman whale who spouts—this big guy coming toward me was preening and ruffing and I said, It must be wonderful to think of the great things you've done—I never met a man like you before—I said, What was the big moment in your whole life?

And he stood still, a-preening and a-strutting, but he stopped to brag, the big peacock spreading all his feathers for the little hen, and he laughed a little spout of laughter and said, "It's strange you should ask me that right now—because tonight—tonight—is going to be one of the big ones. You've heard of Los Angeles Harbor?"

For a minute I didn't know whether to say, Yes or What *is* it—but I thought I'd better know, so I said Yes very low, and I took a big breath and moved back a couple of steps so I could look up at him and also be nearer the door, and I opened my eyes very wide and said, "Nobody knows about that, we have to wait—you don't mean you *know?*"

He began to laugh some more. He said, "I can tell you it's going to San Pedro and I'm the man that's going to put it there—"

I could see how exactly like Chanticleer he was, now he had to crow, and when he crowed little Perilot would see the sun come up over San Pedro at his command—

He said, "You'll read about it in tomorrow's papers—"

To myself I said, If I do I will eat your opals—if I don't read about it in this afternoon's homestreetgreen—timetimetime—time is passing—I pass on to you there is no moment when you say to a man, *What time is it,* but he will look at his watch. I said, "Oh—what time is it?" And the Grand Sachem of all the railroads looked for his watch, which I had seen on the dressing table, and I was out the door and going downstairs like a rattlesnake coming down the mountain. I never did stop for an elevator. Crossing the lobby on a dead run, I saw Johnny the bell captain. He stopped dead and stared at me; he had a girl with him. I noticed her because she had such bright blond hair and she looked quite *young*—but my head didn't have room for it so I broke the four-minute mile between the Alexandria and our office and came up to the city desk like Pepper Martin sliding into second base.

Campbell stared at me with that *So you killed a bear* look he kept for our lower moments. He said, "You say he *told* you the harbor is going to San Pedro."

I nodded. I couldn't get my breath to say it again; one braid had flopped down and I'd lost most of my hairpins.

"How did he happen to do that?" Campbell said.

A strange hush had fallen on the city room. Somewhere a phone kept ringing and ringing and nobody answered it. The presses were going—I must have missed the home edition—but the city room was silent, city rooms are like that, unless they have antennae they are no good. "Well," I said, "what do you care *how*—as long as he did?" I said, "He was kind of bragging about it—"

Campbell looked at me again. "He said the words San Pedro—"

I'd had a nervous morning. I yelled at him. I said, "Yes—yes—he said San Pedro—that's what he said—San Pedro—"

"Take it easy, Sister," Campbell said, and picked up the phone.

"I wouldn't be your sister," I said. "Why would I—"

Breaking a couple of their own records, in came Guy Barham, the publisher, natty and suave, and Sam Blythe of Washington and *The Saturday*

Evening Post, and behind them—dear gods and little fishes hells bells is this good or bad? *Mr. Hearst.* Calmest of them all. This meant that the harbor was important enough economically, civically, politically so that Mr. Hearst had come down to talk it over personally.

Campbell told them. He said, "Miss Rogers says the harbor is going to San Pedro. She got in to see the man. She says he—just let her in and he *told* her it's *San Pedro.*"

This was my first time of working directly with W.R.H.

In a voice of precision he said, "He may have mistaken you for somebody else, though it doesn't quite seem possible. Did you tell him you were a reporter from the *Herald?*"

By this time I was shaking. So was my windpipe. I managed to say, No Mr. Hearst—I tried—but he just said yes yes I know who you are—

"Hmmmm—" said Mr. Hearst.

"Did he chase you?" Guy Barham said. He was a debonair man-of-the-world type and he was by this time wearing a broad *joie de vivre* grin.

I said, "No and he couldn't have caught me if he had. He told me a lot about Daniel Boone and how he himself dug stumps out of—he was—he seemed to feel he wanted to tell me about *himself*—"

"People always do, especially men," Mr. Hearst said. "Did you get the impression that he is quite sure of carrying the Commission with him?"

I said, "I don't think anybody is going to give this character any back talk about where he wants to put Los Angeles Harbor—"

The city room was holding its breath.

Then for the first time Mr. Hearst said to me what he was to say over and over—like when he made the publisher print my Unemployed Women series—"Miss Rogers, are you sure of your facts?"

And I gave him the same answer, "Yes Mr. Hearst I'm sure of my facts."

If a silence can get silenter this one did.

Sam Blythe said thoughtfully, "This is quite a feller. I've met him in Washington. He's always been a gambler. He didn't get where he is however without judgment of what his hand is worth if he's called for a showdown. If I were you, I'd call him—"

Mr. Hearst was utterly immobile for about three seconds then he said, "You know him, Mr. Blythe. Go into Mr. Barham's office and call him—I agree that is the honorable and also the wise thing to do."

So Blythe disappeared. When he came back he had a broad smile. "He's a sport," he said. "He says to tell Miss Rogers she left her hat."

How long I continued to blush I don't know. I remember as though it was yesterday how it felt up my neck and into my hair.

Campbell said, "We better get going—"

I started over to my typewriter and I heard Campbell saying, "She can't write this for chrisake. She can't write her name. She's never written a goddam thing except recipes and symposiums and women's features— why don't we let Sam Blythe—lucky he's here—"

I froze.

I turned all the way around. I saw Ike St. Johns looking at me across the copy desk from under his eyeshade. To the tune of "Sons of the Stanford Red" Ike was holding out a pair of copy shears and this time *I* wasn't going to let old J.B.T. get into any telephone booth and I had forgotten all about Mr. Hearst when his always dulcet tone *carried* like a bugle to the whole room in the silence.

He said, "Mr. Campbell, it appears to me that Miss Rogers has brought us an impressive exclusive story. It showed a great deal of—enterprise—and courage for Miss Rogers to obtain this newsworthy and historic fact. I have always been in favor of allowing reporters to write the stories they get if it is possible—I expect we ought to let Miss Rogers write her own story and I expect she can write her own name at the top of it. Perhaps Mr. Blythe would be so kind as to sit down beside her and make himself available for consultation—"

Campbell said, *Yes Mr. Hearst* with four grains of arsenic concealed in it—

Sam Blythe said softly, "Get a direct quote in the second paragraph—"

LOS ANGELES HARBOR TO SAN PEDRO
By Adela Rogers

My first by-line. I remember when they brought up the wet smelly first editions and I saw this headlined on the front page, I cried.

Guy Barham made a fortune, just as Earl Rogers could have made a fortune out of the Griffith case when his client offered him half of what later became Griffith Park. Perfectly legal, both of them. But the Rogers never got *acres*. On our pilgrimage through this incarnation we get money only for work. The only time I ever got it any other way was at Las Vegas when Farmer Page and Guy McAfee were there and *somebody* had to win.

Mr. Hearst didn't either. Real estate wasn't his game though he told me often to buy Southern California and he did buy some of it for Marion. I think Mr. Hearst was naïve about real estate or he wouldn't have let his pal and No. 1 columnist Arthur Brisbane make such a sucker of him in New York. Getting property is one thing. Holding it is a real estate man's game.

Probably I had been naïve about the man in G.

One explanation must be made. The line between a girl whom the bell captain would supply on request, to keep a lonely man far from home company at breakfast if he wanted company at breakfast *and* a girl like Adela Rogers, was very distinct. As I see her back down through the wrong end of my periscope, the difference was sharp as a razor's edge. In the name of so-called freedom, all those lines are growing less plain to the naked eye or the naked soul. In a free and freeloading society it would be harder if not impossible for a man to know whether the girl had been called from Madame Francis or was a friend of his daughter's arriving for the day.

At first, then, it bothered me a good deal that even in that *blight* of a dress and the ostrich plume such a mistake could be made. I figured out that he was *expecting* the girl he'd asked Johnny to get and we often see what we expect to see. And second that as a newspaperwoman I would from time to time be required to convince somebody that I was somebody else and not a reporter. Or at least as Mr. Hearst said make them forget that I was an interviewer.

I admired that Grand Sachem very much.

He could have denied saying any of it and where would I have been then? Mr. Hearst might have decided to go with me—but that would have been a long chance. Or he might have decided to tell all the papers—industrial leaders had no public relations counsels in those days.

If I hadn't been afraid he'd try to make me take another opal I'd have gone back after my hat.

Mr. Hearst sent me a new one. At that time he had Mrs. Hearst pick it out for me. It was his first move toward keeping me the best-dressed girl reporter.

When I showed up on my beat the next morning Johnny the bell captain had already seen the headlines of the afternoon before—they would have been hard to miss. And the follow-ups in the *Times* and *Examiner* after confirmation.

He said, "I had expected to be back earlier."

I said, "Well—I guess it was good luck for me you weren't."

Will the *real* lady of the morning please stand up? I always thought I'd kind of liked to have a picture of Mister Railroad's face when she did!

One night during the Alfred Landon Presidential convention in Cleveland, John Aloysius Clements and I were sitting around having a few beers and I said, "Do you know it's possible that one experience flavored my whole career such as it is?"

He said, "One experience flavors everybody's career. Or maybe three or four. You just have to figure them out."

I didn't tell him what experience I was talking about.

I wasn't sure about it anyhow.

Except that I did figure out that in those days men had all the advantages—and a girl had a right to use what she could, up to a point.

Even in *pink,* that railroadman should have known better. It was his own fault. He was a good sport but, men being men, it was his peacock feathers that got him into trouble.

CHAPTER 3

This was a breed of *men,* the Hearst city editors.

Often I wonder about the nice, good-looking, photogenic, clean-cut poised and imperturbable reporters on news television. Even on the scene of a story, do they miss having a city editor breathing fire and brimstone down their necks?

One like Walter Howey.

For he was the pattern and paragon of this breed called the Terrible Men.

No one, *no one,* in his right mind would work for Howey, the star team of Ben Hecht and Charlie MacArthur (who married Helen Hayes) used to say. Except they'd rather work for him than any other editor alive and always did and wrote *The Front Page,* the smashingly successful newspaper play around him, to prove it. Singing in a Gravel Gertie voice was Howey's only way of expressing kindly emotion. Many's the time when the city room was going mad on a photo-finish deadline I've seen the great editor fancy-skating between desks to his own version of "Has Anybody Here Seen Kelly" just to tell us he was with us and he *cared.* Otherwise nobody would know how he felt. One of his eyes was glass. We assumed someone had shot it out during the back alley circulation war when he was on the Chicago *Tribune* before Mr. Hearst lured him away. It was hard to tell which was the glass one, Ben Hecht said it was the *warmer* one, and finally Jack Clements, Howey's favorite reporter, asked the undertaker, but that was too late to do anybody any good. He saw more news, more color, more features, got out a better paper with one eye than anybody else ever did with two. He created news.

I always sort of wished that the glamorous bewitching millionaire grande dame Washington hostess, member of the Medill and McCormick families and publisher of the Washington *Times-Herald,* one Cissy Patterson, *had* married Howey, as, morally, I suppose, she should have. Or should I say that the violent, coarse, irresistible musketeer torpedo and dynamo, whom I once heard recite *King Lear* in its entirety without a break, had married Eleanor Medill Patterson. Wouldn't that have been something? Howey *en résidence* as the prince consort in Cissy's mansion in Washington with its staff of eighteen servants. Or Cissy trailing and bejeweled in Howey's New York flat over a grocery store on Forty-fourth

Street in New York so he'd be close to the office and from whose windows Kitty, his girl friend, used to pour beer or worse on him, if he came home and rang after she'd locked him out.

They almost did get married, you know. Cissy and Howey.

I was going to be a witness.

I regret that—I'd sure like to have seen it.

I have to back Howey.

Whatever other titles Howey acquired—and he acquired them all—managing editor, publisher, head of International News Photos, he was never and never wanted to be anything but a glorified city editor.

The prototype of the terrible man was duplicated behind the city desk of Hearst newspapers in New York, Chicago, Detroit, San Francisco, Atlanta, Boston, Denver, Seattle, Los Angeles, Portland, and Philadelphia. And of course in Ray Helgesen of the Washington *Herald*. I suppose it was inevitable that the psychic trauma of my most unforgettable true love should have been one of them.

Helgesen was the very model of an audacious city editor.

Actually, the nearest thing to Howey I ever saw was the aforementioned Jack Campbell, who was crouching behind the city desk when I reported to the Los Angeles *Herald*.

John B. T. Campbell was a native Californian of a fine old family. He was a tall cadaverous lantern-jawed icy-gray-eyed Scotchman once removed. Like all newspapermen he took off his coat immediately on entering the city room, never his vest. Men then wore vests. The sport jacket had not been invented, if a man came to work with coat and pants that didn't match we concluded he was broke or woke up drunk.

Do not ask what the B.T. stood for. B. went without saying. T.? The nominations were varied—Torquemada, Third Rail, Tyrannus as in Sic Semper but Juana Neal Levy won with Tarantula, which she allowed was a large black spider at sight of whom horses in the early West had been known to jump ten feet sideways.

Juana Neal Levy was our society editor and she had what she thought was more reason than most to thus identify Campbell, who was strictly a front page man. Nobody could convince him that anybody bought a paper to turn back and read a society, club, dramatic, or even sports page. Thus he opened Juana's mail, listened on her phone and laid traps to get Society over onto page 1. Since our Juana and those she considered worthy to belong on her pages believed a lady should have her name in the paper only on the occasions of birth, marriage, motherhood and death, she fought her city editor tooth and nail.

Once when she went on a vacation, poor soul, Campbell got the bright idea of putting me in to pitch for her. After all my Aunty Blanche, Mrs. Harry Clifford Lott, and my grandmother, Mrs. Lowell Lynch Rogers, were still in the Blue Book though Papa and I had been dropped. Being myself impregnated with the Tarantula's front page doctrine, I handed over Grace Harvey's engagement to Bernardo deBaker Shorb, a marriage in the Sartori family, and a costume ball at the Childs mansion on Adams Street and when she came back Juana said not even the chairman of a charity luncheon would speak to her.

Old B. for you-know-what and T. for Tarantula Campbell got the clubs into headline contention the time I met Alice-Don't-Sit-by-the-Fireside Winters.

Before me I have a note to J.B.T.—one of the famous ones signed W.R.H. This was preserved by Herb Krauch, an office boy when I was a cub, who in time became managing editor.

> Dear Mr. Campbell; Your front page is excellent. I find pages 2, 3 and 4 lack both substance and sparkle in prose poetry and pictures. WRH

Campbell forced upon us a furious campaign of substance-and-sparkle until we were daffy and dizzy.

Why did we put up with J. B. T. Campbell?

We knew. He was on our side. Always. We knew nobody else from the White House down was ever going to holler at one of *his* reporters. We knew how good he was as a city editor and great city editors make great reporters if they live through it.

Our love for Campbell and Howey was streaked with pain, stained with flashes of hate, but it was love.

I ask you to remember that two things were safe and inviolate.

NEWS.

No advertising man ever set foot in Campbell's city room. EVER. Once when on his way to the Waldorf Bar, he heard the advertising head ask me to dinner and he damn near fired me though I'd said no *instantly*. Badly as at times he wanted to get rid of his first girl reporter he wouldn't allow her to go that way.

We had no *sponsors*. We were as separated from the advertising department as the poles.

Second to this was the *authority* of a good city editor and everybody, including the young, longs for trustworthy authority.

Mostly the publisher of a paper was a fine-looking front man and the managing editor could be overridden without looking. All Mr. Hearst's suggestions or orders, written in the margins of the papers with a large soft black copy pencil, were addressed, not to the M.E. but to the city editor. Lee Ettelson, for whom I worked in the old days, has entrusted me with a priceless collection of these notes, which have never been out of his hands before. They go to prove that while Mr. Hearst was the Commander-in-Chief and could make the decisions, the Hearst Service, when it was the proudest newspaper army that ever existed, believed in the city editor as the Marine Corps believes in the top sergeant.

These margin memos to Lee Ettelson, as the city editor next in genius and power to Howey himself, prove that Mr. Hearst thought so too.

On a copy of the rival San Francisco *News* on September 6, 1938:

> Dear Mr. Ettelson. Our fashions are awful. These are better and not so good at that WRH

On the San Francisco *Call-Bulletin* of April 28 in the margin beside a picture of ten women caught in a police raid:

> Dear Mr. Ettelson. This makes a rather sad and sordid picture. I doubt the advisability of thus exhibiting these poor wretches
> WRH

All around the top and margins of the San Francisco *Examiner* on September 5, he scrawled:

> I would like Mr. Ettelson to go to Chicago and New York and install this make-up on the Chicago Examiner and the New York American. I would also like him to find someone on the paper capable of maintaining it. We need *tasteful* and resourceful city editors, especially on the night side.

In answer to a memo from the Chief evidently making some specific comments on one day's editions of the *Herald,* Jack Campbell wrote his mind on four or five outspoken sheets of copy paper. Nobody ever backed away from telling Mr. Hearst anything. One of the reasons he loved Marion Davies with complete devotion for over thirty years was that she stuttered when she did it, but she sassed him back. This always made Mr. Hearst roar with laughter.

Campbell's irascible letter drew this never-before-published answer from Mr. Hearst, which helps establish the early atmosphere in which I lived and moved and had my being, and the character and genius of *the* man who influenced us all.

Let it be noted that he employed a rapier, never a bludgeon.

> *Office of William Randolph Hearst*
> *Wyntoon, McCloud, California*
> *December 13, 1943*

My dear Mr. Campbell:

If you are not "in the habit of blowing your own horn" you certainly made up in your last letter for any lack of previous practice.

But your letter is not merely a recognition of your own obvious merit, it is largely shadow boxing.

You are repelling attacks that have not been made.

Everybody knows that the Herald-Express is a good and growing newspaper.

It has been while you were editor and please God it will be when you are gathered to your father—which I hope will be many years from now.

Everybody knows, too, that you are a good editor.

If I did not think so, you would not be editor of so important a paper as the Herald-Express.

Everybody knows that the Herald-Express has many good qualities, characteristics and features, and that is the reason we do not want to lose too many of them by inept condensation.

The point is not these obvious facts above mentioned.

The point is that the Herald-Express can be improved, as you very wisely say.

Well, then, let us improve it without so much circumlocution.

I said let you and I improve it, but if you do not like the association, I will assume the responsibility of issuing the instructions.

I hope you will be so good as to carry them out.

Indeed, you have already done so in large degree, as shown by the sample pages submitted to me.

I approve of all the emendations and restorations, but I still do not particularly like "Sergeant Pat".

I think you have better material available.

There is no objection to buying outside comics if you can get good ones.

What we lack is space, not money, and good comics take up no more space than bad ones.

I doubt if you really have to buy comics.

It would seem to me that in condensing four pages of comics into two it would be possible to fill two pages effectively and still lose "Sergeant Pat".

Will you please see if this cannot be done.

In other respects the improvements are entirely satisfactory.

Sincerely
W. R. Hearst

We who became the *Herald* got out a paper that became the biggest moneymaker and circulation smash in the evening field anywhere, matching the fabulous growth of the City of Angels. Our secret was Local News.

We preferred our own murders to those headlined in another city. We'd read about a home-town girl named Clara Phillips, who beat her husband's girl friend to death with a rock, rather than Ruth Snyder, bopping her husband with a sash weight in New York. Between a good name-calling uproar in our City Council or Board of Education *and* a hassle in Congress, the headline went local every time. We took States' Rights for granted, Civil Rights were as undiscussed as space travel. The local readers were interested in where we were going to put Los Angeles Harbor, which would increase values and paychecks, not in any Presidential doings, most of those began in a one-column head on page 1 or 2 and jumped immediately to page 18, Outer Mongolia newswise. What a city official said to his girl friend in some indiscreet and very funny letters (the other fellow's always are, aren't they?) startled us more than whether or not President Harding had an illegitimate daughter.

The place where we got out this paper was called the City Room. In the Movies, on TV, on Broadway, city rooms are shown. They are never true. A city room has to be *real;* the fact that it is real, dealing with real people always, never simulated, the stuff out of which drama, comedy and tragedy are woven is *there* in utter reality, is what makes it different from all else. This tempo, spirit, inner drive got out six or seven editions a day, though a buck would get you a hundred that it couldn't be done.

Not in *that* city room.

Mr. Hearst could have afforded a city room filled with priceless antiques, of which he had $40,000,000 worth in a New York warehouse, with Georgian silver, of which he had the finest collection outside the British Museum, with automatic carriers for copy and clean linoleum on the floor.

He knew better.

Ours was, say, about as big as the fifth grade schoolroom.

Dark, airless, noisy, and crowded beyond anything you would believe. At right angles was the city desk, copy went from the city editor to the copy desk, built like a crap table with one man in the slot and the rest around the rim. The flow got more frenzied as the deadline of each edition approached every hour or so. Behind the copy desk was the door into the composing room, where ink-stained overalled linotype operators set the copy for the big presses and *they* got more frantic too. I have a dim impression of two or three minutes after you heard the presses start to roll and roar when you could relax, but when that edition came up, we took a fast look and went to work on the next one. The spaces in the city room were so narrow you had to run sideways—*walk* we knew not of. No no, we ran.

At each end of the city room were cubbyholes about as large as your pantry, in one of which sat the sports editor, in the other was the drama department, where one day I saw D. W. Griffith borrow $250 to meet his day's payroll for *Birth of a Nation*. We passed the hat.

A door also opened into the darkrooms. Here the cameramen Stagg, Haley, and Blackwell reigned amid stinks and bubbling caldrons and from them carried forth box cameras as big as suitcases. Dark as Tutankhamen's tomb, walls were plastered with glossies of unusual corpses, freak accidents, and girls honestly naked. How any of these three gents got girls to pose in the nude I didn't then understand. Stagg told me he had never known a girl who wouldn't strip for the camera if asked—and a stroll down Fifth Avenue today confirms Stagg's conclusions. Nobody asks them but they're still trying. Haley kept his large white pet bulldog in his pigeonhole. Stagg and Blackwell insisted that once on hearing a most peculiar growl they found Haley with his teeth sunk in the dog's ear. Yet it was this same Haley I personally heard say to the beautiful Queen of the Belgians, *Skirt a little higher, Queenie, you got nothing to be ashamed of* —and with a slightly bewildered but—could it have been *flattered?*—look, Her Majesty obliged. I can see Stagg in puttees like Cecil B. DeMille's jumping from behind a marble angel in Evergreen Cemetery and shouting at a woman kneeling beside her husband's grave to make her look up into the lens—true, the deceased had been shot by one of his three other wives but that wasn't her fault, and I thought Stagg was unnecessarily blunt on that occasion. However we had an exclusive shot of the widow and the grave and that ought to teach men not to go around leading double or triple lives.

Photographers used long metal troughs set on handles in the middle into which they poured Flash Powder. They pulled a chain with one hand and snapped the camera shutter with the other, sometimes it went off and sometimes it didn't. We were trying to get a picture of a cardinal one day. The device would not flash after six or seven times and I started to investigate and nearly got my head blown off. The cardinal was very patient with us, I recall.

If you know cameramen you learn a great deal about the human race.

Let me add reporters.

We owned the earth.

We were the guardians of the Four Freedoms.

We all believed this. I believed it then, I still do. A press controlled by sponsors or advertisers, TV or otherwise, is not a free press, don't let anybody kid you.

The traditions of our country, its glories, its growing culture, its right to protection and explanation from its leaders—since they worked for the people, as we understood it, all these were in our hands. And we were RESPONSIBLE. I never knew a really *irresponsible* editor or reporter where *news* was concerned.

William Randolph Hearst caught us young and taught us young. On the wall of every city room hung his credo—SPEED AND ACCURACY. If you couldn't do the first, or didn't do the second, you got fired. A lot of that was destroyed as columnists took over, but then news couldn't be guesswork, gossip, or speculation.

For a while I didn't have a desk. Only a shelf with my typewriter and telephone on it. *This is Miss Rogers of the Herald.*

One fine day I felt a presence behind me and, looking over my shoulder, I saw Mr. Hearst looming slightly taller than the City Hall. With an inscrutable face he was regarding a big sign the boys in the composing room had made for me and I had tacked up on the wall—VOTE FOR WOODROW WILSON—which I wasn't old enough to do but I wanted to take my stand. The Hearst papers were not for Woodrow Wilson. So I probably turned green as I gave with what I hoped was an imperturbable but cheery good morning to the man who owned them. He smiled down at me and said in a mild voice, "I never expected to buy your vote, Miss Rogers. However I do prefer uncommitted reporters in all fields. They can report the news better if they have neither preconceived ideas nor loyalties."

One more stupendous factor was another long shelf that tied our city room to the nation and the outside world. Here sat the telegraph instrument with Blitzen Benz brooding over it. Blitzen remains a legend in the newspaper world. He was supposed to have beaten Beany Walker, sports editor of our morning *Examiner,* who sported a cane and had 377 stickpins wrapped in chamois which he carried in his pocket, and was alleged to be the best poker player west of Dodge City. The only thing that ever halted the reverberating pandemonium of the city room was a shout from Blitzen. With no radio, no television, we got the great news flashes by wire—also the results of elections, world series, murder juries, and death watches.

Of course our city room was a firetrap. A test tube for breeding tubercular germs. A dust bowl. A wastebasket. An anteroom to the psycho ward. No factory owner would have dared to ask his laborers to work under such conditions nor would the state have allowed it if he had.

We adored it.

We never went home if we could help it.

I suppose it was psychologically sound to say that my initial romances were in this, to us, most romantic of all settings in the world. It also gives me a chance to explain how and for what Sad Seagrove, our courthouseman, became famous, and remains so, even on a street with so short a memory as Madison Avenue.

I can give it to you best by quoting from a book written long afterwards by another rookie reporter of that day whom Campbell brought up to be the Last of the Terrible Men. Or so *The Saturday Evening Post* in a profile labeled him when he was city editor of the Los Angeles *Examiner*.

In his book Jimmy Richardson said:

> Sad Seagrove was a poet and as such he was always in love. He went from one girl to another and celebrated them in song and story which he sold to Smart Set and others. Until Adela Rogers St. Johns came to work on the Herald as our first girl reporter. Sad really fell in love with her as hard as I ever saw any man fall in love. Adela wasn't Adela Rogers St. Johns then. She was simply Adela Rogers, daughter of the greatest criminal lawyer America has produced. Sad tried hard. But he lost Adela. Along came a tall handsome guy, Ike St. Johns, fresh out of Stanford, who became another good newspaperman. Adela married him, and Sad didn't stay around long after that.
>
> "I'm carrying a torch that can only be extinguished in the gentle surf on the beach at Waikiki," he said to me, and took off for Honolulu.
>
> Sad is famous forever. For having written *two* sentences. Among the best known in the United States. He had everything money can bring a man but he told me he'd never been so happy as when he was a reporter on the Herald, trying to kill Campbell and marry Adela. "Now I'm an advertising man," he said, "and it serves me right that my success story is ulcers." You want to know about the two sentences? One was
>
> ALWAYS A BRIDESMAID BUT NEVER A BRIDE
> and
>
> YOUR BEST FRIEND WON'T TELL YOU.

On a clear day, you can see a long ways back. My teen-age romances seem brighter to me now—I was too busy being a reporter to get the full benefit of them then—youth, as they say, is sometimes wasted on the young. My outstanding memory of Black Thursday in 1929 when the market crash brought us down in the Depression, is of Sad. I was staying with Damon and Pat Runyon at a hotel half a block from Madison Square Garden when out of the woodwork it seemed, alone and palely loitering, came a wraith who said his name was Seagrove and he'd just lost a quarter of a million dollars, his life's savings. Sad had always been a tight man with a dime. I remember he had some drinks and sat on the floor and, repetitious as only drunks can be, kept *asking* me, and I kept telling him, "I wouldn't have lived with ulcers on Madison Avenue that's for sure."

In this glorious last half of my life for which the first I know now was planned, I get a little kick out of remembering some of the poems the greatest copy writer of all time composed for me—even if I can't find any of them now.

Hours never occurred to us, Sad Seagrove and Jimmy Richardson and Ike St. Johns and Jim Pope—a superior court judge of fame later on—we worked with dynamic enthusiasm. In my own case when I first went to work on an evening paper there it meant taking a big red electric car from Santa Monica—I always lived by the ocean if I could, I still do—at 4:30 A.M. so I could be in the city room to take the overnight telegraph flimsies Blitzen had put on my shelf—and this was I am sure a better training than any School of Journalism. How lucky I was! I worked through the day on running stories, and stayed until I finished with features for page 1 of the second section, which was Campbell's hobby as it were. I was responsible for the ART there, too. Pretty girls if possible but they had to *tie in* or we'd hear in one of those W.R.H. messages.

> Dear Mr. Ettelson: This is not a good picture, it has display but isn't interesting and has no news value.

> Dear Mr. Ettelson: Query. Is the Call a bit too merely decorative in its illustrations? Should we not be a little more *vigorous?* I am enclosing a Herald. It is just as attractive pictorially as the Call but it seems to have more vigor. Perhaps pictorially we can get a little more *interested* in the News.

Thus along around three o'clock after about nine hours' work and after the last home edition had gone to press and we had only the Green, with sports and any big story break, I turned my attention to putting more vigor on the first page of the second section. I worked on that sometimes until nine or ten o'clock for the next day.

Glee was the word for my response to this.

How young I was. Eighteen going on nineteen. How young we all were. Old man Campbell was all of thirty-two.

We did all this because we liked our work best as *a way of life*.

We stayed and worked late because we would rather be together in the city room than anywhere else on earth.

CHAPTER 4

My first murder case as a reporter was not local. While it took place in Los Angeles, it rocked the nation. The murderer of his pregnant sweetheart was a slight, pleasant-faced youth named Harry New who turned out to be the bastard son of the Postmaster General of the United States.

My copy out of that courtroom bore for the first time:

By Adela Rogers *St. Johns*

I didn't want to give up being Miss Rogers. Papa said I must be Mrs. St. Johns so as not to belittle Ike's feelings. I suppose I gave in easily, at eighteen a girl wants to be *Mrs.* somebody—anybody. Our marriage had startled the city room. A reporter learns early what the copy desk can do to your copy, which, they said, might explain why I married him. The handsome young man from Stanford was head of that desk. The city room had a theory as to why he married me. Miss Rogers' handwriting was illegible. Our typewriters at the *Herald* were three-deckers, one for small letters, one for capitals, one for numerals and punctuation; Olivers they were called, having been invented by a clergyman of that name who couldn't read his handwritten sermons in the pulpit. Learning to type on one was fearsome. When they went next door to the Waldorf Bar, where no female had ever been allowed to accompany them, Jack Campbell, Wes Barr, Hub Collins, and rewrite man McGilverary decided that Ike, who suffered most from the chaotic results in my copy, thought that if he married me he might persuade me to stay home and this would do away with some of the uproar on his copy desk.

It wasn't quite as newspaperese and unromantic as that.

On a moonlight night while we strolled along the boardwalk between Santa Monica and Venice, Ike had told me he loved me and how about getting married? It seemed all right when he kissed me tenderly but I had to say I did not think well of marriage on account of my father and mother. Look at Florence Campbell, I said, married to J.B.T. In the beginning she must have thought it was tender and romantic. And now, Ike said with a grin, Jack Campbell is the most henpecked man this side of the Rockies.

Besides, he said, you're always talking about babies and you can't have babies unless you marry somebody.

That gave me pause. "No, I can't," I said.

If I remember correctly, it was his taking me out to the sprawling white St. Johns mansion in that serene Quaker suburb of Whittier to meet his folks that turned the trick. His father, born in England (where I found when I went there to work for Beaverbrook in London they pronounced the name Sinjon), was dead. His mother, a redheaded matriarch, examined me politely but exhaustively and left me in no doubt that the idea of her oldest son marrying Earl Rogers' daughter filled her with dismay. From all she'd heard of the both of us, she would try to thwart such a disreputable and déclassé mésalliance with all her strength.

So going back on the big red suburban car, I told Ike I would marry him right away.

He was bowled over with surprise, and, it appeared, delight. He'd been afraid the way his mother behaved might have put me off. Naturally I didn't tell him that I had to marry him after that. I couldn't let her get away with forbidding him to marry Earl Rogers' daughter.

Anyhow, my real reason was to have a baby.

I do not think I then understood any other reason for marrying anybody.

So I was Mrs. St. Johns when I walked into the Harry New murder case.

No stage fright could come to me from a courtroom, of course. I'd spent most of my life in them. Setting, procedure, vocabulary were as familiar to me as the palm of my hand. To my utter panic, however, I found I was writing the afternoon feature story while Winifred Black did it for the mornings.

Miss Black was the first consistent star newspaperwoman. Never a reporter in city room parlance as I was, for years she'd done color, feature, profiles and semieditorial columns on big stories. Since the morning papers then had no night-before editions, she could go back to the office, write at leisure, rewrite to add literary touches, quotes, and remove errors. While I on my first courtroom assignment had to do it in pencil, in the press box, on gray paper and hand it sheet by sheet to a copy boy and never see it again.

This is what Papa and I used to call a brillig situation requiring nothing less than your best and that in a hell of a hurry.

I was hypnotized by the sight of the great Winifred Black, sitting in the front row of the press box, wrapped in white Irish lace that for a moment I thought she'd snitched from Bishop Conaty's windows. As the Reigning American Beauty, *Lillian* Russell was only a couple of years behind us and Lillian's hips and bosoms would have made *Jane* Russell look like the paper on the wall. Winifred Black was of this school. The sight of her ample curves made me feel like I'd sprung a leak. A boyish figure was in those days a sunless sea. Ike and I were earning $32.50 a week between us, so my usual tailored suit was an old one from San Francisco days and pretty shabby. Papa's dictum that it was always better to be *under* than *over* dressed was cold comfort to Cinderella amid the ashes.

The last person I expected to play godmother to me was the celebrity in the press box wearing a black velvet hat and ostrich plumes with her lace.

A cop testified to how bitterly young Harry New wept when he surrendered the body of his dead love to the night lieutenant at the police station, and a piece of gray copy paper was passed down to me. Scrawled on it was *I'd make that my lead now if I were you. You won't get anything better this morning. WB.* All through the trial these continued. *I'd jump ahead now to say that New is going to testify that when the girl wouldn't marry him because he was so poor, his own anguish overcame him because of what he himself had suffered as a bastard child. If you do it now in imagination you'll be ahead of us all.* Big things, little things. *Notice his ears.* And *How about all of us starting to see whether we can make the Postmaster General come out to testify, it's all his fault.* Though he did get the boy a lawyer, he never appeared in the courtroom.

I was overwhelmed by all Winifred Black did for me. The big thing I never knew until years later. I was staying up at the Ranch and one day Mr. Hearst sent for me to come up to his rooms in the Tower. As he turned over some papers in a leather box he said, "I've always intended to give you this," and handed me a worn piece of that old gray copy paper.

In black copy pencil was written, "Dear W.R. I know you have been concerned about who is to take my place when I retire in a couple of years. Don't worry any more. I've just seen her. Her name is Adela Rogers St. Johns. Yours lovingly, Winifred."

I can't help it—I still get tears in my eyes when I read that.

The jury convicted Harry New. Next time I saw him he was serving his life sentence at San Quentin, where I was doing some stories on how prison life affected women. By that time, Harry New was secretary to Warden Houlihan and came in to listen to *Amos and Andy* on the radio with us. He told me then he had done the right thing, he'd never regretted it. Illegitimacy carried a stigma, he told me. "I knew the child would suffer all his life." The pendulum may have swung too far the other way in our time, when a mother of enough little bastards can live well on a government subsidy, but that is better than what Harry New called "the stigma" and for which he killed.

2

You want babies, you can't have any unless you get married.
So I got married.
I lost my first one.
Many people did then.

I grieved most desperately. I can still feel, deep down, the vibrations of that shock and pain. It was too early for me to realize in thought that when, at nine, I had said when I grew up I wanted to be a lady with a baby I was speaking the simple truth. But in my stomach I knew it.

I was shaken to the roots of my confused being by a profound perplexity and suspense as to whether or not I was worthy to have a baby. I did not exactly believe in God any more. On the other hand, neither could I believe that *Ike and I* doing what we did *had created a baby*. Nobody in his right mind, I thought, could believe *that*.

Maybe the God in whom I didn't exactly believe didn't think I could be trusted with a baby. Then why did he give me one in the first place at all? Maybe he was a jealous God. A God of vengeance. A punishing God.

No. My grandfather, who had taught me the Bible from three to eight years old, said no. Grace, he said, had come to us by Jesus Christ. The Bible was part of my being, my blood stream, what we now call my subconscious, and in it the Old Testament God was full of hell-fire and brimstone, of which I'd heard a good deal more than of *grace*.

Back from the grooves of my childhood played the word sin.

Sin?

Why did He make us capable of sin and then punish me by letting my baby die?

What was my sin, anyway?

Being fresh and funny about God, saying I regarded Christ's teachings as antiquated for our brilliant young generation? Without meaning for everyday life and its *tears*. Sheep and casting nets and raising the dead! As I look back on me, I wasn't filled with honest doubt of my grandfather's *grace*, just plain self-centered I-want-what-I-want-when-I-want-it, I was not about to be obedient to anybody's eight-thousand-year-old commandments. Get drunk once in a while. Play a little poker. I was *married* to Ike so that was all right.

Look at my mother.

Her own brother once told me he was sure she'd been born of Beelzebub. Whatever she did maybe she didn't know any better. I had come to feel a very little that I didn't understand what her temptations were. But

I knew she had helped to destroy my father, there could be no doubt about that. I knew the hell of her black tempers and—other things.

She'd had four babies and all of them lived.

A slow burn began to come up through what had become indifference about God.

All this came over me with loud bugle notes and harsh drumbeats on a cold and lonely night not long after I lost my baby.

We were living, Ike and I, in a cheap apartment on Fifth Street where the Los Angeles Public Library now stands. I had done nothing to make it any warmer or more homelike, I hadn't the time nor the money nor the know-how. I lay there listening for the telephone to ring, wondering where the hell Ike was. In a poker game bigger than he could afford? Or with some gal he'd picked up when he'd been drinking? Or laid out in the morgue the way by now I'd seen other I-was-right-all-right drivers.

Woman's work as a listener is never done. In a frantic self-pity I thought I'd spent too much of my life listening for some damn man, for my father and now for my husband. My resentment got so hot I forgot I didn't really care whether Ike came home or not, and probably he knew it.

He ought at least to have the decency to let me know.

I ought to do something one way or the other about God. Sooner or later—

What has God done for me, I thought.

Nothing. Less than nothing.

He hadn't come rushing with sword and helmet and breastplate to fight on my father's side against his mortal enemy, John Barleycorn.

How did I know I could ever have another baby?

I sat up, shaking with terror. If I didn't, I'd as soon be dead. A ship that's never been to sea, a plane that's never been in the sky. Might not be true of lots of women, I know it isn't, but it felt that way inside of me.

On the other hand, I knew—I always *knew*—that my grandfather had seen his Lord face to face. I have to keep repeating this, for it was the one light I followed up all Hills of Difficulty, which I could see in the dark Cave of Despair, where I was bound hand and foot by the Giant. Weeping, my father told me when I was a little girl that my grandfather had died with a smile of pure delight on his face. As though he'd heard the trumpets sounding for him on the other side.

Much good that had done him! He'd had to go, hadn't he? When we needed him, as men need guardian angels.

My grandfather had been Mr. Standfast. In his Bible, it said faith was a gift. He had it; I didn't. It might be a myth, at that. I didn't have a guardian angel, either.

I put on an old bathrobe and lighted the little gas grate to try to keep warm and I said to myself, The whole thing is a myth, you keep trying to deceive yourself with it, as men have all these years, on and on, the poor lonesome bastards out there. I wanted to be comforted about my baby. He was so *little*.

Someone to go to for comfort. Papa? Not any more. The boys in the city room? That's what came of letting women into the newspaper business. Ike St. Johns, my husband? He didn't want babies. J.B.T., who never had thought I was good for much of *anything*. Even Mr. Hearst—I could have, but I didn't know it then and we weren't on that kind of terms. Couldn't go to the women in my own family, it'd give them a chance to say they'd been right all the time about the way Papa brought me up. Now here I was with *nobody,* they'd say. I didn't know any other women—nor priests nor ministers—and as far as *Beatrice Fairfax* was concerned, I *am* Grimaldi the clown, beatrice fairfax myself.

If the Lord was tenderly saying, I will not leave you comfortless, I couldn't hear him. I couldn't hear anything but the gas grate leaking and the silence where my baby wasn't *crying*.

If there was a *Father*—comforting, giving you the kingdom—I couldn't hear Him either. All the evidence was hearsay. Historical hearsay at that. Inadmissible in any court. What I'd seen of it in my short life was balderdash and bilge and baloney.

Jesus. What a character. What did he have to do with me all these centuries later? Certainly I hadn't been praying at the foot of the Cross the way the hymn said, or anywhere else. I was too busy listening for the phone to ring or Ike to say I've got three kings or Campbell to yell at me to get a picture of that cute kid that'd been picked up in a rooming-house raid, and if it was done unto me the way I'd done unto her Mr. Facing-Both-Ways or My Lord Time-Server might catch me if I didn't watch out. Music—music had been my comforter—the last I'd heard was the band at the Ship Cafe playing Minnie-the-Mermaid-down-among-the-corals-she-forgot-her-morals—

Musicians who played long with Toscanini say that when he wanted something special, he held the baton still and crooked his finger and put it over his *heart*. Then some divine inspiration seemed to go from him to the members of his orchestra and you never heard such music as they played.

In my deep Ditch of my father drinking himself to death just around the *corner,* the paltry *le jeu ne vaut pas la chandelle* of my teen-age marriage, the sorrow for my baby and the fear that I'd never have another, I put down the baton and crooked my finger and cried out for hope—a little ray of hope—a single note of hope.

All right.

I'll be good.

Have you anything to say to me Jesus that I can understand?

In answer came the thought that wasn't mine.

This is the Cross from which Christ came down. Don't you see that? He will walk with you up and down this stable that smells of leaky gas as he walked the sands of Galilee and comfort you as he did the big fisherman. I am the ray, the light, but you must prepare a manger in the stable for the Way is the Way and there is no other.

Plain simple direct ungarnished thought.

It couldn't be mine. From where in me? No such thoughts were possible to my brilliant reason, a trash basket of materialism and hot work and utter excitement and self self self.

I knew it was truth.

I knew too, pitifully enough, that I would forget it.

I don't remember if or when the phone rang or where Ike had been or said he had been or when he came home if he did.

After a while I got dressed and went to work.

Consciously, yes, I forgot. I expect I wanted to—had to—forget. Under the nuns at the Conservatory of Music at Notre Dame Convent in San Jose, and in the Gewandhaus in Leipzig, presided over by the genius of Nickishe, I had learned that if you accept music you must live by its rules. This is the Way and there is no other. If you rock and roll or folk or soul, you must abide by laws of harmony or rhythm. To play a Mozart sonata, you must accept fingering, development of strength in your wrists, practice, self-denial, reverence for the medium of light to you.

All these things I wanted nothing to do with in those young days, except when from time to time I fell into the Ditch.

Late one night I was sitting in the Troika in Washington with Charlie Michelson, officially Chairman of the National Democratic Committee and unofficially the political public relations genius behind Roosevelt's nomination and elections. We were discussing whether there was a God or not, and I can still hear him shout, "If there is, let Him be God and I'll be Charlie Michelson."

I think I felt a good deal like that during those last matchless no-traffic, no-income-tax, no-facing-civil-rights-crises years before World War I.

I don't believe there is a God but if there is—You be God and I'll be Adela Rogers St. Johns. WhoooopEEEEEE.

No more babies came.

I went right on being fresh and funny about the whole thing. Ike and I lived a poverty-stricken, who-needs-money-we-of-the-press-can-get-in-everywhere-for-nothing, badly overworked and loving it, mad whirl on a merry-go-round. Riotous, uninhibited, sleepless, ain't we got fun! *This* generation, fifty years later, didn't invent the Have Fun! philosophy of existence. We were young, careless, naïve, moving too fast to think, hard-boiled and innocent, and *truly* filled with optimism and joy of life and *tough* of fiber. We drank too much too often. Ike continued to be a born loser at poker. I had to play to keep us anywhere near even, and while I consider poker part of a proper education, six nights a week with red white and blue chips on my dining-room table seemed too much.

Gambling is a compulsion. Did I know that then with Ike? I doubt it. I lived with it and it kept us broke. How well I remember standing on a corner with the last St. Johns dime, figuring whether I'd spend it for coffee and doughnuts, carfare to work, or toothpaste. I got the coffee, walked twenty-four blocks to work, and brushed my teeth with salt.

It came to pass that I was working sixteen hours a day and knew it was because I liked the city room better than home. My low boiling point seems to have been reached because Ike really did enjoy seeing a pal win as much as winning himself. He was a good loser. I never was.

I do so well remember that my last sight of the pawnshop at Third and Main (*before* the famed jewel thief Jack Morgan pawned one earring there) was when I went, in a fury, to hock some of the silver Solly Zemanski had given me for a wedding present to cover a bad check Ike had given the night before.

My fire had been kindled by the simple fact that in a *beeeg* pot Ike had drawn to a pair of deuces ahead of me and caught my fourth nine.

CHAPTER 5

Another suite in the Alexandria Hotel besides G on the fifth held remembered drama for me. There on the third floor I once met a girl named Pansy.

No longer on the hotel beat, I was working on our biggest local sensation—this we may call The Case of the Man Who Pawned One Earring. To the swashbuckling young cracksman we had begun to refer to as the King of the Jewel Thieves, this one earring was the sign of his true love. Just the same, it betrayed him to an army of detectives who for months had been looking for the Phantom Burglar, a gentleman opening up jewelry stores as though they were sardine cans, stuffing his pockets with diamond goodies, and dancing away through platoons of guards and cops who couldn't lay a hand on him.

This story was hot, for weeks the whole town had been in an uproar. Some ladies slept with their trinkets under their pillows in pleasurable terror and scolded the police for their unsuccessful manhunt. But on the whole big jewelry stores who own coal scuttles full of rubies, emeralds, and diamonds protected by electric alarms and armed watchmen do not arouse sympathy in the human breast. The average citizen is on the side of Robin Hood. Also around that time we had a big *Alias Jimmy Valentine* rage going on. A book, a play, a movie, a catchy tune *Look out, look out, look out for Jimmy Valentine, for he's a pal of mine, an educated crook*—all from a short story called *A Retrieved Reformation* by the man who'd introduced to the world a new literary form, the great O. Henry. He had served a term for embezzlement himself, his prison setting for the safecracker who could feel the tumblers with his own sensitive fingertips and opened the warden's safe to save a child's life—this was a sound tearjerker and we whistled it everywhere—and now we had a Jimmy Valentine of our own.

They caught him at last.

His name was Morgan—Jack Morgan—they just called him Morgan, and he was a more picturesque character than *Clyde*.

"Go up to the jail and see this Morgan," Jack Campbell said to me bright and early one fine day. "All the women in town will read anything about these *tiaras*, though what any of them would do with a tiara if they had one I don't know. They are fascinated by tiaras. Women drool over diamonds, find out about this young man that stole several. At that I'm not sure if I came home with a tiara my wife would care where I got it."

Personally I didn't care for diamonds. Papa had been annoyed because I couldn't remember what I'd done with some diamond sunbursts and a couple of big rings we'd taken from a man at the race track as a fee when his wife shot somebody. I *still* can't remember. I put them in a safe place somewhere and as far as I know they are there still.

Years later I was comforted by what Peggy Hopkins Joyce told me. At that point Peggy had more diamonds than practically anybody. Showing me a new forty-two-carat ring, she said, "*Darling,* there are only two kinds of women. Those who love diamonds and those who don't."

I said to Campbell, "They're holding this Morgan incommunicado."

"Don't let that bother you," Campbell said.

When I got to the police station, also the city jail, I found everybody serious about this incommunicado order. Nobody could interview Morgan, who was a cop-hater. He was driving them nuts. "I'll go through the keyhole," he shouted at them impudently, "a man could pick one of these locks with a hairpin, I can take these bars up by the roots." If Morgan was the jewel thief, he'd picked model electric alarms and he had several prison escapes to his credit.

A friend of mine, Lieutenant O'Brien, was on duty. I asked him could I see Morgan and he said no. I said, "Women have the vote now. They are interested in this fellow. If I am not allowed to see him," I said, "they will think you have been working him over with a hose. I might think so myself. I have to write some kind of a story about him."

"I'd have to lock you in his cell with him," the lieutenant said.

So naturally I said okay, and he said, "I'll have to ask him first. He doesn't like reporters any better than he likes us. He says he's had too much publicity already." O'Brien came back and said, "He says he'll see you. You got to remember he's a lady killer—he may try to use you." We got in the elevator and before he opened the door into the cell block the lieutenant said, "I gotta have those hairpins." I said, "You are kidding," and he said, "Morgan claims he can open up the whole jail with a hairpin." So—I took out my hairpins, which I must say were as big as screwdrivers, and my braids came down and hung between my shoulder blades. I thought this very undignified for young Mrs. St. Johns and I said to the lieutenant, "I am now on Morgan's side." He put the pins in his pocket and said, "I cannot think how he came to pawn *one* earring. Without that I do not know when we'll catch up with him—this is a very smart hombre. If he pawns two earrings the chances are the pawnbroker will never call us."

I could see that *if* I had any earrings and *if* Ike St. Johns went down to Zemanski's some morning he would pawn them *both*.

One of the mysteries was that no fence had as yet been located and they hadn't gotten back any of the fortune in loot.

We went along a crummy corridor to a cell in the middle, the lieutenant had a guard open the door, and I went in. This was a young man who knew how to ask a lady to sit down on a stool in his cell. At once my teenage imagination figured that if he was left alone with a girl in spaces larger than this, the invitation to the waltz might come from her. He had on a silk shirt open at the throat and blue denim pants of a type I'd never seen before; they're very common now.

O'Brien said, "I'll be around," and walked off. I could see a guard at each end of the corridor. Morgan saw them too, and grinned.

I felt a need to explain my hair hanging down my back and he sat down on the bunk, there being no place else, and began to laugh and so did I, and a guard came down and peered in at us. When Morgan stopped laughing he said, "They tell me you're Earl Rogers' daughter."

So that was why he'd agreed to see me. He said, "I remember when, if you could get Earl Rogers to defend you—" and I said, "So do I." He stared at me and waited, and I didn't say anything more.

What more was there to say?

Quietly he said, "I'll have some dough—"

I said, "He isn't actually practicing right now."

After a pause, I was trying to come up with the right first question. This is a technique. Jack Paar had it—Mike Douglas, Merv Griffin, and Johnny Carson when he cares. I've never seen any other TV interviewers who did. I knew in my stomach that he was the jewel thief all right but maybe he was going to deny it.

He said, "I think your father would advise me to plead guilty."

"He—hardly ever did," I said.

"I made two mistakes," he said. "First in pawning that one earring. The other was—a post office."

"Oh no!" I said.

Nobody robbed post offices or bothered the mail any more. Nobody. Nobody wanted any part of the Treasury boys.

"If I plead guilty to this diamond business," he said, "maybe they won't catch up with the other—or they'll be content to prosecute one only."

I wished I was back in our old office, with Papa behind his desk, and Bill Jory and Jerry Geisler—and this young man was a client. I wasn't up to advising him.

I said, "It's funny they haven't turned up any fence."

He said, "They won't. It's way outside their territory and I only used parcel post. In shoe boxes."

I said, "You mean you put that necklace in a shoe box and sent it by parcel post?"

"It got there," Morgan said.

I said, "What about this one earring? I have to have some answer to that for my story."

He went to the bars that hemmed us in and looked both ways up and down. Then he swung around and faced me, with his back to the corridor. My knees were beginning to ache and the smell of Lysol and sweat and urine was sickening me, I thought, I'd better get *out*—and then he said very low, "Listen. I don't want to talk loud. I'll tell you all about it if you'll do something for me. She wanted a fur jacket, she'd never had one in all her life. That dope in Des Moines was late sending me my dough—Let's call that earring pride goeth before a fall. I wasn't going to admit I couldn't buy her that goddam cat's tail. So—I rooted around and picked out a good big stone—how did I know whether it was an earring or a finger ring or what it was? I was going to hock it and buy her—"

He took a couple of steps sideways and back and I could hear the breath he drew. He said, "You going to do something for me?"

It's a dreadful thing to see a man in a cell he can't get out of. I am all for putting some of them there, more of them nowadays than we do, such as Yale uppergraduates who advocate in their daily paper selling marijuana to students—and pimps who use fourteen-year-old girls on Forty-second Street—I'd put *them* in jail but it is always easier if you don't *see* the man in his cell.

She—she wanted a fur jacket—that's why he was here. Climbing walls in helplessness.

He said, "She's still there."

Sure enough, she was.

Nobody had caught up with her and she was scared witless and speechless. The only people she'd spoken to were the waiter who brought her dinner from room service and the chambermaid.

One look—and I could see what had happened. She must have been prettier than a white angora kitten. As frisky and as ready to play with the pretty pretty diamonds that glittered when she batted them with her paws. The little veneer of sophistication—young Mrs. Jimmy Valentine—registered as Mr. and Mrs. John Morris of Lynn, Massachusetts—he'd given her that lovely bracelet and the engagement ring—no, they weren't married yet—and now her folks back in Illinois would find out—she was afraid to write to them and she didn't have enough money left for a ticket home.

No man is an island.

Somewhere there's always a girl who wants a fur jacket or a daughter who loves you or a lost baby.

I could see why Morgan had been worried about Pansy.

In one corner of the suite sitting room was a Victrola. He'd told me where to look, and there I found money. Not enough for the furs, enough for a ticket home.

What shall I tell her? I asked him and Morgan said, Tell her I got killed in an automobile accident.

She already knew. The waiter had brought newspapers with him, with pictures. Her confusion was like that of a kitten driven quite mad. The diamonds, the luxury hotels, and plush restaurants, the travel and excitement and lovely clothes, the roadster and the expensive luggage marked J.M. and P.M. She'd lain on her back waving her four little paws —and now he was in jail—they'd never get married—everyone would know.

The bell wasn't just tolling for the flamboyant young man up in the city jail. It was tolling too for a girl named Pansy.

All the time in the city room writing my exclusive interview with the famous jewel thief, I could feel the sweat trickling between my shoulder blades. Never mind my scoop on his confession; if Campbell found out about Pansy he'd burn me at the stake. I mean he would literally burn me at the stake. Just the same, I couldn't do it. I knew we needed a kitten-picture to go with the story. And the girl who was the *why* of the one earring. Oh—I knew. I said to myself, That's *news* and you are a traitor worse than Benedict Arnold. Mr. Hearst would not do such a thing for his own *mother* probably, not if it was news he wouldn't.

We were about the same age—nineteen—twenty—she kept *hanging onto me*. If I put her on the front page, she's doomed, I thought, and girls who look like that and are such nincompoops aren't islands either, they set bells tolling for bored married men with three badly brought-up kids. I got our-man-on-the-courthouse-beat to come up with a marriage license for Pansy Ducommon and John Morris and as I watched the train pull out for Peoria I wondered how a strong, tough, brilliant bastard like Morgan had fallen so hard for her. Now I remember Jack Barrymore's answer when I asked him about Elaine Barry, who rang the last bell for him. *Don't ask,* Barrymore said.

I put extra vigor into writing my pieces about Morgan. While Ike was too tall for the elegant suits tailored by the best on Fifth Avenue he liked the shirts. I always ironed his silk shirts myself—Ike's, not Morgan's, he was in San Quentin—and I remember one jade green with a rich dark green satin stripe that we thought was great. It would go well today, come to think of it.

The warden wrote me about Morgan. Within a year he had become head electrician of what was our biggest penitentiary. His conduct was a hundred per cent, but above and beyond that he had invented ways and things that were a help in fire prevention and insuring safety. Not only would he get full time off for good behavior but the warden himself would give him a recommendation so he could start life anew.

Morgan came out.

I asked screen star Jack Gilbert, who was about Morgan's size, to give me some clothes for him—Morgan's own were way out of date by then— and also transportation to Chicago, where my friend Johnny Cuneo of the famed Cuneo Press had agreed to give Morgan a job. Not long after Morgan arrived in Chicago and went to work, Cuneo wrote me a most glowing report; I'd done him a real favor, he said. Though a cheerful fellow and popular, he didn't drink and, if the girls hung around him, Cuneo wasn't the man to ask a young fellow like Morgan to be a monk. And he had actually put into operation some valuable electrical changes on the Cuneo presses—acres and acres of them, which were to grow to handle much of the country's printing as Chicago became a distribution center.

After that, the next time I heard from Morgan he had escaped from another jail in another big city for another big jewel robbery.

Why do you suppose, I said frantically to Jack Gilbert.

Some people, Gilbert said, react only to life-and-death games. If Morgan had been around during the Civil War, he'd have been one of the Raiders. I still didn't altogether understand. I was sad. Such a waste of talent.

As I write comes back to me another story I covered in financial brackets high enough to rattle Wall and Threadneedle streets. In Volume XX of Who's Who had appeared the biography of one Coster, Frank Donald. President of a huge drug-manufacturing firm, loaded with education, club, and directorial honors, all listed.

However, in Volume XXI appeared what Robert Shaplen, in his classic *New Yorker* portrait of this unforgettable character, called "one of my favorite pieces of prose in the entire language:"

> Coster, Frank Donald. The sketch of the then President of Mc-
> Kesson & Robbins Inc., published under this name is the only in-
> stance during five decades of continuous publication involving
> 77,000 biographies of a fictitious biographer foisting himself on
> the editors of Who's Who. This imposter . . .

Guffaws were heard, but Who's Who could comfort itself by the company it kept. For Mr. Coster, whose real name was Musica, Phillip, had a record mostly police, and he had taken in an incredible collection of wise guys and big organizations. For the *New Yorker* piece further states that while a financial wizard he preferred to be a fast-shuffling, double-dealing crook who lived by his wits.

Hearing footsteps drawing near, Coster-Musica shot himself, and I was sent to Fairfield to see the dark-haired Social Register beauty who was now his penniless widow. I went down to the playroom opening on exquisite gardens where the big-shot financier had loved to entertain his friends. There were billiard and Ping-pong tables, dart boards, half a dozen slot machines, latest Las Vegas models.

All the slot machines were crooked.

Marred pots? I see the big-time swindler and the jewel thief were brothers under their skin. I preferred my boy. At least he took a chance of getting shot.

I don't know whatever became of The Girl Named Pansy, which was the title of the short story I later sold to somebody. Her name, of course, wasn't Pansy.

CHAPTER 6

*I'm awfully sorry, but I don't remember the Korean War.**
In 1967 a girl said that to her dance escort in a *New Yorker* cartoon.
It startled me. The *Korean* War?
I remember so many of them.

My first contact with *war* came in the old Mason Opera House and it
was World War *I.*
My brother Bogart, a sophomore at Stanford, was down from Palo
Alto and we went to see a road company of *The Mikado.* At the first act
curtain, Bogey left me to go across to the Waldorf Bar for a beer. Ladies
then were not allowed in saloons; there was also a city ordnance against
a woman smoking in public. As the curtain went up again, Bogey slipped
into his seat, a vibration hit me in the stomach, and I whispered, "What is
it?" He grinned triumphantly and said, "I just enlisted in the Royal Flying
Corps." I said, "You did not. How could you?" He said, "They've got re-
cruiting officers in the lobby." There, when the play ended, I saw young
men wearing the uniform in which my son Bill was to die in World War II.
In a world where England is finished and dead I do not wish to live. My
brother felt that in 1915, my son in 1941.
Bogart left the morning following his enlistment.
For the first of many times, as it turned out, I said good-by to one of
my own going into battle.
Letters came from Canada, where he trained. From England, at last
from France. Snapshots showed me a swaggering young RFC captain, in
front of a toy airplane made—it looked like—of cardboard and adhesive
tape. This my brother must fly while shooting and being shot at. *He liked
it.* The way he stood, wore his cap, the fighting-man expression on his
young face.
With those letters, those pictures, the war moved into my heart, my
personal life, became a reality to me long perhaps before it did to others.
I moved out of the Isolationist Party. William Randolph Hearst still believed we could avoid foreign entanglements *with honor.* His generation
was closer to Washington's. *It is our true policy to steer clear of permanent alliance with any portion of the foreign world. To the Monroe*

* Caption for a drawing by Lorenz in *The New Yorker.*

doctrine of isolation for our hemisphere. To Thomas Jefferson's *honest friendship with all nations, entangling alliances with none.* We were not to expect to be translated from our deep-rooted policy and platform to an overseas war on, as Jefferson once phrased such a change, a feather bed. Mr. Hearst stood for a time firmly behind Stay out of Europe's Quarrels.

We must be impartial in thought as well as in action.

No more impossible plea than Woodrow Wilson's for neutrality ever came out of the White House. Nobody has ever seen an American who could or can define impartiality, much less think feel or be it. We are all born rooters. Everybody has a ball team. For a little time perhaps there were two sides to that war. I never knew anyone who was pro-German exactly, we distrusted the Kaiser, we just felt there had been differing viewpoints in *Europe,* with the *Balkans,* whatever they were. We soon reacted to the stories that began to occupy the spotlight. The execution of Nurse Edith Cavell for helping Belgian prisoners to escape. Stand a *nurse* up against a wall and shoot her? Surely not! The taxi drivers who went out to save Paris—*taxi drivers* in their old cabs—they aroused in us an admiration and partisanship so that we cheered them as we cheer our team in a World Series. Soon the pacifists who sang an appalling ditty called "I Didn't Raise My Boy to Be a Soldier to Shoot Some Other Mother's Darling Boy" were drowned by our shouts of "It's a Long Long Way to Tipperary" and "Roses of Picardy." For once, the devil didn't have the best tunes.

There is such a thing as being too proud to fight, said Wilson.

There is? we said.

Bunker Hill or Gettysburg, Stonewall Jackson at Bull Run, Tripoli and Ticonderoga, the cadets at West Point who stepped out of the line and marched south to fight their own comrades for Robert E. Lee and Dixie. Too proud to fight? Justice Oliver Wendell Holmes once said we had a Code of Honor that neared Folly. Anyhow, most of us believed it impossible to be too proud to fight for our honor, our principles, our friends. Our country. We saw it that way.

The war began to move daily, hourly, into the city room.

Blitzen Benz screamed as though in pain from the wire desk—the Germans had resumed unrestricted submarine warfare. This ignited our truly peace-loving people as the Japs did again, finally, at Pearl Harbor. *Will you Germans never learn?* the schoolteacher in the White House cried out in one of his rare passions, as he handed the German Ambassador his walking papers.

No radio. No television. Thus we in our city room had in our telegraph desk and open wires the hottest line and things broke first to and for us.

I was in the city room when the President went before Congress on

April 2. Nobody breathed. Nobody moved. Nobody spoke. We knew first, we took his speech off our wires, and John B. T. Campbell, a patriot if ever there was one, stood up tall behind the city desk and read it to us from the flimsies as a boy handed it to him sentences at a time:

> It is a fearful thing to lead this great peaceful people into war . . . we shall fight for the things which we have always carried nearest our hearts—for democracy, for the right of those who submit to authority to have a voice in their own Governments, for the rights and liberties of small nations . . . To such a task we can dedicate our lives and our fortunes, everything we are and everything that we have, with the pride of those who know that the day has come when America is privileged to spend her blood and her might for the principles that gave her birth and happiness and the peace which she has treasured. God helping her, she can do no other.

Great words now in *Bartlett's Familiar Quotations*.

They were greater as they poured out then to us, who *were* America. Cheers welled up and filled the city room. Men banged on the copy desk with the big shears. Out in the composing room we heard marching steps and loud shouts. When the presses began to roll, they had a new throbbing rhythm.

We used what we came to call WAR TYPE to declare war on the Germans.

I hate war.

You hate war.

Everybody hates war.

What's the use of saying that? It's taken for granted, it's a basic truth. But we knew that day, as our forefathers knew, that there are worse things than war. Slavery, for example. Taxation without representation. No free press. No freedom to worship. Being tried by the same people who accuse you. Star Chamber.

Or the cringing cowardice of a man standing by and watching a bully full of hop beat up a child or an old woman.

Or dishonor or a Broken Word.

I hate war.

It has cost me dear. Few dearer.

I still say there are worse things than war.

I remember the smell of the ink as WAR TYPE came up that April day. The smudges of it on my hands and skirt as we danced around the city room shouting snatches of "Yankee Doodle Dandy," my imagination had leaped the sea, I was with Bogey's squadron at the front, how proud he would be that we had at last Come In. Hope would warm the British with their backs to the wall. What a welcome the French would give us as the United States ended what had seemed to them her long neutrality of dishonor. I had friends flying in the Lafayette Escadrille—the boys like Bogey who couldn't wait—they would cakewalk down the Champs Elysée to meet the other Americans who arrived—at last.

I began to cry—we were all crying as we cheered. With joy, with pride, with sheer love of our country and her magnificence as she went to the rescue of the almost defeated countries fighting against the mailed bully Germany. God helping us, we cried, who could do no other. God helping us we will win and the world will still be free.

Not only did we feel God was on our side. We felt we were on God's side.

You can't do any business if you haven't got a band.

George Michael Cohan's "Over There" was the "Battle Hymn of the Republic" for World War I—Yankee Doodle Cohan could always hear the songs his nation needed—

We sang "The Yanks Are Coming" as we marched. Joan of Arc, we are calling you—and once again the Maid of Orleans was with her troops on the battlefields of Mons, too many saw her shining armor, her oriflamme, we were fighting again for the France she had died to save.

A man must die—a girl must die—for that which is dearer to her than life and this is what makes life so dear.

Above all we sang:

> From the Halls of Montezuma
> To the shores of Tripoli
> We have fought our country's battles
> On the land as on the sea.
> If the Army and the Navy
> Ever look on Heaven's scenes,
> They will find the streets are guarded by
> United States Marines . . .

as, under Lejeune and Duckboard Butler, the marines landed and fought the reckless battles of Belleau Wood and Château Thierry and won them to become the most legendary of all fighting forces.

We lost a battalion and found what there was left of it and our faith in our cause rose higher—and our anger with it.

We began to have Heroes.

Somebody saluted a grave and cried, "Lafayette we are here," and we thought it had to be General Pershing.

Captain Eddie Rickenbacker. I defy you to match him for perfect casting in any righteous war anywhere any time. He was the most dashing, fire-eating daredevil and when he tossed his Hat in the Ring Squadron of our planes against von Richthofen's Flying Circus he was our idol. He thought men were born to fight.

We had Sergeant York of Tennessee, who could knock the eye out of a squirrel with a rifle at fifty yards. When his detachment was wiped out in the Argonne, he charged a machine-gun nest by himself and captured ninety men and released forty-two prisoners. Marshal Foch, supreme commander of all forces, said it was the greatest thing accomplished by any fighting soldier in all the armies of Europe.

A little-bitty war, War I.

So many nations involved we called it World—yet the Front was never more than 212 miles long.

My husband went as soon as he could.

After our declaration of war I found I was, at last, going to have a baby and not even for my country was I going to take any chances with that. I quit my job, we moved down to a ramshackle in-the-rear cottage at the beach, and he got more and more restless and steamed up day by day. I had the baby at home and Ike, in a red sweater with a Stanford block S on it, held the ether cone over my nose for the doctor and as soon as the baby was safely in her clothes basket under the kitchen stove, he began to pack.

"I'm so goddam BIG," he said.

I knew what he meant.

By that time every young man of our acquaintance was in uniform. The words draft dodger hadn't come into much use, no one we knew had ever waited to be drafted. The term that was equivalent to any insult ever written on a wall was *slacker*. This meant you hadn't enlisted. This was then a social disgrace and barred you from the ranks of *men*.

As Ike got ready to enlist in 1918, my recollection is that we added up to $5.75 in the bank—about normal for us. While I was nursing the baby, I realized I must eat or she wouldn't.

None of us, the men on the paper who couldn't go, considered this move of Ike's—and mine—a momentous or unusual decision. If we'd had any sense Ike—a Stanford graduate—could have gone to officers' training camp. The point however was to get *over there*.

An odd scrap comes back to me.

I drove him down to MacArthur in our third-hand Ford, with the baby asleep on the back seat. We were too buoyed up to feel either fear or sorrow. As he kissed me good-by Ike threw his big brown overcoat onto the car floor. "Hell," he said, "I won't need that. I'll be in uniform." It turned out to be cold and foggy in San Pedro and the poor guy damn near froze to death before he got his army issue.

This proves how little we knew about War.

In every war, women play the part of supreme decision.

The spirit, faith, love and good will with which they meet the fortunes of war determine the time and place of victory or defeat. In 1917–18 *men* believed civilization had advanced so that the chastity belt was as obsolete in war as the crossbow. As *women,* we felt that to cheat on a man who was away fighting for his country was low, shabby, dishonorable, and unsportsmanlike. I never heard of a Dear John letter in that war. Not until World War II, after the Modern Woman had achieved freedom, been given the vote, knew all the words, referred casually to infidelity as a roll in the hay, did the wives of soldiers become a major problem to our major generals. The problem being that, whether it was the haunting suspicion of what their wives were doing at home while they were far far away, or having their wives following them to camp, it made it even more difficult to make them into soldiers. Never one to be mealy-mouthed, I find it impossible to quote now as it was in 1943 the mildest that General George Patton had to say on the subject. The *Ladies Home Journal* and Army Public Relations had sent me to Fort Benning to find out about our army wives and General Patton said at once that wives who followed their husbands to camp and kept them unsettled and off balance and never let them become *soldiers* were in fact crawling bitches in heat. Those who wrote whining letters filled with their complaints about troubles at home were female rats. Those who began letters Dear John, I don't know how to tell you—should be *shot* as traitors.

Possibly the general judged other wives by his own, the former Miss Ayres of Boston, who was *the* greatest. Under five feet, Mrs. Patton had sailed as crew with the general in the Honolulu boat races, rode jumpers with him for blue ribbons. At Tiger Camp, where he was training the immortal Tenth, our first armored division, he was known as Old Blood and Guts. The troops said the general was Blood all right, but Mrs. Patton was the Guts.

For a future profile of the general's lady, as an example to army wives, I gathered material for *Cosmopolitan.* Sometime thereafter I got a call from Mrs. Patton, whose husband was by then overseas. She said her husband had smacked (her word) a private soldier and there was hell to pay. The army and the correspondents had agreed not to mention the incident. The general had come to visit the hospital from a battle where his men were fighting and dying; he wasn't prepared to take sass from a man who'd shot his big toe off to avoid combat. To a country that didn't know we had a self-inflicted-wound ward, this could damage morale. She wanted me to know this, however, before I committed myself to a story in praise of the Pattons, in case it leaked. Few people are as honorable as reporters, and still it did leak, without the circumstances of the self-inflicted wound. A *columnist,* not a reporter or correspondent, believe me, used it, and the country blew up a storm of criticism, stilled by Eisenhower, who said calmly that he couldn't win the war without Patton.

I was glad I'd gone ahead with my Patton profile.

In it was a story told me by Mrs. Patton's daughter, married, of course, to a West Point officer. When her husband got his orders for France, she was in tears. Her mother tried to comfort her and the daughter said between sobs, "Oh Mother, you're too old to know what it's like to be in love." To this piece of youthful presumption, the general's wife said, "You're too young to have the faintest idea what love really is. When you've lived with a man as long as I've lived with the general, sent your husband to war as often as I have, endured as many days of waiting for news of him, you may be allowed to speak of it."

2

This is the diary of a pilgrimage, as whose life isn't? Here I must tell you of my Mrs. Valiant-for-Truth, who, as it happens, comes into the story of *Pilgrim's Progress* only when the woman Christiana sets forth. *Timourous* tried to keep Christiana from setting forth at all.

> What canst thou, being but a poor woman, do? Consider what thou art like to meet, the bitter goes before the sweet, there will be Mrs. Inconsiderate and Mrs. Love-the-Flesh with Mrs. Lechery and Mrs. Filth, there will be Lions and Shadows and Apollyon himself. You must go through the Valley of Humiliation and the City of Vanity Fair to reach the Desired Country and find on the King's Highway those women who pretend to be the King's Labourers and say they are mending the road a long way ahead but who bring dirt and dung instead of stones for foundation. [circa 1678]

Don't I know.

Do not venture at all—stay in the cave—shouts Timourous.

To this, my Mrs. Valiant-for-Truth could shout that great song:

> No Lion shall her fright
> She will with Giants fight
> She hath a right
> To be a Pilgrim.

Her name in this my life was Mother Meyer, as I have said before.

How such a varied company came to beat a path to her door is still a little mysterious though I suppose when those in the dark see a light they climb toward it.

After Ike had gone to war I went back to the paper and to live with her —the best friend I ever had. Have. Hope to have, anybody ever had.

She was called Mother Meyer by a gaggle of goslings including opera stars, fortunetellers, the founder of a new religious sect, the owner of Hollywood's notorious Vernon Country Club, Baron Long, a society leader of the magnitude of Mrs. Hugh Livingston McNeil, *and* Jack Barrymore. Since her husband was a truck driver and by worldly standards she was totally obscure and without marketable assets, she must have made a better mousetrap.

In writing this now, I have to mix up times and people and places. How else to get her on—or as we call it, to come off the paper—I do not know.

There were other reasons besides the mousetrap of course.

She had been born in Virginia as Frances Lee, goddaughter and cousin once removed of Robert E. At seven, she fell from a horse and broke her hip, by the time a doctor could be brought to do such setting as they understood in those days it was too late, she always limped somewhat. At the end of that war—the Civil War and that one every American remembers—she met a young captain named Jordan returning from the Confederate Army and hot to go West, so she married him and came with him to Nevada, where he got a job on the railroad. A few months later he was killed. The only thing the young widow knew how to do was play the piano. The only pianos were in the dance and gambling halls, so there she went to teach music. The majority of women in that silver rush who could reach a piano and pay for lessons were dance hall girls and whores and so the delicate, aristocratic young Mrs. Jordan taught them. When she used to tell me their stories she felt so pleased that she had helped many of them to make good marriages, she had interest in and compassion for most of them, and cheered them on as they went still farther West. At last the Bonanza was over, the gambling fever died, people moved away. And so Mrs. Jordan and her baby girl Jessie came to Los Angeles and she taught music there and was so good a teacher that the finest families sent their daughters to her. There, too, she met a handsome young German named Dick Meyer, who made a good living driving a truck for Roebling's, and married him.

The girls she had helped in Nevada were settled in Los Angeles, some of them in positions of social prestige, they had the grace of gratitude and the fondest memories of their teacher and came to see her. The mothers who brought their debutante daughters to learn something of music from her made her a friend—both mothers and daughters. Her own daughter Jessie—someday I am going to write a whole *book* about Jessie to vie with *Auntie Mame*—went on the stage for a while and thus in the stock company days of Los Angeles and the Morosco and Belasco theaters Mother met the Barrymores and the other stars and writers. Jessie's best friend was Hazel Gillon, a California beauty who had studied for opera in Paris and who befriended a lot of the bewildered young stars of Hollywood's silent days.

All of us—sooner or later—drifted to find Mother again at 836 Kensington Road.

The house she lived in and where we could always find her was a big brown box on top of a hill in Angeleno Heights, a swank address which had already been left behind in the city's progress out Wilshire Boulevard through Beverly Hills to the beaches. Upstairs were six bedrooms, five large and one just big enough for my baby daughter Elaine, and one antique bathroom. Downstairs, on one side of the big entrance hall, an enormous drawing room with windows at both ends, filled by a Steinway concert grand, some atrocious sets of stuffed furniture, and several exquisite pieces Mother had kept by her all the rugged way from Virginia. On the other side, a blue and white dining room with a Persian carpet and behind that a *huge* kitchen, three large pantries, and a big screened porch. *Room*—lots of *room*. Out back a yard with apricot and fig trees, berry bushes, and a chicken yard where we collected our own brown eggs. In front, a cement porch with pillars and a blue plumbago vine where years later—Mother left me the house in her will—I was to meet Little Augie's boys from Brooklyn in my custody fight for my youngest son.

The kitchen was the heart of the house, as it should be; in it was a sink with long deal drainboards, kept spotlessly polished; in front of this an old piano stool with a wine-red velvet cover; Mother was so small she twirled it up as far as it would go to wash dishes. I wiped and put away. The time passed so quickly we never noticed the dishes. Here also I learned to cook, and beat my own homemade noodles on the marble-topped table Mother had known in Virginia.

At that table, made of a marble slab about ten by three, on sawhorses of dark battered mahogany, I sat out the long nights.

I had a wonderful colored lady named Linnie who helped out in the daytime. She took over just as I finished the morning nursing—the baby had bottles while I was down in the city room—and I steamed off in a frenzy so as not to be late getting there. She *left* the moment I staggered in, having climbed the wooden steps that led up the side of the hill and saved me a few minutes getting home, and *I* took things back, nursed Elaine, helped with dinner, and let the baby keep me awake most of the night. We sat in the kitchen because it was the only place I could keep warm. She was part night owl; as long as I held her and talked to her she was enchantingly content and talked back in sounds neither poet nor musician can equal. My heart was filled with true joy. If she hadn't been so cute there were times, by four o'clock, when I ached with fatigue and for sleep, I would undoubtedly have put her in the oven, which I kept on for warmth.

Sometimes Mother came to sit with us.

When I *see* her now I see her sitting at one end of that table, in a blue and white checked gingham apron with a gimp, a crocheted jacket, and slippers that seldom matched.

And, over the years, at the other end I see Ely Culbertson, who invented contract bridge.

A sheriff, flapping a loose dish towel, having just allowed Clara Phillips to escape from his jail because he'd fallen for her. This escape was causing wild indignation at that very moment, for Clara was accused of a particularly unpleasant murder. They caught up with her, extradited her from Mexico, convicted and sent her to San Quentin. They never did find out who'd let her out. Mother knew.

The woman who should have been the finest actress in the American theater, Marjorie Rambeau, a name that had been in lights on Broadway in its truly greatest—and gone forever—days. Mother was trying to keep her from drinking herself out of her birthright.

Slow to wrath, she suffered fools more charitably than most, but once at that kitchen table she told a governor of California that he was too stupid to be allowed to control our destinies, he mustn't run again. He didn't.

A movie star who was a beau of mine but always ended in the kitchen talking Buddhism, Byron and Beethoven. He can learn, Mother used to say of that fine young actor Dick Barthelmess. And Valentino adored her.

Anybody who could *learn* she would put up with.

She must have thought, part of the time anyway, that I could learn, for here in that big warm kitchen we had the talks, the teachings, the half-awakenings, the glimpses of the light I didn't see then but which came in the moments when I was giving up on my pilgrimage.

Like the Elephant's Child, she was full of 'satiable curiosity. About people. About religion. About life and death, the hereafter and the heretofore. In her search for truth nothing was barred from investigation. This I did understand, even then. Curiosity had motivated all her excursions into the outer world. Once it almost landed my wartime helper Linnie in the hoosegow.

Some of our Hollywood friends, always and ever pursuing the occult and the esoteric, told us fabulous experiences with a new medium. A remarkable gentleman from India—or Mecca—or Jamaica. Anyhow, he wore a turban and could read the past and predict the future and, sitting cross-legged, he held séances that were sensational. Mother wanted to go and behold this phenomenon, so off we went and were greeted at the door of a Wilshire mansion by my old friend Linnie, wearing a long white robe.

The medium was her husband Archie and *he* was wearing the turban. Linnie's face was aglow with *honest* delight. She *believed* him, she always had. But meeting Archie's eyes they looked exactly the same way they had on the occasion I caught him with a pair of crooked dice. He'd known then—he knew now—I wouldn't betray him for Linnie's sake.

So we joined the séance.

I never saw Mother so utterly overcome with laughter, for Archie said almost at once that Mother's aged bull terrier, Jim, who'd passed to a happy hunting ground the year before, was present. "Good evening, Jim," Mother said gravely, "I hope you are behaving yourself."

Mother herself had real extrasensory perception. That's for sure.

Not long ago, some friends of mine asked me to meet a ranking professor of ESP and psychic phenomena who had worked with Rhine at Duke University. I listened with, I hope, polite attention while this goodly academician explained at length how for a couple of years he'd been testing a young man somewhere in Czechoslovakia or Dalmatia or Cairo and that now sixty-two per cent of the time this prodigy could tell whether the downside of a card was red black or green by sheer ESP. No one thought I was sufficiently impressed and I did not feel it was the moment to tell them about the night I took Mother Meyer to Nola Hahn's famous gambling house on the Sunset Strip.

She wanted, she had said to me, to see how much things had changed since her own days in the Nevada gambling halls or hells.

Mother, to the cool but just the same consternation of the blackjack dealers, could tell you not only whether the downside of the card was red or black, but how many spots there were on it. Or whether it was a king, a jack, or a queen. Of course blackjack is a small player's game. Roulette is different. When her *cane* and my chips kept hitting the red or black accurately we were in the upper echelons and I thought it was time to go.

"Things haven't changed a bit," Mother said kindly to Nola as we went out. "The eyes are always the same."

Nola, always the courtier, bent over her hand, but I noticed he didn't ask her to be sure and come back sometime. And later whenever I met him or The Farmer or Guy McAfee in Reno or Vegas they always asked about the lady with the cane.

Another excursion followed Mother's decision that we should walk down to the foot of our hill and hear Aimee Semple McPherson preach in her big white temple, all lit up by electric signs. More talk about *Aimee* there was than any other woman in California, not excepting movie stars. Her following was sensational in numbers, there seemed to be testimonials of crutches and wheel chairs left at her altar.

Nor could anyone overlook her political power, she did not separate church and state, she spoke out on radio to hundreds of thousands, to millions, for anyone she believed in or was against or anything in or out of laws she called evil. Public opinion was split right down the middle about Aimee, half believed she was the most inspired evangelist since St Paul, the other that she had to be a fraud and was a scandal to Christianity.

She certainly stirred up the churches.

Echo Park was jammed with people the night we went. If they couldn't get into Angelus Temple, which stood beside the lake, they heard her over loud-speakers, her shadow might fall on them as she passed.

I had a press pass. Anything with press on it received quick recognition from Aimee's team. Ralph Jordan and Ralph Wheelwright of the Los Angeles *Examiner* kept her covered all the time because she was in that class as *news* and also, both of them admitted afterwards, they were madly in love with her. Mother and I sat in the front row and felt the dramatic sweep of her entrance and, soon, the overpowering hypnotic evangelistic fervor or her—what shall I call it—speech? sermon? performance? Come-to-Jesus, spellbinding oratory?

I looked at Mother for her reaction, she was weeping silently, tears streaming down her soft, delicate skin. Mother had great beauty, and when you find beauty in the old it is beyond anything the young can offer. Oh *no*—I said to myself—she can't fool Mother, we all had complete faith in the radar-for-truth Mother carried, not even Aimee Semple McPherson could jam that.

When the service ended we started to walk along Hollywood Boulevard and Mother took out a lace handkerchief and wiped away the tears. I could contain myself no longer. I said, "Mother, she's got to be a phony. Those costumes and that clothesline with the paper money pinned to it— that henna hair—" Mother stopped in front of a hardware store and her eyes blazed blue fire at me and she rapped the sidewalk with her cane and said, "Who are you to judge—she believes in Christ and what do you know of her temptations?"

I didn't say anything more.

She prayed for Aimee, that I know. When Aimee disappeared into the ocean and the whole country was in suspense I went down with Jordan and Ralph Wheelwright to the sands off Ocean Park where she had gone for a swim and never come back. For days, nights, her followers were kneeling in the sands, praying, looking for her to come back walking on the water. Instead she came up in the desert in Arizona and finally it came out that she had been in a cottage down at the bottom of Carmel with a young organist named Ormiston.

All Mother Meyer said was, "Her temptations were too much for her, poor thing. We forget the teaching about temptation. It is among the few words in our Lord's Prayer. Poor soul. She will die of them." And she did.

Mother Meyer taught me all I was willing to accept about how to live. Her last hours were filled with a sort of *glowing* curiosity about death. "In just a few minutes," she said to me, "I'll *know.*"

This, of course, was how to die. I was too young to pay much attention to it then. I do now.

When I lived with Mother Meyer at the time Elaine was a baby and Ike was in the Army, more people were dying of the flu epidemic at home than were being killed overseas. We had never known what a *plague* was and we were badly shaken. I wrote articles about it but maintained that calm arrogance we put forth when the fear doesn't happen to be one of our own. I wore my gauze mask with tolerance; since it was a nuisance at work I soon sneaked it off altogether.

I remember once going down on the streetcar to Fort MacArthur to see Ike. On account of the flu epidemic no leaves were being granted. So I walked up and down outside a ten-foot wire fence with the baby under my arm and my mask on, and Ike in the khaki uniform of a private several sizes too small, so that the sleeves were above his wrists and the blouse hit high above his rump, walked up and down inside. Nothing more unattractive than the scenery, the barracks, the *dust,* and us can be imagined. Only Ike was in a state of delirious delight. They were expecting their orders to move out for France any minute; he was going to get to the Front in time for a crack at the Huns and a chance to tweak the Kaiser's mustache. I was so glad he was pleased with this ferocious prospect that I agreed I could keep the home fires burning, though personally I was so tired I had little hope I'd manage more than a bed of ashes.

Yet somehow a warmth and sweetness and compassion for these three young creatures comes from that memory. It seems possible to me now that this was the tenderest moment in our years of marriage.

Though that was a very tough year.

I missed Ike more than I had expected. Not just as a man around the house. I had gotten used to being married, it was neither as ball-of-fire nor as distressing as I had expected, it was the only marriage I'd ever had and I'd grown accustomed to it. He was a kindly man, and I found in him some of the good company and trustworthiness that made him so popular with other men and so successful in politics later. I know now how kind and patient he was with me a lot of the time.

I was covering too many funerals of my contemporaries, the flu struck down the young, I remember particularly two brothers with fine Irish names who'd been my friends, they went on the same day.

As the excitement died down, the marching songs became familiar, the young men in uniform were increasing and going off to where the fighting and dying were, the war itself, the *continuing* war, was vibrating inside me—inside us all—as a profound shock.

My brother had been in France a long time. The casualty lists of the Royal Flying Corps grew longer. He was an *ace* now, this meant not only that he got credit for shooting down five enemy planes but that he was in the thick of the air war. I began to wait for his letters with an uptight suspense and to avoid the mere thought of telegrams.

The despair about my father reached its all-time low about then. I hardly ever saw him, I got word of him occasionally, and I had to freeze out my memories altogether. This left me chilled to my marrow on many a night. Once in a while he came to Mother's and perhaps slept there. And this, in spite of promises not to, *was* sitting up with the corpse.

Half the time I was broke. With Ike's salary gone, I only had mine to pay all our expenses and while Mother wouldn't take any rent I had to pay Linnie, buy our food, keep myself dressed and clean, as all career girls do, and carfare became a problem.

I was badly overworked on my two shifts—one at the paper, one at home with the baby, I never got much sleep, and I was so thin my shabby old suits began to *hang* on me.

Any day I expected to hear that Ike had gone overseas—his brother Hallie was there already with the Rainbow Division—it seemed a long way away.

With all this, it was strictly necessary to keep your chin up and your hair combed. What else?

After we had finished some study on the *Imitation of Christ,* Mother had given me a book she was reading called *Science and Health with Key to the Scriptures* by a woman I'd never heard of, Mary Baker Eddy. To Mother, all religions were spokes, the rim was humanity, and the hub was God and what spoke you were on or used couldn't matter less. She was impressed by Mrs. Eddy's efforts to share what she considered a vision of the *return* of the active divine healing of the early apostles with all Christian churches. To Mother, who attended these in turn, she thought they'd *better* show some results or someday people would think God was dead. From this distance, I can see it was natural for Mother Meyer to admire and accept Mary Baker Eddy as part of her beloved Emerson and the New England transcendentalists.

I once took Mother down to Marion Davies' Santa Monica beach house to meet Mr. Hearst. Sure enough, as I'd expected, soon she and Mr. Hearst were in a corner. I am reminded of this here for they were discussing Mrs. Eddy's founding in 1908 of the first national daily newspaper, *The Christian Science Monitor*. A remarkable feat for anyone, Mr. Hearst called it, and more so for a woman and far ahead of her times. Mother said surely Mrs. Eddy must be considered one of the greatest American women and Mr. Hearst said, Most certainly. He had, he told Mother, sent Arthur Brisbane to interview her when she was under strong attack.

Thus though I didn't understand one word in seven in *Science and Health* I so admired Mrs. Eddy as a newspaper editor and publisher that I kept on trying. Sometimes it was the only thing I did try and it probably kept me from debacle and catastrophe in the temptations of Vanity Fair.

I am not as disconcerted by the young woman I was then as I expected to be. She seems—as Edna St. Vincent Millay used to say—to have so done her best.

The armistice came late in 1918.

My first son was born the following November. William Ivan St. Johns, Jr.,—our Bill—weighed twelve pounds and all of it seemed to me to be bone. He was the color of bougainvillea, had long black hair, and had given me as rough a time as you get. I thought he was more beautiful than dawn upon the mountains and when at six weeks old *he slept all night* it scared me out of my wits when I woke up. I thought he had smothered himself.

This may be hindsight. Who knows what is and what isn't? But it seems I did know he was to be my rock.

A few months later, we all moved to Hollywood, so I could be near what, to my surprise and exasperation, was turning out to be *my work that I could do at home*.

CHAPTER 7

Will anybody believe Hollywood? I keep asking myself. Not the businesslike, splendidly organized, well-trained commercial Hollywood of today. Everybody can believe that.

I mean Hollywood as I knew it when we were young together. I myself under thirty billed by Mr. Hearst and the first fan magazine as Hollywood's Mother Confessor. The young, inspired Hollywood that changed the face of a nation, created art forms, gave the United States border-to-border idols, national clowns and America's Sweetheart, the first Movie Star, Mary Pickford.

The Golden Years, the silent days of the universal language pantomime, better understood than all the dialogue spoken in the United Nations, which transported a world population into a never-never land of love stories, far places where none had traveled before, wars that came alive off pages in our history books, true comedy, an essential of all art, whereas before we'd known clowns only on yearly visitations to a circus; which produced the Art Form of the Western, continuing many hours of everyday with *Gunsmoke, Bonanza,* and *The Virginian.*

Can I make anybody believe Tom Mix, who transposed his own cowboy life to make that form so real and, a movie star but still a cowboy, gave his wife a few million dollars' worth of diamonds which she wore to breakfast?

Greatest of all movie directors still, David Wark Griffith, who in the end destroyed himself, his exquisite love story with Lillian Gish, and his art and career for a girl *nobody* can believe. We didn't, and we were looking right at it. Or our dancing daughter Joan Crawford, who spans the cycles, and the army brat, Gloria Swanson, who occupied the DeMille bathtubs and became our first titled lady.

Unintentionally, without being aware of it, few of us told the truth. We no longer saw it perhaps.

It should be told because it is so much more wonderful and so much better drama than what has grown up around us—me and them—lurid tales by those who weren't there.

I was. I was part of it, most unwillingly at first. It happened to me. It grew up around me while I was staying home raising babies. I used to take them with me onto the sets and a star or an electrician took care of them while I got my stories and thus I began to write for and edit the first fan magazine for the first fans.

We were all still so *young*. Younger than anybody.

Will you believe Mabel Normand?

The youngest of us all and we found her under a rosebush.

She died young, too.

The spirit of laughter she brought to the screen, as its fairy godmother, we must believe in. As Peter Pan said, we must believe in Tinker Bell or light and laughter may go out forever.

I hadn't intended to put Mabel in this book.

She *came*.

A big, rough tough plumber named Mack Sennett knew about gadgets such as movie cameras and klieg lights and about laughter from his mother, who, before she left Ireland, was buddies with the leprechauns. He put these together as Clowns and Keystone Cops, Chases, the original Sennett Comedies and Bathing Beauties, and made them a stone of the corner on which the Movies were built.

I met his mother. She never forgave Mack for what he did to Mabel.

Charlie Chaplin always said *inspired* at Mabel's name; when they called him Genius he still said he'd never be as good as she was. Marie Dressler said she was the greatest clown ever born.

And with it she was so beautiful. Hollywood harbored her for a time. Then, being but mortals, they killed her as mortals do gods and fairies.

I've never been able to write about her before. Brought up among men, school days few, living in hotels without neighbors, Earl Rogers' daughter Nora never had a girl friend her own age until she met Mabel Normand. When you are well past threescore and ten, as I am now, some of those who have inhabited your heart all the time come visiting.

My first girl friend Mabel *comes*.

I might as well begin at the Vernon Country Club. In those gold-rush-of-genius Hollywood days, it was the most exciting, exhilarating, enthusiastic, noisy, and colorful combination of the Barbary Coast, a cakewalk dance hall, a discotheque, and a superexclusive restaurant I've ever seen. In its high style, rowdy splendor it was unique. Because of the smashing personality-plus of its early Hollywood clientele, it is difficult to bring you into it. We *lived* there; when we went, it was home as we'd like to have had one. It belonged to us. In those days there was not yet Society. Nobody gave a party, nobody knew how. Nobody yet had that kind of a house, no silver, dishes, servants to handle guests. So every night Vernon was packed with those young people of the movies, on their own, rarin' to go, money to spend, lots of money, fame on their shoulders and around their heads. Before Ike and I were married, when I first worked on the *Herald,* Mabel and I used to go out there by ourselves. We thought it would be more fun to see who was around than to go with someone we already knew. This did not make us popular with other girls and once one of them hit me with a gold mesh bag full of silver dollars she'd snitched from the change her escort got when he paid cash for each round of drinks.

Bill Jones, who ran the place with an iron hand for Baron Long, never wanted to let Mabel and me *in.* Both of us were underage. But along with everybody else, Bill could never resist Mabel. Once we were *in,* he began strategic deploys to get us *out.* Mabel was always cold, so she took a little whiskey and added apricot brandy to kill the taste. This made her harder to deploy. I stuck to crème de menthe—it makes me sick to think of it. We did the Turkey Trot and the Grizzly Bear and the Black Bottom and there is no use looking down any noses today at the Twist or the Frug or the Watusi—*believe me.* My ash-blond pigtails come undone and Mabel's long brown curls flew and it's easy to understand why Bill Jones kept saying plaintively, "You little girls ought to go home now, oughtn't you?" We left alone and sometimes we went straight to work, she to the studios in Edendale, me to the paper or the police reporters' room. I'd come in from Vernon and was asleep on a desk when the Gay murder was discovered in an office building. I was the only one there, the graveyard shift had gone home and the afternoon boys hadn't arrived, I couldn't pool with *nobody,* so my scoop was legitimate.

Usually we went to Mabel's apartment at Seventh and Figueroa, I'd drop off to sleep in my chair or on the floor. I never saw Mabel asleep. If I woke up she was flitting about like a firefly.

As Edna St. Vincent Millay was to say so poignantly, we were burning the candle at both ends all right. And though it gave a lovely light, I can see now that it wasn't a good way of life for young girls, which is what we were. Being tough of fiber, of body and soul, thanks to my ancestry and my spring training, I survived but the candle didn't last the night for Mabel Normand.

In those nighttime girl talks, Mabel told me a story of her life. Looking terror-stricken into a dark past, she said as a child she had worked in a garment factory. A high percentage of tubercular infection in those hellholes I saw later in our fight against child labor, which you wouldn't believe. From the scars she carried, Mabel had been attacked by this consuming fire when she was eight. Soon enough to save her, someone glimpsed her beauty, her charm, she became a salesgirl, the advertising department took a picture, she made her first movie at Fort Lee.

Never once did she mention a family. No mother, father, brother, sister, uncles, aunts or cousins. She never described any house she lived in, school or church she attended. After making *Molly O* for Sam Goldwyn, she became one of the greatest major stars, but no kith or kin showed up to claim her. This is very rare. No former schoolmates, usually there are four or five thousand of these to bear witness.

Maybe we did find her under a rosebush.

When she was not too long out of her teens, two tragedies caught the beloved little clown and put out light, laughter and love, and none of these, I weep to say, have been equaled since on our celluloid records. Nor for me, in any other human being. Those of us—the few who are left—who knew her keep saying that.

First, the heartquake of her broken love, the night before she was to have been married to the man she loved.

Then the shocking scandal of the morbid ugly murder of another girl's illicit lover, of which Mabel was suspected.

Mabel loved Mack Sennett only and always. Yet for a long time she refused to marry him. In our Vernon days, she was a virgin, as most of us were. Mabel danced, flirted, basked in admiration. But she loved Sennett. I had never been in love, but I could recognize this. You couldn't miss it and, as she said, with rueful laughter she was a One-Man Woman.

When she kept putting him off, I asked her *why?* "He loves you, too," I said, and she said gravely, "I know. But he doesn't really want to marry anybody. His mother—you know how old Irishwomen are—wants grandchildren, she talks him into it. But I can't marry Mack unless he wants *me* for his *wife* more than anything in the world."

Chopin could have written her laughter the day she told me she believed he did, and so she flew swiftly toward that wedding; the altar was to be of white lilac and she'd carry lilies of the valley. Would I be her maid of honor?

As bride's gift to the groom she was giving Mack a priceless little chest said to have belonged to Joaquín Murrieta, that leader of the Spanish underground against the gringos, who was Mack's hero. On the night before the wedding Mabel dropped by his house to leave it.

Mack was supposed to be at a bachelor dinner.

He kept pleading to see her, to explain. I honestly thought if she had to talk to him she'd die, so I hid her down at the beach. I kept trying to tell her about the night before the wedding or the wife having the first baby; Pearl Morton told me she would never *let them in.*

At last Mabel said, "If it had been some girl I didn't know, I could make it not *real.* But she was a friend. So I keep on seeing it again and it is real.

Part of my real life, real people. You have to have faith in a marriage, I had it, I don't any more. It isn't that I don't forgive them. Only the magic I thought was to be our wedding night, our marriage, is gone. I don't want marriage to him without magic. Or faith. It won't work."

Two weeks later she jumped off the Nat Goodwin pier in the dark. How the boys saved her in the pitch black as the swirling waves battered her against the rocks and piles, I don't know. I—I wished they hadn't—that the sea had been allowed to take her down to play with the mermaids. It was one of the times I had to learn that there are worse things than death. For in life we still had to go through one of the world's most famous unsolved murders with Mabel in jeopardy all the way.

Briefly.

The victim of this all-Hollywood murder was a front-rank director at Paramount. To me he was a fugitive from Somerset Maugham's tales of handsome, aristocratic English remittance men driven by scandal to the South Seas or the Alaskan Klondike, and ending in Hollywood as a man of mystery. To us, very sophisticated. I thought he was a nice guy because he appreciated the beauty, wit, and rarity of Mabel Normand.

He'd been among us several years when his body was found on his living-room floor in his fashionable Wilshire Boulevard garden court apartment; he had been shot, no gun was found, a houseboy was missing. The last time William Desmond Taylor had been seen alive he was putting Mabel Normand into her chauffeur-driven car in the early evening. Eyewitnesses said he stood watching her drive away, then went back into his house to his death.

The reason it was and has remained such a big, all-fired unsolved number in the murder mystery collections is because the district attorney never made a charge. So much time has passed that I may speak openly of it as I once erupted to that district attorney, Thomas Lee Woolwine, a lifelong friend of our family and, on occasion, my father's opponent in court. Having lost patience, I said, "Innocent people are under suspicion. Among them Mabel Normand. Sure she has an alibi but in the public mind only the guilty have those and Mabel has a reputation for *trouble*. Why don't you solve all this by arresting the person you know did shoot Taylor?"

"You know I couldn't convict her," Tom said in his Southern drawl.

"I'll give you the little pink chiffon step-ins with the monogram on them I've had hidden in my bureau drawer ever since it happened," I said. "There's your motive." He was furious with me for swiping evidence. He kept shaking his head. I said, "If the jury acquitted her on the Unwritten Law of a mother's right to kill the man debauching her child, it'd still take the heat off Mabel and it wouldn't hurt you. There have been others you couldn't convict."

Let me present in truth the Case of the Hollywood Producer, the Child Star and her Smother-Mother and with it the solution to Hollywood's deepest mystery.

As for Mabel, it is true that night after night she'd been at Taylor's apartment. He gave her the man companionship she'd been used to in her work association with Sennett. He was, she told me, her close friend, but they had never spoken a word of love nor exchanged more than a friendly kiss. I believed her because Mabel always told the truth. But to the world it was, of course, a love affair and anything including murder can come of *that*.

The houseboy was a No. 1 suspect. Legally, you don't have to prove motive, but Papa always said you'll play hell getting a conviction without one *and* if you prove that this murder is *against* the interests of the suspect the odds are the jury will think him innocent. Why should he kill the goose that continued to lay the golden eggs of an easy job with extraordinary totin' privileges. Bill Taylor knew about his pickings. "But," he said once to his neighbor, young comedy star Douglas McLean, "I overlook them for his Jeeves qualities as a valet and cook." To which Doug had replied, "Bill, you need a lady of the house," and Taylor said—as did Rhett Butler—"I am not a marrying man."

There we are. In those words lay Taylor's death sentence.

Why did the servant disappear? Cash on hand was a fetish with Taylor. Somewhere, sometime, Mabel told me, he'd been forced to make an emergency take-off. As a result, he kept a roll of five thousand dollars handy. The one person who knew where this lay hidden was the houseman. It seems obvious that he came in early, found Taylor dead—the time the shot was heard was just after seven. He saw a corpse, the end of a job, pickings, and privileges; to use the money for its original purpose of escape, taking along studs, cuff links, and money, must have seemed normal procedure—it couldn't hurt Bill Taylor now.

None of them—houseboy, money, jewelry—have ever been seen since.

The big clue was the monogram. In embroidery done in France three letters floated like butterflies on intimate undergarments. A mother might well demand that the man who had these in his bedroom should marry her nineteen-year-old daughter.

Among my souvenirs I find a Friday night at what we called a Cat Party in early Hollywood, the men being at the American Legion fights. The girls, Lillian and Dorothy Gish, Colleen Moore, Gloria Swanson, were gossiping about this affair and somebody said, "*If Bill Taylor doesn't look out, that girl's mother is going to shoot him one of these days; she ought to."*

Any wonder that we thought she had?

Take it as a basic assumption and go on from there.

I had two close friends living in the court at the time. It was a rectangle of two-story frame bungalow-type houses with balconies, a block square built around a garden. Every window was an observation post. It fronted on Alvarado Street, the three other sides had delivery alleys behind.

After the murder Doug McLean's wife Faith said to me, "We hung out the windows, of course, watching Taylor and his lady friends." She and Mother Meyer's beloved Hazel Gillon, who was to become Mrs. Ernest Holmes and who had an apartment cater-corner, had seen Mabel come and go openly enough, and been surprised to see a little ingenue also sort of fluttering in and out.

On the night of the murder Faith, from her back porch, had seen someone lurking in the alley behind Taylor's back door. Later after she had seen Bill put Mabel in her car, she heard a shot. "It was just after seven. I went to the back porch to see if a truck had backfired. No truck—but—there was somebody sort of scurrying—"

"Who was it?" I said. She hesitated and I said again, "Who was it?" and she said, "—wasn't cold, pulling her coat collar up and her hat down the way a woman does—it was so peculiar it made me sure it was a woman dressed as a man—" "Did you recognize her?" I asked.

A woman of high principles, Faith was silent. "A small, quite thin woman—" she said after a while.

"Under oath," I said, "would you identify her?"

"I'd—have to," Faith said, "wouldn't I?"

Hazel hadn't heard the shot but she'd seen the figure scurry-hurrying around the corner. "A man might have thought it was a man," she said. "Any woman would have known it was a woman. I would swear it was a woman."

That's opportunity. Now for motive. The *only* motive.

In doing a piece for Jimmy Quirk about movie stars' Christmas presents, I found this mother had given her grown daughter dolls. Not a doll, but dozens of dolls. The puzzlement was how she had escaped her nursery long enough for l'affaire Taylor. Hollywood was a matriarchy. No more wise, wonderful, and remarkable women than Charlotte Pickford, Mrs. Gish, Peg Talmadge, Phyllis Daniels ever lived. We had mothers who failed and succeeded, but we had no other mother with a pathological obsession concerning her daughter's life, love, and career until Jean Harlow's Mama Jean came along. Her we forgave. If you were Jean Harlow's mother, you had to be a tigress.

Being murdered, I am sure, surprised hell out of William Desmond Taylor. I've always been convinced his last words were *I am not a marrying man.* Seeing the gun, he must have laughed incredulously, and when the shot hit as he fell he must have had a flash that to be shot by an old lady in man's clothes for the seduction of a theatrical maiden well over the age of consent, and a buxom wench at that, constituted a supreme irony.

We were a very small town. We were amazed to see the police running around *investigating.* In a small town everybody knows everything and we did. We were likewise amazed to find that police public and out-of-town newspapermen suspected Mabel Normand—kept questioning her. *Why?* Because she was there—because somehow she was Mabel and mortals in the end must destroy the elves and fairies.

For that reason I kept the monogramed lingerie. Ike St. Johns had stolen it. My husband was then secretary to the mayor, who had sent him out early to the Taylor apartment to see what was going on. The mayor didn't want any further scandal in Hollywood, already fighting the charge of a second Sodom and Gomorrah. Ike knew also that, without a qualm, I would throw both the girl and her mother into the furnace along with Shadrach, Meshach, and Abednego before I let them touch a hair of Mabel's head, and that was why he brought the step-ins home in the first place.

After a while of course the police and the press knew Mabel was innocent. But for what time was left to her The Public kept on reacting to her as a first-class suspect. *Evidence* never alters that kind of strange stupid somebody-said-so suspicion. Baby face with the golden curls as against the dark smile-when-you're-hurt clown who had already tried suicide—? And Mabel was so light, so nonresistant that she whirled on top of the hurricane but it broke her spirit at last. Scandal, like death, loves a shining mark. Both scandal and death loved the shining mark Mabel was.

When no one was ever arrested it was all registered as an Unsolved Mystery with Mabel still part of it. Other things—she attracted them—a very rich young man killed himself in her car. Nobody ever knew why. "I don't *know,*" Mabel said to me through tears. The Fatty Arbuckle scandal and trial hit us. Fatty had worked at Sennett's when Mabel did, she went at once to see his wife. Buzzing tongues spread this—why had Mabel gone to the Arbuckles' home?

So swift was the pace of this gold rush that a new generation skyrocketing in Hollywood did not know Mabel Normand's glory, her triumphs in Goldwyn classics after she left Sennett. Socially, she was déclassé. We had Society in Hollywood by then—Parties. George Fitzmaurice, noted as the best woman's director in the business, invited Mabel to one of his parties. He told me later he would rather have directed her than

Garbo. Yet as she sat on his stately staircase chattering little starlets gave her only surprised stares.

The one who did the most to save her was a matinee idol named Lew Cody. With half the women in Hollywood chasing him, he made Mabel marry him and when I smugly thought, Well, there's so much good in the worst of us, he said quietly, "It's no credit to me to take care of her, she's the only woman I have ever loved."

Maybe this was true of Mack Sennett also. He didn't marry Mabel, but he didn't marry anybody else either, though he lived to a ripe old age.

If I weep for Mabel it is partly because we lost her gift, such a gift it was! And partly because among my treasure I hold that I should have been Mabel's best friend—it still heartens me.

In our teens we used to talk about whether we believed in God. I was defiant and Mabel was seeking. She wanted to believe, she spent hours on her knees in front of Our Lady. I wanted to help her but—in that piteous yearning I had nothing to give. So as time went by I tried to persuade her to be merry as we had been when we were very very young. She adored merry-go-rounds and roller coasters, there had been none in her childhood, for a little while they would take her right out of the world. Oh—I wish I had known enough to do a small part for her of what I know now she did for me. Teaching me that *joy* can endure in affliction and remain joy-in-the-heart. That happiness is in-spite-of more than because-of.

I'm glad that at last I've had the courage to write about the littlest clown, though it hurts almost as much as it did when she died so gently. For as I have written I've heard once more the angel song of her laughter.

I hope now I never have to lose it again.

CHAPTER 8

The way I got mixed up with Hollywood was accidental, involuntary, and irretrievable. There I was when Hollywood went up like a self-operating elevator with me in it. The only button I pushed was one of the noblest impulses of my checkered career. To make a home for my children.

This phone call came from Jim Quirk, of whom I had never heard.

We seldom recognize a Big Moment and this might not have been one but for the timing.

Coming as it did—

When Ike and I had just had a row ending in dialogue I intended to forget but couldn't.

When I saw in two well-intentioned errors what could happen to my children when I wasn't there.

When a haunting echo awakened me in the night and I heard my grandfather quote again that old proverb *No man can drive three mules.*

When I had no place at all for Papa even for a few minutes.

                                                        —this idea's Moment had arrived.

". . . better," I had said to Ike, an icy edge on my voice, "if you came home once in a while before dawn. I'd like to get some sleep."

"Home?" Ike bellowed. "If I came straight home you wouldn't be anywhere around, would you?" I was going to answer him but I saw he had begun to cry. Only partly from sleepiness and too much poker and that last gin for the road. A big, good-looking young man absolutely filled with heaven-bestowed talent to get other men to follow him. If only he knew where he was going! He could never face anything, when it was there in his path he turned aside. God help me, I knew this already.

I was having trouble with my daughter Elaine. We had Linnie, who'd taken care of her when she was a baby, and Linnie's husband Archie working for us now. Linnie spoiled her baby, she waited on her and talked to her all day whether we got any dinner or not. At three, as she then was, Elaine was a decade pre-Shirley Temple but she had the same effect on her populace. We had no yard in front and less than half of that behind, but into that I had crowded a slide, a swing, and a sandbox for her.

Unless somebody stayed to keep her company, she climbed up the back steps and yelled until Linnie brought her baby in. The Sunday before I had determined in a sort of frenzy to let her cry it *out,* I did, too, until the neighbors who also adored her called the S.P.C.C.

Archie and Linnie had begun holding séances, audible all over the house. They'd then left me so that Archie, as Mother Meyer and I later discovered, could set up in business for himself.

One night I'd worked late, on the Obenchain case, I think, and came home to find every light and the phonograph on full blast, the blond Swedish girl I'd hired was entertaining at a beer bust. Running upstairs like a madwoman, I said to myself, You cannot trust white people ever, my Billy was in his bed with all his clothes on, even his shoes, and I could see the tear marks where he'd cried himself to sleep. He woke instantly and held out his arms and croaked at me—he'd caught a *cold*—

By the time I got back downstairs the Swedish girl had vanished forever, so if I was going to strangle anybody for neglecting my children it would have to be suicide not murder.

One night somebody brought Papa to me and in this horrid cold little house. I'd hardly had time to notice. I had no place for him, I couldn't sleep on the floor and put him in my bed because Ike was in it already.

All these things were present when the voice from New York said, "This is Jim Quirk of *Photoplay* magazine."

I'd never heard of that, either.

Mr. Quirk pinned it down. He said, "I've read your stories in the *Herald* and I'm wondering if you'd care to do a few pieces about Hollywood for me in your spare time."

Spare time? I said to myself. Aloud I said, "Hollywood?"

Mr. Quirk said, "Naturally, you know where Hollywood is—"

"I used to live there," I said. "I went to Hollywood High School—ten years ago. But what—"

"It's becoming a geographic synonym for The Movies," Jim Quirk said. "I've started a magazine for movie fans, there are millions of them already and will be millions more. They're interested in Movie Stars, Mary Pickford and Tom Mix and Charlie Chaplin. They don't know anything about them and I thought they'd buy a magazine to read interviews—stories—" He waited but I didn't know what to say, he went on, "I could pay you thirty-five dollars apiece, I could use two, even three, a month under different names. You're right there. I could also give you $2.50 for anecdotes about them for a department I call Cal York."

Right there, my friends, was born the Hollywood Column. To show you how new this was, we were to publish in this, a monthly magazine, Rudolph Valentino's engagement to Natasha Rambova; the equivalent of this story today would make every front page everywhere.

Here indeed was an unheralded unrecognized Big Moment for young Mrs. St. Johns of the *Herald,* wife of Ike, mother of Elaine and Bill. Big sister of Thorny and Bryson, who were around more and more whether there was room or not.

Aside from everything else, let me say here that no journalism school ever gave a course as valuable as Jim Quirk's assignment to me of *anecdotes.* I would need desperately the extra ten bucks, or even more, that it could mean. But Jim Quirk was a fanatically fastidious and dramatically *comme il faut* editor; my luck in editors held. Having built *Popular Mechanics* into a blockbuster ahead of its time, he was now turning his Irish blue eyes on Hollywood, was to be a vital stimulant in its growth, a witty and often sternly critical voice, again almost prophetically. Most important to me as a writer was his eagle eye and good taste for these anecdotes. His never-tell-it-if-you-can-show-it as an editorial demand I'd met before though not as definitely, but you could no more fool Jim Quirk with a press release or get by with a small fake than you could fool Howey.

Up to then, the only thing I'd done for magazines was pulp fiction. A long long fiction story for the Black Cat to pay the bills for Elaine's arrival. There were, to be sure, Hearst Magazines but to the newspapers those were a sort of never-never land. Howey didn't encourage it. In fact it was through Jim Quirk that I finally met Ray Long, editor of *Cosmopolitan,* and the first story I sold him was Hollywood fiction.

I told Mr. Quirk I'd think it over.

Plainly, as far as I was concerned, I couldn't do it in my spare time for I didn't have any.

It is totally impossible, writing about this now, not to know that here in this decision began in deadly earnest the tug-of-war that is at the core of every modern woman. What I was to come up off the floor fighting with and about in my debate with Mrs. Winters.

Whether or not I knew it at that time I find it difficult to be sure. Some things as you look back you see permeating your whole life, some seem so clear in retrospect that it has to be *impossible* that you didn't know at the moment. Often, nevertheless, you didn't or you couldn't have done what you did or not done what you didn't. On the path, you can see only so far ahead, you are afraid to look down or back, or even up and ahead sometimes.

I remember I sat on the steep back steps with my knees up under my chin and watched Miss Elaine, happy as a kitten in the sandbox, showing her little brother Bill how to build houses on sand. She had on pink rompers and was carrying on a conversation with him about the Duchess' pig, a character she admired inordinately. I remember it was a clear, hot day in from the Mojave Desert, I let down my braids, on about a foot of which I could sit, and held my face up to the comforting warmth.

Whether I knew it or not, my three mules were with me. Capering and prancing about. Getting the harness tangled. I feel, from here, a distinct sympathy for that young woman, sitting in the sun, so desperately wise about so many wrong things, so heart-and-soul anxious to do right, *as who isn't?* So stupid, so spoiled, so bright, so eager, so distraught. This young creature had no pattern, no precedent, no group discussion, no educational investigation, no recognition as yet of careers for women as part of the American way of life. Ninety per cent of the women who were wives and mothers did NOT have nor wish careers or jobs. No psychiatrists, either, thank God; the psychiatrist of that day with his alibis and indulgences, explanations and concentration on *self* would have driven her up the wall.

This goddam house is too small—I hear that from her stream of consciousness. It has been, she thought, for quite a while. It's a horror now that I look at it. The kids in one room and Elaine keeps Bill awake with her chatter. It's too small I can't even find my clothes which is why I never look dressed properly. If I decided to do some Hollywood pieces we would have to move, it is all too far from here.

We ought to move anyway.

To do these, I'd have to quit my job.

I could work *at home.*

Home?

Where? In the bathroom?

If I got, say, seventy dollars for two interviews even one hundred and five dollars for three, and an extra ten dollars for anecdotes maybe more, if Quirk was willing to pay for my gas, it'd add up to almost as much as my salary.

I pinned up my hair, got Elaine out of the sand, put Billy under my arm, and took off.

Better not tell Ike until I'd made up my mind.

A big yellow house set on a corner, with orange trees, we could pick the oranges while they were still warm and *ripe,* the blossoms and leaves would smell divine. Several palm trees, an acacia, and along the walk some jacuarandas that dropped their purple flowers in drifts, in full bloom they had breath-taking beauty. The garden had been allowed to dry up, there were a few rosebushes that could be saved and lots of room for sweet peas if you took the trouble. Out beside the garage that had been a barn were a broken-down chicken coop and two artichoke bushes. All around the house was an old-fashioned California veranda for sitting out on when your work was done and the roast was in the oven. Over one side of the veranda was an enormous old climbing rosebush, the La France, in a waterfall of shell pink and fragrance.

An overwhelming yearning I must have had battened down in the lowest hatches sprang up, clutched at every growing thing, every green leaf. How, I thought, do people *live* in cities, in houses where you don't see anything but the asphalt street and other houses? My longing for the ocean was ever-present, I always knew that, but a garden—trees—growing things—this was there, too. Somehow I'd been thrown out of a garden and I wanted back in.

Inside, the house was enormous. Big, high-ceilinged rooms, bow windows, *three* fireplaces. A house is not a home without a fireplace, in the ache of the modern home there is no *hearth*. The most charming thing in all the world, Victor Hugo calls it. If there is no hearth how can there be a cricket on it? Upstairs were seven bedrooms. Downstairs a servants' wing *with* a bath. And in that sitting room there was a fireplace!

I saw out the window a school, only a block down Franklin, and across the street a drugstore and a grocery and a vegetable stand.

That frenzy of impatience, with which I was so familiar, took over.

I have to have those fireplaces and that orange tree and that *library* with bookshelves right now. Let's go.

Of this I can make a home.

As well as I could I slowed down my thought processes. Nobody will get it before you can. You're *here*. Take it easy. *Think,* for once in your life. This would be a big step. No way to make a home no matter how many fireplaces unless the woman is *in it*. The house's wife. On the hearth. Face that, will you be so kind? The women who came West made homes in covered wagons. A palace is not a home if the queen is off conquering tribes with an amazonian spear.

You have got to become this house's wife.

A home is absolutely necessary to make a family, as a nest is for birds. Children must be part of a family. That's the whole thing in a nutshell. Nothing is so important as for them to know it is their family. All for one and one for all, as the three musketeers said. United we stand, divided we fall. A mother is what makes a home. A mother who is *there,* puts her children first, knows all about them every day, speaks their language because she hears it all the time, hears them evolve and create it, she understands it, she listens to what they mutter in their sleep, what they say when they fall off their bikes, when they scream with nightmares.

Footfalls echo in my memory, in the emptiness of that big, spacious, old, hard-to-run house, with its enormous closets, its spreading bow windows, its fireplaces that would be so much trouble. I said to myself, You never had a mother. Nobody ought to know as well as you do what it means not to have a mother when you are small. Whether because she isn't *there,* or because she doesn't care anything about you if she *is.*

Too late for me to say the wise words of that wise woman, Katharine Hepburn, spoken many years later, but I must appropriate them for this moment of my decision. "I know," said Miss Hepburn, "that if a mother is not at home, available to the child, the child is apt to become insecure. I know that when I realized I was going to lead a professional life, to become the victim of what I did, I very quickly decided I would never have any children."

That decision it was too late for me to consider, it always had been.

About the *job.*

My father insisted all women should be trained for some kind of self-supporting work in an emergency. Admittedly, the emergency of war was over for me. The financial emergency in which we existed had little to do with this. I always earned enough to pay my household for the domestic work I didn't do. The difficulty with that was that then *they* were *there,* and *I* wasn't.

Come to think of it, all the women in my family had been professionals. In those moments of striving intelligence and ever-present intuition, I saw an interesting fact. My grandmother was a college professor after her children were grown. My Aunty Blanche was on the vaudeville and concert road as an accompanist to opera stars, had a musical career, so that she didn't marry until late. After she did and had her children she taught piano, had her chamber music group that gave morning recitals in her at-home studio. In fact, she stayed home. Aunty Madge played first horn in orchestras at the Burbank and Belasco theaters. She had no children of her own but when she married she stayed at home with her husband, taught hundreds of them from high schools, so that the house in which she stayed home was always blowing bugles and sounding trumpets.

Thought, Voltaire says, depends absolutely on the stomach.

My stomach, as I heard my children shrieking with joy as they slid on the polished floors, told me that what had moved my advanced relatives back into their homes was the oldest of all inherited instincts for woman. Handed down from far far back of their Puritan grandmothers in New England, their pioneer ancestresses in Maryland and the South. These women had taken their freedom as human beings for granted. They used partnership as equality, and motherhood as essential superiority, in matters of their responsibility for the character and well-being of their men and their children. In emergency, they did what had to be done, but their accepted pattern was to stay home and see to first things first.

Unless you can drive three mules, you must be content to drive two.

How about a couple of mules and a burro? To be called *working at home?*

First things first. Which would be the burro?

The answer was obvious.

All the jolting rushing thought forces of my stomach showed me that a *family* has to have a *father*.

The name of the game is Life with Father. Mother could be taken for granted.

Men and women began to call each other Father and Mother early. Their relationship to each other existed only in their relationship to their children. What's wrong with that? I said to myself. The Nora-daughter within you at all times knows what a father can mean. Not that Ike could ever be like my father, just the same Elaine had a right to a father—to say Papa—to have that extraordinary affection that exists only between fathers and daughters.

If Ike would consent to this.

Before talkies, when Jack Gilbert was a top-ranking movie star, in a bleak moment after he'd broken off his tremendous love affair with Garbo, he asked me to marry him. I said, "But Jack, we're not even a little bit in love, much less madly." Jack said bitterly, "I hope not. Being madly in love is an agony. Couldn't we form a partnership and live happily together?" I said, "You wouldn't be satisfied with that, sooner or later, lamb, you would fall madly in love with somebody and being what you are you'd be noisy about it, and I wouldn't like that. No no, we'd never be satisfied with a *partnership*." He saw the point, we stayed friends, he left his godson, my Dicky, a trust fund to go through college, like so much Jack did that was generous and loving there wasn't enough substance to set up the trust fund.

I didn't know whether Ike would be content to be Father, dear Father.

I intended Ike should have a happier life, I'd see to that. Not only would I *be there,* but more attention must be paid to him. A good deal less to Mrs. St. Johns' work, now being done—as I was picturing it—placidly at home. His career had grown from his secretary-to-the-mayor success into recognition as a campaign manager for candidates running for the Senate, the governorship. With a wife, a home, a family behind him he could become a power.

Or, said my stomach to me, could he?

Ike, everybody always said, is such a nice guy.

He was, too.

Leo Durocher is one of the men I usually agree with. When he popped off that *Nice guys don't win ball games* it distressed me and I decided to look up the shopworn treacle word. *Nice:* pleasing, amiable, pleasant, agreeable, easygoing, characterized by good manners and language. Leo meant that *just* being a nice guy, always being a nice guy, not having any-thing you were ready to *not* be a nice guy about, meant you weren't fit to win ball games. In those terms of definition, you wouldn't win the tough games you *have* to win. I might be a lousy wife but I knew Ike was a nice guy about ninety-nine per cent of the time.

He was such a *cheerful loser,* and too generous so that he paid more than things were worth, too high a price. When he got a little tight on Friday nights after the fights as most men did in Hollywood, he brought home expensive gifts. Once he brought me a fire-engine-red Rolls-Royce town car, the chauffeur we didn't have was supposed to sit outside. If you drove it yourself, there you'd be come rain or snow or darkest night. One difficulty about that nearest I ever came to a town car was that it was bigger than our garage. Trying to get the rear end in, Ike poked the back wall out. Coming to get the paper the next morning, there was that ele-gant Rolls-Royce wearing my lil' ole garage. But—Ike had traded in my Es-sex coupe as a down payment. I had to spend the time, energy, and pride taking it back and blackmailing the agent into giving me back the little car I could afford and drive by telling him I knew more movie stars who could afford a Rolls-Royce than he did. I suppose no all-nice guy could have been a suitable husband for Earl Rogers' daughter Nora. If there was ever a man who hated to lose, who pulsed with glory when he won, who was never nor wanted to be one-of-the-boys, that man was my father. He never settled for mediocrity in his life.

To be what his ability, his personality, his good looks, his valuable education gave him the right to be, Ike needed something more.

I could have supplied it.
First of all—
I suppose I had to try out whether he'd be a burro.
Suddenly, in spite of the sum of the facts if faced, I had a completely happy moment. The telephone in the dining room had not been discon-nected. I practically floated over to it to call Jimmy Quirk.
Then I told the real estate man I would take the house.
Ike, when I told him, was so pleased he didn't even resent my having done it all without consulting him. *Such* a nice guy.

There we were, spang-bang in the middle if it, at the corner of Franklin and Bronson, where Wally Reid and Cecil B. DeMille, now batting No. 1 ahead of D. W. Griffith as the producer-director, drove by every morning on their way to work. Ten minutes in my Essex, with a baby on the back seat, from Universal City, Sennett in Edendale, Christie Brothers and Griffith on Sunset and Hollywood boulevards, RKO a couple of blocks away on Gower, and Ince down at Culver City, the longest trek and only about half an hour even with a few cross-streets.

Thinking of Wally Reid as the handsomest man I ever saw to this day, I always see him one morning when he drove up in his big dark-blue open roadster to say hello, and Elaine raced down and he swung her into the car before Bill and I and my two small brothers could get there. Instead of his usual gay and amiable greeting Wally stared at me a minute and said, "What the *hell* have you done to your head?"

Trying to be insouciant and sophisticated, I said, "I have had my hair bobbed. Like Mrs. Vernon Castle, the great dancer. It's the latest fashion."

"On her," Wally said, "it may look good. On you it looks like somebody hit you over the head with a broom."

I began to cry. I was really scared silly. Ike had gone to Sacramento for a couple of days and I had steamed up my courage to do this dread deed. Nobody else in Hollywood or anywhere else as far as I knew had bobbed hair. Except the brilliant Irene Castle and she seemed far far away. I said, "I am so tired of all that hair pinned on top of my head. You don't know how wonderful it is. I had sore spots from the hairpins. Mrs. Castle is a great star a lot bigger than you or Mr. DeMille—"

Wally said, "Did you cut it yourself?" and when I nodded he began to roar with laughter. He said, "Get in—at least we can have it cut properly—" so I got Billy and we went over to the Famous Players Lasky Studio on Vine Street and got the studio barber to do it—though I must say he didn't want to and protested without ceasing. When he saw how it looked after we got it done Wally said it was quite an idea at that and brought his wife, Dorothy Davenport Reid, to have hers done—hers was a gorgeous *red*—so we started the new fashion.

It all seemed to have fallen into place. I now had a couple from New Orleans, Prue and Laura Dejoie. They had a little girl named Celestine the same age as Billy—Prue was devoted to Bill. I can hear him now, "No Billy no Billy your mama say you can't have any white bread and molasses," but when Bill came out he had molasses all over him. The Tom Inces—just across the street—were neighbors—real neighbors. Tom was the Ince of Ince Studio. Nell Ince was a wife, mother, and a cultured lady and they had three boys. My two brothers stayed with me most of the time by then, there was lots of room.

Also I decided to pay a little more attention to my *clothes,* the way Papa had tried to teach me. Nothing really made me itch with boredom like looking at, buying, and fitting clothes. But in Hollywood, where now we had to have some social life, not like when I was on the paper, I saw that I had to. My clearest recollection is of a plaid blue-and-green skirt worn with a tailored blue jacket. Looking at it in the three-way mirror at the Unique, the best dress shop in town, I let out a shriek of protest.

"I can't go out in this," I said, "it's almost *up to my knees*." They convinced me, by quotes straight from Paris where all good clothes came from then and by the most blatant flattery, that I could. Lady Godiva never felt nakeder than I did as I went out in public with it on.

I still didn't pay much attention to clothes when I was working at home.

I used the library to work in and one day I was sitting behind my typewriter contriving a piece under *one* of my names—all this, I kept telling myself, was good practice for something, like *real* writing on a newspaper —and I heard a voice speak behind me.

Bill had been a worry. He was two years old and up to that moment he had never said Mama or bye-bye or go-to-hell or anything. The doctor had examined him, he wasn't tongue-tied, and he said boys were much slower to talk than girls; he would, the doctor said, begin to talk when he was ready so meantime Billy smiled with kindliness upon the world and maintained silence.

Now a voice I'd never heard before said, "Mama come look at the lady going by out there—"

My amazement sent me out of my chair like a porpoise. Bill in his own good time was ready to talk. Also, I noted, he had something to say.

The children were all right and I was there when I packed Thorny and Bry off to school and Elaine to kindergarten.

Ike had a new campaign.

My house was run beautifully by Prue and Laura, who were part of our family, our household, and I was the house's wife.

My footsteps were not echoing too much, my memory says, one afternoon when the phone rang as I crossed the dining room. Loud, long, insistent peals—louder and longer and more insistent than usual. My heart hammered against my side, I could feel it, my stomach spun, I *knew* it was going to be Jack Campbell—or Mr. Hearst—a big story had just broken— it would be J.B.T. saying come on in, or Mr. Hearst with I have an idea we might—

Something *real*.

Real life—not cardboard sets and actors pretending to be somebody else.

I said, "Yes, yes, here I am."

It was Jimmy Quirk. He thought we ought to do a new story about Valentino.

I must have hesitated for Jimmy said, "Are you there, Adela?"

I said bitterly, "Oh yes. I'm here—I'm always *here*—"

Until I heard that bitterness and felt it flooding me I'd been able to squash down my hunger for my work. I felt at once on top of it, as I knew now it existed, what today we call guilt-by-circumstance. I hadn't done anything, I couldn't be blamed for anything, I couldn't help how I felt, but I was swamped in reeking guilt. The other mule—the second mule—had given me some kind of jerk on the reins, I knew I wanted to leap onto his back and go galloping off alone to the ring called the city room.

The guilt was in my genes. It was, and I knew it even then. The primal instinct to put children first, to protect and care for a home. Until civilization, if anybody wants to call it that as of now, breeds it out of women it will remain in her genes. I felt that any time I betrayed it, by all the gods and little fishes, I was a renegade and a rogue.

Burro or no burro.

So I put the kids in the car, picked up the boys at school, and went up the hill to interview Valentino once more. The kids played on the enormous king-size black velvet couch and I saw nothing incongruous in what might appear a wasted opportunity for any woman. But as a matter of fact neither would any other woman in Hollywood. Valentino was without that kind of honor in his home town.

CHAPTER 9

Hollywood is always coming into and going out of my life or vice versa. Either way, I am constantly aware of the extraordinary quality of the people I grew up with in Hollywood, so new and all. In the beginning, none of us had any perspective nor could we see the forest for the trees, which were pretty exciting themselves. Memory gives me a skyline, the horizon has a rim. In reconstructing that vanished past I would like it not—repeat *not*—to be the flight from reality so much written about it turns out to be.

Hollywood, a fragrant, idyllic peaceful country village in the midst of orange groves with trails leading to the ocean or up into the foothills. After school, when I went to Hollywood High, we strolled along as kids do ("teen-agers" wasn't yet in our vocabularies) under pepper trees that hadn't been touched since the Franciscan fathers walked that way and the Spanish grandees rode through on prancing horses.

It became the trade name for The Art and Industry of the Motion Pictures, in those pre-smog days, on its rate of sunshine hours per day, for movies pre-lighting were shot outdoors.

As I began to work on and in Hollywood for Jimmy Quirk, I had to shift my own focal point, trying to find the secret of Hollywood personalities and the drama and melodrama that inevitably sprang from these.

The secret was their *exaggeration.*

At a time when The Theater looked down on The Movies, in their infancy, one of its shining Broadway stars gave me that word as the key and it has opened the Hollywood door to me ever since.

David Warfield, whose *The Music Master* had been running in New York for years, came to our road company theater and I was sent to interview him. I found a white-haired distinguished twinkling star so gentle in manner that I decided to ask him a daring question. If I got an answer it might give me a real front page story. In his dressing room between acts I said, "Mr. Warfield, would you consider making a moving picture?"

"No no," he said, "oh no no," he repeated in a shocked tone.

To my surprise I found some sympathy and loyalty in me for the young people I knew who were pioneering this new wonderland and I said, "Why not? Perhaps someday they'll be as big as the theater."

"Of course," David Warfield said. "It is simply that I would not dare. I should make a complete failure. Pantomime is the supreme art of the actor, I know nothing of it." Then, with the golden voice and vibrant power he used on the stage he spoke the great line of his play. "*'If you don't want her, I want her.'* I must have the voice. I could not express myself without words as the movie actor must do. I go often to see motion pictures. Consider this carefully, my dear child. In the movies, you lack a dimension and always will. A painter to make his portrait life-size must make it larger than life so it comes off the flat surface of his canvas. So the actor on the flat celluloid film surface must be a third larger than life. Always he must be an exaggeration. I am not, I am only an actor."

To examine what was to be a totally new viewpoint is to find a profound truth. Brief example—

Shirley Temple was an exaggeration of everybody's little girl.

Marie Dressler was The Old Lady, everybody's, good or bad.

Chaplin the full prototype of The Clown.

Tom Mix—THE Cowboy.

Jean Harlow in black lace panties.

Garbo, mysterious, *belle dame sans merci,* forever unattainable.

Gable. The King. An exaggeration of A Man.

Humphrey Bogart, the Gangster, Mary Pickford, Our Sweetheart. Valentino the Latin Lover whose exaggeration no one has surpassed.

I could see why Mr. Warfield wanted no part of this. We were all so young in Hollywood. Artists perfect an art as it grows, but the initial flame must be there to begin with and we had it in early Hollywood.

2

According to John Mason Brown's *Mirror of His Times,* a biography of the great American playwright Robert E. Sherwood, Bob's contemporaries were perplexed to find this cool sophisticated New Yorker enamored of silent movies. At that time the man who became Franklin Delano Roosevelt's favorite speech writer was reviewing pictures for the original *Life.* In spite of mechanical flaws and rough edges he believed in them as a new art form and predicted they would become the major entertainment media not only of the United States but the world, since in the silents no language barrier existed.

Mr. Brown recalls that I was Sherwood's guide on his initial pilgrimage to the film capital. Our first visit I remember was to Charlie Chaplin, who was in one of his soulful moods and could do nothing but talk about Mabel Normand. Sherwood wanted to meet D. W. Griffith and we did, and at last Douglas Fairbanks, the object of his special admiration. Having met everybody in his first ten days, Sherwood, future author of *The Road to Rome* and the Lunts' greatest success, *Reunion in Vienna,* wrote for his magazine. "Hollywood seems to me to be a normal community, inhabited by regular people who go about their business in much the same manner as do the people of Emporia, Pawtucket, Little Rock, San Diego and Medicine Hat."

As I told him, he had fallen in love with Hollywood. He later married a beautiful movie actress, Madeline Hurlburt. He therefore lacked that perception that later understood F.D.R.'s alter ego, Harry Hopkins, well enough to write a book about that complex character. Like many others who came, stayed briefly, saw the dazzling glamour, he missed the main forces of all that Hollywood was and did. Henry Adams says a newspaperman is, more than most men, a double personality. In that double personality as a reporter *at all times* and a woman who lived with them for years, it hasn't been until I look back now and sort out my observations that I can comprehend most of it.

He had not, Bob Sherwood said, seen any *drugs.*

Hashish? Cocaine? Bhang marijuana LSD heroin?

Very few of those vital, excited hot-blooded high-spirited young pioneers needed such phony stimulants. Sex deviates were practically unknown, they had all they could do handling sex in its ordained orbits.

Meet some of them.

The child-like girl named Gladys Smith of Canada who, as Mary Pickford, was to convince Big Money that Big Movie Star could be Big Business. A grammar school dropout playing child parts in third-rate traveling companies, she, with her golden curls, put the gold into this new Gold Rush. The Gish sisters and their mother, straight out of *Little Women.* On the other hand the original IT girl, Clara Bow, had seen her mother haul sailors into the Brooklyn back room that was their home to earn a dollar to buy food. Colleen Moore, for two years the biggest box office attraction; her uncle, our Walter Howey no less, made D. W. Griffith give her a job when she was sixteen. Shortly she created The Flapper and changed the whole feminine population as no one else ever did until Jackie Kennedy came along. Doug Fairbanks never grew up, he dared to fulfill every man's dream of playing Robin Hood and D'Artagnan and Don Quixote as long as he lived, on and off the screen. He was one of the very few who'd been inside a *theater.*

They'd never been to New York. They had never been anywhere including school, except Joan Crawford, who washed dishes at Stephens College for Girls to get half a freshman year and Jean Harlow, who eloped from a fashionable Chicago finishing school at sixteen to get married. Unless they came over steerage—Chaplin and Valentino—they'd never been to Europe. Garbo was applying lather in a Stockholm barbershop until a Swedish director refused to come to America without her. Finances got frightfully tangled because half of them didn't know what to do with checks. Judy Garland was singing at Elks' Club smokers and Lon Chaney was a kid hoofer in the cheapest musical touring companies, half-medicine shows and half-circus.

Marie Dressler was at the other end of this scale. A Has-Been. She *had been* a Broadway star with Weber and Fields, so *through* that she had rented a place in Paris to start a boardinghouse for American tourists.

It is possible to *live* in a world of imagination as you go back into the past and, as I do, I know one thing that lights up that time and place and all its people. I once asked Knute Rockne what he wanted most in a football player, weight, speed, or brains and he said None of them—a *desire* to play football. Hollywood's first stars were burning with desire. An exaggeration of desire. The personalities, the beauty, the temperament, the lust for life, the *joie de vivre,* the vigor and vitality were exaggerated to include intensification of everything, dramatization on and off, IT girls, matinee idols who aroused nations of women, cowboys, and Indians *being* cowboys and Indians before our very eyes, the wits, wantons, un-balanced excitable irresistible people, all gathered in an area relatively not much bigger than Times Square. You've read of the Left Bank, Green-wich Village when it was not a phony tourist trap, and Bloomsbury of London, remember that on top of all they had, all that made them dra-matic, Hollywood was in and of itself a new Medium.

Do not believe for one second that they were ordinary citizens from Emporia and Little Rock.

I sat one day in a garden with Barbara La Marr, costar with Fairbanks in *The Three Musketeers,* the most beautiful woman I have ever seen in my life. She pointed to the white and gold butterflies among the flowers and said, "Our life is always short, isn't it?" And two days later was dead of what we called galloping consumption. I was with her because I'd known her for what then seemed a long time. The first time I ever saw Barbara her name was Rheata Watson, I was covering the juvenile court on some other story, and the judge sent Rheata home to Imperial Valley because he said she was "too beautiful" to be allowed loose in a big city. I took her back to the paper with me and we had a full front page of The Too Beautiful Girl that very day. God knows she was too beautiful to be loose in Hollywood.

P. T. Barnum invented a language of superlatives, he originated bally-hoo but Hollywood took over where he left off as *we* became The Greatest Show on Earth.

As I helped invent all this breathless excitement my own vocabulary grew from colossal to supercolossal to Colosseum to Colossus to all the words we could find or make up or splash on—as Gauguin splashed his colors in superlatives.

They thought Big—these guys. These Laemmles and Goldwyns and Mayers and Cohens.

Shakespeare? Let's see if we can get him to write for us.

How much will that fellow Dickens take for *Oliver Twist?*

They had no frame of reference at all.

There are still many landmarks to take me back, it's not *that* long ago.

Pickfair is there in Beverly Hills, in an upper room of exquisite beauty lives a beautiful old lady surrounded by an adoring court and watched over by a devoted husband, Buddy Rogers. Her name is still Mary Pickford.

Mr. Mayer's small private dining room off the commissary at MGM where the one-man decisions were made is gone. If it were there who would sit in it or make such decisions? But the main gate and the studio streets are the same. Ghosts walk them with me. Clark Gable swaggering with the sheer joy of living, Spencer Tracy as Father Flannagan, Lionel Barrymore in Dr. Gillespie's wheel chair. For at last of course The Theater's great came West. The Baby—Jean Harlow—getting ready to die gladly at twenty-six.

How odd that it is most often Lon Chaney who walks beside me. That rugged, cantankerous, stay-away-from-me guy who invented screen make-up—and behind him I see as background the crowds that gathered for miles when they heard he was dead. The telephone company going mad as their lines jammed for hours for people to cry it *mustn't be true.*

A *big* star! In electric lights, on twenty-four sheets on Broadway and Main Street, they billed him as LON CHANEY The Man of a Thousand Faces. The face I see as I write is not the Hunchback of Notre Dame nor the Phantom of the Opera, I see his own simple, lined, marred young face with an expression of love on it beyond any I have ever seen. For he is telling me about his mother, he talks to me for hours about his mother.

She was a deaf-mute. An invalid confined to her bed for long silent, lonely hours. No television then, they were desperately poor, she didn't have sufficient education to be much of a reader. Her son saw a nimbus of light around her head. Where he got the inspiration that he could entertain her, bring joy into her life, take her out of that room to meet people, he didn't quite know. It *came* to him, he said. He began to observe, to collect, to create characters and their stories. He began to impersonate for her his classmates, the baseball game they had played at recess, a lady shopping, the streetcar conductor changing the trolley, once he managed to sneak into the gallery of the vaudeville house and saw a dancer, and from that he made up more dances. Old hats, a yard or two of worn-out curtain, a dish towel—he designed costumes. When her face lit up with joy at all this the light that came to him, he told me, was what he thought the apostles saw on the Day of Pentecost. In that room he first *acted;* that frail woman, obscure and handicapped, was his first audience; this training and knowledge and desire he brought forth to reproduce for the world the crippled beggar in *The Miracle Man,* the Old Lady in *The Unholy Three.*

When he died his throat had been closed by cancer for weeks, he spoke his last words, as he'd spoken his first, to his mother on his hands.

In his will, he left One Dollar to Cleva Creighton Chaney, of whom no one had ever heard. I was writing his biography for *Liberty,* as a reporter I had to know who she was. I found a birth certificate, a divorce decree, at last I found *her,* cooking for the hands on a bean ranch near Oxnard. His first wife. She was a cabaret singer with a lovely voice, and he had left her, taking their two-year-old baby with him. Young Lon Chaney grew up believing the second Mrs. Chaney was his real mother but the birth certificate I found said his first name was Creighton. "I tried to see him," Cleva Creighton Chaney said, sitting in her cooking tent, wiping the sweat from her face. "I looked in the windows and he said he'd have me arrested. He thought I'd been unfaithful to him. He was a hard man."

An important man, Lon Chaney, in the development of the motion picture. The Encyclopaedia Britannica gives him many pages and pictures in their section on Make Up and Disguise, the inventions that made it possible for him to be legless, hunchbacked, dwarfed. It seems natural enough that his mind ran on the handicapped. His second wife had been previously married to a man without legs who ran a cigar store in San Francisco.

But—the thing I will always turn to is that look of love I saw on his face.

No no, do not believe that these were ordinary people going about their business as in Des Moines or Upper Montclair.

On the other hand, while Hollywood was wild and woolly and full of fleas and hard to curry below the knees, it was possible, as Bob Sherwood said, to see that it was not the sink of iniquity so-called after the Arbuckle, Wally Reid, William Desmond Taylor scandals. "I have," Bob wrote, "attended no orgies (heaven is my witness, Adela, and I have spared no effort to locate one), I've seen no murders, been offered no opium pipes." It seems to me all our sins were committed in hot blood.

Many of the early scandals were misunderstood and misinterpreted.

I knew the hanger-on amateur call girl who made a practice of tearing off her clothes when she had three drinks and who, uninvited to the party, died in Fatty Arbuckle's rooms. True, the Sennett comic was accused of murder. Pulpits and clubwomen's forums thundered in blind and ignorant horror. In Montana they shot up movie theaters. Ought we not to record and remember not only that he was ACQUITTED by a San Francisco jury but that jury in an unprecedented statement said that Arbuckle should never have been tried in the first place? A San Francisco jury would not be prejudiced in favor of anything that came out of Southern California.

As a comedy star, Fatty Arbuckle had contributed nothing but laughter, maybe a little comfort to those others who had been told that nobody loves a fat man. But my father had said at once that, though he was innocent, beyond question he would be publicly castigated because it was repulsive to think of a fat man in the role of a rapist.

Fatty had a sort of simple integrity. He was devoted to his wife, Minta Durfee. His reasonably ordinary spree in San Francisco became a savage puritanical witch hunt difficult to believe.

Come to think of it, we all had a sort of simple integrity.

Rudolph Valentino went to jail for bigamy. There may have been some simple stupidity in this. Yet there has to be a simple loyalty in his cry, "No no, I will go to jail before I will admit or agree that she is not my wife."

Simple integrity, as he saw it, kept Valentino off the screen at the peak of his fame for an entire year at a time when he enjoyed more personal popularity than any star can claim today. Simply because he would not agree to make the stories his studio picked for him and which he thought to be ugly, immoral, vulgar, and contributory.

Stop and recall how *poor* he was. How poor they all were.

The first time Valentino came to take me dancing he tore the seat of his pants when his pocket caught on the door handle of his rickety roadster. I said, "Never mind, Rudy, I'll wait while you go home and change," and he said wistfully, "I haven't got another pair of pants." So he wrapped a towel around him and I sewed the seat back in.

I know that no money would have persuaded him to any dirty inciting work to be shown, even if our summers were not then so long nor hot nor riotous as they have become.

To be sure, I saw Jean Harlow kidnaped by a real gangster, they shot Bugsy Siegal shortly afterwards. But Harlow fought to make comedies, and she would have been shot along with Bugsy before she played any of the call-evil-good sluts slatterns and she-goats actress of today present as images to teen-age movie fans.

They had integrity—and temperament, artistic and otherwise.

Nazimova—star of stage and screen as TV announcers say—once defined artistic temperament for me.

There are, she said, people who are like big brass gongs. To get a sound out of them you must hit them hard with a sledge hammer. Others—you know Chinatown? she said. You have seen outside the door those little glass bells, lovely painted panels of glass. You do not even have to touch them—a summer breeze—a note of song—the sob of a child—and they will begin to give out music. They will ring sweetly, gaily, sadly.

The brass gong is what most people have, she said, but the Chinese bells—ah, that is the true artistic temperament.

As The Movies swept the country, stories grew in news value. Gold was being panned from Universal to Culver City to the Selig Zoo. And people were behaving the way people do who are panning gold, especially if they did it with spades called artistic temperament.

Our big yellow house was square in the middle of this Mother Lode country.

3

In the library at last I had room for all our books, mine and my father's through the years, he didn't have a place for them any more. He came to visit us there, he liked to sit before the fire waited on hand and foot by Prue and Laura. Everybody always waited on Papa.

His hair was all silver, he still looked elegant in a wine-velvet dressing gown I kept ready for him, but the fiber of him seemed frail instead of tough. Sometimes he himself would sort of fade, the way a light bulb does before it goes out. His heart was playing for time, I knew this though I never admitted it even to myself. *Don't sit up with the corpse,* I'd promised him I wouldn't up at Jack London's Valley of the Moon.

I tried.

Now and then I talked to him about writing a *book*.

"On cross-examination," I said. "Who else can? It would be a help to law schools forever."

"Perhaps it would," he'd say. "I must think about it."

Then we'd go over the art of cross-examination and I'd put down some notes on his masterpieces. How once he made the chief witness for the prosecution practically confess to the murder on the witness stand. The medical question about the spray on his face in the McComas case. Those eight questions he'd prepared and which had taken him four days to ask Supervisor Gallagher when we defended Patrick Calhoun in the San Francisco graft trials.

His heart wasn't in it.

If he couldn't be Earl Rogers he'd rather be dead, he had said that. *Earl Rogers* was a great criminal lawyer in a courtroom defending the underdog. It was like telling a painter whose hand had been cut off to write a book about painting. In a way, it was like my hoping that telephone call would take me back to the city room and not to write articles about movie stars for a fan magazine.

"A book," I said to Papa, "would give you something to leave your grandchildren."

"Better I don't," he said with the old grin.

He was fond of his grandchildren.

There were moments when he was with them when I thought, Maybe he will make a big comeback.

The day Joe Schenck came out to my house with that big check to see if Papa would defend Fatty Arbuckle, I was sitting in the window seat watching him and my son Billy, who could just walk. Theirs was a silent companionship. Hand in hand, they were about to cross the street to the drugstore for an ice cream cone. Our big German shepherd dog, Ali, was following them and they were all three laughing at something. I thought, O God—please—he could *live* here with us and write a book, and my children would know him as I knew him.

I had to give the check back to Joe, I knew Papa didn't have the strength to defend a murder trial the way Earl Rogers defended a murder trial.

One night we were sitting in the library, the brightly burning logs filled the air with the clean spice of eucalyptus. My daughter Elaine came in, she had on a pair of pink flannel pajamas, her hair was still wet from her bath, under her arm was a book.

"What have we here?" Papa said to her.

She climbed up on his lap and his arm went around her.

"You know," she said, "about Mowgli."

"We have just read the whole book about Mowgli," Papa said.

"Begin at the beginning—" his granddaughter said firmly.

It was seven o'clock of a warm summer evening in the Seeonee Hills and Father Wolf had just—

The beginning? I got up and pretended I had to see about dinner. We would always keep the Children's Hour! We would always be beginning again—*It was seven o'clock of a warm summer evening*—it always would be, my children, *my* grandchildren and unto my great-grandchildren—

"Grandpa," Elaine was saying when I came back, "how old do you suppose Mowgli was when Father and Mother Wolf found him?"

"Oh," Papa said, "about as old as you are."

"Good!" Elaine said.

My eyes met Papa's and I knew we were remembering when Mowgli had been about as old as Earl Rogers' daughter Nora.

My eyes were saying, Once upon a time you came first, Papa. I think I would have died for you. Probably not, but I think so. You see it can't be like that any more. I have babies. You can love everybody or somebody most, but babies have to come first. He kept regarding me gravely, all of a sudden he gave me the most radiant joyous smile I'd ever seen.

Laura came to take Elaine to bed.

"We will read about Mowgli tomorrow," Elaine said to him. "Where Bagheera comes in."

But—tomorrow when we woke up, he was gone.

I knew we had said good-by to each other with that smile. So when a few weeks later the city desk called to tell me he was dead I—didn't go to see him. Why should I? Death is always a lie about the one who is gone.

I wore my best dress to the chapel where the underdogs gathered. And though nobody could see it, under my brand-new hat was the red ribbon they wouldn't let me wear to my grandfather's funeral when I was eight. I knew as well as anybody how sentimental that red ribbon Papa used to tie on the end of my pigtail was, but it comforted me a little so who should say me nay?

My anger with a God who'd let this happen to my father flamed up again higher than ever.

On my way home from that sad little service, I was swept by a new thought. It shocked me so I had to pull over to the curb and stop.

If it was true that there was no God who cared for us, then there would be no roll called up yonder, and neither Papa nor I could be there. I had seen him for the last time?

You will never lose me, Papa had said. *You will always know what I would have thought or said. . . .*

But that wasn't the same, was it?

As looking forward to someday when he'd be waiting to welcome me on that farther shore.

CHAPTER 10

Simultaneousness.

Simultaneity is the better word, no doubt.

Things that I know were strung out over years, woven back and forth in time, all too frequently seem to happen at the same time when you look into the past. Now I can see the decades from end to end—like from 1913 to 1932. What decades those were!

When you get to my age you are aware how lucky you are to have a *past*. So many today seem afraid they never will that they discount ours.

Your past shows signs of simultaneousness. Decades appear as tapestries, not video tape replays.

On Setting Forth. When Virgil spoke to Dante going up the hill from Purgatory on their way to Paradise, he said, "Turn your eyes downward; it will be good for you to tranquilize your way to see the imprint of your own footsteps ascending."

Perhaps it's a magnificent obsession but my memory says obstinately so much *was* simultaneous in the long view.

Vignettes.

How I knew that Amelia Earhart wasn't just flying around the world. I interviewed her on radio before she took off and I *knew* she was going on a mission so adventurous it made Mata Hari look like a thimblebelly. He drank, the only man she ever loved. That's why he wasn't with her when she died.

Auctions are bright gold splashes. Of William Randolph Hearst and *Miss* Julia Morgan, Beaux Arts architect of the Castle at San Simeon, who could say nothing more ways than my Great Aunt Betsy Bogart. Aunt Betsy Bogart, having caught Great Uncle with a girl in the haymow, cut her *own* throat, then decided no man was worth it, stitched herself up with a needle from her own sewing box, and, it is alleged, never mentioned it again. Mr. Hearst understood and obeyed what Miss Morgan *didn't* say at auctions. Otherwise he would have had eighty million dollars' worth of antiques in that New York warehouse instead of only forty. He was an auction buff and did the auctioneers know it.

That bright green bit? Mark Kelly and me going to South Bend to put over the first intersectional football game between U.S.C. and Notre Dame.

A dark purple patch. *Chicago*. The real gangster era and area. Johnny Torrio, who told Al Capone what to do, I had tea with Torrio and his daughters at their charming apartment on the lake shore. There, too, was humanitarian Jane Addams, founder of the social settlement Hull House. If we had a hall of fame for American women, as we should, she would be in it. Dion O'Banion, organizer of the alley gangs for Howey in his circulation war with the *Trib*. Mary Garden, prima prima donna of the Chicago Opera, big enough to play guard for the Bears, yet she danced *Salome* with more sex appeal than Brigitte Bardot because she *had* more sex appeal.

The Cal Coolidges (he was against sin and a teetotaler) at the Ranch the day Marion spiked the fruit punch with apricot, peach, and blackberry brandy, crème de menthe, and champagne—in her own defense later Marion told Mr. Hearst, "I *said* it was a fruit punch, champagne is made of *grapes,* you have to admit grapes are fruit, don't you?"

The silent stars move silently, especially Gary Cooper, who came from the Great Open Spaces where men *were* silent.

Automobiles, telephones for everybody, the Broadway Limited and the Twentieth Century, the Chief, and Super-Chief, as exciting to us as jets became to later generations.

Somewhere in Switzerland a man named Einstein talked about a formula—$E=mc^2$—nothing to do with us, this science business.

The Olympic Torch in the Los Angeles Coliseum, the press box in tears as the teams from around the world stood to attention in PEACE.

The Babe. One night at Damon Runyon's apartment I saw Babe Ruth bend over the phonograph as it went round and round. While it revolved at top speed the Babe began slowly but accurately to read the title on the record's label. A fantastic feat of the eye that made him able to hit anything any pitcher could ever throw him.

Don't let them cremate him, a whisper coming over my telephone said to me one quiet day.

Bits and pieces—and *lettering* woven in clearly so I can read it.

From Mr. Hearst
To All Publishers and Editors:

January 23, *1930*
You know I am personally interested in having our papers do all *they can*—to remember constantly to do all they can—to control the evil use of narcotics. The need is grave. I have asked to have news on this matter both from Geneva and Washington adequately covered. Please remember that to stamp out the illegal sale of narcotics and their use is a definite policy of our papers

which is never to be neglected. When articles or signed communications or editorials are sent to you, based on any news or on the general narcotic evil, I should like them printed.

To American Legion Aviators Post No. 743:

February 6, *1929*
Aviation is the most important matter before the people of the United States in this day and generation. Rapid communication in war and peace is now a fact and must at all times be studied and valued.

To All Editors:

September 18, *1919*
The question involved is not the right of organized labor to strike. Every thinking human being admits the right of ordinary employees to organize and to quit work when conditions are unsatisfactory and to be taken back after conditions have been amended. But policemen are not ordinary employees, they are the trusted guardians of the peace and the safety of the public. The man who becomes a policeman must accept this responsibility.

Simultaneousness.
Things existing at the same time. They don't, they can't, *I* know this, but looking back from here it seems as if they *did,* I see them in *perspective* sometimes, as they related to each other. I know who won or lost— and *why*.

On one of my early visits to the Ranch at San Simeon, so often part of my life and the lives of my children, Mr. Hearst showed me his famous tapestries and they are vivid and vigorous in my memory and now, as I still behold them, they remain my best definition of Simultaneity.

2

My first visit to the Ranch came about in this wise.

Joe Willicomb was Mr. Hearst's secretary. A whole Cabinet he was, and a finer gentleman, a saner more loyal counselor never existed as he served for over forty years.

Notice that everybody always stayed with Mr. Hearst practically forever.

It was Willicomb who began "The Chief." The Chief says—The Chief thinks—The Chief would like you to—A short cut, he told me once, in the stream of communication and command he sent forth.

On a certain morning, Willicomb called me and said, "Ray Long is at the Ranch. He wants to see you. The Chief is driving up this evening and he says you may come with him if you care to."

I said I cared to.

An equivocal underestimate.

Ray Long was then editor-in-chief of all Hearst Magazines, and we had many. He raided *The Saturday Evening Post* to get Mary Roberts Rinehart, Edna Ferber, Fannie Hurst, Irvin S. Cobb, Peter B. Kyne. He used Mr. Hearst's bankroll to boost prices higher than anyone had ever dreamed they could go. Mr. Long had bought a short story of mine about Hollywood called "The Tramp," and given me a big send-off in *Cosmopolitan*, then tops in the monthly field. *New Author We Introduce with Pride*, it said, under a full page picture of me with my short hair hanging over my brow in a curly fringe as shaggy as a sheep dog's—or a modern teen-ager.

Thus began my magazine career.

I knew Ray Long wanted me to come to San Simeon to discuss what all editors want to discuss. Can they count on steady production? Nobody, I knew by now, wanted to put advertising promotion and money behind an author unless a certain output was forthcoming. I really didn't care much about this nor about Ray Long, but I did want to go with Mr. Hearst to see the Ranch.

"Who else is going?" I said to Willicomb, and he said, "No one."

To most of us who worked for Mr. Hearst he came above all earthly authority and just below Jove or Jupiter on Mount Olympus, and I was going to ride from Hollywood to San Simeon, two hundred and fifty miles, alone in an automobile with him.

That day, and ever since, I have been trying to find the word for what Mr. Hearst inspired in those of us who *did* work for him a quarter—or half a century. Joe Patterson, who owned the New York *Daily News* and some of the Chicago *Tribune,* came up with it one day at his sister Cissy's Dower House when he suggested it was an Affectionate AWE. I imagine that what called for awe in us was what aroused sheer hostility in so many little men or rivals.

Awe is not fear. Nobody stays to work for a man all those years because he is afraid, especially if he is offered other jobs frequently. As Runyon, Willicomb, Howey, Louella Parsons, Tad and O. O. McIntyre were. So was I, for that matter. No, it was respect and confidence and never being bored or let down. We talked back to him. "But Mr. Hearst I don't want to sell enough bonds to build bridges across San Francisco Bay," I said. "I know," he said, "but we must think of the people who could then live in Marin County—" "It'll spoil everything, no more ferryboats," I said. "Then," he said, "I expect I'd better send someone else." Damon Runyon was of shining courage of all kinds, and as for Howey—he was never afraid of anything except a girl named Kitty White.

Deference we gave Mr. Hearst. We did defer to his judgment, his experience, his integrity, and his kindness. No MEETINGS. No chewing things over until they were predigested hash. No committees where no commitments were reached. Once Mr. Gordotowsky told me the whole board voted NO, and Mr. Hearst voted AYE and the chairman said, "The ayes have it." And thus a gent who shall be nameless got a large loan from the company to cover indebtedness he'd contracted and twenty-seven years to pay it back out of his salary! As Gordy said, "Mr. Hearst knew more so he was the majority that was right in wisdom if not in numbers. A wise minority should be the majority over an ignorant majority." Would to God it were!

As Earl Rogers' daughter, I had been able to get anyplace I wanted to go. By no means the shy type, I had learned humility through suffering before I was in my teens. AWE was something I had never felt. My father had taken me to Mr. Hearst to get me a job, and Mr. Hearst had been real great to me on the harbor story. Nevertheless at the thought of this ride alone with him I shook with the worst case of stage fright I was ever to know. In our many years together I was to learn how shy he was with strangers, how much more often he listened than spoke, how kind his responses were, but I did not know this then.

One thing I had known because his mother, Phoebe Apperson Hearst, had explained it to my grandmother, Adela Andrus Rogers. No one ever quoted Mr. Hearst without mimicking that unique high light voice. The small trumpet squeak of an elephant is a surprise. This same surprise takes you when you hear the high tenor tones of Jack Dempsey, whom to this day most people from six to sixteen to sixty-six mean when they say The Champ. Dempsey explained this to me one night when I was sitting around his place—having been routed out by Howey at two in the morning to catch up with the *then* heavyweight champion, Max Baer, and find out whether he and his wife, Mary Ellen Sullivan, had separated. (I have a special fondness for the memory of Max Baer. He was the only man I ever saw who, whether in his dressing room at the Capitol Theater, his hotel suite, or his training camp, always took *off* his bathrobe when a lady entered—he wanted to be sure she didn't miss anything.) Dempsey knew his own strength and the murderous temper that had given him the name of the Manassa Mauler. The reason he had the most beautiful manners I ever saw was because he felt an inner necessity to be a *gentle* man. Otherwise he might kill somebody. When he first opened his New York restaurant, it was par for the course that every man took advantage of Dempsey's position as host and owner to take a swing at The Champ's jaw in fun. Then he could go home and tell the folks about it, this being the chief reason many people travel. It took spiritual force and character for The Champ not to swing back. His first step was to greet them in a soft, high voice and this, he told me, helped both him and them to be less pugnacious.

What Phoebe Apperson Hearst told my grandmother was that her only son had early been aware of the privileges and obligations of his enormous inherited wealth in gold mines and land, of his position as the son of a United States senator, a member of a First Family of California, which had become a state only a few years before Phoebe Apperson married and moved there. As her son built up his chain of newspapers, magazines, wire services—International News Service, Universal Service, King Features—the cartoons that were so powerful and popular, he recognized and took seriously his dominating inherited position as a public force, a decision molder. No one could fail to give him leadership of that Freedom of the Press which he regarded as absolutely necessary if the people of his country were to be sure of enjoying the other three. His mother said he was careful, even timid, for fear he would use this driving crash-through strength of another kind but as lethal as Dempsey's. So though he carried his wealth and position as a big stick, he spoke *softly*—and so seldom had to use the stick.

He picked me up and we went along quietly beside the Pacific Ocean, which, in the late afternoon light, turned the dancing white caps into as many colors as my railroad president's opals.

Mr. Hearst far in one corner of the big luxurious limousine, me in the other.

As we swung in from the sea toward Oxnard and the stretch of hills and fruitful valley, we were still silent. Later when I was presented to the King of England I was told to wait for him to speak, and once he *had* to wait for him to stop. I had decided for myself it was good manners to wait for my host to speak, he was much older, I was a reporter, he was The Great White Father. Still, I was a lady and he was a man.

I was wonder-struck by the blazing sunset which flamed like the gates of heaven. On the coast of California we have no twilight, one moment the sun is a stupendous ball of orange fire, then it dives into the sea, an instant of thin curved pure golden light, then it is gone. You forget your own little self.

So I spoke. "I don't know whether I could be happy away from the sea. I think I got booted out of Bryn Mawr because I couldn't bear to stay away—"

He turned to look at me with a smile. He said, "I never thought of that as an alibi for my getting booted out of Harvard. I thought it was natural villainy."

I felt more comfortable. I said, "My not being able to do algebra did have something to do with it."

"All you really have to do about algebra, I found," Mr. Hearst said, "is to find out what the problem *says*. You are good at English, you should have had no trouble."

"I never saw any connection," I said.

"That is the fault of your teachers," he said indignantly. "We need better teachers."

I thought of that later when I was writing pieces to get more money for their pay.

We talked, I remember, about Jack London, my godfather by adoption, and I said it was too bad Jack had got cluttered up with ranching in the Valley of the Moon and building Wolf's House and Mr. Hearst said they had done their best to protect his genius, paid off his mortgages, advanced huge sums on magazine serials that were never written. I said the fire that destroyed Wolf's House broke his heart, his wife Charmian never gave him a moment's peace, also he hadn't written the best book on alcohol of all time in *John Barleycorn* from pure *imagination*.

At Santa Barbara, dream city in the gloaming, he said it had been built on the Orena grant from the King of Spain and I said I'd gone to the convent with Herminia Orena. As girls we'd driven in the carriage with her grandmother, Donna Maria Antonia Orena, who had six postilions and wore a mantilla with a tall comb set in diamonds, gift of Pio Pico, the last Spanish Governor of California. I told him I'd always said I was born in San Francisco instead of Los Angeles, it was more picturesque for writers. This amused him, he said like all native San Franciscans, he'd looked down on Los Angeles, but it would soon be bigger. Buy Southern California real estate, he said. People love to believe life can be easy and above all warm. They want to sleep under a palm tree and eat oranges, and after their frozen winters it is not difficult for the Los Angeles Chamber of Commerce to sell that to the Easterners and Middle Westerners.

It had grown dark, the next thing I knew the car was slowing down, and I woke up with my head on Mr. Hearst's shoulder. What with losing my stage fright, his kindness about Jack London, a *minstrel* tale he told of Fra Junípero Serra and the missions, I had drifted into happy slumber and stayed there for a hundred miles or so. I should have been terrified or embarrassed. I wasn't. I had fallen, not in love, but *in affection*.

We went into a roadside diner at Los Alamos and sat on stools and Mr. Hearst said he recommended the ham and eggs *or* the chili so I had both. Then we got back on the road. Coming out of San Luis Obispo, where we took Coast Highway 1 by Morro Bay instead of the inland route to Paso Robles and the Salinas Valley, we ran into a sort of cold corn-soup fog, clammy and cream-yellow, which thickened so the car had to cut it like a knife. We were on a one-lane in each direction dirt road with no lights, no white lines, our car lights were dim. The sea was on one side, a cliff high on the other, the car twisted so Errol Flynn once got out and walked and Dolores del Rio got seasick. Our driver hung his head out though what good he thought that was going to do him I don't know. Then Mr. Hearst said gently, "Here is a shoulder, pull off and I will drive."

Thank goodness I lost my breath so I couldn't yell. This was what *Papa* used to do. Move our chauffeur over and drive himself and for sheer unadulterated bad driving I have yet to meet his equal. Here we have a trained chauffeur, it's his *business,* I said to myself. Mr. William Randolph Hearst owns gold mines and runs 999 newspapers and can tell presidents what to do so he thinks he can drive. He isn't even drunk. That's forgivable, but cold sober? I am not going to have any affection for him at all.

In nearly half a century since that particular coastal fog I have ridden around the Indianapolis track with Ralph de Palma, flown with Amelia Earhart, to say nothing of today's jet BOAC pilots out of a real London fog across the Atlantic to another one at Kennedy Airport. I have never witnessed such uncanny mechanical manipulation as Mr. Hearst's driving that night.

Fifty miles to San Simeon. Though from time to time I heard a car or the rocks bouncing down from the cliff edge, I never saw anything. Our way was as wide as the car's wheels, no wider, and as spiral as a corkscrew. We drove at a steady, fast pace, once or twice we stopped to let a gate swing open under the invisible guidance of a Mexican cowboy, we curved, climbed without a single hesitation or inch of deviation, and came to a perfect stop on the circular drive in front of what we then called the Three Cottages.

From that day to this I have been sure that, whatever his faults, Mr. Hearst could see in the dark.

On the terrace of one of the white-stucco three-story "cottages" that were the only houses then finished, Mr. Hearst bowed and told me a courteous good night and thanked me for my company.

A maid was waiting in my room, the blaze of a wood fire in the huge fireplace was at the moment more important than art treasures and the light gleaming from behind silken shades, and silver sconces gave the peaceful and comforting effect of candlelight. The maid brought a tray of sandwiches, fruit and cake, milk and hot chocolate, and I thought to myself, This is a life I shall be glad to have known. I shall realize that people who have always had it and take it for granted are different from other people; they can be worthy and strong and accept their obligations, or they can be indulgent and selfish but they are *different* from people who scramble for money.

I sat there in front of the burning logs of pear wood from the vast orchards that were part of the Ranch, they smelled like incense, and I recorded on my memory tape my conversation with Mr. Hearst. I am inclined to embellish, to twist to suit my purposes or prove my point, and we all forget some. Certain things I felt it was right to keep clear and exact so you would have them to play back—this was one of those.

3

The fog had fled before the sun when I woke up, in the daylight the room was the richest and most ornate I had ever seen. Exquisite statuettes, priceless brocade hangings, inlaid furniture, the *ceiling* had been brought from a palace of Richelieu's, the Renaissance décor was deep and rich in color. Renaissance is not a favorite period with me, yet that morning I had an amazement I never lost. How in this cinquecento baroque extravagantly colored and ornamented style with all its gilt and carving the Ranch was nevertheless so *homelike,* so natural, so welcoming. Perhaps when the host and the house are one this comes to pass.

My fire was lighted again, I put on a robe and rang, and asked the maid who came—there was twenty-four-hour service of all kinds—for coffee. With a pleasant smile she said I would have to go up to the Castle for that. This was almost the only thing I found difficult about the Ranch. All the years I went there, sometimes I spent weeks at a time, I had to get dressed, walk paths between white statues and flowering trees to the Castle for my coffee; *or* after the big main building was finished and I was usually in the Doge's Suite on the second floor, dress and walk down flights of stone or tiled or marble stairs. At home I had coffee the moment I opened my eyes. I once asked Marion Davies about this incongruous bit amid the luxury, the meticulous service, and extravagant indulgence by which guests were surrounded. She said W.R. did not approve of breakfast in bed. If people did not *get up* and *get dressed* they might frowst away hours that could better be spent *outdoors.* He thought, Marion said, that the wonderful walk through morning dew and freshness with the sparkle of the sea below and mountain air blowing from above the Sierras was a good way to start the day. I'm sure it was but at the time I thought I could have appreciated it more with one cup of coffee under my riding britches or my tennis skirt.

On that visit the Castle, La Cuesta Encantada, or Enchanted Hill, was far from completed. As yet the dining hall, to seat a hundred and fifty, was only begun, so we ate at a long table in the Big Room. No sleeping rooms or suites, not even those two soaring towers, one for Mr. Hearst and one for Marion, were ready for occupancy. Wings were in process, the movie theater was a blueprint, an indoor swimming pool to be connected by corridors was planned. For this reason William Randolph Hearst's architect was in residence.

In this setting and company Miss Julia Morgan had to be a double-take of unexpectedness. For she was a small, skinny, self-effacing lady whose iron will was *fem incognita* and *sotto voce*. Her graying hair was held in a small knob at the back of her head by bone pins, her gray tweed tailored suit was inches too long, and she used no make-up at all. At dinner, with the Queen of Rumania, the Duchess of Sutherland, our ranking novelist Gertrude Atherton, the Marquise de la Falaise de la Coudray (Gloria Swanson), Mrs. Tom Mix in all her diamonds, First Lady Grace Coolidge, Cissy Patterson of Dupont Circle, Washington, Mary Pickford, who really queened it in Hollywood, the governor's lady, and Mrs. Flo Ziegfeld (Billie Burke) present, Miss Morgan, in a blue foulard dress with white daisies, was like a small neat bantam hen among birds of paradise. Except that she always sat on Mr. Hearst's right. She had designed the unforgettable Tower of Jewels for the 1915 San Francisco World's Fair and she designed and built the Hearst Ranch and everything that had to do with it as long as Mr. Hearst was building it.

As I stood in the window of my own bedroom that morning I said a prayer which I didn't believe in to a God I was convinced didn't exist to the effect that IF there was a heaven to which I would go permanently I hoped it would look like this. I never saw anything in Greece, or Sweden, the English countryside, the French château country nor among the Italian villas to equal the Ranch.

Just then the door opened and to my surprise in came a friend of mine from New York. Helena Young was the wife of a well-known jurist and with her, help us all, was the lady of the Castle. I had never before met Mrs. Hearst and I was astonished at her youth and sparkling handsomeness. She had on a pink Irish linen morning dress, no lady had ever heard of slacks or shorts much less worn them. Mrs. Hearst's hair was dark and worn in an elaborate crown.

Helena bounced as usual, we said the usual things about my trip up, what a lovely morning, then Helena said, "You know Marion Davies, don't you?"

I said, "Yes, I know her." I thought I might as well fall off a tightrope as choke on my own bated breath, so I said, "Mr. Hearst introduced me to her." I hope this implied that I hadn't invented Marion Davies. It wasn't me who elevated her to the left hand of the throne. Nevertheless she was my friend, so I said, "I like her a lot."

All right, I thought, I will now be ordered to the Tower and nobody will find me for years. I will probably be beheaded, it seems to me my chances of survival are not very good at this moment.

Helena said reassuringly, "Millicent is just curious."

Mrs. Hearst smiled at me and said, "What does she call him?"

I said, "She calls him W.R."

"And what does he call her?"

"He calls her Marion," and you know at this very moment I can hear him calling, "Mare—eee—on, where's Mare—eee—on?" To the day of his death he wanted to know every minute where she was.

Then we talked about the yacht at the pier below and Mrs. Hearst told me why her husband had given up politics. In the beginning he had thought it was his duty to offer to serve his country in government. Then, he found the people didn't want him. Now, we have the Rockefellers and the Kennedys but when Mr. Hearst ran for governor we were against great wealth for candidates, we were still committed to the log cabin. So there was no obligation to continue. He wouldn't quit, she said, just because Congress bored him—as everything might except his newspapers. And the Ranch.

Mrs. Hearst said she didn't like the West. Not even the Ranch.

Just last summer I went to Southampton to talk to Mrs. Hearst and she said again quite simply that one of the things that had kept her and Mr. Hearst apart so much was that he loved the West, and she was an Easterner. So she kept the Eastern houses and estates and apartments going and he stayed at San Simeon. Of all places on earth the spot he loved the best.

On that summer day in the glorious house at Southampton when he had been dead for fifteen years, Mrs. Hearst told me about her first date with young William Randolph Hearst. Even then, this East-West angle came up.

At that time she was Millicent Willson and she and her sister Anita were favorites on the New York musical comedy stage. Not in the chorus as Marion Davies and her sister Rene were—the Willson girls were featured singers and dancers, both had some talent and a lot of beauty. An old-timer told me they had what is called *class*.

"When he asked me to go out with him," Mrs. Hearst said, "my mother was against it. We were carefully supervised in those days and I recall she said, 'Who *is* he? Some young fellow from out West somewhere, isn't he?' She insisted Anita had to come or I couldn't go. Well, he took us down to the *Journal*—the New York *Journal*—we'd hardly heard of it, and he showed us over it, *all over it*. I hadn't the foggiest notion what we were doing, walking miles on rough boards in thin, high-heeled evening slippers, and I thought my feet would kill me. Of course this wasn't our idea of a good time. We wanted to go to Sherry's or Bustanoby's. More than that Anita kept whispering to me, 'We're going to get thrown out of here, Milly, the way he behaves you'd think he *owned* it.' It wasn't until our next trip that I found out he did—own it, I mean. I told Anita and at first she wouldn't believe me. She said, 'He's like all *Westerners*. All big brag strutting around as though they owned the earth.' But—" Mrs. Hearst stopped to smile, but whether at me or that long-ago young Westerner talking so big I couldn't tell, "I guess I must have fallen in love with him at once, he asked me to marry him two weeks later and I said yes right away.

"For many years I went back to the paper with him every night, from the opera, from a ball, from a dinner or the theaters. In our evening clothes. I thought he wore tails better than any man I ever saw, a man must be tall and carry himself with an air to wear tails."

After a little moment, a little sigh, Mrs. Hearst went on, "I used to call him a prophet," she said quietly. "I used to say to him *You're a regular old prophet, that's what you are.* The longer I live the more I know how true that was. He saw far ahead."

There were, she said, prophecies he didn't live to see fulfilled. Impossible to remember how far back it was he'd begun to warn both privately and in his papers of what he called The Yellow Peril.

A bright smile brought back the young Mrs. William Randolph Hearst, married to the young publisher whose mother had to lend him money sometimes to meet the payroll of his New York papers, and she said, "That and a comic strip we had called 'The Yellow Kid'—everybody was as crazy about that then as they are now about 'Peanuts'—was why they called the Hearst papers Yellow Journalism, you know. He was sure we'd have trouble with Japan and China. And he fought to get rid of coolie labor in California or the state would never have grown as it did. He said to me one night going home after our visit to the papers, 'Millicent, I may not be here when that great slumbering Yellow Elephant called China wakes to its own strength but it will come, it will come.'"

I thought of this the other night when CBS television presented a brilliant special about China and Chairman Mao and his Little Red Book.

4

I know a gentleman named Martin Dunn, who was on the night city desk at the New York *Journal* in those days. As a very old man, he told me he liked to remember Mr. and Mrs. Hearst when they came in at night, he to work for hours, and she sometimes to sleep in a chair. A sleeping beauty, Mr. Dunn called her.

Martin Dunn was on that night city desk when the big story of the Spanish-American War broke. Mr. Hearst wasn't in the building at the time, though one would think if he *started* it, as I've heard tell often enough, he would have managed to be there. Also he would, I am sure, have warned his editors to be ready for it so they could get a jump on everybody. His purpose in *starting* the darn war, according to the version that says he did, was to get circulation. When Mr. Hearst did come in that night he discovered that the managing editor had kept on Page 1 a fairly dull and entirely unrelated story by a big-name English author. After this had been removed and Mr. Hearst had remade the whole front page—he fired the managing editor, who defended himself on the grounds that this by-line feature had been a MUST signed W.R.H. To this, Martin Dunn told me, Mr. Hearst said quietly, "I am sorry, Mr. So-and-So, that I find it necessary to dismiss you. I'm sure you will see that I dare not take any chances on the judgment of a man who doesn't know when *news* makes it essential to disregard my previous orders." Martin Dunn remembered that clearly—and with glee.

That day in Southampton Millicent Hearst was again wearing a pale pink summer frock with a spray of jewels like a flower at one shoulder, a bracelet to match around her wrist, thin high-heeled slippers. Her hair was in little curls and with the delicate make-up she looked twenty years younger than the eighty-six she told me she was. Her eyes were often on the green rolling lawns, the exquisitely tended flower bed, the tiled swimming pool. The charming room with its fragile gilt furniture, the cabinets for priceless Meissen and Sèvres and Ming porcelain, the paintings of the French school fitted her as well as the pink frock and the flower jewels.

Mrs. Hearst was the only one of that triangle still alive. Of her five sons she'd lost the one most of us thought might follow in his father's footsteps, Jack Hearst, but George, the eldest, named for his grandfather the senator, was paying her a visit when I was there. Young Bill, as we still call him though he's past fifty by now—and the twins, Randy and David, come often to see her.

It was Young Bill who had said to me, "My mother wants to see you."

Remembering what his father had taught me about ethics, I said, "Bill, I wouldn't like to enter your mother's house under false pretenses. She doesn't think I can leave Marion Davies out of this book, does she?" And Young Bill Hearst said hurriedly, "No no, no no. She just wants to be sure you don't leave *her* out. As she says, after all she had five sons by him and went back to the paper with him every night for years before he ever heard of Marion Davies."

5

At the time we met at the Hearst Ranch in the Twenties, Ray Long was the golden boy of the art and industry called The Magazines, then at their peak. George Horace Lorimer of *The Saturday Evening Post* discovered as many stars as Louis B. Mayer. With *The New Yorker* the fabled Harold Ross was blazing a new concept, creating a new school of writing and writers. The magazines guided thinking, setting up images, presenting information, building the interests of the American people, an influence almost as great as, and certainly as careful and beneficent as, TV was to become in the Fifties.

If you could sell your article, short story, or novel to a magazine you got cold cash. Books—who knew? Thus the magazine was sitting in the catbird's seat. The magazines financed, underwrote, and encouraged such giants as F. Scott Fitzgerald, Sinclair Lewis, Ernest Hemingway, John P. Marquand, O. Henry, Edna Ferber, Willa Cather, even Mark Twain.

Ray Long was a Pied Piper and he played a golden tune with Hearst dough, and soon star names came over to appear on the covers of Hearst magazines.

I admired Ray because he could get Sinclair Lewis and others to *write* and persuaded Somerset Maugham back to the short story after a long absence playwriting. His series of Maugham's stories, including *Miss Thompson*, inspiration for *Rain,* in *Cosmopolitan* made it the leading monthly publication but I don't forget that it gave us classics that would otherwise not have been written.

In his day, Ray Long was as conspicuous and celebrated around New York as Harold Ross became later, and without the self-perpetuating you-scratch-my-back-and-I'll-scratch-yours of the self-created Algonquin Round Table. I may add he was quite as eccentric as the creator of *The New Yorker.* His Bond Street tailor produced such elegance that most people overlooked the fact that Ray Long was a dumpy little fellow with a potbelly entirely surrounded by the divine right of editors. His assumption of the *droit du seigneur* gave some of his women writers a leeetle trouble but Edna Ferber, Mary Roberts Rinehart, Fannie Hurst, and me, tagging along at the end, were, I daresay, quite able to take care of ourselves. At the very beginning of Café Society our Ray Long was a dashing fellow along Broadway and at the same time under his ruthless, skillful editorial hand *Cosmopolitan, Good Housekeeping, Harper's Bazaar, Pictorial Review, Town and Country, House and Garden, Field and Stream,* and *International Studios* skyrocketed in circulation attended by increase in advertising, advertising rates, and literary prestige.

On the second morning after Mr. Hearst and I arrived at the Ranch, Ray took me for a walk, soon ended on a bench under an oleander tree. Glory, glory, glory blazed and swung around us, but there are people everywhere except in England who do not care for landscapes, seascapes, river mountain or cloud scapes, or gardens, and of these Ray Long was one. He paused sometimes to admire skyscrapers, but Fifth Avenue and Central Park were as far as he liked to wander. His purpose was to say that he didn't think I was as much interested in magazine work as I ought to be and what could he do about it? I said I was interested, having just bought a *ranch*. At this, I may tell you, he glittered at me like Scrooge. Full well did that wily ringmaster R.L. know that once any writer has bought a *ranch*—be it Jack London's Valley of the Moon or Louis Bromfield's Malibar or Hemingway's hills of Dakota or Bud Kelland's cattle acres in Arizona—or even Maugham's small vegetable garden on the Côte d'Azur—*advances* would soon become necessary, then the writer must produce to support his land. This is plainly both good and bad. It sparks a writer to write—it can drive him to overwrite and in the end to kill himself as it did London—or to drink himself to disaster as it did Red Lewis. And me, periodically.

Possibly the Ranch at San Simeon wasn't the best place to talk about magazine work. To tell the truth, Mr. Hearst was never interested in his magazines. When Ray Long eventually ran off to Tahiti (wrong place) with his secretary (wrong girl), Mr. Hearst did nothing about it at all. All these wrongs drove Ray to shoot himself in the end. If he'd been a good city editor on any one of our papers, Mr. Hearst would have caught him by the seat of his trousers, got him a divorce if necessary, and put him back to work.

My only interest in magazines was that I could work at home.

I did believe my work as a reporter was something to be proud of, it held my whole heart, mind, and imagination. Harry Luce finally founded a national school of *news* magazines and the magazine style of covering news by the week instead of by the day and hour. This had superimportance and foresight at a time when, with wars and drama in many places, *non*fiction was assuming such proportions that fiction had to take second place. Mr. Hearst had no such magazines for news, that was one place where his utter devotion to and absorption by newspapers, their power, style, presence, stars, and coverage, blocked his prophetic vision.

In my newspaper work I felt I was learning all the time. To read excerpts from his letters to editors and publishers, or the famed penciled comments around the margins of our daily papers is to produce a formula for Hearst Journalism at its best.

>The backbone of a newspaper is news. In other words, a newspaper must always be a NEWSpaper.
>A paper with the news and without features will circulate. A paper with features and without news will not.
>The happy combination now and forever is a strong NEWSpaper with a proper proportion of entertaining features and sound editorials.
>Even pictures must always be primarily *news* pictures.
>Pictures are only as strong as their relationship to news.
>Please have no time for long stories. Take time to be brief.
>It is the lack of judgment in the use of big type which is chiefly responsible for the protests against it. Big type should always announce NEWS without exaggeration and with exact truth.
>To have good writing you must have good writers. You cannot make a hen lay a duck egg. If you want duck eggs you have got to get ducks. The attraction of good writing is subtle and elusive, difficult to define, yet obvious in every instance. It is not necessary to dilate this point. The thing to do is to comb the country vigorously for the particular people who can do good writing about whatever they are writing about.

As Ray Long and I sat smoking leisurely under the oleanders on that morning of glory, he kept urging me to spend more time on fiction. Especially, he said, Hollywood fiction. These tales were new and Hollywood was an entirely fresh setting and the public was growing more and more curious and interested. I began thinking. There is Bill Hart's wife Winifred, poor darling, the way his sister ran her out of the house—out of Eugene O'Neill, that one. There's the one about the director who no longer wanted the girl himself—I could call it *Dog in the Manger,* which he *is*.

They seemed to me awful, those stories. False and phony and fake—yet they weren't, most of them were built on fact and often became fiction only to avoid libel laws and violation of national security. Fiction, as I discovered then and later, had that one distinct advantage. In some instances it was the only way in which you could print the truth.

Reporters have always written fiction out of and from and because of newspaper experience. Legend says Shakespeare wrote some of the original stick-em-on-the-wall news releases in the time of Great Elizabeth. Charles Dickens was our-man-on-the-court-and-banquet-beat. Kipling's *Plain Tales from the Hills* were written while he was a working newspaperman in India. Ring Lardner's *Alibi Ike,* Damon Runyon's *Butch Minds the Baby,* Willa Cather's *Coming Aphrodite,* and Edna Ferber's *Our Mrs. McChesney* all show direct connections. Paul Gallico's *The Night Before Christmas* was told to him at my dinner table by reporter John A. Clements and was a *factual* experience. Half a dozen of Jim Thurber's classics he himself ties to his newspaper work in Columbus. All these show finer stories, better writing, and stronger purpose than the artsy-craftsy *mood* dwarfs of a shallow period from which we were rescued at last by J. D. Salinger in his *Nine Stories*.

Again, as in tapestries, I see so clearly that fact-and-fiction have been often woven together.

6

Nothing so helped me to *feel* and *understand* (simultaneousness) as did the tapestries at the Hearst Ranch when, on that later visit Mr. Hearst explained them to me.

I got a particular impact out of those tapestries partly because I had never seen any before. Tapestries had been outside my experience entirely.

When I saw the big ones that covered the walls of the Dining Hall they fascinated me utterly, the dimensions, the grouping, the stereopticon depths, they were caught in a wide ray of time where you could see right and left and up and down *all at once*. I would not always have to attempt chronological order, I could show as a reporter how things existed in relation to each other at the same time. Not as a *strip,* as a whole. Often examples, illustrations, proofs did not fit in time, yet they did fit in relativity. It could be essential to show the end even before the beginning. To look at them thus was as valid as motion picture reels run end to end; with tapestries you rose above the flow of time.

I was standing examining one, for which I had been told Mr. Hearst had paid $3,000,000, and for which he could now get $10,000,000 when he came along. Before he could start to tell me I ought to be outdoors riding or swimming or playing tennis and getting fresh air, I said, "Are there many more like these?"

He said, "No no. These are most special. They were woven when the beauty of creative work was understood by the workman who executed it as well as the artist who designed it and by the man who was willing to pay them both for the time to do it. Catherine de Medici was the great-granddaughter of Lorenzo the Magnificent, these were begun the day she was born as part of her hope chest, she took them when she went to wed the son of the King of France in 1553.

"Exactly as we are looking at them now, so did little Mary Stuart, Scotland's princess who had married the King of France, one of Catherine's pitiful sons, stand fascinated by them, as children now are by fairy tales, until she heard behind her the Old Queen's footsteps—Catherine was a formidable mother-in-law—soon she was to accomplish the Massacre of St. Bartholomew—"

After that when I sat at the long refectory table and faced one of those tapestries I always thought of little Mary of Scotland before she grew up to be such a pest to Elizabeth of England. They were like picture books in a way. Of course Mr. Hearst had the gift of making history real, so that when he gave an assignment into the future, as he did when he sent me to Washington, he had steamed me up by the full understanding that *news is history in the making.*

This is why I don't attempt chronological order for looking back I am looking at a tapestry where so much is simultaneous.

The night I sat outside in Evalyn Walsh McLean's car while she went in to be with John L. Lewis, who had called for her when his wife lay dying—the owner of the Hope Diamond to comfort the great labor leader. "A great calamity has befallen the United States," Evalyn said when she came out at dawn. "Mrs. John L. Lewis is dead. She was his vision, his faith in God, his stop-look-and-listen. We needed her as much as he did."

Madame Chiang Kai-shek, the first woman to address Congress since Clara Barton had done so when she founded the American Red Cross.

F.D.R. explaining that he had dismissed General Knudsen and put in a man we didn't like—Donald something or other—sometimes the President said a man who cleared the ground isn't the one to build on it—

These are small exciting bits of my *Washington* tapestry that I have hanging in my soul.

Now unbelievably I see it as simultaneous as on the tapestry on the wall I could see at one and the same time laughing groups picnicking beside a lake; archers in battle; hunters mounting their horses; lovers clinging in fond embrace beneath the greenwood tree; children rolling hoops near a fountain; court ladies in deep curtsies, and picturesque gardeners at work.

I can see my first trip to the Ranch—and my last. I see that through tears always. I loved no other place in quite the same way. It was my ancestral home as though it held my past back to Adam.

I never saw Mrs. Hearst at the Ranch after my first visit. She did not again come West and Marion Davies became mistress of the Enchanted Hill and the Castle and hostess to Winston Churchill, the Coolidges, and Queen Marie of Rumania.

Oddly enough the Zoo, now so much discussed, isn't in my tapestries at all. Except the polar bears, and that only because my Dicky got adventurous once and fell halfway down into the pit and had to be rescued by cowboys with ropes.

Mr. Hearst loved picnics. He could keep us all *outdoors* and there was group conversation around the fire or under the trees. The special treat I see now was in a little valley among fruit trees, where a bright stream sang and danced over seal-brown rocks. A staff from the Castle had gone out by truck at dawn and set up a trestle table, a dart target, an archery range, and Ping-pong. We had cold chicken, stuffed eggs, potato salad, hot dogs, and sandwiches—Mr. Hearst was a traditionalist. I remember Clark Gable, we were doing a blackout program in the Movie Theater, and I'd had to write *All the Brothers Were Valiant* from memory for him, so we went under a peach tree to rehearse.

When shadows began to invade the tall mountains behind us, big black Cadillacs returned.

There were horses, tied to a fence, for anybody who wanted to ride back. Marion was not one of these. She claimed it was farther to the ground from the back of a horse than from the top of the Empire State Building.

That day just the two native Californians, Mr. Hearst and me, rode back. He towered over me, a magnificent freewheeling horseman, he'd ridden his father's ranch at Pleasanton as soon as he could be lifted into a saddle. To understand a person, you have to know his relationship to animals, his dogs, cats, tigers, hamsters, elephants, or boa constrictors. Never trust a woman who can *abide* snakes, I knew one once in Washington.

I was riding alone with Secretary of the Navy Knox the day he fell off into the creek. I got down and pulled him out. We sat on a boulder until he dried off and then rode back and sneaked in through a rear door. Naturally, I watched his career in the Cabinet with the hope he could handle battleships better than he could horses.

The principality of San Simeon was an operating ranch with thousands of cattle on its hills. Orchards that were working units and a factory to can the fruit. I never forget the pear trees, loaded with pale gold delicately shaped fruit. I liked it best when Mr. Hearst told me about it as we rode through. He loved it so.

More and more since he is gone, I've heard of Mr. Hearst's *rages*— charging around through jungles like a mad elephant. I find it difficult to reconcile such tales with our long rides through the land where he was indeed lord of all he surveyed and where he showed such patience and kindliness to the lowliest employee. Or with my years working for him. Not his bitterest enemies ever give any specific instances, produce any witnesses, testify as to where when or why any single one of these furies took place. In the forty years I worked for him, always on call for a story, I did some reasonably fancy sowing of wild oats and never reaped an angry word.

There were, it is true, certain rules and regulations for guests at the Ranch, there are at every big house where I have visited and, as I understand it, at Windsor Castle and the White House, where I have not. One of these at San Simeon was attendance at The Movies. There was a motion picture run every single night come hell or high water in the lovely theater and to this every guest whether exalted or unimportant had to go. And *stay*. Nobody moved until Mr. Hearst and M.D. rose at the end. This was, I think, partly because Mr. Hearst loved movies and partly because he had a sort of paternal care for his high-spirited and temperamental guests and thought it might be dangerous for them to wander about at night, alone or in couples. (It often was.)

The worst temper tantrum I ever saw him throw was after the movies one night. We had all come out into the Big Room and Pepi and Charlie Lederer, Marion's niece and nephew, and Lloyd Pantages and his beautiful sister Carmen, Mary Grace, daughter of one of Marion's friends, and some other youngsters kept playing a record, "I'll Be Glad When You're Dead You Rascal You." Over and *over*. At a point of nausea, Mr. Hearst removed it, broke it in two, and put the pieces in the fireplace saying, "I feel we have heard that often enough. I find it a vulgar lyric and a vapid tune. Let us have something gay." We all cheered loudly.

This incident gave rise to a thrice-told invention that you could not mention the word "death" in Mr. Hearst's presence. How this squared with the charge of Yellow Journalism, having by its nature to lay emphasis on death from the passing of President Harding to the St. Valentine's Day Massacre to the Snyder Gray case I don't know. It wasn't true. When my son Bill was killed in 1943 my first call was from Mrs. Roosevelt, then my neighbor Ethel Barrymore, and third from Mr. Hearst. Within an hour of Gandhi's assassination he assigned me to do a series on the Mahatma, he spoke of Gandhi's death with pain and grief and anger. While I was doing my final stories for him, "The Legends of Hollywood," his own death was near, he knew it and spoke of it to me in a dignified old-fashioned faith. I thought it would be unusually difficult for a man of great wealth and power to realize that perhaps in one breath he would have none of these. I said this once to Mr. Hearst and he said a man could only hope he had laid up some treasure where neither moth nor rust could corrupt.

Once he scolded me for being rude to that GGGGGGREAT columnist Arthur Brisbane. I was prancing into the dining room for breakfast one morning when I saw Brisbane at the long table in solitary splendor. So I said, "Don't let me interrupt your mighty meditations," turned back, and walked right into Mr. Hearst. He said, "You are prejudiced. Prejudice either way is inadmissible in a reporter." I said, "It isn't prejudice to move out of line if you meet what you know is a skunk, is it?" He kept shaking his head and said my grandmother would reprove me for bad manners and I said my grandmother never met Arthur Brisbane. What I didn't dare say was that nobody in the Hearst Service could figure his admiration, friendship, almost hero-worship of that pompous ass. Gene Fowler, who often reverted to Anglo-Saxon, once said that someday Brisbane would die of swallowing his own spit and for all I know he did. This was the large flaw in Mr. Hearst's judgment of men in our book, and when the near-catastrophe of '39 came it looked as though we had been right all the time.

7

Controversy is the Lifeblood of Circulation. Maxim of William Randolph Hearst.

Controversy surrounded, still surrounds him. A more polemic figure exists not in our annals.

One of the most controversial questions was why William Randolph Hearst did not get a divorce to marry Marion Davies. By then, so many people did get divorced.

This is not as complicated as it appears.

Two good reasons.

Millicent Willson Hearst.

Marion Douras Davies.

Magnificent and amazing that the two women in his life always seem to have thought about *him*—what was best for him. They gave him some trouble now and then to be sure, but they always seemed in the end to *act* as they thought best for him.

Once upon a time Clare Boothe was a guest at the Hearst Ranch at San Simeon. By then Clare Boothe had divorced a Mr. Brokaw and was married to Henry Luce, founder of *Time, Life,* and *Fortune,* one of the most creative publishers of all time. Marion Davies, who was not married to anybody, seemed to us to take Mrs. Luce with a slight twinkle. The following conversation between these two ladies was reported to me by Eileen Percy, Dorothy Mackaill, and Bebe Daniels, Marion's best friends, in the ladies' dressing room at the Ranch, where Mrs. Luce never came, though whether her kidneys were stronger or her wit weaker—the competition there was tough—than ours, I do not know.

This is what they told me:

Clare Boothe Luce said to M.D., "Marion, dear, you know my first play, *The Women,* was a great success with no help from anyone.

I value my artistic independence and integrity so after I married Harry Luce I still wanted to be judged on merit, without fear or favor. When my next play, *Kiss The Boys Goodbye,* was presented, I asked Harry to order his publications *Life* and *Time* to deal with it fearlessly, forgetting that the playwright was the wife of the owner of those publications. None of the reviews of the play was favorable. Those in the Luce magazines were vitriolic. They even attempted to make me a little ridiculous. As though they were pleased with the opportunity to take advantage of my high principles. Now I must do something about this. I wondered, dear Marion, what exactly are your arrangements with Mr. Hearst about reviews of your pictures?"

Said Marion Davies to Mrs. Luce, "Dear C-CCC-Clare, it c-cccouldn't come up, ccccccould it? You see, Mr. Hearst l-l-lloves me."

We all loved her.

Even in the last dreadful days, for Marion couldn't drink, no Irishwoman can, thank God I quit trying almost thirty years ago.

We loved her because she never once used her enormous power for anything but good. In the last days of Mr. Hearst's life she ran the Hearst Empire. At one time, she was officially Vice President. This blond ex-Follies girl movie star was in charge of the most powerful press organization in the world as Madame Pompadour once ruled France. All orders— preceded on the phone by "Mmmister Hearst says"—came from and through her. I sat beside her once or twice while she transmitted them.

The answer to the controversy as to why no divorce is fully known to me and I think now it not only could but should be told. Few knew it, some who did had no reason to speak. Now time has passed, the main characters are part of that past rather than the present.

The first reason there never was a divorce and that Mrs. Hearst still wore her wedding ring by right when she was eighty-six was—Mrs. Hearst.

To know Millicent Hearst even somewhat, as I have for over fifty years, is to be sure beyond doubt that she would never hold a husband against his will. A beauty herself, she grew more and more important in the social life of New York and Europe. I vision her in those years wrapped in chinchilla at the opening of the Met or in a box at Madison Square Garden for one of the big fights staged under her patronage for the Milk Fund by the sports staff of the New York *Journal-American.*

All Mr. Hearst ever had to do was ask for a divorce. That's all. He never did.

A couple of times some sort of property division was discussed. Nothing came of it. Once when a Spanish grandee with a historic title became a Penelope suitor of Millicent's, there was talk that *she* might want to be free. Nothing came of that, either.

During my visit to Southampton, Mrs. Hearst did not mention Marion Davies at all. Perhaps she had forgotten her.

The final choice about the divorce was Marion's.

I went over this once with Eileen Percy Ruby, Dorothy Mackaill, Bebe Daniels, Connie Talmadge—her best-loved circle. They confirmed that she had said to them several times in the thirty years she lived with Mr. Hearst what I myself heard her say once in my own house on the Whittier ranch when she and Mr. Hearst came to dinner.

I had been telling him about the new old-brick English house I'd built on the only running water I could find in Southern California and he said politely that he'd like to see it. To my amazement, he agreed to come to dinner. He *never* went anywhere to dinner.

The only other guests I had were Tom and Vicky Mix, Buster Collier and Constance Talmadge, and a banker he was fond of, Irving Hellman, and his wife. I was wild with excitement, I can tell you.

After dinner we wandered about looking at my redwood library and the fireplace big enough to stand in, and the stables, and as we walked back Mr. Hearst and Marion fell behind. She had been on him all evening, something to do as usual with young Jack, the third Hearst son. He was about sixteen then and always in trouble. Marion was saying that he needed a *firmer* hand. People, Marion said, who are divorced are always too soft with their kids, they have a guilty conscience.

"But," Mr. Hearst said, "I am not divorced and I do not have a guilty conscience."

It was the only time I ever saw Marion cry.

She said, "Sometimes I don't know what to do. You know you can't live without me."

"I would prefer not to," Mr. Hearst said gently.

"I won't let you get a divorce," she said. "I've told you before and I tell you again. You're a great man, a great power in our country. You must have dignity. They can attack your politics and throw dirt and all, but you mustn't ever give them anything that could—could make you lose your dignity. It is all right—it's sound historically, or traditionally, and dramatically, if it *is* wicked—for you to have a Follies girl and blond movie star as your mistress. Look at Louis XIV and Charles II and Herod! If you divorce your wife, the mother of your five sons, to *marry* her, a girl younger by twenty years, they can make you look like an old fool. You can live down being thought old-fashioned and even immoral but no man, you say it yourself, has ever lived down being ridiculous. I'd rather take our chances this way.

"But you cannot pretend we are a good example for the boys, though they seem fond of me. You need to keep a firmer hand on young Jack. He's the most like you—he's brilliant, you know."

So when we went inside Mr. Hearst asked to use the telephone in my library and he called the city desk at the *Examiner* and said to Harry Morgan, the night city editor, "Perhaps it would be wise to let Jack stay in jail overnight. We must be firm with these young fellows, Mr. Morgan. Some wise man has said that the ultimate result of shielding men from the results of their folly is to fill the world with fools. We must not be guilty of such indulgence."

Not long after that young Jack married a Los Angeles debutante of good family as the first of several wives and at the wedding I saw Mrs. Hearst again and there was no way to know whether she knew how much her son owed to Marion—as her grandsons did later.

Marion sent a beautiful wedding gift, she was always an advocate of marriage, was Miss Davies. One unmarried couple were having an affair in Hollywood and, visiting the Ranch, continued the romance there. They were told by Miss Davies that they'd either get married or go down the Hill. The girl, a young movie star, had the temerity to say, "Look who's talking," to which M.D. replied, "Mr. Hearst and I can't get married. You and Harry can." What's more they did.

There is a story about the return to America of Charles Augustus Lindbergh just after he flew the Atlantic and of how he came to Hollywood that shows something of Mr. Hearst's respect and care for his mistress-en-titre, how in the smallest matters of courtesy he protected her.

Overnight—this time truly overnight—the Lone Eagle had become the greatest hero the United States has ever had. On his arrival in our film capital a short time after the ticker parade of the century in New York, Mr. Hearst entertained for Lindbergh at a beautiful *thé dansant* at the Ambassador. The guests included every star in the firmament plus all the brass in any field and their wives. Lindy, tall, slim, very quiet—looking back, I am sure he was still in a state of shock from all that had happened —sat at the head table between Mary Pickford and his hostess, Marion Davies. We were fond of *thés dansants* in those days and it had many advantages over the later cocktail party in that soon everyone was *seated* at the flower-laden head table and all the smaller ones around the shining dance floor and Guy Lombardo's music began.

A moment of silence prolonged into tension.

If Lindbergh had ever drunk tea before it had undoubtedly been in a Harvey Eating House and he had no idea he was supposed to open the ball. We saw then that there was also involved a Social Predicament.

If he takes Mary Pickford will this be adjudged an insult to Marion Davies? If he chooses Marion, will this violate protocol that nobody must step on the floor before an anointed queen? Moreover this is a clean young Galahad, idol of American youth, should he so honor the mistress, no matter how much we love her? Even if *we* didn't print it, everybody else would.

Mr. Hearst needed no advice from his columnist Emily Post. With elephantine grace he moved. Before we could expel the breath we were holding he had offered his hand to Marie Dressler, conducted her regally to Lindbergh, and presented him to her. In less time than we got a new breath, the Grand Old Lady of the Movies, the incomparable unequaled and beloved Marie Dressler who was also friend and intimate of grand duchesses and society leaders, and Lindy had taken the floor together. We sat watching them. Gloria Swanson and I were reminiscing about this the other day as one of our shining memories. Recalling how we burst into applause and then cheers as the tall blond hero and the stately old lady moved the length of the floor and back alone in a waltz. Then Mr. Hearst indicated and Douglas Fairbanks, the Prince Consort, bowed to Marion and he himself took Mary Pickford out in royal fashion to join these couples of the dance floor.

You see, Mr. Hearst l-l-lloves me.

CHAPTER 11

Come right down to it, it was an earthly paradise.

My own ranch at Whittier. The beautiful trees in their orderly rows giving us the illusion we were ranchers. Fortunately we had only nineteen acres in walnuts or that hovering bankruptcy would have descended. I felt I'd built this house with my own hands, being there day after day to choose *aged* brick, get the plaster for the living room mixed to the exact adobe shade, stand over a foreman and a carpenter who thought I was mad because I wanted the redwood beams *hand-hewn*. Inside the house I put glazed chintz, Spode dishes, Persian rugs, Early American furniture, and some old English pieces Miss Julia Morgan had helped me get at auction. I was embarrassed about bidding at auctions and never got anything.

The swimming pool was enormous. The tennis court had Cecil Bruner roses growing up the wire before long. The stables had a horse for each of us.

An earthly paradise where I could bring up my children.

They walked a mile each way to a one-room country school on Mission Mill Road. Of the forty pupils in six grades thirty-three were Mexicans.

Mexicans made wonderful neighbors. Decorative, mind-their-own-business, but warm when asked for help, devout, and filled with easy song and laughter.

An omnipresent aggregation of *little* Mexicans with huge black eyes was a difficulty and a blessing. We were the Big House. Bill was their protector, son-of-the-*señora*, it was Billy's pool, his horse Red, his football, but if I opened my mouth because they'd taken *home* all the baseball gloves, or ridden my mare Golden, or jumped into the pool at 5 A.M. on their way to Mass, or trooped into the kitchen for lemonade and ginger cookies—Billy defended them with all-for-one and one-for-all and whatever upset Jose or Pio or Juan upset Bill more.

At eight, Billy was as average as any mother can admit her son to be. Too tall, too skinny, bony, toothless, with eyes more topaz than brown. One outstanding thing about him then—and forever. The opposite of cruelty and meanness is not only kindness. It is *tenderness*. Billy had tenderness. Sometimes I wonder whether his soul knew how short his time was to be.

For a year after we moved to our walnuts in Whittier, Billy had nightmares. Not just childish bad dreams. His began with one wild, high scream of terror, echoing through the house and down to the gardener's cottage. The screams would mingle with sobs that were part attempts to breathe and part pleas to escape some pursuing horror. For that year, I never left the house at night. His legs were so long and bony I could hardly carry him, but I'd manage to get him over to the rocking chair, I'd sit down and rock him and begin to sing "It's a Long Way to Tipperary," I'd tell him stories about Mowgli and his favorite Tin Woodman, I'd keep reassuring him, and finally the sobs were long, quavering sighs and he'd open his eyes and say, "Mama?" and I'd say, "Yes, Billy, I'm right *here*."

He was a big boy when, down in Washington playing the finals in the Hans Wagner League series, he tried to stretch a single into a double so he'd be in scoring position and shattered his knee. *Knees!* I sometimes wish the Lord had thought of something else. We had to operate a year later and, as he opened his eyes after the anesthesia, he said, "Mama?" and I said, "Yes, Bill, I'm right here."

That same year of the nightmares, amiably, smilingly, he *would not eat*. Three quarts of milk and nothing else are not enough for a growing boy. Everything half a dozen doctors, his father and I, our governess-nanny Mrs. Sawyer, his teacher, Robert and Anna, Callahan, the groom who taught him to ride, and his sister Elaine could think of—we did it. He ate in the dining room with Ike and me. In the breakfast room with his sister. Indoors alone and outdoors with *all* his Mexican brothers, every kind of food was served him, set on the table so he could serve himself, arranged picnic style on paper plates. One day, as he had suddenly begun to talk he began to eat. But he always stayed too skinny. I suppose a good high school coach could have made him an end. But he wasn't interested in football, he fell madly in love with baseball and that was it. He was slow, cautious about most things. Elaine got on her first horse, a sorrel I'd picked up at a claiming race, fell off, scrambled back on, whacked the horse between the ears, and dashed about like a cowgirl. Billy waited, watched, made friends with the cowpony named Red, refused to get into the saddle—one day he mounted and could *ride*. To his father's exasperation he sat on the edge of the pool all one summer and wouldn't get wet while Elaine dived, splashed, belly-flopped, choked herself, and nearly drowned but swam. One day Billy got in and swam clear across.

Of all my children, grandchildren, nine great-grandchildren, Billy was the most loving. And lovable. Or—again—do I think this because I had inner warning? Or because I lost him while he was still almost a boy and we never had to make the adjustment of grown-up mother and son?

No no, I don't believe it. Kindness and tenderness harmonize things at all ages.

As for *Elaine*.

A beautiful daughter has to be a joy and a scourge, a blessing and a curse. The lily maid of Astolat was no exception. Chronologically, it ought to come later but it is one of my truest blessings after the pilgrimage into the Desired Country that she has turned out to be such a fine woman, to write books like *Prayer Can Change Your Life*. I do not know how she ever did it. The overcoming overcoming overcoming all the damage done in the years when she was young and against which I truly fought the battle singlehanded—and very stupidly. As much as I had time for, of course.

By the time she was nine, she was so badly spoiled that, though I adored her, I knew she was rapidly becoming a beautiful, dimpled, smiling, overindulged, self-willed pixie princess, who in truth would suffer from too much too soon.

If *I* wouldn't give it to her, *somebody* would.

If *I* said she couldn't do something, somebody else found a way.

If I clamped down with a NO, not only her father whispered yes, so did her uncles and her brothers, her cousins and her aunts. Particularly her uncles, great—adopted—honorary—and contemporary, for my little brothers Thornwell and Bryson were living with us then and they were her willing slaves. Yet now I face it, her aunts were as bad. Mrs. Sawyer and I had strict ideas about the simplicity of a little girl's clothes. Her middy blouses, serge skirts, plainly cut but *so* expensive frocks, her high laced shoes (so she'd have *ankles* instead of ham hocks when she grew up), her short white sox, her smooth Dutch bob. Every time she went to her grandmother St. Johns and her aunts she came back with lace on her panties and crimps in her hair.

Her inclinations, I now see, were always toward the world of science, then so new to us all. We had always been in the arts or professions—it never entered my mind to encourage her or make it possible for her to become a chemist or a physicist. Or a philosopher.

Poor baby. Here I failed her badly, but I think I was also confused, that a good deal of the time it seemed I was fighting for her life and mine.

This is better understood when I explain that she had her first psychic experience in total childlike simplicity when she was four.

Poor baby?—*poor Mama!*

Mother Meyer recognized a real spiritual hunger. I didn't. At that time I was a registered voter in Vanity Fair, and her questions neither moved nor amused only exasperated me, being as I had no answers. Big shot me wanted to have all the answers.

She seeks to be alone, Mother Meyer said. She said that sometimes Elaine would sit perfectly still in the little wood by the stream and Mrs.

Sawyer told me that Callahan worried because she rode off into the hills or down the river bed toward the lion farm and was gone for hours, so I told her she mustn't do that.

At night when Mother and I were talking she'd find a hiding place in Mother's room, and that was when the questions really welled up. *Can I see God?* Can God see me? If He can see me why can't I see Him, I think I can. Is God a Christian Scientist? If God didn't make me who *did?* Is God inside the Catholic Church, Jose says He is on the altar? Who am I?

The thing that disturbed me was that she "borrowed" books off Mother's night table and made marks in them. Things like Juliana of Norwich and once, Mother said, she was starry-eyed over a volume of Emerson's *Essays* though she didn't understand a word of it, she just liked it, she said.

The day I had to deal with her when she came in out of the back yard of our Hollywood house and saw a picture in the paper is long ago—she was only four. It is more real in memory than what is actually going on now.

Upstairs I could hear Bill and the redheaded imp from next door singing forty or fifty times in a row:

> "The sons of the prophet are brave men and bold,
>   And quite unaccustomed to fear.
>   But the bravest by far in the ranks of the Shah
>   Was Abdul the Bulbul Emir—"

From the kitchen I could smell spareribs and sweet and sour cabbage, one of Prue's more heavenly dinners.

Beside me on the floor lay the *Herald* afternoon Green Sheet, with a four-column picture of Ross Snyder, in his AEF uniform. There had been a movement to bring back some of the boys who'd been buried overseas in World War I and Ross had been chosen among them because his father, Pinky Snyder, was Mayor of Los Angeles, to whom my husband was then secretary.

Wearing dirty one-piece blue overalls, my daughter Elaine came through on what was obviously an emergency call to the bathroom, tripped over the paper, said, "Oh—there's *Ross*—" and rushed on.

My double-take took seconds—minutes?

Ross? He'd gone to France with the Rainbow Division before she was born and been killed at St. Mihiel when she was three months old. I myself had never before seen a picture of him in uniform. The mayor kept one on his desk but I knew Elaine had never been to that office. She pelted back and I said, "Wait a minute, lamb. How did you know that was *Ross?*" And she said, "Oh Mama—I guess I know Ross, don't I?"

and I said, "How, sweetheart?" (I mean what can you *do?*) and she said, "Mama, he comes to see me all the *time,* doesn't he?" and took off.

I tried to keep my teacup from rattling and thought, I won't pay any attention. I *won't.* Until about a week later, offhand, she said, "Mama, Ross wants you to tell his mother he can't come to the attic." Now the mayor's wife was a prim and proper Bostonian and the idea of saying to her, *Dear Mrs. Snyder my four-year-old daughter talks to your son who's been dead four years*—I put it off until Elaine said Ross said I *must.* I invited Mrs. Snyder to tea. It wasn't until just before she left that I got up my courage—and then she fainted. It seemed that when Pinky made her break up Ross's room, which she kept exactly as it was when he left for the Army, she'd moved it in toto to the *attic.* No one knew of this—no one, for Pinky wouldn't have stood for it—but she went there to see if she could get some message from her only child. Now she had the message— Ross told Elaine to tell her it was morbid to come there and she should get about being a better wife and mayoress (I guess). He came once more to tell Elaine he wanted his mother to give her the ring with the ruby she'd given *him* when he was five.

We still have it.

As Mother Meyer said, not only were the *evidentials* amazing, but they were blessed in every way. Totally without guile. "This," Mother said, "is not merely a true psychic gift—it's a spiritual gift as well. It won't be easy for her."

It wasn't.

Nor for me her mother.

All gifts have to be protected by discipline and I had little enough of that for myself.

During that interval on the Whittier ranch I tried going back to church. My marriage was in real trouble and I knew it. Like all earthly paradises mine had some small purgatorial serpents crawling around ready to become dragons and I wondered what it would be like to have some *help,* the way Mother did. From prayer, from a shot of spiritual power such as my grandfather used to get. I was full of fears for Ike, and for the *children*—I was sure my sins would catch up with them. I expect it was chiefly fear that moved me. During my whole stay in Vanity Fair whenever I was frightened or felt that tug of guilt I made tentative passes at some church. Very tentative, and I remember once when, very pregnant, I threw up in the aisle of the Mother Church in Boston I was angrily convinced it was *their* fault as much as mine. If it was fear that pinched me, it was fear, too, that sent the leper and the harlot, the man possessed with devils, the blind and the halt and the condemned and the sinner to Jesus.

Why not me?

Who came whole?

Moreover, I really thought *I* was doing any church I went into a favor. Busy finding motes in others, especially the righteous, I was able to shudder at squeaking shoes in an usher, ridiculous hats on a regular churchgoing lady, minor human flaws and intellectual deficiencies enough to allow me to go away as boldly as any Mrs. Muckrake or Mrs. Inconsiderate or Mrs. Light-Mind, forgetting that Mercy is the one companion necessary on this pilgrimage. How could I have so soon forgotten that my grandfather's key was humility-with-God? Yet when I discovered that a high official of a church I'd favored with my attendance walked four blocks rather than pass a church of another denomination I was as ready to throw stones as any guttersnipe.

Ike had worked out simpler methods. Inevitably Sunday morning came after the Saturday night poker game. I made him go to church during these fervors of mine. Big, good-looking, putting on the weight of success both physically and mentally, amiable withal, he felt that it did a man good politically to go to church. I never kicked him until he snored. My stupidity and arrogance soon sent me back to the side of Lucifer with a whoop and a holler, and I gave myself up to the games people play in earthly paradise.

In buying a ranch near Ike's home town of Whittier, I had moved across the Los Angeles River, twenty miles the other side of what was called Hollywood. I wanted to get away from it all. Getting away from someplace anyplace to another someplace anyplace from somebody anybody to another somebody anybody for some time any time long time or short time is one of the false hopes that lure you off the main drag up the Hill of Difficulty going to the Desired Country.

I had other reasons. If I couldn't be on a newspaper, if I had to work at home, fiction seemed a lot closer to my chosen work than another movie script, which incidentally I did worse than anybody in recorded history. I hated doing scripts, *hated* it, I loved some people in Hollywood, I was sick to my tonsils writing about them.

It may be about then I saw myself somewhat as my co-worker Herbert Riley Howe saw me in an article he wrote titled *"Our Adela."*

To begin with, Herb called me "the most temperamental star in Hollywood," and it got worse.

> At six-thirty she is breakfasting. Seven, tennis. Nine, writing a script, sitting in a story conference or, if she can *sneak away,* apprehending a murderess for the papers. Noon, interviewing a star at lunch for Photoplay. Two, whirring off a fiction story for

The Saturday Evening Post, or Good Housekeeping. Five, with all her children and anybody else's she can gather in, swimming at the beach or in Mrs. Wally Reid's pool. Seven, in cloth of gold, bobbed hair rioting, she is fizzing up some stellar dinner party. Retrousse nose, blue eyes shimmering with wit, a too-dramatic imagination, yet you'd never guess her to be an author-ess, her complexion's too San Francisco Irish, her ankles too trim. All of it in a word, *Irish*. And she is given to Irish hyperbole of Gaelic extremes. She storms gaily to sweep everything out of her path. She shrieks hilariously in praise. She "adores", she "loathes", life is too hectic too wonderful.

Not only I myself call her "Our Adela." All Hollywood does, and Howard Strickling and other press agents call her "the most lovable and the most unreasonable woman in the world." When *I* stormed her house to interview *her,* I had to force my way past her colored butler who shook his head in foreboding, warning me she was up against a magazine deadline. I found her pas-sionately strumming a typewriter in a vine-shadowed library, wearing silk pajamas under a Chinese robe and red Chinese slippers.

When I announced that I had come to interview her as ruth-lessly as she interviewed others, she shrieked protest, embraced me in rapturous gratitude and threw me out.

Has there ever been anything more repulsive? And Herb Howe was my *friend.*

It came over me that I wasn't just reporting Vanity Fair-Hollywood any longer. I was *inside* now. Evidently I was getting unreal myself—showing off like that, and at that pace must be doing shoddy work all along the line, not just on scripts.

So off I went over the river and under the walnut trees to write fiction seriously. I did. But Hollywood is like flypaper. Get one leg waving in the air. Try to pick up the next one. If you do, down goes the one you thought was free, right into the glue again. There you are, buzzing in its fatal fascination.

Only a few, as I look back, recognized either the dangers, the signifi-cances, or the power of the New Media at the time.

D. W. Griffith did. "I made them *see,* didn't I?" he said to me one day. "I changed everything. Remember how small the world was before I came along. I made them see in both ways in time as well as in space."

David Wark Griffith.

Conjure with that name. Enshrine it. For no other has surpassed it since he shot *Birth of a Nation.* Even though he worked with inferior tools, as did Michelangelo.

By chance, I had met Griffith one day on Hollywood Boulevard near Musso-Franks and we went in for coffee. I was soon shaking with fury, with embarrassment, he wouldn't let me have any pity. He was broke. He was sleeping on a couch in Mack Sennett's apartment at the Garden Court. As usual with the bright new boys—*it's a business now*—they wouldn't give him a job. They said he drank too much, they couldn't trust him, his last picture with Carol Dempster had been too unbelievably bad. All true. He'd given up his throne for a third-rate actress. Yet—he was *Griffith,* who had made *Intolerance.* He was David Wark Griffith, he was a bum. Trying to swallow that can make you choke to death on your coffee.

"I brought it all to life," he said dreamily. Far far away. "I loved the whole world onto a twenty-foot screen. I was a greater discoverer than Columbus. I condensed history into three hours and made them live it. They still remember Mae Marsh trimming her dress with cotton and putting coal dust on it to look like Ermine when the Colonel her brother came home. *Griffith touches,* eh? They still talk about Griffith touches."

A ham. All right. A ham. But when we see *Gone with the Wind* we are on his same magic beam and Victor Fleming, who made that one, was a big enough man to acknowledge it.

Of course it is easy to see that it wasn't possible to let him play around with the price it cost to make a picture by that time.

Or is it?

Mother Confessor of Hollywood.

Speaking of ham.

That catch line—invented by James R. Quirk of *Photoplay* to give my interviews, profiles, and articles the true-story touch—and that's fair enough, for they were, I was still an honest reporter—was what caused Mr. Hearst to send for me years and years later.

To be close to his doctors, he was living in Marion's beautiful house in Benedict Canyon, behind the Beverly Hills Hotel. I found him in a big chair, quieter than usual, but as usual looking all ways at once. He had an idea for a series in *The American Weekly.*

An incredible combination, *The American Weekly.* A combination of violence, murder new and old, society scandals, documented reports on all that science was doing or trying to do as far ahead as Jules Verne had been with *20,000 Leagues Under the Sea,* inspiring profiles of great Americans throughout history, presentation of new cults, religions, spiritual advances and psychic phenomena, sociological reports from experts and college presidents, sob stories and charity appeals by the best authors in the country—I have always thought that if you could see inside people's heads or had a tape recording of their usual daily reel of thought it would come out very like the contents of *The American Weekly*. A conglomeration of good and bad, love and hate, saint and sinner, past and present, violence and peace, hope and despair and interest in all of them.

Mr. Hearst edited it personally and the conglomeration added up to the largest circulation in the world at the time.

"It has occurred to me," Mr. Hearst said, "that you might do a series putting together the Legends of Hollywood. Much of this may be lost. As you read history and biography you discover how much has been lost about which you long to know.

"The coming of the Motion Picture was as important as that of the Printing Press. Human interest stories convey the truth to more people better than any other method. We might remember less of Napoleon if there had been no Josephine. As I have said before—*biography*—

"There will never again be anything like those early stars. Things—times—have changed too much. When there is no more cavalry, can there ever again be such a dashing cavalry leader as Jeb Stuart?

"In those days my friend James Quirk, a fine editor, billed you as the Mother Confessor of Hollywood."

"I was in my twenties," I said in protest.

"Confidante then rather than Mother Confessor if you prefer," he said, "but you were an integral part of it all and I think we should put it on record."

His enthusiasm as always awakened mine. I began to see that, as an integral part of it, I'd overlooked a lot while it was happening. "Where do you want me to begin?" I said.

"When the world fell in love with Mary Pickford on the screen," he said.

"How many would you think we ought to do?" I said. I had, by the way, totally forgotten I was in the middle of a serial for the *Ladies Home Journal*.

"No limit," Mr. Hearst said. "Let us start with a possible twenty-five."

They ran for fifty-seven weeks, with wild leaps in circulation. In those fifty-seven weeks, I took my copy to Mr. Hearst every Monday and he and Marion and I went over them together. I never was happier than when they made him laugh or cry.

We called them Love, Laughter, and Tears.

CHAPTER 12

David Wark Griffith
Mary Pickford
Tom Mix
Cecil B. DeMille and Gloria Swanson
Colleen Moore
Valentino

As usual Mr. Hearst was right. It had to begin with Mary Pickford.

One thing must be accepted. The identification of the Star and the Person was then absolute and complete. Of the Star-seen-on-the-screen with the Individual who might—and must—exist off the screen. The silver film was Magic.

Mary Pickford WAS Mary Pickford.

The public never separated a human being of whatever kind or character from the girl with the long golden curls in The Movie.

Who the hell AM I? I once heard Valentino shout madly.

Very early Hollywood had this dual existence problem. Today we have a psychiatric disorder known as schizophrenia characterized by splitting the personality; though we'd never heard such a word we had more versions of splitting a personality, NOT splitting it, we had a whole town profession and industry made up of schizophrenics and NON-schizophrenics split in all directions.

Sometimes the star fell entirely under the hypnosis, sometimes they grew together. With each man in her life, each motion picture, Gloria Swanson, the all-time prototype image of A Movie Star, created and accepted a self I watched develop like a character in a novel. Through five husbands, not to mention the man she really loved, one Mickey Neilan, Gloria learned, accepted, grew, absorbed. Gloria was always a Star—but she was herself, too. From a Mack Sennett Bathing Beauty to DeMille's heroine of the bathtub era to roles that were the height of sophistication—she glittered like the planet Venus. Finally when in real life she became the Marquise de la Falaise et de la Coudray, married to one of the oldest and most authentic titles in France, no one who saw her would believe she hadn't been born to it. Both were Star performances.

Garbo, on the other hand, and remember she did make silents, was never at any time disturbed by nor conscious of the Helen of Troy screen star. The mysterious, unattainable she. Never. She wouldn't have recognized her if they'd met on the street. Garbo *acted*. By the time Stiller brought her to America, acting had become her job. In personality, her one-hundred-per-cent Swedish reactions were difficult for us to follow, her slow mind, her fear-dislike of people, the immovable stubbornness. Away from the Camera, she did not wish to be the Garbo created by the Camera, could not be, never was.

Mix Greta Garbo and the Camera, you came up with something that never existed in reality any more than does the Mona Lisa created by da Vinci with canvas and paint. Unmix them, you had the Movie Star, an expressionless, colorless, sulky Swede. This distinction the public would not make. They saw her off the screen, too, as mysterious and mythical.

"You are in love with *Garbo*," Greta once said gloomily to Jack Gilbert, who was her lover.

"Damn right," the dashing Gilbert, then at the height of adulation and stardom, said to her. He told me about it, he said, "I told her yes, I am in love with *Garbo*. I want to marry *Garbo*. She wants to leave the screen and buy a wheat ranch and have seventeen children and don't think she can't. I love people and cities and *conversation*—so I say I will not marry her unless she goes on being Garbo. She says she will not marry me unless she can leave the screen forever. So there we are."

And there they stayed.

As far as Jack found out, her silence was not sphinx-like and scented of the Nile. It was just having nothing to say. Jack was a silent movie star, as a man he was talkative, gregarious to a fault. She was in love with him and when in sheer exasperation he threw her off the balcony and she rolled down the Beverly hillside, she climbed back up over rocks and through burrs and tumbleweed. But she would not move an inch from her determination.

I only saw her when Gilbert roped me in to play mixed doubles against her. From that brief experience and at this distance it is apparent that her famous bon mot:

I Tank I Go Home Now

was merely a sincere expression of Garbo's desire to *leave*. As for this other personality of the screen, Garbo would have none of her in her private life.

With Mary Pickford, the exact opposite was true. She never got them separated any more than the public did.

2

The star who made the Movies, created the Movie Star, brought Big Business from Boston and New York to finance the Motion Picture Industry was Mary Pickford.

Somebody would have, no doubt, but it was Mary Pickford who did.

The nugget that started the new Gold Rush was a picture of hers called *The New York Hat*.

With it she became America's Sweetheart.

I can still say no woman who ever lived at any time in any walk of life ever occupied the position in the United States of America once held by a girl in her twenties, not quite five feet tall, weighing less than a hundred pounds, with long golden curls down her back.

As near a queen as this republic is likely to have and Pickfair, atop a Beverly Hill from which she ruled, was Buckingham Palace.

One of my unforgettable moments in Pickfair's spangled international history was when Joan Crawford finally made it.

Young Douglas Fairbanks, Jr., belonged to the Royal Family, for Our Mary had wed his father, Douglas, Sr. Being thus, it involved his asking Permission to wed a commoner like Our Dancing Daughter Joan Crawford. For a time this was refused. So it was a big night when, as young Mrs. Fairbanks, Joan at last came down the curving stairs in a gown of scarlet, her red hair aflame, her dynamic charm flung at those of us below as though it was a spear. In the stately hall, amid her white-tie-and-tiara guests, Mary waited, wearing soft white with a train, the golden crown of curls, and a smile.

While we were waiting in the wings to do the Merv Griffin Show together the other day, I asked Joan Crawford about the Night. She said she was so frozen with terror that she was sure she would trip and fall head over heels at Mary's feet with her legs in the air. "I even," said the former Mrs. Douglas Fairbanks, Jr., "had on an extra pair of panties. In case. I want to ask you one thing. I've never been quite sure. I didn't kiss her hand, or did I?"

Mary Pickford at her social zenith.

To examine the deal she got from Adolph Zukor when she renewed her Famous Players contract gives an idea of the magnitude of this phenomenon. It has yet to be equaled. It invented Operation Percentage way way back in 1916. Also, Miss Pickford could reject the *finished picture,* a privilege not granted since; a studio must be built for her, she must own it herself so no one else could make a movie there.

The newspapers, in a state of shock, headlined the financial agreement.

(Signed by Adolph Zukor, President and Mary Pickford)

$1,400,000 a year salary.

50% of the profits of all Mary Pickford pictures.

As President of the Mary Pickford Corporation, with her mother Charlotte as all the vice-presidents, she was to get beside a *$10,000 a week* drawing account.

$300,000 bonus for signing. [also a first]

A private car attached to any train if she travelled.

Two limousines, chauffeurs paid by the studio, on call day and night.

Her wardrobe in toto *on and off* the screen.

Two maids both at the studio and at home.

She had been off Zukor's payroll for four weeks while she considered offers from every other picture company and from industrial billionaires who wanted to form companies for her. She now made Zukor pay her $40,000 a week for those four weeks.

I am too ignorant in these matters to enter into the shifting value of the dollar, tax increases, and economic laws, but experts tell me that for take-home pay no one has topped Pickford.

As Mary had such complete control over her own product it is fortunate that her words when she ascended the throne were almost identical with Queen Victoria's, who said, "I will be good." Mary said to her writer, Frances Marion, and her director, Mickey Neilan, "I will make good pictures," and the three of them had a magic formula that produced *Tess of the Storm Country, Rebecca of Sunnybrook Farm,* and *Stella Maris,* one crashing success after another with never a failure.

So that in the end the immigrant boy Adolph Zukor, from Hungary, who had worked up from Ellis Island to President of Famous Players, could crow, *She was worth more.* When, he said, you have only got one of anything it is sometimes beyond pricelessness.

There is, he announced, only one Mary Pickford.

The Presence of Mary Pickford made Hollywood the Film Capital of the World.

But as her fame and popularity soared with *Daddy Long Legs* and *Anne of Green Gables,* Mary Pickford was kept—or kept herself—in total seclusion. Try as I might and did, I never saw her or spoke to her in the years when she was the most beloved woman in the world—nor did anyone else. I was to be admitted to her presence only in an unforgettable moment as a public relations adviser concerning her divorce and remarriage when these were rocking the very foundations of our infant industry.

Was all this cloistered solitude far from the maddening throng to create a nimbus, build a niche? Actually, it was to preserve one. Charlotte Pickford, who had been a widow since the riverboat on which Mary's father was an engineer "blew up on him," as Charlotte said, lived now in Mary's life and she had uncanny intuition and *feel* about people. Better, she told me long afterwards, to keep her little girl out of the goldfish bowl Hollywood was becoming. Already the Pickford curls were the most famous physical attribute ever possessed by a feminine personality. What if her adoring fans discovered that Mary's hair had to be put up every night in rags? "She was a good girl," her mother said, "but they'd got a halo on her and they'd not have liked it if it was tilted even a little bit. Who could have lived up to what they thought of Our Mary then?"

Queen Elizabeth said, "My epitaph should be a line or two and briefly express my name and my virginity and the years of my reign—"

Mary Pickford might well have said the same. In Mary's reign as in great Elizabeth's virginity was part of her power. Therefore in her private life Mary Pickford went to confession, behaved like a little lady, and was never never seen in public. Thus when she met Douglas Fairbanks and they fell madly in love it not only rocked her as a girl-woman and broke up that withdrawn way of life, it brought to the picture industry a threatening crisis.

With Mary Pickford as everyone knew went the control and domination of the Movies. In his definitive history, Terry Ramsay writes, "Without Mary Pickford all other Famous Players were nothing, as were all other players everywhere. Only her name had been up on Broadway in electric lights."

Thus this personal love crisis in Mary's life shook the growing structure of which America's Sweetheart was the Cornerstone. The only guarantee for the gigantic plans, money being and to be invested, theaters and studios to cost billions now in blueprints, legitimate theater talent to be brought over—all this was founded on the love her people, as she called them, felt for Mary Pickford. If she lost her hold, the financial march would halt cold.

Two major factors would be news, if this love story broke.

Very very few if any of the millions who now saw her knew that their idol was already married.

The all-seeing eye of the press was not yet focused on the Movie Stars, no reporters had kept track of Mary down on location in Florida. Even her mother didn't know for months that she had been wed so secretly to her handsome young leading man, Owen Moore. "He must have bewitched her that she'd do such a thing and not tell me," Charlotte kept saying, and by the time the United States was about to go into the First World War Owen Moore was a faint cloud on the horizon of Mary's memory. Shortly, however, he became thunder lightning and hurricane.

Mary had never been in love and there can be no doubt that Douglas D'Artagnan Robin Hood Fairbanks swept her off her feet. But no amount of swashbuckling could conceal the fact that he was married to the daughter of a tycoon and they had a son, Douglas Fairbanks, Jr. So even if Mary's marriage could be annulled, Douglas would be a divorced man. She could never marry him in her church.

Her romance moved to a climax at a mad tempo. Women may wait and weep but Fairbanks was a man of action by profession, he began to press Mary and as rumors grew her Empire showed signs of restlessness and suspense.

This is when, at last, I met her.

Her only close friend, her story writer, Frances Marion, asked me one afternoon to come to her house.

I walked in and—there was Mary Pickford. She was sitting in a big armchair. The long golden curls were looped and tied with blue ribbons and she wore something simple and white. When at last she spoke it came over me that neither I nor any of her fans had ever heard her voice, it had the enchanting lilt of an Irish song.

She was then about twenty-five years old.

Hurriedly Frances explained that they wanted my opinion in my own field. In days to come when Louis B. Mayer or Jean Harlow or Tyrone Power had to make decisions that might affect their careers they would have the infallible advice of Howard Strickling or Harry Brand—but on that day as I stood awe-struck before Mary, there were few public relations men. Mary had no expert professional to advise her.

"If," she said, looking up at me, "I get a divorce and marry Douglas, will anyone ever go to see my pictures again?"

What she was asking—will I be stoned as a witch, branded with a Scarlet Letter, driven off the screen.

"I think," I said, "your chances are better than even if it's handled carefully. All the world loves a lover—a real one—"

She put her teacup down and I heard it rattle in the saucer, she said, "Above all, there are my people to consider." Word for word that was what she said. She had the power and the glory and she accepted the responsibility.

Besides this, Mary faced, I realized, a religious and family crisis. This would be heartbreak to her mother, a devout practicing Catholic, she would be separating herself from the place where in her little white veil she had made her first Communion. All this was beyond Douglas' comprehension or consideration. He was half-Jewish, his real name was Ullman, he had no ties of this nature.

"You think they will forgive me?" Mary said, and when I nodded she gave me her hand and like Joan Crawford later I'm not sure whether I kissed it or not.

After she'd left Frances said, "She's never made a decision before without Charlotte, Mary idiolizes her little brother Jack and Jack can't *stand* Douglas. He says he's a mountebank. Mary's pictures will always—Douglas can only be a Prince Consort. We never invented a story with more conflicts, did we?"

"Do you understand why she's in love with him?" I said.

"I don't understand why I'm in love with Fred Thomson," Frances said.

At the request of President Woodrow Wilson, in the burning patriotism of World War I, Mary came out of seclusion to sell Liberty Bonds across the nation. On platforms with Douglas she was always accompanied by Marie Dressler or Charlie Chaplin. But later when newspapers headlined the divorce granted to Beth Sully Fairbanks naming as corespondent, "A famous unknown woman," Mary had to make a move.

Though she didn't believe Mary could find joy outside her church, Charlotte went along with her to establish residence in Nevada.

In six weeks it was all over and soon, guided by Frances (and me), Mary issued an unprecedented invitation to the press to come to Fairbanks' house on the hill, which she was transforming into Pickfair. On all front pages next day in 12-point Bodini the public was told:

MARY WEDS DOUGLAS FAIRBANKS

They left for England on their honeymoon and people slept in the streets to see her. "I spent my honeymoon on a balcony waving to crowds," Mary said.

The Love Story had won and Hollywood went triumphantly on its way.

You never know the end.

Mary tried to drive three mules, though she and Douglas had no children she had a family—Jack and Lottie had always seemed to me more like her kids than a brother and sister, there was her career—and Doug wanted a wife.

Charlotte at this time knew she was dying of cancer.

On a morning when I went to visit her, I found Mary there, lovelier than ever. Talking to me across the bed where her mother lay propped among the pillows, Mary said, "Adela, you go to the Christian Science Church, don't you?" I said, "Sometimes." I knew Mary had become deeply interested in Christian Science. I waited and she said with a rush, "You believe in the healing power of the Presence of Christ, don't you?" I took a long breath and said, "Oh Mary—sometimes. I try—I try." "That's what I mean," Mary said. "Do persuade Mama to give us more help. She never sees the practitioner unless I bring her. She doesn't read her lesson at all. *You* read your lesson, don't you, Adela?" I was tired of saying *sometimes,* so I said, "Yes. I say the Rosary, too, and read the Book of Mormon, and I was brought up a Methodist and baptized a Unitarian and married in an Episcopal chapel. I haven't made up my mind and I doubt if God cares which road I take, if I ever take any." Mary said a little frantically, and I thought she was trying not to cry, "Mama isn't giving us any help at all—"

At that Charlotte spoke, there was an echo of the old, merry brogue: "Oh Mary, me darling, you're wrong about that. Adela knows there's not anything in the world I wouldn't do to get up and go to Mass again."

Soon it became apparent that she wasn't ever going to get up and go to Mass again and Bebe Daniels called me and said, "My mother thinks Charlotte should have a priest to give her the last rites. We have to do something.

One day when Mary was away for the afternoon, Phyllis brought a priest and Charlotte had the comfort and uplift of her church before she left us forever a few days later. Mary never knew.

Years after that I was writing an article under Mary Pickford's name that appeared as a best-selling book called *Why Not Try God?* and, as we sat working on it, Mary looked up at a portrait of Charlotte and burst into tears. "I have no right to be talking about God," she said, "when my mother didn't have her last sacraments."

Then I told her about what we had done and joy came like an April sunshine.

One brief scene shows better than I can say it the beginning of the end of that Romance we could not believe would ever end.

We were on the sand at Doug's and Mary's beach house in Santa Monica, this one they called Fairford, Doug, and *young* Doug, and his wife, Joan Crawford. In a deliriously becoming white sports outfit Mary appeared, making us all conscious of the whole messy business of bathing suits, sunburn, oil, and sand. Doug jumped up and kissed her hand and said, "Let's go and see this dance marathon on the pier. A couple have been dancing seventy-eight hours—"

Mary said sweetly, "Douglas, love, you know we can't be seen in such a place." She was tiny, tiptoe, enchanting, and yet—we all understood when Doug said, "Tupper, love, the steel hand is showing through your velvet glove."

Prince Consort trouble for a Career Woman. Doug did want to explore the Gobi Desert and climb the Matterhorn and Mary never in her life wanted to do anything but make movies. Doug had the innocent snobbery that dearly loved a lord, so when he went to London, poor Doug was ensnared by the daughter of a stable hand who had married the not-quite-bright heir to a title and could thus be called My Lady. When Mary found out about the Anglophobia flirtation she went quite mad. Unfaithful to *HER? Off with his head.*

Though he pleaded all the way from Albuquerque to Chicago on his knees in a drawing room on the Chief, she wouldn't take him back. The last time I ever saw Doug, at Claridge's in London, he said wistfully, "Have you seen Mary lately? How is she?"

What fools we mortals can make of ourselves, can't we?

3

He was a cowboy. And he made the Cowboy our national hero.

He loved being a cowboy, a marshal, a Texas ranger, a Pendleton Roundup winner, he loved his virile dangerous youth, and he has made that youth eternal in the Nielsen ratings.

He showed us a way of life he knew so well because he was part of it. Not in marble but in pictures that moved, he immortalized the West he helped to win.

He created an art form we call the Western. And he wrote us a code, the Good Guys and the Bad Guys. A code our children know before the Four Freedoms or the Gettysburg Address or the Declaration of Independence.

Tom Mix.

All who came after him then and now follow his pattern. A few variations, some new angles, but they haven't changed much. God grant they never will.

From the standpoint of the continuum, of history and love-of-country, he was the most important star we have ever had.

Also, if I had to name the most attractive man I ever knew from every standpoint—physical, mental, and spiritual—it would have to be Tom Mix.

Debonair. Brilliant. Brave. As Jack Kennedy used John Buchan's words to describe *his* ideal man, they are mine, too.

Debonair. I wish you could have seen Tom Mix in dinner clothes. The broad shoulders, the trim waist, flat hips and stomach, he had the figger to wear 'em. As I look back now, Tom was as elegant on a horse as Fred Astaire on a dance floor, and that's the elegantest there is.

Brilliant. If he left the firewater in the bottle, Mix was brilliant. If not, not.

Remember he was not only from time to time a cowboy on a spree, able to buy his wife sables. He used to say with his cousin, Will Rogers, "My folks didn't come over on the *Mayflower,* they met the Pilgrims when they landed." No all-white man ever moved with Tom Mix's grace—and no quarter-Indian should uncork a whiskey bottle. In the end, it killed him. He tried to ride a combination of alcohol and gasoline in an unbroken Cadillac.

Otherwise, as Mr. Hearst once put it, the sinews of his mind were as impressive as those of his body.

Many stars of early Hollywood came up with fantastic domiciles. The side-by-side drawing rooms in the Mix mansion a few doors down from Pickfair were in a class by themselves.

One side of the vast entrance hall. A room two stories high, redwood beams, huge fireplaces both ends. On the walls Indian blankets, several Remingtons, and two Swinnertons. Around the side sawhorses supporting Western saddles heavily ornamented with silver. Thick Indian rugs on the floor and copper everywhere. The cabinets in the corners held Tom's cups and medals for roping, bulldogging, breaking colts, riding. Tom Mix, his room.

Through an arch, Victoria Mix had created a copy of Marie Antoinette in gilt, French china, Fragonards, and furbelows. Vicky had been a cowgirl and Mix's leading lady, now she kept her diamonds spilling out of a gilt casket when she didn't wear them to breakfast and aspired in this room to be a French duchess before the Revolution. Tom wanted always to be himself and Vicky wanted to be somebody else.

Of all the literary experiences I have ever had, even with my father, watching and hearing Tom Mix read Shakespeare was the most brilliant. Tom hadn't finished grammar school, he had never read one line or seen one scene of Shakespeare. A mature, thoroughly adult, experienced-in-the-world-and-in-battle, victorious pioneer, and he had no preconceived notion, no opinion from somebody who had *studied* Shakespeare. He said if the guy was any good he must have said what he meant to say and it oughtn't to be that hard to understand him.

After he read *Hamlet,* he could hardly bear it that the author was dead. For he was one hundred per cent sure that readers, teachers, actors, and producers had not done right by author, hero, or play.

If I may inject here—he felt the same way only more so about Jesus Christ. The New Testament had always been his favorite reading as story and biography; he saw Jesus so differently that he made me see some of his feelings; in a novel I wrote years later called *Tell No Man* I find in the sermon direct cribs from Tom Mix.

> A master of men was the Goodly Fere,
> A mate of the wind and sea,
> If they think they ha' slain our goodly Fere,
> They are fools eternally.
>
> I ha' seen him eat o' the honey-comb
> Sin' they nailed him to the tree

Tom Mix loved those words of Simon Zelotes after the crucifixion, as conceived by Ezra Pound, and it was about Jesus *the Goodly Fere* he talked.

"That country he was in," Tom said, "it's like our Southern California. Jesus had to be weather-beaten, tanned, walking and sailing and fishing and climbing mountains all the time. Can't do that no way and stay the underside-of-a-fish color some painters make him. I looked it up quite a lot," Tom said, and gestured with a closed fist, "at his age it's unlikely he wore a beard, or if he did it'd be a short trimmed one. Long straggly beards were on *old men*. He wasn't a little bitta guy, either. Those Galilean fishermen were mostly five ten or maybe six feet. Had to be. He didn't wear his hair long, at least not *that* long, it'd have caught in the sails or the fishing lines and he slept outdoors too. You ever talk to Wyatt Earp about Jesus? The old man's been setting on his front porch some years now reading about him. Wyatt says it's all *there* in the Book. But so many other kind of people have interpreted the hell out of it it's hard to read it for yourself any more. There's quite a lot of questions both me and Wyatt are going to ask him, Jesus, I mean."

I don't think I had realized till this moment how much of my own thought of Jesus I owed to Tom—and Wyatt Earp—and I hereby render them my thanks.

The one question Tom wanted to ask Shakespeare—how *old* was Hamlet?

"Burbage who played him first was thirty," I said. "Since then most of the actors have been even older."

"If Hamlet was thirty," Mix said glumly, "it's a lousy play. Man that old took that long to make up his mind what to do about the blackguard that murdered his old man, stole his throne and seduced his mother, somebody ought to put him out of his misery like a horse that's got a busted leg, he's no good no more. After Hamlet had talked to his old man there on the ramparts—"

"You believe in the ghost?" I said.

"Have to believe in ghosts or you're awful narrow-minded," Tom Mix said. "Once in Cheyenne—well, anyhow, if Hamlet was Prince of Denmark and thirty years old what was he letting his *uncle* be king for? It was his father's throne. And he was coming back from *school,* he had to be pretty backward to be still in school at thirty."

"No actor, they say, can play Hamlet till he's thirty," I said.

"Then it was actors done it, not Shakespeare," Tom said. "All that getting Ophelia in trouble and jumping in her grave—that's kid stuff. When I was in China in the Boxer Rebellion there was a girl. I mighta jumped in her grave if I could have found it. I was *sixteen.* Maybe I shot a few men but they wasn't the *wrong* ones. A *man* ought to look behind that curtain —a *kid* don't look where he's shooting."

Jack Barrymore, called the great Hamlet of our time, on his way to Santa Barbara to work with the Shakespearean coach Margaret Carrington, stopped by my house at Malibu and walked about shouting, "I am too goddam *old* to play Hamlet." He was in his thirties.

Mr. Hearst was fond of talking to Tom Mix.

One day at the Ranch he took Tom up to the library to show him the Folio Shakespeare. I tagged along. Somehow in discussing *style* in writing Mr. Hearst said that a good newspaper must have style.

"Gotta be sensational, too," Tom said with a grin.

"Can you define that word?" Mr. Hearst said, and I said I'd heard it so often I'd looked it up, it meant: *Producing a thrilling impression, obsessed with a desire to thrill.*

Tom cut in with a gleeful whoop. "What I've been reading of the Bard of Avon, looks to me like he intended and desired to thrill—scenes *and* dialogue." He found the Folio *Romeo and Juliet* and, though the old type threw him, he shouted, " *'Oh heavens! Oh Wife! Look how our daughter bleeds! This dagger hath mistaken! For Lo! his house is empty on the back of Montague and is missheathed in my daughter's bosom!'* Look—look at all those exclamation marks, will you?"

Mr. Hearst said, "There are quite a number of murders in that best-known love story. And *Othello* is a most sensational account of interracial marriage. Macbeth is filled with sensational assassination."

Mix was hypnotized by the books. He said, "Come down to it, *Richard III* is gang warfare and *Hamlet*—we'd call him a millionaire juvenile delinquent—Shakespeare didn't miss one dramatic invention, or one combination that creates sensation and thrills an audience."

"You may include Dickens' Bill Sikes and Nancy and Bill Sikes' dog,"

Mr. Hearst said, "and the way Aeschylus presents the return of Agamemnon from Troy and his murder by Clytemnestra."

"I gotta get around to the Greeks," Tom Mix said.

I wrote two screen stories for Tom at Fox, one about a cowboy who met an English girl at a dude ranch and followed her home to the hunt country. It was the only time I ever enjoyed working in the movies.

Brave.

The other word Kennedy quoted.

The Boxer Rebellion. Marshal, ranger, cowboy in the early days. Wyatt Earp said Tom went up against the worst of the bad men.

Mix was a pallbearer at Wyatt Earp's funeral along with Jack Dempsey and Mark Kelly and Bill Mizner. I found it brave that he cried all the time he was carrying his old friend's casket.

Tom Mix doesn't have to wait all those years for a monument like David Wark Griffith. You see Tom's monument in celluloid every hour of every day.

He still rides tall in the saddle.

If we have a code of Good Guys and Bad Guys and which are which—and we do, though sometimes we are too lazy to take advantage of it—we find it in the Westerns where Good was not afraid to speak up and fight Evil—and win. If the first Western star hadn't been the real thing, it might have all come out phony.

Anticlimax.

Footnote 1.

Some old-timer may want to know about Bill Hart. William S.

Okay. Bill Hart was a second-rate Shakespearean actor. He had played Messala in *Ben Hur* on the stage and had never been farther west than Jersey City. He had a mean rugged countenance, and so that fine showman Tom Ince, second only to Griffith, made him come to Hollywood and do some Western into which that face fitted.

He was scared to death of horses.

Footnote 2.

I am adding Tom Mix to that group I want to find waiting in the Tavern at the end of the Road. My son Bill, my father, my godfather Jack London, Mark Kelly and Damon Runyon and Tom Mix.

I'm not sure I won't like it better over there than here.

CHAPTER 13

Gracie Allen, bless her, was covering a Presidential convention—in a humorous vein, of course—and we met one night when our tasks for the day were over and had a cup of coffee in the Pump Room. To get away from politics, I said I thought this Sinatra boy had talent, and Gracie said, "Oh sure, everybody's got talent nowadays. But can he wrap it up?" I had asked myself this question when I first saw Leo McCarey looming on the motion picture horizon, for he was the son of Uncle Tom McCarey, the big fight promoter and I'd known him for talent since Los Angeles High School.

By the time he asked me to work for him on an original story he had shown the guts, dedication, and spirit necessary to wrap up *Goin' My Way, Love Affair,* Cary Grant, Mae West, and Irene Dunne and also I needed a weekly paycheck.

This original story of Leo's was to become, he said, THE epic picture about Hollywood. We would use his story *Came the Talkies* to destroy a way of life, love, and finance as Victor Fleming used the Civil War in *Gone with the Wind.*

I'm sorry you never saw this picture.

Unfortunately, our contract was with that destructive-constructive, productive-conflagrative force named Howard Hughes so we never got to make it.

Leo and I worked three doors down the hall from Howard, we never once got to see him. If he was chasing girls he did not chase them down our corridor. (I missed all the *chases* I heard so much about in early Hollywood. I would have donned my pink coat for I dearly love a chase. True, I saw Wallace Beery chasing Gloria Swanson in her Mack Sennett bathing suit around the dry lake at their studio—evidently she got away, for later he married her. I also saw Ava Gardner sock Jimmy Stewart with a chair and guards break down Mario Lanza's door only to find him concealing neither girls nor drugs, only *food.*) As for Hughes, he spent half his time watching Jane Russell's rushes in *The Outcast,* the other turning a deaf ear to his business associates from Texas. He left a couple of glamour girls waiting at the church, nobody knew why; one girl told me that, though he kept her locked in her room for the term of the movie contract and he gave her a huge salary, he never came near her.

Leo was to get no money till he started to shoot, he couldn't start until Hughes okayed the script and cast, he couldn't get to Hughes. At last he busted into the boss's office and his language penetrated Hughes' convenient deafness and they ended in court. Leo won, but we didn't get to make our picture.

The day we went to work on it as a Hollywood epic, McCarey stated our credo. Nothing that could happen anywhere *except in Hollywood* should be in it.

From all the stories I can tell of my Hollywood, *Valentino* is the one that completely lives up to that model.

In his career, Valentino only made twelve pictures.

Only twelve years from the day Rodolpho Guglielmi, an Italian peasant boy eighteen years old, landed from steerage on the shores of America to the day his female worshipers were prostrated by his sudden death and even his male enemies said, Why, the poor bastard, he was too young to die.

For *lover* the thesaurus gives us Lothario, Romeo, Casanova, Don Juan; most people, I discover, give you *Valentino*. When they die young the wounds bleed, wounds that bleed leave scars to remember by.

Valentino comes out of the past loud and clear.

The last time I saw him there was a terrific thunderstorm going on outside my New York hotel, the roars of it shook the building, and I moved back into it, back where the lightning opened the very heavens with flashes of blue.

Valentino didn't seem to notice it. He had appeared in my door from his suite down the hall, found me in the hands of a hairdresser who swooned at sight of him, and regardless began to pour out his troubles.

"It is *Pola*," he said, "she telephones. She can no longer live if we are separated, she comes to join me."

"You're engaged to Pola Negri, aren't you?" I said.

"A myth," Valentino said. "Pola believes her own acting, me—I cannot. To marry *Pola?* In the home, I love quiet. Pola is quiet like the falls of Niagara. Poor poor Rudy!"

In the middle panel of my triple mirror he was framed as the picturesque Great Lover, Valentino, shining gold dressing gown, patent leather hair, hypnotic black eyes. Matinee Idol of all time. Oddly, it was as though in one of the side glasses I saw my friend Rudy, who truly did love quiet in the home, who liked friends in ordinary Italian restaurants and talk with easy laughter and operatic airs played by a violinist in a velvet coat. And —in the other I somehow had an impressionist picture of a very young Italian peasant boy, working in the fields and then racing to sing and dance in the village square.

The peering, hypnotic Valentino stare, most famous physical attribute except the Pickford curls—that was just Rudy refusing to wear glasses so he could see. He didn't want to sweep you into a mad embrace, he just wanted to be sure who you *were*. Not mesmerism—*myopia*. One of the grimmest jests the camera ever played.

He disappeared into my bathroom and shouted, "The bicarb. I do not see heem. Pola, she drive me to eet."

"Also," I shouted back, "you ate three dozen snails for lunch. There isn't any bicarb." Then it came to me to say as he returned, "In spite of the divorce, you still love Natacha."

"She *is* my love," Rudy said simply. "Can I be divorced from my heart?"

Is it strangely Hollywoodian that this flaming representation of all screen lovers carried to his grave, only a few days away, a torch for the woman who had married him without love, and in the end divorced him without mercy, the bizarre, sophisticated, ambitious arty, triple-plated egotist Natacha Rambova, a phony name beneath which she was Winifred Hudnut.

Rudy's worry about Pola was wasted. On arrival she put on widow's weeds instead of a bridal veil. I hoped Rudy, who had a primitive sense of humor, could see the weeping wailing whooping thousands who hour after hour for days walked by his ornate casket. For in it, Jimmy Quirk assured me, lay a Madame Tussaud's wax image. Valentino's body had been shipped to California, nobody was taking any chances of an Edgar Allan Poe horror with hysterical women trying to tear his heart out for a souvenir.

"What happened?" I said to Jimmy Quirk. "I saw him the day before he went to the hospital. He was on bicarb but I had no idea he was *ill*."

"The doctor said he had holes in the lining of his stomach as big as your fingers," Jim said. "The doctor said the boy hadn't taken care of himself."

Taken care of himself!

Much chance he'd had.

At twenty-five, having been a busboy, and by chance danced in a café when Bonnie Glass's partner broke a leg, and played extras, he made *The Four Horsemen,* a picture to live forever. At twenty-seven he married Natacha, broke his Famous Players contract, and by court injunction couldn't work anywhere else. At twenty-nine, she left him. Before he was thirty he was dead of not taking care of himself.

A montage of those five years shows Valentino waking to find himself as famous in his time and place as Lord Byron was in his, and as infamously misunderstood. The word *gigolo,* to describe our first foreign star, and the final insult of the Pink Powder Puff article were the knives that emotionally—and medically, the doctor said—dug those holes in his stomach.

If the Big Three who made *The Four Horsemen* had stayed together it must have changed Valentino's life. Valentino, star, June Mathis, writer, Rex Ingram, director, a combination to conjure with.

June Mathis, actress-turned-writer, a most extraordinary woman, spotted Valentino as an extra man dancing on the Metro lot. She didn't fall in love with the boy; she had already given her heart, brain, and talents to Rex Ingram, the coldest man who ever directed others in passionate love scenes. Having written for Ingram the script of the Ibáñez classic, she went at once to him and said, "I have found our Julio," thereby making it known for all time as the picture that blazed Valentino as a star overnight. They saw Valentino dance the tango and that was it. An extra girl named Alice Terry caught Ingram's fancy, he married her. Casting her peaches-and-cream beauty as co-star of *Four Horsemen* wasn't what shook us— *what would June Mathis do?* If June's heart broke nobody knew it, the picture went ahead. However, as soon as it was over, June Mathis broke up what might have been a potent and protective union-in-art and went to Italy to help Louis B. Mayer with the first (and best) *Ben Hur*. Ingram, furious that his picture had become merely a starring vehicle for Valentino, said he could create another one of those any day and tried it with a young Mexican named Ramon Navarro. So Rudolph Valentino, as inexperienced and darkly ignorant as a coal miner in a space capsule, signed a contract with Famous Players.

Fabulous as he had become, Valentino had true humility and so he agreed to play Armand to Alla Nazimova starring in *Camille* and thereby signed his own death warrant, for on Madame's set he met her designer, a very tall, very thin girl with a turban winding her very black hair, very clanking jewelry, long slinky robes, and too much Oriental make-up. "What do we *do?*" Alla said. "He has before him this stupendous career, she will swallow it and him like a boa constrictor to feed her own ego."

Too late too late. From the moment he saw her.

Now the giant spotlight searched in the corners and found his first marriage, about which no one had cared before. An extra man named Guglielmi and a bit actress, Jean Acker. "Why did you marry Jean?" I once asked Rudy, and he said, "You start to climb an alp, if you see one beside you as alone and lost and afraid as you are, it may be easier if you hold onto each other. Or so it seemed."

Loneliness: stand by to crash.

They were wedded and parted long before Rudy's success, but Jean appeared as a forlorn shadow to give him a divorce that he might wed the object of his grand passion. Pretty soon, since as usual Rudy hadn't the remotest idea what the *hell* he was doing, he landed in jail for bigamy.

When I went down to the jail I found him shaking the bars of his cell— his jailers didn't like the gigolo either—his face wet with tears, he shouted,

"I rot here before I deny our sacred marriage. She is my wife my wife—" "Stay locked in jail, you can't do much about it," I said. "What have I done?" he demanded. "You only got an interlocutory decree," I said. "In California you have to wait a year for a final before you can marry again." When it came to trial, where the charge was dismissed but the marriage declared null and void, he cried, "I would break any law to make her my wife and so she is."

So she continued to be, bigamous or otherwise.

Right after one more smash hit as the bullfighter in *Blood and Sand,* Valentino walked out of Famous Players and refused to work under that contract. The studio got an injunction forbidding him to appear before any other camera and Valentino was out of work—encouraged therein by Natacha who had long nourished an ambition to produce his pictures herself. The studio gave the impression that the trouble was about money but as Valentino said in a letter he wrote himself, "I have done without money so long I will not be a sardine in a can to get some—from my sweetest friend June Mathis I have a promise to make the motion picture as an art and in this my adored wife also joins me."

Actually it turned out this was the shot that started the war on block booking to come to the Supreme Court long after Rudy was dust—but he fought that first battle alone.

Finally his lawyer got a modification of the injunction and he and Natacha were married or remarried and began a dancing tour. The men so detested the foreign gigolo that they locked their wives up to keep them from going to see him dance; they must have broken loose for they turned out in hysterical mobs.

I wish you could have seen them dancing together. This was Love in Bloom. The only other couple I can remember for sheer beauty were Zelda and Scott Fitzgerald at a Beaux Arts Ball.

Finally under public pressure, and the chill of losing so much box office loot, a new contract was arranged and he went back to Famous Players-Paramount, taking his wife with him.

This was Natacha's opportunity to move into the driver's seat. Poor Rudy. She wasn't even married to *Valentino,* only to the Valentino career. With him as star she produced his first picture under the new deal, *The Hooded Falcon.* I was on the set one day when it reached the point of no return. In a motion picture you can tell the writer what to write, the director how to direct, but if you're in your right mind you let the cameraman alone. Natacha couldn't let anybody alone.

The Hooded Falcon was an unalloyed disaster.

The man who saved this fermenting situation, as he did many others, was Joe Schenck. Famous Players had *had* the Valentinos, box office or no, and when Joe, as head of United Artists, offered to take the whole thing, even that prize pain-in-the-neck Mrs. Valentino, off their hands they were delighted. A kinder man than Joe Schenck never lived, nor one more immovable in a righteous cause. His contract offer to Valentino was magnificent. It contained a clause that barred Mrs. Valentino from the studio, the set, and any part in the Valentino pictures. In return Mr. Schenck would pay Valentino's debts and finance pictures for Natacha Rambova *without* Valentino: she could use the shawls and Moorish costumes she'd spent thousands of dollars for in Europe. Rudy struggled, pleaded, and Mr. Schenck retaliated with special advantages about directors writers and stories. In the end, Rudy's debts were so dreadful, time was passing with no income—he signed. Once they began to work, he told Natacha, he would adjust everything and he would be able to give her all the money she needed.

Natacha listened with narrowed eyes. The ambitious Rambova had been divorced from Valentino the star by Mr. Schenck. Without a word of warning, she got on a boat and in Paris Mrs. Valentino was divorced from Rudy the man by a judge.

The separation from *my love, my wife* broke the mainspring for a tired confused young man. She would neither see him nor answer his wild letters. Hope of her return left him and with it all his joy of life. I truly think it would have comforted him if he had known how short the rest of his journey without her was to be.

The final straw must be set down. It may seem silly today but it wasn't then. On the Chief on his way to New York for the premiere of *Son of the Shiek*, he saw in a Chicago paper where some nameless columnist had said:

> A powder vending machine! In the men's wash room! Homo Americanus! Why didn't someone quietly drown Rodolpho Guglielmi alias Valentino years ago. Masculine cosmetics, shieks' robes, floppy pants and slave bracelets—London has its dancing men, Paris its gigolos, now Rudy the Beautiful gardener's boy tries to become the prototype of the American male.

Valentino's rage was appalling. His manners and appearance were Continental, his love-making Italian, his dancing gorgeous, no one who knew Rudy or had seen *Blood and Sand* could have questioned his manhood. But the words that brought him out fighting were those that defamed the slave bracelet. Natacha had fastened it on with her own hands, you'd have had to cut off Rudy's arm to get it.

We all advised him to let it alone. He couldn't, his anger shook loose this letter:

To the man (?) who wrote the column editorial headed Pink Power Puff: You slur my national ancestry, you cast ridicule on my name and doubt on my manhood. I call you in return a contemptible coward. I challenge you to a personal test . . . I defy you to meet me in a boxing or wrestling arena to prove in American fashion (I am an American citizen, you know) which of us is more a man. You have put it in these terms. Hoping I will have a chance to prove to you that the wrist under a slave bracelet can snap a real fist to your jaw that sags, I remain with utter contempt, Rudolph Valentino.

No answer came from the PPP's author.

Rudy brooded, walked the floor nights. "I have not the hide of the rhinoceros," he cried. He ate and ate and ate—

When he collapsed at the party to which he went on the night of that thunderstorm in New York they rushed him to the Polyclinic Hospital. All day. All night. All during the week he was at death's door, people stood or knelt outside that grim building, and hourly bulletins flashed out to the cities, farms, towns, hamlets where others congregated to pray for him.

How could they know he had no desire to live?

He was an object of ridicule to decent men.

Natacha was gone forever.

His dreams as a boy had been of quiet orchards, of green fields in the lovely old countrysides of Italy. His kind do not thrive in cities. He went to America to get money enough to buy a farm! His dream of work was that of the Italian peasant and even in his motion pictures he had wanted simplicity and dignity and strength. This must have been a powerful dream for he gave some of the finest performances ever seen on the screen and he always said he couldn't act, something "took him over"—as St. Martin took over Sidney Poitier in *Lilies of the Field*. His dream as a man had been the One Woman—he had found her, loved her, and she hadn't loved back.

As I grow old, I value friendship more than most things. It was Rudy's friend June Mathis who stood beside his grave and said the last words of blessing for him.

He was my friend, too—a nice, clean, simple friendly young man.

As far as I know he never did any harm to anybody.

You see, on the whole I don't—I didn't—*like* Hollywood.

Hollywood = Vanity Fair.

For me.

None of it ever seems real.

But it is stupid and academically arrogant to dismiss it and its all-powerful offspring television. Surely we know that now. This is the main force of our times—from the day the media began with Thomas A. Edison's pictures that would move, the media has been building up to take over.

Our society as it exists today has been molded by what it has seen and heard coming out of Hollywood. Its movies. Its television.

So was my life.

I wanted to get my work out of the picture business. Myself out of Vanity Fair. Many times I've hoped that now I'd lifted my foot free of that flypaper. I have never succeeded any more than I am going to succeed now. For I must use its power if I can and there are people there I love or have loved. They tie me to that medium and, that place, memories of which I have none dearer. Like Jean Harlow and Clark Gable.

CHAPTER 14

Jean Harlow was known as a nation's Sex Symbol.
In her own home town, her own home studio, we called her The Baby.

I have to set down an explanation of this word as Hollywood and Metro-Goldwyn-Mayer, all-time biggest and most successful motion picture production company, used it as a synonym and pet name for their blond bombshell. There are not too many things out of Hollywood I want to keep forever in any incarnations to come. This is one of them. Meanings of words change so much. *Baby* has become a low idiom. Its connotations are vulgar, suggestive, criminal, and *blue*. As far as Jean Harlow was concerned, The Baby was a *title,* given her by the entire population of the studio where she made all her pictures except *Hell's Angels*. They weren't many. The title was indicative of the depth of our affection—and something more. As Jeanette MacDonald, star on the same lot and a prima donna indeed, once said, it was only fair to acknowledge that Jean had won something no one else ever had, and perhaps, Jeanette and I decided, it was because we knew she needed protection and care and we tried to give them to her and never, never could. Mr. Mayer, Marie Dressler, Joan Crawford, Clark Gable, Lionel Barrymore, Judy Garland, Lon Chaney, Lew Ayres, Mickey Rooney, even Norma Shearer—we called her The Baby. And so did the grips and the carpenters and the electricians and the painters who, in tears, kept the long night watch around her bier at Forest Lawn because, they told me, "The Baby was afraid of the dark."

You cannot do better for any girl—than what we meant by it—let me show you. This is not my witnessing. One of the best storytellers in the entertainment world told it to me. Harry Ruskin wrote for the Follies and for sixteen years fifty-two weeks a year got paid a record-breaking salary by Metro to write the comedies of *Andy Hardy* and *Doctor Kildare*. Those were the years of Harlow's success. Not long ago when we were reminiscing of this and of her he told me:

"You know about the Commissary at Metro the day Jean Harlow died? You knew the Commissary. Six hundred people had lunch there every day. Noise between a parrot cage and a boiler factory. Actors, writers, extras, stage hands—I been there when they threw chicken soup and once Mr. Mayer hit a writer over the head with a water bottle. The Commissary at lunch was where everything went on. Right?

"The day The Baby died there wasn't *one sound* in the Commissary for three hours. Not one *goddam* sound. People pointed at the menu, waitresses tiptoed, people stared at the food and got up and went out. You didn't even hear a footfall." Harry took off his glasses and wiped them and, after a pause, he said, "I liked that kid. I said to her once, 'You know, if you'd been a boy I'd like to have roomed with you.' "

That is what we meant by The Baby and we never found anyone else in show business that merited it.

The Baby had been well born, gently reared. I'd been in the home where her grandfather and grandmother, a family of distinction, lived. I'd seen the library of much-read classics, the music room with its grand piano. I'd seen her on the night her husband Paul Bern shot himself in the next room. Oh yes—she was there. No reason not to tell it now. She'd heard the shot. She would hear it as long as she lived. When Jean called Howard Strickling he consulted Thalberg and they decided to get her out of the house. So Howard picked me up and we took her to her mother's; when the police and press got there all they found was that hideous note that made her—a girl men kill themselves over.

Dearest Dear Unfortunately this is the only way to make good the frightful wrong I have done you and to wipe out my abject humiliation. I love you. Paul. P S You understand last night was only a comedy.

I said much later, "Look, Baby—it wasn't the first time he tried suicide. When he lived with Irving Thalberg in that house back of mine and Barbara LaMarr got married to Jack Daugherty he put his head in the *toilet* and got stuck. They had to get a plumber to unscrew the seat and there he was wearing it like a wreath but he didn't drown, and he said, Nothing is so terrible as tragedy that becomes comedy."

"He must have looked pretty silly," Jean said.

"I wish they'd let him drown," I said.

"So do I," Jean said.

It was the only bitter thing I ever heard her say about anybody.

She was twenty-six years old when she died.

The love of her life was Bill Powell and it was Bill who bought the stately white marble tomb at Forest Lawn, where two million people a year go to see the Thorveldsen Christus, the reproduction of Michelangelo's *Moses,* and the window of *The Last Supper,* the finest stained glass in America. For years they saw too that the only sepulcher never without flowers was Jean Harlow's. Weekly there was a basket from her old friend Lionel Barrymore, who'd been with her at MGM all the years of her short life. There were sheaves of chrysanthemums from Clark Gable, to whom she was "My kid sister." White orchids from her boss, Louis B. Mayer, and every single day white roses from Bill Powell.

2

Agatha Christie has a famed detective called Miss Marpel, who solved murders because they always reminded her of something, someone, she'd known in the village of St. Mary's Mead. In those years in our village of Hollywood I was firsthand with life, with people who were highlighted, who attracted drama, violence, and every possible combination of them. They were *exaggerated,* but they were exaggerated *from* the same things that other people were and the same things that, less often, happened to those others. Thus on my Dangerous Journey, in Washington, Baton Rouge, Flemington, New Jersey, London, the Bahamas, Chicago, Seattle, and Salem, I could figure what the people were really like. Something somehow reminded me of some things I'd seen in my village of Hollywood.

And the Great Common Denominator of this village was Clark Gable.

One day we were leaning over the fence out on his little ranch in the San Fernando Valley having a stormy argument about a story I liked for him but he had dug his heels in and said NO about a thousand times. I made some crack—I was worn out with trying to find a story he'd consent to do after he came back from the war—and I said something about his being the King. "Anybody'd think you believed it," I said.

"Well," Gable said, chewing on a straw, "I don't believe it but I know why they like to think I am." This surprised me and I said, "You do?"

"I'm not much of an actor," he said apologetically, "but I'm not bad unless it's one of those things outside my comprehension. I work hard. I'm no Adonis and I'm as American as the telephone poles I used to climb to make a living. So men don't get sore if their womenfolks like me on the screen, I'm one of them, they know it, so it's a compliment to them.

"They see me broke, in trouble, scared of things that go bump in the night but coming out fighting, they see me making love to Jean Harlow or Claudette Colbert and they say, If he can do it I can do it, and figure it'll be fun to go home and make love to their wives.

"They see life with a high price tag on it, but they get an idea that no price is too high if it's *life.*

"I am not going to make any motion pictures that don't keep right on telling them that about a man. Let's get that understood. The things a man has to have are hope and confidence in himself against odds, and sometimes he needs somebody, his pal or his mother or his wife or God, to give him that confidence. He's got to have some inner standards worth fighting for or there won't be any way to bring him into conflict. And he must be ready to choose death before dishonor without making too much song and dance about it.

"That's all there is to it."

All that Gable said to me after he knew that the plane carrying his wife Carole had hit a mountain and there were no survivors.

But I'd seen him prove it and himself a good many years before to the cold and candid eyes of the younger generation on one of his first visits to my house in the Malibu Colony on our beach beside the Pacific.

My son Bill, then about ten, wished to offer our best to any guests and, observing Gable admire the crested roll of the forty-foot breakers on our sandy shores, said, *Would Mr. Gable like to go swimming?* Mr. Gable said he would only he hadn't brought any swimming equipment and Bill said we had it in all sizes shapes and colors. I protested. Mr. Gable and I had to talk business and Bill said, Well, you can't talk it all the time, can you? Clark gave me a peculiar look and then followed Bill out.

They disappeared up toward the cove where the breakers are biggest and best to ride. I had a flutter of unease.

Bill came back first shaking water out of his ear and said, "Mama, you oughta have told me he couldn't swim," and as I started to say, "Is he all right?" Mr. Gable hove into the room. He had swallowed two whole waves, you could still hear them, his hair was matted with sand, his eyes and ears were running salt water, he staggered a bit, and he had seaweed between his toes. With great dignity he said, "I can too swim! I never was in the ocean before, but I was a whiz in the ole swimming hole back in Cairo, Iowa." And he managed a grin at Bill.

This began a friendship between these two which lasted even after Bill's death.

My first sight of Clark had been in some film Irving Thalberg ran for me to see how I felt about him as a replacement for Jack Gilbert, victim of the talkies, as the gambler in *A Free Soul*. Accurately but ungrammatically I said, That's him, and they cast him for it and soon I was called in by Howard Strickling to meet Mrs. Clark Gable, a rich Texas widow. From being the wife of an unknown young actor Rhea Gable found herself married to the hottest star in the Movies. Although she did most things well for this she needed a little guidance.

Women came fairly far down on Gable's list of life's *summum bonum*.

First, his men friends and man pursuits, hunting and fishing and poker and a little drinking.

Second, his work.

Third, women and children.

He married older women. His dramatic teacher, Josephine Dillon. Then

Rhea. He hoped they'd stay home, run a good house, send out his laundry, keep the bills paid, and prevent social life, per se, from catching up with him. This Rhea did, she had two children to whom he was devoted, and this he truly believed was all he required.

Until he met Carole Lombard.

Mr. Gable had no hesitation about marrying a blond bombshell. He would take care of that. A woman would *try,* he said, but no woman was ever happy in marriage unless the man was head of the family. At the time he married Carole Lombard she had a reputation of swearing harder and talking dirtier than any other girl in Hollywood. A couple of days after the wedding she blued up the air some and Clark said to her, "Mrs. Gable. Around here *I* do all the swearing. If any language that isn't fit to print has to be used, *I* will use it. I don't ever again want to hear any of it from my wife." And he never did.

Young Bill Hearst called to tell me that Gable was dead.

Of course I didn't believe it.

Came the Talkies, came a new royalty, Gable *was* King and this time the picture business was built on the formula Only God can defeat Gable, and He has to use the heavens themselves as in *Hell Divers,* fire, flood, and earthquake as in *San Francisco,* war as in *Gone with the Wind,* and usually they end up on the same side. When Gable finds out his best isn't good enough and not even Spencer Tracy can help him he asks God. Gable agreed when I outlined this formula and said he didn't know just how it had evolved. After World War II when he had lost his wife Carole and I had lost my son Bill, we worked together to see how to get his picture career into a new pattern.

As soon as he got back to America, Clark came to see me. He had seen Bill in England only a week before he was killed; they'd had, Clark said, a night on the town in London. He remembered what they'd laughed at, and some Polish fliers they'd met, and he said quietly, "Remember, he was doing what he wanted to do as few men in this life ever get a chance to do it. He died fighting for his country and for all he believed in and he was a fine soldier." And that consoled me very much.

That's what I meant when I said their friendship, Clark's and Bill's, lasted beyond Bill's death—and I expect it has now beyond Clark's. For it was Clark who asked Mr. Mayer to run for us a picture MGM had made called *A Guy Named Joe*—where there was a hole in the sky for all good pilots. Clark and I saw it together.

When Gable died Bill Hearst wanted me to do some stories about him and I started to say, No, I do not write about Hollywood *any more.* Then I thought, I cannot build my old friend a monument of marble, or carve his face on a mountain, but I can erect a small memorial of paper and ink. For a moment it may recall, for me, and perhaps others, some beautiful yesterdays, bid bygone times return.

So I went to my typewriter—I had trouble seeing the keys—I still do.

The King is dead. Long live the King.

There has been no successor, nor will be. The title died with him.

Is it strange that from the man who was an *exaggeration of life* I learned that death is a door life opens? As happens in wartime, we were confronted with death. His wife, my son, my brother.

The Army didn't want Clark Gable. An Air Force officer followed by cheering mobs upset discipline. Once *in,* the studio fought to keep him out of active service. "He was a soldier," war correspondent Hank McLemore wrote in a dispatch from the front, "an airplane *gunner,* where the mortality rate is highest. He made it like any man had to. A tough guy up there where you know whether a man is really tough or only camera-tough. Facing death."

Most clearly I saw no thought of death nor fear of it would turn him aside from what *life* demanded, or rob him of joy as adventure. Nor would it occur to him to ask or allow anyone he loved to give up climbing the highest mountain, because death might be waiting around a turn.

Everyone has to learn how they feel about death. I learned from this simple sincere man of fiber faith, without spiritual pretense. He said to me that day in Carole's room, "They say in the midst of life we are in death, but I know now in the midst of death we are in life." It has served me well, that honest, unpretending acceptance of a part of life called death.

He had gone to war soon after Carole's death. With the peace, he had to face *everyday* living. Getting up in the morning, going to bed at night, walking where she had walked. He talked about her a good deal while we worked. He lived in what was still Carole's house with her Siamese cats and her hunting dogs as well as his. He wanted it that way. The dark-skinned couple that had been with them were with him now. It seemed, he said, the same fire they'd sat in front of so many evenings— "We liked," he said, "to be alone, just the two of us. She was the best companion."

"She was," I said, "the one woman that always kept you laughing. You are an unsentimental man. The first piece I ever wrote about you I said you had never sent flowers to a woman in your life and you were furious and sent me a carload but you admitted it was true. Whenever you were afraid things would get sticky—Carole made you laugh."

He grinned at me and said, "One day we were looking around at our ranch here in the San Fernando Valley and it was beautiful—one of those California days. We were just—lazy—strolling around—gabbing and I said, 'Mother, we're awfully lucky, you and I—all this and each other—anything you want we haven't got?' You know what she said, standing there looking lovely as a dream? She said, 'Well, I could do with another load of manure for the south forty.' "

He'd laughed then—and laughed again—but a few minutes later he took me upstairs to her sitting room to show me her books. "She'd like you to have any of those you want," he said, and so to Carole Gable I owe my first meeting with *The Cloud of Unknowing* and my big copy of *Cosmic Consciousness*. But I thought she would not like him to keep this room just as she left it. I wondered if I ought to say anything. More Mama Fix than Mother Confessor, and I said to myself, Why don't you mind your own business? Clark Gable is a grown-up man, if there is such a thing, who knows what he is doing about most things. Death, I said to myself, is not new to him any more. He did a great thing; he turned back halfway up that mountain when Ralph Wheelwright said to him, *Carole wouldn't want you to see her in that plane wreckage*. That was *love*. He'll know when to give up this room.

He walked around and looked out a window and then—not turning—he said, "I don't think she'll want me to keep this room any more. If she can ever come back to me at all, she can come anywhere, can't she?"

So I told him the story about Elaine and Ross's mother—and the attic —and it comforted him.

The last time I ever saw the Clark Gable I'd known over those years was one night in that same house at another story conference. To me— well, I didn't see him often after that, I never thought he was the same man. He never could stand loneliness. And Carole had always gone everywhere. He sort of drifted after she left him until he ran into a small safe harbor with Kay Spreckels.

We were working late—he had turned down a story I liked called *Haunch Paunch and Jowl*—and we were trying to make some sense out of a thing later advertised as "Gable's Back and Garson's Got Him"—a *horror!*

The telephone rang, he answered it and handed it to me, and a studio operator said, "Will you call your house right away, Mrs. St. Johns?" I got my house—and when I tried to put the phone back on the table I missed, it hit the floor and rolled, and Gable jumped for it and for me. "What is it?" he said, and I said, "My—brother Thornwell is missing in action over Rabaul—with the Marine Air Corps. I—must go home—" "I'll take you," Clark said, and I said, "No no, I have a studio car outside," and Clark said he'd rather take me himself. "It's quite a long way," he said, "you better have someone to talk to."

Driving over Coldwater Canyon, he began to talk directly, as a man does who has known war himself. To ask me about my brother—and I said he was a young lawyer following in my father's footsteps, he'd played football at Stanford and married a wonderful girl—and then I broke down, I guess, and said, You see he was actually my first baby. I was seventeen when he was born and I took all the care of him, he only weighed two and a half pounds and we had quite a fight to save him and I used to tell people I was his mother when they saw me pushing his baby carriage—

I got straight talk from Gable.

He said, "Go ahead and cry. You're lucky you can. Sooner or later, you'll have to bite on the goddam bullet. You know Carole was on a tour selling bonds and Franklin D. Roosevelt, the President of the United States, said to me, She died for her country as much as any man in our fighting forces— You—women—can be as much a part of our fighting forces—"

I remembered then about Carole, I finished my cry as quick as I could. He pulled up in front of my house and my son Dicky came out and I said, Thank you, Clark, and went in to Adrienne, my brother's wife.

A couple of hours later Dicky came and said, "Mama, do you want Mr. Gable to wait out there any longer?" and I said, "Is he still out there?" and Dicky said, "He says he thought he'd just stick around to be sure you didn't need him any more—"

This is what I call friendship.

When I told that small cherished memory on the *Tonight Show* to make people understand Clark Gable, Johnny Carson said to me, "You sound as though you were in love with him."

I said, "There is a great difference between being *in love* with a man and loving him. I loved Clark—and I always will—and I think he loved me.

"One day, when I had just moved into a new house we called The Hill over near MGM where I was working, a truck drove up and two men in overalls began taking down my front door and putting in a big new one of solid oak. They said it was Mr. Gable's house present. And I remembered that I had admired Clark's front door.

This is what I call lovingkindness.

Late one afternoon my secretary said Captain Eddie Rickenbacker would like to speak to me.

Eddie hadn't then written his own life story but his best friend, Steve Hannagan, had done a fine job of biography under the title *Hat in the Ring,* the name of the famed Rickenbacker squadron in World War I. The rights to this had just been sold to the Movies and Eddie, who knew little of pictures, was upset about a rumor. Recalling that I had once been connected with Hollywood, he wanted to discuss it with me.

"What's the rumor?" I said.

"Well," said the captain, "at '21' today someone said they'd heard that Clark Gable was going to play me."

"It's too good to be true," I said. "Such magnificently accurate casting is beyond the possibilities."

A pause. Then—still with some surprise—Captain Rickenbacker said, "To tell you the truth I—it didn't seem right to me at all."

"You have to be out of your mind," I said. "Not that it is oft given us to see ourselves as others see us, but nobody can be *that* cross-eyed."

He was huffy about that; he said, "Gable is a *gambler,* he's usually cast as an adventurer. A—a swashbuckler as they say—he has no *restraint.*"

It took me a minute to recover, then I said, "There is, they say, a word for everyone—you remember *Valiant Was the Word for Carrie*—are you suggesting that *Restraint* is the Word for Captain Eddie Rickenbacker?"

"Perhaps," Eddie said, "dignity would be better. I am certainly supposed to have some *restrained* dignity—"

I said, "There is only one man in the world who could really play the part of you and that is Gable—I still am afraid to believe you could both be that lucky."

He said, "I'm sorry—I still can't see it—"

I said, "Let's not sell either one of you short, shall we? You are a couple of swashbuckling, hell-raising, looking-for-trouble, hard-drinking, roistering adventurers—direct descendants of Jeb Stuart and Mad Anthony Wayne—and the word for you both is Hat-in-the-Ring—'Restrained dignity' indeed!"

After a second he began to laugh.

Of course I was right—they didn't cast Gable for the part.

Now, on the other matter, I think I was wrong and Eddie was right.

Both of them were an *exaggeration* of the dignity of man.

Of course the captain is still alive and—so is Gable, to me. The heart's dead are never buried.

CHAPTER 15

PRIVATE SCANDAL
From a Letter to Hearst Publishers by William Randolph Hearst

October 1928

I have been asked if there is any justification in publishing
news of a private scandal. None whatsoever if it is private and if
it is scandal. But news about the actions of private persons
ceases to be private when it gets into the public courts.

I once sat next to a man in Washington at a dinner and he
kept annoying me by complaining that some one of my newspapers had printed items about his brother's divorce.

Finally I told him that it was deplorable and that I would
make a compact with him. If he would keep his brother out of
the divorce courts I would keep him out of my newspapers, because so far as I know his brother had no other claim to newspaper attention. A good many people who object to the attention
newspapers give their private affairs forget that their affairs have
become of public interest and public importance through their
own fault entirely and through no fault of the newspapers.

*A newspaper's right and duty are to print public facts in which
the public is interested, whether the individuals concerned are
public or private.*

2

Just the other day Chet Huntley, an old newspaperman himself, said to
me, "Does anyone know whether or not William Randolph Hearst killed
Tom Ince on his yacht?"

I said, "Well—he told me he didn't."

"You mean you asked him?" Chet said.

"He told me—*go and ask*," I said.

I didn't tell him I also asked Nell Ince, Tom's widow, and got for the
first time her own detailed story.

Having handed in my Valentino copy in the *Love, Laughter, and
Tears* series on a certain day, I was invited to a beautiful little table oppo-

site Mr. Hearst. Over the teacups, I was inexplicably moved to ask him this question I'd never dared breathe before nor had anyone else. He was enjoying his jelly doughnuts—Mr. Hearst loved food, I noticed as he grew older he was fonder of sweets—he was pleased at the tremendous success of our Valentino series in the *Weekly* and I thought, Think of all this man has seen of life, now his old age is a big chair from which to look back on it. So on an impulse when the word *scandal* came up about Valentino I said, "There are scandals around all famous men. There's one about you."

"I should think there'd be several," he said. (Watch it, Lee Ettelson said, remember he's a mind reader.) "Are you referring to my alleged murder of Tom Ince?"

I swallowed my doughnut hole and all.

"I didn't murder him, you know," Mr. Hearst said mildly. "I doubt if I could have gotten away with it. I had both opponents and enemies who attacked me on every possible point. But negatives can be dangerous. In an interview I recall you once quoted Madame Montesorri, an inspired educator, as saying, Never say to a child, *Don't* cross the street. Say, *Stay* where you are. If you say, *Don't* shoot it comes out Shoot. If you say, Put down that gun, it might work. Your father asked for affirmative answers. Tell the jury whether you are innocent of this crime? I am innocent of the murder of Tom Ince but if I say I didn't the average reader notes I spoke of the murder and two days later may well pass on the word that I confessed."

He passed me the pastry tray. "I recommend the éclairs," he said, "they have custard, not whipped cream. Not only am I innocent of this Ince murder. So is everybody else," he added with a twinkle.

(I am reminded of an evening at the old Coffee House on Forty-fifth Street in New York. Grantland and Kate Rice had asked me to dinner with Harold Ross, founder-editor of *The New Yorker,* whom I had not met. Mr. Ross said to me immediately, "Bob Benchley once took me to that beach-house-castle of Hearst's at Santa Monica. I was stunned. I expected Dracula and, by God, *he* thought he was *Mr. Chips.* Before I got out of there he made me believe it, too.")

"As I have often told you," Mr. Hearst said, "as a rule I am opposed to denials and retractions. They call the attention of many people who never heard of it to the very thing denied. At the time Mr. Brisbane died, you remember I took over that column, no one else seemed available who had the weight of years to handle it. Also, I must admit I enjoyed doing it. I've never liked being an editor, you know, I prefer a more active part, that's why I covered the Spanish-American War myself—I was younger then. I must admit I enjoyed a place to express my seasoned judgment. A column should be an expression of expert knowledge or of seasoned judgment, and like all seasoning, columns must be used with a careful hand. But even in my column I never came upon a time when it seemed wise, or tactful or entertaining to deny the Ince canard. Better, I thought, leave it alone."

Yet now I feel that under his own instructions it would be tactful and wise to clear up this oft-repeated mystery, in which so many are still so interested; it's a long time ago and since it's about two extremely public individuals it is no longer a Private Scandal. It's been controversy long enough.

And certainly the facts are entertaining.

It occurs to me that I wish Mr. Hearst hadn't mixed up in Motion Pictures. I don't mean Marion. Marion Davies was a Movie Star. Her pictures made money; she had the most luxurious bungalow on the MGM lot; Mr. Mayer gave her casts and directors second to none. As a comedienne she would have been second only to Mabel Normand if she hadn't had to carry Mr. Hearst's romantic ideas. I started a picture with her once called *Zander the Great*. She was a desert waif, daughter of a prospector with a burro. One day she found her shack full of orphan children and one day I found our film's rushes full of M.D. in organdy ruffles in a garden swing! In the middle of a desert? Mr. Hearst had indeed waved his magic wand and for once I wished he'd stayed home.

3

Why did Mr. Hearst kill Thomas H. Ince?

Were you ever on the yacht where Mr. Hearst murdered Ince?

Did W.R. poison Tom Ince for making a pass at Marion Davies?

Do tell us, darling, about Mr. Hearst and Tom Ince, did he shoot him or poison him? I've heard it both ways.

So have I.

For my authentic, documented presentation of the facts I needed only three witnesses, but I checked many more.

The three are:

A. M. Rochlen, now Harbor Commissioner for the City of Los Angeles at San Pedro.

Nell Ince, widow of the deceased.

Marion Davies, alleged motive for the alleged crime.

I call Rochlen first.

In 1926, Rochlen was star reporter and No. 1 bloodhound on the Los

Angeles *Times,* strongest opposition paper to Mr. Hearst's *Examiner.* Everybody called him Rocky. The *Times* had the Otis fortune, a top staff, and a great publisher in Harry Chandler, who had married General Harrison Gray Otis' daughter Marion and founded the vast Chandler family and fortune. Between these two papers was as fierce competition as I ever faced. When Harry Chandler said to Rocky, There is a lot of talk W.R. killed Tom Ince—get the truth about this, he meant with your shield or on it. Moreover the natural instinct of every reporter is to hope the story is true. I promise you, if, when I worked on the Chicago *Examiner,* Howey had told me to go and see whether Bertie McCormick had committed the St. Valentine's Day Massacre my hope would have been that dear Bertie's finger was on the trigger. For both these reasons, Rochlen of the *Times* was not about to whitewash William Randolph Hearst or cover up for him on a *murder.* This, like skiing, would be against all instincts for self-preservation. The thought of a *Times* headline:

HEARST ACCUSED OF INCE MURDER ABOARD YACHT

would send any opposition reporter's heartbeat up to 220.

Last week I asked Rocky, whom I worked against and with for years, to tell me about it and we spent a couple of days. It's not necessary to put the famed

By A. M. Rochlen

here.

I can say that he told me how he covered every moment from the instant Tom Ince left the yacht, interviewed the water taxi driver who took him ashore, and the train crew and from there on through doctors, nurses, undertakers, police, and coroners. He then had to go back and tell Mr. Chandler that there was nothing to it.

I think the best account is that of Mrs. Ince, whom I will first qualify as a witness. Besides, it is exclusive and I have the reporter's pride in an exclusive.

Before the Inces moved to an estate in Beverly Canyon where Ince died, and Ike and I moved to our walnut ranch in Whittier, our big yellow house in Hollywood was cater-corner neighbors to Tom and Nell. My children and the Ince boys went to Chermoya School together. Nell and I sat in our gardens and watched the kids play, thus I knew her much better than most wives, for I was too busy for daytime women's social activities. Nell was a beautiful tiny blonde with wit and humor, executive ability and a seeking soul. Her boys will bear witness that she was also a fighter. Before she wrote for me her version of her husband's mysterious death—she calls it untimely—Nell said, "Do you think I would have done nothing if I even suspected that my husband had been victim of foul play on anyone's part?" The idea that, as a cheap scandal magazine printed, Hearst had "given the Ince widow two old beat-up apartment houses to keep her pretty little trap shut" is evil idiocy. Thomas H. Ince was not only a prominent but a highly successful motion picture producer. Nell was left a rich woman, one of the apartment houses she already owned was The Elysee, then the most expensive in the area. Nell had built it herself on the very grounds where their old home stood.

Sunday December 5, 1965

Dear Adela: [Nell's letter begins and after some kind amenities continues:]

We want to talk about the twenties which when one looks back seem simple compared to today's tangles. One thing is similar: No one wants to be "involved." I am referring to the enormous fable "people" built up about Tom. Many knew and did not speak. I greet your questions gladly, my friend, and tell you that you are the *first* ever to ask *me*. Why? I am glad you felt that I would be cooperative and I would, especially to you. So to answer all the questions.

I was not there so cannot bear exact testimony as to how Tom got from the yacht to the train. I do know that the doctor who was married to Alma Rubens, you remember? was called and only intended to see that Tom got on the train, but changed his mind as Tom seemed to grow worse and went with him, taking him off the train at Del Mar and to the hotel there, where another doctor and a nurse were called. This second doctor called me saying Tom wanted me to come and get him and to bring Dr. Glasgow with me. Which I did, by car, immediately, my son Bill came with me. Dr. Glasgow was a well known physician and at the time was treating Tom for ulcers and had been for a long time. Tom told us that he had eaten quite a few salted almonds before dinner and had some champagne with dinner, both forbidden articles on his diet.

Tom's attacks of "acute indigestion" were well known to those who worked with him. Often in the middle of a conference he would double up with pain, the sweat would break out and drip. This I saw myself.

He said he hadn't refused the champagne because it was his birthday and Mr. Hearst proposed his health. Both doctors at Del Mar told me he would be a week recovering but it was safe to take him home where he'd be more comfortable. We sent the chauffeur on with the car to meet us in Los Angeles, and we came by train and Tom lay down all the way. From the moment we met in Del Mar I was never separated from him for a minute. Tom had been treated by a specialist M.D. for chest pains which were diagnosed as angina. When my son Bill became a doctor, in his medical studies and experience and in many talks with physicians, giving all the symptoms he saw in his teens, Bill says it all fits what we know today as a thrombosis, and the end came at home a week later. He had been improving steadily, the doctors and nurses were pleased—the end was unexpected as with thrombosis it generally is. He died in his own bed in his own home attended by his own doctors and with a nurse present. I was with him and his last word was "Nell—" He overworked always. He did not drink, his ulcers wouldn't have let him but he had no inclination that way. I imagine it was the day after his death that you brought Florence Heifitz (she was then Florence Vidor) to see me. She was my dearest friend and she wanted to take me away somewhere—being thoughtful of me—but I had those three boys asking questions in sorrow and they needed me so I couldn't go. You question as to the Why cremation? Mine is why all this uproar about cremation? As you say, it was not as common then as it is now . . . but it was our considered opinion and belief that it was the best way. We both wanted and had promised each other that we would have a very simple service and cremation—did we not have the right to do what we wanted in this very personal decision? That decision was *not* made after Tom's death but had been made between us long long before. I expect you know that most of those who try to make a mystery of this simply seek what they call kicks. No mystery was intended or carried out. I did not know at the time about the rumor of Tom having been *shot*—which sprang up immediately—but Mr. Carpenter (Tom's attorney and trustee) went with Reeve Houck, our studio superintendent AND the Chief of Homicide of Los Angeles and Dr. Day—of Day and Strother, the mortuary where Tom's body was. They made the necessary legal examination before the cremation—so you see, Adela, all those who wanted the truth could have found plenty of testimony. Why did no one ask me? Do they think, could anyone think, that I would have remained silent if there had been any truth in his having met with foul play on the Hearst yacht? Anything else you ever want to ask I can take it—the only thing I haven't learned to take—it still happens so often even after *forty years*—is to meet someone who says sweetly Are you any relation to the Movie producer who was shot by Mr. Hearst? That one *I* could shoot. Forgive me if I have spouted off too much. When I think of skunks like DeMille and Bill Hart admired still and all these lies cooked up about Tom I do get enraged. I am so glad you will be writing of WR in your book. None I have seen do him justice at all, they give no conception of the dynamic and fascinating man he was to meet and know. A delightful dry sense of humor I found, and such kindliness—and such a splendid *dancer*. Did you ever dance with him? He was *the* best. Of course I only knew him socially—that was a joy at all times. He expected a lot of those who worked for him I know—but like my husband none of them worked as hard or as long hours as he did. Adela, I am writing this carefully because I do hope for the sake of my children and my beloved grandchildren no such belief in such a weird and silly story will continue down into the generations. My best wishes to you and whatever you do, thanks for asking me for the truth —my love and many good memories—

Do you believe that a murder could have been concealed under these circumstances?

The examination in the presence of Mr. Ince's lawyer must rule out bullet holes, for, even saying a reputable mortuary firm might *overlook* this under ordinary circumstances, surely they wouldn't do this in the presence of the homicide chief?

Look at the number of doctors—nurses—wife and son—even saying an attempt might be made to buy or frighten them into silence, somebody would have leaked as the Associated Press added its eagle eye to the investigation. Too many people were involved—too many people saw him —too many of them would be Hearst enemies, or opponents at least.

My father used to point out that on the basis of reasonable doubt we have the right to consider a man's character temperament and record. Some crimes, he would say, the accused is capable of committing—of another you may have either reasonable doubt or complete conviction that none of the many selfs of whom each of us is composed could have done that particular deed.

Alice once said to the Red Queen that one can't believe impossible things. "I daresay you haven't had much practice," said the Queen. "When I was your age I always did it for half-an-hour a day. Why, sometimes I've believed as many as six impossible things before breakfast."

As a rule, I'm with her.

This is the seventh. I can see Mr. Hearst shooting an enemy—maybe even in cold blood. Everybody can shoot somebody sometime for something. But poison a guest at his own table in a birthday toast—NO.

When Jessie Costello was tried for poisoning her husband in the Kiss-and-Tell cop murder in Salem, Mass., most of the press thought she did it. The jurors told us afterwards they couldn't believe *poison*—she was, they explained, a *violent* woman.

Marion's casual testimony is a final word for me.

On our way from the dining hall at the Ranch to the theater a group of us, beckoned by M.D., stopped as usual in the ladies' dressing room after dinner to repair lipstick or comb our hair before proceeding to the nightly movie. This suite consisted of a charming tiny sitting room, with comfortable chairs, a dressing room with full-length mirrors, and tables with triple mirrors and make-up. Besides the usual plumbing. Sometimes we had a wee nippy there out of Marion's secret bottle.

Mr. Hearst did not like her—or anybody else for that matter—to *drink*. Ale and beer were served with lunch, in moderation. Sherry or a cocktail, maybe two, before dinner with copious hors d'oeuvres, especially mountains of caviar. A trusted guest might have a highball after a day's ride or the Movie. Mr. Hearst believed we should handle our liquor like gentlemen or not drink at all and *nothing* got a guest that chill, courteous "A car will be waiting to take you to the night train" as quickly as overindulgence in alcohol.

At dinner when Albert, the butler, sometimes passed behind Marion's chair without stopping, Marion would say across the table, "Oh W.R.— I just want one more glass of champagne. I never get cross with you when *you* drink."

"No," Mr. Hearst would say, beaming at her, "you only get cross with me when *you* drink."

We enjoyed our gab sessions in the ladies' room and often settled down to make serious decisions about people and things. On the night I'm writing of the name Ince came up.

"One of those scandal sheets said W.R. killed him for making a pass at me," Marion said. "Nobody ever made passes at me except Chaplin and everyone knew he was harmless and anyway it was for laughs. Either men worshiped W.R., or they worked for him, or they were our guests and *gentlemen*, or they hated W.R.'s guts but were scared of him. My leading men—they went *whoosh* the instant the camera stopped grinding. Ince would have had to have what Freud called a death wish to give me a wink on a yacht which has as much space and privacy as a barrel. Tom Ince was a very ambitious man. He wanted something from W.R.—you know everybody always wants something from W.R. Even us. I've already got it, so it doesn't count any more. Why would he take such a million-to-one chance? Ince was devoted to his wife and family. If he cheated he was damn discreet about it. No no—I could still recognize it when a man gave me the eye and Tom Ince didn't. Moreover I would not have given it back to him, so why would W.R. get mad enough to murder him? It's plain silly."

We were fascinated, time passed more rapidly than we noticed.

There was a knock, the door opened, nightgowns, slippers, toothbrushes came flying in. Mr. Hearst's voice said, "Mare-ee-on, if you and the young ladies propose to spend the night in there you may be more comfortable if you have these—" Marion's eyes opened wide, she rushed out and threw her arms around him and said, "You are an impossible man to get along with, you know that? I was trying to explain to them that you didn't murder Tom Ince for making eyes at me."

The movie wasn't nearly as interesting.

CHAPTER 16

The cremation of Tom Ince and a whisper that this was to *prevent* an exhumation order and a belated autopsy have to bring me to the day when both these things were true.

And I got back into the city room!

We were living on the Whittier ranch at the time.

I answered the phone myself. It works that way for you sometimes.

I said, Hello—and when there was no answer said it again louder—Hello—Hello?

I was just going to hang up when, faintly, words came to me.

"Mrs. St. Johns—?"

"Yes," I said. "Who is it?"

A silence, but I felt someone there—I heard a long difficult breath.

"Who is it?" I said again.

"It doesn't matter"—I could barely hear this—"but hurry—please hurry. Or it'll be too late."

I said, "Is this a joke?"

Got back a startled gasp, "No no. I shouldn't have waited so long. The funeral is this afternoon at two o'clock at Strothers on the boulevard—oh hurry."

This is for real, my stomach said. My blood began to chill, then to *jump*. Don't scare her. Take it easy or she'll hang up. Just keep her—let her feel you're listening—I said yes very low—

"He didn't die of pneumonia," she said. "They beat him to death."

Distant, eerie, an unrecognizable whisper. In response, the news flash had begun signals in my brain. The flash that transformed everything.

I said, "Go slowly—someone was murdered? Who?"

"They—beat him to death." The voice broke like a dry twig. "You must stop the funeral."

"If you'll tell me who, I'll stop it," I said.

"The two of them," she said.

"Which two?" I said.

"They're going to cremate him. Oh—hurry."

Before I could speak again, I heard the click as she hung up.

My book-lined redwood library had faded away. The lovely garden— through it ran the little clear brown stream—the giant eucalyptus trees marching away—they had all disappeared.

I was back in the city room.

Take too long to trace the call. *Two o'clock*. The clock on my desk said twelve-twenty. Hurry hurry—an hour and forty minutes to go. At least an hour's fast driving from my ranch to the funeral parlor—I was in work clothes, pajamas and a robe—one statement I must check—

"Two o'clock?" a pleasant, grave voice said. "Yes we have. Ray Raymond—you may know the name. A—a theatrical figure. Yes—his wife has requested cremation. Dorothy Mackaye—the actress."

So much was true.

The phone call could be malice, gossip, old wives' tale, neighborhood grudge. Or—it might be the truth. As far as I could remember I'd never met Ray Raymond—came to me he'd done a musical show at a theater on Vine Street. Dorothy Mackaye I'd met and didn't like. Why I couldn't recall. What *about* them?

I picked up the phone to call the coroner.

Put it back.

This is my story.

Call the coroner, he'll tell the press room. Or somebody will leak—his phone operator, a secretary—the boys in the press room must have leaks. With this one, I could make the street edition, the biggest one of the day on an afternoon paper. If I called him I'd blow it wide open. If I didn't and the funeral went on—I was juggling bright balls called minutes as I dressed—if he'd been beaten to death and the certificate said *pneumonia* there was big monkey business going on. The only proof would be the body and cremation is ashes to ashes.

I shoved the copy for my new serial for *Good Housekeeping* out of the way, pages fell on the floor, who cared? I called the city desk.

J. B. T. Campbell could listen. He said he'd have the coroner come down to him immediately. Then Nance—the coroner's name was John Nance—could be at the funeral parlor with whatever papers were necessary. Campbell said he would take care of *him*—nobody else would know. By the time I could get there Nance would be parked across the street from the mortuary chapel. The moment the coroner moved in to stop the services and the cremation on information received, we could go to press. All I'd have to do was call the desk, I could dictate my story to McGillvray.

Information received. My information. Could I still dictate a big story that fast? I'd better!

Who called you? Campbell had asked and I said I had no idea. Or why. Why me, I mean. I wasn't working on a paper any more, worse luck.

As I began to run for the car Mother Meyer came out of the garden. I told her, and she said, "I wonder what made her decide to call you. God go with you."

As I swung the Packard roadster I'd won from Earl Anthony on a Stanford-U.S.C. game, I prayed that there wouldn't be any motorcycle cops between me and there. I could explain, but it took time and I didn't have *any*.

I began going over my files.

When a story broke and you had to pick it up in the middle without any clippings, any morgue information, it was necessary to use your own files that you often never even knew you had. I hit the traffic just before the narrow bridge over the dry Los Angeles River and crawled across, up-tight as a bongo drum. All right. My files—a reporter's files—bits and pieces, odds and ends, scraps of every kind of information, names, people, places, the hodgepodge began to click into order. As I swung around the Plaza onto Sunset Boulevard I sorted it out.

Ray Raymond. Song-and-dance man—second-rate—no great shakes, no great loss. But every man had a right to live out his life.

Mackaye—a *real* good actress. From Broadway. Good-looking, dark, never going to make it to the top, be a first-class heavy, leading woman, character parts. Something harsh about her. Something dangerous if you got in her way? Tank right over you? I thought so.

They were married. Didn't they have a child? A little girl?

I do not know how I knew this, I had heard it somewhere, it had registered itself in my memory file, memory is your stock pile.

Whispers—whispers again—thin and eerie—scandal whispers.

Now it began to come back. Talk about Dorothy Mackaye and Paul Kelly. This was something else again. I liked Paul Kelly. A fine actor, I'd seen him in New York in *Machinal*. Good-looking—had class—what was he doing running with the likes of Ray Raymond and Dorothy Mackaye? One explanation for that. Sometimes a woman can see and understand the sex appeal of another woman—Harlow, Liz Taylor, Gloria Swanson. Then again she can't, as in the case of Mackaye and Julie Christie. On the other hand, an earthy quality—some kind of challenge?

They! The faint voice on the phone had said, "*They!*"

Dorothy Mackaye and Paul Kelly?

Something was trying to come through. I was pushing it back from a warm liking for an Irishman named Paul Kelly. The file card jumped up, facing me. The Lambs. That famed New York club actors, playwrights, managers loved so much, we used to say it could be sued by wives for alienation of affections. In his Broadway days, Paul Kelly had been a member of The Lambs. A frequent visitor after his show. But—he'd been in trouble that had made the papers. For *fighting*. Some well-known figure

—a *brawl*—Paul Kelly had been suspended by The Lambs for violence unbecoming a gentleman.

They beat him to death.

No seventh impossible thing to believe before breakfast, this one.

If Ray Raymond had died of a beating Paul Kelly was capable of it.

Second degree. No premeditation probably.

Nance was waiting in his car all right. He did not look pleased. J. B. T. Campbell must have put the fear of J. B. T. Campbell into him.

"What is this ring-around-the-rosy you're up to?" the coroner said, looking at me with extreme disapproval, though I thought I was appropriately dressed in a navy blue suit by Eddie Schmidt, white collar and cuffs, neat and respectable. Nance said, "He died in the Sisters' Hospital. The death certificate says pneumonia, it's quite in order."

"You talk to the doctor?" I said.

"No," Nance said. "He's a man of good standing—"

"Let's get going," I said. "I've got a deadline."

"I don't like any of this," he said as he climbed out of his car. He was a big man, he towered over me like a thunderhead. "This is a highly ethical and respectable mortuary firm—never had a word—if you're wrong I shall look a fool."

"If I'm right you'll be a hero," I said, "and anyhow your conscience might keep you awake nights if you didn't at least take a look."

The dead can't hear—why is there such a hush? It's our own fear—we don't want to face that sooner or later we will be up there in that box. We will be the main character in this drama—without *faith* we face it without the support of either joy or curiosity. Lights were dim, the organ played softly, the scent of flowers unlike any others wafted from the chapel. A baritone voice began to sing:

> Sunset and evening star,
> And one clear call for me . . .

It seemed singularly inappropriate to me.

The coroner dropped off into a handsomely furnished room. I could see him greet a man in a cutaway and striped trousers. They started to talk. I went on and found a spot behind the scenes. From it I could see a lot of the people. The family pew and Dorothy Mackaye in heavy black; a man beside her looked like a doctor. *The* doctor? Holding each other up?

I didn't see Paul Kelly anywhere.

Only a few minutes to go.

> And may there be no moaning of the bar,
> When I put out to sea . . .

No moaning of the bar if the man in the closed casket under the blanket of white carnations had been beaten to death by his wife's lover? To get rid of him? No no—easy to get *rid* of a little man like Raymond, they didn't have to kill him. Or just momentary madness that takes over when passion and evil are allowed to run loose.

Where *was* Kelly? Pacing the floor somewhere, remembering his past, waiting for this woman to come to him and say it's all over, we're safe?

The countdown to ashes was moving toward zero.

And ten may nine there eight be seven no moaning . . .

—but of course neither of them now, Kelly or the man in the box, could hear the baritone. Under her widow's peak Dorothy Mackaye's face was stark, when she raised her eyes to the man beside her they were black and expressionless as shoe buttons.

Six five four

—Or maybe this was all nonsense. Maybe nobody was strung on any rack of suspense. Maybe this was imagination. They could be innocent but I knew now that they weren't. They might be so sure they'd gotten away with it!

But such a tide as moving seems asleep,
Too full for sound or foam . . .

—In the days everybody lives through between death and the funeral, nobody had cast a questioning glance at the death of the little song-and-dance man whose nimble feet were now quite still under the white carnations.

Twilight and evening bell,
And after that the dark . . .

—You're always taking some *chance*—somebody left around who saw something—who might pick up a phone and whisper anonymously—hurry hurry—

Where was the child?

I was glad she wasn't there. Children should not go to funerals. How well had the song-and-dance man known her—he'd probably been on the road a lot. And of course Dorothy Mackaye was a career woman. Always hard to tell how much time a career woman had for her children and how much she cared about being a mother.

When I put out to sea . . .

We were about to put out.

The rector rose. *I am the Resurrection and the Life. Though I were dead yet shall I live—let us pray—*

One minute to go.

A strange static silence, an immobility fell.

Everybody waited.

The ushers, the pallbearers did not come forward to start the blanket of white carnations toward their final bonfire. The widow turned her head toward a movement in the door. Other heads followed her.

Down a side aisle the coroner and the director moved into the chapel. Now the coroner was standing beside the casket, his hand on the cover, a couple of white carnations fell. The director walked over to Dorothy Mackaye and she stood up. The director seemed to ask her to come with him, but a white flame flared at him. She couldn't turn any whiter but she turned hotter and her eyes were all black.

Autopsy? Her voice—a harsh, interesting, trained voice carried the word autopsy.

My heart had begun to gallop. *What must she be feeling?* So near and yet so far.

I had to get to a telephone.

"He's stopped it," I said, and Campbell said, "You've got about seven minutes—" I began to dictate.

> In the presence of his widow, Dorothy Mackaye, Coroner John Nance this afternoon halted the funeral services of song-and-dance man Ray Raymond and ordered the body taken to the morgue for an autopsy. As strains of Crossing the Bar filled the chapel at Strothers Mortuary, the Coroner moved on information that Raymond had not died of pneumonia but may have been killed in a fist fight—

Information. Well, I said to the mystery woman, wherever you are, we stopped 'em.

If they're innocent it can't do them any harm.

The post-mortem showed that Ray Raymond had been beaten to death.

"What have you got it in for Mackaye for?" Jack Campbell said to me one day when I came down from the courtroom where Paul Kelly was on trial for the murder of Ray Raymond with Dorothy Mackaye and the doctor as accessories after the fact. Campbell was reading the lead on my story, which said that Paul Kelly on the witness stand was his own only hope—a great witness—and that Dorothy Mackaye watched him with—

"What's all this about shoe-button eyes?" Campbell said. "The district attorney asked me to ask you to lay off the woman. She didn't beat her husband and he doesn't think he can convict her."

"She has got eyes like shoe buttons," I said.

"How about ignoring her for a bit?" Campbell said. "He says you made him charge her in the first place—lay off—"

"All right," I said. "You call me off. If you're taking orders from the D.A.'s office."

"You know I do not take orders from anybody but William Randolph Hearst," Campbell said. "I told the D.A. I would convey his request to you. I've done it. I assigned you to the story and you cover it your way. I'm a little surprised, that's all—usually you're on the side of the defense."

I thought of Paul Kelly's landlady, the one who'd run the apartment house where he lived—Mackaye, she testified, had come to Kelly's apartment that morning—weeping bitterly. Yes—she came there sometimes. Often? Well—yes, quite often. Did she ever stay the night and anything more perjured than the woman's NO I'd never heard from the witness stand. But that morning she had been crying loudly—and the people in the next apartment heard her crying and talking to Paul Kelly and then he began shouting and cursing—and that afternoon there had been a phone call, they could always hear his phone ring, and then they'd heard him shout again—and he rushed out of the door and the landlady said he went by her like a hurricane, cursing out loud.

"I am for the underdog," I said, "the underdog in this case is the child. Did you know Dorothy Mackaye and Ray Raymond had a little girl? I don't know but what Paul Kelly is the underdog—Mackaye went and told him Ray Raymond beat her—*she* picked up something and hit Raymond over the head with it all right—*Paul Kelly*. A guy with a reputation for violence, a compulsive temper, bad habits with his fists—"

I knew from the first day I couldn't hope to save Kelly from San Quentin. Nobody could. Maybe he had to learn to keep cool.

But I made up my mind the opening day of the trial he wasn't bigod going alone.

The Guilty Party was going along with him. It made me think of the way O. Henry did it in a short story set in the Court of Heaven.

"Case No. 99,852,743."
Up stepped a plain-clothes man—and by the arm he dragged —whom, do you think? Why, Liz!
"This girl murdered her fiance and committed suicide. She had no defense."
"Discharged," said the court officer. "Come here, Jonesy. How would you like to be on the missionary force in the South Sea Islands—hey? Now, you quit making these false arrests, or

you'll be transferred—see? The guilty party you've got to look for in this case is a red-haired, unshaven, untidy man, sitting by the window reading, in his stocking feet, while his children play in the streets."

Paul Kelly?

The doctor who, controlled by Mackaye, gave the false death certificate?

The woman who used them both?

Never in my courtroom experience have I been as sure who was the Guilty Party.

All three of them went to San Quentin to serve long terms.

Time lapse.

I had been speaking at a midmorning meeting of a woman's club. Afterwards I stood in the hall greeting old friends, strangers, people who liked what I wrote or didn't, and people who remembered my father. A middle-aged woman in a gray dress said, "I—could I have a word or two with you, please?" and then she stepped out of line. She's written a book, I thought frantically, or her life would make a great book if I'd write it.

She was waiting for me on the big side porch. As we faced each other she said, "I've always wanted to explain why I called you—"

I didn't recognize the voice, but the visceral reaction was instant. She said, "I am—it was me—that time about Ray Raymond—"

I had to put my hand on the railing to steady myself. Such a simple nondescript wouldn't-know-her-again woman. She said, "My husband didn't want me to get involved in anything. He said I might have been mistaken and it was none of my business and I'd have to testify if I called the police—but I—I heard him begging for mercy. I told my husband you don't beg for mercy if you have *pneumonia*—"

"Where were you?" I said.

"We lived next door." She was beginning to whisper again, I recognized the voice. "My kitchen windows and theirs—of course they were shouting—" She began to cry, the tears made paths in the wrong-shade powder she wore.

I waited while she got her handkerchief and pulled herself together.

Defiantly she said, *"The little girl*—I couldn't stand it that she let him do it in front of the little girl—"

"Where was the little girl?" I said.

"That's why I called you," she said, "she's not fit to have—the day of the funeral, I saw the little girl alone in the back yard crying. The colored maid had gone somewhere—and the little girl was crying all alone. All of a sudden I just couldn't stand it. She's a nice little girl—"

"Where was she when the—fight took place?" I said.

"Right there in the kitchen," she said, "in her high chair. It—Mrs. Raymond and her husband were yelling at each other and then Mrs. Raymond went to the phone and pretty soon Mr. Kelly drove up and smashed into the curb and ran in like—like a madman. I'd seen him in the house before when Mr. Raymond was away. For a few minutes it was terrible—like wild animals all of them not like *people!* I pulled back my curtain and I could see the little girl in her high chair watching them and crying and crying— that woman *let*—the child was seeing her *father* and the mother didn't do anything—"

She couldn't speak, and I said, "Why me?"

"I'd read your stories and I knew about your father," she said. "I thought if I called you—you'd do something and I wouldn't get mixed up in it—"

"I see—" I said.

"If she hadn't done it in front of the little girl—"

"I know," I said, "grownups are one thing, *children—*"

An old friend embraced me with a gurgle and when I turned back the woman was gone.

I still don't know who she was.

Or if I do I'm not going to tell anybody.

CHAPTER 17

My divorce from Ike St. Johns came while we were at the Whittier ranch. We had been married for fifteen years.

The Ray Raymond trial was one of the things that triggered it. Ike was furious because, as he put it, I'd rushed off to cover it at the mere snap of Campbell's fingers, though he had needed me to go to San Francisco with him on political business and I'd stayed home because I should have been finishing a serial for *Good Housekeeping*. To be sure, we were short of money. But then we always were. We had too much credit and not enough cash. This, as Dorothy Parker would have said, is the history of my life and was more unusual as part of the American Dream then than it is now.

Important scenes take place at odd moments. We had one between sets on the tennis court one day, thank God he could beat me at tennis. We were hot and sweaty and we went to sit on the canvas swing and he *started in* about the Raymond-Kelly-Mackaye case.

A little wildly, I daresay, I seem to remember feeling wild, I said, "Ike— can't you see at all? Now you're a big shot in politics and advertising but you used to be a newspaperman. All these other things we're doing are imitations. What we make movies *out of,* or I write serials *about*—don't you ever want to go back and do a *real* story?"

"You have to grow up sometime," Ike said. "If it's so much greater why don't they pay you as much?"

By that time I'd begun to have some of my newspaper work syndicated and Mr. Hearst and Howey gave me a percentage part of the time. Still, I was making a lot more money out of fiction especially if the picture rights sold. Ike's salary as a campaign manager was fatter and he and Danny Danker, a creative young advertising man, thought up the first endorsement of products by movie stars. Danny got the product and Ike got the stars. Wally Reid, star of racing movies, was photographed in a Stutz Bearcat. Laurel and Hardy endorsed the Omar cigarette. A certain face cream bore a To Her Majesty Gloria Swanson on its labels. A main trouble was that *I* thought Ike was smart about money and should handle all our business. I would have let anybody handle it as long as I didn't have to. It turned out he was a born loser there, too, poor lamb.

We didn't want to be millionaires, we just wanted to live like we were. That's not just a trite saying. It was true of most of us. We were *ignorant*.

Our front was opulent; we must be *rolling*. We just owed more, that was all.

Bill collectors howled on our doorstep.

Socially, we were received at Pickfair. We had our own group who rode together, played tennis on Sundays with buffet suppers afterwards. I gave some spectacular parties for writers, editors, and illustrators who came out from the East and wanted to meet movie stars. Billy had nightmares and said *Mama?* when he woke up, Elaine won cups at horse shows—Mama?

We think of death as the great separator. No no. It's *time*.

I can see my daughter Elaine every day. She is a woman now and my friend. I can talk to my son Dick, who is likewise my let's-keep-Ma-out-of-jail-if-we-can lawyer. My son Mac is a Christian gentleman who has walked with his principles through war, temptations, and some despairs intact in soul and body. If Bill hadn't crashed out of the skies coming back from a bombing mission, he'd bring my beloved great-grandchildren to see me, he'd be their grandfather, but either way I can't see him as he was when he woke up from his nightmares and hung onto me saying *Mama?*

Nor can I see Dicky when he was four years old coming in on top of the big waves at Malibu like a little Hawaiian. I have movies to prove that. Nor the day he came back wearing the white airplane silk scarf and his trousers tucked *in* his boots as only Jim Gavin's 82nd Airborne was allowed to do. I can't see Elaine the day she married Paul Gallico in my Cow Lane house, with Leland Hayward as best man, though he had offered to do it the other way round. Nor my small brother Bryson, when we searched wildly for him all morning and found him asleep in the bottom of the clothes chute.

I must explain here about my son Mac. He was one of Bill's "Oh Mama, look what I found" godsends. Bill couldn't bear an empty *bed,* much less an empty room. Mac was a motherless redhead Bill had known in grammar school and once brought him home because, he said, there wasn't anybody much at his house. His father was a remarkable man, a mining engineer, away a great deal. Later in Cow Lane, Bill said to me, "Mama, Mac wants to be a newspaperman so I told him to come on and you'd get him a job and he can stay with us." So he did, and became another son to me.

We lose them all. Not once. A hundred times. Day by day. As time changes them. And now and then we have to feel the nostalgia of what Aline Kilmer once wrote:

> I'm sorry you are wiser,
> I'm sorry you are taller;
> I liked you better foolish,
> And I liked you better smaller.

Sometimes I miss Bill so *much.* I know all is well with my child—I *know* this. I just *miss* him. Dick is perfectly safe and well in his big office and I miss *him,* when he was smaller—

I miss the Whittier ranch.

Sometimes I miss Ike St. Johns.

I am going way out of time sequence here. Not a flashback, a flash forward. Not into the past, into the future. That is my advantage as I write, I am above time and the river. They run both ways. Sometimes I can begin at *The End,* where at last it becomes clearer whether I was right or wrong.

The best way to tell about my first divorce is in a conversation that took place a good many years later. Ike St. Johns stayed in my life long after we parted. He was there for many events not yet part of this chronicle on my journey through what Dante calls Purgatory. Just the same to get the true story of that divorce of a career woman who couldn't drive three mules we must go *ahead* of it. See its results.

Mr. Hearst always said if it wasn't worth remembering it wasn't worth writing about. I once had finished an interview with the English Prime Minister before the shorthand report of it at a press conference came in and I was only five words wrong. My talk with Ike probably needed to be remembered for I have never been able to forget it.

By the time of this phone call all those years later, I was living in a house on Long Island we called Cow Lane.

The Cow Lane house.

A house everyone speaks of, has tried to reproduce or imitate. In terms of a *house* is a *home,* an unforgettable permanently memorable, beloved house.

At about 3 A.M. the bell rang. It often did. Sometimes for me to go to see what had happened to the *Hindenburg* or to say one of the boys had taken a girl home to Westbury and had a flat tire, or to tell me a plane was waiting to take me to Baton Rouge, where, as he had told me one day at Olney's Inn, somebody *would* shoot, somebody *had* shot Huey Long.

Ike's voice, it seemed to me, had changed little over the years.

I said, "It's three o'clock in the morning here. Isn't this an odd time to call?"

He said, "There are times when I miss you and they're usually odd times. There are times when I miss you so much I make an ass of myself. I can't schedule them. I just got to wondering if you ever miss me."

At three in the morning this is a difficult question to field. I thought— what the hell. This is a man I was married to for fifteen years. He held the ether cone over my nose when I lost my baby. In that fearsome business about the custody of my son Dicky, Ike was my most impressive witness though we'd been divorced a long time. He speaks well of me, they tell me.

I said, "Yes, Ike, I miss you. What I really miss is—the things that never happened. I miss what we ought to have made of our lives, you and I, the man and woman we might be today to each other—"

"Yes," Ike said.

I said, "Where are you?"

"In a Turkish bath," he said. I didn't pursue that. It was midnight out on the Coast.

"I wanted to tell you—" he said. "I know it didn't look like it a lot of the time, but I did love you and I guess it looks like I always will."

I said, "I was so *spoiled,* Ike. In so many ways I was *so* spoiled. I thought I knew it all and a lot of the things I knew were the wrong things. We were caught up in a lot of—of changes that weren't even ours. We were in a new business that was pretty wild. Marriage was changing, it wasn't woman's only business any more; it wasn't even a sacrament. It was becoming a business or a sex partnership. And naturally the divorce rate was skyrocketing and devil take the hindmost. We had no guidelines, no signals."

I said, "Ike, ours was one of the divorces that—ought to have been prevented. I know that now. If I'd known *then*—if I'd had any unselfishness—"

The IF deck?

"Hell," Ike said and laughed, "that can be a forty-two-volume set of the lives of everybody, can't it? You weren't twenty and I wasn't much over that. If we'd had the sense or judgment or character or *anything*—"

"If I'd made a little more effort—" I said. "If I'd put my—my uncompromising female will where it belonged— Oh, I don't know, Ike, whether we could but we should have tried harder. When I think how little patience I had—a drop of it and I could have held our home together. But that's me even now—then I didn't have any patience at all."

"All of it was my fault," Ike said seriously, quietly. "You want to know something? You never had any idea how jealous I was. I got green-eyed too when I couldn't make you jealous of me."

"I'm of an impatient nature," I said, "but not a jealous one."

"The way we lived—the place—there were a lot of attractive people around on the loose," Ike said, "I behaved like a fool. It's awfully late to be asking this question—I mean, did I have any right to be jealous? I've always wanted to know."

"You wouldn't believe me then when it meant something," I said. "You won't believe me now, will you?"

"You were a first-class liar," he said, "but I can't think why you'd lie to me now. I'd like to believe you."

What should I say?

Crossing my fingers, I said to myself, I was faithful to you *in my fashion*. No man, at least none with whom I'd been enough in love to break up my marriage. How could I tell him there were newspaper*men,* one-eyed like Howey or uncategorically unromantic as J. B. T. Campbell at the toot of whose pipe I would follow like a buff after a fire engine? Why should I try to explain what I didn't understand myself? Then in a wave of passionate uncertainty sweeping down on me through the years I tried to catch the beat of what he wanted to hear me say. What you have done to yourself can fester far worse than what others have done to you sometimes. Ike was such a nice guy, so loyal when the chips were down. Would he rather think I'd left him for another man than that he'd destroyed our marriage by the quarrels and naggings and a *phantom* colored green by his male jealousy? My imagination cooked up a couple of yarns—but I had a glimmer, faint then, that truth sometimes carries its own protection.

"I was faithful to you," I said. "There wasn't any other man."

All he said was, "I believe you," and then, "How are the kids?" and I said they were great, Elaine had a beau from *Yale,* and Billy wanted to be a major league first-baseman. "If you're coming East," I said, "let me know. I've got to go to Washington sometime soon and you could come and spend a week or so with them here in Cow Lane."

He said, "Look, I want them to know it was all my fault. I want them to know I was telling the truth that day in court, on the stand, under oath when I told the judge you were my kids' mother and they'd had the finest mother anybody ever had—"

"No," I said, "no. Please don't say that Ike. No."

"Yes," Ike said, "you love them so much more than I ever did, even Elaine. That was part of the trouble. I didn't want Billy, remember? I was jealous of the kids, too. I knew you'd always put them first. You used to tell me so. If somebody has to get off this raft, you said you'd shove *me.* I knew that. They ought to know it, too, because I'd have shoved *them."*

"Ike," I said, "this is costing you a fortune, oughtn't you to get some sleep?"

"I had to call you," he said, "I had to. I don't know why. You tell the kids what I said, will you? I was jealous of your work, too. You tell them it was all my fault. Promise me that. I want to tell you I love you and I always will."

I couldn't go back to sleep. I found I was shaking with pain. And guilt.

Pretty soon, light began to come in at the windows and show me my lovely room in Cow Lane. It was full of ghosts. I thought how wonderful it is that if we have faith the light will come every morning, every single time it will come. It didn't comfort me much. I could hear the birds beginning to make small, confident chirps and a sleepy little wind began to rattle the leaves in a song of contentment.

Oh no. *It wasn't all his fault.* Face that.

In that new light the truth seemed to me so trumpery, so paltry, so shameful. I felt so small I was beneath my own contempt. Not a big, swashbuckling hard-to-resist sin. No. A shabby picayune every-woman-for-herself indulgence. Heads-I-win-tails-you-lose—that's ignominious, that is. Women are *cheats*.

Look at *me,* everybody. No hands. No heart, either.

No other man? Of course not. Me myself and I, that was all. If *I* don't get what *I* want the sky will fall.

Lots of attractive men around, as Ike had said. If I'd told him the truth, I would have said, "Ike, my good and honorable friend, I divorced you because, after fifteen years, you bored me so that for the only time in my life I knew what boredom was. I despise people who are bored but I was. Never before never since. I divorced you, my for-better-or-worse, richer-or-poorer, till-death-do-us-part husband, the father of my children NOT because you were notoriously unfaithful to me with inferior people—I knew that was a gesture; promiscuous physical infidelity seemed to me sort of like not washing your feet. Horrid, but not important. Moreover, *face it,* I always blamed myself. I had never troubled to be a responsive bedfellow. I divorced you, Ike, because you nagged. Women are supposed to be the naggers, men are much worse. You nagged so much sometimes I said to myself, Let him jump in the swimming pool while it's empty if he's going to jump. Next time I won't call the doctor and the ambulance when he says he's taken bichloride of mercury. Then I won't have to listen to him. *Did you get a new globe for my shaving mirror? Did you tell Anna to have my bacon cooked crisper? Did you know what a fool you made of yourself at dinner talking so much? That dress you had on was indecent, way up to your knees. Elaine needs new shoes. Did you remember to deposit that check like I asked you?*

Hell, I work just as hard as you do *and* supervise the household, why don't you get a light for your shaving mirror yourself?

Looking back as I lay there wide awake after the phone call, I said to myself, For all your big talk and the fact you can handle servants, you were a careless housekeeper. You did rush off to meet Coroner Nance and forget to deposit that check. Sometimes maybe she who gets nagged is just as guilty as he who nags. Why didn't you try not to give him so many things to nag about? Why?

Serenity I had never known. When I was little, my mother saw to that. There had been tragedy in life with my father, but the drama and the tempo, the *action,* were there all the time. If pure excitement was the apple the snake was offering the modern woman, life had conditioned me to take the first bite.

Two ghosts, it hurt to look at.

The two who had married each other. They meant so well.

Everybody means well! It takes guts and stamina and—something more —to wrap it up. I didn't know even then what that something more was.

Oh Ike—I wish we could have made it. I wish we could go back and try again. Those two kids who married each other—I was bitterly aware of this after I hung up the phone and pictured Ike three thousand miles away at midnight in a Turkish bath poor lonesome bastard—they're *gone*. All those people, you and me, Ike, in that punk one-room apartment up on Fifth Street where you thought it was a big joke to drive me screaming out of bed telling me you had six toes on one foot—you and me, Ike, as we were, and the children and the cow pony named Red and our big dog Ali—*you* remember Ali, I got him when I made a picture in Canada with Strongheart—and some nights when you came home to Whittier late if you'd been drinking he wouldn't let you in my room. He was fond of you, you'd speak to him so coaxingly and he'd wag his tail until you started for my door, then he'd say *Grrrrrr* and you'd go forlornly upstairs to the guest room. I wonder if Ali knew it wasn't your being a little tight—no woman likes that in her bed to be sure—mostly, it was such a bore to hear for *hours* how you lost all that money on three nines and had I remembered to have a piece set in the sleeves of your new shirts? They were too short. I bored *so* easy. Who did I think I was, I wonder? Why couldn't I think about something else or recite Keats or play Mozart in my head?

It'd be easier, Mother Meyer said wearily one time, if he had a sense of humor. *Now Adela,* she mimicked him. But then she said tartly, "But you are lacking several senses yourself, aren't you?"

Patience chiefly. *Hurry up hurry up hurry up everything please.* Hurry because I say so. No *patience* at all.

In the end it wasn't even that, Ike. I didn't love you enough but I loved you some. I knew you were *kind* underneath. Way back down all those years I remembered how good you'd been to Papa *always*. I did remember that. And way back down those same years I knew, watching the light grow in my bed in Cow Lane, I knew exactly what made the final decision. You went to New York with Danny on advertising business. And it was so wonderful to be alone! *To do everything my way.* To read a book after I went to bed. To do what *I* wanted to do. Ride with the children in the morning and then go to work, if Howey or Ettelson or Campbell called I could take off *without a pang*. No pangs, *please*.

I could drive those two mules at a fine, high-stepping pace.

I'm sorry, Ike, I said to the phone I'd hung up. I'm sorry. And I was.

Even before I got the telegram.

The sun was up by then. I was having my coffee, the children had been in to kiss me before they went to school. I could hear Dicky starting an argument with his governess, Cracker Graham.

After I read the telegram I knew why Ike had called—and he knew, too, by then.

For the wire said that Ike had died at dawn of a heart attack.

I sent his son Bill out to the service in California by air. His first flight. When he got back he said, "Mama, I never saw so many men as were at my father's funeral. He made more friends than anybody, didn't he?"

When Bill was shot down and managed to give all but two of his bomber crew time to parachute out over England I had over thirty cables. They all said *Bill St. Johns was my best friend.*

He inherited that from his father.

CHAPTER 18

The newsboy stood with his papers under his arm outside the players' gate at Comisky Park in Chicago. The big black headline said:

WHITE SOX SOLD
WORLD SERIES

In the first paragraph it named men who had been idols in that town. The one that hurt most was Shoeless Joe Jackson. And when Jackson came through that gate in his street clothes the kid looked up at him, tears streaming down his dirty little face, and said, "Say it isn't so, Joe, say it isn't so."

That may be folklore. I don't think so, I don't think there was anyone around at that moment who could have *invented* it. If anybody did, I wish it had been me.

Sports have grown bigger and bigger, I'm glad to say—but we don't *love* as many people in them as we used to.

At the time I became a sports writer we really *cared*. We called the Yankee Stadium the House That Babe Built, and it took him quite a while to bring it forth from the ashes of the White-Sox-become-the-Black-Sox scandal. But, as Heywood Broun once wrote in the lead of a story about that stadium, *The Ruth is mighty and shall prevail*. He did. Now Mickey Mantle has taken it over and the fact that folks love him keeps its gates open.

Of the things I would like to live over again—

No woman could attend the Baseball Writers' dinner. Bill Slocum sneaked me into the Waldorf ballroom and parked me on the balcony where no one could see me among the shadows. I was to leave as soon as the formal speeches were over.

Mayor James J. Walker was the chief speaker. Whatever darkness has engulfed him, however the Little Flower has overshadowed him as New York's mayor-for-all-seasons, Jimmy Walker was the Favorite in his day, a speaker of such wit and persuasion as we have not heard since. Maybe just as well.

On his right sat Babe Ruth, and when he had the room in gales of laughter Walker turned and spoke to him directly. The lights hit them full, the

Babe's big red face upturned to the man-about-New-York elegance of the slim young mayor. An instant silence fell.

"Babe," Jimmy said clear and soft. "You are the most powerful man in this country. The boys who have got to grow up to be men tomorrow— you are their idol. They would a lot rather shake the hand that hit that last home run than that of the President. I know you're not only the great- est ball player alive—don't get sore—you also have a heart of gold. You're a modest fellow, Babe, you may not know how the youngsters look up to you and love you, and want to be like you. You're an example to them, Babe Ruth." There was a long pause. And Jimmy put his hand on the Babe's big shoulder, where the home-run muscles bulged beneath his din- ner coat, and said, "You've got to stop it, Babe. You see that. You've got to stop all this nonsense and be the man we want them to grow up like—Promise me—"

I saw the Babe point to that center-field fence that day in Chicago and hit the home run over it. I saw him this night too and there are others who remember it well. For the light showed Babe's big face as tear-streaked as the newsboy's and we heard him say, "All right Jimmy—I promise—"

The boys swore the Babe never did take another drink. I know myself he was never in another brawl.

That's the kind of man it's possible to keep on loving and remembering as I find we still do. More than any other name in America—you say *Babe Ruth* and they *remember.*

Other things I'd like to live over again—

A golf tournament at the Los Angeles Country Club, for charity, I recall. I'd gone because the world's top woman athlete, the fabulous Babe Didrikson, was going to play with the men. When I arrived it was to discover that she'd been partnered with George Zaharias, the wrestling champ, all of whose poundage and muscle were in revolt at the idea. A woman? He'd never seen Babe Didrikson, it wasn't personal, he wouldn't play with *any* female! I was standing beside him when he saw Miss Didrikson come across the turf, tall and beautifully muscled herself in a white skirt and sweater, her brown hair brushed back. He just stood there and stared and then in a very low voice he said, *"Why—that's my girl,"* and Romeo's "It is the east and Juliet is the sun" never sounded more romantic. I don't care if it was a wrestler and the queen of the muscle molls. They were married a week later.

The day at the Huntington Hotel in Pasadena when I saw May Sutton Bundy beat Helen Wills a set at tennis. May had been world's champion before the greatest-of-all-women-tennis-players Miss Wills was born!

Our All American All Heel team, on which we voted each year. No- body could make the team if anybody could think of one good thing to say about the candidate. Every year Herbert Bayard Swope turned up as quarterback, darned if I can remember exactly why.

There was, too, the Gorgeous Blonde. She attached herself when we went to see Red Grange play at Illinois. In diamonds and sables, she followed us all around the circuit. Turned out Pegler was the one she really wanted and a lot of good that did her.

The World Series,

The Indianapolis Road Race,

The Kentucky Derby,

The Army-Navy, the Yale-Harvard, the Stanford-California games,

The heavyweight championship fight,

Forest Hills and the tennis championship.

As yet, basketball ranked about like marbles. I never so much as *saw* a basketball game.

An odd synchronization, my divorce from Ike St. Johns and my assignment as a sports writer. Vina Del Mar had written a throbbingly true novel called *Ex-Wife,* showing the peculiar, unexplored wasteland where this modern woman wandered in her new freedom. Virginity no longer protected her as it had done before marriage in that day, but neither body nor soul was as yet conditioned to accept or receive Sex and the Ex-Wife.

Now that I was one, somewhere in all this I found myself caught in a change in everyday living and a pendulum of emotional ups and downs so that, literally, there were times when I couldn't keep anything on my *stomach.* Even gin-and-ginger-ale. There are times when what happens to you on awakening in the morning, the confused flow of your readjustment, the pain and embarrassment even of your own rejoicing and of forgetfulness—are more disturbing than world events or humanity's perils. It was a kind of death. You were a widow—and the gag then was *grass* or *sod.*

Ike wasn't coming home any more.

For fifteen years he had either been coming home or *not* coming home. I was relieved, I was safe, I was glad, *it had to be done.* I was out of orbit, lonely, disoriented, unsure of what I was doing at what time, guilty—and the woman who isn't, at least the first time, probably likes snakes.

On the other hand, I was only a little past thirty and on my own for the first time since my teens. Ike went to live with Howard Strickling on a hill above Sunset Boulevard (now the Strip) and I stayed on at the Whittier ranch.

It was a time before I discovered I hadn't got rid of *the third mule.*

Once during the Second World War a story about evacuated children whose parents had been killed in the bombings had a line spoken by a small boy to his new guardians. He said, *Now I'm nobody's nothing.* This kills me. *I was my mommy's baby and my daddy's pal, now I'm nobody's nothing.*

Something violent and threatening welled inside me after my divorce. My children had no father. I must never let them *miss* having a father. I must never never let them even be *half* of *I'm nobody's nothing*—I'm not my daddy's little girl now—it had no thought basis but it twisted my guts at night.

Once or twice they said things—Elaine especially.

Then I saw with conviction that I hadn't got rid of that third mule, I'd just changed its name. Now the third mule's name was I-have-to-be-*father*-to-them, too.

Just the same, I liked being what I called free. The *St. Johns* was all mine now. There was no *Mr.* St. Johns any more, but I was *Mrs.* St. Johns just the same. It's so long ago—yet I still feel it.

Into this vacuum, at the crucial moment, I got back to my own work.

I can forgive some of the weird things other women do in that loneliness and forced growth for I know I was never put to that test. Joy rushed in and I forgot the perils and difficulties, swaggering around press boxes and getting the first press card ever given a woman to cover the Derby in Louisville. Colonel Matt Winn gave it to me himself.

Mark Kelly was sports editor, reporter, and columnist for the Los Angeles *Examiner,* then the paper right under Mr. Hearst's nose. Harry Morgan said the other day that seldom in all his years on the night city desk did he fail to hear *Mr. Morgan? This is Mr. Hearst* coming from wherever Mr. Hearst was, and then this word had to be distributed to the other city editors in Seattle, both Portlands, Boston Atlanta Denver Detroit and so forth.

On an afternoon Mark Kelly was behind his desk getting out his daily sports column when the well-known voice said, *Mr. Kelly?*

Mr. Kelly.

In his column, Damon Runyon called Mark Kelly the Red Rooster of the Arroyo. The Arroyo being that gulch out near Pasadena where the Rose Bowl is located. Mark was 5'8", weighed 135 pounds, had a crest of red hair, you felt he ought to be entered in a cockfight. Instead I once heard him offer to lick Max Baer, to Max's face.

As to the Arroyo, I best remember the Red Rooster *of* it *in* it on the New Year's Day of the Stanford-Columbia game. A sufficient California dew fell on that New Year's Eve so that the players' benches were floating in the Bowl like cakes of Ivory soap. Never had happened before but about 8:00 P.M. we were notified that there would be no game on the morrow. For many years sports writers assigned to cover this then *only*

Bowl Classic had not been able to celebrate in the traditional New Year's Eve fashion so they would be in shape to do what was always a very tough story. Peering out of the windows of our hotel, we saw torrents sweeping down the Arroyo and with a whoop decided to make up for lost Eves. When the drinking started, I always figured they'd appreciate my absence more than my presence. I saw the Red Rooster take off with Gallico, Corum, Red Smith, and Salsinger from Detroit and made what I hoped was a graceful exit to bed.

At 7 A.M. my phone notified me that with the help of all the fire engines from San Diego to Bakersfield they had pumped most of the dew off the playing field. The game would start on time. Three hours later this was confirmed.

My first thought was *Kelly*. To pump him off the floor might be tougher. He had to do the running story, I would write the feature. With Gallico's help I got him on his feet, but into his clothes he would not go; under the impression that we were the British, he swept by us, snatched Gallico's handsome black fur-lined cape, flung it over his pajamas. Gallico was a good six foot two, consequently Kelly vanished so that only his red crest stuck out at one end and his plaid bedroom slippers at the other as he stalked to the elevator. With him, we detoured through the lobby and out, and the fresh air and sunshine staggered him, but he recovered and we raced down the lovely wistaria pergola to the sidewalk.

At the exact moment, one after another, two long, sleek black limousines drew up at the curb right in front of us. The door of one opened, out got ex-President Hoover. The door of the other swung wide, young men covered with gold braid leaped to attention, between them emerged the many-splendored figure of Rear Admiral William Sowden Sims, United States Navy, returning from leading the Rose Parade.

With a jaundiced eye, Kelly observed them start up the pergola, then flinging Gallico's cape over his shoulder he strode forward, flicked the aides aside, got into the admiral's car, and shouted, "Avant, my hearties" and when the uniformed driver looked not avant but aghast he said, "The Rose Bowl, you corn-fed popinjay." "Have to explain everything," Kelly said to me through the window. Having done so, he went to sleep, his head resting on the best upholstery.

Don't walk—*run* to the nearest exit. There are times when not even your dearest friend has a right to expect you to stay. Then to my horror I saw the official car sweep away with Kelly in it, the aides were leaning limp against palm trees, and when I returned, on tiptoe, they said, "What was it? The Wizard of Oz?" Just then Gallico appeared to join me. In lieu of his beloved cape, he was wearing a bright yellow oilskin sou'wester with hat to match, like those on the Uneeda biscuit box, he said he had found them on a chair in the hall. Now while I was fully clothed and I liked to think in my right mind, by this time I must have looked like Thurber's grandfather. The way they were looking at us, I hoped they thought we were refugees from a Rose Parade float, and if Kelly has a story to cover so have I, so I shoved Gallico, none too steady on *his* pins if the truth must be told, into *Hoover's* car as it stood by, got into it after him and said in elegant tones, "Rose Bowl and please hurry," and away we went and I can prove it.

When I got into the Rose Bowl press box Kelly said coldly, "That's the trouble with women, they're always late."

Mr. Kelly, this is Mr. Hearst.

Kelly wasted no time on the old Oh-sure-and-I'm-the-Emperor-of-Ethiopia routine. He said one word and hung up. He ignored the phone's repeated jangle until he saw the greatest phone operator we ever had making gestures to pick up the phone, so Kelly did and heard, "Mr. Kelly, I understand your qualms. Meantime, consider my predicament. I have a suggestion I would like to discuss with the sports editor of my Los Angeles paper—"

Kelly said, "Go ahead—I wanted to be sure."

"Thank you," said the voice from San Simeon. "Do you think it might be a good idea to have Mrs. St. Johns write some sports stories for you?"

"You mean how a wife or mother feels before the Big Game?" Kelly said.

"No," Mr. Hearst said, "I meant features at the events themselves."

"Does she know more about sports than the average spectator?" Kelly said.

"I hope not," Mr. Hearst said. "Mr. Kelly, not only more women, more *people* are becoming interested in sports. As due to better working conditions we have more leisure, we will have more time and money. Sports will give us places to spend both. Larger ball parks will be built. Bigger and better stadiums. A vast increase in public golf links, public tennis courts, which I hope we will continue to promote. New fans—women, young people—have no expert knowledge of sports. Perhaps we should show them what Mrs. St. Johns sees as well as what you see."

"I see twice as much as the guy in the stands," Kelly said, "I can explain to him what really happened."

"I have just reminded my papers that you are getting out the best sports section in the country," Mr. Hearst said. "I like the imaginative way you use your photographers. It has vigor and variety. However, we may be in danger of expertizing our new fans beyond their present understanding. Your explanations may be beyond their comprehensions. This would possibly cool their interest. My mother was a schoolteacher and a woman of more than average intelligence, yet when I took her to see a football game at Berkeley she found it difficult to follow that when California had *fifteen* yards to go instead of three they had *lost* ground, not gained it. Brilliant sports editing should probably not exclusively describe off tackle plays to readers who do not know a team must make ten yards in four downs."

"You want me to get out a sports page for people who don't know you have to make ten yards in four downs?" Kelly said.

"Could we combine the elements of expert knowledge and colorful description at the level of all our readers?" Mr. Hearst said. "If you like this idea—"

Kelly said, "I don't. There has never been a woman in the press box at any sports event and I'd just as soon there never was. Editorially it may be a great idea, it won't work."

"I am sure you will do your best to see that it does," Mr. Hearst said.

"I'm not going to wet-nurse her," Kelly said.

From time to time, Mr. Hearst was capable of bursts of Jovian laughter. After it was over, he said, "Will you discuss this with Mrs. St. Johns? As your own idea or mine, just as you think best."

I sat ringside at the wrestling matches in the Olympic Auditorium on Main Street, as inconspicuous as I could get under a soft felt hat pulled down over my hair.

Ringside.

Magic Word. Tickets bearing that legend were prizes we seldom shared.

At that time wrestling was a sellout, the Olympic was mobbed though not with what you'd call a high-class sports crowd. This was an integration of Hollywood, Beverly Hills, Watts, Pacoima, and Long Beach. Wrestling to me had been connected with Greece, with sculpture. This place was dark, hot, airless, smoke-filled, violent, and dirty. Nor was it, as Kelly sitting beside me knew and knew that I knew, the assignment on which to start a woman writing sports. Women were to go mad over wrestling later on TV—I was the only woman present at the Olympic that night. I had some trouble keeping my hands steady as I rolled a cigarette, while in the ring, which I was so ringside *of* that I could see the whites of their eyes, two behemoths groaned, splattered, snorted, grimaced and committed mayhem and dismemberment. One of them was a former Notre Dame tackle. If I hadn't known it was impossible I'd have thought in the midst of this blood sweat and pseudo-savagery Joe was rolling closer and closer. A glance at Kelly got me a cloying smile. It should have warned me, but I was as unprepared as a day-old chick when in a flash of frozen horror I saw him launched at me like a swelling rocket and then I got 280 hot sticky pounds of him in my lap. Yes I did—*yes I did*. I was smashed like a stepped-on bug. I screamed. *Yes,* I screamed like a fire siren. Then I blacked out. When I came to, Kelly was looking at me with the smug satisfaction of a man whose quarter just hit the jackpot in a slot machine.

So what do you do? If I chickened out now he'd tell Mr. Hearst no woman could cover sports. Keep my cool? I did that all right, because I was an iceberg and only the tip of me was above consciousness and all it had to say was, *Next time bring a hatpin next time bring a hatpin—*

In the car, I said, "Find an Irishman who is a louse and he is more louse than anybody."

Kelly said, "You want to go to the Brown Derby and eat?"

I said, "No I do not. You might have busted me in half with that big clown."

"I do not have anything to do with how these guys wrestle," he said smugly.

"You are a liar," I said.

Then he grinned at me. This I hadn't seen before, it was wonderful. He said, "What'd you want me to do, apologize?"

So we went to the Brown Derby.

Bill Mizner, the country's most famous wit, sat in his sacred corner in the Brown Derby, which he had founded so he'd never lack someplace to sit. I must have still been green for he said to Kelly, "What have you done to the young woman?" and Kelly said, "I took her to the wrestling matches, she wants to be a sports writer." I said, "I never said I wanted to be a sports writer, *you asked me—*" and Mizner said, "Wrestling is not a sport, it is an inferior brand of Shakespearean comedy. If you had any parts as a sports writer you would close up that fraudulent fandango." "Why don't you write me a piece about it and maybe I will?" Kelly said.

I can't find a copy of that piece of Mizner's. It was a minor classic of invective and one of the things that got the mob on Kelly. Their accusations were silly. Everybody knew Kelly was too mean to take money. He was never beholden to anybody.

His was the toughest opposition to a woman in the newspaper profession that I ever had.

Walking across the campus of the University of Southern California not long ago, I met its white-haired president, Dr. Rufus Von Kleinsmid, with other academic brass, and he stopped to say, "I hope you always get your tickets? You see, gentlemen, it is to Mrs. St. Johns that we owe the first intersectional football game, U.S.C. versus Notre Dame," to which

Mrs. St. Johns replied with *real* embarrassment, "Oh no—please—I just went along for the ride."

However, since this was what finally convinced Mark Kelly that I belonged in the same world, it had a big effect on my life.

And the manner of it was thus:

In a bar where the *Examiner* crowd sometimes forgathered, Kelly one day met up with an *I'm-a-Notre-Dame-Man* who had never been nearer Notre Dame than San Luis Obispo. Before pro football gave every fan a team of his own, a large percentage of those who'd never been to college rooted for the Fighting Irish (Savoldi, Stuldreyer, Carrideo, Malenheivich, and Sasparilla). This particular self-nominated alumnus recognized Kelly, who naturally wrote more about U.S.C. for the sports section of a paper published in Los Angeles than any other team, but it was hardly fair to shout at Fighting Irish Kelly, "You and your Trojans couldn't walk on the same field with Notre Dame—Notre Dame'd lick S.C. 777 to 0—" Kelly said, "Let's be realistic, U.S.C. would win by two touchdowns—" and Those were the last civil words they exchanged. It ended with a bet. If the two teams ever met each of these enthusiasts said *his* team would win by two touchdowns. BUT as Kelly walked out the N.D. enthusiast shouted, "You can open your big mouth—you can afford to—you know them Trojans'll never get in the same *county* with Rockne."

The only intersection game in the United States was the Rose Bowl. But now the Red Rooster of the Arroyo began to brood. He was sitting on that final insult by the Notre Dame fanatic. One day it hatched.

"Why not?" he said.

We were coming home from an early baseball game. "Why not what?" I said.

"Notre Dame versus U.S.C.," he said.

Startled, I said, "You mean play each other?"

"We don't travel by covered wagon any more," Kelly said airily.

Like most big ideas, it looked too simple. Kelly said, "I will talk to Von Kleinsmid tomorrow."

Here I contributed my two cents worth. "He'll leak it to the other papers," I said. "Go to South Bend and get Notre Dame. Break the story from there, we both know Von Kleinsmid will go along with anything that means a buck to U.S.C."

A ripple like dawn light on Killarney shone on Kelly's countenance. Too late, I recalled Kelly's record on trips. Nor was he a favorite son of Van Ettisch, the city editor, nor Fred Eldridge, the managing editor whose toupee always skidded during a big breaking story, which entranced Kelly. So I said, "I have friends in South Bend, a family my father defended. I could visit them. Why don't I come along?" Kelly said, "I told Mr. Hearst

I wouldn't wet-nurse you, but there was no agreement vice versa." So I went.

I don't say Kelly was awed by Father Coughlin, president of Notre Dame. Kelly is recorded in sports history as the man who broke the Black Sox scandal after a gambler named Abe Attell, in bitter remorse, told Kelly all about it. Kelly was not an easy man to awe or scare. I will say Notre Dame took him right back to being an altar boy again and his behavior was exemplary. Two days later under his by-line Mark Kelly broke the big exclusive of Notre Dame's approach to U.S.C. for an intersectional game to be played at the end of the regular season. The first suggested date was December 4 of the coming year and that was when we played it.

Controversy, Mr. Hearst repeated, is the lifeblood of circulation.

With the story I wrote about *that* Notre Dame game I stirred it from all points of the compass. As Kelly remarked as he handed it to a copy boy, "Everybody in town'll be mad at you for this one. Nice going." The first word of praise I'd ever had from him.

For several reasons I'm interested in this column. One, it was written at top speed, parts scribbled as the game was played in the Los Angeles Coliseum before the biggest crowd ever to see a football game up to that time, the rest as soon as we got back to the city room to make a deadline. Also, there is a definite forecast of professional football.

On the front page of the sports section:

By Adela Rogers St. Johns

The old old story. Brains over brawn. The natural order of things wasn't halted out in the Coliseum yesterday afternoon. A business-like Notre Dame team who evidently believed in union hours and didn't intend to work overtime, coolly, calmly and without undue effort beat the University of Southern California by four earned touchdowns. They managed the performance with miraculous efficiency, even allowing U S C to do most of the forward passing for them. It only required half as much effort to intercept U S C passes as to throw their own. And counted the same number of points.

Tested, Troy fell.

Notre Dame proved once more that a team is never a champion until it has defeated a champion.

I am a football fan. I don't mind travelling miles, battling crowds, going without sleep. As a spectator I haven't missed an important western game in years. But that game this afternoon struck a prophetic chill to my soul. It was *so good*—as football it was so great—we are going to demand more of the same and where will we get it in colleges?

Yet it lacked the color, the enthusiasm, the spirit of college football as I have never seen the game lack it. There was better football than anybody ever played before, but the glow and heartbreaking thrill were gone. There was no *heart* out there today and this will have to be replaced and developed again somehow, or football will never hold its followers. Can this be done?

There was to be a time when pro football began that it seemed sparkless and colorless and without the old college try. Eventually they had to develop it. No other football team except Notre Dame ever assembled such delirious followers as the New York Giants, no college fans were ever wilder or noisier than the Dallas Cowboys. My friend Jimmy Brown once told me that to play on the gridiron at Green Bay was like it must have been on the floor of the Colosseum in Rome when the spectators could turn *thumbs down*. Who should know if this greatest football player of his era didn't?

If I were casting Notre Dame's quarterback, the great Carrideo, I'd let him play the bank president. On the football field he has the manner you've encountered when you sat across a mahogany desk to borrow money. Courteous, kind, errorless, exact and ruthless.

I see now that he was the original of a unique breed—the pro quarterback—Johnny Unitas, Bart Starr, Y. A. Tittle, Frankie Layne, Joe Namath, La Monica, Meredith, and Brodie.

I have never seen an athlete like him. He never wasted so much as an *inch,* much less a yard. He never wasted a gesture. He walked with grace, intention, precision. His was the spirit of an undefeated and undefeatable team.
You can't beat perfection.
U S C looked a champion in the eye. They played 60 minutes of football afterwards, but it was all over in the first 3 plays and everybody in the stands knew it.

I can see now why Kelly said everybody would be mad at me and they were.
This—is controversy.

Sports are an outward manifestation of all things inward in man.
Dink Templeton, the supreme track coach, was a great leader, philosopher, and Olympic hero. When NC 4 A records were falling like bowling pins before his Stanford teams, cheers called him the Wizard, but Dink once said, "No no. I can make a man run as fast as he can. No faster! But —I *can* make him run as fast or jump as high or as far as he *can.*"
Charlie Paddock, for years the World's Fastest Human when at last he ran the hundred in ten flat, I swear to you he did it with his heart

and his guts. And his poor, spindle-legged (he'd had polio as a child) pot-bellied body had to come along with him. Ever see a good picture of Babe Ruth? Same holds true.

Babe Didrikson Zaharias—out of bed after a cancer operation to win the woman's golf titles—all of them.

Carl Hubbell—the Meal Ticket—after he struck out the three leading hitters in the American League one after the other—Ruth, Gehrig, and Foxx—saying, "You just have to be a little more careful." And Sandy Koufax, "Your bases on balls in the late innings—they'll beat you every time. It's your own mistakes that beat you."

Ray Barbuti—I was sent to interview him when he came back from winning in the Olympics at Amsterdam. Me: "I have always been told the 440 is the hardest of all track races—it's a *long* sprint, really. How did you do it?" Barbuti: "Oh—I just run the first 400 yards as fast as I can—and then I sprint."

Bill Tilden, the greatest tennis player who ever lived—he was teaching my son Dick among a lot of other boys—and we all went together to Griffith Park the day Dick won the Metropolitan Boys' Championships. In the car going back to Malibu, Tilden never spoke—and finally Dicky said, "Hey Bill—I *won,* didn't I? What more do you want?" And Tilden said with cold fury, "You played *not to lose.* I saw you. Don't you ever dare as a Tilden pupil to do that again. You will never get to the big time playing not to lose—you must always *play to win.*" When Dick's big brother Bill was killed, Dick was to play the day after we got the news in a tournament at the L.A. Tennis Club—and Tilden said, "Of course he will play!" As Dick went on the court, white and shaky, the world's champion said, "You had better *win.* Your brother wouldn't like it if you tried to make an alibi of him." Dick won. There are no alibis in sports!

Eddie Arcaro, whom I once saw the tallest man in the room where everybody else was over six feet—*true*—telling me that Willie Shoemaker was the greatest jockey who ever lived because he had such *patience.* Patience? It seemed a peculiar attribute to say of a great jockey when the time for a mile and a quarter at Churchill Downs is around 2.02. But Eddie shook his head and said, "Time's relative. You got to be more patient in two minutes than two days. Willie's so patient nobody has ever been able to make him make his move until he's ready, and I've seen the best of them try."

Championship heavyweight fights distressed me. *I don't see why you go,* Gallico said to me. *You keep your eyes shut the whole time.* Once, though I *warned* him, Gallico made me eat *dinner* on the way to the stadium to cover the Louis-Baer fight. When Louis knocked Baer to his knees right in front of me and the blood spurted, I lost it in Gallico's typewriter. In a gasp I said, *I told you,* and Gallico said, *Who would be-*

lieve a thing like that? Also, though the *word* image wasn't with us yet, the thing itself was. I didn't think it was a good image for a woman sports writer to cover heavyweight fights, even when there were great fighters who knew the art of self-defense and the rounds were breathless and sometimes as beautiful as ballet dancing.

Yet words spoken to me by Jack Dempsey—*the Champ*—are part of my spiritual philosophy along with Lao-tse and Plato and St. Thomas Aquinas.

"You've known them in all fields," I said. "What is your estimation of the factors that have always been present in all champions?"

"In any field," he said, "you have to be able to do it *then*—at Madison Square Garden Tuesday night at 10:20 P.M. OR in Yankee Stadium at 2:30 the opening day of the World Series. Or that last putt on the eighteenth for the Open on Saturday.

"And of course you have to be able to go on when you can't."

Run 400 yards as fast as you can—and then sprint.

I have found it applies almost everywhere.

There is a national language.

Two strikes.

Big League.

Photo finish.

Hole in one.

The Olympic Games. Long before the United Nations they gave us an international meeting and language—and some hope.

In the press box at the Coliseum the year we had the Games in America, I sat between Damon Runyon and Westbrook Pegler and Damon leaned across me and said, "Peg, this is going to be tough for you," and Peg, bristling as usual, said, "Why do you say that?" and Damon said, "What are you going to write about? The whole thing's on the level and even the gatekeepers are polite."

As the music swelled the opening day and the voices lifted *The Star-Spangled Banner* high in many languages, as the teams marched round the track, the finest youth the world had to offer, as the Olympic torch flamed once more, Damon said quietly, "More than that, much more."

Nearly three thousand years is a lot for anything to endure. The Games were held first in 776 B.C. and though from time to time the Romans or the Turks or the Germans have interrupted them, they *survive*. Until now? In those first Games on the plain of Olympia as part of the Festivals, the youth of all the Grecian states could take part in *peace,* and beyond their skills on running and wrestling and hurling the discus, they had to have civic and personal integrity.

As the tall young man from the United States mounted the steps to take the Olympic oath, Damon said, "They have beaten their swords into poles to vault with and their spears into javelins. We ought to tell people about this. The name of these games is hope, isn't it?"

And to us both it seemed as though we swung out of the present into other layers of time.

When I go back to my sports tapestry, I can see why tapestries cost millions. I wonder if I would ever have sold the tapestries of the Olympic Games or Mark Kelly's funeral even when we needed money most. I mean, never again to be able to look at that day in the Coliseum when we lit the Olympic torch, or to see Dempsey again amid the conglomeration at Mark Kelly's funeral at St. Timothy's?

What would I buy with the money?

Only Runyon, who was there, could describe that requiem Mass for Kelly at St. Timothy's.

Next door to 20th Century-Fox on Pico Boulevard, the guys and dolls (not many dolls at Kelly's funeral, he was a man's man), the gamblers and gimps, the referees and hustlers, the crooks and card sharps, the champs and preliminary boys, the baseball magnates and managers and umpires and bat boys and Joe DiMaggio and Lefty O'Doul and the Babe, who flew out, Jack Dempsey and Joe Benjamin and Maxie Baer in tears, college presidents Rufus Von Kleinsmid and Ray Lyman Wilbur of Stanford, Dink Templeton, and Slip Madigan of St. Mary's, Pop Warner and Howard Jones and Bill Mizner and Granny Rice, gangsters and hoods and medicine men and headwaiters, the fall guys and the call girls—and newspapermen from New York, Chicago, Milwaukee, and San Francisco, editors of rival papers, printers and pressmen, Darryl Zanuck and Louis B. Mayer, Clark Gable and Gary Cooper, John Wayne, who, when he was known as *Duke* and played for U.S.C., Kelly had designated as the lousiest tackle he ever saw on a football field, Eric Pedley, a ten-goal polo player, Eddie Arcaro, Doc Strub, who owned Santa Anita Race Track, Bing Crosby, Bill Tilden, Ben Hogan—

And there I heard the most practical declaration of immortality that has come my way. Dempsey was sitting next to me and he leaned to whisper in my ear, "Kelly is not in that box up there. I don't know *where* he is, but I can tell you now, nobody ever got Kelly in that box."

You have to miss a guy like Kelly forever.

I asked Dempsey the other day and he said yes.

CHAPTER 19

I got married again.

A woman who has just gone bankrupt in her real business, marriage and children and home, may not really be in the best condition to start over, but in shock and panic she almost invariably does.

I ask myself to believe when I remember things. Now I have to ask myself to believe that I have forgotten the name of my second husband. Most of the time.

Not *unkindly*. I saved his life later on.

It seems incredible, doesn't it? I can remember the name of Gloria Swanson's second husband, Herb Sonborn, the pick of the bunch. This forgetting can be a phenomenon of maladjustment, rejection, a sign of age, and of course, as one grows older, there is so much more known and done *to* remember it gets crowded. But—Sister Mary Regis was the name of our second-in-command at Notre Dame in San Jose. Ring Lardner's beautiful wife's name was Ellis. The teacher who tried to tutor me in math for the entrance exams at Bryn Mawr—she kept saying you *can too* do algebra, read what it *says,* four walls, how many rolls of paper, I so did my best I felt sure it couldn't be right, when she picked it up her hand began to quiver and she said, You've papered the room solid—*her* name was Miss Ratliff.

Somewhere I have read that to start an autobiography, which I suppose in a haphazard way this is, the writer should have accomplished something of importance. My accomplishment worthy of recording has been to see, know, interview, hear, and observe people whose very names made *news*. Who did unusual, historic, exciting things. Sometimes to live through momentous, even historic events as an eye-and-ear witness by profession. To relive this, memory must be my chief asset.

Yet here I note an exception.

Elbert Hubbard, author of *A Message to Garcia,* whose common sense philosophy in his magazine *The Philistine* was nationally popular until he went down on the *Lusitania,* says, *A retentive memory is a good thing, but the ability to forget is the true token of greatness.*

I'd like to make this one small claim. For I have forgotten my second husband. Even—most of the time—his name.

As I look back on myself sitting in my redwood, book-lined library with my eighteen-room Whittier mansion and my new second husband on the tennis court, the solemn hush that fell on me had to do not only with the fact that I'd talked myself onto a platform called Modern Woman Is a Failure, at which no one else had so much as hinted. Likewise it had to do with the fact that the mortgage was bigger than the swimming pool, the walnuts grew more slowly than the interest on it, the payments ran much much much faster than my horses, the amusing little deficit they left me now looked as wide as the Grand Canyon.

Ike St. Johns hadn't always paid the bills, but he had a genius for handling creditors. Moreover Ike hadn't minded—since he *was*—but my second husband objected with violence, sometimes public, to being *Mr.* St. Johns.

Along with almost everything else in the United States just then, my second marriage was on a falling market.

Where the words came from by which I had declared myself on the subject of Modern Woman I still did not know. The echoes of my own voice, as of the debate in the Ambassador Theater, now kept me strange company.

Stop   Look   Listen, I had said.

Perhaps I'd better.

Danger Ahead. Road Under Construction.

Woman's road to freedom, I must have meant. *From* what and to *do* what?

> The way women are handling the gift of freedom at this minute has to lead directly to the destruction of a sane and normal civilization. We'd better get out of this sink of liberty-become-license, and get back on the road.

Look homeward, angel. Can you go home again?

Thomas Wolfe, who'd said that first, would say later, You Can't Go Home Again. So would lots of others. But in me some intuitive welling up of emotion had shouted itself in words totally unfamiliar and not my own. All invention must start with intuition and that is in the stomach. But those with the best stomachs cannot always assemble and express their thoughts nor make the invention work. Now I must stop and think this through and see whether it was a warning or a road map or a revelation.

I had started trying to figure out Whence I came and I'd had a fair look at that. I knew somewhat Whither I wanted to go. Papa's *key* question, it came to me, could be Where am I now and what am I going to do about it?

What kept dinging back to me was what I'd said about *husbands*. *The man is the head of the house.*

I had said that.

Ha! Do you, Adela Nora, refuse to take the marriage relationship seriously—

As I'd accused those other women—those modern women—of doing.

I had to repeat to myself that I had let my second husband push into my life for only one reason. Dicky upstairs in his nursery could be neither a virgin *nor* an illegitimate birth. Yet we went around saying women were now independent of men. I'd never given a husband an even break, that was for sure.

Ike, to some degree, had consented to be the burro of my three mules. *Such a nice guy.* This new one wasn't. He was a star athlete. Of necessity he was also a competitor, a winner. He certainly is trying to make you take him as seriously as he takes himself, I said to myself.

> Not only is the modern woman a failure, she must accept ninety per cent of the blame for that failure.

Ninety per cent?

Into my muddled thinking came the word evolution. Totally without formal education as I was, way back I'd read some Darwin with my father and very recently a biology teacher named Scopes had been dismissed for teaching evolution. In the celebrated trial following, William Jennings Bryan had represented the prosecution and Clarence Darrow was for the defense, on the grounds that the man had a right to teach what was now part of the advancing scientific age. As usual, Darrow lost. I had to admit that this lost case of his was an early educational banner, it had stirred public thinking. As I recalled this, I could also hear Papa outlining for me a little of what he called the progress of humanity—how when they came out of the caves the tribes had to stay together to survive. How all Thomas Jefferson's glorious philosophy of government was founded on the Agrarian Age, the Family on the Farm was the center of life, work, education, politics, and religion. He shuddered as the Industrial Revolution wiped this out. He had said, I remembered, that when the Family was destroyed in any civilization history showed that wars and famines and hell in general broke loose. We would, he said, need great leaders to direct our course in a democracy if we were to live through it.

Could this Modern Woman business, godforbid, have anything to do with evolution? Could circumstances be causes that forced people *out of orbit* into a desperate detour that could end in disaster? *It wasn't working.* I'd won the debate with that and I believed it. Guilt, inherited in my genes from 77,000,000 ancestresses who'd put families first and accepted man as head of the house, sent my own fever of apprehension up to 106 degrees.

For as I sat there mulling over what I'd said, quite as new to me as it seemed to be to my audience, all around me I could hear the sounds of my own crisis.

A home is made up of smells; in Whittier I could smell wood smoke and heliotrope and Cecil Bruner roses climbing around the tennis court and, faintly, the stables. Of touch; I would always love the feel of warm bricks, of the smooth redwood railing of the stairs, of crystal glasses and copper bowls. Of sight; through my library window the glint of the shallow stream, the peaceful pattern of garden beds and the orderly rows of the orchards. Sound; the sounds of everybody involved in this turning point to which my *talking* and thinking had brought me. Elaine practicing her piano, rebellion in every scale. The pat-pat-pat of my second husband's tennis balls had ceased. So had the shouts of the kids in the swimming pool. I knew his tolerant superiority as he stopped on his way to the house had silenced them. Aunt Janet, the nurse, walked by on the terrace with my new son Dicky, who was making noises like a small, friendly frog. I leaned over and hit the most-used key on my typewriter—X X X X X X—adding the clicky-click to round out my predicament.

To say peace peace where there is no peace simply leaves you unprepared for either peace or war.

Be practical. This is not working either. Why?

Three mules, or two and a burro. That's what you had. *Now* what have you got tangled up in and yanking your arms out of their sockets? Now you have to be a father to your children, having divorced their father. Now you have to protect them from a stepfather—meaning a step removed—a little step or a giant step—you got him for them instead of their *own* father, who at least was that, now you have to impress them all the time that *you* are on *their* side, and that makes a division with your husband, their stepfather. Maybe not in all cases, certainly in this one.

Then there is the Bank. Ike St. Johns had so many friends at the Bank! Small things, no doubt, but who now was going to keep the books and make out the checks and confer with the Walnut Growers Association? My third mule is *writing,* I am no businesswoman. And write I must as the chief earner of this concern. Charles Dickens managed in such an atmosphere of confusion, children, debt, and a wife who was a disaster, but you are not Charles Dickens by light years and moreover he died at fifty-eight and that seems too soon.

Bill's and Elaine's *step*father is also the *father* of my son Dick.

If I have to walk on eggs now to keep from hurting his feelings, what will it be when Dicky grows up enough to know?

Probably I shouldn't have tried living in Whittier with my second husband, Ike St. Johns hadn't been the best husband in the world, I was now discovering too late that he hadn't been the worst, either, maybe once men are husbands there isn't all that difference. Ike and I had found the Whittier walnut ranch together, built the house together, selected the furniture together, moved into it with high expectations now hanging in tatters. When we parted we'd put the place in trust for our children, with only a life tenancy for me. This could not go unnoticed by a new occupant, Husband Number Two. If it had, my daughter once or twice reminded him of it. Children do. You told them they came first, I said to myself. They believed you.

I should have given her at least a token rod on her small behind or forbidden her to ride for a week. I remembered what Marion Davies had said to Mr. Hearst about his son Jack. "People who are divorced are too soft with their kids. They all have a guilty conscience." I was walking on eggs with my children, too. *Children of broken homes,* rich or poor. They manipulate and maneuver and parents have a guilty conscience instead of divine authority.

And, as my daughter said, you *are*—you and your second husband—living in our house.

Very well. The move is plain. No use *crying* about it.

Maybe the way to make marriage work is to give your *husband*—never mind the number—a chance. A fair chance.

Takes two.

To do this, you have to leave Whittier.

My challenge had turned out to be to myself. The gauntlet I'd flung in the pearly teeth of Mrs. Alice Ames Winters had been picked up by a jury of my peers and flung back at me. Any decision I made would be a direct result of that. Who but myself could come up with an answer to Papa's probable key question—What to do about it here and now?

I heard the gentle tap tap of Mother Meyer's cane and revised my decision not to talk it over with her or God or anybody. When I presented to her my problem she put her arms around me and kissed me on the cheek. Very unusual, she was not a demonstrative woman. She said she thought I might feel like that but she couldn't help me. She said, *You won't believe the answer until you find it for yourself.*

A husband—the dictionary says—comes from husbonda, hus + bonda (OE. *hus*—house, cf Icel. *bondi*—holder). Householder. Then the husband should *be* the householder and it wouldn't work in another man's *hus*.

Sell this white elephant you and Ike created and, with Ike's juggling act with dough and my gift from heaven with servants, had somehow maintained. This new young man, once famous for being on the touchdown end of a forward pass in the Coliseum—he's bright, he's attractive, I guess, he does have a name many remember, he may go far, why not? In time, he may overcome his disapproval of almost everybody and who knows? But time is what we haven't got for him now as a husband. Four servants inside the house, a groom and a gardener and a chauffeur outside—a happy household, no doubt, a husband couldn't be happy if he earned ten per cent of the upkeep of such an economically ridiculous ménage.

I was glad my son Dick had been born on the Whittier ranch before I had to give it up.

Parting with a home you love is leaving some of your heart behind you. Or would be, if you couldn't take it with you. Shelley says that when the soft voices die, music vibrates in the memory. A melody takes possession of you, even without a tune memory haunts you. God creates—memory re-creates. I never went back after I closed the door of my dream house in Whittier, except in memory. At first I couldn't bear to do that, but now I make quite long visits there and find everything just the same and live it over in smell and touch and sight and sound, and out of these things you re-create a time gone by. The *hus* where the children came first. They are still there—

Within the jingle-jangle-jingle of this drastic dreadful move that had become a necessity, I had my old crying desire to get back to the ocean. If I can get back to the sea, I can begin all over again. Worth-while people, I told myself, can always begin again.

Build a house on the sand, where the ocean beats at your door. No cushioning gardens. No peaceful shallow brooks. No softening sighing trees. No growing vegetables or nuts you could eat in a famine. If it is going to be rough, let's do it where the sea thunders and the gales blow from around the globe and the gulls soar in beauty and courage like no other birds ever can, crying harsh sounds of defiance against storm and cloud and wave. If you want to swim, no sun-warmed machine-heated pool. Go out into the cold salt water and fight the crested breakers with your own hands and feet on your own belly.

Be a *wife* now, a *hus*wife, to the *husbonda*.

When I moved to Malibu, in this attempt at a new method of driving three mules, oddly enough it was not, I realize now, because of my second husband. My failure with *Ike* drove me. Now I had made everything more complicated, now I was going to do right by the wrong husband. The fact that I had had no good, honest, unsupportable reason for divorce the first time created a sort of herculean embarrassment at the thought of another one, even if it had all the causes ever listed on the statute books of California. This next one had to be on me. All women who know they are still women are horrified by the common, easy-come-easy-go vulgarity of a second divorce.

The odds were longer now. But I would give it my best try. Settle down. Take care of my husband, my home, my children in what lovingkindness I could command nor did I know then that is never enough. *Your* loving-kindness. Never mind who's on first—or second, I said to myself. Do some of the cooking and take on everybody's day off, give you more time with the little fellow. Also help to cut our expenses (that'll be the day). Establish definite hours for work on your fiction, now your only source of income and always a precarious one. Get your new serial for *Cosmopolitan* going. As soon as the children have gone to school, climb your winding staircase to your workroom, from there all you can see is the sea, as from the deck of a ship. Nothing but that and the inverted bowl of the sky and the distant horizon. At exactly 10 A.M. every day, as I'd seen Jack London do up at Lark Ellen in the Valley of the Moon, *stay* there until you've done a good number of words or pages. *On paper!*

Maybe it would be better to put Bill and Elaine in good schools. Girl's Collegiate—Menlo Park, which prepped for Stanford. The British Empire was built on the playing fields *and* classrooms of Eton and Roedean. Could I make myself believe that?

I wouldn't do it unless I had to.

In my heart they still came first. But this new routine—I must try to make it work. I must. It had an edge of desperation but I hung on. I would be restored, we'd be a family. As much as I could, I was using his name. One reason I had to forget it later.

At night, I went and sat on the sand in the dark and fought my way back to some kind of sanity by morning. I didn't need much sleep, but I needed some. The quality of my work, doing it *at home,* wasn't improving.

I should—and could—have made a success of my first marriage. My second could never have been anything but a calamity, not if I'd been born in a cave.

If you hadn't married him, a friend said to me, Dicky wouldn't have been born. Oh yes, whether I divorced Ike or whom I married, Dicky was himself. He was sent to me as his mother. I don't think children always have to do with heredity, they may even select their parents or parent, or this selection can be made for them as to this particular incarnation.

The telephone rang just after lunch.

This was sometime in 1931 and Joe Willicomb's voice said, "The Chief wants to talk to you" and when Mr. Hearst came on he said, "If it is possible I should like you to come up here *at once.*"

I spun around like a top. "I'll be right up, Mr. Hearst," I said happily, "I can take the night train."

And though I did not realize it as I hung up the phone in that tremble of delight, here at last my Dangerous Journey really began.

BOOK TWO

BOOK TWO

CHAPTER 20

The Telephone, from which came the voice that controlled most of our lives, was the scepter of Mr. Hearst's authority over his newspaper empire.

It seems to me it might be a good idea for you to pose as an Unemployed Woman, the voice had said, and I was hooked.

As Mr. Hearst spent more and more time at the Ranch, more and more telephones appeared. In his own Tower, where his living quarters and offices were located, there were dozens of them. At both ends of what we called the Big Room, now open to the public, were enormous windows and there were phones at each end. Swimming pools, indoor and out, tennis courts, movie theater, stables, gardens, zoo, each had two phones, the one for him had a different ring and was kept open. Only the dining hall had none; if possible they held calls until he'd eaten.

Our great cartoonist TAD once said, "No man is great if you can't make a recognizable cartoon of him. It's the most penetrating of all criticism *and* compliment. Lend it to untruth, and it's an unscrupulous weapon."

On this subject Mr. Hearst said, "If each of us resembles some animal, I concede the elephant may be mine. I *am* large. However, if I were my own worst enemy, I would cartoon me as a polar bear. He is more vicious than the grizzly, and more dangerous because he has such a snow-white coat to hide his black heart. I understand that in the offices of one of Mr. Henry Luce's publications hangs a portrayal of me as an octopus. This I find farfetched."

While I waited to know exactly what he had meant by posing as an Unemployed Woman, I remembered this, and I disagreed with him. Before I go into an Operation Octopus to which he was to assign me, I must give a few illustrations of the method of his reach, that gave him the octopus caricature. He would not thank me for whitewash. *Not only can you smell whitewash,* he said in decrying it, *nothing more perishable exists.* So these are meticulously accurate.

A night call to the New York *Journal.* Al Williams was on the night desk and to him Mr. Hearst said, "Many faults were to be forgiven a man as picturesque as my friend Mayor James J. Walker. Jimmy built a picture of New York and sold it to the world. I think that city deserves and desires someone of higher caliber than its present mayor, Mr. O'Brien. Don't you find it old-fashioned to allow Tammany Hall to continue to run your city? I want you and Mr. Spiro and Mr. Curley to put on your thinking caps and find a way to convey to the public that they can do better than Mr. O'Brien. I do not insist on ridicule, but I feel you may find it appropriate for Mayor O'Brien. There must be instances and it is the one thing no politician can survive. We should begin at once."

Al knew what *at once* meant but Spiro had gone home and it wasn't till morning that he got a quorum. Then they sat staring at our City Hall reporter, Joe Cohen, who must know any possible targets where the octopus could hit the Mayor of New York in the eye. Joe said, "Ever notice that smile of O'Brien's? He never manages it on both sides at once. Very lopsided. If we put a photographer on him all the time and concentrate on pictures of him *smiling*—it's got to look phony—"

The double truck of Mayor O'Brien smiling upon varied and sundry occasions carried no captions. It needed none.

Fiorello La Guardia beat him; now that the Little Flower has been immortalized and an airport named after him it's hard to recall how difficult it was to elect him. The layout of O'Brien smiling was the opening gun in that campaign.

Soon thereafter I was standing in an alley behind a county hospital upchucking the very lining of my stomach. A tentacle of the octopus had sent me inside that hospital, and I wrote an exposé to clean up its brutality, incompetence, and neglect. An exposé was regarded by Mr. Hearst as successful only if it created news that the other papers were forced to follow. Those other papers had to print the news stories about getting a new board, staff, and buildings, but we were on top of it. Of course it put on circulation! Citizens were interested.

As William Randolph Hearst fought for the Hetch Hetchy Dam at Tuolumne to give San Francisco *water,* he needed as many arms as an octopus to drop copies of the San Francisco *Examiner* on the desk of every United States senator in Washington every morning. These held facts and figures to support the bill he needed, and his editorial position. *I am in favor of a life stream owned and protected by the Government, as against a profit-seeking private corporation.* This was one of, if not the first, battle for what he, in his own words, called *public ownership of public utilities.* As Samuel Gompers, head of the American Federation of Labor, and one of its foremost forever leaders, said, "Mr. Hearst gave the full strength of his personal, political and newspaper influence for the passage of legislation to bring about public ownership of public utilities to benefit all of us."

Doggone old octopus!

2

Looking back upon it, I see that it was ironic that I was given the particular assignment to *uncover* the depth of pain and poverty unemployed women were suffering in the Depression at the Ranch. After he and his father, Winston Churchill, had been guests of the Lord of San Simeon, as he called him, the late Randolph Churchill wrote, "The Ranch—for so it is termed *in false modesty—*" Here young Mr. Churchill misunderstood. The Ranch was the Ranch because it *was* the Hearst Ranch, as in Texas it is the King Ranch. Or the Johnson Ranch. It was also erroneous for him to say that it cost $5000 *a day* to run the *Ranch.* It was the Enchanted Castle atop the hill that cost that much and more to run. We thought of it as quite normal for a man to have that kind of money and to spend it any way he wanted to.

After all, it was *his* money.

Up to the Depression, the veryveryrich were the veryveryrich. *Charity* went to the veryverypoor. Sharing was not an active principle. It was less than fifteen years before Black Thursday that J.D., Jr. (whose father had given dimes), intervened personally in strikes led by Mother Jones against the Rockefeller mining companies in Colorado and himself installed the first Employee Representation Plan ever seen in this country. Now we take it for granted that such wealth as Rockefeller and Ford fortunes is intelligently shared, distributed in hospitals, colleges, foundations, grants, and controlled funds as well as higher wages and benefits. We in 1931 had never heard of such things.

Obviously Queen Victoria regarded herself as born to the Throne, a fact of Nature and an Act of God. Mr. Hearst, born with the biggest Gold Mine in the world in one hand and estates as big as kingdoms and dukedoms in the other, felt no more guilt for having all this than Victoria did for wearing her crown. He assumed, as did she, the responsibility for handling it and accepted that though men may have been created equal money wasn't.

The Depression was what altered the face of America as I saw.

Without it, Roosevelt, when he came into office, could never have put over a Share the Wealth program called the New Deal. It took most people a long time to adjust to this new world where a device called Income Tax as well as the swing of power to labor would try to make finances equal. Under it, Mr. Hearst faced bankruptcy and the loss of his papers and this he regarded as unnatural.

Next to the Civil War we saw the Depression as the event in our history bringing about the deepest changes. It had been building for some time but the event itself resulted from the catastrophic collapse of the Roaring Twenties. The insane, unchecked, bogus brummagem spiral that was called Wall Street cannot be blamed on Wall Street since it served the wild wishes of the People. Our rash, headlong, impassioned greed for money and pleasure at any price infected us like a fever, a plague. At its 106° temperature we made full surrender to the underworld gangsters and the Black Hand Mafia of the day. Rather than deny ourselves a couple of drinks until we would repeal an unpopular law, we entered into an era of permissive lawlessness, and the beat goes on. The Depression was our City of Destruction built on the Sands of Sodom and Gomorrah and when the rains came, it fell.

But at the time—

We didn't believe any such thing.

Don't look. It will go away. Dance, little people, dance.

Following October when the market broke and those who had tried to gamble their way into equal riches with the rich were broke likewise, men jumped out windows, women sold diamond necklaces for ten dollars, vice-presidents of big businesses peddled apples on street corners, bread lines formed, factories shut down, veterans marched on the Capitol.

Still, we insisted it was a temporary setback. A crisis in my own personal finances, sheriff pounding at the back door, wolf asleep on the welcome mat, the way to solve this was to make more money even if I had to write for the movies. I always had, we always had, the United States always had. That we were entering into a time of sweeping social reform, as revolutionary as France or Russia but in our own American way, that we were about to start a bravissimo attempt to combine private enterprise and governmental control into a benevolent paternalism and bake it into a form of socialism—who knew it? Who believed it?

As the Depression dragged through its second year, its third loomed, we grew intensely restless and apprehensive. One thing it is vital to understand. With the lack of such visual communications as we now have, with the much lower standards of education and the much slower means of travel, literally and truly millions didn't know, had never known, how the other half lived.

Look how long it took us to outlaw Child Labor. States that didn't have it simply wouldn't believe it existed anywhere.

If you found out, after you knew what poverty was, what shame was like to live with, after you had seen desperation in reality for the present and future of your children, all things changed. They could never be the same again.

My feet grew to be a throbbing menace that swamped my courage, my self-confidence, my belief that by *right* I was safe

and brave and happy and had a job if I wanted one. I think as
long as I live I shall remember the bleeding feet of the unemployed who must walk in worn-out shoes. For mine were among
them.

(That is from my stories as an Unemployed Woman when they were
published.)

And that is why I note the violent contrast of receiving my orders at
the Ranch. The Ranch, when it was Mr. Hearst's home, was my real
Earthly Paradise. Nothing, it seemed to me, could go wrong there. I am
glad that millions of people can now go through the Castle every year as
they go through ducal palaces in England, also outdated, and I only wish
I could put on paper how much I *loved* it, for them to know. What it
meant to me and to all of us to be there, what it was like when it was alive
and not a museum.

Now I wonder if it was the very contrast, the comparisons I had to
make, that were to give me a supersensitive plate for exposure to the
Unemployed Women—as well as the way Mr. Hearst gave me the assignment.

3

Before dinner Mr. Hearst came across the Big Room to me with caviar,
toast, chopped egg, and onion, arranged on a Sèvres plate, and we sat
down in the window facing the sea. A sunset was sheer lucent light leading
into some unexplored infinity and we were silent watching it dim and
then my heart began its usual gallop when I was going to talk story with
him.

"Eat your caviar," he said. "It's very nourishing, and you need it after
your trip." He watched me until I did, then he said, "I have had some of
our papers look into the situation of the unemployed women in their
cities. Until recent years we have not had a high percentage of women who
were consistently employed outside the home, so this question of their
*un*employment is new. I think you must go and find out what is happening to these women. Both public and private organizations have broken
down in their attempts to cope with it. This depression is a national emergency and I think the authorities supposed to handle it must be found
and faced with the facts and called to account and possibly given new
ideas to match changing times."

I said, "I've talked to a couple of the brighter clubwomen, they don't
seem to know what needs doing, if anything, what's their responsibility,
how to handle it if it is."

"No amount of editorial comment can equal eyewitness accounts nor detailed reportorial coverage. We must appeal first to their hearts," he said.

"I'm going to be a sob sister again," I said.

"I hope so," Mr. Hearst said. "It is right that we should sob over this cataclysm that is before us.

"I want you to go out and *be* an unemployed woman. For whatever time you may find it necessary to cover completely all phases and to un-cover mistakes and demand new drive in this emergency. Start under the worst conditions. Conduct yourself as though you were in truth in this tragic state. I do not need to ask your word that you will not violate in any way the role you now undertake to play. *Brother, Can You Spare a Dime?* —this theme song has established the monetary unit of the victims. A dime, therefore, is all you should take with you.

"I want you to tell it exactly *as it is*. Let the chips fall where they may. We have no sacred cows, social, political, religious, nor professional. I know of not one we need consider at this time."

"I'm fairly well known in Los Angeles," I said, "if people recognize me and think I'm doing it for the paper it won't be so good."

"I do not favor disguise," Mr. Hearst said, "but we must not forget how unobservant most human beings are. Glasses, perhaps—a dress that doesn't fit—and one of those cloche hats that make any woman look de-pressed. If you enter into your role as I know you will, they will take you as authentic without a second glance."

I knew now exactly what he wanted. I said, "Do I work out of the *Herald?*" and he said, "I have not told anyone of this as yet. Later I want a photographer to go with you, he can use one of those new cameras I sent back from Germany last year. That will give us on-the-scene pictures as illustrations to confirm and supplement your stories. For this the *Examiner* will be more satisfactory. A morning paper can give us more space, it's read more carefully and has a larger percentage of women readers, we must reach the women with these." I said, "I can start down tonight—" and he said mildly, "That will not be necessary. I don't want you to feel rushed on this."

Dinner was announced and Marion fluttered over in black velvet and diamonds. Some of them were from the dime store, it tickled her to buy the kind of lavaliere she'd seen in the windows and admired when she went to school in Brooklyn, and she never seemed to notice the difference between those and the jewels worth millions Mr. Hearst had given her.

It was *Marion* in the circle of the old Metropolitan Opera House who, when she broke her three-strand strings of matched pearls and they showered at her feet said, *"Jeez, me beads!"*—a line that Bob Montgomery, who was in the box at the time, has made historic.

1. Adela Rogers at the age of nineteen months.

2. Adela at two years with
great-grandmothers:
left, **Mrs. Victoria Greene**,
direct descendant of
General Nathanael Greene,
Washington's second-in-command at
Valley Forge;
right, **Mrs. Allida Bogart.**

3. Young Adela, called Nora, and
brother Bogart with Grandpa,
the Reverend Lowell Lynch Rogers.

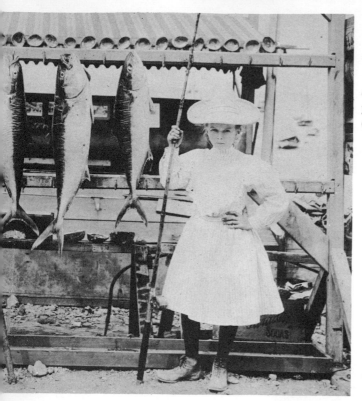

4. Adela (Nora) about eight years old on an excursion to Catalina Island.

5. Earl Rogers with son Thornwell, age one year.

6. Ike St. Johns at about the
time of his marriage to
Adela Rogers.

7. Young Mrs. St. Johns
of the *Herald*.

8. Mrs. Valiant-for-Truth . . . Mother Meyer with Elaine.

9. Mabel Normand, beloved friend.

10. This photograph of Adela introduced her to readers of *Cosmopolitan* as a new author.

(*Cosmopolitan*)

11. Adela's favorite picture of William Randolph Hearst,
taken at about the time she first went to San Simeon, the Hearst Ranch.

12. Adela, with daughter Elaine and son Billy.

13. The wedding party at the marriage of Bebe Daniels to Ben Lyon.
Front row, left to right: **Mae Sunday, Adela Rogers St. Johns, Lila Lee,
Diana Fitzmaurice, George Fitzmaurice, Louella Parsons, unidentified man,
Rita Kauffman, Constance Talmadge, Marie Mosquini, Betty Compson.**
In the rear row, third from the right, directly behind Constance Talmadge,
is Howard Hughes, who was an usher at the wedding. Other gentlemen in
this row are unidentified.

14. Adela with Tyrone Power
at 20th Century-Fox.
(Courtesy Twentieth Century-Fox
Film Corporation)

15. Adela and Clark Gable
coming out of the Commissary
at Metro-Goldwyn-Mayer.

We got up. "What," said Marion, with the familiar gesture of tucking her arm into his, "are you two up to?"

Mr. Hearst twinkled down at her and continued to me, "This eye-witness report must be accurate. It will be attacked by those we find it necessary to expose, by those who do not wish to be persuaded or moved by it. Do them with *vigor,* appeal to the hearts of their more fortunate sisters, but always with *accuracy.*"

"No doubt," said Marion, "I am one of the more fortunate sisters? Come and eat. I didn't cook it but I took a lot of trouble with it just the same."

At dinner I sat next to Louis Bromfield, as always he was witty and heartfelt, I don't remember anything he said. I was becoming an unemployed woman that not a soul in Los Angeles would recognize. If I washed my hair myself I'd look as unemployed as a Death Valley prospector. Bite my nails. No buffer. Ha! Nothing made a woman look so down-and-out as the wrong lipstick. Finally in the distance I heard Louis and Mr. Hearst talking across me about Peter B. Kyne, whose novel *Valley of the Giants* was a California classic, and about Pete's ranch. Pigs, I gathered, were worse than walnuts. "I wish," Mr. Hearst said wistfully, "authors did not insist on running farms and ranches. *The Saturday Evening Post* is trying to persuade Mr. Kyne to revive the *Cappy Ricks* stories and I fear the Curtis Publishing Company will not finance his adventures with pigs. If I wish to read more Cappy Ricks, I shall have to."

That much I caught, but actually I had moved into tomorrow. Background, tempo, other times, ripe and rife and right for the kind of stories I ought to be able to find and write. Ought? I *had* to. I knew it was later than we realized and I could smell change in the very air.

Before long, in hardly more than the blink of an eye, with Mr. Hearst's active help at a Democratic Convention in Chicago, the young man from Hyde Park who was Governor of New York would be nominated, elected to the Presidency, the Roosevelts would move into the White House. The Media has arrived, the Message of Radio is the Fireside Chat. F.D.R.'s *My Friends* spoken to the whole country will sound like a fife and drum, our hearts will jump, some up, some down, but they will all *jump.* Just the same he was never to abandon his first love, the Newspapers. Roosevelt understood the press and all that composed it as no one else ever had or will. He would use it to bring about the American Revolution 1933.

The stories I did get and write on this assignment are among things President Roosevelt said had changed the climate of public opinion for him, it had shown one-half of America how the other half lived. Without this, he said, he would not have had the consent of the People to move by the People upon a New Deal for the People.

When I went to cover Washington in the administration of Franklin Delano Roosevelt, he told me so himself.

A week after I talked with Mr. Hearst at the Ranch I set forth. Horn-rimmed glasses, dress sneaked from the M-G-M wardrobe, coat frayed at the elbows, I was dropped at the uptown entrance to the Third Street Tunnel.

Was?

I am dropped at the tunnel which I hate because it is damp and smelly.

I am what I was forever. To say I am old now and once was young is nonsense. Unless I have forgotten, if I have ever been young I am always young, when I wish to return—*for a time only*—for if I do not forget I cannot be other than I was then or than I shall be as I move into its future or the future of now. I am always a *me*.

When I come out of the other end of the tunnel into downtown Los Angeles on this chill, fresh morning I am a young woman ignorant and filled with hope.

I am unemployed.

My shabby pocketbook holds one dime.

My name is May Harrison.

CHAPTER 21

I approach this through something Ernie Pyle said to me.

Ernie Pyle was the greatest of all sob sisters. A hundred and sixty-one million people read, loved, were inspired and enlightened by him when he was a correspondent in World War II. *One* Ernie Pyle, of which we have none any more, would have made the American people understand Vietnam. We never have.

Unpack your heart, Ernie Pyle told me.

"You know that," he said. "It's the word made flesh. It's the only language everybody understands."

Not long ago on his TV show my friend Mike Douglas said to me, "You are the only woman I've known who admits she was a sob sister," and I said, "No no, Mike, I don't admit it, I brag about it. Nor do I say *used to be*—I pray I still am."

What *is* a sob sister?

One who brings sobs, as it says.

Why not? Who are we that we should not weep for our brothers?

No comic genius from Chaplin to Dean Martin who can't bring tears. Bob Hope's theme song is "Thanks for the Memory," and this touches your heart. Sir Laurence Olivier got the laughs out of the tragic script of Hamlet, and this made him the best. Sometimes Ernie Pyle wrote columns as funny as Art Buchwald. Edwin Newman, Frank McGee, Walter Lippmann, Huntley, Brinkley, Cronkite, Heywood Hale Broun, and Severeid are all witty and dramatic, also from time to time they speak to the heart, you watch and listen through a mist.

Tears and laughter must mingle, they will so often open truth and love to you, and surely open you to truth and love.

I told Mike then, You cannot move people, help them, give them the thing we most need—HOPE—by writing and broadcasting and teaching only above the neck and below the belt. This you cannot do. Above the neck with intellectual arrogance and academic mind-without-heart, sterile and limited. Below the belt, where horizons are obscured and aspirations are degraded by insane overemphasis and abnormal variations. Between these, there is a *heart*. It cannot be ignored.

As a man thinketh *in it,* so is he.

The scientist, paleontologist, priest Teilhard de Chardin says, *It is not our heads nor our bodies we must consult first, but our hearts.*

That's it, Brother, and no matter how much mud and manure they try to kick up to hide that immortal fact, it's still there. *An immortal fact.*

Jackie Kennedy had been around Washington quite a while, nobody swooned at sight of her. As First Lady she was nowhere near as popular as Bess Truman had been, nor as powerful as Eleanor Roosevelt. But when she walked behind her husband's casket that day she took our hearts and became a national idol. So that when she forsook the country of which she had been First Lady in favor of Greek Antiquity it was our hearts she broke. Behind F.D.R.'s brilliance, we knew he couldn't get up and walk, his *gallantry* held our hearts spellbound for years.

Remember an obscure unimportant little girl named Kathy Fiscus who fell down a well in California? Outside war, no other story has so absorbed readers and viewers of America. As her little voice came up from those lonely depths, top engineers from Cal Tech and M.I.T., heroic derrick crews, miners, mine operators, famous doctors gathered to help. The rest of us prayed, our hearts stretched out on either side no wider than the world on either side of Kathy Fiscus, but just as wide.

Corn? I've heard the Kathy Fiscus story called corn and I am given to understand that there are Schools of Journalism that are agin it. If you don't give the people a little corn they will have nothing to eat but husks.

Unpack your heart, Ernie Pyle said, and so no other newspaperman or broadcaster of our generation has come anywhere near him in readership and influence.

We must not forget. They had to give him the Pulitzer Prize for it, practically by public demand.

Also, the idea of a sob sister, unlike that of the objective reporter, was to walk right into the experience. To reach hearts, you have to do more than report facts. Get under the skin, become part of another life, *let* your heart beat with another's heart. *Be* it. Become it.

At the time I put on my horn-rimmed glasses as an unemployed woman this was a new technique.

Later, Ernie Pyle, as I've said, became G.I. Joe. He slogged with them, ate with them, got shot at with *combat* soldiers. Any combat soldier, my son Mac says, knows that no one understands anything about a combat soldier who hasn't been there. Not how his heart beats, anyhow.

Paul Gallico introduced this into sports writing when he faced Dempsey in the ring, caught Carl Hubbell and came down the slopes of Garmisch-Partenkirchen on skis, and still much later George Plimpton brought this to classic heights in *Paper Lion.* To this technique I was assigned as a pioneer. If it takes you over, you are never the same again. Ernie Pyle wasn't. I wasn't.

Never bright unclouded morning again.

In my father's office I'd grown up with all kinds of people. I thought I'd known human nature on a deep wide swing but I'd never *been* it. Now I was. I can bear witness.

A unique experience of the Great Depression. Like a war—you were in it or you weren't. My son Mac was in the Battle of the Bulge—*a combat soldier*. A picture of my son Dick about to make his rookie parachute jump with Jim Gavin's 82nd Airborne—either you have *jumped* or you haven't.

And—have times changed as much as I wish they had? Oh sure, we have Social Security, old age and unemployment insurance, Medicare, stepped up jobs, civil rights. But the War on Poverty beats on and only Christ can feed the five thousand so that they know God loves them.

Unpack your heart, Ernie Pyle said out on the battlefield.

Here we go!

2

Los Angeles, Dec. 14, 1931

By Adela Rogers St. Johns

Cold morning against a red sky. Already my hands were stiff and comfortless in my thin pockets. A new recruit in the army of unemployed women. Courage high, spirit undaunted. You *hear* about women out of work, girls driven to the streets, old women begging for a roof. I didn't believe a word of it!

Now, I'm scarred with it.

One thin dime. By my honor as a reporter that was all I had as I went to seek work. Starting from scratch. No money. No baggage. No friends. The hard way. Over a year after Black Thursday there were thousands of women doing the same.

If I wanted to eat, sleep, keep warm, I had to get work. Not next week, month, when things "got better." Cold and hunger won't stand still. I was to discover that both *those* can be borne with a grin, there are things that happen to an unemployed woman that can't.

The humiliation of asking charity. The yearning for a little brightness and gaiety. But you can from time to time warm your icy loneliness, your *homelessness,* at the beacon fires of kindness and sympathy that spring up.

Nothing, *nothing* seems to take away the agony and symbolic ravage of aching, sore burning feet. Grotesque, isn't it? Oh Lord help me to walk with bleeding feet my guts are bleeding too, listen to the purr of tires, the cling-clang-clang of the trolleys, *I'll be all right if my feet hold out,* they say.

As long as I live I shall remember our bleeding feet as I remember the colored bootblack who lent me carfare to Hollywood when a woman in a fur coat shuddered away with distaste.

The poor are a brotherhood.

That's why there are revolutions.

Some day-before-yesterday impressions come as a reverie, to music, to fragrance, with dreams. Other times the impressions come and call, the people and places are near and real, because they are tuned at the other end of things you now are.

I had to have work.

Simple, justifiable. *My daily bread, by the sweat of my brow.* We got out of Eden with *that,* at least. I can see peering back at me from a shopwindow my own face, the lower lip folded back over the upper, jaw out, eyes narrow, as grim as when I was eight years old and intended to shoot a boy who shot my cat. Americans are not beggars. Baksheesh is a cry never heard in the American streets—the bark of guns, before that.

I wasn't going to be *fussy.* Any kind of work. I was young, strong, intelligent, not repulsive to look at even in those clothes. I began, as I walked in this new world, to grow into the role with inner excitement. To *imagine* myself into it. Imagination is the gateway to reality, my father said.

I am May Harrison.

No roof. I hammer it in. On account of a month's overdue rent, my landlady threw me out and kept my clothes. No references nor foundations, no friends nor relations—I'd never *had* to get work before. Stores would do—it took me a couple of hours to find out there had been no jobs in stores since Black Friday in Wall Street. Said I to myself, I can cook, wash, iron—Grandma was a lady, therefore I can sweep, make beds, darn, sew a fine seam, so I could tell my servants how to do it. I can likewise use a typewriter.

Later a gray-haired woman at the Community Chest said in exasperation, "My good woman, there are twenty thousand cooks looking for work in this city." No office employment agency would even register me.

I will get work! Old clothes, glasses—these things could not alter the Real Me. The hell they couldn't! Let enough people tell you you're no good and your primal soul begins to shrink, to believe it. Maybe your face hasn't changed but the face of the Universe that looks back at you has.

Disassociated from everything I knew, I discovered in a moment of cold panic that first day the simple compelling value of a nickel. Coffee—5¢. Carfare. Phone call. From the phone book, I made a list with my stubby pencil of employment agencies to visit. Then I went and sat in Pershing Square. Where else? As many women there now as men. The women did not speak to each other. Other women might be enemies—out here in this wild free wilderness.

In the first agency I went to I became familiar with "The Board." *A cook.* That's been there since Hoover, a tall girl told me. A waitress? "Can't you read?" the man said, *"Eighteen and snappy!"* I wanted Lizzie Borden's ax for him, and a little Mexican girl said, "They mean it—they made me strip to my panties to see could I wear the uniform." At the next agency the woman was kinder. She flipped through a file, she said, "Here's one for housework. She don't keep anybody long, she'll want you to clean apartments, you might make yourself a stake." She handed me a card. "Good luck, sister," she said. Wherever I was going she'd been there—and back. At the end of a long journey was a pink four-story building. A woman whose hair I could smell came to the door, she looked at the card, not at me, "That's been filled a week," she said and slammed the door in my face. At the car line, I thought, it was a long way out, it will be longer back if I walk. I will take the streetcar. I could not bring myself to spend half of my dime. It stood between me and choppin' cotton. The soles of my shoes began to heat up about halfway back, I asked women for a ride and all they did was step on the throttle. I got hungrier.

After awhile, I got back to town.

Night must fall. I had no place to sleep.

3

Give Ma a house with four beds in it, or eleven beds, there will be someone sleeping in every one of them, young or old, black or white, whether she knows 'em or not. So says my harassed son Richard, who stands firmly against my living in a *big house,* as part of his effort to save enough to keep me out of the federal prison for nonpayment of income tax.

If this were goodness or unselfishness or Christlike love I couldn't say it here. It is none of these, it is an aching memory I cannot *endure.* A shattering guilt moaning inside me. If you have refused to believe something that is *true,* the vibrations of its truth beat on and on.

Were you ever alone in a city at night without money, friends, a bed, with only an empty stomach and burning feet? Until you are, do not consider yourself to be a judge of those who are. Do not stop to find out whether they are worthy. Lots aren't, but who are you to know how much thirstier they are if it's their own fault?

Up to midnight, I imagined it into adventure. A poor, shabby critter moving among crowds who neither know her nor care, all going somewhere while she is going nowhere. The pitiless glare of street lamps and signs is worse than darkness. Never mind—King Cophetua will be along any minute. Brother, can you spare a kind look or a helping hand? For then it gets dark, the lights go out, Eve's deep fear of dark empty alleys outside the Garden of Eden upsurges into your throat.

I must say here that in 1931 our streets were not the lawless jungles they are now when a woman actually cannot go out alone after dark. This was only the primal female fear.

"You weren't afraid, were you?" a girl known as Big Liz said to me the next day, and I said, "At first I was." A park bench cuts you loose even from fear.

When the next night was coming on, after I'd spent a nickel of my dime for a cup of coffee and a *roll* flavored with *ambrosia*, it occurred to me to call the Community Chest. They had quite a lot of my money. Not really shameful to dip into their chest and get a couple of bucks back?

The Community Chest didn't answer. It was after five.

I couldn't get my nickel back.

On a show called *The Match Game* the other day the question was, What can you hit and make it start again? Television, toasters, they said, no one mentioned the coin box of a telephone. But *I* saw myself again standing there beating with my poor fists till they were raw and saying between my teeth *You lousy sons-of-bitches, you conniving swindling thieving no-good bastards, you give me back my nickel.* Close up the Community Chest when it gets dark and then the stinking telephone won't give me back my *nickel—*

"I have been hungry for years, I wish I was dead." When Mario Lanza said that to me long afterwards I knew what he meant—I knew why he could sing "Give Us This Day Our Daily Bread" the way no one else ever has!

The "Y," Young Women's Christian Association. They had a hotel on Figueroa.

The first real step down is the feeling of *shabbiness*. Somebody has to do something about it quick, inject you with kindness and confidence; in the bright beautiful lobby, with bellboys in red uniforms, none of the young ladies in pretty dresses gave a baked potato—the truth is they probably never noticed the cocky entrance of this scarecrow nor the cockier—it's a wonder I didn't break my neck—*exit.*

I remember that I said earlier, you warm your loneliness, your homelessness, at beacon fires of kindness and sympathy, they did spring up or I couldn't have gone on holding up my head.

At nine o'clock, staring into a show window at some *oranges* a man spoke to me. My heart turned over with terror. Oh, not my virtue. If I got much hungrier I'd be glad to exchange it. No—it was just being spoken to after so long. An old man, shabby himself, said, "Like to take in a movie? I always hate going alone to a movie." I said, "Could we—would it cost any more—we could have a visit—if I'd rather have something to eat." He said, "I wish I could manage both in your company but my pension don't run to it." Through a part of town I'd never seen before by night, we walked to a hash house. I wanted to be sure it didn't cost any more than a movie ticket; for fifteen cents I had pork chops and mashed potatoes, bread and coffee. We talked baseball and he told me the stories of some movies he'd seen. Out on the sidewalk, he said, "Where you going to sleep?"

Now it's coming, I thought. For fifteen cents? Well, look what happened to AT and T. "Try the Christ Faith Mission," he said. "They're kind to ladies down on their luck." I stammered the most heartfelt thanks of my life and went. A dark building. I was to know its beauty and faith but not that night. When it was so full there wasn't even a pew left in the chapel, Mother Green shut the doors.

Until two o'clock I walked the streets. *Vagrant vagrant Ahdell-ah's a Vagrant.* I dodged a policeman. I got thirsty. A light shone from a doorway and behind it loomed a big garage. They'd give me a glass of water. A slim dark young man in a coverall met me. "Something wrong, lady?" he said. The *lady* did it. I said, "Could you tell me where I could get a bed—I haven't any money." He didn't bat an eyelash. Matter-of-factly, he said, "That limousine over there in the corner. Got good upholstery. Be out by seven." His last word. When I went out in the morning, rumpled, dirty, disheveled but rested, he merely nodded.

Across the street was a coffee shop. Never will I forget the man who ran it. At the counter I ordered toast and coffee. I shook with the horrid fear that the girl would ask me to show my money but she didn't. A large man next to me had a side order of fried potatoes with his ham and eggs. He left them. Watching out of the corners of my eyes I sneaked them. A big 15¢ was scrawled on my check. I walked to the cashier's desk with hands that trembled. I laid the check on the counter, the man looked at me. "I haven't any money," I said. Never have I seen such a look of disgust on a human countenance. With unutterable weariness, he picked up the check, stuck it on the big spindle, said no word. "I'm sorry," I said miserably, "maybe some time—" "That's only the two hundred and tenth of them I've got," he said, "you might as well owe me another quarter, I'm going broke anyhow. Tell her to give you an egg and another cup of coffee." All the time he looked as though he could cheerfully see me go down for the third time, but as I started out he called me, shame-faced he reached in his pocket and brought out a dilapidated package of cigarettes. "Take a couple," he said crossly. "You dames would get the habit, so you'd be like men. Sometimes the dames come in here want a smoke worse than food."

4

Don't get suckered by any of those jobs as a mother's helper!
I opened one of my stories with that quote from unemployed women of every age, color, degree of education, background, religion, and type.
Stay away from *those,* baby, they said.
Why?
Certain women were too weak for the work, some had kids or mothers and the pay wouldn't cover their upkeep, others had to be home nights. But it was more than that. "Charity's bad," an old woman said to me, "and unemployment's a curse, but those women—they're worse. They're mean."
I had to write it for if we have woman's inhumanity to woman cutting loose like that, then the sisterhood of woman is no nearer fulfillment than the brotherhood of man.
I had to find out.
With Christmas almost upon us, I took a job as a mother's helper.
Eventually—the cold, desperate defeated *eventually* of the guy without a job—I would have to come to charity. But not quite yet.

> As I walked the long road from Los Angeles to West Hollywood—the hole in my shoe let the wet in and then sizzled—to apply for this position at $15 a month, my head swam already. Good luck, sister, that gal in an agency had said—well, sisters, I thought as I trudged—we asked for it. We sure liberated hell out of women. True, part of this is the Depression but where were we when that happened, did we try to calm it down any or spend less or—I am wondering as I walk whether our part of it is part of the price we women are paying for this freedom.

When I hired out as a mother's helper just before Christmas in 1931 I wasn't sure whether I was on my head or my heels. Or who was right or wrong because there seemed to be two sides to that deal.

A simple California bungalow just south of Santa Monica Boulevard —and the lady of the house told me her story. Her husband had been out of work a long time, now he was working again but at less money and they were in debt and they'd lose their home—"I was a waitress," she said, "I can make enough so we can catch up. I'm not asking anyone to do only just what I do myself, when I can stay home. They have a room and good food—what's so wrong with it—the two kids?"

I washed and ironed and cooked and I liked it a lot better than things that came to pass later.

As for the kids—if Santa Claus doesn't ever leave me anything in my stocking again, it will still be full. They were worried—the kids—because I had no home. They spent some of their Christmas money to buy me a present. Toilet powder, it was. Or she might not have *any* present, they told their mother.

I can feel now how I hated to leave. I felt guilty, they liked the stories I told them, they were those I knew by heart, everybody was happy they'd found somebody.

They have to be taught to be stinkers and slam doors.

5

An hour into my investigation of our city's organized charities I hollered for a photographer and they sent Buck Forbes, a genius *no less*. In his chunky sensitive hands he held one of the Leica cameras Mr. Hearst had sent back from Germany. Never before had I worked with a candid camera following me—nor had anyone else—and that may be one reason memory unfolds this in those terms or it may be that Buck produced masterpieces that did as much to sell this campaign as any words of mine, maybe more.

In bread lines. In the act of begging from a lady who withdraws her garments from me, here Buck showed clearly the background of a jewelry store from which she had just emerged. In *waiting* rooms with other derelicts. Hanging by my teeth from the roof of the Y.W.C.A. dormitories. In all of them, broke, shabby, down and out, haggard with physical fatigue from bad food, no place to *sleep,* too much nerve strain, and spiritually sick with the absence of any love at all, I am a forlorn and foolhardy pilgrim until at last I sight the Salvation Army.

There is a force to light the city—or the world.

Let us begin and end this chapter of horrors and humor as sharp as swords with the AEF's old cheer:

HURRAH FOR THE SALVATION ARMY

However, properly I go first to the Community Chest.

A pretty girl says, The Relief Department and I say, *Nine blocks?* I ride like an empress on the token she has given me and clutch in my hand her quarter.

10:00 A.M. I arrive at the Relief Department.

1:15 I feast in gluttony on the two bits—soup beef milk PIE.

4:15 Ushered into a large well-fed lady who gets me straight without delay. We will, she says, have to turn you over to the County Charities, dear. I am holding four C's—Community Chest County Charities and in a trauma I am aware that the Charities *are* run by the County under the Board of Supervisors and have to offer me in my predicament the dread and infamous County Hospital, the County Poor Farm, the jails, asylums, almshouses set up to deal with the dregs of the downtrodden the criminal pauper the unfortunate illiterate sick-unto-death and the foreign born. Once inside these walls you are nobody's nothing forever and ever amen.

How about tonight? I say. I haven't a place to sleep.

She says, You might try the Christ Faith Mission—

The Mission I discover does not receive one thin dime from organized charity.

Maybe Christ wouldn't take it.

The Public Library! Lovely lovely thought. I can kill the hours before bedtime—where who knows—I can satisfy one hunger anyway.

"Hey," I say to the girl opposite me, "you'll get us thrown out. I'd like to know anything that could be that funny." She shows me a slick and shining magazine all full of the *shades* of rouge one must wear of a morning, of an evening, creams for *dry* skin. In war soap is more precious than soup, so it is in our existence—we stare silently at ads for scented soap, we are okay until we come to the *diets* that will give us svelte figgers, our giggles subside under a cold eye from behind the *counter*. We don't get thrown out but Buck and his candid camera do.

Cleanliness is next to godliness but there does not seem to be any godliness around for it to be next *to,* so we smell of sweat, our nails are never quite clean, neither are our necks, no needle marks of drugs but pinpricks of dirt in your pores—

This No-Room-of-Your-Own is a slum of Vanity Fair, sometimes *still* I look into my uncracked mirror and see far down in its quicksilver the cracked-mirror face and frightened eyes of my poverty self. Sometimes as now I walk back into that No Woman's Land where we developed a sisterhood of the damned that took in the blonde I met in front of a drugstore and whom Buck's pictures showed walking the streets by profession and around that I wrote:

To be in the preferred class of blondes the roots of her hair needed attention. She said, "A blonde needs cold cream. You wait right here a minute and I'll see can I get us some" . . . she came out and began her walk up Broadway like a duchess . . . we went into the washroom at the Hill Street bus station and cold creamed our faces and wiped them with toilet paper. . . . "How long," I said "have you been—out of work?" "Quite awhile," she said. "Do you—make enough?" I said. "Well," she said, "they tell me business is bad all over." "Even," I said, "in these *clothes* and I'm older but not a single man has spoken to me." She said, "They don't speak to you, you speak to them. You got a place to sleep? Try the Christ Faith Mission." "Have you been there?" I said. "No—my mother's sick—I keep a place for us—working the night shift—"

Buck Forbes makes lithographs of the Christ Faith Mission when we get there. The dormitory, the chapel—the fifty women I sleep with have to go to the chapel so Mother Green can tell them Who multiplies the beds and doughnuts—well, unemployed women can't be choosers. Mother Green isn't choosers. She never turns anybody away.

But even in the candid gray shots of the County Charities I see nightmare colors, Dali or Chirico, even Gauguin.

A woman's voice like a piccolo echoes still, "They sent *five* different women in *cars* to investigate me—" Buck leans against the doorjamb of the waiting room built to hold sixteen—I count fifty-three. He stops me as I start out, he says, "Where you going?" "I am going," I say, "to ask those women-with-a-vote if they *know* where their tax money goes—" but he persuades me back into line; I mutter and mumble-mumble I have spent time in the city jail, county jail, Folsom, San Quentin, not as an inmate *yet*, as a reporter. Standing here I see worse conditions, sanitation, overcrowding, morale, they would not dare to treat criminals like that, the Mafia would get them—not even the *Lincoln Heights Jail* is as bad as this.

May Harrison? Ticket! I showed her my pink slip. She turned her back. A woman who looked like Irene Dunne gave a sound and went out, we identified her later—*Buck* did—she jumped off the Arroyo Seco Bridge, I always see her when I go to the Rose Bowl—

Saturday at noon, everything closes. The Los Angeles County *Welfare* takes weekends off.

I remember that at this I thought I was going to throw a fit and here I was hit with my roaring temptation. I can go home! Home home home home—these Lady Macbeths cannot keep me from a place to sleep—where

I can hear the *waves*—as a hillman desires his hills so I desire the sound of waves outside my sleeping porch. But *they* can't—the others!

I will never get this spot of Lysol and sweat and vomit and urine and stale tobacco out with all the Chanel 5 on my dressing table, with the whole Pacific Ocean—never—it's the same spot the same smell I must use the same words—of a *jail,* that's where I first knew it, where it always hit me. You can't get it off you—

I never have. Don't think it.

I remember I remember I had to pass the County Jail, the Welfare Building squatted behind it like a venomous red brick toad. I put my head against one of the gray granite *stones.* Papa and I had gone through that very doorway to see a boy named Boyd, maybe that was where I first met the *smell.* I'd said, Papa my stomach says Boyd didn't kill that man. I hadn't cried then; I cried now. Life is terrible, without meaning, a tale told by a Dragon. A man stopped beside me and put a card in my hand—cards cards cards—counters counters counters in hell—Not much of a hotel, he said, run by Japs they gambled on me for a weekend—

Weekend? *Weekend?* By God I am not going to spend any goddam weekend in any slough of a hotel.

I hang on the drab wall of this world the warm rich glow of the Salvation Army Home for women.

Room of my own. Clean bed. Few things I have experienced in the way of physical pleasure like the hot bath with *soap,* towels, and privacy after weeks without them. I don't know how they could love me but they did. Like God. And the Lassies had breakfast with me and cheered me on my way.

The Army was in debt, but they knew Our Lord would see about it. . . .

> No woman who comes to us for help any hour of the day or night has ever been turned away or ever will be. If our own buildings are full, we pay for her room at an hotel. Our Christian purpose is to assure her of Christ's salvation for her.

Hope is the word for Salvation and love—and the red tape of the Salvation Army is all on their uniforms. I like it there.

6

Work, work, I must have work. I shall die of charity in my gizzard, I said to Buck, and he suggested the artificial flowers door to door. Sell or starve? I starve. Salesmanship is a gift I have not got.

The dance hall where I tried later to sell them is not a candid camera shot, it is a record, a record of Bessie Smith or Billie Holiday or Aretha Franklin singin' *Ten cents a dance, That's what they pay me* . . . The lights are dimmed, polished floor, girls lined up against a wall to be shot, girls spinning like tops, always to the moanin' music . . .

Buy my v'lets? My white satin gardenias, my lavender silk orchids? The girls in the dressing rooms Karsh needn't be ashamed of the portraits Buck got there they couldn't afford fifty cents for a flower—the men wanted more for their dime . . . sell or starve, there are those of us who starve.

Ruby. I met her in an agency. She knew all the evil the fallen angels had been able to think up. Sharp, harsh, loving, as long as she could pay the rent she let us sleep on the floor and she said if you behave yourself you can live with yourself anywhere, if you don't you're going to have to anyhow. She had a deal with the Virgin Mary . . . every morning she lit a candle for all of us and told the Blessed Mother that as soon as she got a job . . . any of us got a job . . . we'd pay her back.

All this time I had to keep looking for answers, solutions, ways and means. How much could the organized groups meet of this emergency? What new measure could their more fortunate sisters take? Deeper, much deeper, was this part of the entire problem of a changing world? Mr. Hearst had said that this was a new class in the American Democracy. The Employed Woman brought forth not by Suffrage but, as Marshall McLuhan says, by the invention of the Typewriter. The New Deal. Mr. Roosevelt hadn't yet invented that term, but that was what we were thinking about.

I left Christmas out of most of my stories in this series. Even if Mr. Hearst had the courage to publish them, by the time I'd written them it would be long gone. I didn't want anyone to say how sad, empty stockings at Christmas, for that would beg the real question.

Three Hundred and Sixty-four Other Days.

Naturally, none of them were written until I had completed my weeks of living, or dying, working, looking for work, eating and going hungry, sleeping or staying awake as an unemployed woman myself.

When I felt I had all the material I'd set out to get, all I could use, I went home and wept bitterly in the arms of my children. Shaken with joy at sight of them, of my home, hardly able to believe I was back safely and all was well.

And I had a job a job a job!

Now I know what I scarcely realized at first. Relatively, I had been gone a lifetime. I had moved from one incarnation to another. I was *not* and never would be the same woman who had said a cheerful, excited good-by.

As I ran up the boardwalk into my house at Malibu, it seemed I'd been gone for years. Everything looked extraordinary, incredible, secure, and beautiful as it never had before.

In my own bathtub, physical comforts I'd taken for granted all my life no longer seemed trivial. I'd read of people who had no way to keep clean, I'd said, Tut-tut too bad, I'd assumed they'd find a way if they wanted to be clean. Now I knew better—or worse.

I went around the house touching things, I can feel the satin marble of Mother Meyer's table with the slab on top. My father's big leather chair. My books my books my books—the aching hunger and emptiness for things to read, how did they endure not having *their* books, the ones that to reread is the heart of friendship? Going from room to room rejoicing in ordinary furniture, looking into the refrigerator, the storage cupboards with air drafts for fruit and vegetables my children must have and which Johnny, our vegetable man, brought us fresh from the market each day. *I have children*—they'd said that to me, a-many of them. I patted the piano I kept so Mother Meyer could play when she came—*I have my mother to support, she's been sick*—suppose it was *me* and my Mother Meyer who was old and lame—The painting of the azalea garden William P. Silva had let me pay for two dollars a week—I'd had a *job* so I'd been able to possess it for our joy.

Bursting into laughter at myself, I can remember the tears I wiped away. Who was I to be so favored—and why? I ordered—and I *ordered* all the things I'd hungered for on nights in a crowded dormitory where everyone was still hungry. There was a sizzling steak, a baked potato right out of the oven. I couldn't eat half of it and I began to cry again because there was no way to share it with women I knew were still hungry. I'd *been* hungry. In the morning hot coffee made in a pot would come to me and I'd been *without* my morning coffee as I'd been without books.

Now I seemed unable to detach what I was doing from what I'd been doing—they kept interweaving—

My job. The glory of labor. My background had opened doors, I'd never had to fight and claw and struggle for a chance to *work*. Even when Adam and Eve got booted out of the Garden of Eden they had a right to earn their bread by the *sweat* of their brow.

The benefaction of a *job*. Of *employment*. That had to be the answer.

Thank God for my children and their fresh vegetables and my job that would enable me to pay for them.

Thank God?

Whose God? What was He doing about all the others? What about *them*? The women I could see in my mind's eye, desperate for work, for food for their children, where was God in their despair? All right now for me. But what kind of a God would take care of some of His children and leave others to starve? What kind of a God was that, huh?

Anger, fury—*fear*—simmered in me.

Take away my good clothes, my name, my position in society, my profession, the people I knew, and the world had shown me a different face —oh it had, it had. *You shouldn't have been sent here, go to the County Inferno—No, we don't have a bed for the likes of you*—gratitude for what I'd taken for granted all my life had welled up in music when I got home safely and found all well, now it was drumming out a war song, now it was running red in horror at my memories. Could I ever be the same again, so pleased with myself and my safety and my tinsel success?

Was this what my brother Bogart meant about *combat* airmen?

Never bright unclouded morning again.

If there was a God, if He'd made the world I'd been living in, to hell with Him.

Humanity was all we had. At night I walked the sands again, trying to quiet my stomach so I could think. If I didn't know where God was, neither, I found in cold sweat and tremor, did I know where His church had been in those weeks.

I hadn't seen anyone passing out *manna* or offering any loaves and fishes. Yes—take that back—I'd seen Aimee Semple McPherson, God bless her. Feeding, encouraging, giving hope hope hope to the poor, and faith and strength as they jammed Angelus Temple and slept there if they had no place else to go. I saw her begging for them, insulting those with folding money into parting with it for their destitute brothers. Sick women on the floor of her home, old men in her garage, families sleeping in the pews. And Mother Green of the Christ Faith Mission. The Church didn't really think much of either of *them*. No checks flowed to them from the Churches nor Organized Charity.

Give all your goods to feed the five thousands—Ha Ha Ha.

Had I seen, except for those two unorthodox women, a moment when what the Protestant Church called faith was active?

Oh well—we'd been doing goddam well without it. We'd done it ourselves. We had come through the Red Sea and riotously worshiped the Golden Calf hey hey and now the Golden Calf had given everybody a swift kick in the behind and they'd forgotten how to make it work if they'd ever known.

Well well!

How confused I was I can hardly convey.

Nor how angry. I was shaking again as I went to bed, this time with rage. I called it righteous indignation. It was pure unadulterated Irish rage. Trying to go to sleep I was taken over by thoughts that were not mine but they were vague and senseless and in a language I didn't understand. Even when I woke up after a few restless hours, they weren't at all clear.

That morning, having had a couple of days' rest and two nights' tossing sleep, I went to the beauty parlor where I got my hair washed and set, had a manicure, both the manicurist and the hairdresser tut-tutted over the dirt, *can't get this out,* they said, I could have told them it was there to stay forever. In the mirror, at the end of these rites I looked about as usual.

How amazing to discover in one's self that volcanic changes hadn't come through to the outside.

Or had they? My expression was different. There were *lines.* My first. Not that I objected to that, I'd hate to end up with a face like a blank page on which life has never written anything. Only idiots have no lines—and those women who wipe out all record of living and character ahead of the embalmer. Like pans of shallow milk, they are.

Down at the office they gave me the usual beat-up typewriter in a corner of the *Examiner* city room. I had reported to the city desk, of course, and Van Ettisch said, "You want to write one at a time or finish the series before we start—we'd like to get going as soon as possible?"

I said, "Van—I have a feeling you ought to see them all first."

"How long will it take you?" Van said.

"How much do you want?" I said.

"Whatever it needs," Van Ettisch said. "Buck has all the pictures ready. Unless you think things will change—take your time—maybe two or three thousand words a story."

"Nothing will change," I said bitterly, and Van gave me a speculative look.

I wrote sixteen stories of three columns—half a page—apiece. Imagine! That much space, I mean. It took me almost a week, working long stretches. In the end I threw away more than I turned in. I knew I was pressing like a pitcher in the World Series. *Now.* You're no good unless you can do it now.

I was unpacking my heart on this one the best way I knew.

I put them on Van's desk at last and went to sit behind my typewriter, the sweat trickling between my shoulders, I saw him sit quietly reading, then he got up with all the gray copy books (the pages with the carbons between we call books) and went through the glass door into the managing editor's office. While they talked, I picked up the phone and called home. The children were swimming—in *January.* That'd toughen 'em up.

After *forever* Van came back to the city desk and Managing Editor Eldridge, his toupee at half-mast, went out to the elevator, a tiny Renaissance affair intended to take Mr. Hearst to his apartments on the top floor. He didn't use them any more—he telephoned—so the elevator had been turned over to the publisher's office on the third floor.

After a while a copy boy told me Mr. Young George Young, the publisher—wanted to see me. I couldn't wait for the elevator, I climbed the circular marble stairs and there he was, his smile as far out front as the Cheshire cat's.

"A great series," he said, indicating the pile of my copy on his desk. Ah, the best butter, I thought. Otherwise he wouldn't be a publisher. "But I'm sure you know yourself we can't possibly publish them as they are." I didn't say anything, he went on, "We'd find ourselves in grave difficulties. For example. Consider the power and prestige of some of these organizations both here and nationally—"

"That's why," I said.

Publishers! Let them go to banquets and luncheons and get photographed with the governor and confer with advertisers. I cursed Van Ettisch. What kind of a city editor was he, to throw me to a publisher? My heart yearned for J. B. T. Campbell. Hell, the *Herald* would be on the street by now.

Mr. George Young was saying, "Many of our best advertisers are active in the fund-raising drives—"

"Advertisers!" I said. I was shocked to my toes. Never before had I heard the word used without modifying, descriptive adjectives, but this was the publisher's office, NOT the city room. "As for the important men who raise the money, they ought to be glad to find out what's going on with it afterwards—"

"Not so publicly," said Mr. Young.

Being a publisher must be split personality like Tweedledum and Tweedledee, I thought. I said, "You won't get far saying it privately."

"However," said Tweedledum, "I'm quite sure you can rewrite this so we can publish it quite happily. Those charming stories about the children where you worked as a mother's helper—and the girls in the ten-cents-a-dance halls."

"No," I said.

The smile grew Tweedledee-er. "I know writers dislike rewrite—" he said.

"If there is rewrite," I said, "my city editor should tell me."

"This is a matter of policy," Tweedledum said sternly.

"Mr. Young," I said, "I have never in my life gone over an editor's head. Mr. Hearst gave me this assignment as my editor. I will not rewrite it unless he tells me to. You'd better call him, hadn't you?"

"Certainly, certainly, I will indeed—" he said.

"*Now,*" I said. Before I strangle you, I thought. "I want to go home.

I've been on this story for weeks. I missed Christmas if anybody gives a damn. I've been writing it now for days. We ought to get into print with it—they're hungry now. Call him."

So the publisher got the Lord of San Simeon on the telephone.

What a retroactive joy it is to recall it by retelling it. No meetings meetings meetings, no committees committees committees, no conferences board editorial and sales, just one man who *knew*. May not be democracy but it sure worked. Years afterwards, Mrs. Kettering read about Lindbergh's solo flight across the Atlantic and said to her husband, "How wonderful that he did it all alone." To this he replied, "It would have been even more wonderful if he'd done it with a committee."

To be said for George Young. He presented his case concisely, accurately, and completely. He told William Randolph Hearst all his objections. The probable loss of advertising. The political kickbacks and discomforts from the Board of Supervisors, the mayor, and undoubtedly the governor. He relayed the information that the lady of whom Buck Forbes had shot a superb picture as she withdrew the hem of her fur coat from my weary worn shoes turned out to be the wife of a big department store president. In those days department store advertising was the lifeblood of a morning paper. The use of the candid camera was so new at this time, we hadn't known how it would turn out and here was a picture of the man's wife refusing me carfare. It had turned out! Mr. Young put the dangers in forceful, even lurid, terms.

When he had finished he listened, then said, "Yes—she's here—"

Mr. Hearst said, "Adela, are you sure of your facts?"

I said, "I have a lot of documentation and the candid camera shots are terrific. Yes sir, I'm sure of my facts."

"Let me speak to Mr. Young, if you please," he said.

My knees were shaking, from a great distance I heard Mr. Young's voice, "Yes Mr. Hearst—very well Mr. Hearst—of course Mr. Hearst—if you say so—"

He hung up. He looked at me with extreme distaste. He said, "We will publish all of them exactly as they are."

I wanted to say, Aren't you glad you've got somebody to tell you what to do? but the poor bastard was out on his feet already.

One thing for our Tweedledum. All his dire prediction came true.

Not since the graft prosecutions in San Francisco had I seen a city declare civil war and break up into camps and scurry hither and thither as our town did when the St. Johns series began to appear with front page fireworks, billboards, and trucks.

A salute goes to our opposition, the Los Angeles *Times,* it took one good look and backed us strongly.

We lost some advertising. Quite a lot as a matter of fact.

Our reporters were barred from certain civic gatherings, offices, and beats for a time. Libel suits were filed though not by the department store president. A few sermons were preached about yellow journalism, sensational and irresponsible newspapers ready to do anything to gain circulation.

Just the same, we got new laws about the County Charities, new staff for much of their operation, new buildings, new leadership and wherewithal for emergencies. The women of the city rallied. They organized relief, pressured employers to diversify jobs, forced all-night and weekend phones with emergency workers on them. They set up a program of spare rooms in private homes, of stocks of groceries to take home to the sick and helpless. They took over several vacant stores, wheedled beauty shop equipment out of manufacturers. The Federation of Women's Clubs got a new budget through and devoted some of it to providing decent clothes so that unemployed women were presentable to apply for jobs and drove their own cars to take women to apply for them.

The YWCA clarified its position, insisting it was not and never had been a charity organization, its purpose being to help and protect the health and morals of young women of Christian faith by giving them inexpensive places to live. Once they recognized how grave was this emergency, they brought their policies into line with the needs for the duration of it. Cooperation was then most heartening and only had to be asked for.

This whole circumstance and all the new problems arising from the Depression were faced by the Community Chest. They began to stay open weekends and most of the organizations the Community Chest supported worked out ways and means to deal with situations they were facing for the first time. Our exposé brought all this into line in a hurry.

During this time Mr. Hearst asked me to Marion's beach house in Santa Monica. He told me he'd like to make a donation of some kind in my name as my bonus. Where should it go? Of course I said The Salvation Army and the Christ Faith Mission. He sent them what seemed to me large checks.

I hold this dear.

More than that he gave me the money for the personal things that had entered my heart and were therefore on my mind.

The man at the lunch counter across from the Biltmore didn't look up from the sports page until I spoke. When he did he had no idea he'd ever seen me before. I pointed at the big spike crammed with bills beside his cash register and said, "How much do those add up to?" He said, "What's the difference?"

"You don't remember me," I said. "One of those is mine. I told you I'd come back." His skepticism abated not a jot, so I took a roll of money out of my pocketbook and said, "Please? I'd like to pay mine and all the others." He was still looking for the gag. I said, "I'd like also to give you an extra five hundred dollars so you'd have a backlog for other women who are broke and tired and scared and can't pay their checks. You could stand them a meal and a couple of cigarettes the way you did me."

"Jesus Christ," he said, *"Santa Claus!"*

The checks came to $302.65. Plus $500. Of course it was Mr. Hearst's money.

We set Ruby up in a new kind of employment agency, where she could try to act as mediator between employer and job seeker and fit them together. She did a great job.

I went around and repaid all the girls and women I could find who'd loaned me dimes and quarters and handed them a small emergency fund. They got a big kick out of it and so did Dorothy and Buddy when I took them an armload of books, to fill in for the stories I'd told them after they were in bed.

The Santa Claus part was a shot of sparkling self-gratification, and I loved it. Why not? We are entitled to our rewards. But this was bigger than that, bigger than anything that had come my way.

What had exploded deep inside me and changed my life was the Power of the Press and me as its handmaiden.

How, if I was an honest woman, could I refuse to use it for the underdog?

I'd known that power before of course, to get the Notre Dame-U.S.C. game, to halt a murderer beside the coffin of his victim, to fill Christmas stockings for the poor.

But the results of this Unemployed Series were on a scale that jolted me into a new field of vision. And responsibility.

Looking back over my shoulders I could see that it had been possible for me to attack the entrenched horror and neglect and incompetence and cruelty and injustice of city and county agencies to help the poor, and I had made them do better.

So out of Hollywood I must get and find real new larger worlds to conquer.

Going back to see what my father would have thought—*you'll always know what I'd think about anything*—and there he stood at Armageddon, still battling for the underdog. Papa was a *humanitarian.* I hadn't realized that before. Being angry with God in his compassion for all humanity, Papa had had no faith in Him as a court of last appeal. His faith was entirely in himself and his hope was that man could be saved by his own efforts, was strong enough to re-enter paradise without divine grace.

What, somebody asked Socrates, is the substance of your teachings? and Socrates said Human Affairs. Right afterwards, his little Affairees, subhuman perhaps, handed him the Hemlock Cup, and apparently he was glad to drink it down. A Greek humanitarian had no place else to go, and neither did Papa, though his hemlock was called Scotch Whisky. I could see him so clearly, a little shabbier, a little grayer, still lifting the cup.

Now I had come to believe that if men and women could be told what approached them, if they could be called to account, they would come to see a way out.

My warning to Modern Woman had sprung from arrogance. True, I really had no idea what I was talking about. I had simply been open to a flash that if she wasn't watchful the porpoises would come up out of the sea and take over and I hated the thought of this for my children.

But the women I'd met in the wasteland of unemployment had opened my heart to a new dimension. No use offering these sisters and mothers and cousins and aunts and wives pretty gifts to put in a Christmas stocking that had a hole in the toe.

Years later, I can see that woman I was. So sure, so full of those good intentions with which hell is paved, and knowing as I do what lay ahead I am filled with a compassion for her.

Vanity Fair, get thee behind me! was my cry.

I didn't want to be a Free Soul any more.

I wasn't going to worry any more about which of the three mules came first.

I would be my sisters' keeper, dedicated to her human affairs, to setting them right by the power in my hand.

How could I have taken that first step without knowing it was the first staggering stride toward the Desired Country? How could I have failed to identify it with the beloved disciple's words that we have to *start* by loving our neighbor whom we *have* seen? Or my grandfather's oft-repeated reminder that it was Cain, the first murderer, who first used the first alibi—am I my brother's keeper?

Wherefore weepeth so thy sister?

I wept with her. I can rejoice in that step now. I know there is no progress without it. Christiana had taken Mercy as her traveling companion, now I did the same, and blessed are the merciful for they shall obtain mercy. By hindsight, I can recognize this as a leap *up* on my Dangerous Journey for mercy carries the compassion which turns at last to tenderness. But then I was without the comfort of that knowledge.

Hindsight can be awesome. And frightening. Even knowing the end I wonder where that end might have been if, here a little and there a little,

I hadn't treasured in my human heart some of the love and wisdom that had been given me. I thought I had repudiated and forgotten it all in my blazing self-confidence. The words had been drowned in my loud shout *I am my brother's keeper*. But what my grandfather had proved to me by his love and words, what Mother Meyer had shown me of joy—they were still there.

I wanted to dedicate myself to removing the cause of my sisters' tears. I didn't stop to observe that humanitarianism had killed my father. That it had destroyed the glory that was Greece—and we were twenty centuries more jittery than they'd been.

This dedication was also a justification of full concentration on my career. It wasn't true that nobody could drive three mules—*I* could.

My three mules would take the Hill of Difficulty in stride.

As it turned out, it wasn't going to be that easy.

Finding yourself a white horse doesn't mean you are prepared to save France. You may turn out to be Lady Godiva instead of Joan of Arc.

If anybody needed God as a Co-pilot, it was me.

I had no such maudlin ideas, I would walk loudly and carry a big stick—the power of the press.

I would do my best, my best would be good enough. A lady with a lamp all right, and no dusty answer would douse its flame, no self-conceit lead to destruction.

Look out, Sister, here *I* come. They'll never gain a yard around my end. I'm indestructible.

CHAPTER 22

The tapestry of Cow Lane, where we lived when we moved East from Malibu, was a magic carpet.

It comes to me now that Cow Lane gained brilliance and excitement that dazzled and deep affection as a refuge from my illegal last-minute escape from the Cinema Capital of California.

On the day the Lindbergh baby was kidnaped Howey called me. I went to David O. Selznick's office and said I was leaving for New Jersey on the next train. Mr. Selznick had not yet produced *Gone with the Wind,* he was head of this fringe outfit RKO, a violent aggressive man consumed by ambition and *talent* and the best NON-Marquis-of-Queensberry fighter in town. Under his roaring drive Laurence Olivier, Katharine Hepburn, John Barrymore, and the fashion elegante Constance Bennett moaned, worked, and survived.

I showed David O. the morning paper about the Lindbergh baby, my insides curling as I read. Only gangsters snatched each other. I was livid at the idea criminals had dared to steal an American baby, son of our Hero, and I was so *hot* to do something about it I was running out the door when Selznick grabbed me violently and shouted, "You will go back and finish your courtroom script for Jack Barrymore or I'll have you blacklisted in pictures forever. Have you forgotten you have a contract?"

I had. It was my first. At no time did I ever have a piece of paper with William Randolph Hearst. Who needed it? The way Selznick glared and shouted I thought he meant to call the cops. I'd have chanced that but I'd already mortgaged my RKO salary for months to make payments on the Malibu house. I had seen Selznick in a fight with Gable in a garden one night at a party—Gable took him, but it was nip and tuck—and if he blacklisted me what would happen when I *needed* money for my growing family if I couldn't do a quickie job for the Movies?

I stuck it out until after the Olympic Games.

Then I told David contract or not I was through, and he laughed so much I am pleased to say I got three weeks' salary after I was in New York. He didn't believe I would dare; if this sounds dishonest anyone who could dishonest a Selznick deserved all he could get.

So one day I arranged myself, children, and animals into drawing rooms and baggage cars on the Santa Fe Chief—at the last minute we almost missed the train because Dicky sat on the steps of the Malibu house with his alley cat Joe Doaks in his lap and his large German shepherd dog Michael beside him and refused to budge unless Joe Doaks came too. Since Michael had tried to take an arm off Dicky's governess when she smacked his behind for refusing to come out of the ocean, we decided the better part was to take Joe Doaks. The governess quit, so I took Dave Selznick's secretary in her place, a beauteous blonde named Eunice. I hoped this would annoy Selznick more than finding me gone, a first-class secretary has to be worth more than a third-class movie writer.

At the end of this journey I found Cow Lane, a blessed refuge for me. I was soon sure this could be my Celestial City. Everybody who was ever there felt its magic. When they speak of Cow Lane there is a faraway look, they follow the golden gleam. Friends have told me they tried to copy it and never succeeded. No more did I. Magic is not transferrable. Any earthly paradise takes a combination of time and place and people—especially people—and you *can't* go home again.

The Cow Lane magic carpet comes back as a tapestry of music. The shouting of "Tipperary" as the bus rolled along beside the Hudson the night after the Great Neck Swamp Angels played the Sing Sing baseball team within the prison walls at Ossining and Warden Lawes said to me, *Your son Bill doesn't seem able to hit except with men on base.*

Gay dance music of an operetta staged by Gene Buck, producer of the Follies, moving spirit in founding ASCAP. At the very exclusive Sands Point Club with all the pretty girls, among them my daughter Elaine. Behind it I hear the roar of the presses, for on that night I met Senator Huey Long and was witness to the *fact* that the high-and-dignified *Herald Tribune,* gunning for Huey, went to press with the story of his "drunken brawl" in the men's room an hour before it happened.

At the Old Met. I had taken the top popular singer of that day, Rudy Vallee, who had never heard a grand opera. Having listened with grave attention to the glorious score of *Madame Butterfly* he said in the car on our way to his supper show at a Broadway club, *Very interesting, but it's too long between tunes.*

A little old six-piece band playing "My Old Kentucky Home." We all wept, I wept as I stood there beside Runyon when the thoroughbreds came out to Run for the Roses in the most famous race in America, the Kentucky Derby.

Music from a fairy tale romance on our treasured spinet. The Wedding March. For my daughter, lovelier than any bride I've ever seen. Sixteen seemed so *young.* But she was as self-willed at sixteen years as she'd been at sixteen months in Mother Meyer's kitchen and I was rejoiced to think the famous and brilliant man she was marrying, Paul Gallico, could give her a rich full life.

But I suppose the theme song of the Cow Lane years was "Take Me Out to the Ball Game." On thin ice though we were as across the seas Winston Churchill trumpeted warnings of another war—nobody listened, we were in the process of trying to convert democracy into socialism and still keep private enterprise, I was writing fiction like mad and amid the Cow Lane Magic that shone upon us all our dominating interest seems to have been the Great Neck Swamp Angels.

Cow Lane was just that. A lane for cows.

A French family had owned all the land between the village of Great Neck and the sound, had farmed it since the Revolution, sold it off as suburban living moved steadily out the island, until at this time there were only two aged mademoiselles left, and they still lived in the old farm mansion, with a windmill for water. Since they did not consider it possible to cook without cream, these ladies had kept one meadow, over against the woods, for pasture and every morning a boy herded a file of Jersey cows that looked like deer along a narrow right-of-way the sisters had retained and every evening he took them home. Only four big plots had been sold on this Cow Lane and mine, the last one, marched with the pasture. My terraces and gardens and the cow pasture seemed one. Thus a *spécialité de la maison* became dishes done with, by, and in cream and guests took it in their coffee whether they did or not, saying, "Of course when you have your own *cows*—"

The house was brick painted white. As Cow Lane comes flooding back I always smell the lilacs. The curved front drive was bordered both sides with them in purple, lilac, and white, and there were apple blossoms drifting from the orchard behind the house. Not a big house, exactly, it fitted us perfectly. In the playroom downstairs Bill gathered his ball club. We had a winter closet for skates and sleds and snowshoes and that winter Dicky, aged five, developed a passion for *snow* that persists to this day at Aspen, Colorado, and Alta, Utah. My younger brother Bryson was there trying magazine circulation as a possible career. And Mac and another boy we had acquired named Hugo. His folks are going back to France, Ma, Bill said, he doesn't want to, so I said he can live with us. We had a long living room with rich ivory walls, lilac wall-to-wall carpeting, a big fireplace, a grand piano in one corner, and a spinet in the other. An elegant room, but somehow it never stayed that way. One evening when I had distinguished guests I can *see* Bill and Mac and Hugo chasing each other around the furniture with only one bath towel among them to cover their nakedness. Somebody was trying to swipe somebody's new trousers. We also had an oak-paneled library and a formal dining room with fireplace where Ernest E. Adams, Jr., entertained. And it was Ernest

E. Adams, Jr., who entertained down to the last name on the guest list and the last drop of benedictine.

Ernest E. Adams, Jr., is a member of the cast to be introduced shortly. I behold Cow Lane as a way of life.

Bridge, where I frequently got Nick Schenck, New York head of MGM, as a partner, his exquisite wife Pansy was too smart to learn to play. The star-spangled day when Bill St. Johns spanked Howey's girl, Kitty White, with a racket for walking on his newly rolled clay tennis court in her French heels—Kitty, who quelled mobs and mobsters with a glance. Clarence Buddington Kelland in wild despair telling me it had taken him *three days* to get some of his *Saturday Evening Post* serial characters off the sidewalk and up the porch steps and into the house. Trips to Florida with the Artists and Writers and Mrs. Stotesbury—THE one—giving the Party of the Year for us because, as she said to me, they were so bored with each other. A weekend I have enshrined in a chapel of memory when Tommy and Frances Meighan brought Booth Tarkington to stay. I thought then and now that Booth Tarkington was the greatest *American* novelist—I put *Alice Adams* against all competition.

Sunday buffet suppers at Cow Lane turned into a Group dedicated to persuading or forcing President Franklin Delano Roosevelt to put a Secretary of Arts into his New Deal Cabinet in Washington. Likewise organizing a Department of Art, Culture, and Education. Over-all and in detail we spent riotous evenings of discussion, speeches, facts, figures and historical statistics, and embattled differences of opinion. Our choice for the job of Secretary would have been Bud Kelland, president of the Dutch Treat Club and a most erudite, witty, and violent man. In grave but biting dissent Ring Lardner warned us that we'd get cut up into small pieces by the academic world if we didn't have a few PhD.s and MAs in our ranks. So we talked it over and once invited Dr. Nicholas Murray Butler, president of Columbia. One of our many impassioned letters to the White House was illustrated, with dialogue, by Billy DeBeck, creator of Barney Google. I wish I had that one! Others were signed by our heavy guns, George Abbott, Phil Dunning, Guthrie McClintic and Katharine Cornell, Booth Tarkington, Sinclair Lewis, and O. O. McIntyre.

Though we never got off the drawing boards it may have started future proceedings.

In Cow Lane, we were all together as a family for the last time. Everybody was living at home when we moved into that home. But Elaine married there and Bill went away to college. Mac was promoted from office boy to reporter on the *Mirror* and took an apartment near the city room. Bry went back to California—oh, they would always come home, but there is a moment when you know they've left the nest—and so they should.

Somewhere in Cow Lane my second husband disappeared from the scene. Everything is easier the second time.

My second husband and I hadn't parted friends as Ike and I had done, but I hoped we weren't enemies either.

Optimistically, I forgot about him most of the time and hoped it would be a great relief to him not to have to live with me and my children any more.

I didn't see him again until we met in court.

2

As I said before. The Cow Lane motif was really "Take Me Out to the Ball Game," played *pizzicato con agitazione prestissimo con brio.*

More important than any of Babe Ruth's home runs were those of my semipro sandlot baseball team, the Great Neck Swamp Angels.

In those Cow Lane years I seemed to live in a half-world of protest and paradise, torn between my inner unfolding and my life of Vanity Fair, sort of drifting until I went to Flemington, New Jersey, and Roosevelt's Washington where big things were *happening;* there were stories. Meantime came a few that weren't what I longed for but at least they were *real.* A murder case to cover in the old witch-burning town of Salem where a smashing brunette called Jessie Costello was supposed to have poisoned her husband and we went so far on that theory *and* the preponderance of unofficial testimony that we had to get her indicted or be sued for nine million dollars' libel.

There was the day I went into the Crockford Club to lunch with Ring Lardner and called Howey to say, "A Married Couple Bridge Match is going on here for ten thousand dollars prize money. The Culbertsons, Eli who wrote all the books, and Josephine, his wife, who is maybe the best player in the world, and the Simses, who experts tell me are the best *team* in bridge, are playing. I just heard Jo Culbertson say to Eli, 'Well, of course Eli, if you are going to make up rules as you go along'—just like any wife in Oskaloosa or West Orange or Portland"—and Howey said, "Get it in here." We front-paged a bridge game that day.

I was putting in more work on fiction. I had, I think, always been a storyteller and I liked telling short stories, I did it too fast and too close to reality often, but one of them called, "Never Again," in *Cosmopolitan,* melodramatic though it was, got me high acclaim in that field. Also, it was reprinted in hundreds of thousands of pamphlets, in many magazines as a preventive measure for my unfortunate alcoholic sisters.

But I have to tell you about the Great Neck Swamp Angels.

As I have said, this was a semipro minor league club, not a Little League team. Nor does it make any difference in *feel* whether you are Mrs. Joan Whitney Payson, owner of the Mets, who play Durocher's Cubs and Schoendienst's Cardinals, at Shea Stadium in New York before 56,000 people, *or* a hard-working writer whose Swamp Angels meet the Bethlehem Steel Company or Ruppert's Brewery on sandlots behind the fire house with a hundred and fifty-six people on hand. Mrs. Payson never had to worry about money, but I can only hope sometime she will enjoy her team in a World Series as I did. *Our* World Series, anyhow.

A boy cannot play first base without a ball club.

Summer had come, school was out, now you were supposed to play ball. There were no Little Leagues then, it's one reason I bless them now. I had to try to do the job all by myself. Bill said he had Mahoney at short stop, Armstrong at second, I must come and see Davey Course at third, and he had a battery of brothers, Dutch and Frankie Biltz. They could all play in their gym pants, most of them had gloves, but they only had one bat and that diamond on the Great Neck Playground was dangerous without spikes—

Equipment was the problem. And transportation.

Need I say more?

I nearly went broke but I figured it was worth it when I saw that six-foot string bean Bill St. Johns on first base where he "belonged to be" more than anyplace on earth. I was nearly minus zero when we had to go to Washington, and then Captain Eddie Rickenbacker as president of Eastern Air Lines came up with transportation thereto and some further support and we won the New York *Daily Mirror* series and got a bonus and it was Dan Parker, the *Mirror* sports editor, who arranged a game for us with the best team Sing Sing had ever had.

I sat with Warden Lawes, whose classic *20,000 Years in Sing Sing* was a best-seller. The crowd was composed entirely of inmates, who were in a raw and raucous mood to begin with. Of their few recreations baseball came first. Understandably they didn't want to waste an afternoon on a no-contest game with some kids off the sandlots. When the first three Sing Sing players got on base—two walks and a shortstop error—their worst forebodings bade fair to come true and their boos were devastating and a little frightening. My heart began that dull *thud,* I couldn't bear to see Bill and his boys *humiliated.*

Our pitcher Dutch Biltz was a huge blond youth. His problem was control. He had never been out of Great Neck, Long Island, before not even to see the Brooklyn Bridge. All the team was shook that day, they had been searched and their rubbing alcohol and nail files taken away, this was particularly hard on Dutch, who was attached to his nail file. It was new.

With three men on and nobody out, who do you think came striding to the plate? Alabama Pitts—former star of the New York Colored Giants—batting .821. Bill St. Johns loped over to settle his pitcher down, he told me later he had explained to Dutch that strategy was necessary, the strategy was to get the next three men out.

Dutch struck out Alabama Pitts on three pitches.

A stunned silence fell on the grandstand.

He got the next two men to pop out to the catcher.

The climate changed. En masse, the inmates began to root for the kids. This rooting gave information as to why each player was in Sing Sing and for how long. Very wild it was. We got beat 11 to 9, no disgrace in any league.

Bill drove in four runs.

Our game with the House of David is inscribed in letters of gold for two reasons. That team, practically Big League, was the money-raising arm of a religious order to which all its players belonged, and the order did not permit its members to shave. The sight of a baseball team wearing very long black beards, a shortstop scampering after a double play ball with the wind blowing through his whiskers, a base runner sliding into third and being out by the hair of his chinny-chin-chin was one of the biggest box office draws in the game. With them as our opponents we played in the regular park and charged admission and made money to buy new uniforms.

The other reason was the arrival at game time of Cissy Patterson in a green velvet house coat, bedroom slippers, a sable stole, and an emerald necklace. Cissy, who owned not only the Washington *Herald* but family bits and pieces of the New York *Daily News* and the Chicago *Tribune,* also owned more houses than anybody, one of them next door in Port Washington. Being at loose ends, she drifted over to see Bill play baseball, about which she knew less than Barbara Frietchie. All seats being full, seeing Bill at first base, she trailed gracefully over and sat down practically in the first base coaching box. On this evening, Cissy was on the wagon, as good for her as it was for me, however she had apparently had green turtle soup for dinner and, as she herself often said, green turtle soup unless it was good and *hot* with lots of sherry wasn't fit to eat *or* drink.

Anyhow when in due course the House of David first baseman took Bill's place, Cissy at once suspected that his beard was a disguise, she got up and started toward him for the purpose of pulling it *off,* and I'm sorry we didn't get to see this but the sight of Cissy, her red hair flaming under the lights and her emeralds all aglow like hell-fire, scared the first baseman clear out into right field. It took some time for the umpire, though he was a bartender at the tavern as his regular job, to restore order. Cissy remained convinced that the black beards were the bad guys and her vocabulary should have turned them white in the night. Finally, in a spirit of fair play, Bill persuaded her to sit on the bench.

This produced much good, when we went to Washington to play a three-game series the whole team was invited to stay at Mrs. Patterson's four-story mansion at 15 Dupont Circle. The Swamp Angels may have been a little incongruous amid its Italian and Chinese magnificence though Cissy's famous poodles, Chico and Lily, met them with a complete breakdown of dignity. Only Philpotts, her Arthur Treacher butler, who looked down his nose at ambassadors and Supreme Court justices, served my ball team breakfast with a glassy stare but as long as the bacon and eggs kept coming and the milk didn't run out they didn't even notice.

All this was miraculous for more than just us, the Angels.

Our third baseman Davey Course was a Negro. When the Angels came out to practice they were told they couldn't play him in Washington. Bill St. Johns said the Great Neck Swamp Angels wouldn't play without him. As the deadlock persisted toward game time, Bill took his team off the field and back to Dupont Circle. Cissy, dressing to go to the first baseball game of her fabled career in Washington, was infuriated and her voice could be heard all over the District of Columbia, echoing huskily from the Hill to the White House to J. Edgar Hoover's office.

An hour later the Swamp Angels took the field *with* Davey Course batting cleanup as usual.

As far as I can figure he was the first Negro to play in organized ball in the nation's capital.

The leading member of the Cow Lane cast of characters was Ernest E. Adams, Jr.

I never knew him to hold it against me that I was white and I never held it against him that he was black. I don't think it occurred to us. There was a difference—he was black and I was white. So? Before many days after his arrival he was a member of the family and if I was president of St. Johns Inc. believe me Ernest was executive vice-president in charge of me, the children, the staff he employed and directed, the bookkeeping, the bills, and the social secretaryship he shared with Rae Holmes. Cow Lane's *magic*, composed partly of gaiety, ease, and elegance, couldn't possibly have existed without Ernest, which is another reason why neither I nor anyone else has been able to reproduce it. That ingredient had to be there, and now Ernest, with my family no longer at home, runs ranches and whole *counties* for Mary Martin and Dick Halliday in Brazil with—who should know if not I?—law and laughter. Ernest had *authority*.

Of course Bill could get away with more than anybody, otherwise we had emphasis at all times on manners, deportment, and discipline. Dicky drank his orange juice. Mac didn't walk on newly washed kitchen floors. Even Miss Elaine picked up as much of her room as a lady should. This is also what made it possible for me to take off for England to find out for Mr. Hearst what in the world could be going on between the new King Edward VIII and a déclassé American woman named Simpson. Or to cover the Max Baer training camp in New Jersey or the Costello trial in Salem or eventually to fulfill my new life and commute to Washington by Eastern Air Lines.

He would stand in the door and say, "Do not worry, madame. I will hold the fort."

The fact that I knew he would made my work possible.

He loved Bill St. Johns better than anyone in the world and I have a feeling he still does. After Bill was killed, I got a letter from Ernest, by then a mess sergeant in the Pacific. *There I was,* he wrote, *standing outside my tent with your letter in my hand crying and crying, and the Colonel came along and said What's wrong, Sergeant and I said, "Oh sir, they have killed my boy, they have killed my boy." You and I know madame he could always handle other boys and maybe he was needed over there worse than here at this time but it is hard for us, madame, very hard isn't it?*

The Costello case stands out as a most ignoble memory.

Boston was so hot that after I'd checked in with Jim Noonan, city editor of our Boston paper, Elaine and I decided to move out to Swampscott. I'd brought Elaine to see a little of New England and at Swampscott the breaking waves did dash high on a stern and rock-bound coast in front of the Ocean House.

Knowing the deadlines and difficulties of any murder trial for a syndicate, I went over to the Salem courthouse the next morning, located the courtroom, established my seat, found exactly where my telephones would be, and selected a typewriter in our staff pressroom. As usual, I pasted up the list of how to spell all the names, what the essential dates were, and studied our files, set out on a big table, from the day the story broke. Like a football player watching newsreels of the team in the park where he's to play next Saturday.

On the day, the streets were as jammed as the commons and square must have been for a witch burning. Our beat-up taxi was edging through the crowd when what to our wondering eyes should appear but a motorcycle policeman opening the way for a big black Cadillac. As it pulled up to the curb another uniformed cop moved spectators back, and behind him appeared a reception committee composed of James Noonan, city editor of the Boston *Herald,* another editor in charge of our staff in Salem, the reporter writing the running story, two photographers, and an office boy.

To myself I said, Mr. Hearst must have arrived.

The cop swung open the door, Noonan sprang forward, *everybody* sprang forward, the crowd held its breath.

Out stepped Miss Katharine Brush.

You haven't forgotten Katharine Brush, I hope. She wrote one of the best short stories in English, "Night Club," and a first-class novel, *Young Man of Manhattan.* Petite, darkly pretty, glittering as one of her own heroines, Miss Brush descended, and I thought there should be a band playing "You Ought to Be in Pictures." By the time I got to the courthouse, Miss Brush was installed in the press row, her entourage bowing around her.

Noonan and I met in the corridor.

I said, "Who's minding the city desk while you're away?"

He said, "Howey wanted me to be sure she got settled—" he looked at me and said, "Didn't Howey tell you he was sending her to do the Universal features?"

"No no," I said, "but you know how Howey is, he never lets his good eye know what his glass eye is doing, does he?"

Universal Service, huh? The morning wire, more time to write. Do not forget, I reminded myself, it was your own free will to do this for INS, the afternoon syndicate, you made that choice way back on the Harry New case. So why seethe with indignation at Miss Brush—and Howey? Let's be fair, this is what you get for putting any old punk newspaper story ahead of fiction. Arrive as a reporter, in a bum taxi, like a nitwit, no time to get your hair done, it's not Miss Brush's fault you came down ahead of time so you have no chance to make an entrance. She has a studio decorated by Joe Urban, she is a famous *novelist* so she gets hired as a Trained Seal at a fancy price while you're still nothing but a Yellow Journalism Sob Sister. I chose to ignore my per diem and bonuses, which were pretty hefty.

Taking my seat, as the judge mounted the bench, I nodded, pleasantly, I hoped, to Miss Brush, who was looking confused.

Okay okay. Let *Howey* come up here in this heat and throw her a fish, I said to myself.

A tough trial to cover, as it turned out.

Somewhere, somehow, in the background moved the Peabody sisters, who had manufactured Peruna for home consumption before cocktails; they came to Salem soon after the witches moved out, but it was still their town and there was Jessie Costello, dramatic in black in the seat of the accused. The evidence against her mounted. The cop who'd once kissed her now, in our courtroom, told all and provided for the prosecution a motive for her to dispose of her husband prematurely with arsenic. Nobody likes a kiss-and-tell guy but the D.A. seemed to drag it out of him. The doctors were definite about the arsenic. The dead man's family weren't vitriolic exactly, but as they stared at Jessie they seemed sunk in horror. Yet I knew as soon as I saw her that once she got on the witness stand she'd talk herself out of it. The jury might believe her with Lizzie Borden's ax in her hand, but this woman seemed too violent, too emotionally a tidal wave to use *poison*.

The third or fourth night the phone rang in our suite where Elaine and I were having a late dinner.

Howey's voice was *hearty*. He said, "How's my favorite girl reporter?" and I said coldly, "Why don't you ask *her*?" Howey said, "Listen, Swifty, I got a great idea," and I said, "Tell someone who cares. I don't want to hear it. I left home for this, somebody ought to put some fresh cement in that hole in my head." This he ignored, he said, "You know, Swifty, nobody but you could do this, nobody," and I said, "Leave me alone please— just go away—" and then in a perfectly natural voice he said, "She can't do it, Swifty. She's a knockout and a good novel writer, but the truth is her copy doesn't seem to have anything to do with what's going on up there—" I said, "Why should it? She doesn't know what's going on up here—" "I wouldn't ask anybody but you," Howey said, and in spite of my better judgment I could hear violins beginning to play "Maryland, My Maryland," and I said to myself, He is the Pied Piper, it did me no good, it never had. "What I mean," said Howey, from a peak in Darien, "I can't use hers, why can't you do both? You're there, you know the story, your stuff's sensational. You must have two or three different angles—you could use one for the mornings—"

"Two stories a day?" I said. "Who do you think I am, Paul Revere?"

Well, I must have agreed with him.

I hung up the phone and Elaine said, "Mama are you crying?"

"I ought to be," I said, "I am a stinker. I am a mean, jealous, paltry crumb. I am filled with envy and resentment and most ignoble characteristics. It's worse because I really admire Kay Brush, I admire what she's done, much much better than I do—short stories—and serials—and here I sit wallowing in glee on account of she's failed at something I've been doing for years—because she can't handle a breaking newspaper story—"

"Well," Elaine said—already a gourmet in her early teens she had in front of her frog legs *au* something—"she can't, can she?"

"Did I give her a helping hand?" I said. "Did I lift a finger to show her how to handle it?"

"Why should you?" Elaine said. "She came barging in—"

"No, baby," I said, "here we sat, two women writers in one courtroom. Did I treat her the way Winifred Black treated me? Did I write helpful notes to her the way Winifred Black did to me and in the end to Mr. Hearst about me?"

Elaine said, "How could you? You couldn't write a note to say Miss Brush can take your place as a newspaperwoman because she can't and as far as I could see she has too much sense to want to—"

"Eat your dinner," I said. "I'll never be so mean again, I'll try to be kindly and keep that Winifred Black chain alive—I said I would—"

I did try. Jim Kilgallen's daughter came down to Flemington to do sidebars on the Hauptmann trial. She didn't want even a link of my chain. In fact she informed me the opening day that everybody knew how I got all that headline front page *Adela Rogers St. Johns SAYS* treatment and it had nothing to do with my talents as a newspaperwoman! If she was suggesting I was Howey's girl she should have met Kitty White. As for Mr. Hearst, surely she had heard of Marion Davies? Well, Dorothy was only seventeen then and I suppose it was a temptation to hope you could do it some other way than by hard work.

Soon after the Costello trial, I had a knockdown with Howey.

Nobody but Howey could still have called me Swifty and lived, but then he called Runyon Laddie Buck and Brisbane Tarzan, referring to the column before the Dempsey-Tunney fight when Brisbane said a gorilla could lick them both. Anyway I got back to New York to see our trucks with the James Montgomery Flagg drawing of me plastered on both sides under a banner line THE WORLD'S GREATEST GIRL REPORTER READ ST. JOHNS IN THE EVENING JOURNAL. I said, "You are leading with my chin. I keep telling you and telling you the way things are going I will be a grandmother any minute. I have not been a girl reporter for fifteen years at least."

To this Howey said, "You will be my favorite Girl Reporter when you are a hundred," and began to sing "Silver Threads Among the Gold" in his Gravel Gertie voice to tell me he still cared.

He did, at that. And the trucks did say Girl Reporter when I was a grandmother.

3

The title of this segment can well be:

FRIVOLITY

and I find this a well-paved and crowded detour. Here a woman on her Dangerous Journey meets those lesser aspects of herself known as Mrs. Light-Mind, Mrs. Know-Nothing, Mrs. Ain't We Got Fun, Mrs. Inconsiderate and if she trips its primrose dalliance long enough she will run into even less desirable companions, such as Mrs. Filth and Mrs. Lechery, who will bore her to death, if nothing else.

This is then a Progress Report, a passage of this pilgrimage *showing not only whence she came and whither she goes but what she leaves undone as well as what she does and also how she runs and runs. . . .*

Almost at once I knew one aspect of my Cow Lane house that must be set in order.

A married woman not living with her husband and never intending to do so again is an excrescence on society and a menace to herself. In the early fall I took Dicky to California. My own piece of ocean—that was one of the things I always longed to go back for and that was why somehow I'd always managed to keep the Malibu house. The other was Mother Meyer, but now she had left me and nothing could ever be the same. I've wondered sometimes whether life might have been different, easier, with her still there to help and guide and encourage me. But not long before she died she had said to me that a moment always came when you could do almost nothing for even the one you loved best. She thought that time had come for us. I must, she had told me, do it now for myself. My brother Thornwell got my divorce. I was overcome with pride at his young dignity in court, at the way the decree and custody were handled. To see his name in gold letters on the door of Jerry Geisler's office made me say to myself, *His father's son.*

On that visit I saw an astounding thing. One person there was to whom the magic carpet of Cow Lane, all the swimming pools on Long Island, all the skating on frozen lakes and Long Island Sound, the lilacs in spring, and the home-grown corn and scallions meant nothing compared to Malibu Beach. Dicky reverted to type. He didn't know the difference between land and water. The blue-gray-green ocean, the white-crested roaring breakers, the stretches of sand and rocks, the sea gulls—Dicky's heart was at Malibu, as Bill's was in Cow Lane with his Swamp Angels. Dicky and I went back to Cow Lane that time, but I left my brother Thornwell and his wife, Adrienne, at Malibu to keep the house open, just as well as things turned out.

Dicky insisted on being the ring bearer at Elaine's wedding to Paul Gallico but lost interest *and* the ring, one of a series of disasters that might have warned us. I am glad it didn't. I thought she was too young to marry, but most of our grandmothers did and seemed to have a better batting average than ours. Besides, the line had begun to form—mothers of beautiful daughters know that it's not as rosy as it looks. In those days Elaine really did stop traffic, she was much ashamed of this and bitterly resented anything she got by *Her Looks,* as she called it. Irving Thalberg's offer of an MGM contract was turned down furiously—*He only wants me for my looks,* she said darkly. This was a good marriage, Paul took his young wife often to a Europe he knew well, he taught her a world of music far beyond anything she'd ever dreamed, and let her be part of his work as he became a leading short story writer. Thus we discovered her remarkable editorial talent. He profited by it then and I still do as she edits all my work.

After the wedding the Gallicos went to Tommy Taggart's famed spa at French Lick and then joined us in Louisville to cover the Kentucky Derby.

That was the year when, sitting at dinner in the Brown Hotel, we got the dreadful word that there was a fire at Churchill Downs where not only the Derby entries but hundreds of other horses were stabled. I got in the same car with Runyon and we found ourselves alone in a maddened milling crowd outside the locked gates to the enclosure. The shrieks of terrified horses came to us from the dark and the smoke and the flames of hell and Runyon said, You can't give me a boost so I'll have to give you one—up you go, *somebody's got to get inside.* He not only gave me a boost but a shove, the train of my dinner dress caught in the top of the wire fence and I hung there kicking until it ripped away and I found myself running around the enclosure in rags and tatters, scared witless, blinded and unable to breathe in the smoke, seeing horses go by like terror phantoms from a nightmare, being knocked down and trampled on by frantic men, and witnessing a courage and humanity as those grooms, stablemen, jockeys, owners, and trainers fought the blaze to save their horses. They saved them all and I saved my hysterics until I'd written my piece and then they had to call a doctor.

Runyon never said a word to me and the next day gave me four losers, but Elaine told me he came in that night, disposed of two cartoonists I didn't know and a photographer from Cincinnati who didn't know me but had taken possession of my room in my absence, and later a band someone had brought home that was playing "My Old Kentucky Home" outside my door. Runyon insisted that the doctor had said I needed *quiet.*

This my suite-mates, Quentin Reynolds and Bill Corum, refused to believe but they didn't dare disobey Runyon.

After the Derby I ran back to Cow Lane, the lilacs were in bloom, the peonies were running riot and so were the children. The joy I felt in getting home was as overwhelming as the excitement on leaving it. I missed Elaine but it was rather nice to have a chance to wear my own clothes first, and she and Paul came often to Cow Lane from their New York apartment. I saw Dicky win his first medal in a Sands Point swimming meet, watched the Great Neck Swamp Angels every Saturday, played a lot of tennis and bridge, dined out more often than ever before or since, and made enough money writing fiction to pay most of the bills some of the time.

Wasn't it a lovely life to be caught in this pleasant dream of peace and prosperity and fun and games? *The man that met thee is one Mr. Worldly Wiseman and his potion is sweet as honey to the taste.* Sitting on my magic carpet with family, friends, and frivolity listening to the birds sing and the cows moo was what I *done* all right. What I left *undone* was the humanitarian purpose and responsibility with which I had escaped from Hollywood to find real new large worlds to conquer as a handmaiden of the Power of the Press. All pilgrimages seem to be the same. I note it took Ulysses ten years to get home from Troy and seven of those he spent in the Calypso Isles hearing the song of the sirens and once he ate of Circe's herbs.

On my way from Louisville I stopped in Washington, where Mr. Hearst wanted to see me. He'd started a March of Events page and thought I should do a weekly column for it. I was insulted. Why me? I said. What *about?* He said he had never known me to be without an opinion on any subject, I could express them on this page, and I said I would be the world's worst columnist and after a short and undistinguished career he agreed with me.

Very difficult to explain my violent aversion to writing a column. I felt it was being put out to pasture. Maybe I never had that ability, but I do know I never tried, not really.

How she runs and runs, it says of Christiana on her Progress.

As we recovered from the Depression and prohibition we all, in a mad and merry reaction, danced on a volcano. We ran and ran from the war clouds gathering over Germany and England. In those fevered moments of my own and the Century's Thirsty Thirties I am sure Mr. Worldly Wiseman of Vanity Fair, U.S.A., dug up for each of us a peculiar temptation—everything is funny when it happens to somebody else and we laughed and laughed gaily at each other.

My own little firefly came in a guise I could never have imagined. An opportunity for experimentation in the lighter side of love. Well, surely a suave sophisticated self-satisfied modern woman with three martinis under her garter belt should claim this among the equalities with men she'd won along with the vote. In my youth I'd heard them called flirtations, and they were innocent enough; by our Thirties the word was affairs, love (?) affairs, and they weren't.

During my teens I was absorbed in my father, his work, his life, his battle with John Barleycorn. With the exception of getting kissed by Stanley Ketchel and my tail tanned by Papa's razor strap for it, I recollect few occasions when, like other girls, I met young men. I was invited to a dance at the Stanford Zeta Psi house by the son of a friend of my Aunty Blanche and I was a total flop. Jerry Geisler, to become himself a famous lawyer, asked me to marry him only, I had assumed, because I was Earl Rogers' daughter, I had married Ike St. Johns because at eighteen I was afraid I'd be an old maid and thus not have any babies. After our divorce I was free, but most of the men I knew were actors. Attractive as they are, a romantic foray with one of them was more or less a voyage of Walloping Windowblinds.

Who should be aboard the Super Chief coming back from the New Year's game between Stanford and Columbia but the Crooner himself, Rudy Vallee. Children from eight to twelve years were not permitted by their parents to gather in public places in those days, so there is no comparative sound track of squeals, those began with Sinatra and the Beatles. But percentagewise Rudy Vallee was equal to them all when he had the Number One spot, his records sold in the millions, and "My Time Is Your Time," the theme song of his Radio Show (no television as yet), summoned the largest audience that had ever heard a singer to date.

He and his lawyer, who he usually had along, invited me to dinner the first night out.

In a dirty envelope bearing my name—it's an odd experience to go through file clippings about yourself, there they all *are* still—I find that Louella Parsons says, *Adela Rogers St. Johns back in New York is going round and round with Rudy Vallee. This, their friends all say, will wind up at the altar but Adela tells me No.*

I told her no partly because Vallee never asked me. If he was billed as the sizzling torch singer 'twas for real, for he was the original of a guy carrying a torch as big as the Statue of Liberty for his divorced wife Fay Webb. Brought up in a New England town where it was a sin to whistle on Sunday, he'd seen a picture of a girl on the cover of *La Vie Parisienne*, his half-French-Canuck blood leaped and he kept it under his pillow. Then one enchanted evening years later in the ballroom of the Roosevelt Hotel in Hollywood, there she was, *alive,* a dream come true. He married her a week later and I doubt a man feels like that twice in a lifetime. Rudy and I were interested, things broke conveniently as to time, place, conditions, and we were sufficiently fond of each other to make it fun. Rudy had been graduated from Yale, but he'd put himself through by playing every night with his band, the Connecticut Yankees, and thus had no time for social graces and little for intellectual activities outside keeping up his grades. By chance use of a microphone one evening when he couldn't make himself heard, the coming of Radio, the man and the moment met, he became the Prince of the Air and life moved at such a pace he wore two wrist watches.

One thing Vallee taught me and every time I manage to get through a television show in one piece I say a prayer for him in gratitude. He asked me to interview some movie stars on his show, none of them had ever done any ad lib work, if they'd spoken at all it was prepared dialogue, and they *froze* in front of the mike. Gary Cooper's legs shook so he had to hold onto a chair and Colleen Moore stuttered like a windmill. I was to engage them in snappy conversation and, finding me as icy with terror as they were, Vallee said, "They tell you I have twenty-seven million listeners? Don't you believe it. You know how many listeners I sing to? Four. They are all sitting in one room, never more than those four people. That's natural and easy enough, isn't it?" This was a gift I've valued more and more.

Vallee was a man with a quick, eager, hungry mind and a violent French-Canuck temper (see Hockey Players) and a taste for glamour. I felt he was delighted at having an *affair* with an *author* whose work was then attracting attention. He rather showed me off in night club circles. Hattie Carnegie invented for me some Originals, with tight-sleeved jackets and floor-length skirts, the jackets came off and showed bare back and arms, so this was elegant and outstanding for his shows, dinner and supper, in the night club phantasamagoria, and also quite a knockout at the dawn spots around town. Imagine! As for me, I had never seen more of New York than the city room of the Journal Building on South Street or the inside of the Polo Grounds. I hadn't been in a night club since the Barbary Coast and Vernon. Right then they were the FUN thing to do, and let me face it, I did get a kick out of sitting alone at a table on the edge of the dance floor done up in white with one of those pictorial white fox collars that make anybody look good, while Rudy Vallee sang "Smoke Gets in Your Eyes" to me, though I was sure he *saw* Fay Webb in red velvet and monkey fur. He was pathetically pleased at the dinner parties I gave for him at his Central Park West apartment. One was for Jimmy Petrillo, head of the Musicians Union, and his pretty wife. We filled the table with

Jascha and Florence Heifetz, Clark and Rhea Gable, Joe and Agnes Connelly, and an account executive from Young and Rubicam who handled Vallee's show and came in white tie and tails. He was the first I'd heard of *Madison Avenue* and I must say he impressed us all.

As the first of the stars in the new heavens, radio and television-to-come, there were a lot of rumors about Vallee, among them the constant tale about the first nickel he still had. I admit to walking blocks with him on Sixth Avenue to save him twenty cents on a pair of garters, but the same day when I got home I found a sixteen-cylinder Cadillac with blue lining he'd ordered for my birthday. I couldn't take it. *Ladies do not accept gifts from gentlemen except perhaps flowers or candy or a book.* His generosity came from a warm and kind heart, and his New England thrift was ingrained in him. A better trait than reckless waste, neither of them good, come down to it.

Not to waste all that time and material I did a serial on Rudy Vallee in six parts for *Liberty,* then at the height of its enormous circulation. Called *The Prince of the Air,* it was a first-run breakthrough for an Entertainer in magazine big time. Of course today no magazine can get out an issue without pieces by, with, or about one of them.

I'd learned much about New York by night, that other world where millions work and live, about Tin Pan Alley and the search of the singer for the song and the song for the singer. Above all, I got an early recognition of the growing power of the communications medium called Radio. Though how much this was to change the world I lived in nobody really foresaw.

We remained friends, Rudy and I. I sent him an autographed copy of my novel *Tell No Man* when it was on the best-seller list; he sent me tickets to *How to Succeed in Business Without Really Trying,* starring him on Broadway at the same time. We congratulated each other on still being around though as Rudy remarked we hadn't done it without really trying.

All this has to be another incarnation—for instance *Adela at the Fights with Enzo Fiermonte*—the European middleweight who had married Mrs. John Jacob Astor. Enzo was a friend of Paul Gallico's—Gallico loved Italians—so did Enzo, he took his Astor and pugilistic spoils garnered in America back to his Italian wife and their Italian children and became a real Italian war hero in World War II, driving trucks filled with troops against Rommel in Africa. Italians are filled with the joy of living amounting to a philosophical concept, they have nice dispositions, and if flattery can be sincere they possess the art. A childlike quality also—this makes it possible to follow impulses to leave right then at midnight for Yosemite to see that dawn come to over Half Dome. That dawn, I find, charming to remember.

Eventually, Walter Winchell said to Mr. and Mrs. America and all the ships at sea, *Adela Rogers St. Johns will become a bride in September. As soon as her final divorce decree comes through she will marry Ray Helgesen, city editor of the Washington Herald.*

By this time, I'd had my fill of Mrs. Light-Mind and Mrs. Bats' Eyes and Helgesen pulled me up short of even less desirable companions. Ours was no primrose dalliance, and I didn't know whether to run and run or stop right there.

One of the IFs I permit myself, I can't help this one, is what would things be like now if I had married him and we'd taken over the Kansas City paper Pete Jones wanted to buy for us?

Well—the word IF has no future tense, only the past.

BOOK THREE

BOOK THREE

CHAPTER 23

The Trial of the Century.

Damon Runyon, doing the daily running story out of the courtroom in Flemington, New Jersey, was the first one who called it that.

Every newspaperman still says it.

You mean you covered the Hauptmann trial?

> NATION ITSELF ACTS AS JURY TO TRY HAUPT- MANN—Adela Rogers St. Johns is at Flemington to write a special daily article on the trial of Bruno Richard Hauptmann for the kidnap-murder of the Lindbergh baby. Read her story every day in the New York Journal.

Every day.

The day Anne Morrow Lindbergh was on the witness stand to identify the dingy sleeping suit of her baby son.

The day the Lone Eagle, the nation's hero, Lindbergh, was to stand and say, *Yes,* it was the voice of Hauptmann I heard the night we paid the ransom money.

The day Hauptmann fought to save his life under the merciless grueling of the Attorney General.

As you see, I was there.

David O. Selznick had prevented my getting to New Jersey to cover the kidnaping itself, though I am inclined to tell it as it wasn't, and indicate that I did.

Jack Clements and Syd Boehm of the *Journal* kept me in touch with the long, difficult patient work of the FBI, the New Jersey and New York police, and the newspapermen. In September of 1934 they arrested Bruno Richard Hauptmann, a German carpenter who lived in the Bronx. His trial was set for January 2, 1935, in the small town of Flemington, New Jersey.

Clements called to say he'd have a room for me.

I said I hadn't been asked and he hung up, though whether he was sure I would be there, or couldn't be bothered with me since I hadn't been asked, I could not tell. Began that caged tiger routine of never being out of sound of the telephone and leaping to it on one ring only to find it was a bill collector or a magazine editor.

At last at last it was the extension of the Octopus speaking from San

Simeon. "Mrs. Lindbergh will take careful handling in this trial," Mr. Hearst said. "I hope you are free to be there for us."

"Oh yes indeed I am!" I said.

"We cannot endure the kidnaping of our children," he said. "In this trial I am sure we can produce a flame of nationwide indignation that will deter other criminals. As you know, crime is the most dingdong repetitive thing in the world, we must not allow this to become a *wave.*"

This was the order that brought me back from my detour onto the road of what I can call Human Affairs. I would be up tight again as Mama Fix. This would be real newspaper work, alive and crackling with excitement, I was being handed once more the terrible swift sword of the Power of the Press. This time not just for my sister, but for the safety of her children. We would bar her door against evil and danger, for if Anne Lindbergh's door could be hammered in without mercy none of us should ever sleep in peace.

For thirty-one days, I was to write my by-line every day and sometimes twice a day.

(Copyright 1935 International News Service) *Flemington. January 2.* Bruno Richard Hauptmann today went on trial for the brutal kidnap murder of Charles Augustus Lindbergh, Jr., 20-month old son of the Lone Eagle, the first man to fly the Atlantic. Behind the legal battle beginning today in this little, old-fashioned jam-packed courtroom moves a panorama of past events . . .

Past events.

Without that panorama there is no way to understand now all this assignment, as Mr. Hearst gave it to me, meant. Nor the preparation in the small county seat of Flemington to send forth two and a half million words a day to be published in every newspaper around the world. The fever and the furor, the suspense and excitement and heart-involvement grew out of those past events, they magnified the drama and starred its cast.

This had happened to Lindbergh.

It is part of the history of the United States, of those years between the wars, to understand that Lindbergh was our national idol. He was to abdicate later, but in 1927 he became our Number One Hero, cheered and idolized by 125,000,000 citizens, all we then had.

With him aviation became not only a major industry and means of transportation but literally a new way of life in war and peace. A whole new dimension was added.

I find that I, who had spent so much of my life in courtrooms, wrote:

It was probably the most exciting day ever spent in a courtroom, the day of Colonel Lindbergh's cross-examination.

Undoubtedly the most heart-breaking when Anne Morrow Lindbergh identified the sleeping suit.

Qualify your witnesses Again my father's voice echoes down the years.

They were, those two, the most beloved young couple our country had ever known. Stars of real life romance and adventure, dazzling in their youth and beauty and brilliance, we who were still honest romantics were starry-eyed about them.

Nor let it be forgot, that once there was a spot, that for one brief shining hour was known as Camelot.

I want to show you why in those days the Lindberghs reigned in Camelot.

Lindy's take-off for that most famous flight in history was filled with excitement. Chiefly because among the many planning this attempt he was certainly low man on the totem pole to aviation experts. Deac Lyman, ace aviation reporter of those days, told me that suddenly somehow the press covering him at Roosevelt Field had a hunch—a breath-taking, stirring *feeling* that this big, lanky kid was going to make it. This had to come from their nose for news, realistically the odds were 1000 to 1. Many years later, after Deac had won a Pulitizer Prize for his series on why the Lindberghs had gone to live in England, Deac told me that nothing was ever more forlorn than Lindbergh's take-off. No officials, no crowds, not one band or trumpet. No cheers. A sleepless night, watching for a break in the weather, the young airmail pilot came out onto the field at six o'clock and in the raw dawn he looked haggard yet determined. A lot of negatives came with him, as he walked over to his funny-looking Ryan monoplane, built to his own specifications. No co-pilot, no navigators, no radio, no parachute, guided only by a compass, carrying four sandwiches and five quarts of water, he poured out a sixth—the only reason he ever gave anybody about anything was that it allowed him to carry more gas.

Some kind of *nut*. A most unreasonable young man. The tired reporters weren't sure in spite of all he could do that the plane would get off the ground with that extra load of gas, much less fly to Paris.

At 7:25 Lindbergh vaulted into the cockpit of the Spirit of St. Louis. The weary mechanics, who'd been tinkering with the engine all night, got behind and shoved. Anything funnier *or* more pathetic, Deac Lyman told me, than this waddling doodlebug being shoved so it could rise and fly over the trees had never been seen. Everybody waved an excited farewell as it finally did take off, held their breath as it just barely cleared the trees and saw it creep through the gray skies like a fly crawling out of the milk.

They phoned in their stories, went to get breakfast. Within an hour or two the goddam *country* was humming with excitement, the telephone had begun to ring with questions in every newspaper office in our land,

13

the watching and praying had begun. It mounted and mounted for the next thirty-three hours. That *kid* Lindbergh—we began looking up at the sky—maybe he had a wing and the people were adding prayers to try to keep him up there.

Next stop Paris?

Or a watery grave?

The next stop, as all the world should remember, was Paris.

In the three weeks ensuing after he landed in France, Lindbergh loosed the greatest torrent of emotion ever witnessed in human history, according to historian Fitzhugh Green.

As the President of France welcomed our flying ace, the American Ambassador made a speech in which he put Joan of Arc first, Lafayette second, and Lindbergh third in the newly united hearts of France and the United States.

Nobody ever called Charles Augustus Lindbergh *Charlie*. Luckily he had a nickname that fitted him perfectly. We called him *Lindy*.

Lindy and young Prince Leopold of the Belgians appeared together and cheers of joy crashed to heaven. The Prince of Wales took Lindy to the Derby at Epsom Downs and the bands played *Yankee Doodle Dandy* along with *God Save the King*.

His take-off, I remember, was gray, lonely, and forlorn. But Lindbergh came home to the noblest most gigantic welcome any man in history ever received. A fleet of one thousand ships met him in New York Harbor as the cruiser *Memphis* sailed in under the Statue of Liberty.

Jimmy Walker gave him New York City when New York City was Jimmy Walker's to give.

A Presidential car swept him to the White House, Cal Coolidge, with an enthusiasm that in itself was news, made him a full colonel, and decorated him. At a Press Club luncheon Washington correspondents, the toughest group to impress since the headhunters, called him publicly "This onrushing chariot of dauntless youth, the shining knight of the air"—yes they did—their president, my old friend George R. Holmes, came right out with it.

At a dinner for four thousand in New York when he returned in June, after a parade the New York police record as witnessed by nearly five million people, Charles Evans Hughes spoke this totally unprecedented tribute:

> If we measured heroes as we did ships, by their displacement, Colonel Lindbergh has displaced everything and everybody. He fills all our thoughts in America. He has displaced everything that is petty, sordid, or vulgar. He has kindled anew the fires on

our altars. This is the happiest of all days for America and one finds that she is, in the name of Lindbergh, intent only on the noblest and the best.

Looking back now on the radiant hero-worship it's easy to explain what we soon called the Phenomenon of Lindbergh. A rare combination of the man the moment and the deed which life has taught me to watch for. The conquest of the air was new and news as forty years later the conquest of the moon would be.

The heart is always hero hungry.

I cannot tell you how we *loved* Lindbergh.

2

In a story about her coronation Paul Gallico once wrote that every man in England was just a little bit in love with Queen Elizabeth. So, as the staid New York *Times* put it, the women of the world all lost their hearts to Lindbergh.

Nor was this some concocted celluloid phenomenon. And yet his love story was to follow the classic pattern. After his flight he spent a great deal of time making trips to promote aviation. On one of these he went to Mexico City, where he was received, of course, by the American Ambassador, who at that time was Dwight Morrow, partner in J. P. Morgan & Company, a man of wealth, power, and service to his country.

Believe it or not, this distinguished gentleman had three daughters, all of them were at home. Reporters who always followed the news of our national hero's movements sensed romance at once. To their surprise, it wasn't the eldest princess, the Beauty, with whom Lindbergh had fallen in love. Nor the youngest either.

The middle sister.

Anne.

The little one.

The plain Morrow sister.

The shy one who'd written poetry at school but who could sail anything anywhere in any weather in the waters off the Morrow summer home on the rocky coast of Maine.

The one, it turned out, who was to become the best woman writer in America.

I only saw them once in those days. I was writing in a little house in Carmel when they came to be guests of Samuel F. B. Morse, whose great-grandfather invented the telegraph. I went to a party given for the Lindberghs at the Morses' dream house on the shore at Pebble Beach and they were beyond what I had expected. My first thought was, How tiny she is!

Beside him, of course. The plain one? I found her, then and always, beautiful. As the hand of God had created her you were more aware of the light shining through than of the lamp. I was to think this again when I saw her next on the witness stand in the courtroom at Flemington.

Little Lindy when he came along belonged to us too. His official name was Charles Augustus Lindbergh, Jr., and we called him the "Little Eagle." When he was a little over a year old came his father's flight to explore for a new northern route to the Orient, as men had been doing since Sebastian Cabot.

This time the Lone Eagle didn't go alone. In the rear cockpit of his small monoplane as radio operator and co-pilot sat his girl wife Anne. To know them as they were then, only a few months before their Ides of March 1, 1932, you must read *North to the Orient,* Anne Morrow Lindbergh's first book, an account of this flight. A book of which Pearl Buck once said, "It tells humorously and humanly the story of one of the most extraordinary flights of all times."

Though the plane for this exploration was beyond the Spirit of St. Louis, anyone today who'd fly it from Kennedy Airport to the top of the Pan Am Building, much less over lonely icebound country where nobody had been before, would be considered mad.

Again to Lindbergh the problem of weight was vital and constant. *The weight in pounds we carried,* Mrs. Lindbergh wrote later, *must balance that value in usefulness.* (A sound philosophy.)

Lindy even weighed his wife's shoelaces. They used the baby's white scales, it sat in the middle of their bedroom entirely surrounded by untidy piles of not-yet-decided-on equipment. If despite the pontoons the ship got badly damaged, Lindbergh told his wife they were carrying a rubber boat. "If we come down in the middle of the Bering Sea, Charles," his wife said, "it will be a long row to Kamchatka." This time, however, the pilot told her firmly they would have to carry radio.

Of this Mrs. Lindbergh wrote:

"I can see it coming, I can see just what's going to happen. Turning to me he said, 'You will have to be the radio operator.' The next day he came home with a small practice set of buzzers. When I pressed down the key there was a little squeak which brought four dogs and the baby scrambling into my room."

The young Lindberghs were living on the Morrow estate in Englewood, Anne's father had died, her mother was lonely, moreover they would naturally leave the baby with his grandmother.

He'd be perfectly safe and happy there.

Or anywhere. So we thought then.

On a clear hot day, July 27, 1931, they took off and *this* take-off was covered by everything and everybody, huge crowds and radio. Hearing a radio announcer say into his mike, *Mrs. Lindbergh is wearing a leather flying helmet and leather coat and high flying boots,* Anne Lindbergh said to herself, Who, me? and looked down at a cotton blouse already sticky in the heat, at thin rubber-soled sneakers, and light trousers.

Of course from that minute she missed the baby.

In Kamchatka, where they did arrive at last, she met a Russian woman zoologist, who told her that *she* had a little boy. "He is," she said, "in Moscow."

> I said I had a little boy, too. How old is he? Do you have photographs? I took out my photographs and the woman zoologist and the wife of a Russian trapper bent over them with OHs. They were so gay and sweet, spreading them on the table. The trapper's wife made big circles with her hands to show how big his eyes were and pointed to the photographs she liked best. She made me understand by pointing "Here he looks most like you, his mother," and "This is like his father."
>
> When I left them, my boy seemed nearer to me because we had seen his pictures and had talked of him.

How could it be possible for her young American mind to imagine that only seven months later there would be 1752 *hours,* 105,120 minutes, when she would not know whether her son was alive or dead, frightened or hungry or ill-treated by his kidnapers?

We must move the young Lindberghs to that roof tree in Hopewell where the kidnaper crawled through the nursery window.

The year Roosevelt was elected to the Presidency. The year the New Deal began.

At that time the Lindberghs had been married almost three years. Now they began building a home of their own. Why they chose Hopewell, New Jersey, I do not know to this day. Anne's native state is full of flowing water, waterfalls, delightful woods. The spot in the Sourland Mountains that was the scene of a crime heard around the world seemed to me bleak, windswept, even in summer. I went to Hopewell to try to understand the terrain. The big white house seemed stark, or perhaps I couldn't separate it from the windy night in March any more than it is possible to separate the Tower of London from the execution of Lady Jane Grey. In time of course Anne Lindbergh would have had a garden—they hadn't given her time.

You see, it wasn't really a home yet on that March night.

This is one of the things that was to surround so much of the kidnaping with mystery and ceaseless speculation.

The young Lindberghs hadn't really moved in yet. They had brought the Whatelys, the couple who served them, down sometime before, but they themselves had only, so far, come down for weekends. So that Anne could be there to help settle furniture, arrange curtains, begin to get it ready for their own permanent residence. The nursery was finished, a small simple room, an Early American crib-bed with high sides. A table between it and the south window. Living room, dining room, master bedroom next to the nursery, servants' rooms and sitting room, they were now almost finished.

But up to that March 1 the Lindberghs had never spent a Tuesday night at Hopewell.

That weekend they hadn't brought the baby's nurse, Betty Gow, with them. Often Mrs. Lindbergh enjoyed taking all the care of her child herself. However, on Monday, when, because he had a little cold, she thought it would be more sensible not to take him out in the raw March air, one of the Englewood chauffeurs drove Betty Gow to Hopewell.

That last afternoon Anne took a walk in the woods by herself. Coming back she stopped under the window and threw pebbles up and Betty Gow brought little Lindy to wave at her.

A little later—about seven o'clock—she and Betty Gow put the baby to bed. The scene is universal. They rubbed his little chest with Vicks. Then they decided he needed something *warm* over the ointment, so Betty Gow made a little extra shirt from an old flannel petticoat, and sewed it up hurriedly with a particular kind of blue thread borrowed from the cook, Elsie Whately (neither Betty nor Mrs. Lindbergh had as yet brought a sewing kit to Hopewell) who had brought it with her from Scotland—a thread very easy for Mrs. Lindbergh to identify later. They put this on the baby and over that his Dr. Denton sleepers and then tied the small metal guard to keep him from sucking his thumb. They tucked him in and kissed him once more and then Betty Gow pinned the covers down with those horse-blanket safety pins so he couldn't kick them off.

At ten o'clock Betty Gow slipped in without turning on the light to be sure he was warmly covered still. She tiptoed to the crib only by the light from the open door. She felt for him—then her hands a little frantically began to search down—down—perhaps he'd crawled to the foot of the bed as children do.

Do you have the baby, Mrs. Lindbergh?
No—perhaps he's—he must be with his father.
Do you have the baby, Colonel Lindbergh?
No.
Oh please, Colonel Lindbergh, don't play games with him tonight, he has a cold.

Four steps at a time, Lindbergh racing upstairs.

Everything happening at once. The women began that frantic search of every nook and cranny which every mother knows. Three or four times they went over the same places. Desperately the colonel got out his rifle, he had carried it on dangerous flights over South American jungles, before he went outside he told Whately to call the New Jersey State Police.

He hadn't yet seen the note on the sill of the window.

Not till the second time he went into the nursery.

Don't call the police—a warning!

If you do—a threat!

This is a decision I have seen parents forced to make and the indecision span is spent on the rack. Lindbergh had already called the cops and the FBI. Probably he would have anyway.

We will communicate with you, the note said. In script plainly German.

What was there to do but wait?

In the press box later at the trial we saw that the initial work had been bad. Sloppy, we called it. How could it be otherwise? Every policeman there from Colonel Schwartzkopf down was between two fires. This is true on all kidnaping, but Hopewell was the worst. They wanted to find the baby, yet on the one hand Syd Boehm heard Lindbergh threaten coldly to shoot any policeman or agent who dared make a move. Over and over, enforcing it with his rifle, Lindbergh said, *As far as I can I must obey the kidnaper and wait for his instructions.* On the other, was the police reluctance to endanger the kidnaped child.

And nothing could have changed anything, as we were to know.

While the blankets in the crib were still warm, already in those hours while his father and mother, unknowing, ate their late dinner, the Lindbergh baby had been stripped of his homemade shirt and his woolly sleepers and buried in a shallow grave only a few miles away.

The news of the tragedy struck the nation a blow unmatched in our history.

Remember, little Lindy was everybody's other baby. Or if they had none, their only child. We were shot down from heights that up until then had been serene no matter what else went on below. Our *children* were safe.

Kidnaped? The *Lindbergh* baby? Who would DARE?

Our hearts were tied to the heart of that baby's mother. How could she bear it? And she was going to have another one soon. How we knew that I don't remember but we did.

One woman like millions of others, I remember where I was when I heard the news. In 1932 we had no television, we hadn't learned to listen at certain hours for radio news, thus to most of us it came in headlines so big and black it seemed the type must have been especially manufactured for it.

I came up the steps of the Roosevelt Hotel on Hollywood Boulevard with Gene Fowler. Gene was also working for Selznick and also having script trouble. We stood motionless staring at the headline. I cannot print all of what Fowler said but the essence of it was a Shakespearean oration of horror that one desperate criminal was holding the United States with its armies and navies and even its Marine Corps, the Internal Revenue, the Treasury, and the Federal Bureau of Investigation at bay. He could defy them all, for in front of him he held a baby. ANY BABY. We could focus on the Little Eagle, so this had aroused the nation. But surely the United States was safe for BABIES?

He was right. Nobody—*nobody*—could move.

From the White House, from J. Edgar Hoover, from all officialdom down to the cop on the beat the word would be, *Do what the parents want done.*

Circles on the streets, in stores, back and forth from house to house. Where could the baby be? Of course Lindbergh would pay the money, would it be in time? Everywhere women wept, men cursed, we all offered to do anything. That was how Dr. John F. Condon of the Bronx got into the drama. Throbbing with the feeling every man in America had, the good doctor was the one to put an ad in the *Bronx Home News*. It said to the kidnaper, I am to be trusted. To get this child back I will act between you and Colonel Lindbergh as an intermediary.

We waited with Anne Lindbergh.

From March 1 to May 12th.

It is a very long time.

Things did happen under the dark and dire cloud.

Violet Sharpe, an upstairs maid in the Morrow house in Englewood, committed suicide as the police came to interview her.

More ransom notes, insisting the baby was alive and well.

Evalyn Walsh McLean of Washington paid a quarter of a million dollars to recover the baby in what turned out to be a cruel conspiracy engineered by Gaston B. Means.

A well-known yachtsman made a rendezvous at sea to have the baby returned to him. This was a phony and again brought desperate disappointment.

Then on the night of April 2 a thin dark man with hat pulled over his eyes stopped a taxi driver on a dark and deserted road in Van Cortlandt Park and handed him a package to be delivered to the house of Dr. John F. Condon nearby in the Bronx. The package contained the little shirt and sleeping suit the baby had worn. No mistake was possible. Here was the first contact. Also enclosed was a detailed and carefully written order from the kidnaper, with the same circular symbol that had been used on all the notes. Following this, Dr. Condon and Lindbergh went to St. Raymond's Cemetery and, while Lindbergh waited, Jafsie—as Dr. Condon had signed himself in his ads—met the man who called himself John and paid him seventy thousand dollars.

The baby would, the man said, be returned at once—they would soon be told where and when.

It began again—the nation waiting.

On May 12, 1732 hours after the moment on that March night, a weary, waiting, weeping world would learn that the baby was dead—

A man going into the woods stumbled and kicked away the earth from the tiny corpse.

Lindbergh and Betty Gow identified it. And hope was gone.

Again we began to wait.

For more than *two years*.

The Treasury, the FBI, all the forces of law enforcement moved quietly every day, every hour, never leaving the trail, never once giving up. Out of the careful detective work we got a picture, a dossier, of what the Lindbergh kidnaper was, what he would be, when they caught him.

At last a woman in the box office of a movie theater recognized one of the kidnap bills. Yes—she might be able to identify the man who'd given it to her, but she hadn't been aware of it until she counted her cash.

Then an attendant at a gas station got a bill and he did recognize it in time to get the number of the car as it pulled away.

On September 12, 1934, the quietly moving police went to the home of a Bronx carpenter named Bruno Richard Hauptmann, went into his garage, where, nailed behind boards, they found fourteen thousand dollars of the ransom money. They arrested him for the kidnap-murder of Charles Augustus Lindbergh, Jr.

A grand jury hearing. An unsuccessful fight by Hauptmann against extradition to New Jersey.

Then in 1935 we came to Flemington for his trial.

As I said in the beginning, the Trial of the Century.

CHAPTER 24

Everybody said they were going to bed early.

Our beds were scattered all over Hunterdon County. The Union Hotel on the main street of Flemington had been overcrowded for years if it had more than two traveling salesmen at a time. Now its top floor was reserved for the jury and every other room was taken at prices that enabled them to pay off the mortgage. The fact that there was only one bathroom no longer mattered.

The hotel had hurriedly built on a wing with two bars, to become known far and wide as Nellie's Taproom because of a large mongrel female dog who lay across the entrance at all times ignoring tramping herds of people.

The offices of the Attorney General, David Wilentz, were in the State Capitol in Trenton, now he had set up headquarters for himself and staff and entourage at the Stacey-Trent Hotel next door. At the Flemington Country Club rows of cots filled all the rooms, though the surrounding eighteen-hole course was four feet under snow and there was no heat. However quivering reporters, telegraph operators, and general factotums were glad to have anyplace to lie down, if they ever got time. Private homes had rented their spare rooms and doubled up families both out of honest kind intentions toward the frantic press and to put by a little dough for Johnny's college.

I was lucky. I had a beautiful front room with a big closet in the home of one of Flemington's first ladies. At this distance I have only one complaint. She used to sit up for me with hot chocolate, on the theory that the walk from our office to her house had frozen me. I never got up the courage to tell her that hot chocolate on top of Hildick's applejack brandy would have been impossible to keep on a stronger stomach than mine.

Takes a lot of reporters to send that many millions of words daily to that many points around the globe.

We had lots. The best in the world.

So we were all going to bed early. Get a good night's sleep before the trial opened tomorrow morning. Not even one for the road of icy pavements between us and our place for slumber.

It was now the night of New Year's Day.

Why are big murder trials usually in Godforsaken places like the one-horse, one-street towns of the gold rush days in the West? The answer is county seats. Flemington is the county seat of Hunterdon County, where the crime took place.

When everybody said good night right after dinner, I believed them. So I went to my comfortable diggings and, restless as one fly in a room, decided to go back to the office for a minute to be sure I had the spelling right on some names that would come up.

Nobody had gone to bed. Everybody was in our improvised city room. We had taken an apartment above a store one block from the courthouse. Its living room had been converted into a city room, with typewriters jammed against each other, telephones on the floor, a small table with five telephones on it had become the city desk.

Already this was the center of our lives and operations.

What was supposed to be the dining room had the copy desk, the telegraph instruments, and, pasted on the walls, lists of dates, names, places.

Behind this, a bedroom had been turned into a dressing-room-emergency-ward, if you fainted or passed out or needed to comb your hair or retie your tie. On the door of the bathroom someone had placed a large green sign of metal with the word MEN in white, and under this a more decorous gold-and-blue announcement, WOMEN. So there we were. An outsider would have found it difficult to believe this had been an ordinary flat. The few outsiders who did force their way into these sacred precincts —like that left-footed glowworm John O'Hara—were asked to leave or thrown out, bodily or verbally. The city room had flowed over all like lava, obliterating it as completely as Pompeii. The air smelled of smoke, carbon paper, gin and beer, and hot lead, like a city room. Somebody opened a window, a nasty wind blew off the snow outside, somebody else said an infuriated word and banged the window down, cracking the glass. Even at this hour the telephones rang and rang and rang. Whothehell could be calling at midnight?

Mr. Hearst maybe?

In the Hearst service there was, bigod and thank God, always that possibility. *Mr. Mahar, it occurs to me—Mr. Clements, I hope you—Adela, I think we should remember—*

Nobody *but* Mr. Hearst ought to bother us unless Hauptmann had confessed in his cell and he couldn't do that without Jack Clements, our-man-with-Hauptmann, knowing about it ahead of time.

In a space where twenty people would have been a riot, there were thirty besides office boys.

Nobody except the city editor, Eddie Mahar, had taken off his coat. Everybody else still had on coats, mufflers, ear muffs, gloves, hats, and a few knitted caps. This was because they were only going to stay a minute, then we were all going home to bed. Early. Forcrisake the trial starts at ten o'clock and it's now *tomorrow morning*.

It's now *today*.

There we were and there we all stayed.

The hand-picked all-star team of the New York *Journal* and International News Service.

Mike Claffey humming off key and drumming to it with one finger on one typewriter key, rataplan of "They're Hanging Danny Deever in the Morning." Quit that, Syd Boehm said, and Mike made a vulgar sound and changed to "Wearing of the Green."

Sometimes I think of Mike Claffey, who is probably now the police reporter at the press gate for St. Peter. Then I always think of Joan Whitney Payson, who owns the New York Mets. Mrs. Payson came down to attend the Flemington trial one day. She behaved like a great lady and the boys thought she was, so when she invited us to ride back to New York in her Lincoln or Rolls-Royce or whatever we accepted, which usually we didn't, we wanted to talk about the Hauptmann case, and this we never did in front of outsiders. Mike sat beside her and held her hand all the way and told Mrs. Payson things we'd never mentioned to a living soul before and we gave her a permanent subpoena so she could get into the courtroom any time and this is something nobody else ever had.

Sitting around, standing around that night, going back and forth like a cage full of chimps, it got worse and worse. Shouting *Hello* into telephones that hadn't rung and *Come in* to doors when nobody had knocked and I looked once at Clements and I thought he had two heads but it turned out he was just smoking two cigars.

To myself I was muttering, You know how much time you'll have to get out a two-column feature to go alongside Damon Runyon's running story?

Twenty minutes to get the lead on the wire. An hour to finish it.

Sure sure. Why not? Who needs more than an hour?

Not Damon Runyon.

He felt me staring at him and gave me his tight-lipped smile.

I loved that guy. I never knew a first-class legitimate newspaperman, editor, publisher, reporter, who didn't regard Damon Runyon as the greatest newspaperman-reporter who ever lived. One reason when I started this book I had to dig into morgues and the Library of Congress was because I didn't have *one clipping* of all my stuff. That would have been all Damon needed to eliminate me from consideration as a member of the human race—to catch me keeping my own stories, sure mark of the amateur. He never spoke one word of praise to my face, *au contraire,* but every couple of years someone would repeat to me that Damon had said I was the best. A day came at the third-term Roosevelt convention when Howey told Mr. Hearst he was afraid Damon wasn't up to full coverage of the story. Mr. Hearst said, I hope he will be strong enough to do it, if not ask him whom he would suggest. Runyon said Adela's your best bet, she may make mistakes but it'll be *alive*. When Howey told me that I felt I'd been dubbed by the king. I said I couldn't; no one who hasn't seen a master at work, co-ordinating the news, anecdotes from ten different reporters, events from outside, balancing them with the speed of light, writing even as it unfolds so that this will read perfectly and correctly when a new lead of the last-minute news comes in to be put in front—well I knew I couldn't handle it. Fortunately the doctor said Damon could, this was as well, for that Roosevelt third-term convention was the lulu of them all.

I even loved him well enough to get along with his wife.

All this flickered through my mind as I met Damon's eyes across our Flemington city room that night, I probably wanted to think about anything except tomorrow—today's—morning.

Syd Boehm got up and said, "Well, anyhow, thank God the boss fired Floyd Gibbons." This sent us all into giggles and guffaws.

Mr. Hearst had fired the so-he-said-himself-greatest-of-all-first-war-correspondents Floyd Gibbons, the man who made the black patch famous before Hathaway shirts and Dayan, and it wasn't because he took a floor at the Stacey-Trent and brought his attendant nymphs and satyrs with him. Nor even that he wanted four thousand dollars a story. Mr. Hearst never quibbled about money at that level, what you could bring yourself to ask you usually got. He fired Mr. Floyd Gibbons for speaking ill one day of the American Legion, and that's a fact.

Anyway, we were glad he wasn't with us on the Hauptmann trial. This was an assignment for Working Press, no front-page Prima Donnas.

Syd Boehm then said he ought to be getting back to Trenton. He was Our-Man-with-the-Attorney-General, that good-looking young Dave Wilentz. Syd didn't go, he just got up, walked around two or three times, and sat down again. Syd looked like the man who had taken a gun away from Dutch Schultz and told him to *behave*, which he had. None of us would have been the least impressed if we had foreseen that he would become a top writer-producer in the motion picture business. But we were impressed by the fact that he always knew what was going on in the Wilentz camp.

Runyon came over to me and said, "You'll be all right. Why don't you go get some sleep?"

I said, "Oh sure. Damon, the Lindberghs—it's going to be awful for them, they'll have to live it over and over again—over and over—"

"Just in case he didn't do it," Runyon said, "it must be awful for Hauptmann and his wife. Even if he did."

"Do you think he did or didn't?" I said.

"I do not think either way yet," Runyon said, "and neither should you. Some things I need to know more about."

He still wanted to know some things when Hauptmann went to the chair.

Walking around the extemporary copy desk, I saw Amster Spiro. This was the most terrible of the Terrible Men. Why doesn't he stay up in New York, I thought, and tend to his business as city editor of the *Journal?* We have Eddie Mahar on the desk here and for my dough he's a better editor than Spiro. Spiro was talking to his star reporter, John Aloysius Clements, who had a silver plate in his head from a hand grenade someone had thrown at the marines in the Argonne. Now, Clements was giving Spiro the big-shot ex-marine treatment, as he had every right to do, for he had talked to Mr. Hearst. He was telling Spiro and our rubber ears caught it and we shut up to listen.

"No, Mr. Clements," Mr. Hearst had said to him from San Simeon, "not one penny. You may, of course, suggest a chief counsel for the defense, if you have gained a position of trust with the defendant and his wife and his local counsel in Flemington. Their confidence entitles you to do this. By all means, do so to the best of your knowledge. No doubt this would give us an advantage in covering the case. However, we cannot be in the position of paying money to defend a man who is accused by our public servants, the Federal Bureau of Investigation and the State Police and Grand Jury in New Jersey of the foulest crime of our century. Even so, he has a right to the *best* defense possible, and that, unfortunately, is not always that which our law provides. You, Mr. Clements, have every right to find an able and even distinguished defense counsel and I hope you will do so. I suggest that you may find such an attorney will be glad to take this case without a prohibitive fee. Being chief counsel for the defense of a case giving him more front-page exposure than any lawyer has known before will make up for any inadequacy in remuneration. If you have such a man in mind, Mr. Clements, proceed."

Clements was set up for this maneuver.

First, he was pals with Lloyd Fisher, former prosecuting attorney of Hunterdon County, who as Hauptmann's local counsel could handle Bruno and his wife. Lloyd was smart enough to be willing to accept some big-time help.

And Clements had covered Brooklyn in the days of Uncle John McCooey, days when there was more crime in Kings County than any other spot on the globe and Ed Reilly was its leading criminal advocate.

He still hadn't lost any important cases. Obviously the right man to lead the Hauptmann defense. So Clements brought him in.

As it turned out in the short time since Clements left Brooklyn, the ancient Hibernian weakness had caught up with Reilly and neither Clements nor anyone else had quite realized how his affinity for gin had grown.

At the moment of which I write, partly as a result of a New Year's Eve brannigan, Mr. Edward J. Reilly was sleeping the sleep of the intoxicated just, less concerned about the morrow and Hauptmann's needs on the opening day than we were.

I think it was Mike Claffey who told me this, and suddenly a violent storm of emotion shook me and shook me between its teeth until mine rattled.

What was I doing here in this madhouse?

The thing was to call Mr. Hearst right then. Three hours earlier in California and he was always up late. I had asked him to take me off the Leopold-Loeb trial, I couldn't cover a case Clarence Darrow had anything to do with. He must take me off this because I just plain wasn't up to it. Once—sometimes twice?—a day. *Read her daily articles.* Ha ha, I said to myself, Adela Rogers St. Johns has been sitting around taking two—three—four months maybe to write a six-thousand-word short story, one she made up, not bound by facts or events or deadlines. Nobody cared whether it got written except her creditors.

Mr. Hearst, I would say to San Simeon, *I cannot do it.*

I am like a football player who's been making a lush living selling insurance, now they want him to play tight end in the Rose Bowl. Out of condition, fat-in-the-head, hopped up with the imagination, like all fiction writers.

Besides, I have my own trouble. How can I do as big a job as this with my mind on *I ought to be home,* kidnaping isn't the only thing that can happen to children?

They do come first first first—

When I took the Hauptmann assignment I had sent Dicky and his governess to Malibu to stay with my brother Thornwell and his wife. He'd wanted to stay before; if I wasn't at Cow Lane he might as well. Bill and Mac and Hugo were at Cow Lane with Ernest E. Adams, Jr., who would, as he said, hold the fort.

My work. Here it was. Here I was. I wouldn't be long.

On my way to the phone in the bedroom, I heard Spiro telling Clements about the big shots who wanted to get into the trial of the century just for one day, this included all our big advertisers. Get as many subpoenas as you can, he told Clements. This story was going to break all circulation records. Moreover he had begun to think we ought not to come up to New York weekends, anything might break in Flemington any day or night, and Clements and Boehm and Claffey and everybody grinned and said sure sure.

It made me sick. What is wrong with me? This is what comes of being a woman—don't kid yourself—and having children you carried in your womb which their fathers certainly didn't, actually they had very little to do with it, you can get it out of a tube, and they don't have periods when a woman doesn't know which side the moon is buttered on and those come always at a time when you need to be your best. You were right, the modern woman is a failure, she is trying to spread herself too goddam thin, that's what she's trying to do, and you watch—just *watch*—in time men will get so bloody sick of that and what'll happen then I don't know. Something peculiar, I promise you. (I did not then foresee the result in homosexuality, I just foresaw something peculiar.)

I will tell Mr. Hearst I can't do this, I have to be home to look after my children. Look at all the men around here. Are *they* worried about *their* children? Even if the head of the Boy Scouts did tell me the Scouts had been invented to make up for the neglect of the boys' fathers. Hell no—they weren't concerned. They have wives I hope at home taking care of the kids. Look at them. Even Amster Spiro. He has a wife. He looks bright-eyed and bushy-tailed, and here I am dragging my intestines all over the place, they're all on their *toes,* ready for the whistle.

One of my own children kept me in Flemington. Bill, who was *always* on my side. Bill, who was so proud of me and my work. From the moment he slept all night as a baby, I'd known that Bill would be my Faithful. It is Faithful who, on the Pilgrimage, talks of Heart-work. He says something like *Into the moon's wane he goes, unless he Heart-work knows.* He'd offered me Godspeed in what he believed was my Heart-work, had my Faithful. As clear as if I'd called him instead of the Lord of San Simeon, I heard him again. *Get going, Mama. We oughtn't to have people hurting little kids. You write this story like you can, Mama, it'll save other kids sometime.*

I stood with my hand on the door, *listening.*

Other women's children was what Bill meant.

Every word I wrote Bill would read and show to everybody and make them read it, too. Every night on the phone he'd cheer me on in my work. Also Billy knew that our living came out of it and he was one of the few souls I ever knew big enough to bear Gratitude. I guess Bill had a touch of Mr. Greatheart, too. *Give 'em hell, Mama,* he'd say.

I turned back, I was looking straight at John Aloysius Clements, who'd served under Duckboard Butler when the marines landed, I saw he was saying to himself as his sergeant had said to him at Belleau Wood, *Come on, you . . . do you want to live forever?* and just then he said in his Irish-Kentucky accent, "Excuse me a minute, Spi, I've got some pebbles in my shoe," and bolted into the bathroom.

That cheered me some.

Maybe pregame jitters had no sex.

Anyhow you can't quit now.

Mr. Hearst expects every reporter male or female to do their duty.

You better start memorizing those names. You'll have to write too fast to *ask* how that taxi driver, the one that took the package with the sleeping suit from a man in Van Cortlandt Park in the Bronx up to Lindbergh at Condon's house, the one that said the man who handed it to him looked like a *skull,* whether he spells his name Perronne or Perrone or Peronne or Perone.

Dr. John *F.* Condon. That's why they call him Ja*f*sie. What is he doctor of? He was a high school principal. He is an old guy who was spending his life happily minding his neighbor's business and asking why they made so much noise with the garbage cans at 3 A.M.—until he said he'd be willing to act as go-between for the kidnaper to Lindbergh.

The woman's angle.

What exactly this is I have never known though I am always supposed to be it. When I worked for Pan Berman at MGM I practically had a sign hung round me neck. If you want to know the Woman's Angle ask Mrs. St. Johns, poor wretch.

Anne Morrow Lindbergh.

Her mother, the baby's grandmother. Will I ever live to be anybody's grandmother? Probably not.

Betty Gow.

Anna Hauptmann.

Clements came out of the washroom and Eddie Mahar's voice cut into my concentration. He said, "Bruno Richard Hauptmann looks like this new guy they have got over in Germany, the one they call Der Führer, that Hitler. You got to remember Hitler and Hauptmann had exactly the same experience in the war, they were both corporals in the German Army. They must have learned the same kind of brutality. Same *type,* you look and you'll see it."

Runyon's clear voice said, "That doesn't make him guilty. I think we'd better keep open minds—"

A strange silence fell.

In that stuffy smoky hot room we quit pretending we were thinking of other things. We were edgy and simmering and irascible, opening-night scared, even the copy paper was jittery.

I couldn't breathe, I went out into the cold night and, boy, was it *cold.* Six above zero it was in Flemington that night. Stumbling, skidding (I had as usual forgotten my galoshes, they will never be second nature to a

Californian), I arrived at the white clapboard house where I was to sleep. *Sleep?* I'd go in and take a look at my clothes. Mr. Hearst *starred* reporters. My clothes for the Hauptmann trial were on my expense account, Hattie Carnegie had worked them out as a wardrobe. Somebody had to. I could *wear* clothes but I couldn't always select them. They had to be things Papa would have approved, still they had to be noticeable. In front of the big wardrobe I thought of how he had dressed the part for *his* courtrooms. Hattie had made me five dresses of heavy slipper satin, damn-all elegant, in dark and lighter blue, beige, silver gray, and black. Severely tailored with stitched collars and very wide stitched belts. Coats to match of fine wool, lined with soft fur, moleskin and squirrel, mink had not yet come into fashion. I had a series of soft-brimmed hats I had made at Dobbs, very expensive, tailored but flattering. I left those all over the county and at Colligan's Inn, on the Delaware River, our favorite place for all those weeks.

For twenty minutes I kept my mind on clothes, and that's about as long as I ever could. Then I went back outside. On that chill night in March, the kidnaper must have worn gloves, could he carry the baby and hold onto the rungs of the ladder with gloves on? But without them his hands would be as numb as mine and I couldn't light a cigarette. Taking that *baby* out of his warm bed—suddenly the actual moment of the kidnaping was so real my breath made icicles. A dark night, a strange man on a ladder, a *little* boy, my Dicky always crawled out from under even if you pinned him down. Maybe my second husband was right when he made noises about suing me for custody of my son, saying I was an unfit mother if I wasn't there to put him back under the covers. It could be cold and foggy in Malibu, California, in January.

I began to walk as fast as I dared on the ice. Elaine was married to Gallico, they were in Rome. My Bill was a boy who hit with men on bases. But Dicky—Dicky was still practically a baby. I should be home.

But—everyone had been home that night three years ago. Little Lindy's mother and father. The Whately couple. His nurse. After dinner the colonel sat in the library and the ceiling of the library was the floor of the nursery, that's how close they were. Not a big house like Englewood.

Of course the wind was howling outside.

What was that?

Lindbergh said that to his wife as they sat for a few moments in the living room after dinner.

> *Q.* You heard a sound, Colonel Lindbergh?
> *A.* I heard a noise somewhere around nine o'clock, as though someone had dropped the slats of an orange crate.
> *Q.* Might it have been a ladder?
> *A.* Yes, it might have been a ladder, outside, falling.

Anne hadn't heard anything. But Lindbergh's pilot's ears had caught what could have been the kidnap ladder rungs jammed against the wall of the house. Nobody did anything. Who would think of a murderer crawling into the house with five people there, one of them Colonel Lindbergh?

But—the crib was empty when Betty Gow went up at ten o'clock.

"I never saw him alive again," Anne Lindbergh had said.

Oh God!

I got through to my house at Malibu. Naturally, Dicky was asleep. His governess said he was *sound* asleep. Yes, the door between her big room and his sleeping porch was open.

Could I please talk to him?

Certainly not, Cracker said firmly. Did I realize it was past midnight? Call him in the morning, she said, but in the morning I would be in court for the trial of the murder of Anne Morrow Lindbergh's son. If Little Lindy hadn't been safe, how could any child ever be?

Hard to overcome a Nanny, but I said, Cracker I'm sorry, I've got flimflams or something I won't be able to work—just a minute, it won't hurt him, he goes right back to sleep—

Dicky was too sleepy at first to know who I was but I knew who he was. And finally he said, When are you coming home, Mama, and I said, Oh real soon, real soon—

Actually, it was nearly two months. And what a homecoming!

I wanted to go then, that minute. I wouldn't think of going now, I wouldn't miss this trial for anything, I was up to my eyebrows in it.

In the bar where I went, partly because it was warm, I ran into Jim Kilgallen, spare, dynamic, equal of any reporter but Runyon. I said, "Look, Jim, you've been on this from the beginning. Have we got the right man?"

He said, "We know the Lindbergh kidnaper very well. The taxi driver, Jafsie Condon, Lindbergh himself, they've told us certain things. He spoke with a German accent, that's for sure.

"He wrote in German script. All the notes tell us that.

"He lived in the Bronx. The ad he answered and the Bronx cemetery for a meeting place and he drove a car with a Bronx license.

"He was probably a carpenter, the ladder was home-built.

"Around five foot nine inches. Dark hair, that's from Jafsie and the taxi driver, Perronne—

"If the man we pick up speaks with a French accent, if he lives on Staten Island, if he is fat and blond and works as a waiter—then we begin to wonder if we have the right guy—but everything we knew about the kidnaper before we ever heard of Bruno Richard Hauptmann is *true* of him, the man who had the kidnap money—"

Walter Lister of the *Post* came roving around the corner, he said, "One thing is for sure it cannot be any *gang* operation—the money's too small—

seventy thousand dollars for the grandson of a Morgan partner? Hell, they could have had fifty million—"

"Mr. Hearst would have mortgaged San Simeon," I said, not knowing he already had!

Is this being a schizophrenic? I have forgotten all about my children. I am a reporter, I love my work, work is the first thing as it always is with me, love is of man's life a thing apart, the woman's viewpoint is that 'tis woman's whole existence, it isn't mine, not any more.

I went out again restlessly, I thought I would walk around the block to get some fresh air before I went to bed.

A town filled with ghosts.

Figures passed without speaking. Dark shapes appeared around corners. A man I passed near the Baptist Church was Paul Mallon of the New York *Times*. What did he have to be nervous about? The *Times* would print anything and everything. They always did; by dull writing and duller make-up they'd think they made respectable all the scandal and dirty words and nastiness we of the yellow press didn't consider fit to print.

To my amazement I saw Runyon.

The great Runyon sprinting along as though prodded by a pitchfork. We stopped as casually in a whirling eddy of snow as though we were in the city room and he said, "Even circumstantial evidence must give him opportunity—must put him on the scene of the crime within the limits of the time when the crime was committed."

"The kidnap note found on the table in the nursery," I said, "if Hauptmann wrote that, that would do it."

"Anybody could have put that note on the table no matter who wrote it," Runyon said.

I remember circling around with other muffled figures so I could stand under the jail window. In the second floor corner cell where Hauptmann is confined the light is on. No sleep for him, either. Is he sitting with his head sunk in despair? Is he raving and ranting the way Hitler now raves and rants in Germany? Is it the furies of guilt or of injustice nipping at his heels as he goes back and forth in that cell?

What will he be like when he comes into court tomorrow—today?

What will I *feel* about him when I see him again?

The Lindberghs at Englewood—sleepless too. Must be. Lindbergh had gone sixty-three hours without sleep when he flew the Atlantic five years ago. He could take it. But could he? On top of his sorrow he was going into an unbottomed boundless Valley of Humiliation.

Some also have been maimed there in the Valley of Humiliation and could not to their dying day be their own men again.

As a young hero he had abhorred the glory spotlight, even when he was their idol he had never been at ease with crowds. Now this vast and terrible spotlight would show him flying not for worlds to conquer but at the orders of a criminal, in a senseless horrid hoax.

Hey doktor hey doktor.

A strange voice, the voice of his son's kidnaper, shouting over a cemetery wall. Across the road he sat helpless while the old man, Dr. Condon, paid the ransom money.

Tomorrow and tomorrow and tomorrow would find him a few feet from this man whom the state charged had killed his son, dire and dreadful enough but under the vast spotlight his pride would burn to shame; he had not been able to protect or save his son. Laying bare his soul, his agony, the sympathy of the multitudes was something he did not want.

The Lone Eagle must be dreading his day in court almost as much as Hauptmann.

I don't know why I was so sure of this Valley of Humiliation then—now in retrospect I know it was true.

I never did get to bed. Who needed it?

I bathed and changed my clothes and decided on the dark blue outfit for opening day. I tried to put it on *with an air,* so it would justify that huge ITEM on my expense account. So that, no matter if Mrs. Bryan Foy and Mrs. James J. Girard and Mrs. Astor and her horse and Mrs. Macy and Gimbel and Bloomingdale all showed up, I would still look the way Mr. Hearst wished his star reporters to look. In the mirror I saw that I looked straggly and sleepless and pea-green in spite of my peacock feathers.

I hoped Attorney General Wilentz for the prosecution and Ed Reilly and Lloyd Fisher for the defense were good lawyers. It's hard to make a great trial stand up without first-class lawyers.

At breakfast in the Union Hotel Runyon wouldn't let me have any brandy in my coffee.

So right.

At eight o'clock I climbed three steep flights of stairs to the cupola in the courthouse. Runyon's running story would be written in heavy black pencil on sheets of gray copy paper in the press box. Visconti, who could decipher the Dead Sea Scrolls, would take it across the hall and put it straight on a Western Union wire set up there. A typewriter and teletype machine had been set up for me in this hole under the eaves. As soon as each session was over I'd write there and the operator would get it in takes and teletype it to the *Journal* and INS.

I wanted to find out how long it would take me to climb from my seat at the end of the jury box to my typewriter.

I wouldn't have much time.

Court would recess at twelve. I ought to have my lead on the wire by twelve-twenty.

An unexpected Big Moment took place even before court opened.

We were jammed, packed in there for the first time. Judge Thomas Trenchard, magnificent and stately in his robes, swept from his chambers onto the bench. As he stood there, a figure inside the rail, a thin, ordinary figure in a gray suit stood so quickly that his guards didn't make it and so Bruno Richard Hauptmann and Judge Trenchard faced each other in that opening moment, the only two upright in the packed room.

An ordinary man come to the Bar of Justice to have his case heard by those of his peers who would fill that empty jury box, his rights protected by all the gowned majesty of the Law in the person of the Judge on the Bench.

Then the clerk cried, *Oyez oyez,* and everybody broke out of the trance and the two deputies moved swiftly up beside Hauptmann.

But for a breath-taking moment there had been only Hauptmann, face to face with our justice, which told us that we must presume him innocent.

CHAPTER 25

We lived from that day on in a world called the Hauptmann Trial. As sealed off yet visible as a goldfish bowl.

What the Newspaper Guild, poor things, would have thought of the twenty-eight-hour shifts the Working Press put in I don't know. We worked at many levels behind the scenes as well as under the world's spotlight in the courtroom. We knew that, given this Cast of Characters, this Greek tragedy of story, this dynamic suspense we had going for us a masterpiece, as superlative in its field as Titian's *Entombment* or Wagner's *Ring* or *King Lear*. Our sense of personal responsibility gunned us into superhuman efforts and while no laboratory records were kept I can tell you it is possible to work at the speed of light for six weeks without sleep.

Once at Friendship, Evalyn Walsh McLean's most famed house in Washington, I heard J. Edgar Hoover say to an Assistant Attorney General, one Thurman Arnold, "Never overlook the genius for investigation of top reporters. Sometimes they break a case before we do. Often they bring us invaluable material."

In order to give the seething atmosphere of this Trial of the Century it is essential to reproduce what went on behind the scenes *all the time*. We existed minute by minute at the point of a possible *break*. We had to live geared to handle it, whatever its magnitude. Nobody was ever sure of anything. Clouds of witnesses were lined up by both the prosecution and the defense, any change in the story of almost any one of them would blow the case sky high. For instance, we knew Dr. John F. Condon to be, in many ways, an eccentric old man, suppose at the last moment he refused to identify Hauptmann as the man to whom he paid the money in St. Raymond's Cemetery? Dave Wilentz was terrified of this. Suppose the defense could produce the witness they were always looking for, a *reliable* one supporting Hauptmann's alibi. Or some new documentary evidence from the Wall Street brokerage firm where Hauptmann had parlayed forty-four thousand unexplained dollars into nearly a quarter of a million at one point.

Above all, *a confession*.

How we longed for that, both as the greatest story and as a full clarification of all the mysteries and coincidences surrounding us day and night.

About these, our investigations never ceased. Everyone of the hundreds of experienced, trained, powerful Working Press reporters had his own theory, his favorite piece of missing evidence, the unsolved unexplained puzzles in this labyrinth.

Runyon spent hours over the handwriting. If Hauptmann had written the notes this came close to putting him on the scene of the crime and Runyon, his eyes bluer and frostier than ever, still insisted on proving *opportunity*. He carefully compared the note left on the window sill with samples Hauptmann had written after his arrest by order of his captors.

Singnature—for signature—in all the notes.

Boad—for boat.

All in the rough Germanic script.

Violet Sharpe was always Jim Kilgallen's Thing, as they say nowadays.

Just who was Violet Sharpe that all papers headlined her death by her own hand in letters a foot high?

> *Q.* (by Mr. Reilly) You had other maids besides Violet, Mrs. Morrow?
>
> *A.* Oh yes—six other maids I believe.

Mrs. Dwight Morrow, widow of the ambassador, mother of Anne, grandmother of Little Lindy.

If O. Henry had written it he might have called it "There's a Broken Heart for Every Light on Broadway Bagdad on the Hudson U.S.A."

"It wasn't me. It was the *money.*"

That was the classic heartbreak line Violet Sharpe said to the taxi driver that hooked Jim Kilgallen, so that he had to solve the mystery of her suicide. The driver had brought her home to Englewood in the late late hours of the night the baby was taken from Hopewell. She started to pay him and found she didn't have her purse. *It wasn't me.* Of course she had hoped to slip in without being seen, but when they drove up in the predawn every light in the Morrow mansion was blazing. *It was the money.* The butler had to pay the driver and he let her sneak upstairs, but it would have to come out later. When it turned out she'd been out all that night, she had to be questioned. Four days after the tragedy when Violet looked out her third-story window and saw police cars drive up, she took poison. So the cops couldn't get any answer to where she'd been until dawn—they had a piece of the puzzle that cried out for investigation, explanation, they were sure it must have something to do with the kidnaping.

It wasn't me. It was the money.

With that as his key clue, Jim Kilgallen found out where Violet Sharpe had been that night.

What money? The ransom?

"She looked," the taxi driver told Jim, "what I'd call dazed, like some-body hit her on the noggin." Well—somebody had. A shady hustler whose line was recognizing lonely domestics on payday in New York City. Pin-stripe suit, padded shoulders, fancy handkerchief, tight collar—the uniform then of the petty hustler anywhere between Times Square and Fifty-second Street. He was sauntering in front of a movie palace where a Garbo picture was running. On their day off, domestics went to the movies, Garbo was their idol. Sure enough, a plain girl in a coat with a fur collar, upstairs maid written all over her to his expert eye. Eager, forlorn, and—oh sure, lonely. With practiced skill, this womanizer picked her up, they sat through the show twice. The girl was, he admitted later, swept off her feet so they went up to his room. How the hell was he to know, he shouted frantically, that he'd picked up both a virgin and a gal mixed up in a kidnaping, for if there is anything a cheap crook does not wish to be mixed up in it is a kidnap-ing that turns out to be murder. Everything changes then.

When she saw Colonel Schwartzkopf and his men approaching she faced her *shame,* she'd have to tell about her cheap shame that was her alibi. *It wasn't me, it was the money in my purse.* She'd lose her job. Mrs. Morrow was a kind and generous lady, but she had a strict moral code for the help. And the police. *My mother always told me never to get mixed up with the police.* Poor plain Violet Sharpe from Wales, when she heard police feet pounding up the stairs she said to herself, *I'd rather be dead.*

Sometimes that's true.

A pitiful, corny, cheap little story, isn't it?

It was press investigation that found out where Violet Sharpe was in the dark hours of March 1, but as Jim Kilgallen said, Whatever Violet had done she shouldn't, relative to the kidnaping—if she talked too much? —told something quite innocently?—it had been done long before that night.

The trouble with this case, Julia McCarthy of the *News* said, we are expected to believe too many coincidences both ways.

Joe Mickler, who came of a banking family in Florida, had a hangup about the ransom money—he wanted to trace some other ransom bills.

Eddie Mahar never trusted any police anywhere so he reinvestigated everything they told him they'd investigated.

Mike Claffey was a photo finish ahead of the prosecution, as his over-seas phone bills proved. If, Mike said, he's guilty, there ought to be something in his past back in Germany, huh? Clements had a similar idea in the defense direction—how about Hauptmann's *mother* telling what a good boy he'd always been? He paid for a call for Ed Reilly but when they got through to Kamitz it turned out she could speak no English and they knew no German, so they ran up $176 worth of *Hoch Frau Hauptmann* and gave it up.

As for me, my private eye was upon one facet nobody else ever mentioned. In a story from the courtroom I wrote:

> What about the druggist in Pennington, only a few miles from Hopewell, who says that a man and a woman drove up before his store on the night of March 1, 1932, at seven o'clock, that the man stayed in the car but the woman came in and bought a can of cleaning *chloroform.* Well, he couldn't identify the woman, he didn't see the man, but many of us who knew the Hauptmann trial best never forget this incidence—or coincidence.

My mystery had to do with chloroform.

"I can see no basis for this at all," Runyon said to me.

"You know all about lots of things," I remember saying hotly. "I know about babies. He wasn't a baby, really. He was a strong, active little boy twenty months old. Not helpless. Damon, somebody took him from under those pinned-down blankets, carried him across to the window, climbed out the window with him. The covers of the crib weren't even disturbed and it's not easy to pull a child that size out from under them, it's a weight, they squirm, it would have waked him up. I tell you he would *holler,* he would begin to fight and make a noise. Remember the kidnaper would have to find the ladder with his feet and have one hand free to hold onto the window as he went out—he could hold the baby in the other arm but he wouldn't have a hand to put over the baby's mouth if the baby started to shriek or even whimper—"

"Umm," Runyon said, "perhaps that's when he dropped him—"

"But Colonel Lindbergh was in the room just below," I said, "and I'm one who believes this fiend didn't want to kill the baby yet, he was worth more if the parents had proof he was alive. I tell you—I have a hunch that the man used chloroform—"

Runyon looked at me coldly, "Nobody smelled it in the room right afterwards," he said.

"All it needed with a little fellow like that was a whiff," I said. "If we set the actual time by Lindbergh's hearing something fall, an hour passed before Betty Gow went in, the window was open, and besides honestly Damon everybody running around frantically the way they did, who'd notice a little whisper of chloroform if it lingered that long which I doubt."

To keep you quiet, Syd Boehm told me, so in time we began to scour drugstores in the area though, as Syd pointed out ad nauseam, if anyone planning this crime bought chloroform there's a drugstore on every corner in New York New Jersey and Pennsylvania.

But one evening in Flemington after I'd finished a radio broadcast with Gabriel Heatter about the day's events, Syd and I found what I will always believe was the *right* drugstore. In a small town not far away.

We tried to be casual, we didn't tell the druggist we were reporters. We just sort of asked in a gossipy vein whether he'd been in his store the night of the crime in 1932, and he said yes he was always there, he owned it—hard to get responsible help. Chloroform—? No, he didn't recall any. Yes, they'd have to sign a book; no, no signatures in February or on March 1 of 1932. There had been a woman who bought some hat cleaner with chloroform in it, quite a lot of chloroform, but you didn't have to sign for that and she'd been in a big hurry, he remembered.

We never found that woman. Probably she wouldn't have connected up with the case if we had. This, however, is one of the reasons so many of us fought to have Hauptmann's sentence commuted to life rather than death. We wanted to work together on a number of unsolved bits and pieces that might have fitted into the vacant holes left in the gigantic puzzle. Even to this day.

From where I am now and considering what I proclaimed so loudly I was then, I find it both interesting and amazing that under pressure and in this madhouse, my first article out of that courtroom was headlined:

LET US PRAY FOR JUSTICE

Adela Rogers St. Johns Says Let Us Pray For Full Truth

Somebody kidnapped that baby, somebody killed him, somebody left Lindy and Anne to those nights and days of hell and crucifixion.

Who was it?

Today we begin the trial of Bruno Richard Hauptmann for that crime.

We the jury selected in this courtroom, We the people whom they represent must determine.

Is he guilty or innocent?

If he is innocent, he is a martyr and I know no way he can be recompensed for what he suffers. If he is guilty, may God have mercy on his soul for I don't think any of us are Christian enough to have any mercy on the murderer of Little Lindy. So now we must pray with all our hearts that in this courtroom where I now sit justice and nothing but justice be done. Pray that the judge and the jury may see with clear eyes and pure hearts, that they may weigh the evidence that will be presented with wisdom and honesty, that truth may carry its own power to make itself recognized as truth, and that it may give us a strong light through the coming days of confusing testimony to be given by both sides so that no mistakes are possible.

No one could go into that courtroom even for a day, no one could live with it as we did, without being shaken to the depths. No one did.

You gotta have heart.

If you have heart you are overpowered by this tragedy fate has written. Then how could it be that I was praying and asking other people to pray, in a universe where such a thing was possible? If I had been making a world it would have been one where such grief and disaster couldn't *be*.

Yet that first story, certainly at this distance in time both honest and ardent and sincere, makes plain that in the deeper level of me I automatically began to pray. Anger or no anger, sleep or no sleep, applejack or no applejack—where did it come from? Out of old teachings that were part of the fibers of my heart? Out of human instinct never defeated, a spirit stronger than we are?

I didn't know.

We ate sometimes in the church, where the ladies of the congregation had a dining room and cooked food and sold it, a happy change from the Union Hotel Cafe. They prayed for faith. One said strength, I remember.

Mike Claffey went to Mass most mornings. I asked him what he prayed for and he said *grace*. A word I didn't think about often any more.

Most of us began to pray quite simply that we'd all live through this.

CHAPTER 26

This is not a saunter down Memory Lane.

My return now to the Hauptmann courtroom in Flemington has a poignancy that is painful, exciting, and unbelievably real to me in reproduction. A clear definite total return to another incarnation in which I was young, a star reporter, and lived in that time-space called the Hauptmann trial.

Looking back, I do not think I can match in any remake what I wrote under the gun, so to some extent I will try to do it in reruns.

Under the date of January 3:

> In this small, drab old courtroom, packed with humanity, we are again living every horror, every anguish, every suspense, every dastardly step of the murder of our Little Eagle. And here we are seeing and hearing the real people to whom it all happened.
>
> The impassioned heartfelt eloquence of Attorney General Wilentz takes us back to the Lindbergh nursery—
>
> And there in the courtroom we see Anne Lindbergh sitting in the second row, her fine clean-cut face a medallion of grief.
>
> The squirming moving crushing crowd, the jury, look at her once and then turn away. Lindy's face is down in his hands.
>
> Wilentz goes on, his face glistening with sweat, his shoulders shaking as he swings and points at Hauptmann. The Bronx carpenter sits stolid, hard, defiant a few feet away.
>
> We hear the brutal story as Wilentz tells it, we see this carpenter quitting his job the very day after the ransom was paid.
>
> Now we are told what the State means to prove.
>
> Anne Lindbergh comes back quietly after lunch. Her tight little black satin hat has a bow across the front. Her black silk suit is lightened by a small pattern in white, her blouse is softly pink. But it does not warm her misery.

At the time I wrote:

> One question hammers in my head.
>
> Is Bruno Hauptmann, the young German carpenter, capable of the crime of which he is accused? In every murder it must be determined for me at once whether the man is mentally, morally, psychologically capable of doing this *particular* deed?

I watched him. Then—I knew. I knew in my stomach. In my woman's intuition, in my visceral reactions, in my reporter's sixth sense. If I was as good as Mr. Hearst thought I was, or I wouldn't have been there with the salary I was getting and the headlines on my stories, then I had to take this overwhelming conviction seriously.

"He did it," I said to Runyon.

"Someday," Runyon said, "your jumping to conclusions ahead of the evidence via your emotional tracts is going to get you into trouble."

In the courtroom we had a judge. No one of greater stature or wisdom ever sat on the bench than Justice Thomas Trenchard. He made fewer mistakes in his rulings, the trial was almost without error. We had a jury. As average as any ever seen. Two of them were the fattest women to be found, but I had a personal predilection for Rosie Pill just the same. A lot of my life had been spent telling my father after court how the third man from the end in the back row had reacted to that day's witness. I always watched Rosie Pill. Impossible to deceive Rosie Pill's amiable, tough-core common sense. She had a steady eye, did Rosie Pill.

From the first day, I thought it was a mistake that Hauptmann had Reilly as chief counsel. In Brooklyn, yes. In Flemington, he was a City Slicker. While personally I have always found the Country Slicker much more effective, in this case sandy-haired, freckled-faced Lloyd Fisher understood the jury of *his* neighbors and they understood his Sourland Mountains twang better than Reilly's Irish eloquence. None of this had any effect on the final verdict. It might have made us feel Hauptmann had a better shake.

2

Five weeks. Thirty-one days of testimony.

Some routine. Some ridiculous. From the beginning it was plain that the outcome even more than usual must depend on what witnesses the jury believed.

"The credibility of the witness is your responsibility and you must make your own decision in this matter," the judge would instruct them.

Can they believe it possible for Lindbergh to identify a voice he heard speak only two words?

Will they believe the experts?

Or a taxi driver's identification from one quick look in the dark at a face like a *skull* as an unknown handed him a package to be delivered to the go-between.

The witnesses never to be forgotten by me:
> Anne Morrow Lindbergh
> Charles Augustus Lindbergh
> Betty Gow
> The experts on wood and handwriting
> Dr. John F. "Jafsie" Condon, the go-between
> Bruno Richard Hauptmann

These gave us what in every trial are called:

THE BIG MOMENTS

I would like to give here the story I wrote of Mrs. Lindbergh, who was the first witness after we got a jury and the official identifications of the power of this court to try this case.

> We who sit in this courtroom have seen something we will never forget. When Anne Lindbergh sat on the witness stand we saw a slim young thing in black who will never be entirely happy again but who, a great woman and a great lady, was courageous in sorrow and gallant in grief.
>
> Anne Lindbergh didn't break, she didn't faint. None of the things movie actresses do in big scenes.
>
> I would rather have seen her break than to behold that brave smile. I would rather have seen her faint than watch those pauses when her face grew whiter and whiter and it took every drop of her courage to speak at last. I would rather have seen gallons of tears than the blue eyes looking blindly for help.
>
> Did you ever put warm woolly sleepers on a baby you loved? There is something about them, about the silly, foolish little feet and the feel and smell of them, about the little pants that button across the back that makes your heart go soft in its happiest moments.
>
> The Attorney General of New Jersey took up a pair of those woolly teddy bear sleepers and held them before Anne Lindbergh. She froze at sight of them. She had put them on her baby the night of March 1, 1932. Buttoned them—and you knew that as she did so she'd held him close and kissed the top of his head. And he'd laughed with glee.
>
> "I never saw him again," she said.
>
> You knew how effective she had been as a witness when Mr. Reilly let her go without one word of cross-examination. He wanted to get her off that stand, he knew he couldn't make anybody doubt her.
>
> *Q.* He was a perfectly normal child, Mrs. Lindbergh?
>
> *A.* Oh yes—perfectly normal.
>
> *Q.* He had begun to walk and talk?
>
> *A.* Yes he—had begun to walk and talk.

With those short and simple questions by the Attorney General, enter the ghost of the Lindbergh baby.

Never to leave us again.

I remember it as a bit of irony that as I went out of the courtroom green with anguish I met Lloyd Fisher of the defense bound on the same seasick errand. We had just watched Mrs. Lindbergh leave the stand, walking with careful dignity.

Everyone I have asked for the Great Moment of the trial has, without one exception, said Mrs. Lindbergh on the witness stand. She gave us a new dimension.

Colonel Lindbergh, will you take the stand, please?

There he was, America's idol still, in spite of all he could do to reject it.

The chair on the witness stand must be smaller than a cockpit, he's so uncomfortable in it. His enormous hands—he tries to keep them still. Thirty. Oh no, he's got to be more than *thirty*? A film of fat, just a film, has poured over the lanky boy since May 20, 1927—an Eagle? A caged Eagle!

In the main a repetition of Anne's story, Lindbergh's direct examination held one sequence with which she had nothing to do.

The payment of the ransom on the night of April 2.

This was the second Big Moment.

"I for one," Jim Kilgallen said to me, "am going to have grave difficulty in believing any man can identify a voice repeating two words as the voice of a particular man with an accent it's so easy to imitate."

That epitomized the opinion of the Working Press.

I kept turning it over. Lindbergh himself, writing of his historic flight, had spoken of hearing the clouds move by. That's poetic-space-license, isn't it? I said to myself. On the other hand Captain Eddie Rickenbacker told me that in the war pilots heard things other people couldn't and my brother Bogart said he once got a call for help he couldn't possibly have heard but did, and went to a rescue he wouldn't have made otherwise. Isn't that a sixth sense flyers develop?

Quiet as he was on the stand, you knew what that waiting had meant.

Q. What was the weather like?

A. The visibility was clear.

So he *waited*. Nearby Dr. Condon was following the minute instructions for meeting the kidnaper. And Lindbergh knew that the man who had his baby was only a few feet away. In seconds, they might know where the baby was. In an hour—a few hours— he might be able to take his son back to his mother. Or—something might go wrong. Careful—they had to be so careful. They were in this man's power. Lindbergh is not a good waiter, you sensed that as he described this time. But he was a man of great self-discipline. So he waited silent and motionless. Then came the voice from inside the walls, directing Condon—"Hey, Doktor—Hey, Doktor—" it called in a shrill whisper.

That was all. Condon came back, they would be instructed further that night.

In jail, Lindbergh was taken to hear Hauptmann repeat those two words.

Would he make a positive identification? Nobody knew. Not even, we thought, the Attorney General. Nobody ever knew any more about what Lindbergh was going to do than if he'd been the Sphinx. I have never known a press box so utterly silent and motionless, not even when Wilson asked Congress for a declaration of war. The moment had arrived, it held us fascinated, breathless. Mr. Wilentz asked him:

Q. The voice you heard in the cemetery that night saying *Hey Doktor Hey Doktor*—have you heard that voice again?
A. Yes.
Q. Whose voice was it?
A. It was Bruno Hauptmann's.

For the first time, Lindbergh swung in the witness chair and looked square at Hauptmann. He had done it. He had made the positive identification. He had named *Hauptmann* as the kidnapper.

My first reaction was Lindbergh is *sure*.

Watching Lindbergh today in this ordeal I cannot believe he would swear away the life of any man unless he was sure. Automatically, I looked at the jury, even before I looked at Hauptmann.

Yes.

I think they believed Lindbergh, too. I found out later that I was right about this, the jurors told me that he had convinced them.

One climax after another. Next, the cross-examination of Lindbergh following his identification of the voice in St. Raymond's as that of the defendant.

As he waited for the defense chief counsel to move into the space before the witness stand, I felt there should be around and behind him a dark and stormy sky, a gray and threatening ocean, wildly cheering throngs. Not this background of the shabby old courtroom, the embarrassed jury, the avid heterogeneous craning audience, against these and the attentive press he was *awkward* and incongruous.

To understand the vibration of shame and humiliation that were an aura around him it is necessary to know what he felt about the press.

He loathed reporters and detested crowds and resented both. Now here he was at their mercy.

If he could accept the Phenomenon of Lindbergh, Mr. Hearst had once outlined to him, he could be the most powerful leader in the world of aviation, scientific, military, and commercial. This came to naught, for Lindbergh himself refused it as soon as possible.

An early airmail pilot I met once in Albuquerque told me that Lindbergh had been determined to fly the Atlantic without anybody but a few aviators and airplane factories knowing about it, and the men who put up the money for the Spirit of St. Louis, to boost their home town, and the men in the Ryan plant had to force him to make it known at all.

"He was very naïve about publicity," Amelia Earhart said to me.

Under the diary date of October 1934, Harold Nicolson writes most sympathetically from Englewood, where he was researching a biography of Anne's father, Dwight Morrow: "Lindbergh opened his heart to me on the subject of publicity. He absolutely loathes it. He says the worst of this trial is that he has again become front page news and the persecution is again beginning. He says he cannot walk down the street unless disguised and that it is impossible for Anne and him to go to the theater together. This is all right, he says, for your Prince of Wales and people like that because they have an organization to protect them. I haven't. Then he paused and thought carefully. But then, he said, of course they have to be polite whereas I don't, so it works both ways I suppose."

There was another aspect of it working both ways, as Mr. Hearst pointed out to me. "He is unable to handle the press," he said, "since he believes he has a right of privacy. As with so many other people, he wants it both ways. He wants the benefit of the press to spread his doctrines on aviation, but he will never concede that once ready to support *his* doctrines the people have a right to know him as a man. The gift of handling the press well does not always accompany gifts that make it necessary to handle the press at all. A great statesman like Woodrow Wilson failed in his holiest objective for lack of it."

No, Lindbergh never had the gift—nor wanted it.

So that he came to the terrible publicity of the crime of murder, the manhunt for the kidnaper, the trial in which he had to go into open court like any other citizen with this obsession full-blown. Any father would have had to go through a heartbreakingly difficult ordeal as a witness in the kidnaping of his child. To Lindbergh, with his hatred of publicity and public exposure, his never-ceasing suspicion of everything and everybody connected with the press, this was indeed the *Valley*.

Take the witness, Mr. Reilly.

Here came Reilly, lumbering forward.

Shook up as I was, I was swept by a wave of nostalgic grief and pain as great as any I had ever known in my life.

The smell of this musty courtroom. The sameness of its furniture. The jury so like all juries of anybody's peers. The vibrating hum of excitement, the cool of the press. It became powerful in making my heart lift with a memory and sink with the knowledge that it was only a memory and would never again be anything else.

Take the witness, Mr. Rogers.

Oh—I wanted to see *Papa* so bad my whole being choked with tears. I wanted to see Papa, slim, elegant, shining, coming through with such grace to cross-examine Franklin in the Darrow case or Gallagher in the San Francisco graft cases.

Instead it was Ed Reilly of Brooklyn. A tank of a man in striped trousers and cutaway coat.

Within seven seconds I knew Reilly was a fool, a blundering wet-brained egomaniac, and that what must forever remain an important cross-examination in the annals of American jurisprudence was to be a catastrophe.

> Mister Edward J. Reilly on cross-examination of the Ace of the Air came in swinging.
>
> Why?
>
> You saw a bull-necked, florid, experienced lawyer with a cold blue eye, heavy shoulders, heavy voice. Chief Counsel for the Defense, standing square and glowering.
>
> He made a big mistake, if I am any judge of lawyers and I have watched the greatest of them since I was eight years old. Reilly's hostility hummed in his opening question, his cross-examination was an instant attack. Lindy, held relaxed-by-force, became aware of it with amazement.
>
> *Q.* Didn't you know there was a good deal of antagonism toward you among your neighbors in Hopewell?
>
> As suddenly as Lindbergh got the message of that attack, we in the courtroom knew Reilly was now facing the man who opened up paths in the trackless air and flew unafraid where never man flew before. Mr. Reilly wasn't cross-examining Little Lindy's Daddy—Anne had told us the little boy could say *Daddy* —he wasn't examining the haggard young father who told us of identifying his son's corpse in a dank morgue at midnight.
>
> This was Charles Augustus Lindbergh and we knew why he was a Colonel in the United States Army Air Force.
>
> A champion is a champion is a champion, Dempsey says.

> *Q.* Didn't you, as a father make inquiries about the anteced-
> ents of every member of your household after this kidnap-
> ping?

An accusation, the way Reilly said. Lindbergh's jaw came out.

> *A.* I left that to the police.
> *Q.* Didn't you know the police aren't infallible?

This was the man who practiced in Brooklyn, where indeed Lepke and
Burkhalter and Little Augie proved the police fallible most of the time.

> *A.* I think we have very efficient police in New Jersey.

I have seen a great many witnesses on the stand under fire.

> Lindy shouldn't have been under fire, that goes without say-
> ing. He can be guilty of nothing but a mistake in thinking Haupt-
> mann guilty. Under fire, he was the best witness I ever saw. Even
> the sympathy of the neutral press box went out to him.

When it was over I missed Papa for another reason than my own need
to see him. This case needed a great lawyer for the defense. I couldn't
imagine Papa giving Colonel Lindbergh a chance to reaffirm his identification of the voice that came over the wall crying *Hey, Doktor.* To repeat
that he was *sure* it was Hauptmann's voice.

But of course Papa would never have defended Hauptmann.

We defended everybody except the accused Papa thought must be convicted for the good of all.

"Now you're a smart young woman, Miss Gow—"

"Yes I am," Betty Gow interrupted him.

Pot valiant he may have been with his sixth martini, nevertheless here
Reilly settled down with care and legal acumen. With clean-cut precision
and complete knowledge Reilly was using Betty Gow for confirmation of
what was rapidly becoming a growing defense strength. Hauptmann could
not have done the dreadful deed alone, he must have had assistance from
someone inside the Lindbergh home in Hopewell, the Morrow mansion in
Englewood.

With Betty Gow on the stand on the fifth day, Reilly forced an issue. If
Hauptmann hadn't done it alone, unless the prosecution produced those
guilty with him the jury had the right to acquit him.

During those days there were all sorts of experiments. Some of the
younger reporters tried climbing out the window onto the ladder with a
load in their arms. On the whole, they thought someone had to hand the
baby out to the man on the ladder. We went and sat on the hillside with
binoculars to find out whether we could see a signal from the nursery. We
could. We sat in the library to find out what we could or could not hear
from the room above or under the window.

We had the wood expert, impressive in identifying the ladder rails as having come from a yard where the carpenter Hauptmann had bought lumber.

We had the prosecution handwriting expert, Osborne, as good as an expert can be. Yes, he said, Bruno Richard Hauptmann had beyond doubt written the ransom notes. Though later defense experts contradicted this, I do not think they succeeded in making anyone change the conclusions we'd come to with Osborne's many proofs and examples.

Jafsie. Dr. John F. Condon. A lot of speculation and difference of opinion about Jafsie, who likewise identified Hauptmann as the man to whom he handed seventy thousand dollars of Lindbergh's money that night. He was a bit too colorful to really convince the press. But in spite of the ham in him, I believed him. I believed he was basically a *good* man and I did not think any grandiosity could undo that to the extent of allowing him to testify a man's life away.

3

At my father's knee, I had learned that you cannot acquit a client of murder unless you put him on the stand.

Reilly and Fisher agreed that Hauptmann must take the stand as the first witness in his own defense.

On direct, Reilly got everything out of him that was possible for his cause. For three long, often bewildering, always shocking, sometimes thrilling days, Hauptmann was an excellent, careful, superior and in the main a credible witness.

From her seat in the second row his wife began to glow with pride.

Hauptmann explained everything.

Some of the explanations were admittedly better than the original testimony.

He had fight and drive, he was emotional in the right places and indignant in innocence in others to an unexpected degree.

He was, he said, a first-class carpenter. How could he have constructed so botched and rickety and obviously amateurish a thing as that ladder?

His alibi for the night of the kidnaping, as he told it, was quite plausible. A rambling alibi is often more effective than one that is overdetailed and too precise.

Of course it would have to be supported, but at first sound it wasn't dismissed.

His handwriting was like that of all other boys who'd learned to write in German schools. Moreover—and here he stood up and *shouted*—as to all this about *boad* for boat and *singnature* for signature, the way they were spelled in the ransom notes, in the samples of his handwriting he'd been forced to give in the police station, they had insisted he duplicate the misspelling. If he did not, he kept shouting, they hit him with tools from his own case, they beat him with his own hammer. Had they shown those misspellings in any of his everyday writing?

Arriving on the second day at the forty-four thousand dollars he had invested in the stock market during the recovery years after the Depression, and the specific ransom bills he admitted he had passed and the other ones found hidden in his garage, he spun us what became known in the press box as the Great Fish Story.

Some of it I found obscure and hard to follow.

He and a man named Isadore Fisch, Hauptmann said, had been partners. They smuggled. Fisch brought in furs from Germany without paying any duty. I took it there were other lines, probably drugs. Frequently Fisch took hot money paid him for his smuggled wares back to the Continent. We knew that the Mafia, like Cosa Nostra today, dealt in hot money. If a man had seventy thousand dollars of hot Lindbergh ransom bills, he would not use them in this country—that would be asking for sudden death. He would take them to Germany and trade them for thirty-five thousand dollars (the mark-down on the exchange was about fifty per cent and the hot bills would be sent to Cairo or Hong Kong or Paris). According to Hauptmann on the witness stand, Isadore Fisch had been called back to Germany in a hurry, he had not had time to make arrangements to carry the sum of hot money in his possession, he had asked Hauptmann to keep it for him until his return.

The difficulty was Fisch. He died in Germany soon after he got there.

This money, Hauptmann said, was partly his, weren't they partners? A share of it must be coming to him, and so when he was inspired to play the rising market, he used the Fisch cache.

This does not explain why he gave up his job on the very day after the ransom money was paid and never worked again.

A lot of things weren't explained, on others he did a possible reasonable-doubt job.

"What kind of an impression has he made on you?" Mr. Hearst asked me when I called him that night.

I had to think carefully.

"I know he is guilty," I said, "but I think he has put doubts in the minds of the jury for—an odd reason. This crime is so unbelievable when you're looking right at it, after we saw Mrs. Lindbergh it seems so terrible, we built up a picture of the man who did it as someone like King Kong or Lon Chaney as the Hunchback of Notre Dame, a monster like Dracula. For two days, on the stand we have seen a well-dressed, ordinary man who spent summers boating off City Island, whose wife sits and worships him, who had an ordinary home life in the Bronx, bought lumber, if he came to your house as a carpenter you'd be glad to let him in. At this moment, Mr. Hearst, I think the enormity of the crime works in Hauptmann's favor as we see him on the stand."

Mr. Hearst said, "How will Hauptmann do on cross-examination?"

Again I waited to answer. Speed and accuracy but when I was talking to him accuracy came first.

"I had a long talk with Wilentz," I said. "He asked me to. I told him all the things my father did ahead of cross-examinations. How he knew every single thing so completely, was so familiar with everything the witness had ever said or done, was so informed on all places, people, laws, times, religions, backgrounds that he never had to hesitate. He saw instantly if any answer was a lie, an evasion, a quibble. I told him how my father worked out special questions, and spaced them. Wilentz is not the best lawyer I ever saw in a courtroom, but he is bright, he has a fine courtroom presence, and he will work."

"Good," Mr. Hearst said. "How is Colonel Lindbergh bearing up?"

I said, "Oh Mr. Hearst, kidnaping is such a bestial crime. Of a child, the worst of anything. It leaves everybody destroyed—your *faith* is destroyed."

"Let us keep that in mind at all times," Mr. Hearst said. "It must be stopped. The new law that came out of this crime making kidnaping punishable by death seemed necessary. We must back it strongly."

All the time Hauptmann was on the stand under direct examination the jury regarded him steadily.

"They are making up their minds," Runyon said.

"He may be more than a match for Wilentz, I wouldn't be a bit surprised," said Sid Whipple of the UP. "Whole trial now could depend on this cross, if you ask me."

I'm spinning, I said to myself.

That's what's the matter with me.

We live on three levels in this world we call the Hauptmann Trial.

Past—what was Hauptmann doing on the night of March 1, 1932?

Present—what will he be doing under cross-examination today?

Future—what good can ever come out of all this?

Then for me there is another world, my own life, my children, my home. *Is there?* Is it still there? Oh God help us all get this over with and let me get out of here.

Let me do a real fine story on Hauptmann's cross-examination—that's my work—

I'm *spinning*.

Alert he was. Wary. The rest of us didn't appreciate his status as a Superman of the German race. He looked down on us with much the same contempt that his World War I colleague Hitler had now begun to look down on the whole human race. Out on City Island with his group, to two or three of the ladies who had been making plays for his attentions, Hauptmann had openly declared for Der Führer. Fisch always brought him German newspapers.

How much of this mattered I don't know. Certainly it was the climate which had created Hauptmann as he walked arrogantly, erectly, in his carefully pressed gray suit to the chair where Lindy and Anne had sat before him.

A magnificent-looking man, splendidly built. So Lindbergh described him then to Harold Nicolson. True, he was an athlete, a sailor, perhaps another man was aware of his strength. Trying now to see this witness as he walked toward his last defense through the terribly tired eyes of Lindbergh, I find that I cannot.

What struck me full as he walked within a table width of me on his way to the stand was his self-possession. Self-hypnotic it may have been, not one trace of the precross-examination tremors and tensions, not one sign of I-walk-toward-life-or-death for me, these next hours I go free or I go to the electric chair.

I fight for my life.

Wilentz waited. Shuffling papers, moving pencils, occupied. He let Hauptmann wait a minute—two—before he, Attorney General of the sovereign state of New Jersey, rose and walked around to stand in the space between the end of the counsel table and the jury box.

Both young men. In their early thirties. Wilentz, in direct contrast, showed tight nervousness. An ambitious young man he was, and this was an important moment in his professional political life, he was drama-and-public-relations oriented, but I think this was now at the subconscious level.

Hauptmann had made a good impression on direct. Wilentz wasn't ducking that. Far better than the prosecution had been prepared for. For once, Reilly had stayed cold sober and done his best for his client. The jury—at last and always the jury, what else?—the jury believed Lindbergh's identification of this man. In spite of themselves. They were only half sure about Jafsie Condon. They were worried by the issue raised when Betty Gow was on the stand. If he couldn't have done it alone maybe he didn't do it. This sensible, tough-at-the-core Sourland Mountains jury had not, I felt sure, yet made up its mind on any verdict.

I must shake his story.

Wilentz had said that to me the night before and as I thought of our before cross-examination session, I said with him, Yes, you must shake his story.

Flemington January 26
Lightning struck Hauptmann on the witness stand and he shriveled under it, cowering, gasping, livid.

It struck without warning and those of us in the courtroom shrank from the sight of a man being electrocuted it seemed before our eyes.

As I reread my story for the first time after many years, I have to be back there not more than fifteen feet from the two men who faced each other in this life-and-death struggle. I could hear them breathe, smell the sweat.

We saw a man weak now under the lash, we heard the lash strike again and again and Hauptmann fought back in his chair to get away from it, the death sweat gleaming on his forehead and deadly fear in his eyes. I could smell the fear. So complete was his breakdown that I could hardly bear to watch it and once I actually put my hands over my eyes to shut out the sight of a human being brought face to face with his own acts, his own words, his own past that was so damning—any moment—I thought, he may scream out anything—a confession, an admission—anything to *stop* this. If there had been another hour of it, that might well have happened.

Every reporter felt this.

I would like to say here that sometime later Judge Trenchard told me that he also felt it.

But there was no more time, no more time at all, and not even Judge Trenchard could *in justice* do anything about it. In this the wily old fox from Brooklyn had showed his mettle. He had turned his client over for cross at five minutes to four. Since Trenchard always ended the day's session at 4:30 this would break the cross-examination after thirty-five minutes and give Hauptmann the night to recover. To estimate from the first questions what direction Wilentz meant to take.

So at four o'clock, we began the countdown to the recess for the night.
4:01   4:09   4:21—nine eight seven six minutes to go.
Wilentz had begun gently.

He began with one of the most effective things I ever saw in a courtroom. What the Attorney General actually did was to say as though he meant it that Hauptmann now had a chance to tell the truth, that he could now tell the whole truth, if he wished and gain that much gratitude from all. You felt that this young man was no persecutor. It was his business as a servant of The People to see that the truth came out, if that meant Hauptmann was innocent, why, that was his business, too. To get all the truth he even *suggested* that he would perhaps do his best to get Hauptmann a life sentence instead of the Chair all men so dread.

Hauptmann looked at him with icy contempt. It was the last time in the whole trial that Hauptmann ever looked like that.

As long as I live I will never forget the moment when Wilentz moved closer, in a voice still low, but a voice that rang through the courtroom began a series of questions that had never been asked—even suggested—before.

They dealt with Hauptmann's record.

In Germany.

In the days after Germany lost World War I.

Wasn't it true that Hauptmann had once been paroled on a theft charge but that ten days later he was back in jail for holdup —that he had escaped—that Germany still wanted him back as an escaped convict?

Those had been desperate days of *hunger,* of roving bands of ex-soldiers—we knew that. But—what was bad for Hauptmann— wasn't it true that the crime for which he had served four years in Germany was breaking and entering a house illegally?

"And," cried Wilentz lifting his voice from the routine, "isn't it true that you broke into that house *through a window?* Isn't it true that you crawled into that house through a *second story* window, as you crawled into the Lindbergh house through a second story window?"

Hauptmann wet his lips. His eyes shifted from Wilentz to the jury. To the audience. They passed me in that shifting. A cornered rat?

He said then that always fatal phrase—*I don't remember.*

"And isn't it true," Wilentz said, "that you once held up two women who were wheeling babies in the park?"

"Everybody wheels perambulators," Hauptmann said, and took out his handkerchief and cleared his throat and held the handkerchief to his mouth for a moment. Was there blood on it?

"But," said Wilentz, "everybody doesn't reach into babies' perambulators and take out a pocketbook."

A man, then, accused of the Lindbergh kidnapping as we knew it, had robbed babies—in their perambulators—could break into a house through a second story window—

We dared not move.

It was a blow from which Hauptmann never recovered. It left him groggy and though he tried to fight on he was licked. For you see we had always had to find out whether this man *could* have committed the crime of which he was accused—whether he was capable of it.

It seemed to me We The People and our representatives the jury had found out that day.

The next day I wrote what seems an anticlimax—it *was* an anticlimax. Yet in a way it was the climax of the trial. For it showed so plainly what that cross-examination had done to the Accused Man. By that, we could estimate other results—such as the verdict.

> Hauptmann is desperately tired.
> He is like a slow motion picture of the man we saw on direct examination.
> If he were a fighter on whom you bet money you would now be praying for the bell. It takes him so long now to figure out answers that his explanations are confused and unbelievable.

I do not wish to be unjust to Lloyd Fisher. As far as he could make it so, the defense had been adequate. No room was allowed him for several things he had intended to do to occasion a reasonable doubt. Such as the proof of the corpus delicti. The little skeleton had been found on the grounds of a large Catholic orphanage and Lloyd Fisher knew that in that section of New Jersey, militantly Protestant still, they might be made to believe anything about a Catholic orphanage. Reilly had washed that out by "admitting the Corpus Delicti" one day right after lunch, when he was always at his worst. I think that was the major mistake I ever saw a lawyer make in a courtroom, and it seems only fair to Lloyd Fisher to say that within a few months it would be necessary to take Mr. Reilly away for care in what Harold Ross always called the Bughouse.

Hauptmann's alibi didn't stand up as the defense tried to support it.

They did bring the Fisch family over from Germany to prove the smuggling partnership; unfortunately for Hauptmann they seemed to know less about what he and Fisch were partners in than Mrs. Hauptmann did. Their handwriting experts and wood diviners appeared, nowhere near as believable as those of the prosecution. Some very odd characters indeed—one did imitations of Will Rogers on the witness stand though I cannot remember why—these appeared in an effort to establish the presence of others who had been hanging around here and there at the time of the crime.

A few character witnesses from City Island came to say that before and after March 1, 1932, Hauptmann had shown no signs of nervousness or tension or concern.

Of course there was Anna Hauptmann, poor soul. Dreadful, *dreadful* to love a man, any man, as she loved Richard and not be able to help him as the gates of death and hell opened before him.

To all intents and purposes the case was over at the end of those first thirty-five minutes of Hauptmann's own cross-examination.

As to his *guilt*.

CHAPTER 27

So we came to the last round, the final mystery so alive even to this day among lawyers, investigators, and newspapermen. One of the most amazing and dramatic pieces of legal history that we have.

Reilly rose in a pinwheel flare of brilliance and made a closing argument that included the American flag, the Bible, rich versus poor, some Greek oratory, and a lot of Shakespearean poetry.

When he got down to the one possible ground from which to argue for Hauptmann's innocence beyond reasonable doubt, he did it simply, with fine logic and careful presentation of evidence. It did not save Hauptmann but it put that Doubt into the minds of everyone in the courtroom, so that later we fought for a life sentence rather than the death penalty.

It was the Could-he-have-done-it-alone? question, of course.

Flemington February 10. It was an inside job, Reilly says violently. Colonel Lindbergh was stabbed in the back by a member of his own household. In as hideous a betrayal as the world has known since Brutus stabbed Caesar, this hideous disloyalty by those he trusted opened the doors and windows of his home that night to a fiend.

He sweeps aside the kidnap note, the ladder, the attic boards, the money—all as clever manipulations by the police to get their man—a man—any man—

He bears down on something that as he says has not been answered in the days of this trial. He handles it with reason, facts, shrewd argumentation. How could Hauptmann have done what we know was done entirely by himself? Was it *possible?*

Common sense, the sense we like to think we use every day, is what Reilly asked the jury to use. Think of the Lindbergh house in Hopewell. Rooms, halls, stairs, sounds, windows. He makes it impossible to get into without inside knowledge or out of without inside help.

Yes—he does. For me, too. He builds on one word in the State's indictment of Hauptmann. The State charges he committed this crime ALONE. If he didn't, Reilly says, the indictment is void. Alone alone alone—the word echoes. If this man could not have entered the nursery alone, we have no proof of opportunity.

As Reilly hammered this home, Hauptmann's head went down, tears came from the blank blind sockets, this is the only time he has been touched by any emotion except anger. All his hopes ride on this presentation by his Chief Counsel.

Wilentz was a big disappointment. A mediocre speech, we thought.

On the morning of February 13, we had a two-hour charge and the necessary legal instructions from Judge Thomas Trenchard.

Damon always felt that Trenchard's charge was proprosecution.

Having heard many charges with my father, I felt Trenchard's was not only wise and dignified but impartial and unbiased and gave them all the instruction they would need.

At 11:16 on that morning of February 13, 1935, the jury filed out through a small door on their right. Already worn, drawn, white-faced, they walked on eggs toward that sacred spot whither no man, not the President of the United States, the Chief Justice of the Supreme Court, nor the Joint Chiefs of Staff could follow them.

The jury room.

Only those twelve good men and true could enter, speak, vote there.

Deputy sheriffs stand outside the door to guard them from any possible attempt at intrusion, to fulfill any wish they may have.

Hauptmann got up slowly. None of that panther-like grace which I find Wilentz had referred to several times. His wife followed him with her eyes as he went out to his cell to *await* the verdict, and then buried her poor sad face in her hands.

We had started on the usual *How long do you figure they'll be?*—an hour—till after dinner—till tomorrow—when to our horror and amazement we found that *we* were locked in the courtroom as the jury was locked in their room. The working press was to be held under the same No Communications rule as the jurors. None of us had ever before heard of such a thing much less been subjected to it.

Why? We shouted that practically in unison.

Then what if they are out all night? To this we were told calmly by the sheriff himself, we would be taken under guard to our rooms.

A furor swept like a hurricane. I can still see Joe Alsop's smooth bland handsome young face turning purple with rage.

Only Runyon was unmoved. An expression of slight puzzlement gave way to an *I see* nod, he knew *why* quickest. In a couple of minutes more, under our squawks and hollers and threats, our natural anger subsided. We knew *why,* too. Being locked in was our own fault and was fully justified.

Judge Trenchard had acted to preserve the sanctity of that guarantee that the jury cannot, must not at any time in any way be *Tampered With*. About anything. His was the solemn responsibility to see that their deliberations were secret, inviolate, beyond the possibility of any interference or influence. Or even indication of same.

Certainly there did exist all over the place among the working press plots and plans for Tampering With the Jury.

NOT with the verdict. But no possible chance could be taken that the plans might include one word of *that*.

No. Judge Trenchard always knew everything with judicial second sight. He knew that there were strange schemes afoot, devilish devices disposed, in an attempt to get the verdict *first*.

The name of that game was SCOOP.

The Hauptmann verdict was a nationally-awaited-by-millions story.

People hadn't learned to go to their radios for *news*. Black headlines must carry it.

We had it set up both ways, ready to roll in a split second.

EXTRA   EXTRA   EXTRA

HAUPTMANN GUILTY

By Damon Runyon

Flemington Feb. 13th   Bruno Richard Hauptmann must die in the electric chair.

HAUPTMANN NOT GUILTY

By Damon Runyon

Flemington February 13th   Bruno Richard Hauptmann is innocent of the murder of Charles Augustus Lindbergh, Jr.

Waiting on the word of the spoken verdict—sooner if possible.

My own scoop, the only one it turned out, was entirely *human* and for that reason I believe it is worth telling, since mechanical devices change or falter but human nature, I find, does not.

Nobody knew all the gadgets and apparatus installed over weeks in an effort to bug the jury room. Installed they were, however, and bugged it was. Computers, wigwags, mirrors, tapped line, hidden mikes. A window in the corridor outside the room gave onto a corner of the street. A reporter posted there could get signals from a deputy who had a bug inside. Midnight visits weeks before had set up extraordinary contrivances. As it turned out they didn't work. Much time, capital, and promises were invested. Come to think of it, I had invested a good deal of time, my father's genius with cross-examination, and whatever feminine ingenuity I possessed in one form or another upon the Attorney General. That was the one that paid off.

Meantime in Flemington we had twelve hours to go.

How many of us exactly were locked up in that courtroom together I don't know. Hundreds, it seemed. Maybe it was only the same ones passing around and around in parade over and over again.

> The courtroom presents an appearance of the greatest disorder as reporters, lawyers, court attendants and others who gained entrance by one means or another move about. We pass the long hours of afternoon and evening in a state of almost unbearable suspense.

For Damon Runyon the above is as far as he can go and farther than usual.

Talk buzzed. Nervous laughter grew shriller. Paper airplanes began to fly. A checker game was going on across one of the counsel tables. An AP man had gone to sleep in one corner of the jury box, we envied him. Some wag mounted the judge's bench and rapped a gavel, a near riot ensued.

What the hell are they doing?

Every time we met each other in there, we asked each other that.

Those who had expected a quick verdict—like me—began to figure resentfully. Walter Lister of the *Post,* their super-editor-reporter, said it must be the sentence that was holding them up. Some would object to the chair with so much unsolved. Others would insist a man who had anything to do with this kidnaping, alone or not, ought to burn at once. They were deciding no doubt, he said in a short speech, whether to vote Guilty with a Recommendation for Mercy, meaning life imprisonment. Or Guilty without same, meaning the chair.

They might, somebody ventured, be divided between Guilty and Innocent.

Nobody really believed this.

Around three o'clock in the afternoon we were told somehow that the first ballot had been 9 to 3.

A little later, 11 to 1. Then 9 to 3 again.

Has to be the *sentence,* Walter Lister persisted doggedly.

We kept saying, What the hell's taking them so long? *Forever.*

Don't ask me why, sitting in the jury box, we sang "When Irish Eyes Are Smiling." Nor how that sentimental ballad became the theme song of the trial of the century. So many Irish reporters maybe.

Around four o'clock there was a sudden thrilled silence. A deputy came in through the door from the corridor outside the jury room. A verdict? Turned out they wanted a high-powered magnifying glass. Harry Anderson of the Newark *News* said they must want to examine the handwriting. Or the ladder? I said. Even the thumb guard that had been on little Lindy's finger. Four hundred exhibits had been sent into the jury room with them.

At six-thirty they sent out again. Supper. So did we. Another five-gallon can of applejack brandy milk punch. This served us as both food and drink from 11:16 A.M. to 10:45 P.M. Nobody could swallow anything solid.

I kept thinking about Anne Lindbergh.

I always did.

Many of us wrote reports, fill-ins, new leads for our waiting editions. City editors were going slowly mad. No one had expected it to be so long. I noticed Lloyd Fisher was so green his freckles stood out like polka dots. Somebody said to me, I'm going to be sick and I said Not here you're not, Judge Trenchard wouldn't like it.

Any second.

That was it. Always it was *any second.*

Eleven hours and twenty-nine minutes—689 minutes, 41,340 seconds of *any second.*

It's a long long time.

I was sitting in the seat Lindbergh had occupied. Going over again how he could have sat there for thirty-one days and never had to be restrained from trying to get his hands on Hauptmann four chairs away. I had watched his hands, the pulse under his ears, the knot at the end of his jaw for thirty-one days expecting it. Now just sitting there trying to keep my balance, wishing I hadn't drunk that last glass of brandy milk punch—a foul, sweet sticky mess—I had smoked at least nine packs of cigarettes, I was chain-smoking at that moment. The sweat on my forehead smelled of stale tobacco. My lungs hurt and I thought gloomily that I probably had pneumonia, I was hot and cold at the same time, my teeth had to be held to keep from chattering.

I was blowing smoke hard when one of the counsel involved in the case walked by me.

Close.

Didn't need to be *that* close. Was he staggering? He touched my knee as he passed but he didn't look at me, nor notice me, nor turn his head.

He said, *It's the chair,* and kept right on walking.

I heard it, *It's the chair.* I was sure I heard it.

I sat quite still, looking across at the crap game in the other corner. The dice were bright green and transparent. I carefully blew three puffs from my cigarette. They were quite steady. I saw that Runyon was in his own seat in the press box, his eyes closed.

As I stood up the clock over the door registered 10:09.

Keeping the cigarette in my hands, I walked up the aisle. On the door, with his big blue uniformed shoulders blocking it like a tank, was a tall state trooper. All right, I had invested a lot of time and ingenuity in the state troopers, too. They had made me an honorary member. I didn't scrunch down. I thought to myself, I won't lie to him, I won't try to deceive him.

I looked him straight in the eye the best I knew, I gave it all I had, *everything,* my heart was going like a jet engine of which I'd never heard and it almost choked me, the words had to drill through it.

"Let me out," I said.

For two seconds it was in the balance, then he reached behind him still presenting that immovable front to the milling courtroom, unlocked the door, and turned the handle. I sidled behind him, he was as big as Night Train Lane, I was hidden, nobody noticed. Trying to be invisible I spun with the crowd through the hall, without coat or hat I slid crouching down the broad steps between the stately colonial pillars. Mobs massed in the street as far both ways as I could see, the sidewalks packed solid as sardines, as smelly, and as cold. I know these are the Mobs, the Masses, Crowds made up of the Man in the Street, all great work of the world must be and is done through them. But I am terrified. Mumble mumble mumble is the roar, then sudden yells, then wild song. The flickering light of the brilliant movie flares make them look ghastly, a mob buried and dug up in the City of the Dreadful Night yet they are the People in whose name this case has been tried; We the People versus Bruno Richard Hauptmann—as they saw me, the mumbles nearest stopped, they began to whisper, to ask each other; as I hit the bottom step one of the Hearst News Reel men on top of his truck recognized me and yelled, "Have they got a verdict?" and I couldn't shout but I shook my head. I began to work my way through the crowd, someone said, It's Mrs. St. Johns let her through, they gave me a little breathing room, I was so scared that literally I had to hold myself erect grabbing at one coat after another, if I lost my feet on that slick icy pavement I'd be trampled to death, probably not, but I thought so. Just as I got to the door of our building the bell began to toll, it seemed to me to toll the end of the world for whom the bell tolls it tolls for thee—then yells really rocketed, some of the crowd knew that this was an old custom in New Jersey, when the jury announced it had arrived at a verdict in a Capital Case the bell was tolled.

The jury had reached a verdict and was ready to come in.

It would take a little time to march them in and poll them. But madness took over. I opened our street door, some of them shoved me helpfully, and I went flat on my face against the lowest stair. I didn't feel anything. I was beyond feeling anything.

Eddie Mahar behind the city desk said, What the hell have *you* got? and just as the jury came out of their room, we found later, I said to him, *I am reliably informed it's the chair.*

Literally two seconds later as the jury filed into the box the presses in the Journal Building down on South Street began to roll. And the octopus of INS wires went into high.

HAUPTMANN GUILTY
Must Die in the Chair

I went to my typewriter and began my lead.

> *Flemington February 13*
> Keep Your Hands Off Our Children
> The Lindbergh jury didn't say Guilty, though that is the technical verdict they brought in after eleven hours.
> They didn't only say Put to Death. What they really said was
>> Keep Your Hands Off Our Children
>> Leave Our Children ALONE
>> Keep the Bloody Hands of Crime Off Our Babies
> This is what we tell you now. You Can Never Get Away with It. We will always send you to Die in the Chair *if you touch our children.*

So I wasn't in the courtroom when the jury came in. I wish I had room here for the whole Damon Runyon coverage of that day, that verdict, the cast in the courtroom afterwards. A big triple column on the front page, eight columns inside on page 2. Magnificent, clear, comprehensive, without one mistake, packed with news and poignant drama and full color but never a missing detail. Runyon's prose was flawless, adjectiveless as a whole, sparing of adverb, selective even at that fearful pace of the one perfect word. And it was selling on the street fifteen minutes after he finished it.

I can only give you the lead and the first perfect paragraphs.

> *Flemington February 13th.* Bruno Richard Hauptmann must die the week beginning March 18th for the murder of Charles Augustus Lindbergh Jr.
> He is found guilty tonight of Murder in the first degree without recommendation and immediately sentenced by Judge Thomas W. Trenchard to be executed in the manner provided by law.
> In New Jersey, this is electrocution.
> As the jurors are discharged and leave the courtroom, all four

women are crying. The men look at nobody, they are at the point of exhaustion.

Hauptmann stands erect in front of the chair in which he has sat throughout the trial, receives his sentence without the demonstration many had expected.

Judge Trenchard remands him to the custody of the sheriff, he is now handcuffed to Deputy Sheriff Low and Trooper O'Donnel, they make such a quick start that Hauptmann stumbles as he moves with them, like a man about to go down from a punch. He keeps looking at his wife Anna sitting at the defense counsel table trying to hold back her tears. Lindbergh is not in the courtroom.

One quote, in view of what was to happen later in Dallas, bears repeating.

Sheriff Curtiss announced that he will detain Hauptmann for at least forty-eight hours. "I am not going to tell you or anybody else any definite time when I shall make this move. Not now or ever."

The Trial of the Century was over.

We knew now what they were doing that long time in the jury room.

All twelve votes from first to last were GUILTY. Not one voice for one second was cast for Hauptmann's innocence of the crime.

The first ballot showed three votes for the recommendation of mercy, calling for life imprisonment.

As long as the Bronx carpenter was *alive,* several jurors argued, he might eventually confess and explain and bring the others to justice, if there had been others.

Fourteen months went by while the fight to commute Bruno's sentence on that basis went on. Mr. Hearst took a poll of our reporters who had covered the kidnaping and the trial and those who had done editorial work on it at city desks and copy desks. Without exception, we agreed that Hauptmann had not done it alone, that he should be kept alive to find the other guilty parties and to resolve the unanswered problems.

Governor Hoffman of New Jersey, with the ammunition supplied by Lloyd Fisher and our reporters and other legal lights, did his best—but in New Jersey it was not possible for him to grant this commutation of sentence without the consent of the Board of Pardons. This, most unfortunately, he never got.

Mr. Hearst did his best to the very end to cast some final light on this.

On a certain evening he called John Aloysius Clements, who had led with Lloyd Fisher the battle for commutation, through all its political legal and emotional battles. He wanted the opinion of the reporter on the story, the man who knew the most.

"Mr. Clements," he said, "the time is growing very short. I wonder if you and Mr. Fisher think we might make a last move. Certainly Mr. Fisher knows Hauptmann better than anyone and has some influence with him; Hauptmann you tell me trusts him more than anyone else. And Mr. Fisher has confidence in you. Will you consult with him about a plan I have in mind and call me back as soon as possible so I can make the arrangements?"

Late at night on April 2—the execution was scheduled for April 3, 1936 —Lloyd Fisher and Jack Clements went together to the death cell where Hauptmann sat alone.

In his wallet, Clements carried one hundred thousand dollars.

This he showed to Hauptmann. Fisher said, "Richard, if you will write for us a few pages telling the truth concerning your part in the kidnaping of the Lindbergh baby, if you will answer now three or four questions which I shall ask you—Did you do it alone?—Who helped you?—I will give you my word of honor that this sum will be placed in the Trenton Trust Company as a trust fund for your son Manfred. This is a bona fide offer and I as your lawyer say to you that if you have anything further to tell I advise you to do so now. I tell you that you have no possible chance of escaping the chair tomorrow."

He went to the chair without that word.

Years later I said to Lloyd Fisher, "At that time, was he capable of telling the truth, did he know it any more? There is such a thing as self-hypnosis, beyond any question. Isn't it possible that he determined on the story he was going to tell at all times, including on the witness stand, and then for fear of a slip or mistake made himself believe it? Then he wouldn't know any more what had happened. Hitler certainly hypnotized himself, over and over. Isn't this possible with Hauptmann?"

After thought, Lloyd Fisher said, "Possible, I suppose. Hitler was a neurotic. I never saw any signs of this in Hauptmann. He was always rational and in control of himself. It is possible also," said Hauptmann's very ethical lawyer, "that he had nothing further to tell."

So in April 1936, Hauptmann was executed.

For anyone who was there, the Hauptmann trial never really ended.

It affected all of us profoundly for we had witnessed in reality the most amazing tragedy-drama on any courtroom stage. Partly of course we never gave up on the unsolved mysteries, partly the impact of the people went along in our reference files on humanity.

The last time I saw Damon Runyon I was sitting with him at a corner table in the Stork Club. Runyon could no longer speak after an operation for throat cancer; he wrote on his pad, "I do not believe there was any miscarriage of justice, I wish we knew some answers, don't you?" I said yes. He wrote a name with a question mark and I said yes again and began to cry. Not over the *name,* but to sit and listen to Billingsley and Walter Winchell while Damon sat silent was too much for me. He put his arm around me and wrote, "Don't worry, I've already said everything I had to say."

2

Voltaire has called history little *else* than a picture of human crime. In his analysis of the fall of the Roman Empire Gibbon says it is little *more* than a register of crimes.

Out of this crime came the weeping indignation of a people to prove that we can and will halt crime when aroused. We of the press had a strong right to claim our share in forcing the passage of the Lindbergh Law, which moved kidnaping immediately under the investigative eye of the FBI and the power of the G-men so much dreaded by the underworld. And also with public support we changed what might so easily have become a Climate for Kidnaping.

KEEP YOUR HANDS OFF OUR CHILDREN

I meant that as I wrote it. We all meant it as we read it. We would act upon it and the criminal world knew it.

Are we the same nation?

Has Modern Woman developed more—or less—moral courage in the three decades of growing in her freedom? Is she slumping into self-interest or eager to pick up Carrie Nation's ax in this Armageddon of our day?

Why do we allow the criminal world to put its greedy poisonous bloody hands on our children and sell them marijuana and LSD and heroin in the very yards, on the very campuses, of schools and colleges?

KEEP YOUR HANDS OFF OUR CHILDREN.

Then—over thirty years ago—we said it, we followed through on it. I was overwhelmed with vast and humble gratitude that I had been a note in the Voice shouting this battle hymn of the republic. Giving me the assignment Mr. Hearst had promised, *We will do something about this.* As I had learned that Power of the Press from my series on Unemployed Women—now I learned the Power of the Women from their strength and moral courage after the Lindbergh case.

Even when I warned us of dangers I felt and smelled, I had wanted us to succeed. My own dream that we could do *anything* if we didn't get off the road—if we stood united for good—came true as women faced the criminals of our country and I felt a new sense of pride, of potential, of humility that I'd been able to speak for and to them.

Beware the women weeping for their unjustly dead.

Emerson says there is properly no history, only biography.

Moving into biography as history, how strange it is that the two beloved young men of shining hope and promise who met in 1927 to the tune of "Yankee Doodle Dandy" and "God Save the King" both chose abdication and self-exile at almost the same time.

King Edward VIII abdicated his throne in 1936.

Coming out of the Valley of Humiliation, the young man we had called *our greatest son* chose self-exile and took with him his wife, whom I know to be one of our greatest daughters.

Harold Nicolson and his wife, Victoria Sackville-West, author of my favorite Joan of Arc biography, found for the Lindberghs an estate in a quiet English countryside far from the maddening throng, the searchlight of public interest.

In many ways, this was a bitter thing for the United States.

No country has ever beheld without sorrow the exile of its great sons. Though we saw what Lindbergh had suffered and knew what his fears must be, protest was strong and sometimes loud. Mr. Hearst believed that after the trial of his son's murderer, he could do no other. And with my own eyes I saw those days in the courtroom break him, change him, so that he could no longer carry the part of a national hero.

The truth is he had no desire to nor should we have required it of him. Though many did. He did not foresee it when he flew the Atlantic—he woke as he said to a world with no relation to the one he had known. When we were lunching on a day as she prepared for that round-the-world flight from which she never returned—nor expected to—Amelia Earhart said to me that she believed if he'd known what it was to entail Lindbergh would never have flown the Atlantic.

Born to fly! The man, the deed, the moment—he had not bargained for the fame, the public life, the goldfish bowl in which he would live. For two whole nights Deac Lyman of the *New York Times,* the only newspaper reporter with whom Lindbergh ever made friends tried to explain to me. With aviation people, Deac insisted, Lindbergh was natural, friendly, had humor. That he had not wanted to leave the United States but threats to Jon, the boy Anne had been carrying at the time her first son was missing, had driven him to another country.

Might he have been a voice of leadership in our wilderness when we needed it if he could have stayed the Phenomenon of Lindbergh? If one man plants himself strongly at such times, the big world comes to him. Lindbergh didn't want the big world to come to him. Only the sky.

And there was no successor to the Phenomenon of Lindbergh. Nor has there ever been.

Is it possible that it was his wife who, having walked the way with him, was the one who carried the lamp and from it the light was to come?

3

I carried Anne Lindbergh out of the Hauptmann trial with me. No one I had ever met made so profound an impression on me as this girl whose voice I never heard, whose face I never saw except from the witness stand.

I wondered then—how was Lindbergh's wife, the mother of the Lindbergh baby, going to live the rest of her life?

As a good many people had wondered how Earl Rogers' daughter, Nora, brought up in her father's criminal law offices and friends with madames and murderers, was going to make out.

In the end what the desperately hard work, the madness and tragedy of the Hauptmann trial gave me was my memory of this then twenty-five-year-old woman, Anne Morrow Lindbergh. If Joan of Arc had survived the stake, how would she have lived the rest of her life? I cannot know that, nor can you, but I do know that Anne Morrow Lindbergh in her forties wrote *Gift from the Sea,* the closest to a blueprint for the salvation and happiness of the modern woman that we have had.

Who was she? How did she come to be?

Not as rich as Barbara Hutton or Doris Duke, as most people know money, she was born rich. An ambassador's daughter, she could always have done, could always do, anything she wanted to do. *The shape of my life,* she wrote, *is of course determined by many other things, my background and childhood, my mind and its education, my conscience and its pressures, my heart and its desires.* She had been fortunate in parents who had ideals, discipline, and a simple philosophy of responsibility.

Soon after the trial in Flemington, at a Smith College commencement, she was given an honorary degree of Master of Arts.

In conferring the degree, President Neilson said:

"Anne Morrow Lindbergh, B.A., Smith, 1928, Hubbard gold medalist of the National Geographic Society, poet, pilot, navigator, radio operator, co-explorer with her husband of the unflown air routes of five continents and two oceans, who has proved to an admiring world the compatibility of imagination and practical dexterity; of sensitiveness and fortitude; of modesty and daring; the pride of her college, the glory of her country."

Soon after the trial I was to live in New York, London, Hollywood, and Washington, where I saw women who'd screamed for liberty and equality cracking up under them. If things were rough and they didn't get their way, they crumpled.

With me I carried the memory of a woman who never crumpled or even faltered.

Perhaps I carried it with me to judge the other American woman who was to become the wife of that other shining young man of promise, the one for whom the bands had played "God Save the King."

After the verdict, the world in which we'd lived ceased to exist. Flemington became a ghost town after a gold rush. We scattered in all directions as speedily as voyagers at the end of a cruise. Runyon went back to Broadway to write more *Guys and Dolls*. Syd Boehm was shortly on his way to spectacular success in Hollywood. Over his protests, Jack Clements was to be promoted to head of public relations of the Hearst Service.

I flew immediately toward California and what in all my incarnations inside *this* incarnation seems to be my native hearth. Once more the Bench, the Counsel Table, and, God help me, the Witness Stand.

This time I was the Accused. Not as I had been in my library in Whittier after the Alice Ames Winters debate, where I had presented to myself against myself in private and in conscience a general charge. There I had said to myself, You be the judge, you be jury, you be cunning old Fury, you try the whole case and condemn us to death off with our heads.

Academic, violent, instinctive the charges had been convincing enough to win my case. Now, they had become realities.

Especially the one saying the Modern Woman who isn't there when the children come home from school is an Unfit Mother.

My humanitarianism had begun to confuse me. Mrs. Lindbergh had something she was to distill later; it puzzled me then, I kept reaching for it. All I could get was the inspiration of her courage and her courtesy, and this must have grown out of lovingkindness.

I needed anything I could get.

During those fantastic thirty-one days in Flemington my second husband had filed a suit declaring me an unfit mother. At the time I divorced him, the custody of my son had been awarded to me. Unless the mother was proved to be unfit, this was customary with young children.

Now he wanted that custody taken from me and given to him.

In a way I had something to bear that could never have touched Mrs. Lindbergh, innocent of all possible blame as little Lindy's mother. Of myself, I wasn't so sure. Oh—the charges made against me were exaggerated by malice. If I'd had that many love affairs I'd have had no time to make my living and that of my children.

Every career woman I have ever known has a coward's conscience about her children. Can she be a good mother? Has she *been* a good mother?

The three mules were back.

My own words about the Modern Woman were coming home to roost like vultures.

Could it be that what I'd said was *true?* And that it began with *me?*

I would find out in another courtroom with me as the defendant on another Witness Stand.

CHAPTER 28

Sitting beside Mr. Hearst on an enormous overstuffed divan in the Big Room at San Simeon, I had an overpowering sense of change. Me and my world. A time-stands-still pause in this pilgrimage.

I'd come north to ask Mr. Hearst for help in the fight that faced me and as I sat there I was sure this was—not *A* but *The* Turning Point. A lot of them had come, but this time it seemed to me my feet were slipping, I was hanging by my fingernails, I had a hammering suspense to see what was over the Hill of Difficulty but now I could only go there by meeting this life-and-death moment of truth and going with it.

I might stop *living.*

With my father long long ago I had knowledge that I could not be an island, after he died I'd forgotten this for a while, now it had all come back. I was breathing hard from what I had experienced in the Hauptmann courtroom, there I had realized what life can do to a woman through her children if she is a normal woman. Bringing up Elaine and Bill and Mac and Hugo and my two kid brothers Thorny and Bryson had somehow been an adventure. I could cope. We had our ups and downs, but I had never known *fear.*

Now the cruel *timing* was that my *work* had helped to engulf me in personal fear so deep I was drowning. A great deal has been said of what is called nervous shock and its effects. I remember the tears on the faces of those Sourland Mountains women on the jury. If I *could* have lived through the Hauptmann trial without being shaken to the roots of my soul I could not have written stories that, I now knew, had moved millions, any more than, in time, Anne Morrow Lindbergh could write *Gift from the Sea.*

I can see that part of my haunting fears came from Anne Lindbergh on the witness stand identifying those sleepers.

Going back so clearly in memory to San Simeon, I do not understand how that fireplace, tall as Mr. Hearst, who was 6'5", and wide as garage doors, burning logs big as a telephone pole, could be so homelike. Any more than I can explain how that vast room with four hundred and eighty light bulbs in the ceiling could shut me into measureless content. I felt safe there always. Nothing, no one—bill collectors, kidnapers, malicious ex-husbands, one drink of gin too many, screaming pressure of dead-lines—could get me.

On that day when I was feeling my way toward admitting to Mr. Hearst this custody threat, it was the hour when everyone had gone to dress for dinner. He and I were alone beside the big window on the sea end. This showed us a gray shifting February fog, I could hear a wind that seemed to bring the sound of waves up from the sea, the song of pines down from the hills, this had to be imagination, the walls were too thick, imagination existed in that room for all who wanted it.

Only this moment do I know that to some extent I had put Mr. Hearst into the aching void and need that my father's death had left in me and in my life. I know that Mr. Hearst always wanted a daughter, I believe that the beautiful and brilliant and devoted Frances Marion of his native San Francisco, absolute tops to his feelings in friendship, movie-making, com-panionship, and pride, Frances to a large degree and me myself in a much smaller one filled that longing in him.

As I sat there beside Mr. Hearst, I knew Dicky was safe safe safe—a word never in my vocabulary before, I'd taken safety for granted—upstairs sharing rooms and a governess with Jack Hearst's son Bunkie.

Burned bronze even in February, hair tow-white from the sun, blue eyes unafraid of anything, the very week I arrived at Malibu after the Lind-bergh trial he'd been in a wrestling match with another of Mr. Hearst's grandsons who lived up the beach. When Dicky came out of the ocean minus his trunks Georgie hollered, *Dicky's nakid Dicky's nakid,* which demanded reprisals. Mr. Hearst asked who won and I said I understood it was a tie, and Mr. Hearst said those things were good for Georgie. If Dicky was taken away from me would he have to leave his ocean? Where would he *live?*

Day was deepening to dark around us and I said to Mr. Hearst, "I must dress," and waited, but he didn't move or say anything. He was often silent, I think of him silent and listening more than he spoke. After a few moments while a tall plume of blue green red orange phosphorescent flame ran along the top of the logs, he said, "I have told Mr. Howey to give you a bonus for the Hauptmann trial . . ." (I got that bonus later. Not a check, oh no, not me. *Money?* I had long before fallen in love with a picture of a lion cub we'd bought as a cover for the *American Weekly.* At first Howey gave me the glass eye and said it was by Dan Smith, a brilliant young artist who died at twenty-four, and the picture was a museum item, I could not have it. I said Mr. Hearst said a Bonus and he never traveled cheap, after we had a few drinks he asked if my car was there and we carried it down in the freight elevator and all *hell* broke loose when it was discovered missing next morning. It now hangs in my son Dick's house at Malibu.)

I didn't want to talk any more about the Hauptmann trial then, I was trying to forget it, but I was having trouble bringing out my danger, my terror, I had my mouth open to pour out the tale of this Unfit Mother suit, coiled at my feet like a rattlesnake, when Marion came in.

She was dressed for dinner in a sweeping gown of blue velvet with a jabot of rose-point lace worth about five hundred dollars an inch. Her hair was in short graceful golden curls—every time I pass Van Cleef & Arpels on Fifth Avenue I look at the fairy-diamond crown Napoleon once put on Josephine's soft curls and I *know* how she looked to him or he would not have designed that Queen Titania type of tiara for his love. Marion's soft dancing feminine curls could have worn that dainty crown. This is odd for I knew that Marion always wore little wigs—many women do now; then I think Marion was the only one. They were made on silk string caps and sat in rows on her dressing tables, coiffured for different times and places. A short one for tennis, longer and rakish for sports clothes, elegance for evening gowns. *I'm not going to spend half my life sitting there to please a hairdresser,* Marion said; *they can do just as well without me.* When she took the wig off—and no one ever knew when this might be—her own hair was very short, and it gave her even more the look of a pixie on the loose.

That particular evening she had on a necklace of tiny diamonds made into roses to match the lace and I said how charming, she took it off and said, "Seventy-five dollars at that little place in Beverly Hills," she gave Mr. Hearst a grin and said, "To prove I could buy my own diamonds if I had to," and she came and sat between us, her hands full of place cards, which were the bane of her existence. She began to run through them, she said to him, "You will have to have the Secretary's wife on your right whether you like it or not. I will have to have the Secretary next to me! He is a Pismo clam. But I will put Adela on his other side—do you speak clam, sweetie?"

"I had Sam Goldwyn last time," I said. I was glad of this delaying action, it seemed almost as though I were delaying the thing itself. "He told me his wife reads more books than I do. Why don't you put Cissy Patterson on the Secretary's other side, she's from Washington?"

"Her columnist, Drew Pearson, misquoted him," Marion said with a shrug. "What's more, W.R., I will not have that pudgy executive of yours on my left. He tells *jokes*—and I have been studying my Shakespeare all day and I am addled as eye of newt and toe of frog—"

At this time, Talkies had come to stay. Marion's pronounced stutter appeared fatal to her future as a Movie Star. Never a man to give up easily, Mr. Hearst wouldn't accept this. I had a hunch he foresaw difficulties with a Marion who had nothing to do all day long. He had therefore hired a famed Shakespearean coach to come up and work with her four hours every afternoon to overcome the stutter and teach her an approach to dialogue.

"I'm beyond the *Romeo Romeo wherefore art thou Romeo?,*" Marion said, putting the place cards in my lap and standing up. "Now I am where Bloody Tybalt is green in the tomb—where I say, *I'll madly play with my forefather's joints and pluck the mangled Tybalt from his shroud*—wait a minute—what comes next?—*what with loathesome smells so early waking and shrieks like mandrakes torn out of the earth that living mortals hearing them run mad and I dash out my desperate brains*—W.R., I am about to dash out my desperate brains with all this—what makes you think I am ever going to have to say things like that?—I think they're indecent myself."

He was laughing so hard he couldn't have told her anything. An inspired clown—if he would have let her be that on the screen!

"Those were pretty bad little kids I was brought up with in Brooklyn," Marion said, "but they knew a lot of language in Verona at fourteen *we* wouldn't have been allowed to use. And those kids in Verona—sticking knives in each other and taking things that made them pass out for two days and if my old man had caught me playing with my forefather's joints in or out of his tomb he'd have given me what-for with a stick."

She came and sat down, and said to me, "What's wrong with you, Lady Macbeth?"

I said gloomily, *"My mind is trubled like a fountain stirred and I myself see not the bottom of it,"* and Marion said, "Never *mind* any more Shakespeare, say it in English."

"I am in a jam," I said, and told them the whole thing. As I told it, I knew all my courage had evaporated. I could not make it answer to my will. I kept thinking of Anne Lindbergh and how she must have imagined in an actual *present* her child in the hands of kidnapers, and I was imagining in an actual *future* my child in the hands of this man I'd left. I could see a little boy—six seven eight—teen-age—growing up bewildered, scared, lonely.

Now I'm Nobody's Nothing.

Marion said, "What can we do?"

Desperately I said, "I need to know what's going on. Jerry Geisler is a fine lawyer, but I'm not sure he knows how to find out about lies like the ones in the complaint. What they're based on. My going off on a yachting trip with Gable—?"

"Did you?" Marion said.

"Of course I did," I said. "We're old friends—there were other people—"

"No gentleman ever so much as invites me to have a Coke in the commissary," Marion said. "Bob Montgomery brought me roses when we finished our picture and that man *there* took them and told him a long story about how I took all flowers out to my mother's grave. That'd encourage a fellow. All this hiss and rattle about me and Chaplin. You know Charlie has no more guts than a Japanese beetle. He'd be afraid W.R. would clank him in the Tower until *he* festered in *his* shroud. That's what it's like to be the lady friend of that terrible William Randolph the Hearst who poisoned nice honest blue-eyed Tom Ince." She leaned over and kissed him and said, "Now do something for Adela—"

"Can he prove any of the accusations?" Mr. Hearst said.

I said, "Not really—you know when you work with men as I do some things look—unusual. I don't know what he's *doing*. What's going on."

"Who would you like to have try to find out what is, as you say, going on?" Mr. Hearst said.

"You know Jack Clements," I said, "he was in Flemington."

Mr. Hearst went over to one of the phones. In the mist outside I could see the white marble statues like fugitives from ancient Greece dancing in the wind with the trees and flowering bushes. We trailed after him and Marion put her arm around me and said, "You're lucky to have a son to fight for," I can still hear that little-old-New-York-Irish stammer. That is the reason I know, I've always known for sure, that Marion Davies did not have twins by Mr. Hearst as the story is so often told. She would have fought for them, she would never have let them go, they would have been right there right then. In that great many-roomed castle with all the cottages and guest houses around it, on top of a hill amid three hundred thousand acres, with cattle gates and guards protecting them, they'd have been there as were Charlie Lederer and his sister Pepi, children of Marion's sister Rene, and her sister Rose's little girl, and Mr. Hearst's grandsons and everyone's children including mine and the cook's. There are other proofs of course—but what did Marion Davies have to lose if she had twins?

There was not, had not been for many years any concealment by anybody that Marion Davies was Mr. Hearst's mistress *en titre,* hostess at his castle to most distinguished guests who knew of the relationship and didn't stay away, since it was all in what might be called the historic manner and, more than many marriages, was a relationship conducted with love, loyalty, and dignity at all times. In more modern times of all-out promiscuity and permissive arrangements this may seem an outdated type of affiliation but it worked for centuries and families were maintained, positions fulfilled, and children born on the wrong side of the blanket were made princes, dukes and, as Marion's pal Shakespeare pointed out, in several instances they inherited the thrones of their fathers.

Believe me, Marion's children if any wouldn't have been farmed out. Why should they be?

Into the telephone Mr. Hearst said, "Mr. Howey? This is Mr. Hearst. Will you be good enough to send Mr. Clements of the *Journal* out to Los Angeles? We have a valuable asset in Mrs. St. Johns and I have some plans for her I have not yet discussed with you. She is certainly too upset to work and will be, until this custody matter is resolved." There was a silence and then he said, "That may be true, I can see in your manner of speaking it might have value. I do not think Mrs. St. Johns will see it that way. Send Mr. Clements out as soon as possible." He hung up and said, "Mr. Howey feels that the names used in these charges made against you, he mentions Mr. Gable and Mr. Quentin Reynolds, and Mr. Rudy Vallee —he thinks these might increase your by-line worth to us and make you, as he says, better known and more glamorous."

"I don't want to be more glamorous," I shrieked like a mandrake. "The whole thing is ridiculous. I covered the Derby with Quent—we were *working*—as for Gable—"

I stopped.

News.

Suppose he says, This is *news*.

Right in this room I'd heard little Carmen Pantages, whom he loved, ask him to keep something out of the paper when her father got into serious trouble and he said, I'm sorry, but that's *news*.

Two things saved me.

We still had the Unwritten Law that newspapermen were never news to each other.

And Marion said, "It has to be *true* to be news, otherwise I've heard you say yourself it's not much better than blackmail. If anybody threatened to use something as *news*—if it wasn't *true* it would be blackmail. You wouldn't think anything of a woman who didn't fight for her child and Adela says it isn't true."

"Most of it," I said.

I forgot myself long enough to wonder what it would have been like if she'd married some nice young guy and had a big Irish family making their first communion—but then I saw the way she looked at him and I knew she loved him. She always did.

I am always surprised that this is usually overlooked.

"I might lose Dicky," I said.

"We will not pursue Mr. Howey's ideas," Mr. Hearst said. "It will be difficult for anyone to take a child away from his mother in California."

I couldn't be sure. I had never been really frightened before. Not even about Papa. Not even when they shot at us in the Presidio. That was a straightforward kind of war, they hit you or they didn't. This time I was a squirming mass of fears.

Not to know, not to be there, to try to go to sleep at night thinking maybe he was crying himself to sleep all by himself. *All is well with the child,* the prophet told the mother. All couldn't be well always with any child, there were things, and imaginations, but—if he stepped on a rusty nail and got hives between his toes and in his ears, if you were *there* you could put wet soda packs on and that helped. You couldn't stop some defeats and disasters and disillusions in his high school days, for instance, but you'd be *there* to give him back confidence. He would know there was one person who was on his side all the time, so all *would* be well with the child. For any mother the claw of the sea puss would be not knowing—either of you.

I might lose my child?

Nor could I see a way out. Fear distorts everything.

2

There I stood running a temperature saying to myself, *This can't be happening.* I knew it was, I said to myself as I'd done ever since I was a little girl, *I must remember this exactly.* Or I won't believe it.

Through the screen door I stared at the two men. They were dressed like twins. Both wore black overcoats too tight for them. Leaning forward a little, their gloved hands—gloves at nine o'clock on a sunny morning?—hung motionless. Their derby hats—derbies in California?—were tilted at identical angles. Their faces were masked in the same indoor green—their lives were tales told by the same idiot, for there were no lines on their expressionless faces.

What a pair, I thought. Against a curtain of blue plumbago vines they were incredible on the front porch of the old house Mother Meyer had left me. We were staying there because it was near the courthouse.

What were they doing here? What did they *want?*

Upstairs I heard Dicky yelling to get his own way, then his big brother Bill took the situation in hand, I went out onto the porch and closed the heavy front door behind me. A chill tremor suggested that whatever these characters had come for, I didn't want the children to hear it. I didn't want them to get *inside* the house. This could be part of the enemy attack, couldn't it?

I was ready to go downtown to court, wearing a severe tailored suit with a plain white shirtwaist to look older, more sedate. So that the judge would say to himself when I took the witness stand, *Impossible that this woman (lady?) in the plain dark suit with her hair combed so severely, and no make-up, a plain woman really, should have been bouncing around on yachts with Clark Gable or skithering hither and yon with Quentin*

Reynolds in Louisville or consorting with crooners like Rudy Vallee to an
extent that would make her an unfit mother, she looks sisterly to me.

If the judge said *that* we were safe.

Unless these two men came to throw a monkey wrench? Neither of
them looked at me, they looked right over my shoulders. They looked so
incongruous I wanted to die laughing and I suppose quite a lot of people
had—

"I'm Mrs. St. Johns," I said. "You want to see me?"

The one on the right said, "Little Augie sent us."

I let my breath out in a honk. Well now, I said to myself, that's all right.
They're friendly. The name Little Augie Pisano might curdle Brooklyn,
Crime Capital of the World, but he was a friend of mine.

Without moving his lips the other said, "Little Augie heard you were
having trouble."

"Well yes I am," I said, "but—I don't see—"

"He said to tell you we'll take it off your hands, lady," he said.

No. No no. Here I am simply having a legal fight with my ex-husband,
but I was on my way to court to take care of it *legally*.

If I won my case I would soon go back to New York, to Cow Lane.

If I didn't—aye, there's the rub. I couldn't bear to think of it, I thought
of it all the time. If I lost my case I would have to stay in California, work
in Hollywood, fight it through every higher court forever, from *hell*.

"Whatever it is," the man on the right said, "Little Augie says tell you
we'll take it off your hands."

The words hit me.

Gangster talk. I recognized it, I'd investigated to be sure I was right
before I made a nationwide speaking tour for Mrs. Charles A. Sabin to
convince the women of America that the Prohibition Amendment must
be repealed. It was unenforceable; breaking that law consistently, we were
handing the country over to lawlessness. When the tragic farce finally
did end, J. Edgar Hoover faced an established underworld with four million active operators; powerful and well led, they turned to dope, prosti-
tution, Murder Incorporated, infiltration of unions, communist political
activities, and of course blackmail. We were still in that valley of death
with J. Edgar's gallant little band outnumbered 100 to 1.

My two gentlemen callers from Little Augie's left-over-from-
prohibition-mob, were easy to identify though they'd left their guns in the
long black car, those particular long black cars that were by Limousine out
of Hearse.

Little Augie is fond of me, I said to myself. He truly wants to help me.

Seymour Berkson was then a top foreign correspondent, our-man-in-
Rome, and he once got me a rosary blessed by the Pope for Little Augie
to give to his mother. His mother did not approve of Little Augie. If he

came with a rosary blessed by the Pope in his hand she might let him in. With it in *her* hand, she'd ask the Blessed Mother of all to save Little Augie's crime-crumbling soul from hell. Well, she did let him in and me too and she cooked us a dinner fit to be compared to Mamma Leone's.

Little Augie's mother wouldn't approve of what he'd sent these two preposterous little subhumans to tell me.

Or would she?

She'd had the guts not only to fight the devil *for* her son, but to fight the devils *in* her son. That's harder.

Come come, Swifty, I said to myself, don't kid yourself, let's get down to it.

On my pilgrimage I had personally met a lot of temptations. My average of resistance wasn't anything to brag about. Only my grandfather's friend Jesus had resisted them all. "Never forget," my grandfather had said to me when I was very very young and me and a dog named Samson used to listen to him, "Jesus was tempted. He was not a character in a morality play. If it had been a mere allegory, it would be a vicious fraud. *He was tempted like as we are.*" All these years later this echoes back to me; I suppose I said to myself Grandpa meant *you name it* and it faced Jesus sometime somewhere. This one too?

Even in the Garden of Gethsemane Peter had cut off their ears. *Kill*—kill 'em—must have been his action pattern as he drew his sword against his master's enemies—*kill 'em.*

Through the morning sunshine came the scent of sand and sage from the desert beyond the purple foothills. My nose more than anything, even music, starts a memory track. The sand and sage must be the same fragrance that was around my grandfather's church in Globe, Arizona, where Wyatt Earp heard him preach. The same scent that in those days before smog still came to the old Rogers house on Hope Street where he gave me lessons on the front porch and made me memorize all of Peter's Epistles. Now it came to this other old house where we were sort of hiding and where Mother Meyer still was.

I found myself putting up a hell of a resistance against these memories of Peter, who as I recalled it had finally eschewed evil and gone to heaven, where he was now sitting on the right hand of God.

I took a deep breath and heard myself say:

"No, I'm sorry. I—you see he's my son's father, he has his own problems, poor man. I must have been a horror for him to be married to." I was babbling, trying to clear my own mind. They didn't hear me, for hours after I tried a tommy gun in the basement of the FBI I couldn't hear. Maybe these two little men had shot off so many tommy guns in their time they couldn't hear at all any more. So I went right on saying, "Something called Eugenics was the rage when I married him, the science of improving the quality of the human race by careful selection of parents. My picking him to be the father of my child was cheating. He had a right to a *wife* and I never intended to be one, I was too busy, there's an old Irish saying about a man can drive two mules—" I didn't go on with that, I was fed to the teeth with its imbroglios. I said, "He's a man of good intentions, his character—it's moral enough though his *disposition*—and it's disposition you live with around the house twenty-four hours a day and twice on Sunday. The stepfather part was what was hopeless—but you can't go around getting people shot because you don't think they'll be the proper stepfather for your children. A good deal of it was my fault for marrying him, so I can't just hand him over—"

They may not have understood a word of this but they knew it meant no.

"We'll be around if you change your mind, lady," they said, and went down the stone steps like a pair of Baird's puppets, maybe they were a pair of Baird's puppets, I was so overwrought with trials—and there's a grim pun for us—and six weeks without any sleep and coming West to get on my own witness stand.

Whether they'd been there or not, I'd never see them again.

I was wrong.

If he wanted to do a pal a favor, Little Augie didn't give up that easy. At the courthouse when I arrived stood the long black car in front of a No Parking sign and nobody, not even in Los Angeles, said it Nay.

3

So long ago.

That little boy who wouldn't speak to me all the way from San Simeon to Malibu because he wanted to stay and ride ponies with Bunkie—a man now. I no longer wake in the night with the ice of apprehension trickling through my veins, only when I write about that time long long ago as it is, I have to stop. My hands begin to shake.

I am an overprotective grandmother and great grandmother.

After we came back from the Ranch, I received a wire.

ARRIVING 3:15 PLANE DON'T WORRY PAPA FIX CLEMENTS.

Thus bringing into the St. Johns circus what amounts to an institution still in operation as late as this morning when somebody needed help in getting a visa fixed up for an English nurse. True, this is a man who isn't really interested in people who haven't any trouble to *be* fixed. His enemies, he's bound to have some, he knows too much, say he'll get you *in* so he can get you *out*. His functions as reporter extraordinaire and Spiro's right hand on the *Journal,* up to head of public relations for all Hearst Publications, have included and still include watching over the biggest brass in it. What we would have done in our thirty-five years of family difficulties getting out of jail or into the 82nd Airborne, predating marriage licenses and postdating checks, persuading judges and dissuading creditors, finding jobs and losing undesirable camp followers without Clements' Papa Fix I do not care to think. My great-grandchildren call him Uncle Papa Fix and what they are going to do growing up when by due process of nature he is no longer around to fix, I can't imagine. He and Howard Strickling and I were trying to figure out what happens to the last man out and who is going to fix *his* funeral? There is always Howard's line to the famous undertaking firm who arranged all the majestic services in the synagogue and out for Louis B. Mayer—after all religious, musical, and floral and other details had been settled Howard said automatically, "And what time do you want me to have Mr. Mayer there?"

I keep skirting around that custody trial, but get into it I must.

Every detail of that courtroom is vivid to me. I can walk right into it. Everybody in it still exists for me. Then is now.
Of all the courtrooms where Earl Rogers fought to save a man's life—
No no no no. I've got my incarnations mixed, my memory channels crossed. I'm seeing this on a split screen. The one I'm talking about *now* isn't fifty years ago, it's only thirty, I am not Earl Rogers' daughter, I am Dicky's mother. But all courtrooms are the same to me, every detail of all three courtrooms, Papa's and the one where Anne Lindbergh was, and this one—two of those were old and shabby and dark and this one is new and light and polished and center field is 407 feet instead of 320—they're all exactly *alike.*
I can *see* the people again.
Dicky wasn't there any more than the Lindbergh baby had been. Dicky was safe at home with my brother Thornwell and his brothers Bill and Mac and his sister Elaine St. Johns Gallico, watching over him. Jerry Geisler had insisted I have all my children within call. Everything is *about* Dicky so he is there. Geisler looks like a fourth-grade schoolteacher, sandy hair, large Adam's apple, baggy gray suit, not like the criminal lawyer who has come closest to taking Earl Rogers' place. Ike St. Johns is there—all this of course takes place long before my last telephone conversation with him which I recorded out of sequence. We look at each other and remember that we married each other when we were very very young and I was Earl Rogers' spoiled daughter Nora.

A Japanese houseboy. On the stand. A Japanese houseboy? Whose? I don't remember him but he's testifying. Something about a black lace negligee he found somewhere. *Black lace?*

All the time, I had trouble breathing.

Everybody assured—reassured me—no judge, they kept telling me, would take so small a child away from his mother.

I couldn't believe them. I couldn't be sure.

Another thing that made the breathing difficult. It is strange and terrible to be hated to your face. This was malice, the hot brush fire of hatred, while it rages it sears your lungs and your eyeballs.

I must have done something to earn it.

Sitting there in my old blue suit, I thought, This is indeed a pitiful sight. Two people who once felt kindly toward each other, now sitting in open enmity trying to do each other dirt.

Why did he *hate* me?

I was to know a man named Lyddane in Washington not many months hence whose wife was charged with assault with intent to commit murder —she had tied him up in a cemetery, a little prematurely as it turned out. He didn't die of the beating, so this became another case where the corpse was present to testify as Mrs. Col. Griffith Park had been in a case of Papa's. Talking with Mr. Lyddane all one afternoon, I took away his astonished self-accusation. What had he done to make her hate him enough to want to kill him? All the rest of his life, even when he was playing third base for an industrial ball club, he would regard himself as a man who'd done *something* to make his wife hate him.

I felt the same. What had I done?

I'd tried to be fair; I'd kept warning him, Keep your hands off my children, don't force me to a choice, that's one you have to lose.

Come off it, Swifty, I said to myself finally.

That wasn't it. He knew he came third. His whole life and personality had been coming in first. He'd heard the one hundred thousand in the Coliseum stand to cheer him as a Stanford All American halfback, he'd scored against the Four Horsemen of Notre Dame in the Rose Bowl, he'd been the star of the American Rugby Team that won the Olympic Games in Paris; he'd been a forest ranger and spent winters high in Yosemite all alone; it took a *man* to do that, Tom Mix told me, mountains reduce a man to size, Tom said.

Could this man have had some right in trying to discipline my children? The biggest row we'd ever had was when he sent back an expensive dress I'd ordered for Elaine to wear at her first West Point Hop. And I'd said icily, After all, it wasn't *your* money.

Small wonder he hated me.

This caught up with me some, but I couldn't let it enter into the fight I was having in this courtroom. I saw Cracker, Dicky's devoted governess, and Ethel, who'd been housekeeper at Malibu, and my friend Ivy Sawyer Santley, whose little girl Betty had played with him on the beach. All there in the courtroom to testify for me.

Take the stand please, Mrs. St. Johns.

It cannot be true that I am on the witness stand again.

My heart began to thud against my side as Jerry Geisler came around in front of me. My old friend Jerry. Why, we'd been kids together in Earl Rogers' office, listened at doors, peeked through keyholes at my father and Clarence Darrow as they planned his defense for jury bribery. In my father-incarnation I thought he had been sorry for the girl Nora, because I think he knew what was coming to Mr. Rogers long before anybody else was sure.

How had we come together in pain and terror again? What was so awful was that as he stood there, my lawyer, he seemed to me vague and confused, I thought, He won't *fight* for me, we're going to lose this.

If you can get Earl Rogers to defend you—

Oh, Papa, where are you?

Do you want to go on with this farce? That was what my father had asked me in that other trial when doctors had advised me, If he won't help himself to conquer the Noseless One we must help him whether he likes it or not. In spite of himself, the doctors had said. Now I actually heard *myself* using his very word.

"Do you want to go on with this farce?" I said to the man who'd declared me an unfit mother in the courts.

He knew my children came first. Or did they? Then what had I been doing in Flemington, in Louisville, in Chicago? I had to earn a living, that was coming out now in this courtroom in my defense, one of the things that told mightily with the judge. I paid for the house at Malibu, the best governess, Cow Lane, Long Island, his small shoes, even the Kleenex when he had a cold and his big shepherd dog Michael, though actually Gable had given him Michael. Cracker told the judge I'd written daily and telephoned every single night.

BUT—I had been making a good living at home in Cow Lane.

And I had married a man *I* knew couldn't as yet earn money in the bracket in which I chose to live.

Why didn't we cut our losses? You can't win 'em all.

So I said to him, "Do you want to go on with this farce?"

He didn't answer. I don't blame him.

How wonderful for me that the man who did more to help me than anyone, even Clements, was Ike St. Johns. Ike sat beside me all the time and if I had trouble finding under the mountain of flesh the hand-some young man I'd married, I found instead a rock. Why hadn't I known he was, would always be a rock? Because I didn't want a rock. I wanted to go over Niagara Falls in a barrel. In the courtroom he kept pat-ting my hand and when the Japanese houseboy said the black lace negligee was mine, Ike said loudly, But you never wore a *black lace* negli-gee in your life. He indicated for all to hear that I could never have fallen that low.

Ike testified for me. Big, middle-aged, impressive. He said I was the mother of his children, he had of course allowed me to keep their custody and he kept closely in touch and knew that at all times I had been worthy of it. He said he was fond of the boy who wasn't his, about whom this suit was being fought, and that he always took him along when they went on trips or expeditions or to ball games and come right down to it he hadn't seen his *own* father doing any of these things. He said he was proud of the way I brought up our children and in fact, he said, with a grin, he'd be proud if I'd consider giving him another chance as a husband. Even the judge laughed at that.

Too late, Ike knew that as well as I did.

I like to remember how *pleased* Ike was when my son Dick took my St. Johns name a little later. It was Dicky's own choice. He and Ike were fond of each other, and so as a family we are and have been the St. Johnses and I'm sure Ike thinks of that as the memorial he would like best.

The judge's decision came down at ten minutes to five. I might as well say here that Ike had helped to elect the judge, this did not mean that he would be influenced to rule in my favor. It might and often did make him lean over backwards to *prove* he wasn't paying off for past favors. We knew this all the time, he was a judge of grave rectitude. But once he had ruled, it was too late for them to slap an appeal on me. I had to get back to New York, and an appeal would tie me up for months, the way the Appellate Division was jammed it might be years.

IF the ruling was in my favor. IF I was to keep the custody and be allowed to take my child out of the state.

We won.

The decision was more than in my favor. Much more. I still held it to me on cold nights of despair when my doings seemed to consist largely of doing those things I ought not to do and not doing those things I ought to do. The judge ruled that I was more than a fit mother, he even read aloud from some letters I'd written my son from Flemington (*when?*). Since the work by which I supported my child might be out of California I could take him wherever and whenever that work required it.

16. The house built on the walnut ranch in Whittier, California, by Adela Rogers St. Johns.

17. Mrs. St. Johns on Chief, the Irish hunter given to her by Tom Mix, at the Whittier ranch, with the expensive walnut trees in the background.

18. Adela with Warden Halloran
and his wife (standing)
and their daughter (seated
beside Mrs. St. Johns)
inside San Quentin Prison
on an assignment.

19. Mark Kelly,
the Red Rooster of the Arroyo.

20. Adela with her second husband at the Whittier ranch.

AMES MONTGOMERY FLAGG

21. Walter Howey's favorite Girl Reporter, "Swifty."
This James Montgomery Flagg drawing
was used by Howey to promote Adela and her stories.

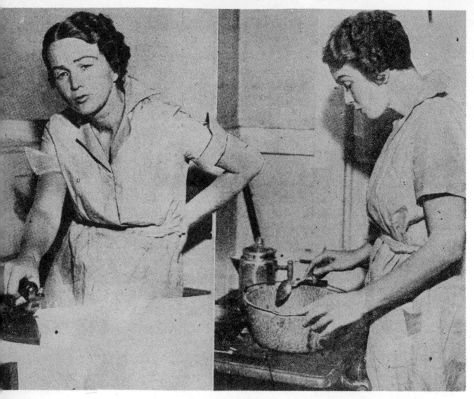

22. Adela working as a mother's helper to obtain
first-hand facts for her series of articles on
Unemployed Women.

23. Adela with
Louella Parsons at the
Roosevelt Third Term
Convention in Chicago,
1940.

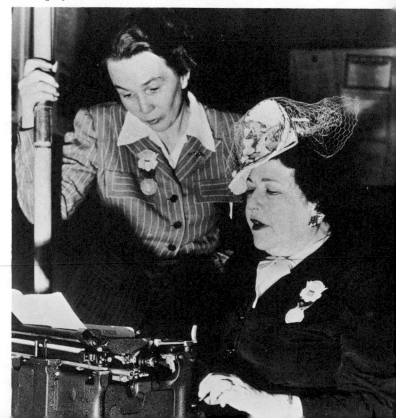

24. Adela with the Duke and Duchess of Windsor in the garden at Seagrist, the house they rented in Nassau.

25. Pilot officer
Lieutenant Thornwell Rogers, USMC
Adela's brother,
lost over Rabaul,
World War II.

26. "The Skipper," Pilot Officer
William Ivan St. Johns, RCAF,
somewhere in England.

27. "Grammy" Adela Rogers
St. Johns at The Hill, her home
near Metro-Goldwyn-Mayer in
Southern California,
with her grandchildren,
left to right: Sunny, Winkie,
Diane, Koko and baby granddaughter, Kristen, in her lap.
On the wall in the background
is the cherished painting of
the lion cub by Dan Smith,
which she chose as her bonus
from William Randolph Hearst
for her coverage of the
Hauptmann trial.

28. **A recent photograph,** left to right: **Adela, Joan Crawford and
Virginia Graham** on *Girl Talk* **TV show.** *(M. Jaffe)*

29. A cherished photograph of William Randolph Hearst, inscribed: (M. Jaff
"Dear Adela: Why don't you come around and see a lonesome old fellow
like yours faithfully W. R. Hearst."

30. A contemporary photograph of
Adela Rogers St. Johns
on the beach at
Malibu, California.
(Engstead)

Gravely, he also said he considered some of the testimony against me to have been perjured, I could handle this as I thought proper.

Another thing was repeating itself. As in my case against my father, in this, too, the press had never mentioned anything that went on in the courtroom. Not a line of testimony got into print. The Unwritten Law of Honor Among Reporters held. There would be small ordinary stories on inside pages saying that Judge Valentine had awarded me custody of my six-year-old son. My reputation, such as it was, was undamaged.

As I've said, when Little Augie set out on a project he never gave up. That afternoon I found the big black car in front of my house already packed with luggage, dogs, children, and Cracker with the little men in front. We were a procession, with Thorny conveying Clements bringing up the rear. We took off for Colton to catch the Golden State Limited of the Southern Pacific—I didn't want trouble at the Santa Fe Station in Pasadena. Before court convened the next morning, when an appeal could be filed, we would be across the state line into Arizona. Exhilaration throbbed along with the big car's engine. Just the same my conscience was sick and got sicker.

People keep saying to me, You've lived the most fantastic life, haven't you?

It never seemed like that to me while I was living it.

I thought of it as perfectly normal, as I suppose people do who think they are Napoleon or Puff the Magic Dragon. As I put Little Augie and his boys on paper I can see people have a point. Perhaps they weren't exactly normal in a woman's life. On the other hand, might they not simply be exaggerations of things that do occur in all lives? What is normal I don't know—this, like a blood pressure that never goes over a hundred, seemed to be normal for me.

I was dizzy with relief.

Yet as we made our way out into the desert I stared at the backs of the two *derbies* and had a feeling growing stronger at every turn of the wheel that this might be a warning blinker to tell me *I* was off the road even if the big black car wasn't.

Certainly I know now it was some kind of a beginning of a major turning point. Life would never be quite that carefree highfalutin' swaggering rodomontade I'd been concocting—never again.

This time I'd been saved. By grace? Nonsense. By Jerry Geisler's courtroom tactics—so different from Papa's but very effective I saw. By the way Ike St. Johns stood by me. By my own innocence. Enough innocence to make it look good.

As we got on the train and once again I began to stow us aboard I heard something telling me, Nothing ever stands still. Things move. They get more or less, if not better or worse.

Do you *know* what you're doing?

You better watch your step.

In the night, as we moved out through the Mojave Desert and the stars were desert bright and very close, I sat upright, yanked off my pillow by a thought.

Suppose the ruling had gone against you?

We'll be around if you change your mind, lady.

What would you have done then, Nora?

At dawn I was still awake facing myself.

I knew what I would have done.

I would have said, Little Augie, you are a true friend, always ready to help a chum in a pinch.

Ye have heard that it hath been said ye shall not kill but I say to you that whosoever looks at a man to lust after killing him has committed murder already in her heart. Something like that it had said in my grandfather's Bible when he preached in that town we'd just left behind us— *Colton.*

Would I have turned *thumbs down,* if the ruling had gone against me?

We do not hear the word conscience much any more. It's there just the same, the internal recognition of right and wrong as regards one's actions and motives. The faculty which decides in reason, in fairness, in truth on the moral and spiritual values within one's own soul.

The decent thing that's possible to do.

I know it's there because mine rode with me that night.

I had been confronted by two subhuman killers for the purpose of murder.

My conscience found homicide impossible to consider in the dawn's early light.

BOOK FOUR

BOOK FOUR

CHAPTER 29

The years in Washington seem cut off with swords from those before and those that came after.

Washington is always in danger of becoming an enormous ivory tower where people talk to themselves and politicians and even statesmen talk only to each other. Like Hollywood and the TV empire, they must have Gallup polls and Neilsen ratings and Crosley checkups to find out what is going on in the rest of the country, in the millions of minds and hearts of those who set them in power. None of these can be consistently accurate. They lack a way to touch the incredible variations of our land, the little farms in New England and the Wyoming cattle ranches, the cities from Detroit to New Orleans, the states from Florida to Utah to California to Maine, of our people with the background and blood of every nation that caused us for a hundred years to be the Melting Pot. Mr. Nielsen's "swatches," as he told me he calls his devices on a few hundred television sets, cannot possibly record all this. So develops not only a credibility gap but a Washington provincialism, an isolation and insulation that can be deadly.

Even though I flew thousands of miles from Cow Lane (New York) to San Simeon (California) to Washington (D.C.), it was Washington that engulfed my imagination. After its tempo and power power power other things seemed flat stale and unprofitable.

I haven't covered Washington since the world-shaking exaltation of the Thirties and early Forties.

Politically, I have never been able to stay put in a party. *The Man!* In my time, I've been a Democrat, a Republican, a Mugwump, a Bull Moose, and I'm almost sure I would have voted for Socialist Eugene V. Debs, of the Brotherhood of Locomotive Firemen around 1908, as a teen-age rebel should.

From being a follower of F.D.R., I came to the Republican Party as a Democrat for Nixon. But in 1969 I thought I might switch again as a Republican for Bobby Kennedy. Remembering how I felt when I cast my first vote for the second term of that rebel-intellectual college president Woodrow Wilson, my heart ached for the young people who saw in Bobby the one man to lead them out of the wilderness we had created for them. But— Bobby wasn't to run, God give him not rest but plenty of work for others where he is now. Nobody could know Bobby Kennedy's genius as well as an opponent on the press side, as I was when I campaigned for Nixon in '60.

On the wall of my workroom is a photograph in grateful appreciation, it says, of *your wise counsel over the years*. I keep hoping my grandchildren, *and* great-grandchildren will *listen to me* when they realize this sentiment is signed by Richard M. Nixon, now President of the United States.

As a writer, the words I treasure most are those in the Introduction to his best-selling book, *Six Crises*. Three people, he says, exerted particular influence in changing his mind when it was made up not to write a book. Mrs. Eisenhower, who said only the former Vice President could tell of certain events in her husband's administrations. John F. Kennedy, who on their first meeting after Kennedy took office said every public man should write a book to elevate him in popular esteem as an "intellectual."

And "The one who had the greatest influence on my decision was Adela Rogers St. Johns. From the time I entered public life as a Congressman she has been a close friend and adviser. Through the years she insisted I should write a book and when I returned to California she took matters into her own hands. [*Mama Fix!*] I received a call from her informing me that Ken McCormick of Doubleday was flying out the next day to see me. . . ."

It has been part of your life that you knew a boy when he delivered your groceries on the Whittier ranch, that you watched him defeat Alger Hiss in one of our triumphs over Communism, that you saw him get up off the floor after being knocked out in 1960—and that makes him a champion— and that you can go back to Washington to visit him in the White House— *news becomes history*—and you were part of it.

At the time I covered it Washington had a Star, a Superstar for a long time. If you had lived there and worked there when he was President, Washington without Franklin Delano Roosevelt wouldn't be Washington. And we must remember that everything that takes place today in social progress is the result of the level of socialism with democracy which came about through our Man of the Moment, that aristocratic benevolent dictator F.D.R. and his wife Eleanor, whose deep concern for all of us when she was First Lady made her not only the most beloved and respected woman this country had known but also the one who actually played the most real and enduring part in shaping our ends. She was the President's second self.

In a press conference one day at the White House, the President used the words *a liberal*. I said, "Mr. President, there are so many meanings to that word nowadays. Would you be kind enough to give us your definition?"

"A liberal," the President said, "is a man who wants to build bridges over the chasms that separate humanity from a better life."

Whether his bridges were the right ones, whether they have been the way to a better world, I have always been sure that this was his aim in all that he did. The hydrophobic quality of his opposition, frothing at the mouth as it did, the fanaticism of his followers who, if they hadn't been Americans, might have knelt in the street as he passed, increased the velocity and intensity of our lives.

My time in Washington was not Robert Sherwood's time nor Jonathan Daniel's time nor Walter Lippmann's time, nor Arthur Krock's. The history of the Roosevelt years has been told by historians, economists, military leaders, statesmen, eyewitnesses and noneyewitnesses, visitors, reporters, academicians, friends and enemies and will be forever.

My time in Washington in the days of Roosevelt can best be pinned down by the nature of the assignment as Mr. Hearst gave it to me when he sent me there.

2

This time Mr. Hearst led me to the window that gave on the mountains, towering purple against a night sky of stars.

"I would like you to consider going to Washington," he said.

"Washington!" I said. "What's going on in Washington?"

"Everything," he said, he hit it *staccato* for him, driving points into his left palm with his right fist. "I have always put local news first. Washington *is* local news. It has become every American's home town.

"Not too long ago a large percentage of Americans knew who was their Governor. Not who was President. Even in our times Washington has been on page eighteen, a week could go by with no mention except on the editorial pages, which most readers do not note. Today the New Deal is the hottest local news in every city and hamlet. We used to write of little except the Tariff, in these precarious times when we walk a tightrope from one war to another we hope to avoid, everything the President and the Congress do is vital to our daily existence. Our jobs, bank accounts, schools, a new branch of local news called Taxes each must pay.

"Taxes?" I said. "Does Congress—I am appalled at my ignorance. Papa was always interested and Ike elected a senator—but now—I don't even know what Congress is *for*—not exactly—"

This made him instantly gleeful. "Neither do our readers," he said. "I always hope Congress does. O. O. McIntyre is the most read columnist in the world today. Why?"

"You think about your dog when he tells stories about his dog," I said.

"He wrote about New York," Mr. Hearst said, "not as a jaded New Yorker who hasn't been to the Statue of Liberty, but as he'd written for his home town paper in Indiana. *Too bad Susie Vanderbilt and Johnny Astor won't get married this year better luck next time*—his human interest stories of the Big City and Broadway were told as he'd told those of the Small Town and Main Street. The reader recognized them."

After considering a moment, he said, "*Woman.* In your series on the Unemployed Woman we dealt with the Modern Woman. Now she has the vote and it may become the deciding factor in our national life. Therefore she must give care and concern to the candidates she elects and follow them to *Washington* to see that they do their job for her as she used to count the laundry or check up on her grocer's weights. Already in *Washington* they are working on a minimum wage and maximum hours bill for *women.* We have a captive readership of women if we can make it entertaining to them."

"How?" I said.

"With the growing importance of Washington news," he said, "we must have more and better features and that is your business."

"Come to think of it," I said, "I've never even seen the cherry blossoms."

"Then you will not take them for granted," Mr. Hearst said sternly. "There must be many many good stories and unusual women in Washington. Mrs. Patterson is a great publisher for my paper there but she moved to Washington when she was very young. I doubt she knows its personalities at all levels. The wife of a first term congressman has a new and unfamiliar job almost as important as her husband's. The Cave Dweller wife of an old senator may be as powerful or more so than the senator himself. Many girls are now employed by the Government. So we are not limited in scope to Mrs. Patterson herself nor the First Lady, nor my friend Evalyn Walsh McLean, Washington's social dictator who owns the Hope Diamond. Are you too young to remember Teddy Roosevelt as President?"

"He made Heney special prosecutor in the Graft Cases my father defended in San Francisco," I said, "so I remember him well but I forgave him because he got Owen Wister to write *The Virginian.*"

"Since the Roosevelts came to the White House they have indeed become our First Family. Everybody is interested always in Family Doings. This is an exciting, dramatic, show-off magnified Family, it is now *Ours,* they may have family feuds and disagreements, scandals and failures, but they will belong to all our readers."

After a pause he said, "One other thing." I thought, *Here it comes.* I knew I wouldn't be peacefully writing descriptions of cherry trees nor ballads about congressmen's wives. There would be *news* around some-where. "I wish to speak to you about Senator Huey Long of Louisiana."

"Even amid orange blossoms and sunshine I have heard of the King-fish," I said.

Mr. Hearst said, "When the senator from California, Hiram Johnson, came to San Simeon last week he said to me that today the United States Senate, the most powerful body in the world, is composed of ninety-five forgotten men and Huey Long. Senator Johnson said our constituents when they come to Washington use us only to get into the Senate to hear the Kingfish. Mountebank, genius, whatever he is, Senator Johnson told me the Union regards him as The Senator." Mr. Hearst paused for em-phasis. "Therefore, Senator Long is national-local news. At this mo-ment, he will not speak to anyone in the Hearst Service."

"Why not?" I said, and Mr. Hearst said, "He and Mr. Brisbane have had a difference of opinion," and I said, "I'm with Huey," and Mr. Hearst said, "I have warned you about your prejudices, when it is a matter of news we cannot afford to debate who is right or wrong."

He held me with a glittering eye, all right, and the merry din of the dinner guests filling the huge room receded to nothingness. "Mrs. Patter-son believes," he said, "a feud is brewing between Senator Long and the President. Let us not forget that the senator from Louisiana had a major part in Roosevelt's nomination in 1932, and Roosevelt was grateful. Now Mrs. Patterson feels sure Huey Long means to make every attempt to get the nomination for himself in 1936. This puts the President and Senator Long, once close friends, at open odds."

"The idea of Huey Long trying to get nominated for President—isn't that pretty fantastic?" I said.

"In a free country, a spellbinding soapbox demagogue who has proved himself a wizard as a vote getter, who can tell?" Mr. Hearst said. "Our George R. Holmes is the best and most popular bureau chief in Washing-ton, however in the matter of Huey Long he is not as helpful as he should be. He is married to Stephen Early's sister. Besides being Press Secretary to President Roosevelt, Mr. Early and his sister Mrs. Holmes are de-scendants of General Jubal Early of Virginia, who never took the oath of allegiance to the United States after the Civil War. They regard Senator Long as poor white trash. An upstart or not, Huey Long is the hottest news in Washington, running nose and nose with the President himself."

"You want me to get on Huey's good side," I said.

"Mrs. Patterson tells me," Mr. Hearst said, "that the senator never goes out socially. He will not accept an invitation from her nor Mrs. Mc-Lean nor anyone else and no one knows why."

I found out. He wasn't sure which fork to use.

I found out quite a lot of other things, such as the name of the man he thought would assassinate him. Huey was wrong about a lot of things but he was right about that.

"Yet," Mr. Hearst was saying, "she also tells me he likes feminine society. We must at least explore the possibility that you may be a source of news to us in this."

Slowly, I said, "I liked him the night I met him at the Sands Point Club. He wasn't all that drunk, you know. I danced with him, and even sober men have difficulty dancing with me. He didn't."

"Then I am sure you must go to Washington as soon as possible," Mr. Hearst said. "Mr. Brisbane is convinced that a soapbox spellbinder who can hypnotize the Senate of the United States as no one has done since Daniel Webster—might take the country as Napoleon once took France. No one believed that could happen either. Napoleon at the time he became First Consul had little more to offer France than Senator Long has to offer us—true, France had just been through a revolution but so have we. We know now that Napoleon was only an inspired gangster and showman who struck at the right time and could lead men. All this, as you must see, makes it vital that we should be in contact with Senator Long. I am running *news*papers. I suggest you report to Mr. Holmes in Washington as soon as possible."

"I'd rather work out of a city room," I said. "I never like bureaus. Can't I go to the Washington *Herald* for Mrs. Patterson?"

Thereby sealing my own future in a measure, for in the city editor of the Washington *Herald* I met my fate or as near as makes no difference.

Every woman tells me there was only the One Man she ever really loved. Joan Crawford told me once that the only man she really loved was the rather dull, middle-aged vice-president of a soda-pop company and when I reminded her she'd said this to me about Doug Fairbanks, Jr., and Clark Gable and Greg Bautzer she looked incredulous. Then she said quite simply, "There is always only one though, isn't there?" And told me. It wasn't the vice-president.

I will now join the ranks.

If I hadn't gone to Washington on a Sunday to get my expense-account wardrobe unpacked and myself settled so I'd be ready to lay siege to Huey Long on Monday, I wouldn't have found the city editor of the *Herald* alone at his desk when I called to check in. On a long, lazy Sunday afternoon he said, "I'd better come round and take you to dinner. I've been waiting for you, you know."

Fifteen minutes later I opened the door.

I know it doesn't. No such thing as love at first sight.

But it did. Even now, looking back across those many years, I know it did. In a strange way, it still does. For him. Not for anyone else.

Of course Ray Helgesen had everything going for him. He was a city editor. Howey had told me about him. If he doesn't kill himself in that car the way he drives, Howey said, he'll be the best in the service. He can handle Mrs. Patterson, too. Women! *In droves!* Last time I was down there a senator's daughter used to wait out in front of the paper for him and half the time he went out the circulation alley. He's quite a guy, Howey said.

I'd said, "A romanticized version of you and J. B. T. Campbell, no doubt. It sounds awful."

It wasn't.

He was over six feet, lanky and balanced, like a good end. He had thick blond hair, a shock of it swung over his forehead, and he flung it back with a furious gesture. Blue eyes—not Irish blue, his were like northern lights, they were a challenge, they didn't light up for just anybody. If they grew warm for you alone that would be a victory.

He sat down, he didn't say anything, just looked at me, and his eyes did grow warm and I lost my breath. He said, "Howey told me you were coming but I didn't quite believe it. I used to wait by the wire every day for your stuff from Flemington. You broke my heart a couple of times. I'd like to tell you I thought it was the best job any woman ever did."

"It was the best material any woman ever had," I said.

"They all had it," Helgesen said.

Shop talk. The same shop talk but now it was different. It moved between us like a shuttle, weaving us together.

On a Sunday the Carlton Grill was quiet, we sat at a small side table with roses and pink candles and what we ate I do not know, but I do know that somewhere something was playing "Stardust." Very softly. He said "Stardust" was like the Schubert *Kunstlied* his mother had taught him back in Minnesota and I told him I'd heard Lotte Lehmann sing Schubert in London once, and so "Stardust" became our theme song and once high up in the Blue Ridge Mountains we sang *"Du Bist Wie Eine Blume"* —nobody to hear us but the pine trees and the stars. Later we used to go and sit on the bank and listen to the symphonies from an orchestra on a barge out on the Potomac.

When we'd had our coffee and brandy that first Sunday he said, "You've never seen Washington. I'd like to be the one to show you some of the places that belong to you—and you belong to them."

We drove in his big open roadster. I remembered what Howey had said, but that night he drove slowly. We parked in front of the White House, quite close. I felt it belonged to me. That was true. So that to this day when I go back I stay at the Hay Adams in a room that lets me look out at it and I hear Helgesen's voice reminding me that Lincoln walked there and I could almost see him. So we went to the Lincoln

Memorial, where he *is*—Lincoln *is*—he comes there to visit us—and then we drove high high up above the Tomb of the Unknown Soldier.

"But," Helgesen said quietly, "it doesn't say an unknown soldier. It says, *Known but to God.* Here rests an American soldier known but to God."

I hadn't known that all Washington lies below him. The tomb seemed poised in the sky and below spread a vast city of quicksilver. A living soldier walked back and forth, very young, with a stern round face. But I knew it was the Soldier known but to God who stood guard over Washington. Young and fair and faithful he was, the starlight turning his helmet to silver, standing guard over those things for which he had died to keep us Forever America.

Looking back, it seems a little unfair that I saw this side—this facet— *this* Helgesen *first*.

As we drove down through the shadowy trees I wondered if I was having a dream. If I was, *why not?*

I was bruised and battered out of sense and shape by my encounter with what can be done to you when love turns to malice; and by the sore and still festering conscience I'd brought out of the custody suit. As for men, I'd been sure I was through with them. That was the third mule, the one *I* couldn't drive. My work. My children. Love, I said to myself—and husbands—I am through with.

I suppose a rebound was inevitable.

More than that, I hadn't known or hadn't wanted to know that there was within me as it were a cup of loneliness, which I suppose all women have when there is no man in their lives. To love, to be loved by. Male and female created He them, it says.

At going-on-forty this had to be there whether I'd named it or not.

We stopped at the Occidental for coffee. He put vanilla ice cream in his and I thought this was boyish and endearing. I knew this would be our favorite place for food and drink and talk talk talk, but that first night I hardly spoke. I was thinking so frantically.

Could this be the answer, please God? To find a man who thought my work was the best, so that there wouldn't *be* three mules, only two, if in our work we were *one*. My children—my-work-and-my-husband—makes *two*.

I was to find out soon enough that in the city room his voice had the traditional whiplash. But that night as we drove back to the Carlton it was low and sure and the things he said were sure, too.

Therefore we did not meet in the city room as strangers, though no one there knew we'd ever seen each other before. We could see they were watching us. How we'd react—the tough city editor and the new star reporter—and this filled us with secret laughter. We were already *a team*.

He looked so right behind the city desk. He had style. Even the inevitable blue vest looked elegant on him. His hair was blonder than ever under the lights.

When a few years later he committed suicide, I went away by myself and lived again that one most spectacular night of my newspaper career when we had been so desperately in love, and I wept bitterly.

Some IFs you carry as long as you live no matter how hard you try. I try to think of Ray Helgesen as an *incarnation*. Separated from all else. I can't. If my phobia against cruelty had not sent me into a headlong dash to escape from it and him, might we have founded a great Middle Western newspaper, a power for good in the land? Or did the fact he had it in him to do that unkind act *on purpose*, like pulling one wing off a fly, mean he wrote his own end without reference to me?

I wondered how it would have turned out if I had taken the other way at the crossroads. He might be alive instead of dead.

I didn't wonder long.

In that case, he would have shot me first.

The only man I ever really loved?

Yes, I think so.

CHAPTER 30

As I moved back into the world that is the Washington of Roosevelt I have the same magical experience that happens when you go to Valley Forge or spend a day at Gettysburg. Whether it is George and Martha who receive their guests upon the terrace at Mount Vernon or Jack and Jackie —the Washingtons or the Kennedys—everything changes but nothing's different.

Washington is timeless. A state of mind, a pulse of heart. A city that lieth foursquare.

Such a variety of stories I can construct to make you know that Washington is the granddaddy of all Main Streets. An old song of Bing Crosby's says wistfully, *It's easy to remember but so hard to forget* and I feel a pang of anguish that some of my beloved ghosts, some tales that made me laugh and weep, cannot populate Washington as I once knew it for it would take many books to hold them all.

So that you can be told but briefly of how I went to dine with the Russian Ambassador soon after the United States had recognized the Soviet Union. How, having rushed from my day's work, I'd hurried into a gown I'd never worn before only to discover in the dressing room at the embassy that there must be *something* which I should have put on underneath. To my horrified gaze into the triple mirror this thin wool dinner frock seemed nuder than a topless bunny. All of us were more conservative then, especially embassies. I put my coat back on and was edging out the front door when the ambassador came by and it was necessary for me to explain my predicament to him. This he greeted with shouts of Russian laughter and I was glad for I figured it was the first good laugh he'd had since he came to America. I allowed him to persuade me to return to a cloakroom. Here he brought me a tray of dinner from the buffet, showed me a pair of dice, and said, "Who do you shoot with these and how?" I spent the evening on the floor teaching the Russian Ambassador to shoot craps as a newsboy named Farmer Page, who later founded Reno and Las Vegas, once taught me. You can tell a lot by the way a man handles dice and when the ambassador and his wife were recalled to Russia and *never heard of again* I had an inner conviction that he was too reckless in believing he could make a six the hard way.

Nor can I give the amazing details of how I again found the power of the American woman when J. Edgar Hoover asked me to go to Tulsa, Oklahoma, to speak to the General Federation of Women's Clubs on the subject of *parole*. The director of the FBI said there was too much parole going on and we found that when we put it squarely up to the women they got off their complacent chairs and set up committees and did the job.

How I got in at last to ask Henry Morgenthau, Secretary of the Treasury, why he was plowing under all the pigs can be told in full, for it is short. This was one of those high-level, supply-and-demand gimmicks like deficit spending. IF fewer and fewer pigs were allowed to grow up the FARMER would get more and more per pound for bacon since there would be less and less of it. Contrariwise, a lot of mothers-of-the-race thought if there were more and more pigs there would be more and more bacon costing less and less per pound and thus she'd be able to give better and better nourishment to her children and the farmer's profit would add up higher and higher since he had more and more bacon to sell. The Secretary said it wouldn't *either*. I did not understand his explanation. The millions of women who read my story didn't understand it either. I wasn't sure the Secretary did and now it would all be totally incomprehensible. However when the interview was published all over the country, the Secretary protested that I hadn't *understood* him but as I'd said that myself in several hundred well-chosen words it didn't help any.

How I became part of some of the dramas, tragedies, and drawing-room comedies that took place at Friendship, Evalyn Walsh McLean's glorious house-and-garden, would take another book and many have already been written, especially Evalyn's own *Papa Struck It Rich,* telling of days when her father was a miner and her mother kept a boardinghouse, before the millions Papa dug with a pick wafted her to her position as Washington's first and greatest hostess with the mostest. A spotlight or two, however, will pick up the notorious Elsa Maxwell, who at an Evalyn Walsh McLean dinner kept on and on with quotes from "my dear friend Winnie." Fell upon the glittering beflowered table one of those silences that do fall, and into it the most beautiful voice in the world said, "Anything less likely for Mr. Churchill to have said I cannot imagine," and we felt that Miss Ethel Barrymore, having been engaged to Winston Churchill in their youth, knew better than La Belle Maxwell. Or fall upon a young G-man who asked Evalyn to let him hold the Hope Diamond. Evalyn always wore that ill-fated million-dollar jinx, for she said that everything had already happened to her, but she never let anyone else touch it. Once she laid it on a coffee table while she was on her knees repairing an electric wall socket, I automatically reached for it and she hit my outstretched hand with a screwdriver so hard it nearly broke my wrist. Yet after looking at this young man gravely with her strange gray-green penetration (she sees more than the rest of us, J. Edgar told me of that lady, whom he telephoned every night of his life the last thing) Evalyn gave him the diamond. It lay in his palm winking like the Evil Eye itself. The next day he shot himself. I said to Evalyn, "You believed in its sinister power—why did you?" and quietly Evalyn said, "It's better for him this way," and that's all I know about *that*.

How I came into Cissy Patterson's 15 Dupont Circle mansion with the transcripts of the much-discussed Behind-Closed-Doors Testimony under one arm *and* Gloria Morgan Vanderbilt and her twin sister Lady Thelma Furness under the other. This started when I broke my rule against attending the most abhorrent of all evils, a Cocktail Party. I can't remember why or where. I do remember well that the first person I saw was Gloria Vanderbilt.

By that time, young Mrs. Vanderbilt had lost to her sister-in-law, Mrs. Harry Payne Whitney, the guardianship of Gloria's ten-year-old daughter, Little Gloria, heiress to the fortune left by her father, Reginald Vanderbilt. Drop those names—Payne—Whitney—Vanderbilt—Morgan—and they spelled Wealth to us, especially as this was before the Rockefellers took the lead with the Kennedys coming up on the outside.

I had watched this trial in the Supreme Court of New York from afar. The Society Scandal of our decade, that was. My fascinated horror grew as it mounted to the point of Greek Tragedy in the appearance of Gloria's mother, Mrs. Harry Hayes Morgan, on the stand where she testified as to the moral turpitude of her own daughter. And thence to climax when the judge closed the doors of the courtroom on the further testimony to be given against this young mother and barred the press. No challenge like a closed door, and when the judge took the child and her vast fortune from her mother and gave them to Aunt Gertrude, the press was indignant, for no one knew what the testimony could be that brought such a decision to pass.

The change in Gloria Vanderbilt since the last time I'd been with her at the Hearst Ranch startled me. She was too thin, there was a new streak of silver in her dark madonna hair, it was as plain that this was a woman carrying a mortal wound as any physical death warrant could have been. A woman having looked on the head of the Medusa, unless God gives her grace to bear it, will not care to live any longer. So it was with Gloria Vanderbilt. Yet she set up a vibration of suppressed excitement at that moment that set off within me the inner summons, the what's-going-on-here of the reporter.

Her lawyers had filed an appeal from the Supreme Court's decision, and so they had been obliged to provide him with the record of the Behind-Closed-Doors Testimony. This record Gloria herself had never seen before. I said to her, "The real disserve of the trial was when the judge closed those doors, the public turned loose their lowest imagination and came up with Roman Orgies and French postcards."

"But there isn't anything in them," Gloria said; she took both my hands and hers were hot. "I've read them. Backstairs tittle-tattle—servants' gossip at its worst and bought and paid for—you could *tell*—my dear, there wasn't any *reason* to have those witnesses testify in that courtroom behind closed doors."

I wondered then if Beauty must always bring about the Trojan War or its equivalents. As famous as, *more* famous than movie stars, the Social Register Morgan twins were the daughters of a career diplomat, they'd been born and educated entirely in Europe where they spoke French, Italian, and German but no English until they were eleven and never saw the United States until they were twelve. By that time it was evident that Gloria Morgan was going to be a Beauty.

Today we have reduced this to a mean average so that every woman young or old who isn't cross-eyed and some who are can rate the term *beauty*. In one Society column it is possible to find the ladies who attend hairdressers' balls or a charity romp described as that pretty little beauty, that dazzling beauty, that decorative beauty, that best-dressed beauty with the infinitesimal waist, that striking blond beauty, that chic beauty, attractive piquant beauty, that Ghana-Malaya-Israeli Egyptian princess duchess shiekess Spanish-glamour, Italian-romantic, petite French, extra-special splendid sexy beauty—all these referring to different ladies of every ilk and stripe which can all be very gala indeed.

In the days of the Morgan twins we had Beauties as a special group tracing directly back to Helen of Troy.

I've seen lots of the above types but only six women who possessed the memorable beauty to launch a thousand ships.

Madeleine Carroll
Elizabeth Taylor when she was young
Lady Diana Manners
Barbara La Marr
Vivien Leigh
Gloria Morgan Vanderbilt

So as I looked at her I wasn't too surprised that she was in trouble. As far as their mother was concerned, this beauty had spelled Rich Marriage. The Harry Hayes Morgans were Fine Old Family but not Fine Old Money. Soon all her hopes were fulfilled. Thelma, who was stunning and witty, married Lord Furness (British Steamship Lines). At *seventeen*, Gloria became the wife of Reginald Vanderbilt and, before she was twenty-one, his widow. Not being of age she couldn't be legal regent for their daughter, Little Gloria, the heiress. It had to go through court. In my articles later I said:

> Let us regard these women, the antagonists in this battle of the century. On one side Mrs. Harry Payne Whitney, nee Vanderbilt. There is no use trying to add up what Mrs. Whitney represents in the way of money. I can't count that high. Mrs. Whitney with social prestige and power as great or greater than any woman in the country. Added together her money, social standing and connections give her influence socially politically and financially which believe me she can *use*. So—in this corner, Mrs. Harry Payne Whitney nee Vanderbilt, sixty now, sculptress, social dictator, horsewoman and power. In the other Gloria Morgan Vanderbilt, twenty-eight, a beauty, subject to all the talk, envy, and curiosity that follow Beauty. A girl brought up with continental standards and ways of life, who is now called an unfit mother by this desiccated in-law *and* her own mother Laura Hecuba Agrippina Clytemnestra Morgan.

No question that I was biased. I had myself experienced what can be concocted by an enemy out of pretty innocuous stuff. Moreover, I was against any doors closed to the press.

Holding a glass of champagne in her hand, Gloria said, "Do you know what it was—that testimony? My maid said she came in one morning with my coffee and I was in bed reading the paper and Lady Milford Haven, who was visiting me from England, came in and bent to kiss me—the maid admitted I didn't even put down the paper, and I had rung for my coffee. I had broken my engagement to Prince Hohenlohe because I would not and could not take my daughter Gloria to live in Germany—so I had sometimes as an escort A. C. Blumenthal and his chauffeur said I stayed in his apartment two hours—have you ever *seen* A. C. Blumenthal—?"

As the elite guests, glasses in hand, swirled around in whosoever's bedazzled and bedecked drawing room it was I was *seeing* A. C. Blumenthal. I knew what she meant.

Gloria's faintly French-accented voice was saying, "It wasn't that I would deny my child a *dog*—no no—only *that* dog. He had a bad disposition, and that was the first time my daughter was angry with me—they told her I would not let her have a dog!" I felt sorry for both Glorias. I looked again at Gloria's too-thin face and silver-streaked hair. What do you do with the rest of your life after you've heard your own mother call you a moral danger to your child under oath for all the world to hear? I'd only had *fear,* fear of loss, fear for my child's future, no such pain as this. Betrayal by those you love builds the hottest fire to consume you at the stake.

Somebody jostled my arm, a spilled martini seeping coldly down inside my dress instead of my throat startled me anew. I tightened my belt and remembered I was Mrs. St. Johns of INS. I said, "Where are those transcripts?" and Gloria said, "In my jewel safe," and I went to look for Lady Furness, who as much as she could took care of *her* Helen of Troy.

An hour later we were in a big Rolls-Royce bound for Washington. I had persuaded the sisters of what I believed. If those pages were published, the petty persecution trick of harmless testimony Behind-Closed-Doors would be exposed, Gloria's innocence of those imaginary debaucheries would be proved, public sentiment would change in her favor, even her child's poisoned mind might be healed.

Gloria and Thelma wouldn't be parted for one second from the big blue-bound books of evidence, they wouldn't go to the *Herald* so we brought the *Herald* to them. The following hours with Cissy herself moving on the outskirts in black net and diamonds—Cissy ordering Philpotts and his staff to turn the magnificence of 15 Dupont Circle into a replica of the Washington *Herald,* the library became the city room, Miss Burney's secretarial suite the telegraph desk, and the shining mahogany table in the dining hall was soon both a copy desk and a place for the experts who transcribed the transcripts to work, so that we could announce:

COPYRIGHT BY INTERNATIONAL NEWS SERVICE
EXCLUSIVE TO THE WASHINGTON HERALD

—these hours cannot be told in detail, only as a hum of frantic activity.

Page by page on the spot where Mrs. Roosevelt and the British Ambassador and Secretary of State Hull had dined, experts copied testimony at a dizzy speed.

> *Q.* She still had the newspaper in her hand when the Marchioness of Milford Haven bent to kiss her?
> *A.* Oh yes, she never put down the paper.
> *Q.* How long did she stay at Mr. Blumenthal's apartment?
> *A.* Oh sometimes an hour or more.
> *Q.* Did you ever see anything out of the way?
> *A.* Oh no, they just sat and talked and played the phonograph.
> *Q.* Did you ever see Mrs. Vanderbilt walk nude through the drawing room?
> *A.* Well, not to say nude, no, but in a sort of robe you could partly see through.
> *Q.* Were there any gentlemen present?
> *A.* Oh no sir—no—not any gentlemen.

Ray Helgesen came back and forth, pleased with his Exclusive; all the papers that published it, and there were hundreds, had to say *Credit to the Washington Herald.*

On the soft-scented morning of the first of May, the front page of the *Herald* carried these headlines—so terribly important then:

MILLIONS HEAR HITLER TELL PEACE PLANS

ROOSEVELT AGREES TO NRA REVISION

FRANCE SIGNS WAR TREATY WITH RUSSIA

DEFICIT GROWS TOO LARGE

HUEY LONG DEMANDS ACTION ON CRIME REPORT

And right in the middle with pictures:

GLORIA GIVES FIRST INTERVIEW

VANDERBILT WIDOW IN CAPITAL

TELLS ADELA ROGERS ST. JOHNS

THE STORY OF SECRET TESTIMONY

The innocuous pages of the Behind-Closed-Doors Testimony did bring about a warm wave of apology and sympathy all over the country. The public reacted to the truth with applause and approval. Sentiment, having condemned the mother, now swung in her favor. She became a public idol.

Presumably, in time, Little Gloria read saw heard and felt this. And she is the only one of the principals in this sensational story who is left. Gloria the beautiful is dead, Mrs. Harry Payne Whitney in spite of her financial and social pinnacle of power had to go the way of all flesh and the Greek-Roman mother has testified in a sterner court I hope.

Lady Thelma Furness I see from time to time, always looking lonely without her twin.

I knew Little Gloria had first married a man old enough to be her grand-father if he *was* Leopold Stokowski, as indeed he was. Then a young movie producer, Sidney Lumet. Then I lost track. So at this point in my memories I called up Her Who Knows All, the brilliant Society-Satirist of the New York *Daily News* SUZY. She told me that after striking out twice Little Gloria married a writer-actor named Wyatt Cooper. They live in New York, a place in the country of course, the union is blessed with four sons. For the past year Gloria Vanderbilt Cooper has had One Man Shows of her paintings. It shows her strength of character to have survived into normal happiness. I hope her mother knows of this happy ending. Even in heaven it will be welcome news.

Gloria was a memorable woman. She is one of the ghosts of my Washington who is *easy to remember and so hard to forget.*

Also, how I got out of Washington now and again as I thought everyone should, and thus found myself in Canada covering the Dionne Quintuplets' first birthday. On the way back the train stopped in the middle of the night and a violent knocking on my drawing-room door woke me out of a sound sleep. When I opened it there stood an harassed conductor who said, "You have to get off here," and I said, "Get off? I'm going to Toronto—" and he said, "I got orders from the head of the Canadian Pacific to put you off here at the Junction." There I was with my polo coat over my nightgown and the conductor threw my suitcase and my clothes after me. Though it was late May there was still snow on the ground, I seemed to be on a prairie. The station was so small I could hardly see it and in its one dim light looked completely deserted until an individual in a parka loomed and said he was the telegrapher and had a phone call waiting for me. My heart climbed out of my chest. The children! But when I picked up the receiver a very annoyed voice said, "Adela? Why are you going East?" and I said, "Why, Mr. Hearst, I'm on my way back to Washington," and the voice said, "I am amazed that I have to think of everything myself. Kindly proceed to Chicago. Howey will have you met, you should be on your way West to *Tacoma*," and I remembered that was where the Weyerhauser kidnaping had taken place. I managed a truck from a farmer, and finally we found a hedge-hopping private plane and in Chicago Howey's man handed me five thousand dollars in cash—in kidnaping you need emergency funds. There is no room to tell you how I bought a motorboat with this—we were told little Georgie had been taken to sea—and how I stood in a dark wood with Joseph E. Patrick Dunne of the FBI and saw two hundred thousand dollars in ransom put on the seat of a dark car and driven away by a faceless figure or how I put a one-hundred-dollar bill on the door of a taxi and the driver told me all Georgie had said on his way home. Nor how I saw Georgie restored to his mother and then telephoned Mr. Hearst *wildly* and said, "I cannot cover any more *kidnapings*."

You will remember that Marion Davies had told me the cause of the feud between Cissy Patterson, now my publisher, and the Princess Alice, and I go back to that now, for I had to be thinking of it one day when I was lunching with Mrs. Nicholas Longworth, who had been our American princess in the White House long ago. The Mayflower was so crowded that every time the man at the next table picked up his fork he got his elbow in my soup, and Alice Longworth has a Barrymore voice that carries even when she whispers and she never whispers.

"—Eleanor is my cousin, different branch of the family but we were both born Roosevelts. A shy plain little girl, I was amazed she made such a good marriage. Franklin was handsome as a Greek god and an only son. A *catch*. Even though she's in the White House, I cannot say I really care for her, but hear me, she is a great lady and I do not allow any of this buzz buzz about Franklin and the Princess Martha to be repeated in my presence. True, the Princess is a beauty and that Eleanor is not, but I tell you Franklin loves Eleanor and has never really loved anyone else—men are unaccountable, aren't they?"

This of course is the Mrs. Longworth, the great lady of Washington, whose description of Thomas E. Dewey as looking like the bridegroom on a wedding cake is said to have cost him the Republican nomination for the Presidency in '48. But Alice said once to me that it wasn't that she *said* it but that he did.

As she discussed this rumor of a royal flirtation going on between the President and the Princess from Norway I slid down in my chair. Alice Longworth was a Roosevelt and she could say what she pleased, but I was a commoner and a reporter besides, and I didn't feel comfortable listening to discussion so public. We believed—the press—that a romantic friendship existed, and most of us hoped it gave him a few hours now and then of rest and relaxation, because he was always sending Mrs. Roosevelt to do a job for him somewhere—but we were quiet about it. So I said to Alice Longworth, "You know Cissy's been ill? I'm staying there and she knows I'm having lunch with you. She'll ask me a million questions. Why don't you come back with me? I think she's often lonely for someone who remembers the same things she does."

They weren't the kind of women who fly into each other's arms, but this historic feminine feud ended when Alice said, "I should have believed you about the champagne—that was your weakness, not men." And Cissy said, "I don't remember how old you are, lovie, but you don't look it," and they began to laugh and laugh.

I heard that laughter so often in the days after I truly believed Cissy had been murdered. But—I wasn't able to prove it, so there I was.

CHAPTER 31

Now I come back to tales I must tell one at a time. Some of these are known only to me, some are bits and pieces of the New Deal jigsaw puzzle.

Looking back those days are too crowded to live through, and I see too that it wasn't the same me living through them—not even after that Sunday afternoon when Ray Helgesen came to take me to dinner to keep me from being lonesome on my first evening in Washington. It was Ray who on my own pilgrimage gave me the illusion sometimes that Washington was the Desired Country.

With a burning passion Huey Long intended to become President of the United States. He had been Governor of Louisiana, was now its senior senator, and "In 1936," the senator said to me, "I will be President or I will be dead."

Sitting at a table on the veranda of Olney's Inn as the Potomac twilight merged into moon over Maryland, Senator Long said, "Unless he has me shot first, I will be President."

By "*he*" Huey meant, and eventually said publicly, his former hero Franklin Delano Roosevelt. No hate so terrible, so active, as that generated by what a man sees as the clay feet of a fallen idol. Revenge becomes a lifework.

Over fried chicken and corn fritters, the senator said, "You don't believe me?" and then on the back of the menu he wrote three names. "One of those," he said. "You think I'm imagining things, but remember this, will you?"

True, I had begun to be bored with his preoccupation with assassination and his cordon of bodyguards. As we set out that evening I'd said, "You've proved you think you're important enough for somebody to want to shoot you. You've got all the front-page mileage out of it you're going to. Leave these blunderbusses home, they're more apt to shoot us by mistake than keep anybody from shooting you." Well—their machine guns mowed down the assassin in the rotunda of Huey's own state capitol in Baton Rouge, but too late to save his life.

Remember this, will you?

I do.

The first name on that list the Kingfish wrote was the name of the man who killed him months later.

Weiss, the name was. Carl Weiss.

"Who is he?" I'd said, to humor him.

"A fanatic," Huey said. He was silent a moment, his pudgy face morose. "I was one of them once."

Oh yes, Huey meant to be President, unless they shot him first.

He not only told me this. He told Roosevelt.

That most astute, most skillful, dexterous, now-you-see-it-now-you-don't, shrewdest, ablest of all practical practicing politicians—F.D.R.—got himself elected FOUR TIMES against all our traditions and all odds—that genius took Huey's declared determination to run in 1936 (a year away) with gravity. Roosevelt never forgot anything. Well he remembered that in the close 1932 election Huey Long had campaigned for him ceaselessly, had carried Minnesota, the Dakotas, Nebraska, and had strongly influenced other Middle Western states that hadn't gone Democratic in years. Some men have *vote-getting* power as Willie Mays has home-run might. No one recognized this in Huey more than Roosevelt. In the convention that nominated him, in the first year of his administration to get his bills passed, Roosevelt had used the Southern senator's spellbinding hypnosis. When Huey easily beat off a carefully planned and financed move by anti-Long leaders in Louisiana, the Master in the White House must have said, Here is a tool to my hand. Later it would become a foeman worthy of my steel.

F.D.R. knew that Huey Long had a Share-the-Wealth Club in almost every city, town, and hamlet; to a fraction he knew their total membership. Others might—and did—laugh, Roosevelt knew them as a formidable fanatical hard core of any wild drive to steal the Presidency. Roosevelt was too smart, too intuitive, too experienced not to realize that by '36 the first glorious hope and promise of the New Deal would be altering fast, chilled into the cold reality of a long fight to make it all come true; it would face an organized opposition as the People came out of the daze of its first surprise. To our objections when he fired General Knudsen as head of the OPA he said to me, "There comes a time when the members of the wrecking crew, no matter how fine, have to give place to those who can clear the ground. Those who wrecked the old way have created too much hatred and opposition to be builders of the new. Sad, but true." As '36 drew near, Big Business and Labor were impatient. Each would demand more, they would be ready to listen to new attacks and promises, for they saw now that the changes Roosevelt had put into operation required patience and sacrifice and steadfastness to bring them to completion. A nervous exhausted country might listen to the siren voice of Every Man a King as put forth in dazzling pyrotechnics by the Kingfish.

In Germany an even more remote possibility than Huey Long, a house painter named Schicklgruber, had been put in jail for what came to be called the Munich Beer Hall Putsch, had come out with a book called *Mein Kampf,* and in a few short years of raving lunacy had become Adolf Hitler, Der Führer. In Italy there was Mussolini; in Russia, Stalin; in Spain, Franco—all before our eyes. Roosevelt, a student of history from Boots Caligula to the Little Corporal, knew that the book soon to be published by Huey Long held the same hypnotic drug as *Mein Kampf.* Huey called his *My First Years in the White House*—yes, he did!—and it held what Hitler subtitled *My Declaration of My Battle for the Poor People.* What Huey said he would do as President contained all the same pie-in-the-sky promises.

But—Woodrow Wilson once said, "When you come into the presence of a leader of men you know that you have come into the presence of fire, that it is best not incautiously to touch that man, that there is something that makes it dangerous to cross him, that if you grapple his mind you will find you have grappled flame." No question, I saw, that when he began to tell people he was laying plans to run, Senator Long had dared incautiously to touch Franklin Delano Roosevelt's mind. An oft-repeated maxim of Roosevelt's was the trite Never Underestimate Your Opponent. (Others he told me were Never Mention Your Opponent's Name. Never Meet Him Unless You Can Stand above Him.) A wise, farseeing man, he estimated Huey Long as a danger to the country, and F.D.R. loved his country with depth and fire and vigilance. The country, he once told us, had survived, could continue to survive only in deep spiritual integrity. Its strength lay in abiding by the truths of its foundations. As a sum total, he would say, America is greater than her parts.

In "Forever America," a short story Franklin Delano Roosevelt gave me when I told him I wanted to do some fiction about Washington, I used a direct quote from him: "Washington," he said, "this wonderful city, the hub of the world. A marble city. Marble's not the stuff of death, it's the stuff of eternity. Under all the mud, by God's good grace there's a solid marble foundation. We preserve what our hearts can't stand to have destroyed."

To him, Huey Long was not only a dangerous opponent but a menace to that survival. Roosevelt, at least, knew the conflict could be of deadly danger and thus Huey Long would find he had grappled fire and flame.

2

All that is now to be told here happened before I sat in Senator Long's office, terrified eavesdropper, and listened in on his phone call to President Roosevelt and explains how I got to be there.

I had told Mr. Hearst I would rather work out of the city room before I ever met Helgesen, nor was that choice made because George R. Holmes, the fabled head of our wire services in Washington, actually thought a woman's place was on the Home Page. A city room always had held for me the tempo, pulse, drive of newspaper business. A story broke there, its first impact caught you, there was an exchange of ideas. Also you worked for a city editor, not by yourself in an office. Helgesen as a city editor took full advantage of this. If I was going to work out of *his* city room, I would take his assignments if he considered them important. This was not entirely what Mr. Hearst had sent me to Washington to do. On the other hand if I could do both, the *Herald* was the only Washington paper that played local news for local readers and our circulation was soaring. Also even for the national stories I worked best in this kind of pressure, having only a little to do with the fact that I was in love with Helgesen.

A few weeks after I began to work out of that city room I was a member of its working staff in good standing.

Coming in from a session of the trial of Mrs. Lyddane for attempting to kill her husband, present as the witness for the prosecution, my first glance showed me Helgesen white with rage behind his desk. Nobody spoke to me. Nobody was speaking to anybody. No office boy moved upon that painted ship upon a painted ocean. I went over and said to my city editor, who by this time was also the man I'd promised to marry, "What's wrong?" He threw back the lock of blond hair, glared at me in frozen speechlessness, and pointed to the bulletin board. The letter posted there began:

> *Dear Mrs. Patterson,* You need more depth in your political news. Your desk is too easily persuaded to glorify a group of young congressmen calling themselves the Mavericks, who are of no importance so far. St. Johns does not belong on page 1. so constantly. On occasion I find this occurs twice in the same issue. She is a front page of the *second section* feature writer.
>
> Your sports department needs improvement in editing and writing.
>
> ARTHUR BRISBANE.

My first spurt of fury was that Bob Considine was then our sports columnist and I considered him as good as anybody in the land. Then came a take-over of anger so violent it was as beyond control as Niagara Falls. To this, I was not given. A flare of Irish temper—but life with my father, both personal and professional, had taught me a measure of control before I was ten. The man who gets angry in a fight usually loses. Nevertheless, there I was reading Mr. Brisbane's missal through a red mist. It now took in Mrs. Eleanor Medill Patterson, known as Cissy. Mrs. Richbitch was allowing that pompous columnist to insult us as though she'd bought us with thirty pieces of silver and to hell with *her*.

Maybe I didn't know what I was doing. Anyhow I took the letter down. All eyes were upon me as I tore it into pieces, put the pieces in the big metal wastebasket, got out my matches, carefully set fire to them and watched them ashes to ashes and dust to dust. Then I went to my desk, took off my white gloves, laid them carefully beside my typewriter and began madly to pound out By Adela Rogers St Johns nowisthetimeforall- goodmentocometotheaidofthepartynow is the timetotakeArthurbrisbane- out and drawandquarterhim andputhis head on a poleinLafayettePark

A quiet voice said, "You need a getaway car I'm standing by," and there was Les Sommer, who later nearly got me shot by an irate old lady with a Civil War musket down near Charlottesville when we were helping Wild Bill Donovan to recover a lost child. "She'll fire you," Les said.

"I don't work for her," I said through my teeth, "I work for William Randolph Hearst."

An office boy said, "Mrs. Patterson would like to see you."

She was behind a desk too, everybody was behind a desk. She wore a Chanel suit and the emerald clip on the lapel was real and matched her eyes, her hair looked redder than usual. In that drawl so low it was hard to hear she said, "I understand you destroyed a letter I posted on my bulletin board."

I said, "I have to file a story for the 1:10 wire. I won't work in a city room with that insulting claptrap on the wall in plain sight."

Her small face, like a distinguished capuchin monkey's, was quite still. Then she said, *"It was by Arthur Brisbane."*

"Come off it," I said. "He's a columnist who ought to be in the real estate business. What has he got to do with your city room and your paper? I don't care if you're Queen of Rumania and Empress of India, you don't insult the captain in the presence of the troops. More than that you haven't any right to put such temptation under the noses of the men who work for you. I'm broke myself, at the moment."

"Temptation?" said Mrs. Patterson.

I said, "You have to be able to guess how much any of these men you underpay could get if they took that letter across the street to Mr. Eugene Mayer who has just bought the Washington *Post*. WHAT ARTHUR BRISBANE REALLY THINKS OF THE HEARST *HERALD*. A good front-page headline and if it's illegal Brisbane could sue but he won't. It makes us ridiculous and that nobody can afford to be."

At my desk, shaking still, I thought about her and her Chanel suit, the emeralds, and the private car waiting to take her to Florida and Wyoming, but I was sorry for her. I thought, You had to *buy* a paper. You wanted to marry that one-eyed fire-eating polecat Howey because you knew he couldn't be bought by you or anybody, and neither can I, worse luck.

She came out into the city room. Except Isadora Duncan she was the most graceful woman I ever saw. Confronted by icy silence, she stood in front of the city desk. "I have come to apologize," she said, in that falling-away melody voice that reached the remotest corner. "Ignorance is no excuse, but sometimes it's an explanation. I thought Mr. Brisbane's advice would help us to get out a better paper."

Helgesen's eyes were very bright, he said, "You stick with us Mrs. Patterson and we'll get you out a better paper, without any help from Mr. Brisbane." The troops couldn't cheer, they grunted, except me, I was still choked. A second-section feature writer! Mrs. Patterson noticed this, she said, "Now that you have met Senator Long, Mrs. St. Johns, do bring him to Dower House some Sunday. I should be the envy of every hostess in Washington."

In that mood, Cissy was irresistible, so I grunted too.

I had, as she said, met Senator Long at last.

I must have been working to the point of the red corpuscles taking over. The Lyddane case, writing Behind-Closed-Doors interviews with Gloria Vanderbilt, and four or five front pages on Maxie Baer, then the flamboyant and popular World's Heavyweight Champ, and his troubles with his bride Mary Ellen Sullivan, a Washington girl.

Moreover, settled at the Carlton, I commuted to Cow Lane where Ernest E. Adams, Jr., as usual had Bill, Mac, little brother Bryson, Hugo, and the Swamp Angels under control. Most of the time, I had Dicky with me in Washington. I was never quite happy if I didn't know exactly where he was. My baby-sitters, tutors, governors, and guide-philosopher-and-friends for him consisted of the *Herald*'s own taxi driver, Minnie the Moocher, who had his stand in front of the paper, and of the entire staff of the Washington *Herald*. Dicky's favorite was Les Sommer and they saw Washington! Once Les lost him at Pimlico on the day of the Preakness and found him after a frantic half hour sitting in the judge's stand, where Dicky averred he could see better. Bob Considine took him to a ball game when the Yankees came to town with Babe Ruth. Besides swimming in Mrs. Patterson's pool at Dower House he could ride horses on that lady-farmer's hundreds of acres so his life was a happy one.

Mine had dilemmas that had grown new horns.

A second look at the man I'd fallen in love with at first sight got me in deeper. Always before I had felt hostility or separation between the men I knew and the work I did. Now I had a newfound joy. Helgesen's life was his paper, as a musician's might have been his orchestra. I was the best first violin he'd ever had, and this was inseparable from what he felt for me as a woman. Just the same that second look terrified me. I could see the sadistic edge, when we went back to play hearts at my apartment after we put the paper to bed. That flick that found the one place that would hurt. Les Sommer shrugged it off and said, "He's got a cruel temperament, Swedes have." But in the city room once or twice I saw big Waldrop, who'd played tackle at West Point, wince when a sort of white savagery caught him if he was too slow. It was different from the newspaper brutality of the Terrible Men. About this time John Aloysius Clements came down on some Papa Fix business for the Hearst Brass and I told him I was going to marry Ray Helgesen. Silence can be other things than golden. After minutes, Clements said, "How long have you known him?" and I said, "I've been waiting for him all my life," and Papa Fix said, "No one can fix a woman who has decided to fall in love with a bastard, especially a cold-blooded Swedish bastard. The dumbest thing on earth is a smart woman. Come on and I'll buy you an applejack." But Clements knew more about men than anybody and a little chill came upon me.

And all this time my first concern had to be Huey Long.

His news value skyrocketed daily. Even the conservative Arthur Krock of the New York *Times* now conceded that Senator Long was more than just another Southern firebrand and along with the rest of us recognized "the possibility of a conflict which would pit against each other the two best known figures in the United States for the virtual sovereignty of this nation" as Hermann Deutsch puts it in his invaluable *The Huey Long Murder Case*. George Horace Lorimer had ordered a three-part serial on the Kingfish for *The Saturday Evening Post*. Senator Huey Long's mail daily was greater than that of all other senators put together. Neither invited nor admitted to his press conferences we in the Hearst Services were hurting worse and worse. We had no warning of his spectacular moves. I'd called, reminding his secretary that I'd met him at Sands Point. He continued to ignore me.

George R. Holmes continued to be dour about my chances. He said, "I've been studying this gent for a long time and I'll give you three things to go by.

"No Mata Hari technique will work. Women aren't his weakness.

"Alcohol is.

"He has never been to a Washington party, embassy ball, Cave Dweller soiree, Press Club dinner, White House reception, or senatorial dance. Nor put his foot inside the F Street Club. No bait of social lionosity lures him.

"He has always been cagey about money or they'd have been able to put him in jail in Louisiana long ago, his enemies have tried hard enough. So bribery will get you nowhere.

"You take it from there."

I took it to Helgesen and he came up with the move that got him. *Both sides,* Helgesen said. "Mix it up, and down, on both sides."

So on a day of April showers in 1935 under:

By Adela Rogers St. Johns

Take a look at The Kingfish.*********Traffic jams****Senate elevators like a department store on a sales day****S R O in the Galleries*****The Greatest Show on earth is about to begin*****The Senator from Louisiana is about to speak*****I saw him in action for the first time*****

Dangerous Demagogue? Using every small trick to tear down the difficult and heartbreaking work of the Roosevelt Administration? Crackpot*****Madman*****OR a statesman trying to stem the recession of The New Deal Roosevelt promised the world, and which Huey Long shouts Roosevelt has now abandoned*****His clenched fist waves aloft*****He is not an orator. His printed word is bald and unimpressive and will not go down with the deathless words of our leaders. His acting and tricks are those of a Poverty Row Ham actor.

But he is one of those men who can pour himself in white heat of emotion, he sells the Gallery*****the other senators dislike him look down on him*****yet he sells them too. . . .

His clothes are awful beyond all possibility. Faun suit, purple shirt, brown and red tapestry tie, brown and white shoes. A racetrack tout*****But the rest of the Senate is now a slow-motion picture of elderly statesmen who have nothing to do with LIFE*****Huey is the best, that is why he is the most talked about man in America*****

Listen to me for this is vital to our country. I know the secret of Huey Long.

He is the Medicine Man*****right or wrong good or bad dangerous or wonderful*****He is The Medicine Man.

Both sides that was, with a vengeance. I wrote my piece in takes in the Press Gallery and went back to the paper to smooth it out. *Both sides,* as Helgesen had said. It went out over our INS wire and appeared on Page 1 of the Washington *Herald* the next morning.

A phone call from Long's secretary, Earle Christenberry, awakened me. The senator, he said, would like to see me as soon as possible.

In the dark paneled dignity of that Senate office, Huey was standing behind a huge littered desk in a white linen suit already crumpled at 9:00 A.M. I try to remember him *sitting down,* but except for rare restaurant meals and at his Senate desk, I can't. When we ate in his office, which we mostly did, he walked up and down gnawing on a chicken wing or waving a wedge of pie to illustrate a point. My picture of him on that first face-to-face encounter, when my story had flushed him out of his I-Hate-Hearst hole, is of a short, squat, tubby man, with very thick crisp curly brown hair, brown eyes alive with something anything everything except fear. I never saw *fear*. My old friend Captain Eddie Rickenbacker would say this showed a lack of *sense,* and maybe it did.

I have still an impression of a too-fleshy pudding face. I had yet to learn the full range of mobility of what he could do with it. Huey's face was putty for molding into most of the thousand faces Lon Chaney shows in the Encyclopaedia Britannica. Twice I saw it carved as though in Washington's own eternal marble—once after that telephone call on which I so reluctantly listened in, and again when he was dead. The rest of the time he used it as a gargantuan clown, a *Hail-*Caesar*-Jail-*Caesar gangster, a shrewd political boss, an Iago for intrigue, sometimes for anger grief disdain contempt.

As Earle Christenberry brought me in, he gave me a quick look. I had put on my favorite suit, a straight navy-blue wool skirt, a tweed coat very tailored of mixed dark and light blue, a scarf of yellow tied in an ascot. One quick look was all I got. Possibly I'd squandered Mr. Hearst's gold as far as this women-aren't-his-problem lion in the streets was concerned.

Without preliminary, he waved Earle out and me to a chair. We were already in the middle of whyever it was he'd sent for me. His impatience was painful. And finally fatal. He picked up the paper, I saw he'd marked my article heavily in red pencil. "You've hit the combination I want," he said.

After he was dead by an assassin's bullet I find this in the farewell articles I wrote about him:

> On the day I met him he showed me an article in the Saturday Evening Post. Here, too, he had used a red pencil to underline. To my surprise, the damning fault-finding and censure, not the praise and recognition.
>
> With his roar of laughter, he brought from his desk a carbon of the manuscript. *Look,* he said gleefully. All the bad things he'd underlined had been written in by Huey Long's own hand. With jubilation, he shouted, "I knew the Saturday Evening Post wouldn't print an article about me without some hard knocks. The old ones have got whiskers, so I asked the guy who wrote this to let me put in some new ones. I don't care what the SEP says about me as long as they mention my name in 30,000 words. That changes my stature. Gives me new dimensions of

dignity and importance. And they'd have to put in a few good things or it wouldn't be an article The Post would use. It's entertaining, this mixture. You did the same, called me some names but you take me seriously. Your story's entertaining."

As I read over this photostat from the Library of Congress I see hear feel again that jubilation, that germinating mischief, that excitement and plunging love of life when he was getting his own way. This is what I miss in all the novels, biographies, and historical chapters about Huey Long. There was so much of the boy, bad boy perhaps, hoodlum, street urchin, *gang,* show-off, look-Ma-no-hands—but still a boy's daily excitement.

Because of Helgesen's brilliant editorial figuring there was Mrs. St. Johns of the Hearst Services in Senator Long's office. With Huey walking, talking, laughing, shouting, pounding on the desk, zooming from one subject to another. "No *money*—my mother had to figure how to give us enough to eat. I went to bed hungry, remember that. She had guts, she was going to see her kids had a chance to grow up equal, and no one of us ever spoke a word back. She told me when I was three I'd be an artist, but by the time I was eight or nine she stared at me bleak as a March wind and said, You're too wild, Huey, an artist's life'd be the ruin of you. You've got the gift of gab, you'd better be a lawyer. In Louisiana then you didn't go to law school and I passed my bar in seven months." He began to laugh heartily, he said, "I was a big boy when she said to me, I catch you guzzling on that whiskey bottle, I'll break your fool neck. You was pretty well born drunk, she said."

One day I said to Helgesen, "I'm getting myself between two fires," and he gave me a surprised look and I said, "Huey trusts me. I'm getting the breaks and we're putting on circulation because he thinks I'm on his side and I'm not. He wants me to agree to give up my job and handle the woman's part of his campaign."

"What did you tell him?" Helgesen said.

"First that I had to *eat,*" I said. "Then he showed me—he's raised a lot of money. Mostly from younger sons. But—that's what I *mean.* If I tell him right out I think he's crazy, I wouldn't touch his campaign, then we'll be back where we can't get Huey Long news. If I just kid it along and say I'm a newspaperwoman not a politician, that's pretty two-faced, isn't it?"

Helgesen said, "He asked you in after he'd read a piece you wrote in a newspaper. You've never been there except as a newspaperwoman. Have you?"

"He forgets," I said.

"As long as *you* don't," Helgesen said.

"It's a fine line sometimes," I said.

"That's his lookout," Helgesen said, "he's been around quite a while. Has he been making passes at you?"

"You Swedes are low fellows, aren't you?" I said.

I couldn't tell him, or anybody, what had happened a few nights before. Huey had asked me to stay for dinner. His secretary had it sent in, then he said did I want a drink and I said I could use one so he mixed me a gin and tonic. I took a swallow or two and relaxed and closed my eyes. A *sound* made me sit up straight in my chair, my eyes popping. This time Huey was almost *running*—he came under the big lamp beside me and I saw the sweat on his face, it looked like a greased turnip. He stopped at the desk and held himself upright by pressing his fists on top of it.

"I want a drink," he shouted at me. "Do you know what that means? I have a lust for likker—a man's *lust*—" He made that sound again and I can only describe it as a *groan*. He wiped away the sweat with his sleeve, it came right back, he said, "I used to look forward to the end of the day when I could relax and settle down to *drinking*. To feel it warm up my blood, to feel it make me breathe easy so I could rest, to get drunk, roaring *drunk* so I'd know I was the greatest man on earth—when I was governor I could do that every night. Like hot glory that was—wanting that drink, lusting for it, then satisfying my lust."

His breathing was like that of a pneumonia patient.

He faced me and said, "I saw that if I am to fulfill my destiny, if I am to be *President* as I was born to be, I had to give up likker. All men are born with lusts, some for women, for power, for money—for likker. I know that. Do you think that highborn iceberg in the White House knows what it's like to hang by your thumbs?"

I had to say, "Oh—I think so. When they didn't know whether he'd ever walk again, when they told him he wouldn't—I expect he hung by his thumbs then."

Literally, he didn't hear me any more than if I'd been a fly buzzing, he said, "I had to lick my lust for likker and I've done it. But sometimes I think I'm going to die of it, you can't understand that—"

Who should understand if not Earl Rogers' daughter, Papa had lost that battle and I had to feel an admiration for Huey, who was winning it for his country, so he believed.

He said, "*God*—I can't stand this—" and picked up the gin bottle and crashed it through the window. I was on the end of a big leather divan, he came and sat down beside me, he was shaking and I put my arms around him and he began to sob and curse and I held him the best way I knew how. Can you hold a little fat man in your arms and try to comfort him on this rack I knew so much about and remain just a newspaper reporter?

He's been dead over thirty years now, he won't mind if I tell of that moment for in it I felt he was a courageous and honest man.

At the time I couldn't tell Ray Helgesen about it. As a city editor *and* as a man in a most unpleasant Othello rage, I felt sure he'd try to find some way to publish it.

The only person to whom I ever spoke about it was the President.

On a day when Steve Early said, *he* wants a word with you, I saw as I sat down in the chair at the end of *the* desk *he* had spread before him the front page of the *Herald*.

BEWARE HUEY LONG'S MEDICINE
Good or Bad He Means It, Says Adela Rogers St. Johns

Directly, very gravely, the President said, "Perhaps you can help me. Huey and I used to be friends. I had hoped to continue our teamwork as long as I am in office. You will understand when I say I wanted him as an end to pass to—he is a man who can make a lot of yardage." The smile came slowly; when it arrived in full it was brilliant. "Now he will not wait for me to set up a play, or to call a series so we can deceive the defense and perhaps get him in the clear for a touchdown. He is so impatient that he wants to call the plays himself. There cannot be two quarterbacks on a team."

"He admits impatience is one of his faults," I said. "We are, he says, at a place where there is no time left to wait."

Speaking more sternly than I had ever heard him, the President said, "It is not in his charge to make that decision. That is mine alone." After a pause, he said, "Could I persuade him to another way if I asked him to come and see me and talk it over?"

I said I was afraid not, I thought hate had poisoned him, it might only aggravate matters, and then I felt so sad for Huey I said, "Oh I don't know, Mr. President. You are a most persuasive man, perhaps you ought to try."

He was weighing it, his eyes were cold, I knew he would deal ruthlessly with the man who had been his friend. *"Do you understand the lengths to which your duty to your country can sometimes drive you?"* he said.

I said hurriedly, "He's stopped drinking. Sometimes he seems very *young*—younger than his forty years and that's not very old."

The President said harshly, "He can't learn patience any younger, can he? I will think this over. If the opportunity occurs you might tell Senator Long I often have to say to myself, *Patience, Mr. President, patience.*"

I stumbled into the back corridor. The door of Bill Hassett's office was open. Bill's job was assembling all the ideas, bits, and pieces suggested by the President's staff, everybody's version of a Roosevelt speech or Fireside Chat, and molding them into a coherent whole to be submitted for the President's own unmistakable style and choice of words. Bill always checked to be sure they had at least eight good quotes for a *Box* on every front page. Bill's typewriter was going so hard he didn't hear me until I began to make noises like a hen that has just escaped being run over.

For the first time, it had hit me *personally* that Franklin D. Roosevelt couldn't even stand up to say good-by to a lady as would have been natural to him. He couldn't walk to the door with anybody, talking, saying the last thing as most men do. He had been *wheeled* to the place where we found him, he was chained there until someone helped him out of it. That lofty dashing arrogant and audacious leader had been elected governor of New York *after* he'd been felled by infantile paralysis, the politicians had then counted him down and *out,* he'd risen above not being able to walk to become President and the most powerful man in the world. I'd *known* this, of course, we know the world is round but we don't realize it when we're walking down a flat street—so powerful was the *activity* of this man's personality, so strong the *movement* of his spirit, his voice, his words, his hands, the light in his eyes. I had forgotten he was *immobile* until I turned back from the door and for one moment saw him sitting there alone, and I got it full in my viscera.

Patience, Mr. President, patience.

This man had a *right* to tell Senator Long to learn patience.

His overcoming, his accomplishments in spite of this handicap, his good cheer in face of *frustrations* that must be beyond belief, his ability never to let this show in his disposition, his expression, his voice—how did he do it?

No wonder as I somehow got all this in one moment I was stirred beyond silence. Bill Hassett came and stood looking at me. He was no doubt the man who had written the final draft of such immortal words as *We have nothing to fear but fear itself—In the field of world politics I would dedicate this nation to the policy of the good neighbor—The test of our progress is not whether we add more abundance to those who have too much, it is whether we provide enough for those who have too little—I see one-third of a nation ill-housed, ill-clad, ill-fed*—words like that had been typed on that typewriter. Bill looked like Mr. Chips but he had Roosevelt's full confidence as few did. Probably it had been years since a female broke down in his cubbyhole and he was flustered. He said, "What's the *matter?*"

How could I tell him? My personal moment of vision about the President—but there was more than that. The White House stirred my spirits and quickened my pulse and fanned my imagination. *That One House.*

Upstairs was the Lincoln bed. In that room over there Woodrow Wilson had given the German Ambassador his walking paper. Under this roof the fate of our country and the world was decided. And I myself was *in* the White House. I had been talking to the President of the United States, it might be corny but I couldn't take it for granted. Just then I couldn't get the newspaper viewpoint that in my own person *I am one of your four freedoms,* Mr. President, I was too moved. Maybe that was what Mr. Hearst meant by not experting the reader, my naïve sob sister approach was what any woman's would be.

To Bill Hassett I said, "Never mind. Just give me a cigarette."

He said helplessly, "I don't smoke them. I haven't got a drink either. Here—have a pinch of snuff, it's much more soothing." It was one of the supreme moments of my life. I was in the White House, with the President's favorite speechwriter holding out to me a snuffbox that had belonged to Benjamin Franklin. I took some and damn near choked.

3

I must have been just back from the Weyerhauser kidnaping for somehow the heart-stopping beauty of the roses in Olympia, Tacoma, and Portland seemed to blend with the beauty of this countryside as Huey Long and I drove out to Dower House at last.

Of all the houses I have ever seen I would rather have lived in Dower House as Mrs. Patterson had restored the period, mood, hallowed warmth, and stateliness of the past to it and still added every modern convenience.

It lay among the sweet and friendly hills of Maryland, surrounded by meadows and streams, a fair land, at peace. It seemed impossible it had ever been anything else. Often enough before I'd seen swimming pools and gardens and tennis courts, from Beverly Hills to Lake Forest to Palm Beach and Back Bay, but the farm acres gave additional charm and Maryland that day was suffused in a glow of loveliness from the past I've never seen elsewhere.

Dicky took off toward the stables. Les Sommer would pick him up and take him back to town in time for his dinner. Huey and I circled the house to find our hostess. The senator was followed by the eyes of all the women and the whispers of all the men, he thought he was presenting a front of danger and defiance, beans, and blarney but actually he was a man who was sure he was being led into a trap. He always plunged ahead with steps too long for his short legs, now he was accelerated with terror.

Gracious, flattering, ready for mischief as a Siamese cat, Mrs. Patterson put a hand wearing an outsize emerald on the senator's arm and though she was taller succeeded in looking up to him. Gay, kind, welcoming, seconded by Evie Roberts, the Glamour Girl of the New Deal on one hand and a Supreme Court justice on the other, Cissy was putting the senator from Louisiana at ease.

None of it did any good.

The senator from Louisiana had no small talk. He didn't have any medium-sized talk either. He had no social graces. All the discomfitures and minor perils and gaucheries of social intercourse yapped at his heels.

Huey was no good on a level of exchange. He had to speak TO.

As the afternoon drew on, most of us went indoors. The room was long with windows on one side. On the other walls pictures and a wide door opening on the hall from which rose *the* most beautiful staircase. At each end there was an enormous fireplace. The spring air was chill enough as the sun went down to permit in each a wood fire of many colors. I steered the senator with Cissy to one of these. In front of the other down the room I saw both Richard E. Berlin and Thomas J. White, officers of the Hearst Corporations, along with a couple of other senators, two generals, and an ambassador. I whispered in Cissy's ear. She gave me a startled look and shook her head. I said, "I do this six days a week and now on Sunday. You insisted I bring him here, you better see he has a good time, lovie, that's all. He isn't. Do as I tell you, will you?"

I made my way through the crowd, when I reached the other end I stopped beside Dick Berlin and literally shouted the length of that long long room. Cissy with a gesture quieted everybody, and I said, "Senator Long—do tell Mr. Berlin how you feel about Ickes—" The Ickes issue is long gone, but I saw the man who hypnotized the Senate take on and conquer a social gathering such as he had never seen before. The *crème de la crème* of Washington. Nervous as a mother whose child is about to *recite,* I watched Berlin, who had no use for Huey Long personally or politically. To begin with, out of courtesy to his hostess, his handsome Irish face was expressionless, then it began to break up in humor, in interest, in excitement as Huey shifted into a plan he had to preserve States' rights from encroaching on Federal Government. As the little man in the badly cut, badly rumpled white suit began to let his voice play, I saw him carry all before him.

The blazing triumph on his face as he ended was indecent.

At dinner, I sat on Huey's right, which turned out to be just as well.

Those asked to spend Sunday at Dower House could enjoy lunch outdoors, ride, swim, play tennis, stroll in the gardens, have cocktails or champagne or beer. At seven o'clock by tradition they were to leave. Cissy abominated buffets, dinner was sit-down elegant. The Chippendale dining table at Dower House seated only twelve, so that chosen number were asked to remain. Secretary of State Cordell Hull and Mrs. Hull. Assistant Secretary of the Treasury Lawrence (Chip) Roberts, husband of Evie, and Evie of course, one of the justices and his wife, Dick Berlin, Tom White and I. With a little shuffling of protocol, Cissy had Senator Long on her right. After his triumph in the drawing room, he was the bad little boy at the children's party. To my apprehension I saw he was looking with the rolling eye of a paint pony at the silver on each side of the gold serving plates. Nowhere could there be a more beautiful table. Crystal, linens, masses of flowers from the garden, tall silver candlesticks once adorning the board at Lord Baltimore's mansion, called His Lordship's Kindness. The flat silver had come down to Dower House from George Washington's stepson, young Custis, who was married there. How many pieces were at my plate I've forgotten, but shortly Huey said with gusto, "*I* don't know what all these are for. Where I come from we use one knife and fork to eat all our vittles with," and put everything else in my lap. His putty face was furrowed into the clown mask, it was impossible not to laugh.

At once Huey began a speech about Section 213 of the Economy Act and told Mr. Berlin that he was helping me prepare a series about it for the *Herald*. This section, he said, held that no two people in the same family could work for the Government at the same time. With the golden tongue of minstrelsy he gave them a medley of iniquities this wrought. A young woman in Government Printing, mother to support, her husband couldn't resign from the United States Navy, so she had to. Couple with three children, she was a filing clerk and the only job her husband had been able to get was substitute letter carrier—they lost their house when 213 forced him to quit. Two young things living in sin—*we can't live on one salary*.

He gave me a smile and said, "After you do the series, honey, I'm going to get it repealed for you," and I hoped Berlin knew that Huey called all women *honey*.

This held the table spellbound till the salad course.

For this, the lettuce was grown on Cissy's own farm, but Huey took one bite with his one fork and said to Mrs. Patterson, "My dear friend, you must let me come sometime and teach your cook to make salad dressing," Cissy was game, she said, "My dear Senator, why not now?"

I thanked God that *Philpotts* remained at Dupont Circle, *Philpotts* would have clapped the salad bowl over the senatorial head and himself gone forth baying into the night. The colored gentleman serving at Dower House listened, left in silence, returned in dignity bearing a tray on which were a bowl, implements, mustard, orégano, white and red wine vinegar, cayenne, paprika, sugar—*May I have this sugar in a sifter?* Huey said. *One grain too much is fatal*—salt, olive oil, Worcestershire sauce, a small bottle of almond extract, and two cloves of garlic, per Senator Long's instructions. As he rubbed, measured, dissolved, mixed Huey discoursed with wizardry, on the origin of salad, on hot-and-sweet, sour and spiced from the Pharaohs to Escoffier, interrupting himself once to say to the butler, "We must dry this lettuce more thoroughly, improperly dried lettuce ruins more salads than careless cooks."

Finally we saw him dunk a leaf in the bowl, taste it with the expression of Aladdin rubbing the lamp, pick up another leaf, and ram it into Cissy's mouth, which, fortunately, was wide open and had been for some time.

"How about that, honey?" said Huey Long.

Cissy swallowed it. "Another of your miracles, Senator," she said.

She was right, his dressing was the best I ever tasted. If it hadn't been I am sure Richard E. Berlin would have strangled him with his bare hands.

Going home I said, "See? You were a great success."

He turned on me in an insane fury. "A court jester!" he yelled. "God damn them."

The rest of the time as we drove through the night he didn't speak. One of those moments of depression engulfed him.

I knew he was the only person at Dower House who hadn't had a drink. My imagination boggled at what it would have been like if he had.

With fanfare and fandango we were getting Section 213 repealed. I got a citation from the American Federation of Government Employees somewhere along the way, addressed to the Editor of the *Herald*. But Huey Long had done all the work.

So we come to the stolen letter and that telephone conversation to which I was a terrified eavesdropper.

The offices of the senator from Louisiana were always Hurricane Huey, but when I arrived that afternoon it was a Disaster Area. It sounded as though a dozen radios were turned on full blast to different stations.

Earle Christenberry, as loyal and intelligent and good-looking a senatorial secretary-assistant as ever was on the Hill, stood at the door of the senator's private office. Through it came the second most famous voice in Washington, a baritone gone tenor, screaming like a man at the stake who has seen the fagots lighted. Some words I could understand, some were indistinguishable—*Betrayed* came out clearest—"I am *betrayed*—that low-down worm, that filthy cockroach—where did he get the *combination* of my safe?—who betrayed me—?"

Raving blind with rage, he came into the outer office. He couldn't see me or Christenberry or his staff or some constituents in a corner, he could not see where he was going, finally Christenberry and two of his bodyguards herded him back—he never stopped yelling—"You and I," he cried out to Christenberry, "and the president of the bank and that company in Akron that installed it—by God on the mountain who else knew that combination?" and Christenberry said, "If you're implying—" Huey halted to stare at him with blind eyes. "No—I could smell it on you—no, *this man* has the power to stretch forth to Akron, into any bank—with all his teeth showing—the Roosevelt Smile, bigod—his *minions* creep and crawl, they know without him *telling* them—who dares oppose Franklin the First —he'd squash them like stepping on a bug—"

Christenberry had motioned me to follow as Long plunged into his private quarters. If Earle thought my presence either as a woman or a reporter would cool or calm him he was wrong, but I might turn his thought or occupy him—I stood with my back to the door. About one thing Huey was right. The President had eyes and ears everywhere. For the sake of the President of the United States and a United States senator, I didn't want anyone to hear or see what sounded as though Roosevelt was Hitler—so when someone outside pushed I shoved back with all my strength. Also if this was going to explode into *news*—*N*orth *E*ast *W*est and *S*outh—it was *my story*. I didn't want UP or AP nosing in.

Now a sort of terrible pause fell. Huey sat on his chair in some dread suspense of indecision, the way Napoleon must have sat in his tent at Waterloo waiting for Blücher. History says his bowels hadn't moved that morning. Huey looked now as though his had been congested for *weeks*. That makes babies scream and writhe and lash out, I knew that.

In one of his incredible changes, he turned a new-made face to me, the face of the little boy outside Comiskey Park the day the White Sox Scandal broke crying, *Say it isn't so Joe say it isn't so.*

Tears running down his face, Huey said to me in a bewildered *young* voice, "You see, he wrote me this letter. He said he agreed with all my ideals. He wrote he'd fight for my Share-the-Wealth program as hard as I would. He said we'd do it together, he was *for* the downtrodden man— the *forgotten* man, I called him that first—as much as I was. I've never showed that letter to anyone. It was sacred, the gentleman's agreement between us. He asked me to do so many things—on the floor of the Senate . . . and I did them. I knew how close he and I were in our ideals—" He choked to a stop. Oh—I know, I knew Huey Long, all about him, just the same he had molded that putty into a death mask of a man who had died for his country. He said, "Lately—just lately—he's begun to back down —*compromises* all the time—"

I broke in then. I said, "Oh Huey! Do try to make sense. I know you have ideals, but you're a politician. You say you remade Louisiana, and I'm sure you did, but you know you had to make compromises and set up deals, and you used *power* in some unscrupulous ways—They say the British ruled longer than anyone because they best understood the art of compromise, the wisdom of the serpent, to walk softly, sometimes to crawl, always to wait patiently—"

I am sure he didn't hear a word. He said, "I began to realize he doesn't call me any more. Now he had all the power. *Upon what meat doth this our Caesar feed that he is grown so great?* When I tried to remind him, when I mentioned what he'd agreed to in the letter and the bills I wanted —he gave me the Roosevelt razzle-dazzle, the old F.D.R. flumdedum, I didn't want to believe it—"

Say it isn't so Mr. President say it isn't so.

God on the mountain, as Huey put it, this man must be a thorn in the flesh to Roosevelt, who with power and patience and compromise and strategy and prayer and poker face was trying, he believed, to remake a world nearer to his heart's desire. *Do you understand the lengths to which this can sometimes drive you?*

I said, "But Huey—think a minute, he's the President—don't say things—"

He said, "The letter is gone." Over his shoulder, the door of the wall safe swung open. He said, "I went for it this morning, I was going to read it to him, it's gone. Shakespeare knew everything—*We petty men walk under his huge legs and peep out to find ourselves dishonorable graves*—oh yes, I'll find myself a dishonorable grave. He won't be anywhere near it though. When they look for motives they won't find any, his cabal acts on the other end of his power ray without his having to order a dishonorable grave—"

I said, "Huey, you know this is *really* nuts—"

He walked over and peered into the safe, "I've got photostats," he said, "it's never the same." He went into his bathroom.

When he came back, he had combed, washed, brushed, tied his tie. I had never seen his face more natural and composed. He sat down behind his desk and said, "I am going to get my letter back. Watch me."

This might turn out to be a story after all.

Into the phone he said, *"Get me the President.* You understand? Get him!" and then to me, "Get on that extension. You don't believe me, missy, I want someone to hear this, you sit there and *listen.*"

I can be sent to Devil's Island for this, I thought, I can be dropped in an oubliette, my hair will turn white in a single night, I don't want to be the one who heard this, I am a reporter I have to stay right here, I have to use both hands to hold the receiver, all that does is make it shake twice as hard—Mr. Hearst will expect me to reproduce this conversation word for word whether we can print it or not—this steadied me. It wasn't Helgesen or Howey or George R. Holmes who'd expect me to know what the senator from South Louisiana said to the President from Hyde Park, New York—as usual it was Mr. Hearst.

In silence, we waited while Christenberry got through to the White House, insisted Senator Long must speak to the President *at once,* in that wait my thought scurried to the different backgrounds of these two men, their bloodstreams, the echoes of their reading and education and childhood and mothers, the language heritage—all the things that make a ME, an I. Were any two men—Daniel Webster and Henry Clay, Hamilton and Burr, Lincoln and Robert E. Lee—*any* two men—

I nearly jumped out of my skin when I heard the Haa-vad voice. The first thing it said coming up from the White House was, "Good morning to you, Huey. I hope you're keeping well?"

The first thing the hush-puppy voice going down from the Senate said was, "I want my letter back."

I saw that Huey was trying to *sit tall,* I knew the Man in the White House sat tall by nature, but he was *chained.*

The President said, "You go too fast for me, that has always been one of your troubles, Senator. You go too fast for many of us."

"Plenty of folks can follow me," Huey said coldly.

"You have me there," the President said, chuckling. "And now, Senator, what letter?"

"You know," Huey Long said. "The one with the promises you made me before I'd agree to go out to campaign for you. The letter that proves how you're betraying those promises now."

"Would you call them campaign promises?" the President said lightly. "When a man becomes President, Huey, sometimes he finds it necessary to readjust the promises. Sometimes he has to work to redeem them, it takes time. I thought it was a pretty fine letter as I recall it. What's amiss with it now?"

"It's a-missing, that's what's a-miss with it," Huey said, the anger jumped against the harness, the Southern accent welled up. "You listen to me, you yellow-bellied, white-livered, double-crossing two-timing bastard. I want that letter back. I know you and your slippery ways, I know you. Who else'd dare to have it stolen? Hear me! If I don't get it back I'm going to release a copy of it to the press, by God on the mountain I am—"

My guts twisted like pretzels. My story! But—you can't print a letter, even Brisbane's, without the consent of the *writer*—a letter from the President?—still, there might be *ways* if I'd read it—I didn't want even me to print it—not now—

"—it tells about how much confidence you have in me," Huey was shouting, they'll hear him through the window, "when you *wanted* something from me—I'll show you how it'd look in print—"

"Senator, you are talking political blackmail," the President said a little wearily, but *patiently.* "You don't mean it, but you shouldn't say it nonetheless. Not everybody understands you as well as I do. You have me at a disadvantage, since I don't know anything about your letter and so—"

Whom the gods wish to destroy they first drive into such *ravings* as I heard then. I cannot put down the words, they were blasphemous, obscene, terrible, mad as Lear and as violent. None of the blasphemy was ordinary, nor the obscenity pointless. I clutched the receiver, I wanted to throw the phone out the window, I was in a state of shock, no one can talk to the President of the United States like that, no one can hurl such insults—why doesn't the President hang up on this babbling lunatic—?

Patience, Mr. President, patience.

You cannot close the door on your past, you must deal with it. Huey Long was part of his past, he was dealing with it.

The President of the United States was dealing with a spellbinder, Hitler in Germany, Mussolini in Italy, *it can't happen here,* we aren't Germans or Italians or *Russians,* we're Americans, our President can handle this bomb even if the fuse is lighted—

Huey said, "Send me back that letter. You're not going to let me live until the election anyhow, so what'd you want with it?"

A Niagara of laughter—rich, full, royal, masculine laughter—*utterly natural*—came over that phone. One man to another. Kindly, friendly, a sober man trying to handle a drunk he's fond of—Huey was drunk with rage and hate—this was one man trying to keep a friend from making a tragedy of himself—

"Now Huey, now Huey," the President said. "You know better than that—you know I am your friend—"

"I know you for a treacherous and deceitful man," Huey said in a chill whisper. "God damn you for a treacherous and deceitful man—"

"No," the President said, "no. I know you don't mean those things, Huey—"

From far far away it seemed came Huey Long's voice saying, "I mean them, I hoped maybe you didn't."

Then he hung up.

He sat pounding the desk with both fists. He looked ravaged and desperate.

I knew—*I knew*—that the Man in the White House hadn't turned a hair.

Only a ruthless, patient man with a single aim has any right to be President.

I knew I ought to stay and talk to Huey. Only I couldn't. I was in a new agony. I had no philosophy to meet this with. I had no strength or comfort to offer this mangled form that had just been run over by a tank. I was myself in the ice-hell of the ultimate of all frustrations, mere human effort.

Well, if *they* could quote Shakespeare in the pinches so could I. *It went much against my stomach.*

In the taxi on my way back to the *Herald* I thought, I wish I ever had time to think except between times or when I'm on my way somewhere else, I wish I had time and quiet to sit down and think and find out if I have a philosophy, half the time I do not know what I'm doing much less what I'm thinking. Hollywood is a sham and a make-believe, I wish I was back in Hollywood where it's all Box Office and No Consequences, not my country at stake, my children's country, and what good is a woman without thought or philosophy? Will my children arise and call me blessed because I sent them to the best schools and put shoes on their feet? Don't think about the President and Huey Long *any more.* Think of some poetry like Anne Lindbergh did over the frozen north—*Guns aren't lawful nooses give gas smells awful you might as well live why is it no one ever sent me yet one perfect limousine do you suppose? Ah no it's just my luck to get one perfect rose and they're hangin' Danny Deever in the morrrrrning. My candle burns at both ends—shoot if you must this old gray head—but spare your country's flag she said*—that's culture for you when I feel like a plugged nickel anyway.

Helgesen was behind his desk, he always was, if I married him I would marry the city desk, we could spend our wedding night on the rim. He didn't look up from the copy he was penciling hell out of, he just said, "What've you got?" but when I didn't answer he finally did and I knew full well what he saw. I'd started out all crisp and clean in blue linen with a red belt and a big straw hat and whatever became of *that,* and now I am a crumpled sweaty *reporter* who's been upchucking in the senator's can.

A pretty sight God wot.

"What's wrong?" Helgesen said.

"Not here—" I said. Mrs. Patterson wasn't in so we went into her office. I wanted to rush into Helgesen's arms and weep and say, *I wish I hadn't heard it,* but he said, "Let's have it," and word for word I told him. He lowered his chin and stared at me, behind what I was telling him so carefully I knew what a *cold-blooded* hot man he was. How can I deal with him? He does hot things in cold blood.

Mrs. Patterson came in and he said, "We have something to tell you," and to me, "Go back to the beginning," and in anger at last I thought, I can't, I won't, I don't want to go over it again, the President patiently following his single aim to serve and protect his country at any price, his country which is his as it has never been anybody else's except all the Presidents that have gone before him. And Huey, impatiently going mad before my eyes, hate has him by the very testicles of his being, he can't stop now, what will happen to him?

Training held good. I tried to outline what I had heard. I was too tired; Helgesen supplied most of it. Mrs. Patterson chain-smoked and her little marmoset face tightened. "He is a menace," she said in the end, and I thought, Which one is a menace or both to *you,* you economic royalist, "I must talk this over with Joe" and I came back to life, I said, "No, you will not." She gave me an oblique glance and said, "I cannot publish any of this without consultation," and I said, "You and your brother and your editor will have to consult Mr. Hearst, because I do not work for the Pattersons. And you cannot publish any of it because I am not going to write it."

Nobody had asked me to sit down. I put my hand against a chair back and then Helgesen put his arm around me, he would have done as much for fat old Waldrop. You're going to out-Swede yourself one of these days, I said to myself, but I put my head on his shoulder to have someplace to put it and come down to it, I would have done as much if the only shoulder had been fat old Waldrop's. I kept thinking—no no—*feeling* about that poor egomaniacal, mixed-up wretch, my little ol' friend Huey all alone—doesn't he know how badly he's outmatched? Up against a man who has everything and will stop at nothing? That's too much weight to give away.

Huey had missed greatness maybe by only a hairsbreadth. That was the trouble. So had Trotsky and Richard III and Aaron Burr. The guys who miss by an arm's length nobody ever hears of.

Mrs. Patterson seemed to *see* me. It shook her. She said, "Ray, why don't you take this child out to Dower House, she looks all in. There's nobody there. I'll call and you can walk in the garden and have a quiet supper and a good night's sleep. I'll stay, and Mason Peters can handle the desk for one night."

Mrs. Patterson, never able to believe a man loved her for herself alone, had a passionate participation in vicarious love affairs.

The guest suite had been prepared. Roses filled the lovely sitting room with color and perfume. A small fire, not hot but very bright, had been lit in the fireplace beneath an Adam mantel and against gathering Maryland mist outside. Before it a table was set for supper. Going in to wash and comb my blown hair—this time Howey had been right about Helgesen's mad driving and I hadn't drawn a breath between Washington and Dower House—I found in the bedroom the famed four-poster that had belonged to Martha Custis Washington and a filmy gown and chiffon velvet robe had been laid on one side, and on the other pajamas and a necktie silk dressing gown.

If ever a woman looked at prepared premarital bliss, I did then.

For brides to be, I had believed in virginity, not only morally but artistically. Girls who jumped the gun in the back seat of a car didn't know what they had missed in tenderness which in the end is the immortal part of love. And marriage. This vicarious wedding night set by Cissy came under no such disqualification. I was in my thirties (late ones at that), I had been married twice, I had recently in public court fought the charge of being an unfit mother with a dozen correspondents, I had been a reporter since I was eighteen. My femininity had, I hoped, survived. Virginity obviously had not. To pretend otherwise smacked of a Victorian coyness. There could be no scandal. No one but Cissy knew where we were and I was going to marry him and make an honest woman of me. To take a shower, put on the robe, relax over supper and champagne—who could grudge me that after the day I'd been through?

Nevertheless, I put a comb through my hair and went back to the fireside the way I was. We had clear soup, crab Louis, and Lanson '21 in silence. The bubbles of the champagne weren't strong enough to lift me. Looking back it emerges as a simple, clean-cut, rather charming scene from a play. The two of us in the beautiful room, the elegance of the food, the colored houseman in white coat disappearing rapidly, and me—ruining the whole thing by staring with abysmal horror, like a Russian heroine at myself as a reporter. I was fed up with being a reporter. With Mr. Hearst and Front Page Howey, with the blind bitter passion and ambition of Hurricane Huey, the terrifying magnanimity and death-dealing idealism of that *tough* paternal despot, Franklin the First, with all his panache, and his *teeth*.

For I had come upon the stark reality that I couldn't occupy the widow Custis' four-poster because I didn't trust them. Not Martha. Nor even Huey, nor Franklin, they'd grind you to powder between them, those two.

I didn't trust my friend Cissy.

With the taste of arsenic in my soup, I didn't trust Helgesen either.

Not to say *trust,* the way I had Bill Jory when I was a little girl, or my father even when he was drinking, or Mr. Hearst or my son Bill or J. Edgar Hoover or for that matter Johnny Torio, the real boss of the underworld who told Capone and Colesimo what to do.

That day I had heard what I ought not to have heard.

I did not know what was in the President's mind, who did? But in a moment of double vision I knew why he had been patient with Huey Long.

I put down my champagne glass and started for the door.

Old Bright-Eyes Helgesen said, "Where are you going?"

Still going, I said, "I've always been in the little guest room at the end of the hall. I seem to have gone all to pieces. I'll sleep better there."

He watched me, saying nothing.

Let me put this as simply as I can.

This was not to be that quiet moment for thinking I'd been yearning for. But it was all I could find. Even people who are just trying to be worth while are always beginning again, and I had that day made a discovery that set up a new life amid my humanitarianisms. Through the buzz of champagne and the twittering of my nerves from that idiotic Helgesen *speed* on top of everything else I thought *They were all with one accord in one place and the Holy Spirit descended upon them*. Did anybody believe that? Franklin in the White House. Huey in the Senate of the United States. They're going to promulgate a disaster, you watch and see. They're not going to blend brotherly love for the best way of using their talents.

I lay down in my clothes. I felt black and blue all over, mentally, morally, and physically, with fatigue.

Everything was very quiet out there in Maryland. In the dark room at Dower House smelling faintly of potpourri, with my too tired too busy brain chasing its tail in my aching skull, I had an impulse to get off the bed and go on my knees—Marie Dressler used to say, Life knocks you to your knees because that is the position that leads you to pray—I decided with sudden vehemence that I would NOT let life knock me to my knees. Where I would have to try to pray.

In some sort of gibberish I said, Whatever—None of this is any good. What are *You* doing? If You exist at all, why don't You take better care of people? That man in the White House—Mr. President. He wants the brotherhood of man, that's what all this is about, he wants the Good Neighbor policy, but he wants to be God himself. You'll ask Huey, What did you do with the *talents* I gave you? but it's no good giving talents without character. That's why so many die young like Keats and Mozart, or is it?

Here we all are. The President with all the power. Cissy with all the money. Huey with all the talents. Me with everything—children, work I adore, sometimes twice a day on the front page, now a man I could marry and he'd be a *husband* to me.

And all the time I knew Cissy was as empty as the old oaken bucket, and Huey was about to die and power corrupts, and I slid off the bed and buried my head in my arms.

The door opened, I suppose he could see me from the hall's shaft of light, I'm sure he didn't think I was on my knees trying to pray, he was as sardonic an agnostic as Pilate, he knew too much about women, that big blond Swede, for his own good and mine, he probably thought, This is the way a woman flings herself down when she's emotionally upset and too tired to undress. Very quietly, he said, "Come on back by the fire—it's turning cold. I won't bother you, I do love you, you know."

So—I went.

What difference did it make?

Rationalization, I thought, is the premature child of all this Freud business!

In the dawn's early light I had once been quite able to rationalize murder.

Why should I stick at a spot of adultery?

And it's not even that. Neither of us is a married person. Only married persons can commit adultery. A bit *loose,* maybe. Better promiscuous than *puritanical.* I am a big girl now; very soon, let me tell you, you will be too old for anybody to ask you to be anything else. Have fun while ye may.

It comes way down on the list. Seventh, matter of fact. And you are not staying awake nights about the first six, are you?

4

I was home in Cow Lane when Ernest came to say Mr. Howey was on the phone.

Howey said, "They've shot Huey Long."

"Who shot him?" I said, stupefied.

"Young doctor," Howey said. "Fellow named Weiss."

"*Weiss?*" I said. "Are you sure?"

"Sure," Howey said. "You better get going, our plane's waiting for you at Newark."

I said, "Is Huey dead?"

"Not yet," Howey said. "He will be soon."

He was.

A low, messy, bloody, disgraceful business it had been, as any assassination must be. The marble corridor of the state capitol Governor Huey Long had built for the citizens of Louisiana and of which he'd been so proud must have looked like the garage in Chicago after the St. Valentine's Day massacre. The blunderbusses hadn't been able to protect Huey, but they had assassinated the killer. Nobody had any idea why Dr. Carl Weiss, a young German-Jewish-Catholic doctor of spotless reputation, happy home life, pleasant personality, and professional prestige should assassinate the Kingfish. Most people still haven't. Assassination is a distorted crime as a rule. An idealistic, sensitive, patriotic young Jew—everybody said that about Weiss. Madness to be sure, yet there must be method in it somewhere. He'd never been to Washington, belonged to no political group, never had been known to discuss Senator Long. His friends told me he was quizzical, pensive, perhaps a little fanatical in his patriotism and gratitude to America.

I wish I could tell why Huey Long wrote his name on that menu at Ol-ney's Inn. I don't know. My best guess is that Huey, knowing everything that went on in Louisiana and some things that didn't, knew or believed he knew of a secret cabal of Roosevelt devotees. And of the superpatriotic Weiss as a member of it. By remote control, Huey had said, If they just think our Caesar wants something done, they do it.

So a violent man had come to a violent end. One night he told me the story of the time he'd locked bank presidents and officials and financial powers of two states in a hotel room and kept them there for twenty-four hours at the point of tommy guns. So they couldn't close the banks, or some such thing.

Well—a man who lives by the tommy gun must die by the tommy gun. Unfortunately when violence grows too powerful, a lot of us who didn't also die.

I only stayed a few hours in Baton Rouge. My stories about Huey were written after I flew back to Cow Lane.

Death had given his face a nobility I'd seen in it only once in life, but that wasn't the only reason I was willing to stand up and be counted in headlines that said:

ADELA ROGERS ST. JOHNS' STORY OF FRIENDSHIP WITH HUEY LONG

It would have been easier to join the throng calling him other names and forget him.

But—in the first place, he had let me in and trusted me as a newspaper-woman when my service needed him as a big news story. This when no one else could get him for us. Also, I found a lot of good in my memories of this man. I'm not sure about speaking nothing but the good of the dead, but I am sure we'd like to have what is good not interred with our bones.

Oh—he had to go. We can't—or couldn't then—be ruled by tommy guns, or Demagoguery, or Mob Oratory or Bumbledom or Medicine Man-ism. But I believed Huey Long meant his Share-the-Wealth dream, a project that disappeared as the breath left his body. His desire to help the down-trodden out of whose ranks he had fought his own way was sincere, but his methods were immature and dangerous. From those stories I wrote about him soon after he was dead are a few paragraphs that go to prove that there's so much good in the worst of us—I hope I hope.

In an April twilight in Washington he once quoted to me a
story out of an old book his mother had given him.

"An Army was marching through conquered territory. They
came to a big house and told its master they wished to take
corn for troops and horses. The master said I will show you
and led them through two beautiful cornfields to one at a distance and they thanked him for his aid and said Now tell us
why when other fields were so much closer you led us this long
journey. And the master said The first two fields were not
mine, they belong to my neighbor."

And Huey Long looked at me wistfully and said, "I wish I
could build my life on that story. I hope I can but I don't expect
so."

He never really had time to find out in Washington. That marble city—
the stuff of eternity which we had erected ourselves and intended to preserve at all costs.

About that, President Roosevelt knew.

5

They won't let me live till the next election.
Huey had kept saying that.

When the 1936 election did come around, some months after Senator
Long had been interred in a white marble memorial in Louisiana, Mr.
Hearst asked me to go to Kansas and report to him what I thought of its
governor, Alfred Landon, as a possible Republican candidate for the
Presidency. The Republicans are so politically naïve.

"We must," Mr. Hearst said as he bought me a ticket to Topeka, "keep
the two-party system always in full operation. It is quite possible that a
Democracy won't work at all and that a Republic is not a practical form
of government—one thing however is certain. If one party can perpetuate
itself through patronage and plums, like Tammany Hall, we are done for.
We must always produce a first-class and electable candidate in each
party so that the people have an honest choice."

So I set out for Topeka.

The real reason for including this brief bit is that Mr. Hearst was so
pleased with my report, on one page and in one paragraph.

It said:

Dear Mr. Hearst; I have spent three days with the Governor and
Mrs. Landon in the Governor's mansion in Topeka, Kansas.
My best estimate to you of him as a possible presidential candi-
date can be summed up in his own words and I quote, "I believe

I am an efficient governor of Kansas. My dealings with the state legislature have been satisfactory and productive. As an opponent for Franklin D. Roosevelt I am manifestly ridiculous. I hope it will not be required of me." End quote. I can only agree wholeheartedly with the Governor.

Adela

I covered that year's Republican convention in Cleveland and it was required of him and he turned out to be absolutely right.

CHAPTER 32

The night of the bus crash began like any other on the *Herald.*

As a rule, news did not break late in Washington. The big beats—the White House, Congress, the departments, the Supreme Court, the embassies—closed in the late afternoon. When we went to press with our eight-thirty edition we carried the main news of the day.

That day in April had been routine for the times.

From Stresa, Seymour Berkson had written a brilliant story of the historic three-power meeting—England, France, Italy—and its attempt to bring Europe into a new peace system. It announced that Hitler, the missing fourth power, would be invited to a parley that summer—too late, but we wouldn't know that for four years.

U.S. leaders, our front page said, were rushing to end the Dole by July 1.

Bob Considine picked Detroit to win the American League pennant and the Giants in the National League.

The bus crash in Rockville, Maryland, in which fifteen high-school children were killed *and* the little man, Mr. X, bent on suing the Washington *Herald* for libel, came out of the fog and rain and met head-on in the city room like strange and explosive elements in a test tube.

The little man who, for reasons you will understand, I have called Mr. X came first.

After the early edition went to press Helgesen and I decided to have dinner in my suite at the Carlton. There was to be a rehearsal later for the Gridiron Dinner. The President was guest of honor at this annual National Press Club event, traditionally it gave the Washington newspapermen their chance to rib him without fear or favor. F.D.R. wouldn't be at the rehearsal but he had sent word that on the Night he wished to present a skit of his own, so everyone was triply excited and Cissy was having a supper after the run-through for George R. Holmes, president of the historic Gridiron, hoping to get some advance information. I had to change for this, though as it turned out I never got there. While Helgesen ordered food and drink sent up I put on a black and white print dress with long sleeves, pleated collar and cuffs of white organdy, and the tight skirt and two-foot train Hattie Carnegie had invented as a fashion for that year.

As we sat down, the phone rang with violent urgency. Ray had left Mason Peters on the desk, as I handed him the phone I said, "That boy's getting old enough not to call you unless it's a matter of life and death," in two minutes I knew it was. For Helgesen said in a voice I hadn't heard before, "What did you say his name is?" and I felt real apprehension popping through his icy control. As he got to his feet he said, "I'll be right in," and to me, "Come on." I said, "I'm supposed—you don't need—" and he said, "*Come on!*" In the elevator I discovered I still had my drink in my hand, I didn't drink it, somehow I thought I'd better not. This wasn't just an office crisis. I felt somehow it had to do with Ray personally, and therefore with me.

Now, the night was fogbound. The rain broke through and seemed to follow us into the taxi. A drab dingy fog, I hated it, I didn't know that it already lay thick on the railroad crossing near Rockville, an hour more and it would be thicker and clammier. I didn't know that twenty-seven students from the senior chemistry class of Williamsport High School and their teacher were comfortably viewing a Chemistry Show at the University of Maryland, their bus waiting outside, the driver dozing. While at sixty miles an hour an express train from St. Louis was tearing through the dark, foggy rain-swept Virginia countryside on its way to Washington. *Fifteen feet, fifteen feet more,* the weeping engineer was to say to me later.

"Oh what *is* it?" I said. Helgesen wasn't going to break the silence in the taxi to put me out of my worry.

A little man had appeared at the city desk on the boil to sue the paper for twelve million dollars for libel. A good round sum, and Mason Peters' reaction had been a guffaw and, "You and who else, buster?" and to this Mr. X said, "Me and Mr. William Hogan, young feller. Mr. Hogan says I can collect it."

Hogan was as good a lawyer as there was in Washington, no client of his could be some kind of nut. So Mason called Helgesen. "How are you supposed to have libeled him?" I said.

Mr. X had explained to Mason that he owned a motion picture theater, a prosperous business enterprise. He said the *Herald* had printed a story that he ran Communist Propaganda films the other theaters wouldn't touch, and Mr. Hogan said this was equivalent to calling its owner a Communist. In those heated days this was considered an evil thing to call a man.

"Did he run the films?" I said.

Helgesen got furious. He said the man's lawyer said he had not.

I had to know. I said, "Did you let the story go through?"

Helgesen didn't answer. This told me it had gone over his desk. As city editor, he was solely responsible for its appearance in the paper. If it turned out to be professional libel, the worst kind for a jury, and if Bill Hogan took it to court and won a big verdict, it would ruin Helgesen's career. He'd wind up editing a weekly in East Pottawatomie. A libel verdict convicts a city editor of carelessness, lack of judgment, and plain stupidity. It says he is irresponsible and not to be trusted in a crisis. Howey was promoting Helgesen and Howey had a *thing,* rabid and malevolent, against libel. Swimming in a pool on a country place Howey had taken in Jersey as I came up after a dive I found myself face to face with a snake lifting its head above the water and Clements yelled from the side, *Howey must think you committed libel to send the snakes to get you.* Moreover, at this moment Mrs. Patterson was annoyed with her favorite editor. Helgesen had got arrested at Atlantic City for speeding into a shopwindow, we'd had to persuade the governor to squash it. This was not the moment for a libel suit.

I put my hand in his, it came over me that I couldn't bear to see him humiliated. Always it is more difficult to see a cocky, conceited, swashbuckling blithe spirit like Helgesen hung from a tree than some more worthy fellow, and unjust as this may be to the good brothers a number of movie stars have become idols on its technique.

Waiting for us on a chair beside the city desk sat the portentous little man who threatened to sue the *Herald* and Mrs. Eleanor Medill Patterson for the largest sum we'd ever heard mentioned.

I went and sat down and decided to be an unprejudiced spectator.

Helgesen took over the desk with what looked like his usual self-confidence. He ignored the little man entirely for some time. I thought these were wrong tactics. To me, Mr. X could be Jeremiah announcing doom. I had a high opinion of Hogan. At last *Jeremiah* arose, a difficult feat if you are only five foot four, but he managed it impressively and we heard him all over the city room when he said, "Mr. Editor, do not try shoving me around. My lawyer did not wish me to come here, but I said to him it is only fair and square to give them a chance to settle out of court and if I personally speak the truth of my situation to them—"

Settle out of court? The words gave me the creeps. In Earl Rogers' office we took a shot, however long, at a trial and a jury verdict.

If we settled this suit for one dollar, the admission of guilt was implicit. While Cissy knew the difference between twelve million dollars and a thin dime as only the very rich do and would be glad to save $11,999,999.90 it wouldn't save Helgesen. An admission was a moral defeat for him as great as a cashier who'd made good his stolen money.

Words thrummed in my head.

Who can foresee worse days than he that yet living doth follow at the funeral of his own reputation? Francis Bacon, who said that, was a genius who did indeed walk behind a coffin carrying the bones of his stupendous good name and his future usefulness. That would happen to Helgesen. The Helgesen cult would vanish from Cissy's future plans. I saw dislike growing on the furrowed countenance of the little man. His voice grew louder, Helgesen inspired the extremes in people he dealt with. I must break this up before he talked his way to the gallows. I got up—

The phone on the city desk rang with a long imperative snarl.

Helgesen said, *"City Desk."*

After a moment he said crisply, "All right. Take it easy. I've got it. Exactly where—how far out—do you know yet how many were killed—all right—any of the rest able to talk—? All right—we'll be there—"

He spoke to a tense, silent city room. "The express from St. Louis hit a busful of high-school students at the grade crossing just east of Rockville. Some of the children were killed—the rest are being taken to hospitals—" then he began to give specific orders, clear, concise, and definite.

The little man with his libel suit was standing isolated, angry, shouting amid the din as the troops moved into action. He couldn't comprehend what was going on. He began hopping up and down and making gestures, Helgesen said, *"City Desk"* into the phone again, his eyes on Mr. X; fury shook him and he started to order him out and I said, "No no—you can't just let him go away mad like that—he'll go find Bill Hogan and have a suit ready to file when court opens in the morning." Helgesen said, "Keep him out of my hair—" and I took him back to my desk. I said, "Sit down and *wait*. Don't you see he's too busy to hear you?"

Waiting.

I was on edge waiting for my assignment.

Mr. X's voice ran on like the old mill stream in an obbligato—an American citizen—a patriot—boys in high school—if Papa was called a Communist their friends would spit on them—if he didn't make any money the boys couldn't go to college—people would not come to his theater—just redecorated—*what it cost*—

I saw Jackie Martin, head of our photographic department, come in wrapped in a trench coat, her camera over her shoulder, then Happy Robinson of circulation, Helgesen told him to get the photogs and their equipment and drive them out in a circulation truck—the wreck was in the mud, Les Sommer said—and he told Happy to bring back the first pictures.

The little man began to run down—he was almost weeping with rage and chagrin—but he had begun to listen—Jackie stopped and said something to me and he stared up at her, his eyes popping.

Helgesen shouted, "St. Johns"—and I got to the desk and he said, "Minnie's waiting for you—take a look at Rockville and then go back to the Georgetown Hospital, they're bringing them in there—get a move on—" I turned and bumped into my little man and in a gasp I said, "What'll I do with him?" and Helgesen said, "Hell, take him with you—" in a nasty voice, so I said, "All right—" and I took Mr. X's hand and yanked him and said, "Come on—get a move on will you?"

2

The Dante's Inferno I found east of Rockville comes between me and this paper. It starts a set of pictures that race like a film before my eyes.

The roads, the grade crossing, the morgue, the hospital, in the rain and fog and mud. The sound track of voices screaming and wailing, the sirens coming from all points of the compass and from the sky and the earth and the trees.

The roads were solid with traffic already, thousands of cars converging on that fatal crossing. Ambulances and fire trucks and police rescue squads fighting their way through. Minnie's car had a siren we'd put on it, it never *stopped* never never never, we were off the road in a ditch, we skidded up onto a cow track, and took a gate with us back to the road. We passed all kinds of cars, the entire population of Williamsport was surging like maddened refugees toward that pinpoint of accident, fathers and mothers and crying little brothers and sisters who didn't know yet what had happened to *their* boy, their girl, who had gone forth in the school bus to a school function, they were crying out, they were in white silent suspense— *where is mine?*—who had survived? Had any? A miasma of fear, every mother knows some miasma of fear about *busses,* the Great Neck Swamp Angels had ridden to a game in a bus in the wild uproar of a hurricane's tail. Now with the siren's shriek never letting up in my ears and the faces in the passing cars and the rain and fog I slipped a cog and it seemed to me it was the bus with the Great Neck Swamp Angels that had been hit and wrecked and *broken* smash by a fast express train—

Minnie said, "You gotta get out and walk the rest of the way." I was up to my knees in *mud.* Slime crawled around my ankles and I couldn't see through the dripping witch-locks of hair in my face. Minnie moved in ahead of me as my blocker, and I tried to follow in the holes he made and behind me pushing and shoving someone was holding *on* to my wet velvet coat.

A cop who recognized Minnie helped us through a barrier. A man was sitting on the ground weeping hysterically. He kept saying, Fifteen feet more would you believe it? He shouted into the air, Jesus Christ Almighty didn't they have a signal at that crossing don't they have to have a signal at that crossing for Chrisake? The cop said, They got a watchman there— I don't know what become of him. It turned out he was due to stay till midnight but he got sleepy and went home and I wonder if he ever slept again.

First aid stations under glaring ghastly lights—mangled bodies that must be part of a nightmare how could they live through mangled bodies, those parents in those cars coming along the roads *not knowing* how could they live through it?

Her name was Miss Funk, she was a tall, pretty, very young teacher. She stood at the door of a first aid station and the doctor kept his arm under hers.

"It is my duty," she said over and over, loudly, to be heard above the sirens that blared out of this flame-lit hell. "It is my duty." The train had hit the rear end of the bus and sheered it off, she had been in front with the driver. "It is my duty to identify my students. I was in charge, I am responsible. It is my duty."

As soon as possible.

Put the fathers and mothers out of suspense, into or out of misery.

This is Leroy Campbell, she said.

That is his brother Howell—no no, not two of them, not two brothers— *how weak and fruitless must be any words of mine—*

I'm afraid to say—Bertha—I think this is Bertha Castle—

A small body in a worn raincoat. Miss Funk touched the coat with her fingers and then saw that the body had no head.

She fell as though she'd been struck by lightning.

Where was the watchman why didn't they have a grade signal goddam them they ought to be hung I will see that they are hung I can do that at least I will hang them myself the careless cheap bastards I will make them put in grade crossings—

Les Sommer, wild-eyed as a bedlamite, met us on the sidewalk outside the Georgetown Hospital. "They won't let you in," he said, "nobody from the press. The nuns won't let anybody in."

I got out and stumbled, I had lost both my shoes. The skirt of my dress looked like a quarterback's towel. I was clutching Mr. X with one hand and trying to get the hair out of my face with the other.

They were taking a stretcher out of the ambulance and I heard a girl-child's voice high and squeaky with hurt and terror calling, Mama Mama Mama.

I have to tell this as a double thread. It is a double thread. Twisted together but true.

I was a reporter. *My* story was inside that hospital. To talk to one of those kids who had survived. An eyewitness account. That was news and it was *my* story, my feature. This meant I had to get inside somehow.

I was a mother. Why do they always say, *Mama* when it hurts no matter if they are four or fourteen like this girl. I reached down automatically and her fingers closed on my hands and seemed to go through my flesh to the bone so that I cried out, what I looked like shoeless, muddy, soaking, walking beside that stretcher with the girl clinging to my hand! The nun on the door never looked at me. We were inside going down the corridor; a nursing sister spoke to the stretcher bearers and we turned and she came with us.

We passed two stretchers. The faces were covered but muddy shoes stuck out at the other end. So quiet. Nothing at the grade crossing's inferno had been pitiful as those quiet shoes that had started the night at such a clatter, as a boy's shoes do.

The operating room was bright, white, it smelled of drugs, it was terrifying but hope came, too. The sister in charge was going to put me out, when I tried to pull away my hand the child moaned, the doctor peered over his mask and said *Keep her quiet* so I stayed. While he set her fractured shoulder and broken arm, she kept crying out and I said wildly *Can't you give her anything* and he said *I don't know how deep she is in shock an anesthetic might kill her.* Now, we have discoveries they could give but then thirty years ago they didn't.

So I kept talking to her as best I could, *I'm right here baby,* I said, I couldn't stop shaking, the sweat on me was icy, I did manage to keep talking, *The doctor's going to fix your arm good as new,* I said, *you're going to be as good as new my lamb,* once she opened her eyes and when she said, *Mama?* it had a question mark after it, so I said *Take it easy, sweetheart, your mama'll be here in a minute, just hang onto me till she comes, will you?*

Back in the corridor so they could take someone else fast, she whispered, "You aren't my mother," and I said, "I know. Can't you pretend I am till she gets here? I'd be very proud. You've been so brave—" She said, "I'm not scared for me, it's Mama—she always *worries* so much—" "Can you tell me your phone number?" I said. When she did I still couldn't get loose my hand and I'd forgotten about my twelve-million-dollar companion. I was beyond being surprised when I found him sticking closer than my shadow, white and wet. I hissed a number at him and said, "Tell anyone who answers—"

When she finally slept—her name was Thelma—the sister had to get my hand loose from her grip.

It was still numb when I sat down behind my typewriter.

3

At about 3:00 A.M. that morning we rolled for the last time.

A beat crew such as I'd never seen. Till we got the paper away we'd been reporters keyed up like dervishes, intent on *work* that was a shield, all of a sudden we were pea green and it was Jackie Martin of the inspired camera who was sick and photographers aren't supposed to be sick. We couldn't go home, we were afraid to go home. Nobody would dare to go to sleep for fear of nightmares. We had to make a lot of *noise* so we'd be sure we wouldn't hear again and again the cries and pleas and weeping of mothers for their children and nobody could make a lot of noise cold sober at three-thirty that morning, not unless they were a hyena.

Helgesen was still at the phone. We couldn't be sure he was still shouting, *City Desk get it in here it's no good to me in Rockville,* or whether it was the echo from what he'd been shouting all night and, of course, we'd left a couple of men out there.

Everybody had a couple of drinks. It was the day before payday, I got some money off the little man to pay for coffee and whiskey and some sandwiches, $39.85. Then the paper came up hot and smoking. It was a masterpiece of death and tragedy but it *was* a masterpiece. Of coverage. The paper was a classic. We knew it, Washington would know it, Mr. Hearst would know it. That knowledge exorcised the howling demons that pursued us from those hours behind, some of us had deep incurable wounds that would haunt us forever after. Yet yet yet—a man's work is the core of his being, the glory of war is hell, a battle won is hell, but it has its glory! We were trying to salve our wounds in whiskey and work.

Helgesen came and sat on my desk, he looked more than half dead. I began to tell him loudly that I wanted to do a series right away to do away with grade crossings, while everyone was shuddering at *this one,* while Rockville was a word that made them weep. We could hit the State of Maryland and the railroad and get some crossing protection. Helgesen said, Go ahead, we can start it the day of the funerals.

How that big cop got into the act we never quite knew. He said we had been reported for disturbing the peace. In fact he got tough with Helgesen, who was brittle; it was whale-ass Waldrop who threw a punch that traveled so fast we hardly saw it. As he knelt over the body on the floor, Les Sommer said loudly, I know! You're the Waldrop who played tackle ahead of Red Cagle for the Army, and we laughed but a hush fell then. A dead cop on the floor of your city room could prove embarrassing. He wasn't *dead,* so Waldrop and Happy Robinson put him in a truck of papers going to Richmond, he never told anybody. How could he?

I hadn't had time to notice our little man. I was just sort of half aware that he'd been running my copy, sheet by sheet, from my typewriter to the city desk and once I heard him protesting to Helgesen, who was only trying to put in some subheads. I couldn't do anything about him now.

Helgesen picked up my gloves that had been white and were wet and caked with red Maryland mud. He looked at them with distaste and dropped them in the wastebasket and said, "I'll get you a new pair tomorrow." He pulled me up on the desk beside him and at one point in the emotional frenzy told everybody that we were going to be married. Some of the brotherhood looked at me in terror mixed with admiration and others looked at Helgesen with admiration mixed with sympathy but we all drank a hearty toast out of our paper cups.

That was, I suppose, the high moment of our love.

The phone on the city desk began to ring and ring in long shrill demanding blasts. Nobody paid any attention. Nobody had strength left to answer it. What would we do with it anyhow?

And then my little man sat down in Helgesen's empty chair.

He picked up the phone and said, *"City Desk."*

He listened a minute and then we heard him shout, *"Get it in here, it's no good to me in Rockville!"*

We never heard any more about the libel suit.

It seemed rubbing it in to me that he not only never got a penny richer out of his sure-fire suit, he ended up $39.85 cents in the red.

Once a newspaperman always a newspaperman. If ever the sea puss had a chance to get her claws into a man it was the night of the bus crash.

I flew home that morning to see my children. I had to. They were all in fine shape, so I took the next plane back to get on with my series.

MAKE GRADE CROSSINGS EVERYWHERE SAFE FOR OUR CHILDREN

That was the headline on page 1.

ADELA ROGERS ST JOHNS SAYS TALK WON'T END GRADE CROSSING TRAGEDY LET'S DO SOMETHING NOW

I find I kept right on saying that for days.

I remember that Mrs. Roosevelt called me, she was a very thoughtful woman and always had *time* to speak a word of praise or say a kind thing.

As always in sorrow and horror and guilt, we moved. Around Washington and Maryland anyhow grade crossings were made safe for the children of democracy.

4

The sharp edges of old reticences are softened in the autobiographer by the passing of time. The incomparable irreplaceable James Thurber says that.

Reticence keeps you silent from shame, guilt, fear, or some deep-seated respect for the canons of good taste, as you were taught them, as long as there is personal identification. Years later when it has become impersonal and the subject of the autobiography is only someone you *used* to be, you merely say, Could this have been I—or me, if you prefer. You do not hide your head under the pillow in chagrin nor hear the telephone bell with distaste or panic. If these are the things that lead at last to the Desired Country they remind you that you learned your very life from them and if the pilgrimage is to be recounted the truth alone will serve. Without, as Mr. Thurber says, reticences.

In thinking of *my time* in Washington, in thinking of Helgesen and Cissy Patterson and Evalyn Walsh McLean and J. Edgar Hoover and the Roosevelts, I wish I could be with them again as I thought they were then. This would naturally include myself as I thought I was then. Otherwise of course they would look quite different. Especially me. Especially Helgesen.

The end was laughing with tears in my eyes, but I know now, as a final verdict, that I did the best *I* could.

Our final act began when Steve Hannagan came down from New York, bringing his client millionaire Pete Jones, head of City Service. A paper was for sale in Kansas City. If Helgesen and I were interested in running it, Hannagan told us, Pete Jones would buy it. In these changing times, the Chicago *Tribune* shouldn't forever be the controlling voice of the Middle West; more liberal policies were needed.

Every newspaperman talks about the time when he will own his own paper. He wants a small town weekly, in a beautiful countryside somewhere in New Jersey, New Hampshire, or New Mexico. He'll settle for a small city paper that can become a Power like the Emporia *Gazette*.

Here it was.

We had several sessions. Helgesen and I said we would think it over and let them know and Hannagan and Pete Jones went back to New York.

Why Helgesen chose in that particular interval of decision to do what he did I cannot explain any more than I can *how* an alcoholic comes to do *what* he does *at* the worst possible moment in the hottest spot *where* it can do him the gravest harm and *when* it hurts most those he loves. All violences and neuroses can become compulsive unless they get Help. Any two people who felt less need of a Higher Power to help us than Helgesen and me, I can't imagine. We weren't sure there was anything higher. Than *us?*

The event itself passed without much to-do. Inevitably, I was in the city room when, by a blunder, Les Sommer revealed to me that it hadn't been one of Helgesen's careless twists of cruelty but had been done *on purpose.* Malice aforethought changes any casualty from manslaughter to first degree murder. This one could indicate a whole series of petty meannesses, belittling abuses, verbal harpoons, and glittering gags with *intention* to hurt. I stood stunned, staring at Les, and only now as I write this down does it occur to me that it wasn't an error on his part. Les Sommer is as highly intelligent and psychologically oriented about human beings as anyone I've ever known and I am sure now, knowing us both, he meant to save Ray and me from a fate worse than death.

I remember my eyes finally left him and focused on my new hat. I'd taken it off and put it on my desk. A dark straw, rolled back and held in front by a light blue feather laid flat, to be worn pulled over the left eye. I picked it up, put it on top of my head like Queen Mary, and walked out. A plane was leaving for New York in three minutes. There were no seats, but I knew the pilot. He let me sit on the floor in the cabin.

A couple of hours later I was home in Cow Lane.

Phone calls mounted from surprise—to city desk *orders*—to kidding and then anger and at last *please.* I note that please is merely pleas with an *e* added to them, that added *e* makes it easier for a proud man to say.

I kept walking around my garden by night like an automaton.

As far as Washington was concerned, I was through there anyway. Huey was dead. I'd done all the features including the cherry blossoms and the piglets.

Kansas City?

I couldn't see Helgesen anywhere but Washington.

Women fall in love with men in a place. With a background and surroundings and a caste. Helgesen was the city editor of my Washington *time* and Washington was the hub of the universe and the setting of the incredible Roosevelt era that had style and class and world-shaking drama.

As I walked around in the starlight and the thunderstorms I could hear the faint sound of Mozart, whom at least I did admit to be *higher* than anything human. His G Minor seemed to enter into my grief and despair and then I would remember that Mozart to eat had had to try to please all the wrong people and now that he pleased the whole world he was as dead as Huey Long. This ceased to comfort me, it began to discomfit me.

This decision would be final.

There wouldn't be another man I could love.

With a click like an adding machine all the *little* meannesses, the unkind words, the moments of hurt made a column on that side. The speed driving; speed terrified me—I'd had too much of it with Papa. Going up to our mountain resort Ray had driven the narrow curving trail at a death-defying madness per hour. In spite of *my* pleas that time.

On the other hand, there had been stardust when we walked among the dark pines in the starlight.

Hell! I said to Mozart. Decisions decisions decisions like the time you wrote that dance for the plumber to pay a bill. That day we got out the Vanderbilt Exclusive and he was blazing rude to me in front of Gloria and Eddie Rickenbacker, that wasn't cruelty that was just showing them who was boss. But—it's not only me. Poor Waldrop has no more card sense than a Sherman tank and at our games of hearts in my apartment Helgesen makes fun of him, he belittles people.

Some people have sinking spells, some hate high speed driving, or can't stay in a hotel above the second floor or think they are being followed. I cannot stand cruelty. I go to pieces. I scream and yell and writhe *inside*. I see it where it probably isn't anything but stupidity. Or lack of understanding. To this day I regard *cruelty* of any name or nature as the sin against the Holy Ghost. I am sure we shall be judged at last only by the rule of *kindness*.

Also, people ascribe to others what they feel themselves and this works both ways. Thus Helgesen, who was pathologically arrogant with male vanity and masculine pride, was jealous if I spoke in a friendly tone to Minnie the taxi driver who wore his belt below his stomach. The plot was that when I came upon him and the senator's daughter I would be as murderously jealous as he would have been had he found me with the best-looking senator in town. When I got back from New York and went up to his apartment there he was, saying a hurried but fond farewell to the magnolia from Mississippi or somewhere, with the tender intimacy that usually follows hard upon the heels of. But it wasn't jealousy that came of this incitement to violence. *Show me my rival and I will show you what manner of man you are.* The senator's daughter was a little overripe, she said Pardon my Southern accent, and giggled in the wrong places, so if she could displace me in Helgesen's affections he wasn't the man I wanted anyhow. I had thus, not being jealous by nature, ignored this scene with equanimity until Les Sommer told me it had been staged for my benefit.

Then I found myself in a cold emptiness that began to fill up with fury. And in this another truth faced me. Helgesen had seen the Great Neck Swamp Angels play ball in Washington. He really didn't care much for sports and the Swamp Angels were no exception. Paul Gallico and his young wife, Elaine, my daughter, had visited me and Helgesen like every other newspaperman had Gallico at the top of his list. But it didn't occur to him that they might soon make me a doting grandmother. It wasn't age that bothered me about this, it was what to do with the grandchildren if Elaine called up and said, Ma can I leave Junior with you while I go to the World Series, which wouldn't be in Kansas City, it didn't even have a major league ball club then. Dicky had used Helgesen's staff as guides and his city room as a skating rink. Not once had Helgesen seen my children as part of our lives. He wasn't jealous of them nor against them— But a home that stayed the center of *a family?*—Such things hadn't occurred to him.

Did I want to give up everything in Cow Lane and Malibu and go to live in Kansas City and run a paper with Helgesen, who would get worse instead of better if he was my *husband?* That was the question.

While I was still walking around to the sound of Mozart, he telephoned one night to say in cold, definite tones that we must talk things over face to face. We had to give Hannagan and Jones an answer. Moreover we were making ourselves ridiculous. If I wouldn't come to Washington he would have to catch a plane as soon as he finished work. It might be late, he said, and late it turned out to be. Ernest let him in a little after four. I'd put on a housecoat and tried to catch some sleep without success.

When I saw him again there in my bedroom door just as he'd stood that first Sunday I thought with the speed of light, *Oh we can make a go of this.* Of course we can make it work. Why not? We do love each other. All the rest is just temperamental differences; somewhere in him there is a generous soul and he does have honesty of thought and he needs me.

I went over and put my arms around him and said, "Darling, this place is full of people who are asleep, not only the people who live here, Bill has four members of the Swamp Angels asleep on the floor so they can practice *early,* and some friends from California are in the guest room, you look tired to death, come on into your room it's the only one I have left and we'll both get some sleep and talk tomorrow."

I kissed him without getting any response, so I took him across to the room that had been Elaine's. I'd always loved that room, Early American maple and spring-green-yellow-crocus chintz, and I pushed him *lovingly* through the door and it might have been revolving, he spun out before I finished saying sleep well, and he was breathing fire.

I don't suppose I need to know why Helgesen regarded that large Shirley Temple doll as the insult *morte.* It was just *there.* On one of the twin beds where Elaine had left it when she went off to get married. Probably Gallico wouldn't let her take it with her.

Holding it in one hand Helgesen was making noises like a demented siren—I got phrases—goddam*airs*—high horse—and sorrow began to well up in me in a spout of shattering truth and I said, "You'll wake the whole *house*," and with that he took the doll by both legs and hit me over the head with it.

Now this doll, sent to Elaine by its original, was as big as a two-year-old child, and its head was hard but so was mine. I wasn't really *hurt*, it was unhappiness that made me want to cry and then the sight of Helgesen his hair on end swinging Shirley Temple like a shot putter jolted me out of my sorrow. I knew if I laughed he'd probably kill me, but you can't live forever and I began to laugh till I cried and at this point a phalanx of apparitions in pajama pants came tarryhootin' down the hall swinging baseball bats, Bill at their head yelling, *Ugh ahfg gugh here we are Ma.* Helgesen gave them one look and went down the stairs like a boa constrictor. I'm sure he thought he'd strayed into a madhouse.

I wished it had ended on a Mozart note in G Minor but even then I knew if it had it wouldn't have ended. Better the final curtain came down to the tune of Cohan's "Always Leave Them Laughing When You Say Good-bye." Actually I never got to say good-by to Helgesen at all.

Easy come easy go. I tried to tell myself that defiantly. It didn't work very well.

It had been a long day!

The years are short, but sometimes the days are long.

I knew I didn't want to spend short years made up of long days in Kansas City. In that moment of sorrow I had known they would *be* long days. So I went and called Steve Hannagan, who lived at Delmonico's and was in love just then with Gloria Swanson, as who wasn't?

I said we had decided not to do it.

Steve said, "My suffering aunt, did you wake me at 5:00 A.M. to tell me that? Why the decision at this ungodly hour?"

"Well," I said, "Helgesen doesn't want to marry me, so I wouldn't be comfortable out there, would I? It's my fault, really."

"You have our Irish love of martyrdom," Steve said. "It's always your fault, but you never do anything about it."

"Like what?" I said.

"How about not getting into it in the first place?" Steve said. "You have a rich, full life, you already have your children; moral standards for unmarried women are less rigid than they once were. What do you want to get married for?"

"It's respectable," I said. "With the children I can't go around just living with people. Besides, marriage is the happiest thing for a woman. It was meant to be that way—two by two, wasn't it? I keep hoping."

"If I let Pete buy that paper will you go out there and run it with me?" Steve said.

"No!" I said.

"I've always wanted to run a paper," Steve said. "Why won't you?"

"What do you know about running a newspaper?" I said furiously. "You're like the people who could write a book if they had time. Helgesen is a great city editor. Oh Steve, don't scold me. I am very unhappy, I think my heart is broken."

"It's not the first time," Steve said.

"Worse," I said, "it's probably the last."

"I don't see why," Steve said.

"Pretty soon I'll have *grand*children," I said. "I can't stand silly middle-aged women, they're the worst. No—it was my last chance and all last things are lonely."

In the sardonic and cranky voice of a man who has been awakened at five o'clock in the morning by a weeping woman, Steve said, "There there little girl, don't cry, they have broken your doll I know—" but at the words *broken your doll* I *cracked* up and Steve *hung* up.

Shamefaced I sat by myself until Ernest got back from the airport and brought me some coffee. The next line of that sentimental doggerel Steve had declaimed at me from Park Avenue to Great Neck kept roaring into my head. *Heaven holds that for which you sigh* was all very well but heaven seemed far far away and it would be a long time to wait.

Women who are not sentimental are, I always feel, the kind of women who like snakes.

As it turned out I was right about one thing. It was the last time.

BOOK FIVE

BOOK FIVE

CHAPTER 33

Upon a midnight, Mr. Hearst called me in Cow Lane and said, "I would like you to go to England tomorrow."

Stupidly I said, "What for?"

I was settling down to fiction, working very hard, doing well at it. I was there when the children came home from school. Cow Lane had become the center if not the circumference of my existence. I was reluctant to disturb it.

To my *What for?* Mr. Hearst said, "The most popular and famous man in the world today is the new King of England. He has invited an American lady named Mrs. Simpson to a dinner at Buckingham Palace."

Two months before this, I had awakened my household at dawn to listen to the voice of this new king. This, I told them, is a Historic Moment. When your children read about what a great king Edward VIII has been, or your grandchildren study all he did for his people, you can say, *We heard* his first speech to his subjects. As we gathered around a leaping fire and his words rang from the radio I believed what I had said. All the world believed it.

> I am better known to most of you as The Prince of Wales. As the man who during the war and since has had an opportunity of getting to know the people of every country in the world under all conditions and circumstances. And though I now speak to you as The King I am still the same man who has had the experience and whose constant effort will be to continue to promote the well-being of his fellow-man. May the future bring peace and understanding throughout the world, prosperity and happiness to the British people and may we be worthy of the heritage that is ours.

Around the world, men listened. Englishmen listened everywhere for in those days the sun never set on British possessions of which he was now King and Emperor. Not one of them knew that the King had practiced that speech before the lady he had invited to dinner, Mrs. Simpson, and that "I am still the same man" had been her contribution.

He came to the throne at a time when every reactionary in England, of church and state, was trembling. The old order was going, going forever.

Ever since that World War I of which he spoke the spirit of unrest, the demands of labor, the awakening of the poor to ask more light and life had been growing apace.

At this moment when the old order needed to defend its privileges and purposes as never before there came to the throne a young king who said, "We must do something for the poor. We must work hand and hand with Labor even beyond what my father has done." Actually, he had appeared in the coal mines of Rhondda Valley, he had visited London slums, talked with the men women and children who lived in them. This was a king beloved not only by the nobility and the Circle of his personal friends, he was the living idol of his people, the symbol of hope to the lower classes. There was no television yet. But on the screens of their imagination—and we used this more when it was all we had—the people saw him with his bow of burning gold attacking those dark satanic mills of Birmingham. His sword would not sleep in his hand till England was a green and pleasant land for more and more of them. If anyone could make this a successful and peaceful revolution, Edward VIII could. He might keep the best of all possible worlds in unity.

Remembering that morning by the fire in our own living room as the first speech rolled out from three thousand miles away, I agreed with Mr. Hearst that after two months as King he was the most popular and famous man in the world.

"When I was a young girl," I said, "we didn't have movie heroes or aviators in uniform to worship. Most of us concentrated on His Royal Highness the Prince of Wales. I had his picture in a silver frame on my dressing table. The dream of every American girl was to dance with him. Millions of us still remember that dream."

All this was what came into my mind when Mr. Hearst said on the phone, "I want you to go to England because he is entertaining a beautiful woman from Baltimore and that is important news. I admit to some surprise at finding the name of Mr. and Mrs. Simpson in the Court Circular, among the mightiest in the land."

Lord Beaverbrook, Mr. Hearst's opposite number in the English press, was to say later on that he had warned the King that Mrs. Simpson ought not to be in the Court Circular, that daily paper which announces to the British Empire the doings of the Royal Family, their travels, residences, and social life. Dickens calls it the most exclusive publication in the world, it was also royally official. Certainly the mention therein of this American Woman was the Clue, the Tip-off spotted that early by old Chief Eagle Eye William Randolph Hearst.

"I think," I said, "Lady Furness, who was Thelma Vanderbilt, presented Mrs. Simpson to the Prince of Wales. Thelma told me that these fancies of the Prince's come and go. If this *is* one—and he's forty now."

"A dangerous age for gentlemen," Mr. Hearst said. (He himself had been in his forties the first time he saw a girl named Marion Davies in the chorus of the Ziegfeld Follies.) "Let us," he went on, "recall another English king who was near the same age when he determined to marry a maid of honor and make her Queen of England."

"Marry!" I said, and heard the phone wires jump across Kansas. "To begin with there is a *Mr.* Simpson—you just said so—"

"In the case of *Henry* the Eighth there was a Queen Catherine of Aragon," said Mr. Hearst, "and she was the daughter of Ferdinand and Isabella of Spain, goddaughter of the Pope, niece of the German Emperor. Yet Henry said, I am going to marry Anne Boleyn. To do so against such overpowering opposition he got the divorce which altered history as few single events have done."

"I've always wondered what Anne Boleyn was like," I said.

"I am wondering what Mrs. Simpson is like," Mr. Hearst said. "I think you had better go to England and make some inquiries about her."

I said, "Young Doug Fairbanks wanted me to go over and work on a movie for him but I said no."

"Good," Mr. Hearst said. "You can use Mr. Fairbanks' motion pictures as a cover to find out what is going on and gather material for a life of Mrs. Simpson in case it is warranted. The King will soon be under pressure to marry."

"Well," I said, "he certainly can't marry Mrs. Simpson."

"His popularity is a mighty structure built over many years," Mr. Hearst said. "Royal marriages are arranged as alliances for the benefit of the country. They always have been. We may begin to suggest that an *alliance* with an American woman would, at this time, have decided advantages. They may need us soon. And," he chuckled a little here, "it would sell papers."

Much as in this particular story I came to dislike, then to disagree with and finally to disapprove of the use he made of it, I am still amazed at Mr. Hearst's prophetic sense of news. At that moment I could hardly believe he was seriously hinting at a marriage between the King of England and an American woman who had a husband. Although *Mr.* Simpson seemed to be going along with the tide, if there was a tide, and nobody cared too much if *Mr.* Simpson didn't, she would have to get rid of him if there was to be any question of marriage.

I didn't know then that she had already been divorced once!

Marriage?

Through my head, as I began to be hit by the excitement of such a fantastic idea, went words that trumpeted denial. True, Edward Albert Christian George Andrew Patrick David of the House of Windsor had had at least two previous lady friends who were American. Lady Thelma Furness and another who had returned to her native land to marry into the Field family of Chicago. This had been taken only as romance. He had not then been King.

By later testimony of cabinet ministers, press lords, family, and friends, at the time Mr. Hearst spoke that word to me only two people in the world had even thought of it in connection with the infatuation of the King for Mrs. Simpson.

One was Mr. Hearst.

The other was the King of England.

As for the "Other Party Most Concerned," as the King was to call her, I do not believe that when I arrived in London, before the story had broken into print by a single word anywhere in England, she entertained even secretly any such mad ambition. One bitter past experience may have helped to condition her to instant rejection of such a possibility. There is a most ironic touch in what we may call the Case of the Two Ambassadors. Wallis Spencer, as she then was, had for some time been the constant companion of the ambassador from the Argentine. And he had attempted to have her invited as his lady guest to a dinner at the British Embassy in Washington. The British Ambassador refused. I daresay later that ambassador thought of shooting himself, for it was this refusal that convinced Wallis Spencer that Felipe Espil had no intention of marrying her. Thus she fled her defeat to England's greener pastures where she met first Ernest Simpson, a jewelry salesman, and second the King.

She married Simpson after his divorce from a New York wife.

But—the King?

Such an *alliance,* as Mr. Hearst was pleased to call it, would certainly make news. A valuable alliance, I granted that. In the future. And that was the future as the King, and incidentally Mr. Hearst, saw it.

The truth was to be different.

There are stories that have unbearable suspense because we do not know the End. And others hold a different but equal suspense because, while we do know the End as well as we know that Joan of Arc was burned at the stake, it works backward and always will. We want to find out how it happened, how it could have happened.

They are still alive, the hero and heroine of this story, stars who played their tragedy with the world as its stage when the British Empire was its greatest power. God helping us all, who could have foreseen, imagined, been made to believe anything so pitiful and paltry as their End? The End that stares me in the face as I re-create days I lived and saw and shared.

What can be more tragic than a world that ends not with a bang, not even with a whimper, but with a hey-nonny-nonny?

Wormwood for every soul, that is.

Julius Caesar crying, *Et tu, Brute,* as he saw the dagger. *Re-enter Macduff with Macbeth's head.* Or Socrates lifting the hemlock cup or Napoleon at Waterloo—

But, to quote Suzy's famous social column of 1968, what could even Shakespeare have made of:

> After dinner everyone repaired to Maxim's, where a crazy party was in progress for Cerutti, the Italian designer of men's clothes. The place was alive with French pop singers, most of the couturiers, the Duke and Duchess of Windsor, Connie Crespi over from Rome in her short dark curly wig and on and on. Paris wouldn't be Paris unless you mixed the bag.

Cleopatra whispering to the asp, *Be angry, dispatch me,* Queen Anne Boleyn putting her head on the block in the Tower and saying with her famed high laughter, *You will not need to strike hard, I have such a little neck.*

But:

> The Duchess of Windsor, international hostess nonpareil, says that forty-five minutes of drinking before dinner is quite enough. If she never said anything more brilliant in her entire life somebody should hang a medal on her for those wonderful words.

Which? The Victoria Cross? Or her own country's Medal of Honor perhaps?

How could such things come to pass?

How could it be possible that this glamorous, beloved, gifted man born to rule the most powerful empire on earth, this shining prince trained to grace a throne, found himself "the promoter for a winter resort called the Bahamas" as his duchess-wife told me he was being described far and wide when, later on, I spent some weeks with them there to get their own story, at long last?

Early in 1936 what Mr. Hearst wanted me to find in London was not the End but the Beginning.

"Let us see," Mr. Hearst said to me, "if we can make her Queen of England."

In Cow Lane we had a farewell dinner and my family came down to see me off at the midnight sailing of the *Berengaria*. There were as yet no transatlantic air flights so no one had to apologize for enjoying the gaiety, beauty, and rest of crossing that ocean on a luxury liner.

When it came to saying good-by to the children and the Great Neck Swamp Angels I nearly got off the boat. The reason I didn't was the same that had overcome my reluctance when Mr. Hearst called me.

I wanted to *be there*. This is what makes reporters reporters.

Long before I knew what a reporter was, I read history with this passionate desire to have been there and gotten the real story. All history was journalism once and some bad journalism has distorted a lot of good history. I have always wondered what would have happened to history if there had been some good war correspondents with Richard III, certainly he couldn't have been betrayed as he was by the Stanleys. A few competent reporters could have prevented the Tudor king who stole Richard's throne from also libeling him down through the centuries with the false tale that he murdered his nephews, the little Princes in the Tower. I wanted to be the reviewer that night when teen-age Aristophanes' play *The Clouds,* ridiculing the educational methods of Socrates, opened in Athens and caused riots, and I wanted it to be possible for Mr. Hearst to send me to Paris when Benjamin Franklin was our Ambassador to France so I could see how this elderly Philadelphia philosopher with his long unpowdered hair had become the favorite of the ladies of that French court. I'd like to have done a feature on the wife of Pontius Pilate, how she felt after her husband washed his hands of a young rebel named Jesus of Nazareth, whose follower she had become. I wanted my city editor to have sent me to find out if the birds really listened to St. Francis in his garden.

Years, experiences, times, and places within this progress I call my life have seemed to me separate incarnations, with a new cast of characters including a different me. One, however, goes back four hundred years, but I can see, hear, smell, and feel it as vividly, so that I know, *I know* that I was on the beach with great Elizabeth when she made the speech to her troops at Tilbury as the Spanish Armada approached. I *heard* her say, *I have the body of a weak and feeble woman but I have the heart and stomach of a king and a King of England, too,* and I knew she was the daughter of Anne Boleyn, the second of King Henry's six wives. The one he really loved. This fascinated me, so I read about it in the history books, but I couldn't seem to *know* Mistress Boleyn, nor why she, of all women in the world, had so captured this beautiful and talented prince. I wanted to have *been there and talked to her and the people who knew her.*

Even Mr. Hearst couldn't arrange for me to write:

THE REAL MISTRESS BOLEYN

But he could and did send me to London to write:

THE REAL MRS. SIMPSON

2

My London assignment was clear and simple.

To estimate the situation we already called the King-and-Mrs.-Simpson from the standpoint of Mr. Hearst's then sensational prophecy that the King desired and intended to marry this woman.

To discover all I could about Bessie Wallis Warfield Spencer Simpson with a view to writing a Life Story that might help the King to make her Queen.

The movie treatment for Doug Fairbanks, Jr., was necessary camouflage. When you are doing on-the-spot research with living people and issues whose consequences are still in doubt and can be world shaking, it is necessary to walk more carefully than when you're rooting in libraries about people already in their graves.

I hadn't been in London long enough for the maid at the Savoy to unpack me before I found one Rock-of-Gibralter fact. The man who as Prince of Wales used to conceal his deep diplomatic doings behind a playboy front, play poker with newspaperman like Frazier Hunt, trip the light fantastic with beauteous babes, and set men's fashions for the good of British trade was now *expected to settle down.* As Falstaff's rip-roaring Prince Hal had become the warrior-conqueror King Henry V, so this prince must now become the people's potentate-liberal leader King Edward VIII. Mrs. Simpson might regard him as "the same man" and so, perhaps, he was. His role, however, would be different indeed. I remembered that, according to the Chinese, after the first Lord of Man had ruled for forty-five thousand years and introduced clothing, shelter, and agriculture he thought it best to appoint kings and emperors as his assistants. They were the first earthly rulers. A king was still, in England, head of his nation by *divine right,* his appointment by the grace of God to rule was part of an Englishman's being. This acceptance of the divine right of kings may not be easy for an American to understand, but the reality of the tradition seeped into me and went with me as I began to pick up on several levels bits and pieces about Mrs. Simpson.

To the people of England she was more an atmosphere than anything else. *This Mrs. Simpson,* they called her.

They speculated about her.

Who *was* she exactly? This woman whose name was borne on every breeze in connection with their king? The people plucked it out by a sort of osmosis peculiar to the doings of Royalty. Seen about with him, dancing, was she? He'd always been a one for *dancing,* had the Prince. Now he was King, she entertained for him in her home and they'd heard he dropped in there quite frequent. Been to visit him at Belvedere? Well, everybody knew that was the castle he loved, he'd done it over so 'twas home to him and nobody had ever seen anything nicer than the gardens he had there. Was this Mrs. Simpson a gardener, like?

Ah well, as Prince of Wales he'd been a lad with the ladies, as had his grandfather Edward VII before him. By his dashing ways and style once that Prince Edward became King, after the old Queen's long and glorious reign, he'd brought the Crown closer to the people. He'd been already married to Princess Alexandra of Denmark, a fitting alliance for the good of his subjects and the power of his realm. He'd not had a chance to wed to please his own heart, therefore no one censured him for having a Favorite. Anyone could understand how it was when he saw that beauty of all English Beauties that ever were, Mrs. Langtry, the Jersey Lily, and later *dear* Mrs. Keppel. It was known over every back fence and in every pub in England that when the King died she and Queen Alexandra had comforted each other. Of course the new King's father had been George V, and he had married their beloved Princess Mae, who became Queen Mary, the idol of all Englishwomen, and that had been the ideal marriage and such a family as everyone could wish for themselves. Whether there were any such royal princesses about now—but he should look for one. A bonnie lassie like his brother's Scottish wife, the Duchess of York. The divine right of kings included the right of his subjects to a Queen and a Royal Family, a glorified version of themselves. As always they desired and demanded this. Once they knew Edward VIII intended to fulfill this tradition, no one would censure him for a Friend. The King's Friend might become their friend, too.

This unknown face they'd seen beside His Majesty at his father's funeral. A woman's face, the whisper said, very white and still. Very close to him. That couldn't have been this Mrs. Simpson, could it now? If it was, they must take this as more than a flirtation. *Death*—that called for respect and seriousness, that did.

Was there any reason this American lady shouldn't be a proper Friend to their young King? She had a *husband,* as was proper; it had never been otherwise within the memory of man. With all of this, they were deeply concerned. For it was impossible for me to miss in the air I breathed the special, all-pervading indulgence they had for this, their King of Promise. In their eyes, he could do no wrong. Not if he did it the right way.

London, March 1936, I found nobody by faint whisper or gesture would admit that Hitler had evil designs and was preparing to execute them. Those were the days of a myth called the Maginot Line. Behind it, France was to sit safe from German aggression. I have to say that except for that old warmonger Winston Churchill, in disfavor with both parties for his tiresome war *warnings,* no one would mention war or listen to evidence of the ominous clouds forming over Europe.

Strong proof of this came into my personal experience. At the request of Mr. Arthur Christiansen, editor-in-chief of the Beaverbrook papers, I was doing for them a series comparing their film capital Elstree with our Hollywood. While I was actually writing these, my friend John Monk Saunders, a famed American pilot of World War I and author of the first aviation war film *Wings,* came back from Germany, where he'd met his former enemy German ace Ernst Udet. As pilots do, they foregathered and Udet told Johnny Saunders about the underground airfields, the millions of gallons of gasoline stored in buried tanks, the creation in deepest secrecy of the biggest air force the world had ever seen, all under personal command of Der Führer. "I believe he meant me to tell England," John Monk Saunders said to me. "Udet was not Hitler's man. He didn't ask me to keep it secret, I think he felt if England knew in time it might prevent another war." Mr. Christiansen deliberated long and long before he printed my story, revealing *for the first time* figures, facts, names, and places, on the front page of the London *Daily Express.* Highly probable that this decision to publish hastened Udet's execution by Adolf Hitler, though Saunders said Udet knew this was inevitable. He had told Hitler he wouldn't serve under Goering. But the publication didn't gain me the white plumes I'd expected and felt I'd earned. Not one soul except a titled gentleman named Campbell, head of Prudential Life, ever mentioned this story to me and he only asked where I got it. I suppose it would affect insurance rates.

The King of England was as much a victim of this incredible illusion as any other Englishman. The wisest men in his government had assured him there would be no war.

A lot of this I gathered as I began to work for Beaverbrook and got to know men who worked for his *Daily Express.* These papers along with Northcliffe's London *Times,* Rothermere's *Daily Mirror,* which I must note was a voice crying in the wilderness to get Britain to rearm, the *Evening Standard,* the *Amalgamated Press,* and the *Penny Dreadfuls* were totally *ignoring* the King-and-Mrs.-Simpson. The arrant nonsense that their King was serious about this middle-aged *who-is-she* American woman was nothing but gossip. Some of the staff had picked up the name of a husband prior to Simpson, one Lieutenant Spencer, but what became of *him* they didn't know, probably a war casualty; since to publish any of this would be totally irresponsible why should they care? They warned me frankly, even in the far-out field of, say, a mistress *en titre,* to suspect anything serious was sheer sensationalism.

I began to suspect they might be wrong.

I had another contact of inestimable value. Before coming over, I'd been broadcasting daily in the United States, a Woman's Viewpoint of the News. I carried to London a letter to Fred Bate, head of National Broadcasting Company in Europe.

Fred and his chic and charming wife Jebbie had been invited to Fort Belvedere and this, I already knew, was the accolade of In-ness. Very thrilled I was therefore when the Bates gave a dinner for me to meet Alistair Cooke and other members of the press and radio, both British and American. All the way to their house in the cab, exhausted as I was because the Boots at the Savoy had carted off the only slippers I could wear with an ice-blue satin dinner dress and I had to use force to find them, I tried to figure ways whereby I could slip the subject of Mrs. Simpson past the protocol of my hosts' position as Friends and Guests of the King.

I could have spared myself the trouble.

They asked *me.*

Politely prefaced with Did I know Clark Gable? Had I ever seen Babe Ruth make a home run? Came Did I know an American woman named Mrs. Simpson? I *didn't?* Obviously they hoped all Americans knew all other Americans. Did I know anything about her? Not much, I admitted. Who *was* she? Replying to the English definition of this phrase, I said she wasn't anybody as far as I knew. In a sort of gay mischief Alistair Cooke said, "She is now. Before long, she might be the most talked about woman in the world," and everybody laughed.

All attempts to get useful reactions out of Fred or Jebbie, whether direct or indirect, were fruitless. Yes, Jebbie said, they had met Mrs. Simpson at Belvedere. What was she *like?* Well, Jebbie said, not a beauty, the King's word for her was charming. Was her husband there? Not, Fred said, as far as they knew. How had His Majesty met the lady? As far as they knew, Fred said, he'd seen her when she was presented to his father and mother, the King and Queen. To be presented at the Court of St. James, I said, she must be *somebody.* To this, a noted author informed me, there were levels; Lady Furness, whose husband was a baron, had arranged to present Mrs. Simpson and Mrs. Simpson had actually worn Thelma's veil and Prince-of-Wales Feathers. On loan. Jebbie said carefully that later the Prince, as he still was, had been weekending at Thelma's and the Simpsons were fellow guests. *Quite* casual. Somebody claimed that Lady Furness had jokingly asked her friend Wallis to be sure His Royal Highness wasn't lonely while she—Thelma Furness—went to New York to see her sister Gloria.

Yes, it was an amusing story that Mrs. Simpson walked through a door ahead of the King; this according to royal protocol, even his mother, Queen Mary, wasn't allowed to do. And that His Majesty had roared with laughter—oh, she made him laugh—and of course, both Mr. and Mrs. Bates reminded us, Mrs. Simpson wasn't only American, she was Southern, *very* Southern. Wasn't there a new book just out called *Gone with the Wind* that gave all the secrets of what a Southern belle was like? So used to gentlemen adoring them, expecting always to be waited on, using their Southern accent to mesmerize men.

"I hear," one guest said sardonically, "she drops her handkerchief and waits for the King to pick it up."

"That's too silly to be worth repeating isn't it?" Fred Bates said crossly.

As I had gone to the Bates with an ulterior motive so now I went everywhere else I could with the same.

Cecil Gibbon was the rage with his band at the Savoy; when he and his lyricist Jimmy Dyrenforth had made a movie in Hollywood they'd been my house guests so they came to see me in London and were actually in my rooms for a chat when the call came asking Cecil to go and play for the Duke of York, who was fond of an hour or two of good piano playing in the popular vein. Cecil said, Come along. From my corner of the music room at York House I was called to be presented to the young Duchess of York when she joined her husband. So, I thought, as we exchanged a few sentences, this is the royal manner, this combination of by-divine-right graciousness, and interest. Later in Nassau when the Duchess of Windsor still referred to her as the Dowdy Duchess, although by that time she was the Queen, I felt sure the former Mrs. Simpson was seeing her through green eyes. Neither as Duchess of York nor wife of George VI nor mother of the present Queen Elizabeth would Elizabeth Bowes-Lyon ever make the best-dressed list, too true, her clothes belonged to *her,* the couturiers didn't dictate them.

Then one day at a charity garden party I was allowed to make my bow to Queen Mary. All I know about her is that like Mother Cabrini and Helen Keller and Eleanor Roosevelt, she radiated a light.

I didn't get any news of Mrs. Simpson on either of these occasions. I did see and appreciate the competition in *Queens* as the English people knew them and expected them to be—the standard the American woman would be measured by if Mr. Hearst's guess was right and came off.

She'd make a mess of it!

At Elstree I met Douglas Fairbanks, Jr.'s producer, Marcel Hellman. Fantastic man. At Boulestin's or Claridge's the staff hovered while he tasted a dish. If he frowned, or yelled, saying there were two grains of salt too many, the manager and the maître d' and the headwaiter and the chef appeared, wringing their hands. He tore up Dolores del Rio's contract and sent her back to America; a woman, he said, who ordered a chicken sandwich for lunch in the Savoy Grill had no soul. I said if she ordered *chiles rellenos* or *frijoles refritos* she wouldn't get them, and Marcel said, Ah, but it would be *distinguished*. Even, he said, the hot dog has character. My impression was that concerning the two ladies of whom we'd been speaking Lady Furness was *très distinguée;* could the Simpson of the liaison be a *faux pas?*

Young Doug, an Anglophile like his father, was a favorite with Royalty, a friend of the Duke of Kent, he knew everybody. Through him I met Captain Cinningham-Reed *and* a great-grandson of Queen Victoria whom even at this late date I don't feel I have the right to quote. We were, I had said to him, so *curious* about Mrs. Simpson, an American woman, about her position in England. No facts came out of this, only opinions, at this height they were more oblique yet more serious. They also took Death conventionally. They were a little surprised that he had been so attentive while still in mourning for his father. Not—*quite,* was it? No one seemed impressed or breathless or apprehensive about *this Mrs. Simpson* who did not suggest a time bomb ticking under the Throne. At this upper stratum it was more as though the King had been caught eating with his knife.

Her claim to beauty, I was told, lay in her coloring. The photographs I got hold of were black and white. Striking, a little too posed, they told me nothing I wanted to know.

In person, I saw her first at the theater. The audience did not recognize her at that time.

"I was not attracted by her style of hairdressing," Lord Beaverbrook said when at last he *had* to look at her. A letter of mine sent home says, "I don't think the madonna style of hair-do is becoming to her. As I saw her she seemed to me a more sophisticated type, *very* clothes-conscious, however I don't suppose she cares what anyone else thinks of it as long as His Majesty finds it entrancing and more and more it appears that he does."

I had not belonged to the great Alexander Woollcott *cult* existing in New York and the rest of America in the Thirties. But when I found he had dined at Bryanston Court as a guest of the Simpsons—Mr. Simpson was still in residence—and the King had been there, I knew I must talk to him. On radio as a commentator, in newspapers and magazines as dramatic critic, columnist, in books as an essayist, he had a penetrating judgment expressed with a remarkable flair for the single sentence and the pointed phrase. *Shouts and Murmurs,* as a dazzling feature of *The New Yorker,* had pulled no punches and gained distinction. I had to know what he had seen and felt when his flashlight fell upon the King and Mrs. Simpson. *Go and ask*—so I did. The wit of Wit's End, as Dorothy Parker called him, agreed that Mrs. Simpson had wit. "Of a purely topical variety," Aleck said, "it will not travel. She was remarkable with the King. She was gay and he was in high spirits and rare form the entire evening. He talked mostly to her but from time to time they included the rest of us. She did not deliver one *bon mot* that I can repeat to you yet I enjoyed her society." As Mr. Woollcott's gallery of feminine friends included Beatrice Kaufman, Edna Ferber, Neysa McMein, Marcia Davenport, Dorothy Parker, Lois Long, and Margaret Case his standard of witty women was impossibly high.

He stared at me and suddenly snapped, "Do you expect me to do all your work for you? Take the trouble to go and see her yourself, you ought to be able to get in."

Here was a point that I found embarrassing and unmanageable. Nor could I confide it to Mr. Woollcott, who might be venomous indeed about the ethics of a Hearst reporter. Yet mine were extremely inconvenient just then. Several people had offered to arrange a purely social meeting for me with Mrs. Simpson. I could not do this without telling her that I had come to England to do a life story of The Real Mrs. Simpson, if conditions warranted it as I now felt they might. Mr. Christiansen had told me he was sure there was a Policy of Silence, probably originating in the Foreign Office, and that if I did tell the truth to Mrs. Simpson I would be refused a meeting. The fact that she was never interviewed during the entire time of her life in London seems to confirm this. Later, the King spoke emphatically of his desire to shield her from "publicity." In France, afterwards, she met an old friend who was a journalist, but actually until I went to Nassau at long last and they both talked to me fully and freely, nobody had ever had an interview with her.

My ethics certainly stood between my meeting her under the false colors as a friend of her friends and then quoting her.

For I did in time find my way into her social circle and could have set this up. I had crossed on the *Berengaria* with Tanis Guinness Montagu, a social beauty who was said to have fled England to escape the too persistent courtship of the sixth Earl of Carnarvon, son of the discoverer of King Tut's tomb, the opening of which had let loose a historic jinx. She and Douglas Fairbanks and John Monk Saunders and I enjoyed the voyage more or less together. In London, Tanis gave a party for me where I met such social lights and leaders as Lady Cunard, Lady Colefax, Diana Cooper, and Margot Asquith, one of whom said to our hostess, "Dear Tanis, your friend Mrs. Sinjon will have a success in London, she is quite as rude as we are." My rudeness consisted in quoting Captain Rickenbacker to Tanis' brother Loel Guinness to set him straight on some facts about night flying in America. As Mr. Guinness was Under Secretary for Air, I thought he should have accurate information. I then tried to become invisible and anonymous, for it was plain that this was the company where Mrs. Simpson was known. They were people who should have been at ease everywhere with everybody and yet they seemed to me wary and watchful. On tenterhooks when the subject came up, as it did. I longed for one big, rootin' tootin' *It's quite plain to see why he's so mad about her,* or *This is really a grande passion* instead of reservations and, I supposed, some envy.

As a result of this Tanis felt free to take me to Lady Colefax's and there I did meet Mrs. Simpson. Terribly thin, the perfect figure for clothes, she wore an effective black-and-white print, she had the most beautiful blue eyes I ever saw—perhaps that was all she needed. I was surprised to see that her hands and her feet were large. I listened to her—amusing—gay—her slight English accent was beginning to lie as a veneer over the speech of her native South. I felt that I was trying all the time to see through a mask, though whether that was because of her position at finding herself the center of this spotlight, the waves of curiosity vibrating around her, I couldn't say.

Brilliant, elegant, popular, tops at his job Joseph Kingsbury-Smith was then head of the Hearst Services in London. I had not been told by Mr. Hearst to report to him, this was unusual, therefore I was wary and so was Joe Smith. If trouble came, I'd be as unofficial to the service as a secret agent, in no wise to endanger Joe's news position with the King, the Court, and Parliament. Joe, who knew a lot, passed some of it to me offhand, having no idea why I was there. But he did say that nothing about Mrs. Simpson would ever be published. What could they say? That His Majesty was infatuated with an American woman? They don't, he said, publish things like that about His Majesty. Moreover, Mr. Kingsbury-Smith reminded me, His Majesty could get goddam *regal* in a hurry. You'd be shooting craps with him all hail-fellow-well-met and if you put a syllable wrong you'd find that cold blue eye upon you and hear yourself calling him *Sir*. It was well to recall that he was an *obstinate* man.

And that was the first time I heard a word that was to recur over and over about Edward VIII of England.

"If the King takes his time," Joe said, "in England, you have to learn to let people get used to things."

"Would it be better if Mrs. Simpson got a divorce?" I said, having after all Mr. Hearst's fish to fry.

"A *divorce?*" Joe Kingsbury-Smith's voice skipped up an octave.

"What would she do that for? What put that into your head? Better she has a *husband*. If she filed for divorce the papers would probably have to print it. Not that they'd connect it with the King. Very thoughtless thing, for her ever to have been in the Court Circular."

"Males," I said coldly, "like to show off. Nobody else could have got her in the Court Circular."

On every story you are entitled to a piece of sheer luck.

Mine came one day at the Elstree Studio. A girl playing a bit part had known Ernest Simpson, *the husband,* soon after he had come to head the London branch of his firm's jewelry business. Glad to gossip about such exalted personages, she told me that *he* had to get his first wife Dorothea in New York to give him a divorce so he could make Mrs. Spencer she was then into Mrs. Simpson, but *she*—Mrs. Spencer as she was then— already had *her* divorce, she got it in America in a place called Virginia. From her *first* husband. He was in the Navy, that was how she'd been quite a traveler as a young Navy wife, been to China and all.

This, with a sinking heart, I cabled to Mr. Hearst.

No one I'd known in America had noticed the divorce in Warrenton, Virginia, of a Wallis W. Spencer from Winfield Spencer. Why should they?

Certainly no one in England had known of it. Otherwise Mrs. Simpson, a divorced woman, could not have been presented to King George and Queen Mary at the Court of St. James, on an occasion when His Royal Highness the Prince of Wales was in attendance on Their Majesties.

It all seemed strangely—*impossible.*

Nevertheless, Lieutenant Spencer had *Entered,* like the ghost of Hamlet's father, divorced but not to be forgotten, he was to be part of the drama from this time hence forward.

Over our elevenses, that strong black tea in thick white cups passed by copy boys around the city room, I heard one day that Ramsay MacDonald, former Labor prime minister now in charge of plans for the awaited and anticipated Coronation of Edward VIII, King of Great Britain and Ireland and the Dominions beyond the Seas, Emperor of India and Defender of the Faith, was slowly going mad because he couldn't get His Majesty to set a *date.* Almost wistfully, Mr. MacDonald had told a *Daily Express* reporter who asked him about it that the King kept putting it off. And there were many many things to attend to surrounding this regal pageant. The reporter added to me that MacDonald then reminded him that it wasn't possible to *push* His Majesty, both because one *didn't,* and also as everybody knew he was an *obstinate* man and if you pushed him he dug in his heels.

Here my mind spun off into pure fantasy. Among the *many things* to be

arranged, the idea of Ramsay MacDonald being told to start having souvenirs made with pictures of Queen Wallis of Baltimore, U.S.A., on the
cups and ashtrays, and her consort crest on the silver spoons sent me
into spasms. True, her fellow countrymen and women would spend billions of dollars for these mementos of an American Queen, and the British
had a sharp eye for Trade. I just wanted a glimpse of Ramsay Mac-
Donald's face.

Then it occurred to me that it might be *possible,* in Mr. Hearst's focus,
that the King was putting off the Coronation because he wanted another
chair placed beside the Throne of Edward the Confessor when that sacred
ceremony took place in Westminster Abbey. In spite of the *hoots* of
crowds, *Henry* VIII had placed a crown making her Queen Anne on Mistress Boleyn's head before he cut it off. Far from hoots in the spring of the
first year of his reign *Edward's* popularity was at its peak. Ramsay Mac-
Donald had said that the growing interest in, excitement about, hurry-up
demand for the delayed Coronation had mounted from the day His Majesty opened Parliament. Could it be that the King's *timing* was for such
a *coup de grâce?*

Plainly I was trying to get some support for Mr. Hearst's project.

Not only was the King ingratiating himself with the people but as near
as I could make out, he was also gathering about him certain leaders who
would be his men in any crisis. I was too ignorant to know how fatal *this*
could be.

About then I went down to Devonshire to visit my former son-in-law,
Paul Gallico. He and Elaine had arranged an amicable, even tearful,
divorce. The age difference, Elaine's desire for *children,* Paul's for a *wife*
who wouldn't think of anything but her *husband* had brought this about.
The three of us had decided no cause had been given for breaking up the
friendship Gallico and I had known for years. *Au contraire.* I found him
settled on a cliff above the Channel where he still was when a few years
later Dunkirk took place. He'd been in our navy in World War I; his part
by small boat in the rescue of British troops inspired him to write *The
Snow Goose,* one of the classic stories of our time.

Through him I met Lady Astor, a fan and friend of his. At once I
thought of her as another American woman in England, one whose influence might bolster Wallis Simpson's cause. As Viscountess Astor she was
hostess at their country seat to the famed and powerful Cliveden Set. She
had succeeded her husband in the House of Commons when he went to
the Lords.

I had another think coming.

Her vote was a loud NAY.

"Can't you make her see she ought to be loyal to her own countrywoman?" I said to Gallico. We were in his garden on the very edge of a White Cliff, on an April afternoon. "How can it do any harm to have an American woman as the King's best friend? In case anything happens, this might be a helpful alliance for England—for us—for the world." I didn't speak the word marriage for fear he'd go and fall on his fencing foil.

Looking across the Channel where soon planes would be flying death and destruction, Gallico said, "Her Ladyship thinks it's bad for Anglo-American relations for people like the Simpsons to be invited to Buckingham Palace. You must remember Nancy Astor was a Langhorne of Virginia." "Well," I said, "I am told that Mrs. Simpson was a Warfield of Maryland so Her Ladyship ought to give her aid and comfort in a foreign land." "Who are the Warfields of Maryland?" said Gallico. "That," I said, "I don't know. But Alexander Woollcott says Mrs. Simpson is very good for the King." "That old horror," said the former sports editor of the New York *Daily News,* and I said, "Nevertheless he says she keeps the King happy and she doesn't even *smoke.* In America, we have heard that His Royal Highness the Prince of Wales used from time to time to overimbibe at the Ritz Bar in Paris. I know Lady Astor is against *drink.* I once wrote a column when she made a hell of a scene with a sailor over the Navy's tot of grog. Now I get it from Tanis' friends that Mrs. Simpson confines alcohol to vintage wines understood only by connoisseurs." "I don't think," El Gallico said gently, "Lady Astor approves of the present relationship." "All right," I said, "perhaps Lady Astor would be satisfied by a morganatic marriage." "A morganatic marriage!" said Gallico. "I beg you will not say any such thing to Lady Astor." "They *used* to have them," I said. "Where does Lady Astor get off to be so fussy? She was divorced herself before she made this big international marriage." "But since then," Gallico said, "she has become fanatically religious. She disapproves more and more of anything that suggests sin."

There didn't seem any more to say after that.

Sitting there in silence as the soft English twilight came and the thousands of sea gulls below us grew quiet, I realized that I was missing Elaine. I wished that her marriage to Gallico had worked, then she would be here now, safely the mistress of this English country house. Paul had wept on my shoulder about how much *he* missed her, needed her in his work, she had always helped him with her warm editorial gift and critical judgment, as she helps me now. In that spring garden in England I felt a familiar pattern beginning to unfold, I didn't like it. Generation to generation, I wondered if I'd been to blame for not teaching her to be a better wife. Paul didn't want more children then, he had sons by his first marriage. Perhaps if I'd persuaded Elaine to put a *husband* first, she might have become a full and happy partner, finding her work in sharing and protecting his writing talent. But—with three thousand miles between me and my children—what could life be like to any woman without them? My mind kept racing across the water to them, worrying, missing them, imagining what they were doing at that very moment. When on this assignment my mind shouldn't have been anywhere but on my work, gathering material for a Life of Mrs. Simpson that would bring her country's support to her in the remote case that the King wanted to make her his queen.

So I wasn't sure whether my sense of storm blowing up was on the ocean between me and *home*. Or across the Channel where Udet said Hitler's invisible air force awaited *Der Tag*. (I hadn't realized until that moment that you could *see* across the silver sea that served England as a moat to the shores of France.) Or in the crisis my every instinct and intuition told me was approaching the King and Mrs. Simpson. Or within myself where I was trying to fly amid my own growing uncertainties and doubts without a compass.

3

What were the alternatives?

There had been no morganatic marriage since George IV had attempted something of the kind with Mrs. Fitzherbert. Nor had a favorite been elevated to be Duchess of Cleveland or Portsmouth since the time of that merry monarch, the second Charles.

At an after-theater supper at Quaglino's, where Marcel Hellman persuaded me that the only proper thing to order at midnight was rare roast beef, that amazing man explained to me many things that I needed to know. Not having been born in England, Marcel could not take things for granted, so he had carefully studied and made himself familiar with not only the written laws of Old England but the unwritten ones called tradition and custom, often the more powerful and important.

The Dominions, he said, were already beginning to express themselves loudly in favor of an immediate marriage for this first bachelor king in centuries. They would have a most important voice and influence upon what lady should be selected for the high office of their queen, they must be taken into serious consideration.

Technically, Marcel said, we must remember that the King could marry anyone he wanted to marry, though the law gave him the right to deny what he judged to be an improper marriage for any member of the Royal Family. (This came up many years later when Queen Elizabeth II as Defender of the Faith refused to allow her sister to marry Peter Townsend, who was a divorced man. The Princess would have had to renounce her royal position to wed the man she loved.) All this had, of course, to do with the succession to the Throne.

"If," I said, doing my best with that rare roast beef of Old England, "we suppose—just for the moment as a supposition—that Mrs. Simpson got a divorce and the King decided he wanted to marry her, and his Cabinet and Commons and Commonwealth were all against it, yet he can marry anyone he pleases?"

"Yes," Marcel said, "he *can*. But there would be a number of other things involved."

Marcel then did make me understand one thing. The Sovereign cannot —must not—bring the Crown into Controversy.

That was why the forming around Edward VIII of an active group of liberal leaders wasn't a good thing. Someday someone would inevitably call them the King's Party and that would upset the applecart. In a constitutional monarchy, the King must at all costs refuse to allow the Crown to be the center of conflicting factions, or a point of contention about anything whatsoever. Even Queen Victoria hadn't been able to get away with anything like that; part of the two periods of her grave unpopularity during her long reign had been first when, soon after her accession, she entered into a controversy about Tory or Whig ladies-in-waiting and second when she disputed on foreign policy with Lord Palmerston. Unlike the Presidency, which is elected by a party, the Crown is a divine right and its business is to remain above party, to maintain always neutrality in party battles and its highest right is to dissolve the House of Commons if the Crown feels that it is no longer representative of the voters who put its members in office.

All this the present King understood full well, for his father, Marcel said, would go down in history as possibly the most knowledgeable constitutional monarch who ever lived.

This much I followed.

But one word he spoke I am sure I didn't take in at all.

He *can* marry anyone, Marcel said.

But he *may not,* as lesser persons do, make his own choice, for upon it depends the future and the welfare of the State.

Suppose, I said, he insisted anyhow?

No matter what the rules about marriage, he would, Marcel said, have brought the Crown into Controversy and he would have to go.

Go? Go where?

That this meant he could—would—be thrown out of the ball game did not get through to me.

"Perhaps," Marcel said, "His Majesty has not thought this through."

Nor could I.

"Love is like a dizziness,
It willna let a poor body
Gang about his bizziness,"

concluded Marcel with a grin.

The drums were beating, they carried the news of the King and Mrs. Simpson more swiftly to the slums, the counties, the Dominions, the Houses, the upper middle and lower classes than newsprint or radio tubes could have done. But I *know* that not even the words *marriage* or *abdication* sounded in the constant roll and ruffles of those tom-toms.

Why, they were just getting used to rejoicing over him as KING.

I saw that. Even if I had let GO, with its dread synonym, enter either my waking or sleeping consciousness, it would have vanished when I saw Edward VIII in his city of London and heard the love-chant with which his people greeted him.

I couldn't see him when he entered the Abbey on that morning of Holy Thursday in Easter Week to bestow the Royal Maundy in person upon some of the poorest of his subjects. As a custom this almsgiving by the King's own hand to real sufferers from among London's poor had lapsed for centuries but George V had revived it as a symbol of Christian charity and humility in memory of that occasion upon which Christ washed the feet of his disciples. Now to the joy of the vast crowds that surrounded this cathedral his son was following in those footsteps.

Standing on the curb, the young man from NBC who had kindly brought me remarked that it was rather as though he renewed his Prince of Wales motto—*I Serve*. Inside, he told me, the Precentor would open this almsgiving with the words *A new commandment I give unto you, that ye love one another*. Outside I was being shoved. I clutched a stranger to keep from falling. The sun was trying to battle through but the day was still chill when there fell a silence. Out of the west door walked a very young man in a dark overcoat. In one hand he carried his hat and in the other a small nosegay, with herbs to keep off the plague and flowers to fight the stench of London's streets, as Charles II had done. Suddenly the clouds yielded and he walked out into the sunshine and never did I see anything so golden as the close cap of his hair. I had heard many crowds give many cheers for many reasons, but not such a sound of possessive love as came from the subjects of the King of England. For this young man was the King of England.

On another occasion I was taken by a young friend named Fisher, a much-decorated officer in the Royal Navy, to see the King review, as Colonel-in-Chief, the Royal Horse Guards called the Blues. It would be open to the public but Dick Fisher also had tickets to something called the Enclosure, into which we were not able to get for the vast throngs that surrounded us. Picturesque as a fine painting, Hyde Park hung in the sunshine as it had century after century, and the Blues were there, the gleaming breastplates, the helmets with waving bright red plumes, and the horses were black gold out of a picture book. On the most spectacular of them all sat a slim young figure in uniform, white-gloved hand lifted to receive the salute and the Blues famous band began to play *God Save the King.* All around me everyone began to sing.

> God save our gracious King,
> Long live our noble King
> God save the King.

I sang it too—only I put in some of my own words—*My country 'tis of thee—Send him victorious happy and glorious—sweet land of liberty—God Save the King*—the tune was the same—they were entwined—the woman beside me and I smiled at each other through our tears—*happy and glorious long to reign over us, Of thee I sing—*

So there he was, God save him in Arthur's seat. Maybe with God's grace—a *gracious* King—he could fill it with more panache and honor than anyone since.

They thought so—the people in Westminster Abbey and Hyde Park.

4

The Savoy in London remains forever a place you must go back to.

Nevertheless, in an elegant suite on the river side I spent one of the most dread nights of my life. One of the most wonderful.

I was to sail the next day so I'd come in early. I knew that when I said good-by to Fred Bates and Mr. Christiansen and young Doug they would ask me if I meant to try to write anything when I got back to America and if so, what. I was beginning to show through my camouflages. What was I going to answer these, my good friends?

When I stood at the big windows looking out at the dark gleam of the Thames, I was overcome by a tide of foreboding. The people who have twigs that bend to indicate water underground are called dowsers. Mrs. Sinjon, as a reporter, sat over a pink gin she would have been better without, still in a silver-blue dinner gown with a long train, and the twig of her nose for news began to gyrate in a dance of death. A story was there, dark, muddy turbulent, perilous. Unquestionably part of this is hindsight but not all. *Not all.* I use these words for the feeling of them was there.

Whatthehell is the matter with you? I said aloud, and began to get ready for bed. Get some sleep, you fool, I said to myself.

By values as I estimated them I should be in a state of euphoric exhilaration over this opportunity, instead I was jumping with jitters. My story,

I was now almost convinced, was that an ordinary average American Cinderella had captured the most romantic and eligible prince in the world. What I should be doing was breaking this up into installments, selecting quotes, anecdotes, scenes, and acts, planning where to go to get the opening chapters for it.

I should be dwelling on how to build this as the Romance of the Century.

The American Girl and the King.

But—the American Beauty was Mrs. Simpson.

And she wasn't a *girl*. Nor a beauty.

With sickening impact I knew that the Romance of Henry VIII and Anne Boleyn hadn't seemed glamorous or dazzling, all the world *hadn't* loved a lover when that royal dizziness swept Catherine of Aragon from her throne and put her lady-in-waiting, Anne, upon it. So heartbreaking had it been that sainted Sir Thomas More had gone to his death rather than *consent* to such a marriage. The Pope had excommunicated Henry and in retaliation Henry had destroyed the churches and the art of much of England. The daughter of *that* Romance of a long-gone Century had been Great Elizabeth, but she had refused marriage to the kings and princes of Europe, denied her desire for children, and when her last lover, my Lord Essex, threatened her throne had beheaded him, crying always to her people, *I am married to England.*

I am as American as you get, my ancestor General Nathanael Greene and his wife Kitty were at Valley Forge with Washington. Being Irish by ancestry, I am English by descent, for the Irish are merely England's professional rebels, the family bad boy, everybody puts up with the Irish, even their traitors, because of a genius for living they have.

Walking the floor, carrying in my hand a pair of blue satin slippers I was too shaken to remember to put down, I felt that it wasn't my lineage that gave me this unexpected passion of pain for *England*. Man does not live by bread alone. Reading books has been the food of my mind, my memory, my soul, my spirit—or whatever you call the inner man who is not sustained by material things—since I could see the letters ABC. Our reading is where we *live* and out of it we make our world; it makes molds mars us. What we hear on radio or see on TV never reaches as high or deep as what we can read and reread; none of it stays as long within us. What I had read all my life, in dawn hours when everyone else was asleep, carrying a book bag wherever I went, a book in hand to every appointment I kept, all my reading was *England*. Shakespeare ran in my veins. Four hundred years before Freud he knew all there was to know about people. No one except Jesus has so influenced the English-speaking world.

Queen Victoria was Empress of India when I began to read. In India was the Jungle where Mowgli came to Mother Wolf's cave, and all those stories I had known by heart before I was ten. From England blew the Wind in the Willows and in England was the hole down which Alice followed the White Rabbit into Wonderland. As I grew up there were first and foremost—and still are—Dickens and Jane Austen, a lady who had such faith in her island's isolation that though she wrote some of the greatest novels of all time in the days of the Napoleonic wars she never mentioned them.

The poetry of my mind's music came from England.

Shelley wrote, "Thou paradise of *exiles, Italy.*" He may have been driven forth, but his skylark flew in an English sky and when he was from it he was in *exile.* Browning, with his adored wife at his side, still cried out, "Oh, to be in England, now that April's there," the heartache of parting never leaves them, and it gets into the reader's heart, too. Keats began his work standing "tiptoe upon a little hill" in Surrey. It was *Chapman's* Homer that filled him with glory, the marbles Elgin brought back to *England* that gave us the *Grecian* urn, and where does the nightingale sing but in England? Rupert Brooke had cried to us, *England's the one land I know where men with splendid hearts may go* and at the last the immortal *If I should die, think only this of me that there's some corner of a foreign field that is forever England. . . .*

Their ghosts walk in an English lane.

We fought our way free of her, as children do when they think they are old enough, big enough to live their own lives—but our initial idea of wit and humor, wisecrack and fun still came from Gilbert and Sullivan and *Punch.* Today the very fact of an English accent on TV convinces us that it's wit and a sense of humor.

This—is London.

This London that lay outside the window of the Savoy that night. In that London I could see Master Willie Hewes walking to the Globe Theater to play Juliet for the first time on any stage. David Charles Dickens Copperfield passing on his way to Dover. Disraeli carrying a spring bouquet to his Fairy Queen, the Widow at Windsor, who owned half of creation, and with it he is about to bring her the Suez Canal as a present—*It is yours, ma'am.* Here Robinson Crusoe tries to make good a bad check, Kitchener is on his way to Khartoum, Sherlock Holmes lives around the corner in Baker Street.

It amazed me to find how much I *cared.*

Whether or not the King believed war was coming to England, from the moment Johnny Saunders had told me what Udet had said, I believed it. His people would need all their faith and the Defender of that Faith was their king.

Long long ago in a prison nearby this room in the Savoy a man named Bunyan carried his faith in Christ and his king so high that, locked in his cell, he wrote the *Pilgrim's Progress*. I was thrilled when John Buchan had his famed Richard Hannay say, *"Pilgrim's Progress* was one of my working tools and I had to get it by heart," at a time when he was working for some branch of the Foreign Office. For when I was quite small I'd had to get it by heart, too, and I could still remember most of it, so I could ask myself the questions Hope had asked Christian—What is the manner, Hope asked, what could be the manner of this Going Back, the manner of this sliding backward, of this danger and despair descending now upon many?

And Christian answers:

1. They draw off their thoughts, all that they may, from the remembrance of God.
2. Then they cast off by degrees private Duties, as Closet Prayer, and the curbing of their lusts, and such.
3. They shun the company of lively and warm Christians.
4. After, they then grow cold to Public Duty and the like, they begin to play with little sins openly and soon become hardened to the big ones.

Would this—could this be the King's Progress?

I told myself not to *judge,* but to try to see ahead on the story I had been sent to get. It was no longer a matter of who's right to me, but of *what's right.* Right for *England.*

Had the King begun in a little way to cast off his duty to be alive first and only to the well-being of his people? I am married to England. Could he cast off the duty of being their *morale?* Was he shunning the company of such warm and lively and doughty Christians as his mother, Queen Mary, and his brother, who was up to now his heir and the little princesses who so adored their Uncle David? As head of his church and Defender of their Faith did he no longer go into the closet and pray to be delivered from little sins, and so these might harden into putting his own life ahead of theirs, or soften it, which would be worse?

All these things hammered at me and in my stomach I was beginning to fear that his conduct was what Peter Arno used to call Unethical and Lousy.

Mrs. Simpson on the other hand had no allegiance to that Crown.

An Unemployed Woman.

That was how I saw her that night.

No job. No children. No home except a place in which to entertain.

Unemployed Women are always dangerous at any level, rich or poor.
The Modern Woman.

Mrs. Simpson was, for all her Southern accent, one version of the
Modern Woman. Only she was the most to be pitied, the most to be
feared as a member of civilization today, for she had no mules at all to
drive. None. In her case it wasn't what she'd done with her freedom, it
was what she hadn't done. Not what she was, what she wasn't. Mother
Meyer had talked about the *vacuum* but she hadn't made it clear to me.
I knew she thought I wasn't yet where I could understand any explanation,
but I knew there was a vacuum and Mrs. Simpson had filled it with frivolity and clothes and jewels and now with a romance that was causing a
good deal of speculation. At any rate, whatever it was Anne Lindbergh
had in the Trial of the Century, that was what Mrs. Simpson didn't have.

Or had she?

If I was at all honest I must admit I didn't know.

I didn't know *her*.

The first story ever published in a national magazine about a Movie
Star I'd done on Greta Garbo. I'd played doubles with her against her
lover, Jack Gilbert, spoken with her beside the swimming pool afterwards,
a few words. When I got the assignment I knew Garbo wouldn't let me interview her—she never let anyone—so the best I could do was to interview
everyone who did know her, and Jack Gilbert could tell me more than
anyone. Out of this I got what added up to as good a piece as possible on
the mysterious Swede.

But she was only a movie star, and in no wise held in her hands any
international destiny or future of humanity or such. And certainly I hadn't
presumed to judge her.

I made myself sit down. I struggled against this niggling dislike of Mrs.
Simpson and all she stood for. Since I hadn't even really met her, this
prejudging is prejudice, I said to myself. I must do as much for Mrs. Simpson as I did for Garbo. I had gathered all I could in London. Now I must
go home and dig in Washington and see her family, whoever they were,
and thus have, by *just* and fair and full investigation, material for an honest
biography.

This was all simple. Routine. My profession.

Why, then, was I in a cold sweat about the King and Mrs. Simpson, as
though in them hastened toward me a doom that was to be England's?

Was it because of Mr. Hearst's prophecy, now put together with what
Marcel Hellman had explained to me?

On many things I have images that are blurred around the edges, seen
through gauze, sometimes a face or figure is highlighted alone in the
center of a dark square. But of that horror-stricken night in London, every
detail is clear.

As though once again I had been taken over by something beyond, out-side, myself.

Christian spoke to me loudly, in my grandfather's eloquent voice.

> Then they cast off by degree private Duties, as Closet
> Prayer . . .

Closet Prayer?

> Thou, when thou prayest, enter into thy closet and when thou
> hast shut the door pray to Thy Father which is in secret and thy
> Father which seeth in secret shall reward thee openly.

Just an old-fashioned way of telling us to seek light in quiet asking. Calling upon us to find a spot where in meditation we could *seek,* a closed-in-silence amid the whirring neon mechanics of our age, so that we might hear the truth, a truth, half a truth, as a reward of faith and obedience. Something to try to reach beyond our pitiful limitations or reason, riot, rags, and riches.

Never *you* mind about the King and *his* Closet, what about your own? Why do you always put first the thing you aren't doing? Now you are in a welter of guilt about your *children,* because you are totally absorbed in your *job,* to the point of getting messages of death and danger. What's England to you or you to England compared with that little plot of ground called Cow Lane? Since you are on a job, do the job! You are NOT putting your children first, you are only feeling guilty because you aren't.

Maybe it was partly the pink gin.

It too often was.

Life had knocked me to my knees again. I went and knelt down in one of the big old-fashioned closets of blessed memory.

I felt the hair lift on my head.

I couldn't pray.

The art of meditation I had never possessed, though I knew it was available to Mother Meyer, but I used to be able to *pray,* to holler for help, whether I believed in it particularly or not. Now even the knack of casual prayer thrown up by so many of us at odd moments of distress or fear or superstition was gone. Neglect anything long enough and it atrophies. It withers. Fail to water or feed it and it won't grow, it wilts. It becomes a lump in your gizzard.

Teach me to pray.

Somebody teach me something, for Christ's sake.

Our Father—

There I stuck. Blocked. Words my grandfather had taught me before I could speak them—I couldn't find them any more. All right, if I can't do this myself that upright judge, that learned judge, that fiery pilgrim Oliver Wendell Holmes has assured me that the first two words of the prayer our Lord gave us are all we really need. *Our Father.* There is a God. He is to be prayed to. He loves me like a Father. If there is and He does He ought to know what to do about *England.*

If they catch you praying for the King of England they'll probably lock you up.

Let the King gang about his bizziness. Oh Lord.

Let me gang about mine.

Let Mrs. Simpson find some bizziness to gang about.

Is all I ask.

Next day Joe Kingsbury-Smith and Marcel Hellman, young Doug, and John Monk Saunders saw me off at Southampton.

What, Joe Smith wanted to know, was I going to tell Mr. Hearst?

"What I always tell him," I said grimly. "The truth. As I see it."

"Do you expect to publish it?" Joe wanted to know.

"We can't be part of this conspiracy of silence, can we?" I said. "We're newspapers."

CHAPTER 34

My meeting with Mr. Hearst on my return from England was not comfortable.

He and Marion were in New York at the Ritz Tower. He owned the building and kept there a palatial apartment with a private elevator. (He always had a private elevator; that's why the Beatles stayed in a hotel he built in New York called the Warwick. At first I was unhappy to have them using his suites but then I knew he'd approve, the Beatles were *news*.)

I'd been invited to come to dinner and report on London and go afterwards to hear *Iolanthe*. Mr. Hearst was a Gilbert and Sullivan fan. As soon as we sat down I told him the unsung Mrs. Simpson was a *must* as a life story. He said, "Very well. Where do you start finding the material?" I said, "Washington, I think," and he said, "Let us move with all possible speed, and plan any length you feel the material justifies."

I didn't answer. The silence was thundery.

When he spoke it wasn't to ask me what *I* thought about Mrs. Simpson. As always, he'd read my mind and my stomach. This had nothing to do with the pink champagne served at dinner, I would have eschewed *that* even if I hadn't resolved never to let him see me take a drink. It was a favorite of Marion's and while Mr. Hearst looked down on it, he made no protest. I think he figured *nobody* could drink enough of it to do any harm.

Firmly, he said, "I must emphasize that you are never to write about Mrs. Simpson except as an American woman who may become Queen of England and one worthy of that high position."

Marion said, "What he wants is a clean-cut All-American girl with a bit of *Gee Whiz* added."

"It's difficult," I said. "She's almost my age."

"If we can place the emphasis on her early life for five or six installments," Mr. Hearst said, "we can create a girlhood impression. I find she comes of good Southern families, Warfields, Montagues. Much of her childhood was passed on a plantation near Front Royal, Virginia. The family home, Wakefield Manor, was built before the Revolutionary War. She made her debut at the Baltimore Cotillion."

I was about to bring up the mother who kept a boardinghouse when Marion said, "Class, huh?" and poured herself another glass of the pink.

"Mare—eee—on!" Mr. Hearst said. "That will make you sick." Then to me, "We can show her wedding to a young midshipman at Annapolis, under crossed swords, the British are partial to the Navy. We may even find a picture—"

"And," said Marion, "leave the impression that he went down with his ship when Dewey captured Manila," and Mr. Hearst smiled at her and said, "Your dates are wrong, but the general idea is what I have in mind."

I had to face him then. I said, "Lieutenant Spencer is alive, her divorce is on the record. As far as I found out over there, no one has ever thought of his *marrying* her. If he attempts that, there will be powerful opposition. The Church of England is against anybody marrying a twice-divorced woman, which she'd have to be, much less the King, who is head of it. The influence of his mother, Queen Mary, is powerful. She has, I'm told, made it clear to her son that she will not again receive Mrs. Simpson. He sneaked her in once before his mother knew anything about her. The women of England always side with Queen Mary."

"You underestimate the hold this man has on the heart of his people," Mr. Hearst said, but the voice of his people as I'd heard it on Maundy Thursday was still echoing within me, and I said, "No I don't, but it's more complicated than we can understand. They will not like an American, who really can't know what *a queen* is—and one too old to bear children—"

"We must get in ahead of that," Mr. Hearst said. "The English are a sentimental people and they are on his side. They will accept this romance if they can and if we show it as a grand romance for him."

"There's going to be a war," I said a little desperately. "I keep feeling we dare not let anything happen to England, to their courage and—and *faith*. It's harder to fight with a broken heart. It could threaten all of us, couldn't it?"

"It could indeed," Mr. Hearst said. "My conclusion is that the best way to prevent any disaster is to give the King what he wants, what he needs. He will not do so well for them if *he* has a broken heart, will he?" He patted Marion's hand, and I thought, He has known what it means to want and need one woman all these years. He said, "If he tries to compromise, by making her a duchess and continuing the liaison, there will still be pressure for him to marry someone else. They want a queen."

"I had dinner with Mrs. Langtry's daughter," I said. "In view of Mrs. Langtry's relationship to King Edward VII, her daughter wouldn't take a narrow view of Mrs. Simpson. Yet, she didn't like it. Nobody who knows about it likes it, Mr. Hearst. I can't tell exactly why, they seem to feel the whole thing is vulgar, second rate—"

"Not up to the Jersey Lily's standard," Marion said.

"If we're not going to miss the curtain, Marion," Mr. Hearst said, "we must go. Adela, if the King can be persuaded not to make any drastic moves and you handle the story of Mrs. Simpson so she is a sympathetic figure, we may win their hearts to this royal romance and present a case for it as an alliance. Some of His Majesty's ministers must know a war cannot be avoided. His Cabinet—the Prime Minister—might not be inclined to oppose a closer understanding between Great Britain and the United States, if we show that Mrs. Simpson's country is behind her. Another point in our favor, the King's brother and heir, the Duke of York, is married to a commoner and the people are prepared to receive her as Queen."

"She's Scotch," I said. "She had never been married before; she was the Lady Elizabeth Bowes-Lyon and that's a family older than Macbeth."

"Let us show," said Mr. Hearst, "that if George Washington had accepted a crown at the end of the Revolutionary War, Mrs. Simpson— whose first name is Bessie—would probably be the Lady Elizabeth Wallis Montague-Baltimore-Warfield. You can create that aristocratic picture."

As he rang for the elevator, he seemed to fill the hall, I thought he had put on some solid weight, anyone meeting him for the first time would think of him as a Grand Old Man. This increased his impressiveness. Just the same, I had to speak.

"A lot of this may have to be fiction," I said.

After a moment, he laughed and said, "Wasn't it Whistler who commented that if we used only facts as they are before us without interpretation the king of artists would be the photographer? You tell me her photographs do not do Mrs. Simpson justice, so let us paint a portrait to perform our miracle."

Iolanthe was never my favorite Gilbert and Sullivan so I said I ought to go to Washington tomorrow so would they mind if I went home now?

As Ernest drove me out the Long Island Parkway I thought, Here I am going home and then I'll be leaving for someplace again.

2

A fire was always laid in my bedroom at Cow Lane, more for light than heat, it was such a comfort that, except in a heat wave, it was lighted. Bill came in wearing a ragged red bathrobe, he was so hard on clothes. Now that he was over six feet and *skinny,* I had to have his clothes made and they seemed to disintegrate on him.

By that time, I had learned that I had to look up to him. That was one of the reasons I was so sure he came back to visit his sister and me the day on Eileen Garrett's terrace. Eileen, a medium of high standing and

my friend, had turned to look toward the door as though she heard footsteps I couldn't hear. When she saw what I didn't see, she suddenly lifted
her eyes by inches, as people had always done with Bill, and said in wonder, "I had no idea he was so tall."

Faithful, it says in *Pilgrim's Progress,* has to die first.

The best of us.

No matter what time I got home he would waken out of a sound sleep
and come in to say, "You all right, Ma?" That was what he said now,
blinking at me from the doorway.

"Not altogether," I said.

After he put a match to the fire, he folded himself into the other chair.
He had big, golden-brown eyes, thick dark hair, and, proportionately
speaking, the enormous hands and feet he'd been born with. He never
quite got time to grow up to them. It wasn't only the flames of the little
applewood logs that brought a glow. Bill had a glow. I think it was his
kindness that grew out of his love of people and all the creatures God
had made. As Ernest E. Adams, Jr., used to say, "I don't know where he
gets them." He said the same thing to me when he came visiting last week.
"If it wasn't stray dogs or wet cats, it was *boys,*" Ernest said. "No matter how big our house was, Billy always bulged the walls."

The Christmas before Bill went overseas he brought twenty-nine RCAF
cadets to our house in Larchmont because they were too far away to
get home. He took it for granted I'd be delighted to see them and I was.
I was also broke. I don't suppose many houses are equipped for twenty-
nine unexpected guests to Christmas dinner. The miracle of Bill's source
of supply held good. A young man who was very very rich but had no
home called up to ask could he come to our house for dinner if he brought
the turkeys. Ernest and I were up all night, but we managed. Canada's air
hero, Air Marshal Billy Bishop, loved to tell me how he once saw my
Bill at the station in Toronto towering over a group of young men in
RCAF uniforms, handing out tickets and money and directions. Then, the
air marshal said, "There he was all alone looking puzzled, so I went and
asked him what I could do for him. He was kind of sheepish, and it
turned out he'd forgotten to leave a ticket for himself." So the air marshal
lent him enough to get home. That was his last leave.

This all comes later, I know, but I cannot tell you how difficult it is
now for me to separate times about Bill. It was all so short.

The night I hadn't gone to *Iolanthe,* he poked the fire and said
kindly, "What's going on, Mama?" and I always had to smile at him
when he said, *Mama,* sometimes he shortened it to *Ma,* but he never used
Mom or Mommy. I told him what Mr. Hearst wanted me to do and that
somehow I felt it was dishonest. I thought the King should be Mr. Stand-

fast. I thought such a marriage might lessen his power and profoundly upset the people of England who had such confidence in him.

"Like Carl Hubbell says, the only thing you can give a pitcher is confidence," Bill said. "If the Swamp Angels come up to a big game like with Bethlehem Steel and they are confused about whether I know what I'm doing or not, they get rattled. If they do not trust me to know what's going on it can give them a hole in their guts."

Ernest came in with a tray on which was a glass of Ovaltine for me and a pot of chocolate with whipped cream, he was determined to put a few pounds on his boy Billy, he said, "Don't you keep the Madame up, Bill, she needs her rest."

"Okay Ernie," Bill said.

I said, "I think the King may be *overconfident*."

"That makes you reckless," Bill said, "like trying to steal home. Mama, what's so wrong with this Mrs. Simpson? Would it do all that harm if she put on her crown crooked?"

"Crowns," I said, "and halos, they have to be kept straight. I wish it was someone else."

"*You* wish that," Bill said, "and some other people, but maybe he wishes it to be Mrs. Simpson. He's no kid. He's been around from what I've read. She must give him confidence or something."

"That can be true," I said. "Do you remember that Puss in Boots you had on the Whittier ranch? It was patent leather and stuffed with cement. I tried to get you to settle for a nice teddy bear before you got your teeth knocked out in your sleep, but you kicked the place apart if I wouldn't let you sleep with that granite pussycat."

"I liked him," Bill said, "I felt safe when he was there."

Just then Dicky came through the door. He was always afraid he'd miss something. He was a young demon whose roars could shake the house, but under his arm he carried a doll called Softy. Restuffed eight times, new covering four times—how can you tell, I said to myself, hard or soft, what makes a child feel confident in the dark? Dicky climbed up in his brother's lap and we looked at Softy and began to laugh and Dicky joined in. He appropriated Bill's chocolate and said, "I heard you carrying on. Tell me however what are you laughing at?"

Bill punched him gently on the chin and said, "The King of England."

"What's the matter with him?" Dicky said.

"If he gets what he wants perhaps he can live to be as old as King Arthur," I said. "Come to think of it King Arthur's Queen Guinevere wasn't a howling success either."

"However," said Dicky, wiping some whipped cream off his nose, "he had the Round Table."

Distantly I heard the phone ring, Ernest came in and said, "It's Miss Davies." Marion's voice said, "W.R. wants me to tell you he has decided to go to England to see the King." I was *dumfounded*. I said, "Can he do that?" and Marion said, "He can do anything. He says to tell you he will do his best to get us more time." I said, "He must think this is urgent," and she said, "He won't even wait for me. I can tell you, he wants you to create Helen of Troy and Cleopatra out of Wally Simpson. For once even Gilbert and Sullivan couldn't make him forget the news."

After all, I thought as we hung up, who created the face that launched a thousand ships—*Homer*. Who put Cleopatra and her infinite variety on her barge on the Nile—*Shakespeare*.

How else would we have known anything about them?

3

It has to be awe-inspiring when a Power speaks to a Throne.

Secret as it was when they did meet at Fort Belvedere, nothing could stop my imagination following them into some big, book-lined, oak-paneled room and, as did Herodotus the king of history, making up their dialogue on this hot subject.

Plainly, for the first time that anyone ever broached it, the Power of the Press must have asked the King if his intentions were honorable concerning this daughter of America. The answer must have been Yes. I have to know this, for when Mr. Hearst got back his instructions that I write about her as a future Queen of England were more emphatic than ever.

Only by what came of it do I deduce what passed between them, for not even to Marion did Mr. Hearst ever reveal what the Throne said. When I got to know the Throne well enough to ask him a good many questions, I never brought that one up.

An immediate result was that as soon as he set foot again in America, Mr. Hearst took the *it's-no-good-to-me-in-Rockville* pressure off my work on Mrs. Simpson's biography. I could hear the deadline behind me but it wasn't breathing down my neck any more. I felt relieved to find that if I was to put this lady on paper to the best of my journalistic skill I was to be given *time*. This had to come from Mr. Hearst's conviction that the King had accepted his advice on what we would now call Public Relations. That His Majesty would halt any reckless, headlong, headstrong, obstinate course. "You must move as in a chess game to be sure you are in no danger of losing your queen," would be Mr. Hearst's advice.

The thing which Mr. Hearst would not see was that it was only a royal courtesy which made the King seem to agree politely to this change of pace.

I knew—I always knew—that never for one moment at any time did His Majesty have the slightest doubt that he could *get his own way*.

He always had!

It never occurred to him that he might fail.

Here is the key to the puzzle. He never saw any need for this caution, this pussyfooting, this diplomacy and tightrope-walking, in view of what the past had taught him. His dizziness had put him in a mood for dash and devil-may-care derring-do in this bizziness—and by the time the danger was apparent to him, it was too late.

Not having his dizziness—other men could not see or believe what might develop.

I had reached my own decision in my talk with Bill in front of the fire.

I could of course withdraw as I had from the Leopold-Loeb case and the San Francisco Bay bridges. I could say, I am not with you in this, you better get somebody else.

But I rationalized to myself that we might best serve this way.

Truth is sometimes trite, things get trite because they happen so often. Two and two continues to make four even if you do them in New Math. In many men, there is Peter Pan who never grows up. In some cases it is a bad little boy who keeps on shooting people with real guns. Or—Abe Lincoln in the White House gaining courage to fire McClellan by telling everybody he'd been the best broad jumper in the State of Illinois. Teddy Roosevelt got what he wanted and rode up San Juan Hill at the head of his cavalry regiment shouting like the cowboy he'd been as a kid, the Rough Rider became the Trust Buster and got what Teddy wanted for his country. I now tried to believe that if this man whom England looked to with such hope got what he wanted he might turn out to be the man who could deal with the Germans and the Italians and the French. He knew them as no other Englishman had. His charms might be effective to bring about councils that would prevent war.

He'd be at his best with them. Mr. Standfast, when trouble came.

What difference can it make if she does put on her crown a little crooked?

For Cleopatra's own person, it beggared description.

By the time Bill put me on a plane for Washington to find the burnished gold and the lovesick winds and the amorous strokes of the silver oars concerning Wallis Simpson, I had decided it was to be *my best description* of Mrs. Simpson's own person and nothing was going to beggar it. The challenge had begun to sing in my veins. I was as jittery as a tightrope walker in a strange tent, but the assignment was my chance to bat clean-up in the World Series.

How was I to know how deeply all this about forever England in front of the fire that night was to go into the heart of the boy who shared it with me? How could I foresee that when he was a foot taller I'd put *him* on a plane and let him go forth to help England, standing fast alone that long year against the Hun?

4

At the moment of entering the door of Mrs. George Barnett's drawing room in Washington, I revised my judgment of Mrs. Simpson and drew my first breath of optimism concerning this biography of her designed by Mr. Hearst to stir the women of America to want her as somebody else's queen.

All Washington including Cave Dwellers agreed that in any terms, Mrs. George Barnett, widow of the commandant of the Marine Corps, was a Great Lady and it turned out she was a *cousin* of Wallis Simpson's. It was at her plantation in Virginia that little Bessie Wallis had spent so much time in those years when her mother Alice ran what might be referred to as a boardinghouse.

It took a little time, after I had announced my business, to get invited to Mrs. Barnett's house on Massachusetts Avenue. Even more to be asked to Wakefield Manor.

In that intervening time I began to work on meeting and getting to know people who had known Mrs. Simpson. How long this was going to take, whether I'd have to fly to San Diego or Hong Kong or transfer myself to Baltimore, I didn't know. It was strange to be back in Washington. It hadn't changed at all, for me it had changed so that I seemed not to recognize anything about it. Places to me are people. The Roosevelts were still there but now I was working in a totally different time and space. Huey Long was dead, the waves had closed over him. There was no need for me to go into the city room of the *Herald* and since Helgesen seldom came out of it, we never met. Sometimes I regretted those days of lost adventure, once or twice I was tempted just to go in and say hello, I knew it would be like falling on my sword so I never did. But without Helgesen and Huey it had to be another world.

I wanted to commute, but it wasn't possible so I went home weekends, sometimes a late night plane gave me an odd day off in Cow Lane.

Lady Luck was with me to begin with, while I was trying to figure where to settle down and hang my clothes I met Evalyn Walsh McLean at the embassy in an incredible gown of floating green wearing the Star of India on her forehead and I can re-experience my excitement when she said, *Dear child, do make one of my guest rooms your* pied-à-terre, *you won't have to be troubled with luggage and hotels in Washington are mad-houses.* Besides the charming room in the ground-floor guest wing open-ing on the pool and Evalyn's incomparable companionship and knowledge, Friendship was the center of Society in the capital. Except for Mrs. Mc-Lean's prim proper and prudish provisos, so that no one with a breath of scandal ever got one of the coveted invitations to her parties, sooner or later you met everyone who was, might be someday, or ever had been anybody at her block-square estate. It still tickles me that the guards who patrolled the glorious gardens and terraces weren't there to protect the Hope Diamond (now in the Smithsonian) or any other of Mrs. McLean's famous jewels but to see to it that the hundreds of guests at her parties didn't misbehave (her word) in the shrubbery.

There at Friendship I met the young man from the State Department who certainly at one time had been the heart interest of a little-known Mrs. Spencer.

Here I must make clear to my reader that this was a real and somewhat complicated investigation. Few had heard much more than a rumor about the King's Mrs. Simpson and since he had had friends before, they attached little significance to this one. And nobody at all had connected the Royal Favorite in London with a Mrs. Spencer who had been in and about Washington a few years before. None of the information I needed came bubbling up in conversation about Mrs. Spencer in Washington as it had about Mrs. Simpson in London. My research began to uncover a modern divorcee no better but no worse than others I knew, including myself. But I was puzzled then, and still am, by the enormous reluctance to talk about Mrs. Simpson when she had been Mrs. Spencer that I found in almost everyone who had known her. Washington is never reluctant to talk, that's why such rigid Top Secret and Security Priorities are in force. Talk is Washington's chief recreation. Either they had forgotten Wallis Spencer, or what they knew could not be revealed without disloyalty to her, or they just didn't understand her and so didn't know what to say.

Any man who was part of foreign affairs for the State Department must know about the King's Mrs. Simpson. One who'd been a close friend to Mrs. Spencer was doubtless aware that they were one and the same. All this one ever told me was that, at one time, she'd lived with Dorothy McNamee.

I well knew that Mrs. McNamee was considered by art circles to be a fine painter of children's portraits. I had always hoped sometime to have her paint mine. Her husband was a ranking admiral but mostly Dorothy stayed in her unforgettable house-studio and painted unforgettable pic-tures. To find that she had shared this with the Mrs. Simpson I'd heard of in London had to be out of character for one or the other. Dorothy Mc-Namee wore smocks, loved flowers better than jewels, and had an *other* worldliness about her. My sessions with her were deeply rewarding about art, children, and modern painters. They yielded little about her former housemate and that only defensively. I was soon sure that, somewhere between San Diego and Hong Kong, Mrs. McNamee had been sorry for the young Navy wife Wallis had been. Wallis, I gathered, was very attractive.

Bessie Wallis Warfield Spencer had a passing strange fascination for men. Not all men. Not the Jean Harlow universal sex appeal. Not even to a sufficient proportion to make other women regard her on the whole with envy, fear, or revilement. But when a man, be he an admiral in the far Pacific or an ambassador from a South American country or a king, when a man fell in love with her, that was it, Brother. Every emotion, every other factor in his life, work, condition, or rank fell. He was determined to have her at all costs.

One evening at Friendship—it had to be evening, Evalyn McLean seldom got up before five o'clock—in her famed upstairs private sitting room, Evalyn said, "Dear child, it's come to me quite suddenly that this Mrs. Spencer was a family connection of Anne Suydam's. I never met her myself but I—I seem to recall—of course Anne is Lelia Barnett's daughter. Didn't Anne do some poetry for Cissy's paper? If she is a family connection of Lelia's—your Mrs. Simpson—dear child, Lelia was a *Montague,* she married a Gordon, Basil Gordon, he left her a very young widow with a fortune and it was from him of course that she inherited Wakefield Manor. Then she married General Barnett—when he was commandant, so she had Cabinet rank—and she's a cousin of Bessie Merryman—they were rivals in a way of the Langhorne sisters—but the real beauty was the youngest of them—Alice. I think she married young Warfield of Baltimore and, dear child, the Warfields own Seaboard Railroads. I don't quite understand why Mrs. Spencer—I've forgotten—it's so long ago I think there was some *cloud* around Alice. But it makes it an entirely different story for you, doesn't it? Don't forget my husband owned newspapers, too! Why don't we ask Anne Suydam to tea if you like?"

I did like. It did make a different story, beyond anything I had hoped to find. After the tea with Anne I began to have a woman named Mrs. Spencer who was a reality. I remembered the glorious blue eyes I had seen in London—and the white face under the dark madonna hair—and the strange big hands that didn't fit in anywhere. I was, of course, moving backwards but now I felt I would arrive.

Mrs. Barnett had, in her own stately time, invited me to tea. And as I say when I entered that door I revised my judgment. The heirlooms, the family portraits, the treasures of antique family furniture, rugs, silver, wallpaper that could have been in the American wing of the Metropolitan

Museum, all added to a gracious welcome—somehow my impression of the King's Favorite as the daughter of a boardinghouse keeper had to be wrong.

As she poured from a teapot given her by the Dowager Empress of China, Mrs. Barnett's first reaction to my explanation of the situation as I had found it in London was surprise that Bessie Wallis had caught the fancy of the King. Cousin Lelia hadn't expected a king.

As we talked, it was plain that her memories of Bessie Wallis went back—back to childhood, school days, first proms. And I was fired with the certainty that Cousin Lelia would have *pictures*. Of course she would. Girlhood pictures—school pictures—debut and wedding pictures—of this woman no one had ever *seen* who might, as Alistair Cooke had remarked, become the most famous woman in the world.

What would it have been like to sit in Trois-Islets and have a cousin show you baby paintings and little girl miniatures of Rose Tascher de la Pagerie? Would you have believed that this little Creole would grow up to be Napoleon's Empress of the French?

At a moment when she was describing Bessie Wallis' first prom at Princeton I mentioned pictures and Mrs. Barnett agreed she had some, and then a smiling aproned colored woman brought albums and envelopes and even one or two desk drawers. Studying them as illustrations of the background of a queen, especially one of a small girl on water wings in the moss-grown pool at Wakefield Manor I said, "When did you know she was going to be a beauty?"

"Bessie Wallis?" Cousin Lelia said, handing me a group shot of schoolgirls. "Oh she's never been a beauty. Too much jaw, don't you think? And then all the Montague women were noted for their hands and feet. Her mother, Alice, had the most exquisite ankles. I've always thought Bessie Wallis got hers—and her hands—from her father's family. They were in railroads."

Passing me a large cabinet photograph of a bygone period, Cousin Lelia said, "That is her mother. The loveliest girl ever born."

By then, soft-footed servants had pulled curtains against Washington nightfall full of summer rain, candles had been lighted and the silver glowed, in the soft silence Mrs. Barnett swung away from the world's whispers beginning to hiss into a storm around a younger woman of her family. In memory she had gone back completely, to tell me the sad little love story of Mrs. Simpson's father and mother. Oh, from the time she went to dancing school Alice had suitors, soon they were advantageous offers of marriage. At seventeen, she fell in love with eighteen-year-old Wallis Warfield, high-born heir to the Seaboard Railroads. Eligible enough. Yet both families tried to prevent the marriage. Death had a hand on the boy.

With what was almost a sob, Mrs. Barnett handed me a picture of a baby, wide-eyed, foot in the air, on a white fur rug. She said, "That is the very picture Alice showed her husband a few hours before he died. They couldn't bring the baby to him—tuberculosis was contagious—so she showed him this, and the boy asked her if they couldn't call his baby girl *Wallis*. He said, 'Then I wouldn't have lived just for nothing.' "

So the baby in the picture became Bessie Wallis and in time Wallis Simpson.

"The Warfields wouldn't give Alice a penny unless she stayed in the Warfield mansion in Baltimore," Mrs. Barnett said, "dark as a tomb and filled with plush draperies and mahogany furniture. They wanted her to keep on wearing widow's weeds. Alice wasn't yet *twenty*. She was like a sunbeam, always dancing. But she didn't have any money and I was away and some young friends persuaded her to rent a house and they'd all share expenses and she could run it as her share. The baby knew just as much about running a house as Alice did. It didn't work. When Alice married again, Bessie Wallis came to live with me at Wakefield Manor."

So that explained the Boardinghouse Keeper's Daughter. For years Bessie Wallis had been like another daughter to Lelia Barnett.

Looking at family photographs, I said, "I do hope I may have them to go with my life story of the real Mrs. Simpson."

Drifting along on this cloud, I was beginning to believe that with this background, with the episodes, color, quotations, anecdotes, reminiscences, and especially with the pictures, I could make this *life* what Mr. Hearst felt was imperative.

Cousin Lelia's voice hit me like an icy shower.

She flatly refused to give me any of the pictures.

At midnight, Mrs. Simpson's Cousin Lelia and I were on a train bound for New York. William Randolph Hearst was waiting for us at the Ritz Tower.

This time, I really saw him at work.

When we arrived at the door of his apartment at 8:00 A.M., he was there. He never had to prove anything but keeping people waiting. He was wearing a tweed coat, a bright tie and his eyes weren't the cold light blue that is so often written about and which I *had* seen, they were warm with interest as he ushered Mrs. Barnett to a chair. The room had been filled with Renaissance treasures. These were his best setting always, and he was urging orange juice and coffee, toast, and Danish pastry upon us—and himself.

Immediately we were deep in Mrs. Barnett's recollections, opinions, and prognostications about *China*. I do not think Chairman Mao Tse-tung's little red book would have surprised Mr. Hearst. As Millicent Hearst had told me he was acutely aware of the Yellow Elephant as early as 1904. On this morning in 1936 of which I write he was enthralled by a woman who had known the legendary Dowager Empress when she ruled all China from her palace. As they talked *I* was acutely aware of Mrs. Barnett as representing a generation before mine, ultrafeminine, gracious, hard-to-break as a rapier blade, deeply cultured, facing danger with such style. Things would somehow be simpler, I thought, if her cousin Bessie Wallis had the half of it.

Of course what Mr. Hearst was doing was what he'd taught me to do. Ethically, you are there as an interviewer, but your purpose is to make the interviewee forget about it. I doubt that Mr. Hearst had had to do any homework on General Barnett after my call the night before. Nevertheless, he was moving with ease about the Boxer Rebellion, which the general had been sent to control. And about the Empress and all her works. His memory was in depths and space and accuracy beyond any I have ever met, even my father's. He could do on the instant the same thing about Sparta or Spinoza or King Solomon's mines.

His glance was my cue to pose the question we'd come to settle.

I said, "Mr. Hearst, Mrs. Barnett is the only one who has all the pictures we need of Mrs. Simpson. She feels she cannot let us have them without certain assurances that only you can give her."

The big big man, with his big big stomach, his Roman emperor head, his majestic air. The tiny frail old lady from Virginia, as exquisite and poised after a night on the train as a lady must be. I thought they were well matched.

"Mrs. Barnett," Mr. Hearst said—I never in my life heard him raise his voice and he did not then, "I feel it would be a good thing for the world if the King of England married this lady who is a member of your family. I am making it my special concern to see that she becomes known to her compatriots. I want her to have our support and good will." He picked up the huge envelope I'd placed on the coffee table, took out the pictures, began going through them, smiling and nodding at one of Wallis in her graduation dress, another in the elegance of her debut in Baltimore. "We want to endear Mrs. Simpson to millions of American women. I want popular sentiment to be stirred, to reach our government, to force them to indicate diplomatically to the power of England that we want this matrimonial alliance."

After the war had started Prime Minister Winston Churchill was to tell the House of Commons, "The British Empire and the United States will have to be somewhat mixed up together in some of their affairs from now on for the mutual and general advantage." In a manner of speaking, this was what Mr. Hearst was saying to Cousin Lelia in 1936.

"Naturally therefore," he told Mrs. Barnett, "nothing Mrs. St. Johns writes nor I publish can contain any indignity to Mrs. Simpson."

"Dear Mr. Hearst!" Mrs. Barnett said. "But I was in the Marine Corps too long not to know what can happen after a story leaves the writer's hands. Captions under pictures, headlines, subheads, what is known as rewrite, all these can cheapen and place wrong emphasis, can they not? For instance, her mother always so disliked to have her called *Wally*. It sounded, she said, like a chorus girl. If I give you this picture of Mrs. Simpson's mother therefore—"

"The camera is kinder to her than to her daughter," Mr. Hearst said.

"Too much jaw—Bessie Wallis," Mrs. Barnett said. "If Alice's first husband had lived—you see Alice was so young, she had been sheltered, she was indiscreet and easily duped. Perhaps it was hard for Wallis to understand her mother. Yes, I can give Mrs. St. Johns early stories of Wallis to make her romantic and endearing. Only I must know that Alice's dear name is beyond anyone's reach. If you could give an order to headline writers—"

"I will do that," Mr. Hearst said. "You must understand, however, I can guarantee nothing. As soon as Mrs. St. Johns gives us a few installments, we will offer this feature to thousands of papers. The purpose I hope to fulfill needs the widest circulation. What papers outside the Hearst Service will do about captions, subheads, headlines—I cannot give you any assurance about that."

Mrs. Barnett got up quickly and took back all the pictures.

My heart sank. I hadn't known how desperately I was counting on them to make my story stand up. Sunshine had now begun to pour into the room where we sat, I resented it, it didn't need to shine so brightly on Mr. Hearst's leaning over backwards to undo all my hard work!

"These pictures are invaluable if we are to present your kinswoman as we wish to do," Mr. Hearst went on. "If we do not have them, Mrs. St. Johns will be obliged to write a different kind of story—"

Here it comes, I thought, and shrank a little. I was now going to hear one of those blasts I'd been told of over the years. See a ruthless power play, a threat. The ammunition was there. It wasn't Mrs. Barnett who had told me why Alice Montague Warfield Raisen had been fired by the country club where she had been housekeeper. Nor about her third marriage. These I had found on my own as any biographer might. Unless Mrs. Barnett put me under ethical obligation to her by co-operation, there was none.

Mr. Hearst was going right on. "—I know, a great deal of press experience in the corps. With those pictures and your help, Mrs. St. Johns can present a definitive life story of a possible queen that will not be challenged. So I do not deny that we want those pictures badly. One thing I wish you to understand. Whether we get them or not, Mrs. St. Johns will write the best, the most just and laudatory story of an American woman named Wallis Warfield Simpson that it is possible for her to write. We'd like to do it with your assistance. Even without it, we intend to protect her at all times."

Cousin Lelia handed the pictures right back to him.

5

With what Howey was later to advertise as "the active cooperation and collaboration of members of Mrs. Simpson's family, by whom Mrs. St. Johns has been given authentic information available to no one else," I worked on, more and more absorbed by this series of just and laudatory articles.

For now the time bomb planted under Edward David's throne was ticktocking for all it was worth.

Tick

He became King Edward VIII in January. As early as February, Jim Thomas, General Secretary of the National Union of Railwaymen, speaking to Harold Nicolson, British statesman and author, paid tribute to his great friend George V, to whom Jim had given long and loyal devotion. Then on a topic beginning to buzz in labor circles, the Labor leader said, "And now that King George is dead, 'ere we 'ave this little obstinate man with 'is Mrs. Simpson. Hit won't do, 'Arold, I tell you straight. I know the people of this country. I *know* them. They 'ate 'aving no family, like, at Court."

Marriage between the King and Mrs. Simpson had not occurred to Jim Thomas. His fear was that the King's growing friendship with 'is Mrs. Simpson might keep him from giving them a "family, like, at Court." This fear was ticking, too, all through the country.

Tock

That summer of his reign came the Mediterranean idyllic interlude aboard the *Nahlin*. Pictures showing the King in a bathing suit flipping about in the water, at dinner on the luxury yacht, in small boats at Cannes, were published, but no name was printed for the lady always beside him, though everyone on the Côte d'Azur knew her as Mrs. Simpson. But in France, Italy, Spain, Germany, Japan, and Russia we knew the eyes of Hitler, Mussolini, Hirohito, Stalin, and Reynaud looked upon the bemused couple with cold calculation. I wondered if already they were speculating about unrest in England, even as to a hole in their guts.

Tick

Again, I was staring at the Court Circular.

Still no word in the public press but here I saw that the lady who hadn't been invited to the British Embassy in Washington was a guest at Balmoral Castle in Scotland. Balmoral was the castle that had meant to his great-grandmother Queen Victoria what Belvedere meant to Edward. Very sacrosanct. When I sat having tea with Cousin Lelia in Washington, Mrs. Simpson was one of a party made up of the King's brothers, the Dukes of York and Kent with their wives, the Duke and Duchess of Marlborough, of Sutherland, of Buccleuch, the Earl and Countess of Rosebery and Mr. and Mrs. Herman Livingston Rogers, American friends of Mrs. Simpson. Plain to my eye this party at Balmoral wasn't a gathering of the intimate personal circle surrounding the King and Mrs. Simpson in London. This was serious.

The hum of talk started by this Circular and the speculations to which it gave rise, along with a burst of gossip relaying that the King himself had driven fifty miles to meet the lady and bring her to the castle, filtered down through the entire population of the Empire.

Ticktock

Now Mrs. Simpson took a final fatal step.

Whether or not she had tried at this point to slow the pace, as I heard from Tanis in London, I am not sure. It is possible, as many thought and as she herself told me later, that at that time she did not know of his intentions to move so swiftly in the matter of marriage.

In October, *Mrs. Ernest Simpson filed suit for divorce.*

And not to put too fine a point on it the fat was in the fire.

She had to go into the witness box herself. From what the papers published, without any mention of His Majesty, from those who covered the story and sent me sidelights, in that Ipswich courtroom she was not the radiant bejeweled, couturier-costumed Favorite of the grand party at Balmoral. She showed the terrific strain under which she was laboring, and, they said, looked white and haggard and unhappy.

When the justice granted the King's friend a decree nisi as Kingbury-Smith had foreseen, reality of a terrible kind broke in on this romance, the whole thing changed, took on a new aspect, had new dialogue.

Romance or no romance, here blame fell strongly on Mrs. Simpson. Many believed, still believe, myself among them, that here Mrs. Simpson might have acted otherwise. Lady Furness, who had agreed to talk to me about her friend Wallis, to help me fill in my backgrounds of the beginnings of this love that was now ticking so loudly, had been discretion and good taste at all times. She believed that perhaps Wallis was the woman His Majesty had been looking for all his life. But when she was told by me of the divorce she made a swift gesture of protest. For the sake of her old friend David, I felt that Lady Furness wished Mrs. Simpson had not taken this action.

The King had seemed to agree politely with his friend Lord Beaverbrook, leader of the British press, who gave him exactly the same advice for care, delay, and circumspection that Mr. Hearst had done, but at that time His Majesty had added an amazing line. He was anxious, he told Beaverbrook, to shield Mrs. Simpson from publicity. This was more than dizziness, it was plain lunacy, coming from a man who had been involved in publicity from the day of his birth. This official court action on Mrs. Simpson's part might remove his last chance to manage the news.

Now I felt that it was getting late—very late.

I wrote in extreme suspense as I prepared my series—I felt as though I was handling not a typewriter but a Yo-Yo.

The fatal words were about to be spoken and I *knew* what he was feeling and planning.

If you look now at the pictures of the King walking in the gardens at Fort Belvedere with the woman he loved it is impossible to miss the relaxed monarch-of-all-he-surveys air, which, remember, he was. This I said as soon as I saw it, this is *imperial*. This is the victorious, the conqueror, swinging along in kilts on the stately terraces, his head high. His Majesty wasn't thinking about abdication. My dowsing rod told me he was thinking about the Coronation with Queen Wallis at his side.

Impossible to believe that he thought his words would be a chanticleer trumpet of triumph—*I am going to marry Mrs. Simpson.*

I began to write as though it was possible, for I knew that he did.

Time was short.

For now the Prime Minister, Stanley Baldwin, found it his unavoidable duty to speak to his king. Unofficially, he had spoken before the divorce—as man to man, even as man of the world to man of the world perhaps—but now he had to tell His Majesty in private but officially that he and the King's Cabinet and the leaders of both houses of Parliament were much disturbed by this increasing public intimacy with Mrs. Simpson, with the new house in Regent Park, with the recklessness of behavior on the *Nahlin* and the nature of the visit to Balmoral. The divorce following so quickly had caused the country to begin to seethe with concern, consternation, curiosity, criticism and soon it might be discontent. They were asking questions. Thus it behooved the King's first minister to do likewise.

The most minute reports came to me as I worked on my story of this woman who was rapidly becoming news, and BIG news, the biggest.

According to the copy I got hourly from INS, the Prime Minister had gone to Belvedere and was still there. The man born to rule and the man elected to rule *England*. I felt sorry for Baldwin, he had been a friend of the Prince of Wales. He must be a friend and adviser to the King, it must be heartbreaking to try to reconcile the roles. He and the King were closeted together for hours—and hours—

What did they say?

Did the Prime Minister ask him what lay between him and Mrs. Simpson, and what were his plans concerning her?

He must have done so.

So began the last act of the tragedy.

For the King said, *I am going to marry Mrs. Simpson.*

Now, with the beat of distant drums, he had said what no one in England had ever believed could come to pass.

And I am prepared to go, and thus he had made it a choice, an issue! GO?

What did that mean exactly? *I am prepared to GO?*

As the words stared up at me from a wire sheet, they set off a chain reaction backwards. I knew that I had not really comprehended the word GO when it was first mentioned to me. Yet I realized that it had been with me ever since, beneath my conscious mind, that was what had caused my constant apprehension, my nagging anxiety for England. I didn't need to summon up Marcel Hellman's quiet voice from a night in London that now seemed so long ago but was actually only six months. *If the Sovereign brings the Crown into controversy he will have to GO.*

GO had not been to me a synonym for *abdication.*

It was now.

I told Howey so when he hovered over my shoulder and Howey snorted and said, "He's King, isn't he? He doesn't have to let them shove him around, does he? He'll stay—"

I could remember so clearly how Marcel had spoken of this king's father as the greatest constitutional monarch. He knew what a king meant to his people. "If I may be regarded as in some true sense the head of this great and widespread family, sharing its life, sustained by its affection, this will be a full reward for the long and sometimes anxious labors of my reign." George V had said that. Also he knew what he could or couldn't do, under the British constitutional and parliamentary system. What powers he had, how he could use them, when to speak, and when to remain silent. Always as the father and representative of his people.

He had taught his son that the duty of the King was to remain above party, above dispute.

Now the Crown itself was in dispute. The dispute of the King's marriage was before Parliament. The Holy of Holies to the British, the Monarchy, was in jeopardy, with meetings between the King and Baldwin, the King and Churchill, the King and his staff, his family, his heirs, the jeopardy spiraled and tightened.

Remembering Marcel, I said to Mr. Hearst, "You know if his ministers divide, if there is formed a King's Party and an Anti-King's Party—that makes it a party fight and he's lost—it has nothing to do with his freedom to marry. He will have to GO."

"He can't have brought it to such a pass," Mr. Hearst said, still warm with hope. "I am sure he will save himself in some way. You did not believe he intended to marry Mrs. Simpson, yet that has come true. Let us not despair. He has the support of his people."

"Not the women," I said.

All kept moving like a film put on the wrong way, the figures came at you in huge close-ups and moved in gyrations, characters you didn't know appeared and disappeared, for a moment you saw clearly then it rolled so fast the scenes began in the middle without preliminary and nobody had explained the plot, so much of the story was unfamiliar to my readers everything had to be so clearly explained when I myself wasn't sure what was happening. Mr. Hearst had kept on believing the King would keep his word to move as in a chess game to save his queen and we were late late late.

A Romance. A Great Romance. The Romance of the Century. The King of England had fallen in love with an American Woman? He would marry her? He wouldn't be allowed to marry her? He might abdicate over a woman named Simpson? Or were they forcing him off the throne because he was too liberal? The people surely wouldn't let that happen, they'd rise up, the King could do what he wanted—the Romance of the Century began to absorb them all. Abdicate? Nonsense!

The King would wave his scepter like a wand and win his will and his way.

I am going to marry Mrs. Simpson and I am prepared to go but you won't let me go, you will never let me go, you will let me marry the woman I love, and make her your queen because I want to.

Even his strongest supporter, Winston Churchill, could not believe the King would force this issue to the point where abdication must be required. He would somehow move off that spot and still have time to accomplish what he wanted.

Men who were there described to me Winston Churchill's plea in the House of Commons. So short a time later he was to stand on that same spot and cry, *I have nothing to offer but blood, toil, tears and sweat.* On that historic day he was stern, controlled, the powerful leader of England under attack.

When he rose to speak long before that for his beloved King he could hardly finish for the sobs that overcame him. Let us keep our King, he cried, wiping away the tears, we must find a way to keep our King. He sat down then, his head in his arms sobbing, and—some of the other members thought and said he made a spectacle of himself.

At no other time in his many years there did Churchill yield to such emotion. *I have not become the King's First Minister,* he was to say with asperity when he served George VI, *to preside over the liquidation of the British Empire.* Could it be that with the infallible divination that had warned them of their "feckless" refusal to face the coming war with Germany he knew that the abdication of its Emperor, Edward VIII, had to be the first step in that liquidation? He believed in the Empire, but could there be an Empire whose Emperor was prepared to *go?*

It is not possible to know how far ahead this Englishman with his ever-prophetic sense about England saw—felt—knew.

But the fact that Winston Churchill was heading the King's cause was a menace to the King—there should not *be* a King's cause!

The King had waved his magic wand. He had spoken the Open-sesame magic formula.

I am going to marry Mrs. Simpson and I am prepared to go.

Mrs. Simpson fled to France ahead of the gathering storm, rocks had been thrown at her car in London, she was now in seclusion with her friends the Rogerses on the Riviera, she spoke with the King by telephone hourly.

Crowds were in the streets reading, at long last, the news of this Romance of the Century. All new to them, it was.

The King moved as the doomed move. Deaf, dumb, and blind.

A moment of strange silence seemed to sweep around the world.

I know it swept into our big INS city room high up above the traffic and the river and the buildings of New York on Forty-fifth Street. They had given me a small office to myself next to the INS cable desk, and now Howey and Seymour Berkson and Joe Connelly and Barry Ferris and everybody were hollering for more and longer copy, day and night.

It had been from the start the most difficult story to sort out that I had ever had to handle. To move smoothly between the lady's past and her present and now, for some time, her future, without confusion. I sweat it out to keep my weaving between Washington and New York and London in a clear picture. Sequence is practically everything always; in this present-day *biography still happening* it was as though I wrote without knowing whether Henry was going to cut Anne Boleyn's head off or keep her forever as queen. To keep any sequence was nerve-racking, backbreaking. To separate the women—Mrs. Spencer of Washington and the woman who now had the world—England—the Parliament in an upheaval of destiny was such a tightrope that I seldom drew a comfortable breath; that time bomb ticking tocking away; the expectation of some explosion moving closer every minute; my typewriter drumming an obbligato make-her-queen-make-her-queen-make-her-queen; four or five installments of my

Real Mrs. Simpson already *out* over King Features Syndicate and INS wires, and papers around the globe publishing them:
Beginning:

THE REAL STORY OF THE KING AND WALLIS

Once upon a time—so all good fairy stories begin—a prince looked down from his place beside the Throne and saw bowing before The King his father and The Queen his mother, a slim dark woman with eyebrows like the wings of a swallow.

So—all good romances did begin—but now this might be a tragedy instead of a love story—or a love story as tragic as Antony and Cleopatra—or Henry and Anne Boleyn—This could be disaster for me, too, you know. A monumental goof was possible in any edition. The pressure on me built higher and higher.
People do not get ulcers from pressure. I never had any.

I was working at the office and sleeping around the corner at the Elysee when I got time to sleep. On that particular afternoon I was going through the copy that was still beside me.

Wallis Warfield Simpson. The woman of destiny, the woman who was to be the one great love of the Prince Charming, of the King of England—the woman for whom today he battles those graybeards of his empire who may demand that he sacrifice either her or his throne. What manner of woman is she?

Well, I thought, that's not deathless prose to be sure but it's safe enough, it's difficult to write well when you have to do it around a pretzel. And then my Bill came in—he came faithfully to say, *You all right, Ma?* and bring me news of what was going on in Cow Lane. He said, "Ernie had to come in to do some kitchen shopping so your car's here and we thought we'd let you hook a ride home for dinner."
A wave of sheer blind homesickness swept me. I got up and marched into Howey's office and said, "I have had it! I am going home to dinner. My damn typewriter does the King and Mrs. Simpson *by itself* without me touching it. I need a breather—" and Howey said, "Now, now, not tonight, Swifty. I've got a very peculiar feeling—" From behind me Bill said, "All right, I can stay in and we can eat next door at the Pen and Pencil, if you'd be closer, Ma. Ernie'd just as soon wait for me." Howey got up and went around to reach up and give Bill a wallop on the back and said, "Good boy, Bill, and you charge the dinner to me. Here—I've got some tickets for the Coward show that just opened—you take your mother, just be sure you leave your seat number at the box office. How about that?"
So—Bill and I went next door and ate prodigiously. I couldn't actually remember when I had *eaten* anything. I forgot to eat. My stomach also

was busy with other things such as *sixteen installments* already finished that could look like washday stew if the *news* changed.

Bill tried to take my mind off the King and 'is Mrs. Simpson, who was now somewhere on the Riviera and what was she doing—saying—thinking —How could you guess? Nobody would ever have expected anything like this, the Las Vegas odds would have been a million to one against. Alice's daughter Bessie Wallis? Bill was talking about *Christmas* and I felt myself turn bright red, I'd never had time to think of it. Bill grinned at me and said, "Don't worry—we've got lots of time—what is this? the tenth or eleventh—we've got two-three weeks—this time maybe we can make Christmas for you—you been Santa Claus for us quite a while—" How he loved Christmas and Easter and the Fourth of July. He always put on a sheet to howl outside the windows to scare his little brother Dicky on Halloween, I expect he misses Dicky more than anybody, but of course there isn't any little brother Dicky any more, he's wiser and taller. We couldn't keep away from the crisis in England that night of December 10 in the Pen and Pencil, it blew off the wires next door like a hot wind and Bill said, "I can sort of understand how the English feel, can't you? There was some scandal about Andrew Jackson when he was president, the *wives* wouldn't speak to Peggy O'Neale and they forced her husband to resign from the Cabinet in spite of all Andy could do. So we can get in a tizzy, too!"

To-Night at Eight-thirty with Noel Coward, who looked a little like His Majesty as to type at least, singing "Has Anybody Seen Our Ships," didn't take my mind off that *obstinate* little man who was commander of the British Navy, that's for sure, so I didn't jump when the usher put his hand on my shoulder and said, "Mrs. St. Johns, your office wants you."

I scrunched up the aisle. In the dark Noel Coward and Gertie Lawrence were singing something so like "Some Day I'll Find You" that I thought it was "Some Day I'll Find You" and always have and it was following me every step of the way and breaking my heart as I said into the phone, "What now?"

Howey's voice came over the phone in an explosion. The abdication of England's throne by England's King indicated to him a lack of both courage and loyalty. And this he expressed in language quite unprintable. He ended up on a shout of: "Come on in!"

Howey was a hard man!

So Bill and I found Ernest and drove like mad back to the paper and all the way I kept hearing Coward's "Some day I'll find you, moonlight behind you"—I am hearing it again now, he had found her and it hadn't done him any good, I am back in that city room that was the all-time madhouse, *names make news,* don't you forget it, the bigger the names the bigger the news, this name was Edward VIII, King of Great Britain and Ireland, Emperor of India, he has *abdicated,* no other English king ever abdicated *voluntarily,* I am back at my typewriter staring in frozen horror at my tomorrow's installment, which is now senseless, I am trying to re-write it, I am like one of those acrobats that go up and up bouncing off the nets higher and higher and then do double twists that ought to break their backs or snap their necks as they come down.

Moreover I am crying so hard that it is like coming down all in a heap, crying so I can't even see the keys.

What's England to you or you to England, you fool, I say to myself, and my typewriter clicks out Some day I'll find you happy and glorious *long to reign* over us *God Save the King* poor lonesome devil out there I gotta feel sorry for—I don't think you wanted to leave your people, either way you had to be lonesome for something don't we all, you had to know you couldn't make her queen, only you never did know, did you?

> What manner of woman is she? Now that she has become the
> center of a battle around the greatest throne on earth. . . .

But—the battle is over! It is lost.

Aye, there's the rub. I am stuck with what has already been published, the glamorous installments about the American Girl who may one day be Queen of England, I can't eat 'em now. I mustn't say Queen of Eng-land any more, forget that. The women of England knew she wasn't an American girl, if she was she could be Queen of England, but the women of England say they won't have a Queen of England with two husbands still living, maybe bellying up to bars right here in London and in Wash-ington telling about how Her Majesty brushes her teeth or what she's like when she wakes up in the morning—a Queen of England with two ex-husbands living?

When they put up another throne beside the one for their new King at the Coronation on it will sit a Commoner, all right, but she will be a Scot and a lady and was a virgin when he married her.

As King he had of course been bound by the constitutional rule that no member of the Royal Family may defend or discuss anything about him-self. So now, as he himself said, at long last he could for the first time speak a few words of explanation and defense to his people, to tell them why he had left them.

WORLD STIRRING DECISION
ALL FOR LOVE OF A WOMAN

By Adela Rogers St Johns

I suppose as long as we live my heart and your heart will carry within them, vibrant to some touch, the farewell of King Ed-ward VIII to his far-flung empire. The flag of England, whipped by the winds from Trafalgar Square to the farthest outpost of the Dominions must have dipped low as that gallant voice broke upon "God bless you all" and then recovered the ring like a trumpet—"God Save the King." Brother to brother—

No more magnificent piece of spellbinding was ever heard and so I began my story the day following the abdication with the above words. With our harrowed hearts, our confused minds, our overdramatized nerve centers, our romantic desire to believe the world well lost for love, none of us faced up to the fact that it was also empty, self-indulgent, irresponsible, and, let's face it, hammy. He sure quit being a king in a hurry! There wasn't any *We shall defend our island, we shall fight on the beaches, we shall never surrender* such as Churchill used later to plug the hole in their guts. King Edward's farewell to all his greatness was the very best butter, but butter it was and in the heat of the passing terrible years it melts away.

We want the King. We want the Queen. We want the Princesses—and the King was *there,* the King of England. "The Princesses will not leave unless I do, and I will not leave unless the King does, and the King will not leave under any circumstances whatever."

In time of war, with bombs falling on London, so would speak the Queen of England and probably Wallis couldn't but have made a mess of it.

Just the same at the moment of abdication the heart of England was broken—and the continuity of the divine right of kings was shattered.

And just the same I had to go on writing the Real Mrs. Simpson for all those papers who'd bought it.

But I felt let down as I had never done before. Through this, the worst emergency of writing and rewriting of my professional career, Mr. Hearst steered me with a few words.

I went into Howey's office and called him after I'd thrown away sixty or seventy attempts at my next day's and day after that and day after that stories. Days following all that radio eloquence.

"I'm sorry we failed," Mr. Hearst said.

"Oh—" I said, "I know he had to, he got too far out. He said the magic words and nothing happened. But—why did he do that? Why did he behave so—recklessly?"

Slowly and carefully Mr. Hearst said, "I have discovered that it is a grave injustice to overestimate a man. To expect more of him than he is able to give."

I can make a man run as fast as he can but no faster.

Would I ever learn that? Probably not.

"I can't help thinking how someday—oh Mr. Hearst, someday, won't he have to regret it?" I said.

Through my tormented mind flitted a character called Adam the First whom Faithful met at the foot of the hill called Difficulty. Adam offered Faithful work. And that work, Adam told Faithful, was many delights and also he, Adam, had Three Daughters, The Lust of the Flesh, The Lust of the Eyes, and The Pride of Life. Faithful could marry all three of them, if he liked. Not everybody could see the words writ on Adam's forehead, made from the dust of the ground, nor know that even as a three-time son-in-law nevertheless Adam would sell Faithful to be a *slave*.

I must fairly have babbled this episode from *Pilgrim's Progress* to Mr. Hearst and I said, "Not everybody can be Faithful and refuse that temptation, can they?"

"Very few," Mr. Hearst said. "My mother was fond of *Pilgrim's Progress*. Few can be Mr. Standfast either, I fear."

"The Real Mrs. Simpson. I'm having trouble with it now. Everything's so changed. He isn't even a king any more."

"I see no difficulty in sustaining the story," Mr. Hearst said. "I agree the series is much less worth while now. However, if you shift to the Real Mrs. Simpson as the woman for love of whom the greatest king on earth gave up his throne I think you will find it quite as dramatic and our readers will be as pleased with it. She is, true, no longer a possible Queen of England. She has, however, become 'the Woman I Love, without whose presence I cannot carry my burden as King.' That is quite a love story and Mrs. Simpson is still its star."

"I suppose it'll sell just as many papers," I said bitterly. "It's certainly news."

"For the time being, yes," Mr. Hearst said. "The Woman I Love is news now and of course she always will be, even as a has-been, and so will he. But over the years the American Queen would have been bigger."

So my third or fourth piece after the abdication said:

They cannot, of course, see each other until her decree nisi becomes final.

As I think of her today upon the Riviera, worn and weary with the strain of the past weeks, I know that her thoughts are with the man she loves, the man who is now in exile for her sake. She has brought him the most difficult choice a man ever had to make and he has said that as "the other party most nearly concerned" she had tried at all times to persuade him to another choice—to stay with his country. Her agony must be increased that she should be for him the cause of this heartbreaking decision, she who so much wished to be only consolation and cheer and laughter to him.

I didn't like it then and I don't like it now. Like the other party most concerned, I wanted him to make the other choice.

That is probably why when the wedding of the ex-king and the American woman he loved took place a few months later I refused point blank to cover it. I told Mr. Hearst I knew exactly what he wanted and that probably as things were he was right. I was too prejudiced to do a good reportorial job. My pieces on Mrs. Simpson had been finished after the abdication in pain, tears, bitterness, and guilt.

"I am the wrong girl to send to France on this sentimental journey," I told Mr. Hearst gloomily.

I think I added that I had written my last word on the Romance of the Century—this proved to be a gigantic miscalculation.

However, he did send Louella Parsons to the wedding. She'd been writing about the movies so long she couldn't tell the difference.

It was four years before I was to write *At Long Last,* their own inside story of the King and the Commoner.

By the time I met the Duke and Duchess of Windsor in the Bahamas, I myself was a different person.

CHAPTER 35

My brother Bogart owned an invention called the Photochart Camera. This takes pictures of the horses at the finish line of a race at big tracks. On my walls are the charts Bo used to explain this device. Same race. Same moment. Yet as the horses come under the wire the pictures can be different. To the judge on the right, the outside horse is ahead. To the one on the left, the inside horse wins. To the Photo Finish Camera on the wire it is a dead heat. The cybernetics of this operation produce truth. Honest opinions, interpretations, mistakes, background, knowledge or lack of it, what you heard saw or read *last,* who told you what, all these produce what you see from *where you sit.* Bo's charts are a help to me philosophically.

By the time I went to Nassau to meet the Duke and Duchess of Windsor face to face, my point of view had been changed.

The Germans had invaded Poland, World War II had begun in Europe, in spite of that vast Luftwaffe about which Udet had warned us the few of the RAF had won the Battle of Britain for the many of England.

My Bill had married his high school sweetheart, a beautiful black-Irish girl, and my first grandchild was born. His father had grown taller and taller but he remained Wee Willie, so his son was Wee Willie's *Winkie* in his cradle. A first grandchild is a moment never equaled and unforgettable. *The world stands out on either side no wider than the heart is wide,* a grandson stretches it into a future, that time-space he will live in, and so you gain a dimension and a responsibility for what kind of world it will be.

Elaine, following a round of *New York,* excessive popularity and theatrical and matrimonial offers, refused a brief job as a story editor, married a white picket fence, a garden with a lily pond, and a house with green shutters near Cow Lane. Having divorced Gallico to have a family, she began by giving me another grandson known to us as Koko.

I married Francis Patrick O'Toole of Cleveland and we moved back to Malibu. Pat was obviously an Irishman, with wit and charm; he played good bridge and better tennis, and as an airline executive had business experience. We wanted to make a go of a modern experiment in companionship, with Pat also trying to run *Adela Rogers St. Johns Inc.* along businesslike lines and with a little less of the fantastic expense of a career most women go through. Jan Boissevain had done this successfully for Edna

St. Vincent Millay. But—Boissevain was a European. He had another seat from which he viewed marriage. Edna Millay was a poetess, withdrawn from the world at her Steepletop home, and there were no children, hers, his, or theirs. There was only the flame of her genius to tend. Pat was an Irish-American in days when it was still a man's part to support his wife; A R St. J Inc was a practicing newspaperwoman and a struggling second-rate fiction writer, with a large family entirely *hers*. At this time there wasn't any output to handle on business lines or otherwise. Once again my hunger for the sea had betrayed me. Slave as I would I couldn't *work* beside it. I did a few newspaper assignments of neither merit nor meaning and no fiction at all.

Also, Pat was a devout Catholic. His mother was one of those irresistible Irishwomen who'd never missed Mass except when she was having a baby and not always then. She could get Sunday dinner for three different tables—adults, teen-agers, and small children—and never let you see what her right hand was doing and I still treasure her recipe for Wash Day Stew. Her devotion to the Blessed Mother had given her a *radiance* of joy. Of course she was unhappy about her son's marriage to a divorced woman, but she showed me nothing but mercy and grace. It wasn't *my* fault, and if she rebuked Pat it was outside my knowledge. I loved her and envied her the radiance, the faith, and the peace amid the tumultuous turmoil of a huge family. Pat had believed he could handle marriage to me and I didn't understand what it meant to him to be deprived of the Sacraments. Neither probably did he. It was a dark night of the soul for him, so we parted with regret and God-Go-with-You. Because of the irregularities of our marriage according to canon law, Pat was able to marry within his church and I have never been more touched than by the lovingkindness of his present wife Betty when a television show took me to Cleveland. It must be that Pat had spoken well of me as a friend, if not a wife.

All this took place in the years leading up to the moment when, on my Progress as a Modern Twentieth-Century Woman, I recognized Mrs. Great-Heart. My conversation-interview with Eleanor Roosevelt at the Third Term Convention, where the First Lady pleaded the President's cause, was a full-scale revelation. Certainly it created the viewpoint for Nassau a short time thereafter when I saw before me Mrs. Worldly-Wise, alias the Duchess of Windsor.

Both were women. As I saw almost with shock, Modern Women. One ten years older, the other approximately five years younger than I was, so we covered the quarter-century span that had produced the New Woman. About then I was falling into the Castle of the Giant known as Despair, I saw his club coming down to smash me like a worm, but the lamp held by Mrs. Great-Heart finally illumined the way out, or I might have been hypnotized once more by Vanity Fair and never have tasted of the Honeycomb at all.

And this brings me to Mr. Hearst's battle against Bankruptcy. If he hadn't fought and won it he couldn't have sent me on those two top soul-searching life-changing assignments because there wouldn't have been any Hearst newspapers to publish the stories if I got them.

2

I once disappointed the press box at the Rose Bowl by not having my last baby *then and there* on the New Year's Day Reigels ran the wrong way. Though imagination boggles at Runyon as a midwife, I'm kind of sorry I didn't. So much of my life took place in press boxes, I'd like to have been the only woman who did. It would have rounded things out. Press boxes, in gardens, stadiums, parks, courtrooms, Congress, conventions, clubhouses, and even such approximations as the Duchess's office at Government House, had for me the irresistible urge that the Theater had for Moss Hart, as he describes it in *Act One.* With respect for that classic, I still think *his* was cardboard carousel and mine was naked truth.

This tale of High Finance, which victory enabled me to go into a press box in Chicago where I got my scoop, "The Voice from the Sewers," and to the Bahamas where At Long Last and for the first time the Windsors told all, has been set forth in many books but never with anything like the full facts or the star New York cast.

At the time, the structure of the Hearst Service trembled, foundations rocked and rolled, over our heads in the city rooms the rank and file could hear footsteps clumping and pussyfooting in the seat of the mighty. In the years of and right after the Wall Street Crash we had seen business and industry crash likewise. Some of our vast army of employees now had to wonder whether they'd soon be without jobs. Yet I must declare the strong emotions were concern and disbelief. We were concerned about the Hearst Service, our papers, and what we believed they meant to Freedom of the Press. The idea of Mr. Hearst as a Bankrupt—*Mr. Hearst?* If J. D. Rockefeller, Sr., had been down to his last dime or Henry Ford to his last cylinder, we wouldn't have been more incredulous. Also we were furious. How dared they?

But actually we knew little. When I came to put this and its offstage impact on my life down for this book, I saw that much of it was new, therefore *news.* I would have to go and get it. Whereupon I was overcome with my ignorance and stupidity in this field. One reason the telling had hitherto been awkward and muddled was because so many witnesses had refused to testify, so many documents been hidden from enemy eyes. I wasn't sure

I'd know what questions to ask on a story of Finance and Business if I reached the right people, nor whether I'd understand if they gave me the answers.

As will appear the only person who knew less about Money than I did was William Randolph Hearst.

He knew less than anybody since King Louis XV.

Also I started on this late self-assignment fearing I might have lost my ability to get news against strong opposition.

It turned out I had advantages denied others who'd tried. Witnesses had been anxious to tell the truth but had gone back into their shells after distortion, misquotation, and misunderstanding. Fortunately, they trusted my training *by* Mr. Hearst as to accuracy and my regard *for* Mr. Hearst as proof that I wouldn't louse it up if they gave it to me.

Thus I, who thought Money and Finance and Business dull, have three unimpeachable, amazing, and entertaining gentlemen with stories never told before, and some secret documents as exciting as a World Series box score.

My witnesses waiting in the on-deck circle are:

Richard E. (for Everything) Berlin, head of all Hearst enterprises then and now.

John R. Haynes, former Assistant Secretary of the Treasury under Roosevelt.

Serge Semenenko, The Boston Banker. You have to believe Semenenko. Nobody, certainly not I, could have invented *him*.

These men are alive as I write, subject to cross-examination, though I don't recommend it. As you will see all three of them, the San Francisco Irish Catholic, the Southern gentleman who rides to hounds, the Russian Immigrant who became a Proper Bostonian, all of them are tough customers.

Begin with:

At past seventy, in 1936 Arthur Brisbane died.

As long as he lived no one could get through to Mr. Hearst on some things any more than Cardinal Wolsey let them get through to Henry VIII. Foolishly, Mr. Hearst had kept secret, as a man smiles blandly after a bad day at Santa Anita or a woman tears up the bills, things he and Brisbane had done. The picture of investments, indebtedness, gambling fliers, and utter chaos was known to nobody, especially Mr. Hearst himself. Only after Brisbane was gone did anybody, even Mr. Berlin, get a good look and that was the beginning of what had to be catastrophe, collapse, and confusion.

The big question—was it too late to save him?

How much of that accumulation and burden of real estate, with no interest and less judgment, he bought to keep Brisbane happy and *writing* what Mr. Hearst considered the most important column in America is hard to tell. He did fantastic things for all of us. Bought ranches for Peter B. Kyne, paid off mortgages for me, invested in inventions and patent fights for Howey, staked Louella twice at least, averted danger for Damon Runyon of which Runyon never knew, financed trips to Egypt for Gene Fowler, who was sure in previous incarnations he'd been a Pharaoh and he *looked* it.

Or did he merrily buy all four corners of Fifty-seventh and Park Avenue at Brisbane's know-it-all recommendation as a wistful gesture of friendship? A man of Mr. Hearst's position, presence, and power finds it difficult to make *friends*. Those lonely people aren't all homeless in the Haight-Ashbury. Brisbane's bustling ego considered itself Mr. Hearst's equal, he behaved as such, and Mr. Hearst accepted this. The bankruptcy threat to his vast holdings of gold mines, real estate, art treasures, and newspapers is too complicated for me. I would make too many mistakes. I did know Roosevelt taxation, intended to level wealth, was making a New Deal all right for millionaire industrialists of whom, though we didn't think of him in those terms, Mr. Hearst was one. This contributed to the earthquake that rocked the Hearst Empire. Also he lived for years in an extravagant and princely style known to few if any other Americans, certainly not to J. D. Rockefeller at Pocantico Hills near Tarrytown on the Hudson. But I can to my witnesses add my own small personal experience and stories Marion Davies told me at the time.

Richard Berlin is, according to those qualified to judge, a businessman of skill and strength. His mild manner and omniscient ease deceive you, the same way Bart Starr's winning ways deceive the defense. One of his first moves when he saw what Brisbane had left behind him was to bring in John R. Haynes to see if this unwieldy mess could be organized. Mr. Haynes had proved himself a magnificent organizer in F.D.R.'s cabinet and Mr. Berlin needed the best.

We heard of Mr. Haynes, in the Hearst Service, most of us never saw him.

As I began I knew I had to talk to him or I would not be able to put down as reality what Mr. Hearst did for all of us in that reorganization. Now, as president of Olin-Mathieson, biggest Chemical Corporation in our chemical organization, Mr. Haynes' stature can best be proved by the fact that he has *his own elevator with an operator* in a tall new building in self-operating New York. This is a status symbol beyond owning your own jet.

Over months Mr. Haynes, victim of some evil misquotes, refused to see me. He would never never talk about Mr. Hearst any more. Until one day Bob Montgomery came to have his tea-and-an-apple lunch in my apartment at the Dorset just after I'd been turned down *again* by Mr. Haynes' polite but firm secretary, and I was fuming with frustration. Bob, who has always traveled in these exclusive circles, picked up the phone and I heard him say, "John, I understand you are giving my dear friend Adela St. Johns a bad time. A hundred times I've heard you say you wished people could know William Randolph Hearst as you knew him, here's your chance through a trustworthy writer who worked for him for forty years and you are acting coy. See Mrs. St. Johns, let her at least explain what she wants."

Mr. Haynes said he'd spare half an hour the next morning at ten and I said to Bob, It hasn't changed. *Contacts* like you are still the answer and Bob said, You know I knew Mr. Hearst very well, too. I'd like to see the truth about him told myself.

The quote I liked best was when Mr. Haynes said, "Most men call a business expert too late and then do all they can to circumvent him. They don't listen, when they do they don't follow the advice. Mr. Berlin asked me to go out to the Ranch with him. Mr. Hearst listened. 'I am not myself a businessman,' he said to me, 'Mr. Berlin controls all Hearst interests at that level. I would like you to help him plan a more businesslike basis for us and then Mr. Berlin can carry it out.' I agreed to this." Mr. Haynes told me, "I did not wish things to be disorganized as they were for this man whose greatness was so plain to me."

As John Haynes lived over those days he soon saw that I was no brighter about organization or *dis*organization than a glowworm, so he sent for and showed me the original *charts* and his face shone with the glory and satisfaction of an artist beholding his creation. A kindergarten child could understand the meticulous picture. The old chart, ragged and confused with thirty-six companies (every time he had a new *idea* Mr. Hearst started a new company), then his new chart with the elimination of waste, overlapping expense when nine outfits were doing the same job. I couldn't take it all in but it fascinated me, I could hardly believe it when Mr. Haynes let me take them home to study and to reproduce to explain his story. "The point is," Mr. Haynes said firmly, "when we showed these very charts to Mr. Hearst he studied them and then agreed to them at once."

Three hours had gone by while we talked together and then he said, "The one man you must talk to, of course, is Mr. Semenenko. I have always thought Serge understood Mr. Hearst better than anyone I ever met. You have in Mr. Berlin the businessman, I was the organizer, but it was Mr. Semenenko who put up the money to make it all possible."

I said, "I understand he won't talk of Mr. Hearst with anyone."

This was a God-Bless-Alexander-Graham-Bell chain, for Mr. Haynes picked up a phone and I heard him repeating Bob Montgomery's words— "I want you to see Mrs. St. Johns," he said, and then to me, "Friday or Monday?" and I said, "Oh Friday, he might get run over on the week-end." I hadn't met Mr. Semenenko so I didn't realize no one would *dare*.

On Friday at five I went to the suite in a Fifth Avenue hotel where Mr. Semenenko has pleasant but quite unpretentious quarters. Certain financial powers have been pictured as working behind a nameless door on the top floor of the Empire State Building in one room—that's not Serge Semenenko. On the other hand relatively speaking his simplicity and lack of show-off are unusual. The room in which I waited—*for not more than five minutes*—was obviously the dining room. Then the only secretary led me into a small, impersonal sitting room where Mr. Semenenko received me courteously but without enthusiasm and, when I said I didn't drink, ordered tea and macaroons for the both of us.

His age? Younger looking than he could possibly be considering how far back I knew him to be saving studios, helping to make movies, rescuing motion picture stars, companies, ventures. His face to me was, in this order, gentle, friendly, and *utterly* disciplined.

I told him that both Dick Berlin and John Haynes had given me to understand he was really the man who saved Mr. Hearst and his newspaper empire.

"No no," said Mr. Semenenko, putting much more sugar in his tea. "Only one man saved Mr. Hearst."

He paused and gave it drama. "Mr. Hearst."

This pleased him, he repeated it vigorously. "No one can save anyone from anything. One can sometimes provide an opportunity for a man to save himself. *If* he has the guts to do it. You can lead a man to money, as it were, but you cannot give him the strength of character to do the other things that make it triumph or disaster. This character he has himself. That is why I could lend Mr. Hearst any amount of money he needed."

"Exactly what do you lend money on, Mr. Semenenko?" I asked. Then he gave me his answer. *"Character,"* he said, *"is the only thing on which anyone can safely lend money."* Further, he said, "All other things are subject to change. Real estate values shift for unforeseen reasons. New inventions make an industry obsolete. Medical discoveries alter the whole pattern of existence. Fashions change violently, fads take over, skills become outmoded. Only character withstands change, resists attack, and rises from defeat. As it is the only foundation for any lasting happiness, so it is the only security for a loan.

"I have never known so strong and fine a character as William Randolph Hearst.

"His word was good, his promise inviolate, what he said he would do he did."

At this I spilled my tea. A good thing I didn't have to speak.

It meant so much to me. Men of such stature, neither his rivals nor his opponents nor his dependents. Only love and loyalty had kept Berlin at his post in the days leading up to the almost inevitable shipwreck, his offers to go elsewhere had been frequent and tempting. Here, too, was Haynes speaking from the chair of power in a vast corporate structure. Now the man whose very synonym was *banker*—1967—and you know what bankers have to be to stay up there.

After listening often enough to crass ignorance and self-serving wisecracks and sheer venomous jealousy, to hear them all speak with such affection and admiration about Mr. Hearst filled me with joy.

Mr. Semenenko went on, "The causes of the gigantic financial catastrophe about to engulf Mr. Hearst when I was called upon were complicated and long-standing.

"Let us face the simple cold fact as I faced it then.

"Mr. Hearst knew absolutely nothing about money. Cared even less. Had never *thought* about money, as Berlin and Haynes and I understood it, for five minutes in his entire life.

"Always it had been there, as much part of his life as breathing. The adjustment to the New Deal changed every life in the United States. This effort to level off wealth he had not faced and more than that he had an accumulation of mismanagement, some of it bordering on treachery. He continued to live at a rate and in a fashion no other private citizen in the United States had ever attempted. I found it had never occurred to him to ask whether he could *afford* either his generosities, his art treasures, his investments to satisfy others—if he wanted to use the money he used it. Where he got it from his innumerable enterprises was his own business."

Much of all this wasn't good business, any more than the extravagant sums he spent on Marion Davies' pictures—which she would have been one hundred per cent better off if he hadn't—were good business, but not even L. B. Mayer had the courage to tell him that.

"I told Mr. Hearst—" The gentle, A-flat New England voice was saying those words to me in the small sitting room of the Hotel Pierre in New York City on a date in the Sixties—by the magic formula that Mr. Semenenko was transported back himself to the Hearst Castle in San Simeon under a ceiling that had cost three million dollars and had belonged to Cardinal Richelieu, he took me with him and as he told it I saw and heard it.

Those two men facing each other.

The tall form of Mr. Hearst wearing flannel trousers and a leather jacket as big as a tent. Silver hair in a crest. The listening expression I had seen most often on the cragged face. Big man, used to command.

Serge Semenenko, Boston-tailored, not much taller than I am actually. It didn't matter that Mr. Hearst would make two of him, any more than it mattered when I saw Eddie Arcaro talking to a 240-pound tackle.

The New England voice took up the story.

"Mr. Hearst," I said to him, "it is simple. You can save your real estate, bound to be worth billions in time.

"Or you can save your newspapers.

"Not both."

By the way he himself paused now, it was plain he had expected, was accustomed to a moment of truth in the Valley of Decision. He didn't get it.

"He said," Mr. Semenenko told me, with a smile, with his eyes dancing, "he said, 'That is not an open question, Mr. Semenenko. We must save my papers.'

"I told him that I accepted that, the real estate was heavily mortgaged, and I told him I would make the best deals possible. Then I told him there was one other thing I had to explain to him.

"He said, 'Please do so, Mr. Semenenko.'

" 'No matter what had been your choice,' I said, 'it can be accomplished only if you are willing to make sacrifices. Mr. Berlin and Mr. Gordotowsky have been told to permit Mr. Haynes to reorganize the business and economic side of your papers. There is another side to it. What you have chosen can be accomplished only if you are willing to make sacrifices, to change your way of life as we are all having to do, so that you can reduce your personal expenditure.' "

In all his life the Boston banker who had said a big yes or no to governments, prime ministers, movie moguls had never felt his heart and breath so out of control. It had taken all the courage he had to say that with *authority*.

This time, though the Great White Father's expression did not change, he did hesitate.

I wonder if in that flash into the future already he saw the one tragedy that, *except* for losing his papers, this new world of the New Deal and his own old mistakes might bring to him. Loss of his life at the Ranch.

To Mr. Semenenko he said, "Will you be more definite?"

"I told him," Mr. Semenenko said to me, "that he would have to reduce his living expenses by about seventy per cent."

He did not give me any exact figures then. But I recall that he said in passing that of course five thousand to ten thousand dollars a day was what it cost Mr. Hearst to live at San Simeon. It staggered me. Like Mr. Hearst, I had always thought that San Simeon *just growed*. The papers were in trouble. When a dime was a monetary unit of the post-Depression years people no longer bought both morning and afternoon papers. Advertisers had been forced to cut appropriations. Under the new circumstances everyone was going to have to cut their outgo to fit their new income—what they used to have wasn't as big and it was now cut beyond our comprehension by taxes.

As he often did in a crisis Mr. Hearst went to the window. From it, he could see the blue swimming pool with the Greek columns and statues, the smaller houses in their exquisite circle beyond the gardens and colonnades, and the distant acres. Around him he could feel his *home,* a man can love his home when it is a palace like San Simeon as much as though it were a shanty in old Shanty Town or Cousin Lelia's Wakefield Manor.

When he turned to his new banker, he knew he had lost it.

He said, "I have asked your advice in a field where you are expert and I fear I am most remiss. I will follow your advice as to what I must do."

Mr. Semenenko said, "We will liquidate your assets, pay as we can, and Mr. Berlin I am sure can gain time from your creditors."

According to the only eyewitness left, the tears were in *his* eyes, not in Mr. Hearst's. The Great White Father, Mr. Semenenko told me, met this loss and humiliation and challenge with a rueful twinkle and with a promise he never broke.

Once upon a time I owed seventeen thousand dollars to a lot of people—the laundry, the gas station, the department stores, the butcher the baker and the candlestick maker.

Trying to switch entirely to fiction and/or *movies,* I hadn't been able to work. As Dickens has told us, nothing keeps creative thoughts, such as they may be, from germinating and gestating like the growl of the wolf on your welcome mat. This is not living picturesquely in an attic on a sardine a day. It is the baying of collection agencies, the refusal of a charge account you've had for twenty years at a moment when the kids need shoes, the finding of the telephone shut off. This particular deadline pressure did not spur me to fiction heights any more than it did Dickens—and though I was a whole Swiss Alps away from that greatest of all I was far enough up the icy trail to *freeze* there like a mountain climber in shock.

Then my young brother Thornwell, who had passed his bar, took it upon himself to visit each and every person to whom I owed money. If, he said, they could see their way to give me time, to leave me alone, not worry nor harass me, not undermine my confidence so that I could work, I would be able to pay them back and since they knew me to be honest I would pay them back a hundred cents on the dollar.

But she has no assets, my little brother told them. I should have had, no doubt of that, but like Mr. Hearst I assumed I had to live in certain accustomed ways. Ups and downs to be sure, but there were some things you had to have and do. Also a lone career mother has to fill her absences in other departments with paid help. Good help in these brackets comes high, as it should. Someone had to help me care for my home and my family. Particularly *someone who would always be there when the children came home from school,* who would keep them from ever feeling neglected. A Nanny as good as a mother.

In my born-and-bred, pathological, and immature ignorance of money, I'd had neither the chance nor the brains to gain assets. My childhood and youth had been lived in flamboyant extravagance and debt. Papa thought he was doing them a favor to owe them money and so did they. The idea of suing *Mr. Rogers* or shutting off his credit was so preposterous that I had never encountered it. In this, as in all else, I didn't have my father's magic.

It hadn't occurred to anybody—it never does—that a writer whose name is seen often in print has no assets. Today they usually do. The tax structure encourages them to have business managers and lawyers and tax experts to handle their money and keep them at peace with the Internal Revenue Service. These able gentlemen also invest and accumulate assets for them. In the Thirties neither I nor anybody else had such help and protection. When Thorny grew up enough to take this over and explain to my creditors that unless I was allowed time and peace of mind enough to allow me to *earn* the money they could whistle for it, they were kindness itself. Thank God I was able to pay back every penny. Soon my credit rating stood at Very Slow but Absolutely Good.

Came a cloak-and-dagger trip across the border into Canada on the part of suave, smiling, and sagacious Richard E. Berlin. A large percentage of the mills where they bought the paper to print Hearst newspapers and magazines were situated there. What William Randolph Hearst owed them was a fair-sized national debt. With the same line my brother Thorny had used, Mr. Berlin as business head of the Hearst enterprises persuaded them not to file any suits. Not to withhold any stock. If they harassed him unduly and prevented him from having the means to get out his papers in time they might get ten cents on a dollar. IF they gave Mr. Hearst time to recover they'd not only get a dollar for a dollar, they would still have their biggest American customer.

He got them to wait.

Meantime began and continued the liquidation of Mr. Hearst's assets. The real estate, now worth the billions Mr. Semenenko told him it would be, went often for the mortgages. His warehouses full of fortunes in antiques and art treasures, piled up against a rainy day when he might not have enough, were emptied. The contents were put up for sale at Gimbels and Macy's, at auctions, and to private collectors.

They were still short of what had to be *paid* to the government and to debtors who would not or could not wait.

Then there was truly a midnight when Judge Shern and Mr. Haynes and Berlin and Gordotowsky were gathered around a big table to see if there was anything else like old manuscripts probably—on which to raise *cash,* when in walked Miss Marion Davies. On that cold businesslike table she laid a glittering heap of jewels, worth several millions, *and* her deeds to some of Columbus Circle *and* two Boston papers and the Ritz Tower.

Literally, all she had. It helped, but it wasn't enough. Like that ninth trick at three no trump when you can see eight, or the final thousand on a down payment, *they* needed a few more millions. Hardest to come by.

Abby Rockefeller to the rescue may seem apocryphal.

I don't really know the one sister of the five Rockefeller brothers. One of them, Winthrop, now Governor of Arkansas, was a great friend of my brother Bogart. At a cattle sale at Winrock he confirmed the story I'd asked Bo to find out about. As Marion had told it to me.

It seems that after piling her jewelry on that table, Marion had gone home to bed, but not to sleep. For worrying. Dreadful beyond words it was to think of Mr. Hearst spending the rest of his life on St. Helena. The bigger they come the farther they have to fall and often it's harder to watch them.

In that hour before dawn, M.D. got up, put a sable coat over her night-gown, walked around from the Ritz Tower to Fifty-fourth Street, and awakened her long-time friend, the Rockefeller sister. (The nearest I ever got to that was that once when Win was young and wild and took a trip to Hollywood, Marion had been a help.) Tomorrow morning, Marion told her, Mr. Hearst is going to be seven million *or* $459.25 *or* that ninth trick short. If he doesn't have it they may force him into bankruptcy. Would Abby mind lending it to her?

Abby said, Not at all.

I hope it is true. A friend helping a friend. Money will always be the test. Only two people in the world I've ever borrowed from. Maggie Cousins and Colleen Moore Hargrave. That two hundred dollars or five hundred dollars looked as big to me as a million or so did to a Rocke-feller or a Hearst or a Marion Davies.

Of course what passed back and forth between Papa Fix Clements and me, or Ernest E. Adams, Jr.'s, salary and me, or other reporters and me I do not consider borrowing nor did they. Whoever had it—

When the Boston banker finished telling me his story, we sat in silence, thinking of our friend.

"Few men would have had the courage or the stamina or the self-discipline or the thought of others. All these were needed to do what he did," Mr. Semenenko said. "He kept his newspapers and as long as he lived you all kept them on top. He had *character*."

"Doesn't it also take the temperament to go with it?" I said a little hesitantly, for it seemed to me I had seen people of character betrayed by their temperament.

"Yes—yes," Mr. Semenenko said, "he had that, too. He loved life— and the other reason I loved him more than any man I have ever known —and made every excuse to go to see him at Wyntoon or in Beverly Hills after he left the Ranch was that he was a remarkable companion. He knew so much about almost everything. He had the most stimulating and broad mind, he was the most thoughtful friend, he never let me down on his promise—"

Suddenly, Mr. Semenenko let out a roar of laughter. "Yes, he did," he said, "yes, he did. We put up his collection of famed Georgian silver at auction at Christie's in London. We got fine prices, many belonged in museums, not in private hands. There was one rare and historic candlestick with many branches, the most beautiful I ever saw. We got a top price for it and everyone was delighted." He stopped to roar again. "Until some time later," he said, "when we found that Mr. Hearst had bought it back himself."

With that breathing space, realization on real estate, what Marion put in the pot, the capital placed at his disposal by Mr. Semenenko, the new Hearst regime began. The various abilities of Berlin, Haynes, and Semenenko served as a kitchen cabinet extraordinary.

We still had the Hearst papers, money to run them in the hard times, renewed credit, till the war spiral in business came.

The only difference was—we didn't go to the Ranch any more.

Nor did he.

CHAPTER 36

I go back to the Third Term Convention in Chicago, where Franklin Delano Roosevelt was nominated as I went forward to it in 1940.

From here, I see clearly that it was the turning point in my life. I didn't know it while it was going on, and it was some time before I was willing to recognize or accept it.

To begin with, who knew that on the fourth day of that baked, sizzling, sticky, unbearable heat Jim Farley of New York would say to Jimmy Byrnes of South Carolina, *Tell Harry Hopkins,* in his eyrie at the Blackstone, *to tell The President to send Eleanor.*

Who knew that?

There had been possible dangers to the *Third Term* nomination, but as it turned out nobody but Carter Glass of Virginia had the guts to stand up to the platoons of Mayor Kelly's men, at the head of every aisle, and use those words.

Otherwise nobody reminded anybody that this was a Third Term.

But after that nomination was safe the delegates dug in their heels, all the hidden protest and shame and uncertainty raged into a hurricane to be called Down with Henry Agard Wallace, we will not advise and consent to his being Vice President even if he is Roosevelt's choice.

They won't have him, Byrnes told Farley.

So the President sent Eleanor again. This was again and again and again, as he had sent her from the day he was stricken with polio and she emerged from ten years of childbearing, homemaking, and husband-tending to save his life and reason by convincing him and the political machine of New York State that, crippled as he was, Franklin D. Roosevelt still had a political future.

My conversation with Eleanor Roosevelt at that convention was in three parts, during the hours from late afternoon until midnight that she was at the convention. They may not have been connected in Mrs. Roosevelt's mind, on which she had a good deal at the time, but something beyond her *mind* worked for her all the time. I am amazed at my questions, how or why I dared ask them. It is my impression that we had all gone at least a little berserk, as people are said to do in the tropics. Lightning and thunder from the dark skies over Chicago and from the darker floor of the convention—I had lost my direction. Otherwise, I couldn't have asked Mrs. Roosevelt questions having nothing to do with the case, and Mrs. Roosevelt might not have so simply and kindly given me answers. My pivotal indication of grace and its first gift, *hope*.

I made the story I'd have to do about her my excuse for these questions, flowing three in one.

1. A few moments when she sat quietly on the platform waiting to speak to the now completely-out-of-hand convention. "Did your husband send you, and do you see your work here as his alter ego as Your Job?"

2. After she'd finished her speech, I knelt beside her in the dark. "Do you put your husband, your children or your work *first?*"

3. The final question came not *from* but *through* me, and it was at the impromptu press conference she held before she flew back to the White House and a probable third term as First Lady.

That one and its answer I myself can understand and believe only by going over all that led up to it, as I had done actually while I was watching the slim figure so elegant in all the wrong clothes, so distinguished in plainness, so unbelievable in simplicity. For it was as a climax that I suddenly saw her as the Modern Woman of our century, and I thought with intensity that she might have the Answer.

Otherwise, with all she'd been through, with all she must know lay ahead, how could she be so shining and serene that she had brought that moment of unforgettable silence, as though we were on another star, to the hell of the convention floor?

So we will go over it together for that answer was my Gateway.

It is an oversimplification to see light as coming only to those in rags, in gutters, in failures and poverty. When at last any success, any fame, any money are empty and powerless and you face it, that for what you love most your best isn't good enough—then you know how vital it is for a camel to thread the postern of a needle's eye and for rich men to find that Gate.

I hit the peak of my own professional career during those days in Chicago with "The Voice from the Sewers" story, about which *Time* only recently spoke words of praise. Still one of the historic scoops. Yet it was there, too, that I asked Mrs. Roosevelt my three despairing and troubled questions.

Taking me out of intense doldrums at Malibu to send me to the convention, Mr. Hearst explained that I was to cover it as news, with honesty and without prejudice, but our editorial policy supported Thomas Jefferson and George Washington and this was against a third term.

It is repetitious but necessary to say that a Presidential convention becomes a senseless, witless, can't-see-can't-hear monster, stunned into inertia then into frenzy, no more representing the People than a pot of boiling oil. A system devised for thirteen small colonies on horseback, not for fifty huge states in jet airplanes, we'll have to come up someday soon with a new method, but in Chicago in 1940 in what we designated historically as the Third Term Convention, the old was at its worst. The only one of its kind.

My copy, as I've dug it out of the Library of Congress, shows how desperately I had to feel my way for any color, action, features, even personalities. Having once said the stadium was policed and cowed by Mayor Kelly's hoodlums, I couldn't go on with it forever. We had Howey, who knew Chicago as well as Mrs. O'Leary, but he was in our city room on the seventh floor of the Stevens and most of the time it was impossible to get in an elevator. Climbing the stairs took longer than the Matterhorn. Telephones, even to William Randolph Hearst, were hours behind in completing calls.

Up to the Presidential nomination I talked things over with Runyon, on one side, and Inez Robb and Gracie Allen on the other. I did my best, after seeing that Louella Parsons knew where she was, to convey to our readers, who were the voters, what was going on.

One of these read:

> The absence of President Franklin Delano Roosevelt, intended to make the heart of this Democratic Convention grow fonder, today faded before the grim presence of James A. Farley. The heart of this great gathering, which on the floor of the Stadium beats sluggishly at these opening sessions, beats secretly, shame-facedly with and for the tall, bald-headed Irishman who is here fulfilling his last task for the man he has served so many years. The delegates know that this man, the greatest campaign genius of our time and the one man in Washington who never broke his word to a newspaperman, is through. Farley didn't believe in a Third Term. Now they have started to fight to get him back, because when the Republicans nominated Wendell Willkie they threw a new young monkey wrench into the well-oiled steam roller the bright boys were sure would sweep Roosevelt back into The White House without trouble. For this campaign, they'd like to have Farley.

All the time, I remember, Farley kept reminding me of something, somebody I'd covered before, and finally I knew it was Doc Kearns at the Dempsey-Tunney fight in Philadelphia. After Doc had been discarded by the man he'd made champion. I remembered Doc telling me then that those weren't tears on his face, they were raindrops.

Without an editor, I came up with:

Courageous, old, ill and alone, his white head like a banner, Carter Glass of Virginia rose to cry No Third Term! *No Third Term! Jefferson who in his wisdom laid down the fundamental principles of Democracy, the father of our great Party, said I beg that you will never elect any man to a third term. When you do, the heart of democracy will cease to beat.* As he cried, I saw the Kelly boys on the convention floor begin to hem in the Democratic delegates; to move toward the tough cocky fighting old Senator from Virginia. And I said to myself What men are these, who wear their guns in parentheses, and I went down on the floor. With my badges and credentials waving I asked them for theirs but they had nary, they told me openly We're Mayor Kelly's men, he sent us, Chicago doesn't want any trouble about Roosevelt getting in.

I reproduce this here for the simple reason that we published it under my by-line in our Chicago papers and got no word of denial. As back in the press box I began to write it, Runyon said, "Why don't you stay out of that? It isn't healthy," and I said, "I'm not going to let that old man do it all alone, I'm a poor weak woman but I've got a little stomach, I don't like to see them push Carter Glass around." "They're going to," Runyon said, "however, if they push you into the lake I will see they hang for it," and I said, "That's nice of you." But it did encourage me for then I wrote:

Just the same, to all Americans everywhere, I say I'd like to see Mayor Kelly go into a room alone with Carter Glass. I will take all bets that if only one of them is going to come out alive it will be the 82-year-old Gentleman from Virginia and not the youthful husky who now heads Chicago's Machine. Feeble, ill and old as the Senator is, Glass has more guts, indomitable, deathless, unconquerable, than Kelly and Bathhouse John and Hinky Dink put together. It looks as if he lost last night, doesn't it? The old Senator from the Old Dominion of Patrick Henry, while the delegates from the smoke-filled rooms let the Kelly goons Boo BOOOO BOOOO the name of Thomas Jefferson for the first time in any Democratic gathering.

I tell you he did not lose. He's tough, the little old man, name of Carter Glass. He goes down shouting No Third Term. As I look down now from The Press Box I can see the gallant old man *trembling* but undaunted. I tell you I'm going to live to see the day when he didn't lose—when he WON.

I have lived to see it.

Refusing a third term, Washington set a precedent. Jefferson spoke a tradition. No law forbade a President as many terms as he could get. BUT eleven years after Carter Glass cried in the Chicago wilderness America passed the twenty-second Amendment, making No Third Term a *law*.

So I win my bet that Carter Glass would be the one to come out alive, for where is Ozymandius Kelly now?

Finally I caught up with Howey in his suite at the Ambassador East and wished I hadn't. A fearsome sight in topless pajamas, he looked at me with equal disfavor and said, "You still have poor and unhappy brains for drinking," and I said, "This convention is driving most of us to drink. Horsing around with a dim platform, no interest, no enthusiasm, like flying in a pea-soup fog, it's a bore and stories about boredom bore me." He said, "You were a flag-waving suffragette, now a lady political boss is director of the Woman's Division of the National Democratic Convention, you oughta be able to wave some flags when she speaks." A few hours later I wrote bitterly:

> Mrs. McAllister is a first-class politician in skirts and that's ALL she is. She sounds like the President of the General Federation of Women's Clubs making the same speech we've been hearing since the Convention opened, expert, grooved, flowing in well-worn cliches . . . *human betterment . . . strengthening our social and economic structure . . . renewing in each American a sense of his moral and material stakes in the future . . .*

You know.
On a sheet of copy paper I scrawled Edna Millay's *Was it for this I uttered prayers, And sobbed and cursed and kicked the stairs, That now, domestic as a plate, I should retire at half-past eight?* and passed it to Gracie, who sighed and said, *Yes, isn't she?* as our Mrs. McA. went on and on—*women have 1500 volunteer directors . . . 850 Speakers' Bureaus . . . 2000 Discussion Groups*—Gracie was muttering, "What do they discuss? We got the vote but can we wrap it up?" We listened to Harry Richmond sing *God Bless America* and she said pitifully, "With the lack of oxygen and all I am bogging down, will they get this show on the road?" and I said, "Well—they always have—"

They did and I got my most exclusive story of all my time.

As best I could I had homesteaded a couple of feet on the steps leading up to the speakers' platform. I pulled splinters out every night, but underneath the steps was a room like a caboose and there on a couple of shelves were the Telephones. FROM the convention leaders, floor captains, state and delegation heads TO Harry Hopkins, at the Blackstone, in charge of Everything and through him to the Man in the White House. Sooner or later I was bound to hear something to my advantage, so, ear to crack, I made myself as small, limp, and inconspicuous as possible, people going up and down to the platform walked around or over me, if I moaned they never looked down to see whether I was a crocodile or a three-toed sloth.

Until the day Bill Slocum, once a *Journal* reporter, tripped over me. In his embarrassment, he tried to make up to me by saying he was now working for one of the big radio networks and would I like to come and see their broadcast setup? I remembered that Mrs. McA. had bragged about seven hundred women *radio* chairmen so I thought I ought to take a look.

I am sure Mrs. McA. knew nothing about the Voice from the Sewers, nor, in all fairness, did Bill Slocum; he wanted to start me at the bottom and show me the whole operation and we stumbled on this deep dark secret.

Down down down we went into caverns measureless to man. I felt the drip drops of foul water and soon I heard ancestral voices prophesying war. The hair lifted on my scalp, as in the bowels of Chicago this demon wailed, magnified and eerie:

ILLINOIS WANTS ROOSEVELT
NEW JERSEY WANTS ROOSEVELT
THE WORLD WANTS ROOSEVELT LADIES AND
GENTLEMEN OF AMERICA I WISH YOU COULD SEE
THIS CONVENTION HALL HERE IN CHICAGO ITS
BEDLAM HAS CAUGHT FIRE WITH WILD ENTHUSIASM
FOR ROOOOOOSSSEEEEVVVVVELLLLLLTTT.

I put my hand against the damp wall. When Slocum and I had left the hall minutes before it had been sunk in a profound lethargy, a lethargy, I'd overheard it said on the phones, was keeping Farley and Alben Barkley awake nights. They didn't want to go into a campaign against the wild, new enthusiasm of Wendell Willkie off this lukewarm halfhearted showing. Nothing could halt Roosevelt's nomination, but apathy or a browbeaten air of intimidation, along with the third-term issue, might cost them the election.

Nobody seemed to have any idea what to do about it.

They had forgotten Mayor Kelly's methods. Or used them?

I turned back as though a fire alarm had sounded at sea. It floods back around me, I can hear my fleeing feet, I wish I could transport us to that time when we knew so little about *Radio,* when it was still a sort of chimera, an audio illusion, and as that disembodied voice pursued me up stone steps, through a little tunnel, I tell you frankly I thought I had gone nuts. Then there before me was the same vast smoking glaring stadium caught in the same flat listless silent movie, you know now from television that a north delegation has no way of knowing what a south delegation is doing, and east and west never the twain shall meet, but now they could all *hear* a traumatic bray describing them to each other:

NEW YORK WANTS ROOSEVELT
NEW YORK IS ON ITS FEET WAVING BANNERS
NEW YORK IS CHEERING MADLY FOR ROOSEVELT

Under the rail where I hung gasping the New York delegation was looking over its shoulder to see if anybody was following them. I shuddered with relief. At least it wasn't ME. The delegates from New York didn't know either, the whites of their eyes were beginning to show, they began to react, to obey the *suggestions,* I slid off the rail and as I hit the corridor and heard the same voice reverberating I thought *the porpoises are coming out of the sea to take over.* Bill Slocum wasn't around any more. By all the gods, I said to myself, if I have any courage at all I am going to see what is behind that door! The door where dwelt the phantom voice bellowing in galvanic waves. I took a deep breath, said, *Jesus Mary and Joseph* as the nuns had taught me long long ago, and banged open the door.

Before me I saw a small doss-like chamber. On the table were black boxes of mechanical equipment and a pair of large feet. Behind it a man —they were his feet—leaning back with eyes on the ceiling, on his face an expression of sheer creative bliss. As I took two steps forward the door shut behind me, he shouted, LOOK AT PENNSYLVANIA, and I jumped out of my skin.

We were alone.

Four damp walls with no windows.

No periscopes.

Only the equivalent. A radio microphone in his hand reaching up up up to the floor and out out out to the United States of America and all the ships at sea.

I had no way of knowing he was another of Mayor Kelly's men but at least I knew he was *human.*

As fast as I could, I was nearly out of gas, I raced back upstairs and sat quietly in the press box watching it happen.

I got to our city room by climbing the stairs and there behind the desk sat Howey. He said, "What've you got?" and I told him.

"Who was he?" Howey said.

Slocum had been guiltless; just the same if I didn't snitch on him I'd had a right to ask for the name. I passed it to Howey.

"Geeseezzzz!" Howey said. "That's Kelly's Superintendent of Sewers."

He sat looking at me. Between lolling on the steps, running the relay, and watching the spectral drama of The Voice from the Sewers, the sweat had rolled and then dried on me like garlic in the mud. I must have looked like one of the porpoises with a low blood count. Howey's glass eye estimated I might be too distraught to be trustworthy and he said, "It's too goddam good to be true. Are you sure?"

With what sounded to me like a sob I said, "YES."

Howey said, "All right, all right, step on it," and began to yell at the telegraph desk.

Repulsive as he was, I loved him. No other editor would have had the guts.

He said, "Hold it to fifteen hundred words—"

Here are some of them. Written hot. I stepped on it.
Nobody else—nobody at all—had so much as a syllable.

By Adela Rogers St. Johns

From the sewers of Chicago came the wild phantom voice whose mounting hysteria guided the destiny of America in her hour of national crisis.

Over the public address system in the Stadium, in the first of the staged Draft Roosevelt demonstrations the voice shrieked crescendoes of:

"Illinois wants Roosevelt. New York wants Roosevelt. New Jersey wants Roosevelt. Pennsylvania wants Roosevelt. The World wants Roosevelt."

If you happened to be listening far from the smoky, jammed glaring convention hall you may have thought the delegates from those states were standing on their hind legs and doing high pressure stunts in a throbbing demand for a Third Term for Franklin Delano Roosevelt.

Nothing, my friends, could be further from the truth. The delegates were standing flat-footed. The scheduled whoopee was flopping like a hooked catfish. . . . A few very young men were marching in the aisles with banners trying to stir up some noise.

In this greatest emergency of the convention one man was rushed to the mike, in the basement, with orders to needle the convention into something that had to sound like a wild and roaring and heartfelt demonstration.

The man who was ready to die—and sometimes sounded like he might of apoplexy—for the dear old Democratic Party was Tommy Garry, superintendent of Sewers for the city of Chicago, a staunch henchman of Mayor Kelly. He came leaping to the mike. . . . The way he bellied up to the open channels of the Public Address system and stayed there, driving himself up and up in a sort of Aimee Semple McPherson frenzy as he'd been trained in ward caucuses. The stunned and bewildered delegates were suggestible with anxiety and fatigue. They stared in all directions to locate the phantom voice. It seemed to me to be coming from the ceiling, from the floor, from all four corners of the vast flag-draped room.

✦ ✦ ✵ ✵ ✱

The boys on the floor began to be sure they'd missed their cues.

In India they say that the natives are spellbound by the purr of the tiger and will walk straight into his mouth to be swallowed in one hungry gulp. So the three thousand delegates who couldn't see each other were hypnotized by the phantom voice and made its pictures come true.

* * * * *

I have not met Mr. Tommy Garry, they say he is a very nice fellow indeed, so I couldn't have recognized the voice from the sewer—I beg your pardon, the basement—where alone and single-handed Mr. Garry put on a one-man show that in my long experience I have never heard equalled. But I had a fleeting glimpse of him at work in that underground section of Chicago which as its superintendent he knew so well.

Well, it was something to have heard. Those of you who listened in your living rooms all around America may have thought there were many voices, many men hollering wildly—the mechanical device made it sound like that from the beginning and in the end of course it had roused the delegates to cast off uncertainty and inertia and join the gag. But the voice that saved the Roosevelt convention came from the Sewers of Chicago and don't let anybody tell you otherwise.

The nomination went through with the impression that wild enthusiasm had swept Roosevelt into a third term. Inez Robb and I, sharing a suite at the Blackstone belonging to Lee Lyles of the Santa Fe, began to pack. We had a few farewell drinks with Louis Bromfield and Pearl Mesta in the Bali Room in a daze of relaxation and serenity.

All hell broke loose!

This was authentic, an inside-the-park home riot. Chairman Barkley, usually omnipotent, found himself chasing around in the outfield unable to catch up with the ball.

Everybody wants Roosevelt, Runyon commented. Nobody wants Wallace.

George R. Holmes, head of our Washington Bureau, had just come from there. He said, "Nobody but the President of the United States. I never saw him more set on anything than having Wallace for Vice President and you gotta know Roosevelt is a pigheaded Dutchman and he won't budge."

I had been circulating on the floor and I said, "Neither will they."

The anti-Wallace flood grew. As though a dam had burst all the hostility, the pent-up opposition to a third term, the animosity generated by being manipulated had smashed through and was seething. By God and Thomas Jefferson, they were going to have their way about this one. The TEXAS WANTS GARNER young man was hollering once more, Garner had been Roosevelt's V.P. for two terms, and this time Texas and several other states were listening. I saw Paul V. McNutt come down the steps after saying a few words, his handsome face covered with tears, he kept saying, "But if the President doesn't want me—" and the men with him shouted, "*We* want you, buddy," and walloped him on the back.

From our city room, I called Mr. Hearst. I felt this was a delicate matter and Howey had the delicacy of a hula dancer. To any Vice Presidency there has to be the aspect of the possible death of the President. One-heartbeat-away. I said, "It's been customary to soft-pedal that. I never heard so much loud talk about it before. No tact. They're so hot against Wallace, partly because they think after two hard terms and the war he's sure is coming, they think Roosevelt won't live out a third term and that one-heartbeat-away—"

Mr. Hearst said, "I'd like to keep Mr. Wallace more than that away from the Presidency. On the other hand if Roosevelt is elected, as we must face that he probably will be, we must not frighten the people, who will then be in constant concern about his health deteriorating. That would be equivalent to crying fire in a crowded theater and that we have no right to do. Mr. Howey and Mr. Holmes assure me they won't nominate Wallace."

Jimmy Byrnes had raised his voice in exasperation and emphasis, so I could hear him plainly from my post on the steps. "*I'm* here," he shouted, "and *he's* in Washington. *I* say that unless the President comes himself, we can't nominate Wallace for him." He listened, he said, "Wait a minute—Farley just came in—" I couldn't see into that dark tiny cubby-hole where these statesmen were conferring but I could imagine them, tense now and furious, as Byrnes said, "Harry says the President can't come—" and Farley said clearly, "Tell Hopkins to tell the President to send Eleanor."

                                  2

We waited at the airport, Inez Robb and I. Our friend Bess Farley, Jim's beautiful blond wife, had told us Mrs. Roosevelt's arrival time. Bess's fury against the President for what she thought he'd done to *her* husband did not extend to *his* wife. She's all the heart he's got, Bess said.

Only Farley was there to meet Mrs. Roosevelt and they met as friends.

Friends. She makes them, I thought, she's brought them along with her. *And* enemies. You can tell quite a lot by the enemies a woman has made. I hope! I feel some of mine do me credit.

We followed the big black limousine through Chicago's hottest hour. The late afternoon had accumulated humidity, the asphalt, cement, and brick had heated to an oven, as yet not a breath of cool came off the sullen gray lake. All we could see in the rear window of the car ahead was the man's bald head and the woman's wrong hat, dark blue with something white astern, worn high on nondescript hair. Inez remarked that he was doing all the talking. In my imagination I could overhear him telling her that as nominations progressed her candidate was getting booed.

I soon left that. Mrs. Roosevelt and her coming appearance at the convention—no First Lady had done such a thing before—were now my story. When you are working on a story you write it in your head all the time. Awake or asleep, drunk or sober. At all levels of consciousness.

In a courtroom, you wrote possible leads for any of ten witnesses that could be called. At a ball game, any sports event, it was second nature to assemble all the color, plays and players, possible scores, anecdotes, or quotable lines ready to hand. As my father had memorized the *direct* examination of a witness so he could move with perfect ease on the cross, without fumbling or hesitation, so I had learned to tabulate and then memorize all that went with my story, so that the gearshift, the brake, throttle, and *maps* were automatic.

In Washington, I had filed in my memory a fairly complete one-line political and personal biography of Eleanor Roosevelt, nee Anna Eleanor Roosevelt, including the dates of her birth, wedding, children's births and names, where she went to school, how she and her distant cousin Franklin met, how close her close family ties were to Teddy Roosevelt—closer than Franklin's.

To this I'd added my vivid portraits of our personal contacts.

Always there would come back to me—does now—the day I called the White House on the telephone to reach her and she answered herself. Recognizing the famous voice, I said, "So they've got you answering your own phone?" and with a warm laugh, *real* as it could be, she said, "The world is full of people who can let a phone ring but I'm not among them. Are you? I don't see how any woman with children can be—we're such fuss-budgets."

I'd interviewed her and been at press conferences as smoothly handled by Lorena Hickock.

If I put my brush to palette for a portrait now, I found a color I hadn't been too conscious of. The bright iridescence of humor. Eleanor Roosevelt with her *reforms* and her *humanitarianism,* and her intellectual writings and her epic events? Surely not. Yet in my few personal encounters there it was. A sort of humorous way of putting things and perhaps putting up with things. Wasn't this necessarily so, or how could she handle as many kinds of people as she did? The soul of America laughs; we had our superb days with Thurber and Benchley and Dorothy Parker and our present dull, gray, dripping, dreadful, cultural difficulties of only one minor note, of no *story,* no *melody,* no *picture,* began when we accepted as true a play pretending to be about an American family in Brooklyn without one laugh in it or one member of it with a sense of humor.

Send Eleanor, said Farley. Without expecting enough humor to face this sticky situation toward which we were driving? Never.

Got to talk to Eleanor. Witty, wisecracking, brilliant Louie Howe—could he have said that every time? And moreover wanted her presence beside him for those long months on his deathbed in the White House, could a newspaperman like Louie Howe have *worshiped* any woman who couldn't laugh with him?

The stately mansion she occupied was always on the front page, but I knew that to her children it had been home, and all her projects hadn't swamped the tears and laughter that made it possible for her to reach so many people about so many things. Louie Howe told me once that she did it by getting inside their skins. "She's thinking about them, not herself," he said. But—you have to have humor for that!

Today the leaders in Chicago had asked her husband the President to send her in his stead. To speak for—or about him. Had any other woman borne such a responsibility?

I knew the story I must write should be:

By Louie Howe.

Louie Howe, the forgotten man, the man who had started the career of that handsome young Roosevelt heir, the squire of Hyde Park, the heir to the Roosevelt and Delano millions, the bearer of one of the most illustrious names in politics. Dead now, Louie had been F.D.R.'s first inspiration, mentor, instructor, companion in those early days before the catastrophe of polio struck him down.

By the time I was privileged to know him, Louie Howe was a bedridden gnome of a man, and in the beginning of his impairment his bed in that back room in the White House was a center for advice and know-how. Often he talked to the President about the big decisions as they came to that oval desk where, as Truman was to say, *the buck stops.* Then, quite literally, the President got too busy. He had *no time.* A modern disorder—*No Time.* Steve Early, the White House press secretary, had for his old side-kick affection, admiration, and anxiety. But—Steve had no time either, he seldom got *home*—

Only Eleanor was never too busy.

How does she do all she does, I asked myself, as we went through crowds gathered around the stadium for news. Not only three mules, but the biggest ones. The ones that pull hardest. Run fastest. Are most difficult to handle. Money, of course, and servants, and help of all kinds—*but that never does it.*

I had asked Louie Howe one day and he said, "You wouldn't believe it if I told you. She—tunes into something."

As I followed behind her into the big ugly building, showing my four or five badges—Press, Floor, Gallery, Speakers' Platform—I realized in a daze that for the first time I was seeing that *Mrs. Roosevelt—Send Eleanor*—was a career gal—a *woman* with a *husband* who was a *man* as well as a President—a *mother* who had lost her first son so she knew that agony, who had five *children* no better and no worse than other women's children, though they seemed more of everything, magnified as they were by their position. I felt that not only the story I was going to write had taken me over, as you pray it will, but *myself,* the Modern Woman, was interwoven with that writer. This had begun to respond to the woman I was watching in a new way.

Here comes Mrs. Roosevelt—surprise surprise—there had been no time to tell anybody? Or maybe Farley wanted it that way. Gasps—whispers—necks craning . . .

Here comes Eleanor—Pegler's vicious hate called her sometimes Queen Eleanor, or Eleanor the First, but as I stumbled in the darkness of the stadium where only the great spotlights were on, nothing could have been to me more otherwise—I was muttering to myself, Here comes a wife, mother, careerist. Would anyone just looking at her think her anything but a very ordinary middle-aged badly dressed *woman?* With that hat and that hair!

I could not know this was the woman who was to be a guiding power in the United Nations, one of our country's most active philanthropists, that this was the woman who would go to all the war fronts of the world to bring back firsthand news to the Commander in Chief of our Armed Forces—his most trusted emissary everywhere.

What I knew in the brief exchange of greeting as she took a quiet seat in the darkness of the platform around the speakers' rostrum was that unexpectedly she related to *me.* When we spoke, she would communicate to *me.* She had moved just ahead of me into a slight activity of woman's suffrage in its earliest days; she had taken part first in public affairs when Child Labor was still a national disgrace; when all that the

New Deal she helped to create was unheard of—racial equalities and civil rights and poverty program! We hadn't even heard the words.

She was a Modern Woman.

One of the first.

The career had happened to her. Louie Howe told me she had not sought it. At twenty-one, she had married and Louie Howe kept emphasizing to me that it was a love match. More on his side than hers, for the young squire with his money, good looks, social position, and future could have married anybody, while his distant cousin Eleanor was an ugly duckling of a girl, too shy and retiring to be a belle. Think more of him because he chose her, Louie Howe said to me. A good thing for him, Louie said, or the last you'd have heard of Franklin Delano Roosevelt was that he got beat when he ran for Vice President in 1920.

In my life, I decided, as I tried to figure how Mrs. Roosevelt could sit so still, I never saw a face light up the way Louie's did when he spoke of her. As I thought of that early courtship and marriage he'd told me so much about, I imagined that she had then what she had now—the exquisite hands, the grace of movement and youthful dignity to sit still, the air of self-forgetfulness, the well-bred speaking voice equal in music and memorability to Ethel Barrymore's. Still, in a young man of twenty-three it showed taste and values to choose these rather than more flamboyant charms.

One day as I sat beside his bed there in the White House, Louie Howe said to me, "Let me show you what she did. For ten years Roosevelt had been in political life. Everyone saw his potential. He became state senator—there's no better school than the cat-and-dog fight in Albany for experience. In 1913 Woodrow Wilson noticed him and made him Assistant Secretary of the Navy and he served brilliantly throughout World War I. He was nominated for Vice President on the Democratic ticket with Cox and they were defeated by Herbert Hoover. So that one defeat every politician should have was behind him. All that time—those ten years— Eleanor had been childbearing, homemaking, husband-tending. She had— let us be honest—a mother-in-law problem. A grand old lady, Sara Delano Roosevelt, but she was a queen-mother type with the money and Franklin was her only child. Eleanor learned a lot about handling women in politics in dealing with that.

"I tell you something else, for I see it as part of her greatness as a woman. While he was Assistant Secretary of the Navy, their marriage almost went on the rocks. Busy with her home, her children—he fell in love or thought he did. Well—he talked to Eleanor about a divorce. She had to overcome her pride and don't misunderstand me, she had a lot of that. She asked me if a divorce then might cost him the fulfillment of those ambitions she knew had been dear to his heart since he was a boy. Would it destroy his work? I told her it would. I'm not sure we were thinking of the White House yet I mentioned there had never been a divorced man in the White House and never would be. So she told Franklin to wait, to let time prove whether he was sure of what he wanted. Like many another ten-years-married peccadillo, nothing came of it. He was glad she'd been patient with him.

"So there isn't much she hasn't been through—you know about her father and brother."

"Only one thing she's never known," I said, "poverty. How can she understand so much about the poor and their needs and feelings?"

"I told you," he said, "she gets inside their skins. She can feel for and with others and she always wants to help—

"The big thing to remember about Eleanor Roosevelt is the Years Between. Between 1920 and 1928. Remember, she had to start with him, a big, fine, strong, healthy young man not yet forty years old. Used to ride, to walk, to dance, to go where he pleased. He was struck down, he would never walk again, he was to be a useless crock. She had to convince her husband over and over that this need make no difference to him as a man—or a husband; she had to keep up his spirits in a glow of hope and faith and she soon saw that she couldn't do this if life's work was over.

"That's when her work really began. With me as a partner, she fought to keep his name before the politicians of New York State, fought never to let them forget F.D.R.

"Ten years of being in the home, a wife, a mother, never expecting or wanting to be anything else. Then she had to come out into an active and crucial moment, an entirely new and unaccustomed role. She worked with me as a committeewoman, she did a dozen different things, she entered all kinds of organizations, charity and educational, her one object always to convince everybody that she knew Franklin Delano Roosevelt still had a future in politics. All this was new to her, and difficult for her. She was very shy and she'd had no real experience of public life.

"She added that backbreaking job to the one of inspiring her husband, taking care of her children. And always creating for him the new ways, the new atmosphere to convince him his life was ahead, not behind him. Remember that."

Dear Louie Howe, I remember, I do remember. I remembered as I sat there listening to the frenzy on the floor, staring at the glaring lights as they searched and watching the woman of the Years Between you had made me know so well.

Because I remembered I got up, moving like a shadow—we were not assassination conscious then; come to think of it the First Lady had no secret service bodyguard with her on that trip that I could see, I never recall one at any time—I moved quietly and after a moment she looked up and smiled at me as though she was glad to see me and I said, "Mrs. Roosevelt, did your husband send you here to represent him?" and she said, "No no. I came to tell the delegates something that perhaps they don't know. And that only I can tell them." "Your *work,*" I said, "as what sometimes we call his *alter ego,* that is your job, isn't it? Your *career?*" She thought a moment and said, "Yes. In our day it seems that the President's wife is a career. Such a responsibility has to be called your job— your work, doesn't it?"

A few moments later the chairman began his introduction and Eleanor Roosevelt moved into the spotlight and stood on the very edge of the platform, not bowing, just smiling at them, reaching out her hands to them. Think of the biggest ovation you've ever heard or seen and you will be in the stadium in Chicago as the three thousand delegates rose to greet her. How could she smile at that braying Monstrum Horrendum with such love? Could she take it apart and see it one by one as her neighbors? We all have one Father? The love was true—you cannot fool the people in a moment like that.

A short speech.

Somewhere in the archives of the Democratic Party are the words. They did not matter. The amplifiers did not harden or sharpen the pure gentleness of her voice as she said she had come to speak to them as the wife of the President of the United States.

She showed us all, without using any of the words, the Man in the White House.

Are you faced with the problem of leading this nation in unending conflict? Is it your charge day in and day out, night in and night out to be concerned always with the fear that if you don't do just the right thing they'll destroy the country that has been entrusted to you with all its hopes and all its future? Such a great country, dear friends, meaning so well and hoping so much and trying so hard to do the right thing and being nibbled to death by friends and enemies alike and you realize if you fail— not somebody else, but YOU—that it may be lost forever—do you have any concept of what that means? Do you understand at all the lengths to which it will drive you—

No, she didn't use those *words;* those are Allen Drury's, years later, in *Advise and Consent,* the best political novel we've had, but they are always the same words and, as all Presidents have said, no one but another President can understand them; yet that day I believe Eleanor Roosevelt came nearest to making our hearts feel them.

The man in the wheel chair.

The man who *must have* whatever help *he* believes will make it possible for him to do the job in the terrible years of war ahead.

If it's Henry Agard Wallace then it's Henry Agard Wallace.

What's the use of words? The appeal she made to them, the love she sent and asked them to send back, is written on my heart and it was on theirs.

She came back to sit on the same chair, the noise rose like mighty waters, at last Barkley took over, he got quiet in time, and the balloting began. Mrs. Roosevelt sat easily, she did not seem exhausted, her son came and spoke to her and she nodded, a hand on his sleeve, and he went away.

To this minute I do not understand how I had the courage to go to her, nor understand how she picked such an extraneous question out of the tumult, and the tension of silence, the pulse of triumph. Perhaps she could turn off when she'd finished a task that hadn't been difficult for her, she was so joyous to be able to do it, or perhaps it was never an extraneous question. She may have been conscious of it at some level always in thirty-five years of marriage.

Shaken to my roots if I had any, I blurted out, "Mrs. Roosevelt, which do you put *first,* your husband or your children or your job?"

"My husband," she said, without a second's hesitation.

If she'd used one of Kelly's sawed-off shotguns to fire that answer, it couldn't have hit me harder.

"Your *husband?*" I said.

"A woman must always put her husband first," Eleanor Roosevelt said. "This doesn't mean she puts her children second, does it? She and her husband are one, and *they* put the children first. All for one and one for all."

"And her job?" I said.

"She must never do a job except with her husband's full and happy permission—" said the First Lady.

"But—" I began. The spotlight hit us and she turned away—I didn't get a chance to ask her about *divorce,* some of her children were *divorced,* the parents of some of her grandchildren—

That would screw up the whole thing, she had to know that.

The convention nominated Henry Agard Wallace to be the candidate for the Vice Presidency on the ticket with Franklin Delano Roosevelt.

It was not what she said to them. I do not actually remember one word or one line of it. It was what she *was.* That spoke to them!

All right! What was she?

Louie Howe's voice on the tubes of my memory turned on loudly—loudly, I tell you. "She is a virtuous woman," Louie had said, and was saying again as clearly—more clearly—than ever.

Remember, he said.

We were in a sort of impromptu press conference by then—she stood quietly, with that poise that marked her always, that gathered her forces into focus—she fielded the questions as though it was a friendly meeting in her own home, and so I got the courage to move through and ask my third question.

Is being your husband's alter ego your career? Yes.

Who do you put first? My husband.

This time I said, "Mrs. Roosevelt, has anything ever happened to you in your life that made you doubt there is a God and that He will answer prayer?"

Inside, outside, I don't know, she had picked up a lamp somewhere, and without hesitation again she gave me a most remarkable answer.

". . . made you doubt there is a God—He will answer prayer?"

"No," she said.

She had made that same answer, I *remembered* as Louie Howe had kept insisting, to him once. When they prayed together. But then he told me she had added, "I think we doubt sometimes because the answer isn't always *yes.*"

The plane disappeared into the sky, homeward bound to her husband, and we went back to the Blackstone.

I found a Bible. A long time since I'd carried one around with me. Why? I'd more or less stopped reading it. I had the most peculiar feeling—here it was, the same Bible, Gideon it was called but it was the same, the one my grandfather had used in Globe, Arizona, to preach his sermon out of I Peter. I can't explain how—how miraculous or *something* it was to find it here so many years—miles—feelings—lives and incarnations of mine—away. I Peter was here, too.

But I knew that it had to be Proverbs I wanted.

A virtuous woman.

Good old Solomon. King Solomon whom the Queen of Sheba went to visit—Solomon and King David lived merry merry lives with many many lady friends and many many wives—by the time old age came upon Solomon he was known as the wisest man who ever lived and apparently he knew from experience how to write Proverbs.

Her price is far above rubies.

What, no rubies? Some of the modern girls wouldn't like that.

Incredible, I was thinking, when Inez came in and, seeing me sitting in a huge chair with the Gideon Bible on my lap, naturally asked me what in the world I was doing instead of packing?

I said, "It's incredible that some unknown scholars selected by that appalling son of Mary Stuart's, James the First, wrote more magnificent English prose than Shakespeare. Listen to this—*Who can find a virtuous woman? for her price is far above rubies.*"

Inez said, "Are you looking for a virtuous woman?"

I said, "I was wondering if that is what it was about Eleanor Roosevelt. It was something, wasn't it? It *is* something."

Inez agreed to this. I said, "It's amazing how modern it is!" She said, "The Bible is the most modern book in the world. I know that much!"

I made a sort of list out of that last chapter of Proverbs—for indeed Solomon wound up his book with this definition of a virtuous woman.

I didn't mention my *questions* to Inez but I sort of took them in the order of their asking.

"It says here," I pointed out:

> She considereth a field and buyeth it; with the fruit of her hands
>   she then planteth a vineyard—
> She perceiveth that her merchandise is good.
> She maketh fine linen and selleth it.
> She openeth her mouth with wisdom . . ."

I stopped there and said, "That could be a daily column, couldn't it? Yours or Mrs. Roosevelt's—it's a career, the whole thing, isn't it? In the real estate business and ranching—vineyards—and selling fine linen, maybe she had a decorator's shop or something."

Inez said, "Would you like a drink to wash some of this down?" and I said, Yes and she said, What? and I said, A martini—which, from first to last, was always a mistake—

I began pointing again:

> The heart of her husband doth safely trust in her, so that he can
>   have no need of spoil.

"Even in politics," I said, "he can be an honest man."

"An honest politician," Inez said, nodding without a quiver.

> Her husband is known in the gates when he sitteth among the
>   rulers of the land.

"If," Inez said, "you are thinking of Eleanor, her husband doth."

> Her husband praiseth her . . .

"That he does," I said, "I will never forget the way he *chuckles* when he tells you something she's done. He's so pleased."

"And," said Inez, showing the boy where to put the tray, "he certainly does trust her. He told me once she was the one person in the whole world he could completely trust."

> She maketh herself covering of fine tapestry, her clothing is silk and purple.

We let that fall into silence.

Then I said, "Well—that blue foulard she had on today—it was sort of like a tapestry—those little white flowers—and you know one thing, she takes a lot of pains with her clothes and they're like the royal family—nobody else would wear them. At night in the White House she's pretty *elegant* at that."

> She stretcheth out her hand to the poor, yea she reacheth out her hands to the needy . . .

"That is for sure," Inez said. "No other woman—not Jane Addams nor Clara Barton—has ever done more."

> She looketh to the way of her home and eateth not the bread of idleness.
> Her children shall rise up and call her blessed.

I thought of Franklin, Jr.'s, extraordinarily handsome face as he bent over his mother—and I remembered how we all thought Jimmy listened to her more than to his father and how, though Anna was "her father's daughter," you always had the feeling that she and her mother worked as a team for him—to protect him, to bring sunshine to him.

> All her family are clothed in scarlet—

Then King Solomon summed it all up:

> Favor is deceitful and beauty is vain; but a woman that feareth the Lord, she shall be praised, give her of the fruit of her hands and her own works shall praise her in the gates.

"Those, my love," I said to Inez, "are the last words ever spoken by Solomon, who had many many lady friends and many many wives—and whose name you will agree is the synonym and symbol of wisdom."

"It sounds like she was a very happy and successful dame," Inez said, "Exactly what—come to consider it—does *virtuous* mean? It obviously didn't mean to Solomon just somebody that didn't go around sleeping with people."

Lee Lyles had a dictionary, Lee always had everything, including the Santa Fe, then our favorite luxurious, restful, beautiful means of transportation. "They find us doing this," Inez said, "they will think we are crazy," and I said, "A lot of people are tonight. They have a horrible illusion that they nominated Henry Agard Wallace."

"Ha!" said Inez, and went to answer the phone.

Goodness. Uprightness. Rectitude. Chastity. [fourth in importance here] *Espeeially in women.*

That was one of the equalities we wanted—not having to be *chaste*—men had never been chaste, had they? But then they didn't bear the children. Inez came back and said it was her office, and I said, "Listen to the rest of this definition of virtuous—"

"Isn't that a fairly moldy old-fashioned dated word for the Modern Woman?" Inez said. "She's not going to like it."

"It's what Louie Howe said Eleanor Roosevelt was, a virtuous woman," I said. "She's a Modern Woman and look what she did today. Listen—*'The cardinal virtues, which are justice, prudence, temperance and fortitude,* and *the spiritual ones faith, hope, and charity.'* " I thought about that, I said, "It says here the antonym is vice. And the opposite of virtuous is vicious."

"Come come," Inez said, "that's an oversimplification, isn't it?"

"The temperance is," I said.

Maybe Mrs. Roosevelt had given me *the answer.*

I didn't like it. To be honest—I knew inside me that this was the answer though I couldn't exactly apply it.

I thought of Pearl Morton, who ran a house of ill-fame, and Mabel Normand, and Mother Meyer and Anne Morrow Lindbergh and Pat O'Toole's mother and Eleanor Roosevelt. Virtuous women!

There is a strange thing here too. I have searched every morgue in the Hearst Service. My blessed Dorothy Hertz, who does my Library of Congress research, has combed them.

We cannot find the story I most certainly should have done on Mrs. Roosevelt's appearance at the Third Term Convention. There is the one on the Voice from the Sewers, and Carter Glass's crying No Third Term and Jim Farley alias Doc Kearns and the Fog over the Democrats—but the one about Mrs. Roosevelt's speech and how she got her husband's selected candidate for V.P. nominated when everyone said it was a hopeless task is not there anywhere.

I do not remember writing it that night.

Perhaps in my despair at the size of the Mountain before me, the length of the Journey ahead before I could see the Gates of the Beloved Country—before I could know even a taste of the sweetness of the Honeycomb—perhaps I went out and fell headlong into the Slough of Despond, beyond the Town of Carnal Policy where things seemed so easy—and there I was overtaken by the Perils of Darkness called too many martinis.

Could it be that for the only time in my life, in a vast discouragement, I failed to file my story?

I can't think of anybody left who would know.

Yet somewhere I know sounded a note of hope—for it *was* the answer. I had an answer. When I got guts enough to face it, I could sort it out.

CHAPTER 37

I had thought I was through with the King and Mrs. Simpson and/or the Duke and Duchess of Windsor.

Then there I was again.

Gentlemen, the King.

This time it was another king, but the man who proposed the age-old toast that had held the Empire together was the man who had been King. Among those memories that are my life it seems to me that no imagination in all its glory could better this scene of Theater-in-the-Real, and it is as real to me today as it was when I wrote:

> *Nassau November 16*—This is one story that will be important one hundred years from now.
>
> Over the radio upon a day millions will never forget I heard the voice of a man introduced as Prince Edward say "And now we all have a new King, God Save the King."
>
> Four years later.
>
> A little tropical island thousands of miles from that other island called England now fighting for her life.
>
> A man rose at one end of the dinner table. Opposite, a fragile woman in floating white stood watching him.
>
> The unmistakable voice spoke, "Ladies and Gentlemen, The King."
>
> The Duchess of Windsor touched her glass to her lips. And I stood opposite her while we drank the toast this time proposed by the man who had been King of England to his brother who was King of England.

They used to break glasses in which it had been drunk and for a moment I was tempted by the quixotic sentimental and moving drama around me to throw mine.

The Duke said to me and I quote, "I had been given a promise that if I abdicated I would serve the King, my brother, George VI, as I had served the King, our father, George V."

This promise was broken and in my time with this famous pair I came to believe it brought catastrophe, though I could understand why it was impossible to have two men in England who had been saluted as:

There was more to it than those amazing words but it comes later in the story.

When, shortly after the Third Term Convention, Mr. Hearst asked me to go to Nassau to write *At Long Last,* the Windsors' own story, I had the most disturbing dilemma of my many years as a reporter, for an open mind, an open heart, a reporter *must* have—and a woman *ought* to have.

Did I have either?

Since Alice in Wonderland days I had never cared for duchesses. *If everybody minded their own business said the Duchess, with a hoarse growl, the world would go round a good deal faster than it does. And talking of axes, said the Duchess, off with her head.*

I knew under what restrictions I would fly to the Bahamas. "You will have the complete co-operation of the Duke and Duchess," Mr. Hearst said. "You may send for our photographer when you are ready."

This was the deal made long ago at Fort Belvedere between the then King of England and the Power of the Press as exemplified by William Randolph Hearst, who had hoped I would be getting those first and only exclusive interviews with King Edward and Queen Wallis at Buckingham Palace.

"If we thus champion the cause of your marriage," Mr. Hearst may have said to King Edward, "we shall regard it as our story to whatever extent it is possible for you to make it so."

"I understand that," His Majesty would reply.

And the Duke of Windsor as Governor of the Bahamas would keep the King's word.

Thus I was to have full co-operation, even to exclusive pictures, whereas all other newspapers, magazines, and book companies had been turned away.

Here I must stop long enough to explain something that readers of newspapers, magazines, even viewers of news and features on television, do not appear to understand.

A doctor takes the Hippocratic oath. A lawyer swears to uphold the law. Bankers, heads of brokerage houses have moral obligations as well as congressional rulings to abide by as they offer a new issue of stock. Without these basic rules of honor and ethics beyond and outside the legal framework, no integrity would be maintained.

Under the moral code of honor, a member of the Free Press, protector of the United States of America, giver of truth so that people may make decisions so influenced, a reporter has *ethics.* Clearly defined, well understood by all honorable members of the Fourth Estate.

A reporter who gets a story *on his own* may do with it as he pleases, write anything he has dug up, subject only to accuracy and laws of libel.

On the other hand, if he is *admitted* to an interview with a leading news figure, whether in the White House or the Death House, under any kind of an agreement, he is obligated to respect whatever the terms of it were. Surely it is easy to see why, for both sides, this must be true. If the reporter is given exclusive, newsworthy, important inside information or quotes, or a news story, and the public is clamoring to read this, he must use it only within the terms he accepted in order to *get it at all.*

Half a loaf is better than no bread. The best butter, if it's only a few dabs, is more than no butter at all. Three sentences of *nothing but the truth* aren't to be scoffed at because you can't get *the whole truth.*

Unlike Cromwell, I was pretty sure the Duke and Duchess did not want to be painted warts and all. Who does? Mr. Hearst was sure what his readers wanted. If I went to Nassau he'd hope I'd be sitting in a seat where it looked to me as though Happy Ending won the Love Story of the Century Handicap.

"To start with the truth," I said, "I've lost my taste for the Windsors."

"Surely not your curiosity," Mr. Hearst said, chuckling.

"With very little effort—" I said.

It came over me that it was *odd*—I had written thousands upon *thousands* of words about them, I had never really met either of them. I couldn't help wondering a little what they were like.

"What people are curious about makes news," Mr. Hearst said. "Before you wrote The Real Mrs. Simpson there were not five hundred women in the United States who had ever heard of her. Now I doubt if there are five hundred who will not be deeply interested in what you find out about their life today and especially in what, for the first time, they have to tell you about their own love and about his abdication."

My breath had begun that old occupational hazard—ta-pocketa—pocketa —pocketa—Oh, I had curiosity. Of course I had. I had pride, too, and we would get the inside on a story everybody in my profession wanted. But—under an honorable agreement. *No warts. A Happy Ending.*

"Mr. Hearst," I said, "will I be allowed to write the truth?"

Very quietly, he said, "You need not write anything but the truth. Let us cross the bridge of what is the truth in this case when we come to it."

I found Runyon at his usual table at Lindy's.

I said, "Bill Shirer says Hitler started the war with one desire, to humble a British duke to whom he will always feel inferior. The English who stand between us and the Huns were belittled and humiliated and snickered at because their King left them. All right—all right—they have a New King. And Queen and Princesses. Just the same how can I write any glowing Prisoner of Zenda Old Heidelberg As You Like It romances about the one who deserted them?"

"Who asked you to?" Runyon said.

"*You* know—" I began.

"Has Mr. Hearst asked you to be judge or jury?" Damon said. "I thought he wanted to send you to the Bahamas as a reporter. Have you got yourself so emotionally involved you can't do your job? Nobody asked you to *think*. You were a flop as a columnist, because those are supposed to be *think* pieces. This is a Love Story, always news, bigger in time of war. If Mr. Hearst has picked you as the best reporter he has to cover this one, why don't you just go and do it?"

"What about the truth?" I said.

"What about it?" Damon said, pouring us more coffee. "Write what you see and what you can't print put away and use in your autobiography."

"My autobiography," I said in horror. "That'll be the day!"

How was I to know I was going to outlive almost everybody?

"You hollered to keep Hauptmann from the chair, as long as there were questions to be answered," Damon said. "Nobody cut off Mrs. Simpson's head. She can still answer a lot of those we'd like to hear. What did he see in her? Was it worth it? Would they do it over again? Are they still in love? Why did she get her divorce in the first place? Did the King's mother try to persuade her to go away? Did they consider morganatic marriage? What was her thought of the best way out of this dilemma? With the war going on, have they a sense of guilt? Do *you* realize—" he fixed me with a cold eye and said, "do you realize that they have answered no questions for any one? You will hear their own story of things everyone has asked questions about. Go and report."

Just then Arnold Rothstein came and sat in his corner where nobody could get behind him, a lot of good that did him, they got him on the back staircase as he sneaked out of the Park Central Hotel around the corner and Runyon wrote his classic short story "The Brain Goes Home."

I thought to myself even Rothstein quails before Runyon's cold eye. All good reporters have that eye. Certainly *I* never talked back to Runyon.

2

Tall, handsome, aristocratic, a sprinkling of silver in his hair, Major Grey Phillips, chief aide-de-camp to the Governor of the Bahamas, His Royal Highness the Duke of Windsor, met me as I stepped from the clipper.

Finding me a place to live (under the circumstances I hadn't wanted to be a house guest) hadn't been easy. Out of season, all the huge resort hotels were closed. Obviously, Major Phillips didn't approve of the American Consul's choice, a combination inn and boardinghouse, but it was a lucky one for me. Run by an enchanting old woman—a *character* in colonial British—I forgave her a pack of what seemed twenty or thirty dogs who greeted me with growls and yelps morning noon or night, because nothing went on in Nassau or the Out Islands she didn't know about. She could tell me what the ladies said at the last Red Cross meeting, who of the best families had a touch of the tarbrush, the number of people who would like to murder Sir Harry Oakes (one of them eventually did), and the reaction of every one of Nassau's fifteen thousand population to the arrival of their former King and the woman for whom he'd given up his throne. This was helpful.

The major said the Duchess would receive me immediately. If he came back in an hour would that give me sufficient time?

Within five minutes, I knew that the Tropics are a reality and different from mere heat like a Washington summer. I showered *again,* before the icy water was dry I was wet with sweat. My clothes adhered when I tried to put them on. My powder mixed with perspiration and looked like a mudpack. Later, the Duchess told me to ice my face, but this was ineffectual so I eschewed make-up for the duration.

Nor did it help my temperature that I was wrestling with an ever-mounting excitement. From the moment we took off from Washington, where I'd stopped for international briefing, I'd felt myself growing more and more tense as the meeting with the Duke and Duchess grew closer.

Runyon's questions were a tom-tom in my head.

What *did* he see in her? Why Anne Boleyn? And though Nelson's Lady Hamilton was a beauty and posed as statues of Greek goddesses she hadn't been the British cup of tea. Considering all I knew, all I'd said, all I'd heard since the abdication four years ago, as the flying boat swept down from the skies and the tiny brilliant island of Nassau appeared, I was *afraid.*

This man has done more harm to the British Empire than any man who ever lived. Ramsay MacDonald had said that.

Save our King at any price, Winston Churchill had cried with tears.

A friend had asked Wallis Simpson why she hadn't gone away sooner, and Mrs. Simpson had answered, *He would have followed me wherever I went, it wouldn't have done any good, he would have followed me.*

He had followed her.

From King of England to public relations in a Winter Resort?

Or from hell to heaven?

Bluntly, it was my business to find out.

Major Phillips drove me through Nassau up the little hill to Government House, through narrow too picturesque streets filled with natives and animals. I saw large land crabs sashaying up the sidewalks, we passed small dilapidated buggies drawn by skinny horses, and far far beyond rose the tourist hotels, shimmering in the heat.

I looked instead at the major's profile. Forbidding was the word for it. Nonetheless, said I to myself, you are the head aide-de-camp, you've been sent to help me, not make it any hotter.

"How do I address the former King, Major Phillips?" I said pleasantly.

"You will address him as Your Highness or Sir, as you please," said the major, "and refer to him as His Royal Highness."

"Do I curtsy?" I said.

"As you please," he said.

"And the Governor's lady?" I said.

"You will address her as Duchess," he said, "and refer to her as the Duchess."

"Not Her Grace or Her Highness or *anything?*" I said.

I knew of course that soon after their marriage, at which no member of his family was present, King George VI had informed his brother by mail—with regret—that the Cabinet had decided that while the Duke should continue to use the title of Royal Highness, this belonged to him by birth as a prince of the House of Windsor, it could not be stretched to include the Duchess, his wife. Since it had been customary in the past to extend the title, I had been told making an exception of his wife really hurt the Duke. He was, I had been warned, very *touchy* about her and resentful of any possible slur indicating that she wasn't as good as anybody else.

All this I knew but I thought I'd better begin to remind this haughty aide that I was there by His Royal Highness's invitation given while he was still the King.

"She does not share his title," Major Phillips said. "You call her Duchess—that's all."

"How about this island?" I said. "Do I call it Nassau or refer to it as St. Helena?"

The car slithered, natives scurried, the major's glance at me revealed that in spite of all efforts I still looked dangerous and unpleasant to him. I had put on, it being now barely ten o'clock in the morning, a white cotton dress, with a brown belt and low-heeled brown shoes, and a brown chiffon handkerchief in the pocket as a *touch,* I thought it correct and rather fetching myself, plainly the major disagreed with me.

He said, "His Royal Highness is governor of a British possession, the Bahamas. Nassau is the capital."

After that, we drove in silence unless he could hear my increasing heart-beat, drumming away, or the perspiration trickling down my back like Niagara Falls.

The Windsors. No longer the King and Mrs. Simpson. He *had* married her. As soon as her divorce was final they'd been married in a rather horrid château in France, after difficulty finding a clergyman to perform the ceremony, they'd lived in Paris and left with the other refugees, they'd rented a villa on the Riviera where Somerset Maugham entertained them at dinner.

My mind passed this in review as we drove through the sparkling day, amid such lush tropical green as I'd never seen. Against all this, Government House was tall, columned, white, and glistening; it must have reminded the Duchess of her childhood, of Wakefield Manor and other Southern mansions in Virginia and Maryland. It looked cool from the outside but inside, I soon found, it had no more air-conditioning now than they'd had.

The whole place, not to put too fine a point upon it, was a *mess*.

While I had not exactly expected the Duchess to be surrounded by perfumed lovesick waves like Cleopatra on the Nile, it still seems odd to me that the smell that most reminds me of Wallis of Windsor is wet paint and damp plaster. Major Phillips explained hurriedly that the Duchess had started to do Government House over and found termites and dry rot so that it had necessitated a complete rebuilding and redecorating job. She was supervising the whole operation and so had an office there, though they were living in a rented house called Sigrist.

Was it for this I uttered prayers, and sobbed and cursed and kicked the stairs that now, domestic as a plate, all I do is decorate?

Yet—*he* was here. They were together on this Calypso Isle and as we drove along the waterfront I had heard mellow native calypso song.

Had it been worth it? Was this the best answer to that tragic choice— My throne or the woman I love?

I got an answer to that soon enough. Unexpectedly, without having to ask a question, straight from the shoulder.

What is she really like?

I walked wide in the corridor to avoid going under a ladder and I got the answer to that, too.

What did he see in her? took longer.

A bare little room, streaked, white plaster walls, a cracked ceiling, wooden floor, a large modern desk, upon it telephones, inkstands, pens and pencils, and long sheets of paper with figures.

Behind it sat the Duchess of Windsor.

When I came to write my articles on that initial presentation—*Duchess, this is Mrs. St. Johns*—I wrote, "One of the things I remember best about it is the fact that I cannot for the life of me recall what the Duchess wore. This woman who has been called one of the world's best-dressed, who has set styles, who has been the pet of the great couturiers . . ." That's what I wrote. It was true. Later when my photographer Sam Shere came down we went back and took pictures of this room and she wore for those a white suit with large dark polka dots and a dark blouse with large white polka dots, but what she had on *that* morning, I donknow.

What was she like? I ask myself now, thirty years later.

I saw an American woman forty-two years old, she looked young for her age but I was instantly *aware* that she looked young for her age. The madonna hair-do was gone, the dark fine locks were brushed up and back and fell in a few ringlets on her neck. She looked like any other good-looking, well-groomed American woman of my generation, wearing the usual amount of make-up, and a very large corsage of jewels on her shoulder. Exactly like, no different. Any day I could see dozens of American women of her age, style, and general effect at Quo Vadis or "21". I was sure nobody would have followed her from Fifty-second Street a block in either direction on Fifth Avenue.

My *At Long Last* look at the Woman I love—the Real Mrs. Simpson.

Second glance. As she indicated a chair for me, I enjoyed the lightness and poised grace of her movement, she was thin—clothes-horse thin—I saw that she had a witty mouth, as so many women of her class do, and a punishing jaw line, Cousin Lelia had mentioned that.

At third look—it was my business to stare and she obviously was used to that—I realized again that she had really the most beautiful eyes I had ever seen in any woman's head. They were the same blue as her magnificent sapphire earrings, or maybe a little bluer. Under winged eyebrows, darkened lashes, they were beyond belief.

She had ugly hands. I thought of Cousin Lelia's *all the Montague women have beautiful hands.* Ah well, the Warfields were in railroads.

Perhaps that might also explain that while she had a look of breeding— she *moved* right—she did not have what we call *class,* and if you can find a real substitute or synonym for that please let me know.

As she asked me to sit down, asked about my flight, made me welcome, there it was. A lovely voice, the *English* English as the English speak it we now know so well, but the Southern accent got all mixed up with it. I was to discover that one or the other predominated according to mood or situation, and now I wonder if that was one reason she gave me *always* a slight feeling of artificiality.

"I did everything I could to prevent the abdication of the King, even though it might mean I would live to the end of my life—alone. I was not a young girl. But I would have chosen to keep him on his throne, where he would serve his people and the world." She said that hotly, definitely, with meaning. She said, "Someday you will know, you will understand what was done to him, the sacrifices he made. This man is—you will know—is almost a saint."

In those first hours she dwelt upon this theme. Her deep concern that this man, almost a saint? who had been Ambassador Extraordinaire, instead of being used in a world-wide position only he could fill, for which only the former Prince of Wales had been trained, he was wasted on this rock in the ocean. She was bitter. He would, she felt, be even better as once more a roving diplomat, with all his experience, than he would have been as King, for his experience had not been within the narrow confines of constitutional monarchy. That this man should be worrying about the failure of the sponge crop—"We are determined to do our duty like good soldiers and he—he bears it like a saint—but it is the world that suffers his loss."

Oh yes, this was St. Helena all right.

This time Josephine was there too.

At some moment in this conversation—interview—research—the Duchess stretched out her hand on which she wore only her plain wedding ring, and pushed a buzzer on one of the two telephones and into it she said, "Darling? Have you time to come in a moment?"

In my story that day I wrote, "I have seen it printed that these two famous lovers call each other 'dear.' They don't, they call each other 'darling' and the way they say it makes that much-abused word all new again, and fresh and sweet and personal. When he speaks of her to anyone else the Duke now calls her The Duchess, though for several years he did say Her Highness. Or if he is speaking to a friend—and later to me—he refers to her as Wallis, she *always* speaks of him as His Royal Highness or The Duke. She calls him David."

She turned from the phone to me and said, "The Duke will come in for a moment," and then I saw an expression I liked best of anything about her. Her face was simply a little brighter, her mouth was amused, but in her eyes there was a light, an expectation of happiness.

Outside, the sound of a hammer went on, a workman shouted, a telephone rang somewhere. It could have been any office anywhere in the building trade. Here I waited to meet the man who had been King of England, who had abdicated for this woman sitting beside me. I knew I still hadn't made up my mind about this man and the feeling in my stomach was a mixture of *hope* that I would see him as she had presented him—did I really want to see him as a sort of *martyr?*—and of dread that he would be what Howey had thought him on the night of the abdication.

No wonder my knees shook when I rose at his entrance.

He came in with eyes only for her. A man who, poised for a moment in the doorway, was the Prince of Wales. The King of Promise still. In the glaring tropical sunshine of that bare room what had happened—what would happen—made my heart skip a beat and as far as he was concerned I knew it would be my heart and not my head that wrote my story. When he smiled as I curtsied, as the nuns had taught me to do—I had not curtsied to the Duchess, how petty women can be—the personality that had held France enthralled, that had enraptured South America, that had blessed the poor on Maundy Thursday, cast a personality glow that I felt from tip to toe. In high spirits, the charm of his smile was as it had ever been, young and joyful. He stopped smiling. He was a haggard, almost middle-aged man.

He should not be kept here, where his genius is limited to sponges, she had said. "What are they afraid of? He *was* KING. All he had to do was stay." Surely they must summon him to bigger things.

Did he have a chance for this? Did he *hope* he had a chance?

At dinner that night in the rich, beflowered hall at Sigrist as he stood in the candlelight and said:

Gentlemen, the King!

I felt that he still had hope, he must have, the last ray was not yet out. Then the next minute I was sure he didn't, he knew he didn't have a chance to be recalled, who should know if not he? I could not make up my mind and it came to me that perhaps he couldn't either, that he still swung back and forth, he did, he didn't, he had, he hadn't—and what about her? *Surely,* she had said. Not perhaps, *surely.* So surely sometimes she had hope that they would summon him back to bigger things—but hopelessness is the most bitter of all things and she was bitter as wormwood.

I couldn't be sure of myself or of either of them.

3

As I read over the many full-page installments I wrote that carried this report, these accounts, to England and the Dominions, to all our states, to many countries, I found myself bewildered and puzzled by myself. My own reporting and writing.

I did not so much mind that it was not the whole truth. Within the terms of our agreement I never tried to get that.

I once explained this to Major Grey Phillips. I needed the help and good will of all His Highness' aides. Captain George Wood and his Viennese wife, Rosa, who gave me the full story of their flight with the Duke and Duchess from Paris as the Germans poured in. Captain Drury, the aide in charge of press relations, as well as the major, who continued to want no part of me or any other reporter. The major didn't like exile, either, and he made it so tough for me that one day when I'd waited for a confirmation of my appointment with the Duke, I sought Major Phillips out and said, "Please listen. In my first hour alone with the Duchess, in that office where you took me, I had quotes from her that would have rocked the British Empire. All I had to do was board the clipper that brought me and go back to New York. Ask the Duchess. You must have heard her opinion of the present Queen of England—the 'Dowdy Duchess.' Her witty and amusing speculations about the family life of the Royal Family. She is not discreet, Major Phillips. But I am keeping to our bargain, I didn't go. I am bound by my editorial word not to write anything that would prejudice the Duke's position at home. Mr. Hearst made that agreement, he will abide by it. Do relax and help me get an entertaining and glamorous story that is both news and a romance and will be true and help, not hurt, England."

While he thought this over I blurted out, "Will they ever let him return to help his brother?"

Major Phillips said, "No."

"But why?" I said.

He did not answer.

After that, though, he did help me and gave me final instructions on royal protocol, what I needed to make me comfortable with the Duke in any circumstances. I must not open a subject or ask questions until he had given me permission. I must never turn away or end a conversation and I must answer any question he asked me. Unexpectedly, this proved a most important thing for me to know.

So it could not be the whole truth I wrote.

Nothing but the truth—that is the point. For the only time in my life, as I read the photostats from the Library of Congress thirty years later, I was terrified. For myself. For my integrity as a reporter. For any value my reporting of major events might have to those coming after me, or in retrospect as an eyewitness account to form thinking or opinion of that time.

Here I say the Duchess has winged eyebrows and the only sapphire-blue eyes I ever saw. This is the whole truth and nothing but. In the scene I used to open this chronicle of my trip to Nassau—the *Gentlemen, the King* scene—I speak of a fragile woman in floating white and follow thenceforth with gushes of adjectives, which I dislike per se.

Frail—tiny—delicate—floating—graceful—dainty. My memory forces me to say I saw her like that at the first dinner.

Yet my deepest recording insists I always had the impression that Wallis Warfield Windsor could play tackle for the Green Bay Packers.

What happened to me?

After several all-night sessions with myself, researching my own copy, my spirits began to lift. At last my subconscious or whatever that innermost life force guarding our own truth—our hearts maybe?—showed me that instead of having betrayed that truth and my work, here was the true mystery of good reporting as I had tried to find it, as near as I ever got to it. To get inside the skin of the person the reporter is covering. To hear what he hears, feel what he feels.

What fooled me was that though I spent more time with her, it was getting inside his skin that was important and that I tried to do. I never tried to get inside hers, actually I couldn't have cared less.

Let me be honest.

From the moment Major Phillips presented me to her, I did not like the Duchess of Windsor.

I am sure the feeling was mutual.

Time did not alter it for me. I just didn't like her.

I think I can safely say that she did not win popularity in Nassau.

She made mistakes. You can't afford to make mistakes with British colonials.

They in Nassau had been quite satisfied with Government House. True, it turned out to be filled with termites, but they didn't think it was *her* place so *soon,* without consulting any of the island's long-resident ladies, to take the portraits of the Duke's ancestors, Queen Victoria and George IV, down from the walls and get a New York decorator to match their color to *her* powder puff.

"Put 'er in a 'ole, it did," my landlady said.

In church the first Sunday I was there I sat directly behind the Duke, who was having trouble in a cutaway and striped trousers trying to scratch prickly heat between his shoulder blades. Words that didn't belong came thumping into my head to the hymn tune we were singing:

> I am sick of the endless sunshine, sick of
> Blossomed-burdened bough,
> Give me back the leafless woodland
> Where the winds of autumn range,
> Give me back one day in England, for
> It's fall in England now.

My landlady lent me a hat to go to church in and came along with me. In my ear she expressed the same thought in simpler words, "I expect he gets a bit homesick now and then, poor fellow," and as the service ended she said, "*She* didn't come to church, did she?" I said I hadn't seen her.

As we were walking home, it came to me that unless I could show the way of this man with this maid my story would limp. I had never known the Real Mrs. Simpson. Now I was having the opportunity to know the Duchess of Windsor, to talk to her, attend Red Cross meetings with her, dine with her and her husband.

So far, I saw what *I* saw.

This wouldn't be good enough!

This wasn't the point.

The one fact I was sure of from the beginning was that this man loved this woman. Therefore he did not see what I saw. To make this story flow with romance and tragedy, the One Woman must be believable. So I must see her as he saw her, I must see him as he looked at her, hear his tones as he spoke to her. *Here she is.*

I am she.

Only poetry speaks truly of this.

> That not impossible she
> That can command my heart and me.

Is a man lucky to know this no matter who she is or what the price? Only if I could get inside his skin could I see her so and make my readers understand why he had given up everything for her, sacrificed country, family, work, friends to be at her side day and night, night and day forever.

All this came clear for me upon a night in Nassau when I attended an exclusive ball at the famed Emerald Bay Club. It was given for the Bahama Red Cross Air Raid Fund under the patronage of His Royal Highness the Governor and the Duchess of Windsor. There I saw them dance together.

It comes back in beauty under a tropical moon. They opened the ball—she in white chiffon showered with roses, yards floating from her shoulders like wings, billowing in clouds under her feet, not her style in the past—nor in the future of Suzy's devastating columns. Moonlight outside, lanterns within, flowers and perfume everywhere, music to make a man dream. She moved lightly enough, but the Duke's dancing was as elegant as Fred Astaire's. He had again the air of a conquering hero, he had her in his arms now forever, and in that awed silence filled with music his head was thrown back and the close cap of golden hair was bright and he was the King again. Nobody moved or breathed.

Fading sweetly, the music was gone, they came back and he sat down beside the wife of the American Consul and the consul whispered to me with tears in his voice, *It does seem such a shame, doesn't it?* For now, close up, a little weary, we could see the ravaged face of the ex-King, and a calypso song drifted up to us from the beach.

> Last night I dreamt I saw
>   the King of England going to war.
> In his left hand he had a banner, in his
>   right hand he had a sword,
> And that's the way we conquer Germany—
>   some Sunday soon.

We were seeing strictly a Musical now, but across those seas was that old isle where the King of England had gone to war and was fighting to save its life from Germany some Sunday soon.

I hoped no one could see that I was crying.

"To the very last," he told me, *to the very last,* the Duke of Windsor told me as we sat in his office-study, "until it actually happened, I simply did not believe it. I was sure that humanity, remembering the last war, having seen the horror and the waste, would find a way to avoid this war. With all my heart, I believed that. Nor was I alone."

At his feet lay the boxes—the red leather and the blue leather, the rectangle outlined on the covers in gold, and the lion and the unicorn were fighting for the crown above the gold letters that spelled *THE KING.*

These he had taken with him that dark night when he went aboard a Navy ship and sailed through the fog into exile—that ended here. I wondered if the thought was in his mind, too. IF he had stayed, IF the papers of destiny had come to him in those boxes, IF he had made that visit to Hitler not as an ex but a crowned king—

Our eyes met in that silence; they had to. Yes, we were both shuffling that IF deck. I knew a reporter must read minds as well as lips and eyes and upside-down telephone numbers.

I could not ask him—not just the protocol in which Major Phillips had instructed me, at the moment I would have dropped Major Phillips and all his works into Mount Popocatepetl—I could not ask this man so terribly sad sad sad all the time under the high spirits and the unchanged smile whether IF he had known there was to be a war he would have stayed on his throne—how could you ask that question? No man can turn back the clock, not even the Defender of the Faith.

I knew the answer.

And so the next time I saw the Duchess I felt even more antagonism, though I believed utterly that she had tried to prevent his abdication.

We are happy together, she said to me often.

I got my divorce, she said, because I came to believe that the King would go quite mad if I did not. If I had gone away, run away, even tried to hide, he would have followed me and found me. When I finally did go to France to stay with my friends the Rogerses, as seemed wisest in the crisis, he was afraid for me in London, he telephoned me all day long. Remember it was while we were separated, in spite of my public plea and my offer to withdraw, that he abdicated.

All that she told me. I remember now that the night at the Emerald Bay Club he had kept moving seat by seat around the table until at last he sat beside her.

I am she and I am here and you must follow me.

Completely different was a dinner at the home of Captain Wood and his wife Rosa. That night we dined on the balcony overlooking the shining water and the blossom-burdened bough. I sat on the Duke's right, with Mrs. Wood on his left, and the Duchess down the length of the brilliant tropical cloth-and-wood table and the masses of fruit and flowers in brilliant colors. For the opening hour the talk was general. The Duke was interested in the Movies; the Duchess said, leaning toward him, "Darling, Mrs. St. Johns knows Mickey Rooney," which indeed I did, so we discussed the Mick and the hours of joy he had given us. Then I told them something of Wakefield Manor, the Duchess' ancestral home in Virginia, as I'd seen it recently. His Royal Highness was honestly curious, too, about why we Americans cut things and transfer our fork back to the right hand to eat it, while I, regaining courage from his ease, admitted that *we* thought it odd to make a brick of your food on the back of your fork and eat it with your left hand. The Duchess, I wrote later, was that night in floating pale blue organdy, so very small and lovely in the candlelight, a tiny fairy crown of diamonds in her dark hair.

Good for me! *That was the way he saw her.*

Then he asked me a point-blank question.

"I have never understood," he said, "why there was such a hostile reaction and response to my broadcast to the United States from Verdun. Do you remember that?" I said that I did, of course. He said, "Do you know why it was received with so much antagonism?"

I glanced at Major Phillips, sitting beside the Duchess. Answer any questions he asks, he had instructed me. Now he gave me a faint grin.

The former King's eyes were on me. He said again, "Do you know?"

I said, "Yes, sir, I know." I was having trouble with my throat, it closed up tight. He said, "I would like you to tell me."

All right, he asked for it. I saw both Major Phillips and Captain Wood staring at me in wary concern. My embarrassment had alerted them.

"In my country, sir," I said—*damn,* my voice is too *loud*—"we have a tradition of enormous sympathy for a pinch hitter. A pinch hitter, in case that sports term isn't familiar to you, sir, is a man who, when a star is injured or out of the lineup or in a slump, is sent in for him. He bats for him in a pinch, when the game may be won or lost. He is a substitute. He is on the spot. All American hearts go out to someone who is, let us say, pinch-hitting for Babe Ruth. We are rooting for him, poor guy, to do well, get a home run, win the ball game."

"I understand this," the Duke said quietly, he had turned all the way toward me, his eyes intently fixed upon me.

"To us, sir, your brother King George VI was, in our eyes, a pinch hitter. When you left the game he came in as a *substitute.* You were a great and popular star, sir. He, with some handicaps we had heard about, and without your build-up, was suddenly called on to take your place." I took a long breath, I wasn't sure I'd ever get another one, I said, "We felt it wasn't right for *you* to appear in an heroic role and speak from a battlefield in *France* when he was trying so hard to bat in your place, to get a hit—as though Babe Ruth ran up and down the sidelines hitting fungoes when a pinch hitter was at the plate in his stead."

I ended in a vacuum of silence. I couldn't turn away. I'd been told that, but after a long moment he did and he spoke to the whole table, smiling at his wife. He had a constant sensitivity about her, he was super-attentive to her at all times, he always took pains to include her at once, he said, "Do you know that the Duchess was the first woman who ever spoke to me about my *work?*" He mentioned then the speech he made after he became King, he said, "I used to discuss my speeches with her even then—that phrase *I am still the same man*—that was hers. The Verdun speech, we thought that any man who had an opportunity to speak for peace should do so. It was meant only as a plea for peace."

It flashed over me then—that phrase "The woman I love—I cannot carry my burdens as King as I would wish to do without the help and support of the woman I love," must have been hers, given to him, perhaps, in one of those long phone calls to France. I had never understood that sentence. It seemed strange for one of England's royalty to refer *in public* to the woman he loved in those words.

It's not done.

And when *it's not done* they don't do it.

From the violation of this English attitude of understatement and reticence might have come some of the antagonism to this woman at the end of the table who was his wife but not his queen. His farewell broadcast reached us in America and touched our hearts. Why not? He wasn't our king.

Major Phillips walked back with me through a glorious scented night. I was glad of his arm down the steps, for I was still shaking with emotion, with exhaustion. If my frankness had offended him he would have something to say about it, so I opened on an offense, "Why not make him Ambassador to the United States? We've always loved him and now he's got an American wife. Or—the French don't love the English, even when the English are fighting for them again, but they did adore the Prince of Wales, why not send him to *France*—wouldn't these be strategic moves?"

He said, "You say you lived in the time of our great Elizabeth, then you must know even that puissant and propitious princess had to cut Mary Stuart's head off in the end. Mary was a thorn; troublemakers, fanatics, those who opposed Elizabeth's strong financial policies, her

Protestantism, formed plots and parties to depose the Queen, and put Mary on her throne. Remember the War of the Roses—red or white, York or Lancaster? Our history is full of such things. Two kings in England will not do."

"*Of England you mean*," I said, "he wouldn't be *in* England, he'd be in Washington or Paris—"

"Very well," he said, "of England. You will say things such as Richard II and Bolingbroke, or Richard III and the Stanleys and Richmonds cannot happen in our time, but the blood of every Englishman tells him differently. Only a year ago we were sure a war could not happen in our time."

My heart sank, I could see what he meant. I thought he was wrong, there must be a way to use this man, but I could see that it was more difficult than I'd known and I had to fight off a chill of apprehension foretelling the end of all hope for His Royal Highness and '*is Mrs. Simpson*. The woman he loved.

Write what you see, Runyon had said. This turned out to be what I could understand of what *he* saw.

What you can't use now or haven't room for, Runyon had said, put away for your autobiography.

And I do find bits and pieces, things you tuck away because you can't quite bear to throw them out and are sure you'll find use for them someday.

Often these etchings or Currier and Ives prints or friendly mezzotints make a living room come to life.

The work at Government House was in that dreadful period when you are sure it can never be brought together again. As we came down the still stately front steps the Duchess said with feeling, with vehemence, "Don't you see I must make a home for him? That's why I'm doing this place over, so we can live in it with comfort as a home. All his life he has traveled and a palace to come back to is not always a home. The only one he ever had he made for himself at Fort Belvedere, he had to leave it, you don't know what that meant to him. I must make him a home—"

After a Red Cross meeting at which the Governor's lady had presided, a poster in Red Cross uniform, she took me along the waterfront and showed me what the Duke was trying to do for the natives. "He will always," she said, "want to improve living conditions, wherever he goes. That was why he went to Wales, you remember. He was their prince and he wanted to improve the conditions in the Rhondda Valley coal mines."

Chuckling, that night after they had opened the ball at the Emerald Bay Club, he said, "It was nice dancing with Wallis again after a whole year.

But of course when I waltz with her, I have to reverse so often I don't know where I am—and in a waltz you're supposed to keep on twirling and twirling." The Duchess said, "But twirling makes me dizzy." "Not dizzy, darling," said His Royal Highness, "*giddy*." "It may make you giddy," the American Duchess said, suddenly going all Southern accent, "but it makes me dizzy." "Oh quite quite," said her husband, "but either way one can't twirl, can one?" "No darling," said his wife, "one can't." And they were laughing.

I always have a vignette, and I treasure it, of them leaning against each other, laughing.

There were pictures of his mother, Queen Mary, in jeweled frames, in the triptych with Queen Victoria and Queen Alexandra. Never at any time did His Royal Highness speak of her. I knew that in September of 1939 the Duke returned to England with the Duchess. I believe he saw his mother, and Princess Elizabeth, who on his abdication had become heiress to the throne. He was her favorite uncle. But as far as I could find out the Duchess did not accompany him on these visits and never saw Queen Mary but once—and then only on a group visit.

Over and over and over, the former King spoke of his father, King George V. "I am going to write a book," he said, "to show what a great man and great ruler he was. As a diplomat, as head of a nation, I do not think there has been his equal in this century. You remember how he tried to tell President Wilson that the true task of the head of a nation was to inform and instruct his people, to keep them aware of all issues, to protect their interests. My father dissolved Parliament when he thought it was not serving the people's interests and desires. That was why he warned Woodrow Wilson that he must not go to Paris and enter into contest, he must let ministers battle and fight for gains and advantages. The head of state could not enter into heated negotiations or make deals, as it is called. He sent his prime minister, Lloyd George, to the conference table. So that when His Majesty spoke it was the final word. If the President of the United States had not so involved himself in the controversy, all history would have been different."

Here again—how could this man have so betrayed everything his father had stood for, everything his father had taught him? When I listened to him as I did as he spoke with *reverence* of that dedicated constitutional monarch George V, I always turned to look at the Duchess. I still had trouble believing it.

Samuel Shere, our best photographer, was with me in Nassau to get our exclusive pictures in this setting of these two, who had been so much photographed and newsreeled. His Royal Highness *always* stood behind the camera, watching, suggesting, overseeing when Sam was photographing the Duchess.

One morning when she stood against a mantelpiece in the library wearing a blue flannel suit and a vest of bright coral, nothing seemed to satisfy Mr. Shere. Finally, he turned to His Royal Highness and said, "D'you see, sir, if you'll look, I'll show you why the Duchess has been—well—practically libeled by cameras. Her high cheekbones make a shadow that isn't really there and those shadows make—that's what makes her *nose*—look so—as if it was out of proportion—I want to get rid of those, I've got to, or the people who look at them won't ever see her as she is." The Duke got behind and peered, he said, "Quite—quite. How extraordinary! I've always wondered." Then he began to move reflectors, and finally he stood up on a table—"Do take your shoes off, darling," Wallis said—and held a huge spotlight lamp at an extraordinary angle, if you like.

Could it be that he had always wondered why the people didn't see what he saw?

When we began to take him in color he appeared at once in his kilts. "I thought," he said, smiling shyly, "if we're going to do color we might as well have lots of it—and these are nice, aren't they? They're handwoven by the Scots. D'you think they'll photograph?"

He brought down his own camera, he was fascinated by the mechanical aspects, but when Mr. Samuel Shere started to explain something that the Duke said he found a bit bothersome the Duchess said, "David darling, you two run down to the other end of the porch and talk about *that*. It only means trouble for me, as you have just expounded I am not photogenic, but I shall have to pose endlessly while His Royal Highness tries it all out. Of course I will, it amuses him so much, but I do get tired."

That night Sammy came to me and asked if he could telephone New York and have them send down by air such discoveries as an expert realized the Duke needed for his color photography. I cannot remember now what these were—new color film, new cameras, new lenses—they arrived and no boy on Christmas morning was ever so pleased as the Duke of Windsor. Probably Sam Shere now looked to him like Santa Claus and that may be why he once said to Sam a few lines that answered questions I might never have had the courage to ask. They'd gone to the golf course for some shots of His Royal Highness and as they strolled from hole to hole Sam, who had photographed literally *everybody,* told him that often he found people different from the way gossip painted them.

"Quite, quite," the Duke said, "I myself was never in the Ritz Bar in Paris in my entire life. Yet to hear the tales told I spent a fair proportion of my life there. As Mark Twain—your great man—once remarked the stories of my overindulgence in alcohol have been greatly exaggerated.

The bags under my eyes, y'know, are not alcoholic, they're hereditary. Look at my sainted great-grandmother Victoria."

We did—and they could have been hereditary, they certainly could.

The Duchess was making out her daily menus one day—she made them out every day—*I must make him a home*—when Rosa Wood came in. The Duchess was called out and Rosa Wood, a delightful and distinguished European, watched her go and said, "She is not easy to know. But whether you wish it or not, you get to know anyone extremely well in the terrors and discomforts of such a trip as we made together in our flight from Paris when the Germans came. They were wonderful, both of them. Never a complaint, never a protest, nothing but courage and trying to help others."

I thought how pleased Cousin Lelia of Virginia, where the Montague women had endured the many battles of the Civil War with courage and spirit, would be to hear this when I got back to Washington. And she was.

"Do you think it has been worth it?" I said to Rosa Wood, and after a moment she said, "I don't think that has much to do with it, do you? He could no more have helped it than the tide can refuse to obey the moon."

Leaving Nassau, I had come at last to believe that the King and Mrs. Simpson, the Duke and Duchess of Windsor, were real people, not characters I'd made up as Margaret Mitchell made up Rhett Butler and Scarlett O'Hara.

Most of the questions had been answered at the time I wrote my final installment:

> George VI is sure now of his hold on the hearts of his people whose dangers in war he has shared. Why not the Duke of Windsor in his old place, which he himself believes better suited to him than the Throne he gave up?
>
> He has found that support from the woman he loves without which he once said he could not go on. I know he is willing to serve the Empire "in any capacity" but I think history will record it with pain and sadness if his gifts are wasted when humanity needs them.
>
> If they had it to do over again, they would do exactly as they did then. But he was sure then that there would be no war, had he known I believe it would have changed his decision then.
>
> I have seen a man and woman who bear each other a great love. I am sure he still hopes that the English love of fair play will grant him a chance to serve them to the full once again.

That was The End at Long Last of the Windsors Own Love Story. It sold far beyond our expectations and it comforts me now to see that I wrote it from inside his skin as much as I could.

I came back to America filled with anxiety. The Duke and Duchess intended to come to the United States soon. I felt a cloud of dark foreboding concerning this visit.

For if he sometimes had ebullient hope, I felt sure that little by little she was losing hers. The endless enervating days without any word showed her the winds were against them. She would never be called Your Royal Highness now.

Perhaps that explains what she did when they arrived in America.

4

DO	*DON'T*
Land somewhere other than New York.	Go to a big New York Hotel.
	Bring much luggage!!!!!!!
Go to Wakefield Manor, the Duchess' ancestral home, as the first stop.	Have too many servants.
	Wear Jewelry.
Wait for the White House to move before making any social engagement.	Attend any parties in either Washington or New York unless guests are carefully checked.
Keep very strictly to all war-time regulations.	Same about Wakefield Manor.
	DO NOT GO to cafes or restaurants at first.
Bring as small a staff as is possible to do with and as little luggage.	

BE SURE TO

Consult the heads of our Press, this as Press is an international matter in war-time and they will wish to help and advise you. William Randolph Hearst, Roy Howard, Kent Cooper, Sulzberger, Ogden Reid, Roy Roberts, Colonel McCormick

I found these scrawls among the few notes I kept, the DO in black, the DON'T in red ink. They are suggestions I worked out with Captain Vyvyan Drury—who, as the Duke's aide, came to handle press in New York—both before I left Nassau and when he arrived in America shortly after I did. Their purpose was to establish good public relations for the Duke and Duchess of Windsor in the United States, her homeland.

The negatives didn't register. Or, as I feared, she had already made up her mind, for she did those things she ought not to have done, and left undone those things she ought to have done. In full command of all plans for her return to her native land for the first time since she had become the most famous woman in the world, free to determine the course they should take, she went to the Waldorf, where they took an entire floor, brought more trunks than the harassed customs men could count, *all* her dogs, maids, a full staff AND all her jewels, including those the King had personally inherited from his grandmother, Queen Alexandra, whose oldest grandchild he was. These were his to bestow on his wife and she brought them in her jewel cases and wore them as soon as possible.

Though at one time he had expressed to me, in the Duchess' presence, much interest in her home—"I do so much want to see where Wallis spent her childhood, and to meet her family," he had said, perhaps not being able to present her to his family he felt they should have *somebody* —in spite of this eager interest on his part they did not go to Wakefield Manor. In New York they began almost at once to go about in what was then known as Café Society and though the British Embassy did its best and His Royal Highness Prince Edward was received by the President, the Duke and Duchess of Windsor did not receive an invitation to the White House.

Mrs. Roosevelt had been willing, but the Secretary of State and the President had vetoed it.

The Duchess was neither color blind nor stupid.

Yet definitely, defiantly, she went against everything that was calm, discreet, patient, tactful wise and proper to win the approbation of her own countrymen and women and gain her the recognition at the White House that was essential to any chance the Duke had of a return to England for service like unto that of the time when he was the idolized Prince of Wales. Much later the young Queen Elizabeth might invite her favorite Uncle David *and* his American wife, a family gesture with no real meaning, but this was the end of any recognition there.

The *Waldorf?* Not the type of hotel the Carlyle was to become—the Waldorf was theatrical, movie, front page, the spotlight upon it. Big movie companies kept suites there for visits their stars paid to New York. All this the Duchess was told. Captain Drury had shown her the lists he had finally made up and explained them to her.

As I think of it my heart sinks a little.

I am ashamed that I didn't like her, who am I to have such likes and dislikes? Yet for the first time I felt a profound sorrow and sympathy for her. Plainly, she knew that the promises of which she had been told, if they were not merely vague hints blown into promises, would never be kept. She knew as clearly as Major Phillips had explained it to me.

There could not be two Kings of England in the days of war and the crash of postwar madness that must follow. Red Rose White Rose— Great Elizabeth and Mary of Scotland—Richard and Bolingbroke.

But I believe there was much more to it than that.

Her bitterness, dark and real and terrible, against the waste of this man's gifts, was partly for herself. They had sat out St. Helena as good soldiers—that wasn't her idea of a *life*. Now with years and years ahead of them, growing older years, what would they do with their lives, with the days? The world may be well lost for love but it isn't *lost*, really, it's still there to be lived in, still there with its leaden hours.

Going back over my the Real Mrs. Simpson, I have to find Mrs. Worldly-Wise herself, long a popular twirling resident of Vanity Fair. A debutante in Southern society. A glamour girl at her level in Washington, where it was long rumored a South American ambassador would have married her but for the religious obstacle of her first divorce. In London, again a romance that eventually led to her marriage to Ernest Simpson, the goal of presentation at Court arranged by her friend, Viscountess Furness, then again the most worldly success of the King's love. Maybe she didn't like publicity, as the King suggested when he said he was trying to shield her from it, but it was a heady mixture just the same to be the most famous woman in the World of Vanity Fair. I remembered eight-year-old Little Gloria Vanderbilt looking out a window and saying, "Where are my photographers?" Now for years the Duchess had been the center of the stage, of a spotlight, of clamoring crowds—the hottest news any American woman had ever been.

She was NOT the woman to be willing to serve by standing and waiting on some isle where the crabs walked up and down on the sidewalks and the only people were British colonials who looked down their noses and they have very long noses to look down, British colonials do, and hordes of natives. No no, not the woman to live in semiretirement, a world well lost for love. To serve in remote parts of Empire if there were any left. Never. She followed, as most people do, her own tastes and desires. Her chief interests were clothes, jewels, parties, society that glittered, a place where her charm and her wit and her gift of Southern hospitality were important.

Once to Rosa Wood I said, "Did you ever hear her speak of children?" and Mrs. Wood said, "She was kind to the homeless children in France." I never heard her speak of a child; she'd been an only child herself; by three husbands she'd had none of her own, so *that* part of a Modern Woman's Three Problems had not come her way.

Nor had I ever heard her speak of any kind of religion or spiritual life. Or prayer. If his position as Defender of the Faith never got through to her it must have made it easier.

Philanthropy, charity, public welfare were not possible, I believe, to her as a career, a way of life, as they are to some women of leisure and fortune. *Always interested in improving living conditions,* she had said to me of the man who, as Prince of Wales, had promised so much in those fields.

Most women—all women?—at some time find themselves in Vanity Fair. Some get out, some don't. I passed this way myself so I know about it. Neither Mrs. Simpson nor the Duchess of Windsor ever get beyond it. In the end, the Duchess embraced it, settled for it, perhaps she'd always preferred it. She never got out as Mrs. Roosevelt had done even in the White House or Anne Lindbergh proves she had in *Gift from the Sea*. Mabel Normand, I could feel now, had died rather than stay in it. Mother Meyer had entered mostly to pull others out.

If there had been left a chance that he might be Ambassador to the United States, or, as a strong rumor once had it, be made Viceroy of India, each day and hour had diminished his chances, and they were left forever dancing to a hey-nonny-nonny in the streets of that Town called Vanity.

So we come again to an end as inevitable as $2 \times 2 = 4$.

Crazy Party—Cerutti Italian designer of men's clothes—the place alive with pop singers couturiers the Duke and Duchess of Windsor, Connie Crespi with her short dark curly wigs and on and on—*a mixed bag*—

No antagonism for *'is Mrs. Simpson,* now the Duchess of Windsor, in a mixed bag in Paris.

You pulled back from this as from the body of Richard III flung over the horse for which he offered his kingdom.

Not with a bang but a whimper. Is it possible I was so sad because I seemed then to hear a faint faraway whimper from the king who *did* leave his country under circumstances that grow more ignominious as time passes?

God help all poor sailors on a night like this.

Perhaps my prayer for England that night at the Savoy was answered with more wisdom than I'd known. For when peace came at last—We want the King, We want the Queen, We want the Princesses—in that cry the people meant the pinch hitter George VI and his wife the Dowdy Duchess and their children, who had never left England. They, and Winston Churchill, had given them Great Heart to save themselves in their finest hour.

But—today—as I see the Empire liquidated and England in her *lowest* hour, I wonder if that heart which had been broken was like a mended pitcher. Four years of deadly warfare, it had held those. But then the crack began to show, in the terrible postwar years it could hold no longer. And I wonder if it all began when their King-by-Divine-Right broke the sacred continuity and betrayed them for a woman.

I was very weary when I left Nassau and on the plane I realized I was wearying not only for home but greatly for my son Bill. I had no real premonition of how short my time was. How soon the talk Bill and I had that night by the fire was to send him forth to battle with Apollyon.

> *Last night I dreamt I saw*
> *the King of England going to war . . .*

another king, oh yes, but I had given him *England* as our mother, as our front line of defense:

> *In his left hand he had a banner, in*
> *his right hand he had a sword*

—a man couldn't wait any longer and see England stand alone on the field of Armageddon against spiritual wickedness in high places, against the rulers of the darkness of this world—a man could not—was he a man already? Taller—wiser—skinny and lanky—a man who must pick up a sword and fight for truth as he saw it?

> *And that's the way we conquer Germany—*
> *some Sunday soon.*

Soon?

Look Ma—it'll be us next—we don't want them coming over here, do we? We can't let England go down, can we?

I'd done this. To myself. I myself had done this to myself.

If you sell your son that something is worth dying for you must abide by the consequences.

On the other hand, if you sell him that nothing is worth dying for he may be stuck with the consequences for half eternity.

The best of the pilgrims. There is a price to be paid.

> Sing, Faithful, sing, let thy name survive;
> For though they kill'd thee,
> Thou art yet alive.

BOOK SIX

CHAPTER 38

I must get this ambulance ride in proper perspective.

I had no recollection of how I got into the ambulance, nor why. If you do not know why you are in an ambulance abject fear engulfs you. To a woman's subconscious, an ambulance is going to or from death or carrying death on a stretcher.

For me, these were the seconds when you are going down for the third time and your life passes before you in review with more than the speed of light. As often as I'd heard of this phenomenon I'd never believed it until, disorderly, out of sequence, more poignant than in the hours of their reality, past present and future marched for 3600 seconds, door to door, with bell clanging and siren shrieking from Malibu to the Hollywood Hospital.

"Step on it buddy," the intern said, "the sooner we get her pumped out the more chance we got."

It changed my entire Way, though until the end how was I to realize this was as near the Road to Damascus as I'd ever get?

For at the beginning, as a portion of me came up out of *complete* darkness, I found myself face to face with the question I'd put to myself in the library of my Whittier ranch long ago. There on what I thought was my deathbed, in clear stereopsis, was Alice Ames Winters, robed in lavender crepe de chine as became the president of the General Federation of Women's Clubs.

With her came visions of our terrifying debate, Is Modern Woman a Failure?

The Universe, I felt sure, could well tremble at the question for if Woman is out of orbit what the moon is made of won't matter much. I had shocked myself as well as my audience when I waved a red lantern of warning that no matter how fast you travel if you are on the wrong road it will not bring you to the Desired Country.

I'd promised myself I'd find out whether this outburst that had come through me was right. It was important to me, but I certainly wouldn't have expected it to be the first thing I encountered in my final delirium.

Besides, this was the wrong ambulance. It smelled wrong.

As if I were going in and out of an anesthetic, the swing confused me. I wanted to dig back into oblivion where I would not have to face past present *or* future. I screwed my eyes tight shut but there they were, these last-second television screens inside my eyelids; from flat to luminous gray, to flashes of vitriolic light; to action of unrelated scenes like switching channels. One of those was Alice Ames Winters. I made at once an incoherent demand for sensible progression of my progress as a Modern Woman, for this was a fact of *my life*. But these are the only memories I have, I can get no others now, I do not want to waste time on Alice Ames Winters! As we scorched wildly along the Pacific Coast Highway a voice spoke to me as definitely as an announcer calling a take-off, saying, You promised to find *whence* she came and *what* she is now, and whither she goes—the Modern Woman, not A.A.W. If that lovable old cynic Diogenes stops here to look for an honest woman who makes a success of holding the reins over three mules with style and ease—will you be one?

I say an honest No. *You are about to die in an ambulance, nothing could be more vulgar and dishonorable; your children will be humiliated and your name will be trash and serves you right.*

I blacked out again before I could remember why it served me right. Down where I went it was no longer completely dark, it was dim and dreadful and slimy things crawled and I began to fight with fury; I will not crawl with you, I said. The Modern Woman has seventy thousand years of true Evolution; she is only out of orbit, she took off for the moon and landed in the wrong ambulance and her unhappiness is what we are passing on to our joyless children. Nothing joyless or phony joyless or stimulated joyful is anything like God.

Just what this had to do with it I seemed to know well but I could not arrange it to suit me, so I said, There are Modern Women who are successes, who are joyful. What have they got that the rest of us haven't got?

Mrs. Winters was gone and well she might be, for there in my delirium was Mrs. Roosevelt, a woman who must surely have something tremendous to be joyful about *in that hat*. She was holding her hands out to the mob—the crowd that goes silent and tearful with joy before her.

Mrs. Lindbergh! Words I had written showed in letters of flame, *She had something in that courtroom, it puzzled me then, I kept reaching for it,* do I get good marks for reaching? A woman's reach must exceed her grasp—*all I could get then was the inspiration of her courage and her courtesy.* Who said courtesy is love in little things? If I have not love I am become as a clanging bell and a shrieking siren.

Mother Meyer said, You won't believe the answer unless you find it yourself.

The price of a virtuous woman is beyond rubies. And there was I reading a Gideon Bible over a martini with Inez Robb in a hotel room in Chicago and we were discussing, Could it be *rubies* and not diamonds that are a girl's best friend? Had we been selling short?

Dear Mrs. Roosevelt, as long as you are up, can I ask you a question? With all you went through, did you ever doubt God? No. Is that part of the answer I'm looking for? When I lost my first baby I asked for a ray of hope. I must have received it for I went on and had other babies. When I was a little girl my father told me my grandfather died with a smile of True Delight on his face. Now I am about to die in a Cave of Doubt tied hand and foot by the Giant Despair and a loathsome fellow he is.

Clearly, firmly, and for real I must put down here that I am not going to raise the curtain upon that sector of my journey between my return from the Windsors at Nassau and the moment of what looked like my last mile. Dickens says the remembrance of the blacking factory was so fraught with pain he could not mention it but with abhorrent reluctance, so this span of time is to me.

Dear Mr. Semenenko, on what do you lend money? Character, dear Mrs. St. Johns. Then you would not lend me a plugged nickel. Grant me poetic license to say I have shot my Character full of holes, it hangs about my neck like the Albatross.

Most of the world's treasures and pleasures were mine and I had everything, as we say. On the whole, the Modern Woman pointed to me with pride. We can too do it, she cried triumphantly; *you're* spanking right along, aren't you? When Howey plastered trucks and billboards with my picture, I had a mild measure of fame. The ability to make money and the optimistic ignorance to consider it Capital. Security I had never known, I honestly didn't believe it existed, so I didn't miss it. I loved my work as a reporter. If dedication is necessary to a full life I was dedicated to the press.

No husband? I'd had husbands, this must be the way I wanted it. What more do I want? How can I be empty?

Emptiness comes in times of growing pains, the absence of Good leaves a vacuum. This can be filled by the scum from the Slough of Despond and knickknacks from Vanity Fair. The only thing to make sure that this vacuum will be filled with evil and unhappiness is for good women to do nothing. If there aren't any good women, then, Genghis Khan, here we come. The vacuum will be filled with boredom and sloth and avarice and fiends that go eeekk in the night and love affairs that go clunk in the morning and martinis that go whoops in ambulances. And women will never never know the glory that was meant to be theirs.

Mother Meyer—my Mrs. Valiant-for-Truth—always kept on saying all that to me. Still was. Then why had my pilgrimage ended in this charnel house?

Bitterness clanged and shrieked inside me.

This time Life had not knocked me to my knees in a gentlemanly fashion. It had laid me flat on my back and no dignity was left to me. No woman can survive without dignity. Dignity is the measure of her honor and value. Weep for the girl or woman who has lost all dignity. On her knees, the way Helgesen found me that night at Dower House, a woman can be trying to pray, asking grace to pray even if she doesn't know what grace means, no matter who or what she is. A woman on her back amid the reek of vomit and worn-out chloroform *or* in the back of a Ford for that matter—and who cares?

Que la pasa a usted?

Spanish? What's with you? When I was drunk I often insisted on speaking French, many women do, but Spanish must go all the way back to Doña María Antonia Orena. She still hated gringos who had stolen her California so we weren't allowed to speak English. And did the Señora have dignity! Even without the vote.

Cómo está usted hoy? The Díaz president's daughters from Mexico City used to say that with dignity in the convent at San Jose.

Well, *hoy* to you, and since you ask, I am not feeling at all well today.

The Modern Woman, Señora and Señoritas, has everything. The vote, the bank account, inventions you would not believe, she has shed the responsibility for her children and wherever possible castrated her men so she may be equal to them. She has no dignity any more and nobody loves her in spite of bath oils, deodorants, hair sprays, hand lotions, face creams, lipsticks false eyelashes and perfume—so *hoy* to you and what I must know is if we are out of orbit can we find our way back? And *Cómo está usted?* as you will see.

"She swallow something?"

I got one eye open and knew from the back of his neck that the driver of this ambulance was back from Tripoli and Château-Thierry and *he* didn't want to live forever.

"She says so," the white-clad young man beside me said wearily. "They tank up on gin and go swimming and swallow half the goddam ocean— Jesus, how I hate women. I am thinking of becoming a homosexual."

A riot of horns and shouts as we slithered around a corner raised protest. The driver ignored this, he said, "I knew a girl in Corpus Christi,

Texas—my mother said a woman who drinks gin is headed for perdition; she was a Baptist, my mother not the girl in Corpus Christi—*hey, you stupid jerk where do you think you're going, that's a goodwaytolose-yourass that is.*"

The swerve kept me up there long enough to get the *smell*. It is not the antechamber to Hell, it is the seals in their little puddle at Las Flores. They're civilized seals now, they smell worse, and as I go down—maybe it's only the second time?—I have a hot sense of triumph. I knew this was the wrong ambulance, now I am in the right one, the driver is a kid and I'm not much more, he's trying to scare me. Listen, buster, anybody can drive an ambulance, what I want to know is how many mules can you drive? This smell isn't seals, it's toadstools, and I am Earl Rogers' daughter Nora and I am a police reporter and you and I are going to find all those lovely people on the floor, papa and mama and four kids, I keep telling the doc they did not eat toadstools, people do not eat toadstools, they eat what they think are mushrooms, that's the whole *point*. That's life. That's why it's harder for the Rich to get through the Eye of the Needle Gate into the Promised Land; they can buy more mushrooms that turn out to be toadstools.

That's my problem!

What kind of a God are you, God, not to tell me the difference between mushrooms and toadstools and love and lust and True Delight and mari-juana? *Keep all poisons out of the reach of children.* Children are curious. *Be not curious about God, you need not understand him—Walt Whitman.*

Suddenly I was sure I was wide awake in the now, the intern was look-ing at me with concern and I put my hands over my eyes for fear the picture on the inside might show through and he'd see it.

My secret shame, blazing in color.

Had to be secret. Must keep it down where I'd buried it deep.

Remember! Remember to take your sense of humor seriously. The all-excusing philosophy of our time; if it's funny it can't be immoral, illegal, or fattening. In time it will become so familiar and easy that if you *won't* whatever-it-is you have no sense of humor. Merely getting *drunk* and going to jail for stealing a taxi might be shameful. BUT boast of it with Humor, have a couple of real funny lines and a jape gesture or two and it can be passed off as a Joke. With a Jest you are safe and sophisticated not square.

What I had done didn't need to be kept secret. *It was that I was ashamed of it.*

Look, buster, let me explain.

What do I want with a taxicab? I have a Cadillac sitting in front of the Ritz. Dinner with Cissy Patterson, she has a floor at the Ritz-Carlton in case she should be in New York. She is On the Wagon so we eat our forty-proof sherry with a spoon in hot green turtle soup of the evening, beautiful soup, and we are Reeling and Writhing all right. Two modern women. Eleanor Medill Patterson, A.R.St.J. If there is anything they don't have, they can buy it? They can go anywhere, they know everybody; as frosting on the cake Cissy owns a newspaper. Everybody has problems, psychiatry will diagnose them, then what do you do? Mrs. St. Johns' problem is that *she* doesn't own a newspaper and the work she can do at home confusion has now made its masterpiece—that work seems to be confusion worse confounded. Now that she cannot go romping into the city room any more.

After a couple of steps in front of the Ritz I got tired of looking for my car so I took a taxi and Away we went. We crossed the Fifty-ninth Street bridge and the driver said that when he left the island of Manhattan he had to phone in, so I said, Avaunt, *mon garçon,* and found myself sitting alone watching green-red-yellow lights blinking QUEENS BAR AND GRILL. This got a little dull and I thought, Why that drunken bum, he is not *telephoning,* he is in the bar *drinking liquor.* It is very dangerous to drink liquor when you are driving. I wish to go home to see my children but I do not wish to drive there with a fellow who has been guzzling gin—

I did not blame the motorcycle cop.

A lady in blue velvet and sables (paid for or not) driving a yellow cab is an unfamiliar sight and if she ignores red lights along Queens Boulevard even a modern man must interfere.

Walter Winchell in his largest-in-the-world column said, *Our Adela has done what every red-blooded American has always wanted to do, stolen a taxi and driven herself home. Congratulations, Adela.*

Well, congratulations to you, too, dear Walter. And any of the other kids that want to steal a car and go joy riding, so we all laughed and laughed and my children said probably I hadn't been drinking—that was just the way I *drove.* I had not been ashamed of Papa when I went to Oakland to get him and Jack London out of jail for brawling drunk but mothers are different they are they are they are they are they are. Women are different or are they?

The key that turned in the lock of a cell door in the Long Island City Jail with me inside is one of the scars I carry with me.

The boys from the paper came and got me out next morning.

I had to telephone Mr. Hearst. I had a serial running in *Good Housekeeping.* The editor, Bill Bigelow, wasn't going to give me the Good Housekeeping Seal of Approval for this night's work. The serial was entitled *Field of Honor.* Mr. Hearst would be surprised. He'd never seen me take a drink.

I could hear Mr. Hearst's voice then as I had heard him, kept hearing him, don't think I couldn't, no siren ever drowned him out.

"I had no idea you were so important," the voice said. "You made the front page of the New York *Times*."

Fathers, provoke not your children to anger lest they be discouraged. The tone of the voice suggested he felt it wouldn't take much to discourage me into the gutter about then.

With the taxicab business I thought I'd hit bottom for all time, but as the marines and I charged up the hill off the Ocean Front to the top of the Palisades where David Bruce Brown had been killed in a Santa Monica Road Race I was covering, I knew I hadn't because this was fathoms down below that. We'd get killed too and I'd make the front page of the New York *Times* again. I hate the New York *Times*, I hate spinach, I hate broccoli, I hate grandiosity, I hate hypocrisy, I hate political double-talk, I love Arthur Krock. That won't get you anywhere in this world or the next, I told myself. Ah well, God had doubtless washed His hands of me sometime back.

The God you don't believe in has washed His hands of you—all your life God has been trying to get into the act, *following following after,* often I heard those footsteps behind me, following after, and I fled them down the nights and down the days. Even then—now—what?—in this dark wood where my straight road is lost I can hear them and I am asking the God I don't believe in not to wash His hands of me, to give me a pillar—a ray—of light to lead me.

I do not want my empty soul to be filled with ice and scum and knick-knacks and *shame*.

Nobody admits it, but we all say it—in foxholes, in ambulances, in nightmares, in jails—please God-I-Don't-Believe-In please help me—

An answer came. Profiles in Heart began to march before me.

Clear on my half-inch screen there was Amelia Earhart's bright head. A modern woman for you. She had decided never to have any children. She had a husband but he was a straw man; she had been able to say of her job, "There's a hole in the sky for all good pilots" and her soul found it. I knew that.

And Charlotte Pickford! Her children had been her life, her children and her church, her church and her children, what I was seeing now was the joy on her face when Phyllis Daniels brought a priest to her deathbed to open the door of Paradise to her. Where in the world had I ever seen *joy* like that?

The women in the church at Flemington, praying for faith. I saw them get it. Mrs. St. Johns on the front page that day prays for Justice, but Mrs. St. Johns is kidding herself, she dare not want Justice. What she wants is Mercy with a drop of dew in it.

Ruby, who was Unemployed; her rent was paid and she shared a floor where we could sleep and she loved her neighbor—she loved her neighbor who was me and I slept safely within that love.

My heart began to expand with warmth.

In that second I knew—and knew I knew—the answer to the Whence and What and Whither—a landscape was clear and unmistakable in a flash of Jersey lightning—I saw it with full conviction—then as the arc of illumination tailed off I couldn't hold it—as it disappeared I only knew with a pleading sense of loss that it was something I didn't have, I was left with only me once more. Moments of illumination leave the darkness blacker—but I had seen and some time I would have to go back and find it.

These women had fortitude and joy.

I had to figure this out later, it was gone now.

"You say she's a writer?" the driver said and interrupted me in my dark recesses. "What does she write?" "She used to write for newspapers," the intern said. "My wife reads her in magazines—the kind of magazines women read. *I* don't know. All I know—she's some kind of writer."

All *writers* of all kinds have sinking spells, Harold Ross said.

I am sinking for the third time, I told you that in the beginning, and if driving three healthy mules is a challenge when one of them is in a coma it is Tophet, which is a place in the Valley of Hinnom where children are offered as sacrifices to Moloch by their own parents.

My third mule was in a coma. Age is as relative with reporters as with pro football players. Their legs go first—*knees* mostly. Christ Church Mission by night, walking back from jobs I didn't get, and in Hyde Park on Maundy Thursday, Flemington in the snow, and the Rose Bowl in the rain, thrown off a train in Canada to run around after airplanes to fly to Tacoma, up and down stairs to the playroom the day Mrs. Musica's husband shot himself, oh yes real reporting is a young man's game. I didn't want to be a rewrite man sitting around while other people brought me news. Or a *columnist.*

You can work at home.

I had sold the first story I wrote and all thereafter for a lot of years. Now my ambulance walls were plastered with rejection slips from all the best editors. This is obviously assbackwards I told myself. These you are supposed to get when you are young and bounce and the baby doesn't need shoes. I never belonged to a Browning Circle but dear Mr. Browning would you be ravaged if I invaded an obscure nook of your privacy to say it should not be the *last* of life for which the first is planned? No no—the *middle,* Mr. Browning, the last will then take care of itself, the middle of the road, middle class, middle age, middle course, the middle mind that purrs and never shows a tooth—you get shot at from both sides.

My agent, friend, guide, and severest critic, Edith Haggard, the lady Robert Nathan once called the toughest rose petal in New York, along about here, the day after the heartbreak of losing the Low Lane house, looked me in the eye as she did Mr. Nathan himself *and* Sinclair Lewis *and* DeWitt Wallace *and* Joyce Carey, and said, "You've been getting by. But nothing stands still." Like the tip of an iceberg those words chilled the ambulance and I cringed when I thought how outraged our rose petal, tough as she was, would be could she see me now. Nothing stands still, honeybun. As I recalled her words I could feel the hoarfrost on my damp hair. Nothing stands still—not sirens nor sarsaparilla nor wars nor Winsocki nor creative art nor ingrowing toenails—

Heart, Ernie Pyle had said. *Heart.*

I kept saying it myself all the time.

I had not given my whole heart to the work I did at home. I was sulking because I wanted to work in a press box. I may be giving myself the worst of it, but when you are cold and dank on the way to get your stomach pumped out if you live so long your judgment is warped.

Bottom. *Rock* bottom. This time you can be sure. Why, I couldn't even get a job in the Movies. For years I'd been putting my hand in the movie till right up to the elbow, dishonest as a working wife. Never done a conscientious day's work in what I'd contracted for. They'd caught up with me now.

There is no greater pain in purgatory than to recall a happy time. I was shaken with a great need. I needed a friend, this I knew and felt the sweat break out with the impact of that need. When I saw him it was so clear I cried out—can this be only memory? I do not know either whether I called *him* or he was the one who heard me—Tom Mix will not pull any punches, you'll sweat worse before he's through with you. He regards four-letter words as illiterate and retarded but he knows how to put all the other words together. But I'm stuck with him; he is my Mr. Standfast.

He will expect me to behave at all times with fortitude, which means you can take it.

I tried to hold the figure still, the horse kept dancing and the figure moved with it. It was too bad Jesus hadn't had anything better than an ass's colt to ride on into Jerusalem, Tom said. He could, Tom said, have ridden anything. *What a character,* Tom always said of Jesus.

A big man from the wide open spaces, but Tom was not silent. A great one for singing he'd always been, for quoting poetry, for reciting a whole poem, by Kipling, Shakespeare, Robert Service, or R.L.S., in any company anywhere so now he was filling my ears with that poem of the Goodly Fere, which he loved because it was a word-picture of Jesus as

Tom Mix pictured him, and as his flat Western drawl filled the space around me it became the dawn on the desert where I used to ride with Tom.

> A son of God was the Goodly Fere,
> That bade us his brothers be,
> I ha' seen him cow a thousand men. . . .
> On the hills of Galilee.

> A master of men was the Goodly Fere,
> A mate of the wind and sea,
> They think they ha' slain our Goodly Fere
> They are fools eternally.

> I ha' seen him eat o' the honey-comb
> Sin' they nailed him to the tree.

The honey-comb.
That was what he had to say to me.

Briefer than breath, I was inside Helgesen's mind, I remembered him best in the glaring light that beat upon the city desk, now there was not even a hope or promise of light. *We had everything,* it wasn't enough, everything never is, in two seconds he will pick up that gun and use it— *trees die at the top.*

Running like an obbligato as I thought of this, I was deeply aware that my grandfather had taught me that the Far Country was not necessarily a mess of pottage as Helgesen had come to know it. God had made a world full of the beauty of gardens and the glory of stars and moon and sun and the joy of love and Grandpa said that it was His pleasure to give this kingdom to me if I would take it. On His terms it may be, but it takes coming to terms to fly across oceans or eat a frozen dinner or tune in a TV show. Doesn't it? But my grandfather knew the joy of obedience to those loving terms and he died with a smile of True Delight on his face *because* he had seen You, His Lord, face to face.

Now as I came back Mr. Standfast had gone. I cried out after him and the intern said, *Take it easy,* but I cried out the more. I said, I'm not guilty because my best wasn't any better. Most people do their best; you must let us taste of the honeycomb so we have strength from its sweetness to do Your best.

I'm sorry, no no, that's no good either. . . . I will not have remorse. Though I die here in the splendor and stink and squalor of Sodom where sin is so victorious people think it is good and the Lord may have to rain fire and brimstone upon me to destroy it—remorse is a death word— *mors*—moribund—remorsus, to bite back and at yourself, what help is that? Repentance is something else again, to change one's mind—*pense*—

with regard to a Way of action in consequence of dissatisfaction with it. I am dissatisfied with the bloody works. I repent me of my unkindness; I am disposed to change my life for the better, everybody is but who does? *Who can?*

Be quiet, my heart, my first wound that left a scar I was carrying right there in you. I can almost feel it hurt, the one when I knew Papa wasn't going to win his fight with John Barleycorn and my best sure wasn't good enough—

Who can overcome fear as I know it now without comfort or encouragement?

I will send you a Comforter that He may be with you always though you make your bed in hell—my grandfather's Friend the Savior had promised that. No?

I had a scar too because I had gone on hating my mother, my poor stupid tortured mother, who could grow roses and begonias.

Who can love her enemies without Your help?

Ike St. Johns—a wormy performance that had been all too often petty and ungenerous, impatient and filled with female vanity—that one wasn't yet a scar, it was still an open sore.

And how could Anne Morrow have made her marriage shine without some grace You sent her?

Why even The Baby, Harlow, that night at the Hearst Ranch wept so bitterly because she wanted the man she loved for a husband to believe she was the woman who loved him, *my* best must have seemed to her a mockery. I needed something more now as Mozart had needed something beyond human music when he wrote *The Magic Flute.*

My child, I thought that you were dead.

Plainly I did not die on my bed of nails. The point is I thought I was going to. Strangely enough death did not preoccupy me. I was concerned passionately and profoundly and unexpectedly with life. *Your task is happiness, what have you been about?* Who said that? As the pace of the wheels increased without, the speed of the emotion-thought-memory-dementia accelerated within. More and more I could make nothing of it. Then—in one fell swoop as Shakespeare says—the pieces of my life, all the lives mine had touched, all the lives I knew through history and poetry and music became a coherent whole and there emerged a stark and simple Truth.

The story of every man's life is nought but the resolving of his relationship to God.

Gutter or cathedral, brothel or brownstone, the cave at the source or the wings to the moon, whatever the century or country, language or kind of language, whether we know it as it takes place or not or have ever heard or spoken the word God, whether we're grinding it out a yard at a time or throwing seventy-yard passes, some go fast and some go slow, some the hard way and some with leaps to the stars—but the longing for the Desired Country whose clouds of glory we trail is there.

> Bethink thee then, and if thou art not blind
> Thou'lt see thyself a woman sick with pain
> Who on the softest down no rest can find,
> Tossing and turning weary limbs in vain.

Dante! I'd as soon have Don Quixote. Dante's friend Beatrice may have had the softest down but in my bucketing tragedy I have a canvas bed with nails as I've mentioned. The result seems to be the same. Always *the same*.

It is true and true that man's life story is a Pilgrim's Progress and I am recording my own Journey with candor as I speak it to myself from memory, and this was one of the times when Mercy held out a hand to help me—to help me to be *silent*.

Not of Gennesaret but Thames.

That was all I could think of as a prayer.

So I was silent—I thought I was silent—voices from outside spoke and I tried to shut them off and out—I began to speak to them myself and tell them to be *silent*.

"What's she talking about?" the driver said. "Hang on, I gotta get by this old tortoise somehow he won't move over—" "She says she wants to cover the Sermon on the Mount," the intern said. "She's delirious," the driver said, he went around the man who wouldn't move over by going into the lane where the people were coming in the opposite direction and, after he bent the damn ambulance in the middle like a pretzel and we were back on our own side, he said, "What's you figure she meant by that, for Chrisake?" The intern said, "She's got a fever of 104 and she's a writer besides, whatyawant, cheesecake?"

I tried to tell them. I could hear myself, but I knew my voice wasn't coming through. I kept saying, No, no, it's not crazy, I want to cover the Road to Emmaus, too, and the Day of Pentecost and I'd like to have interviewed Jesus and Peter and gone out into the desert to find Paul— it's the greatest news story of all time.

Then
There was silence.
I felt myself in silence.
A desperate longing took possession of me.
Others better qualified than I can ever be, whose words come from

inspiration, the Apostles and the apostles of the apostles and the poets touched by divine fire and the seers who see what we cannot—

Just tell it, Howey said, don't try to *write,* for Godsake. Just tell it.

In the silence, I knew that God is and that He loves me.

I don't see how He can but He does and that is grace.

Anyone can know.

Seek, it says, and ye shall find. *Seek!*

Through the window I saw the firehouse. On the night Dicky had an emergency appendix I'd looked out at the fire engines all the time Dr. Branch had him upstairs, so I knew we were coming to the hospital. Here for me is the strangest thing of all; as we went by it I did not lose the joy, I held onto that world yet I was perfectly organized in the one where the firehouse was and always had been.

We pirouetted into the emergency driveway and they lifted the stretcher out. In spite of all they could do I would not let them carry me. If I faltered or fell on my face *nevertheless* I must take the first steps on this new Way on my own. I must choose it as the Way and walk into it myself.

So I stood up somehow and walked into the hospital and inside the door; waiting as he always was when you needed him stood Dr. William E. Branch and he said, "What's the matter with you?"

I said, "Think of all the lousy banquets we covered and nobody was at the Last Supper—" and then I fainted, but as I went down I thought, So that's why Helen Keller comes toward you moving more sweetly than Pavlova; she moves on a beam of joy that is light.

My marks and scar I carry with me for I felt now that they proved I had fought His battles as best I know, even though I'd lost a lot of them.

When Dr. Branch examined me there was a vivid angry welt across my back, like the mark of a lash or the mark of a shark's teeth or the burn of the poisonous tentacles of an octopus. Nobody, not even Dr. Branch, who knows everything, knows to this day what it was. I might, it seems, have died of it.

Instead I carried it with me into my new life as I started up the Highest Mountain. In the far distance I could see the Desired Country plainly, and the faces of some of the shining ones who had been allowed to enter and I sang and shouted for joy as I climbed, hanging onto a brand new rope of faith.

It never occurred to me to ask myself if the rope would hold. I didn't know how steep the road was ahead of me nor that faith is not enough.

CHAPTER 39

The telephone rang with an insistence that told me it was long distance.

Any ring of any telephone holds the potential of all drama. In studio story conferences, which I had loathed, when we hit a block in the script some wag would always murmur, *Ah, there's the telephone now* as a way of getting on with the action.

Yet so often it *is* the telephone.

As it was in this case, though at the moment I had no way of recognizing it, it was the signal for the curtain to go up on the last act of my life.

I had been sitting by the beach windows at Malibu. Until the telephone invaded and interrupted me I was pleased with my conviction that I was going to be able to reconcile the best of both possible worlds. Nature is our connection with Creation and dawn and sunset over the ocean move me to breathless adoration. That afternoon the sun had decided to go down in full splendor, an experience equaled only by seeing the Crown Jewels in the Tower of London. And this, combined with the mystery of the waters staying in their appointed places, which I did not understand any more than I understood many of God's doings, was added to the afterglow of joy from my moment in the ambulance. This brilliant sun was over the yardarm, as we say, so while I hummed "God and Sinners Reconciled," a favorite hymn of Grandpa's, I sipped my martini; being my first, it became a lovely crest that lifted me into the realm of self-confidence. Whatever it was to be, I could do it!

When I bought this little cocktail shaker sitting at my elbow it was because it held two martinis and anybody can drink *two* martinis, though 'tis said nobody can drink three. This frosted silver miniature proved my intent henceforth to abide in moderation. Moderation was to be the word for me. I'd wrapped it up and carried it home declaring to myself—no more *extremes.*

Because you believe in God and have been granted a glimpse of what Grace is—is this a valid reason for now becoming inhibited about normal human pleasures? Watch yourself, if you make goodness unattractive and prohibitive—who needs it? Above all, dear girl, let us not lose our sense of humor.

Congratulations on stealing a taxi, dear Adela. You were very fun-ny last night, what could be funnier than bringing home a horsie? After all fun is fun, some people call it Fun—have Fun—Fun City—fine three-letter-word Fun—if you're going to take all the Fun out of life this is a return to Puritanism. Naturally, you are never going to use gin to excess and thus risk perdition as the driver's mother suggested, but she was a Baptist. Need good and evil be in such violent opposition? Let them be friends. If you get goody-goody how will you hook any teen-agers to feel the need of and joy in the spiritual life? You dampen them right off by showing there's no fun and they'll barge off at a high rate of speed.

The sunset had begun to fade into rich gold. At the horizon was a line of clear unbelievable green, reflected on the ocean right to the shore. This was before the telephone rang—the telephone was silent as though it had paused to watch the sunset with me—I saw that my cocktail glass was empty and I filled it with an air, nothing could have better style than to drink a second martini and stop!

Nor could it be all that difficult.

Look at the flat often vapid dolls who drink two martinis every night of their lives. Surely your will power is as strong as theirs. Lots of people much brighter, much *better* than you drink like ladies and gentlemen. You are always squawking because Republicans and Protestants talk only to themselves, now you're planning to be just as inflexible.

For my higher self, let us call it, was talking back to me, saying, Indeed indeed all this may be true, but you have always known that abstinence is possible to you—temperance is not. Is it or is it not true that as your drinking increased your work-you-could-do-at-home decreased? Has this also happened to a number of finer writers than you'll ever be? Is not drinking an occupational hazard? And what about the abominable places you have wound up in, like a jail cell where they locked the door?

To this my lower self said, Ah, none of this was on the first or second martini. That's the *point d'appui*. Since I am never going to take a *third*— and don't tell me you've heard that before. This is totally different. This is part of a new life, and I want to reaffirm and warn you that if you get smug or holier-than-thou nobody will listen to you. Or read you any more. Maybe nobody will even publish you.

Remember Ray Long always said you could be quite *daring* in the tales you wrote for *Cosmo*—not quite as much a lady as Edie (Wharton) but it enabled you to get away with the first Hollywood fiction.

Also, said the devil using Scripture aptly and inaccurately but humorously, remember that Jesus turned the water into wine—no no, not *gin,* of course not, I never said he did, *wine*—and probably not the kind winos drink on Skid Row—do not put the worst construction on everything.

I took a sip of my second martini and then shook the drops that were left in the shaker into the glass so that it was full once more. A few *drops* couldn't be regarded as part of the third—that would be quibbling—waste not want not I always say.

The telephone rang.

It was across the loggia so I lit a cigarette, picked up my glass to take it with me, and went to answer it. I felt great. Everything was coming my way. I was home at Malibu in peace, the gift of faith had been given me, I was actually humble before it and if I was broke—ah well, that was a recurring season like winter.

Picture me if you care to, *I* care to, as I sauntered back to the phone. Long blue pajamas, Chinese slippers, cigarette and cocktail glass in hand. For this is the last time *she* is going to appear in this act—or any other.

The voice that spoke to me was my son Bill's.

His calling was not unusual. *You all right, Mama?* This time he went on from there without giving me a chance to say yes. "Ma, listen, maybe Mr. Roosevelt knows what he's doing but it looks to me like some of us ought to go and give England a hand. Will you hold the fort for me while I'm gone?"

I said, "Why—of course, Billy. If you feel you must go."

They were faithful and they fought.

My temptations have been many and some of them too big for me. In that moment I had no temptation.

A man must do what he thinks is right.

Nor did it occur to me that anything bad could happen to Bill.

We *all* said that.

The thunder might leap and the lightning flash but nothing bad could ever touch Bill.

He was, he told me then, going to Canada the next day.

As I hung up I saw the full martini glass on the telephone table beside me.

Only my second—and I needed it.

Before I realized what was coming to pass within me, I cried out, no more possible to prevent that than a geyser in Yellowstone Park can check its spout.

Unless you are going to start calling evil good that glass smells like toadstools and seals in a puddle. I promised—I promised my son. *I'll hold the fort while you're gone.* Gone? To *war?* Do you mean to try to tell me a woman can go right on drinking—no no drinking doesn't get cuter or safer or more sophisticated when the pressure is on. You know better. You promised. You know you have those poor and unhappy brains for drinking. Have you ever seen any woman who gets stronger and more trustworthy and brighter and more faithful and all her faculties working to their utmost on *gin?* You or anybody. While the mind is in alcohol it is driven hither and yon by an impulse, a sunset, a sleepless night and cannot add two and two. Then a woman becomes a sort of Broadway Rose even if she does her staggering in the IN places. In and out of sanitariums, jails, remorse, horrors, all that for myself and broken hearts for my children, as face it, Papa, and forgive me, you broke mine. I will be a nuisance and a disgrace. I lived through that with you, Papa, because I loved you so much but I know what it is and I don't *want* my children to know.

Suppose I can't do it?

I've said never again before and before.

I've done my best but I'm not to be trusted—I might let Bill down—I might not serve my country—

God help me!

I tell you I saw that cocktail glass sitting there all by itself. I knew so well the warm exultant life inside me it would produce if I reached for it. And all of a sudden it wobbled, like a dancer out of step, it gave a little shudder and fell quite slowly. The contents made a little puddle on the brick floor.

The power and the glory, I said to myself.

Over a quarter of a century later I know that was answered prayer and answered prayer is the greatest thing that can come to pass in any life. And it always comes.

I know it was answered prayer, that renunciation had been beyond my best. I knew I had given the order to my hand—only the *second* one—as it turned out it was the last. I have never had a drink since, but the miracle is that I have never wanted one. No struggle. No falls. No desire. The choice which was to determine the rest of my life seemed to be made by a power that wiped out all the horrors, betrayals, tragedies of my life and my father's, as though this evil not only no longer existed but never had.

Oh, believe me.

Sunk without a trace.

This is the miracle.

2

Almost at once I realized that the fort to be held was nowhere near the peace and quiet of Malibu sunsets. I should be closer to where the action was—or would be. New York, or maybe Washington.

I telephoned Elaine to find a house somewhere at the lowest possible rent. This time I wasn't just broke, I was penniless. When she wired she'd managed to find a place in Larchmont, New York, without putting up even the first month's rent I wasn't sure whether we were headed for a sod hut or a log cabin. All Elaine said was that the house was on Long Island Sound, not an ocean to be sure, but at least I could see water.

Dick and Ernest loaded up the car with Michael, our German shepherd dog, cats Fuzzy and Wuzzy, books I regarded as vital, a few household gods such as iron skillets and Dutch ovens, the family pictures, and my collection of Mozart records. Cadillac or no Cadillac it looked like a gypsy caravan. Ernest had our gas card and fortunately enough money he'd saved to *eat*. I borrowed my fare from Howard Strickling and took off on the train.

Through my whole grown-up life I had regarded these trips on the Santa Fe as vacations, cruises, luxurious little times of peace where I dropped all responsibility. No telephones! No one could ask me to raise money, come to dinner, pay bills, speak at any gathering, go over anybody's script, consult me on how the house ought to be run, drive me forth to do a job I didn't want to do, because I needed the money. No plumbers, dental appointments, deans of high schools to be faced and placated, no creditors—none of these endless visitants could intrude. I could sit reading all day if I liked without any sense of guilt, allow myself to do absolutely nothing in comfort since in my hideaway aboard the Chief, now the Super Chief, there was nothing else I could do.

Three thousand blessed miles between Pasadena and New York, three days and three nights!

Now as we came rhythmically to our first stop at San Bernardino I opened the leather bookcase my son Bill had designed for me the Christmas before and began to check my traveling library. *The Bible, Pilgrim's Progress, Imitation of Christ, Science and Health,* a book I had a hunch we would catch up with someday, John Buchan's *Mr. Standfast,* than which no better spy story has been written, *Pride and Prejudice,* and the new Agatha Christie. As Maugham says you get in a panic unless you can *see* enough books. In case you are shipwrecked on a desert island or snowed in among the Rockies for a couple of weeks.

As it turned out I did less reading that trip than usual. In San Berdoo I took out my Bible, for I remembered that my grandfather had preached my favorite of his sermons, founded on Second Peter, here. Slowly I read again the things I was supposed to *add*—to my *faith virtue; and to virtue knowledge; and to knowledge temperance;* that I knew about, then *to patience*—patience?—*and to patience brotherly kindness*—

This dawn of a new day was going to be more complicated than I'd remembered. And I was astonished to find how desperately I had wanted a little time to myself, a little time to think without constant interruptions from outer life.

By the time we got to Barstow I was face to face with trying to catch up with whatever it was that had come to me about the modern woman while I was going down for the third time. Afterwards that flash had escaped me as completely as a melody will escape a composer and so it now stood at the head of my Unfinished Business.

The art of meditation was still far from me, but this attempt at quiet thought was not the frantic insistence of my time in Whittier following the Alice Ames Winters debate. I was still diligently searching and trying to connect up when we pulled into Flagstaff. My curtains were not drawn and somewhere out there not too far away I could picture the little church in Globe my grandfather had so loved. All this Arizona landscape reminded me of him as a circuit rider, Bible in hand, ten-gallon Stetson on his head, so I was not too surprised to hear an echo of his voice telling me that St. Paul had written his epistles to *us*. Never forget that, my child, he used to say. Not just to the Corinthians, to the Californians as well. Not to the Romans only, to the Arizonans they are blessed and timely. Not only to Timothy and Titus, to Lowell Rogers and his granddaughter Adela.

At the time I'd been too young to take this in, it was to me one of Grandpa's *stories* out of his beloved black Book.

Now I examined it.

Could they have been written to me? Would they be relevant *now?* Were human beings and problems the same in Flagstaff as in Galatia?

I took up the Bible again, shut my eyes, and opened:

> *To Titus Grace be unto you speak those things which will be-*
> *come sound doctrine—to the aged women that they be in be-*
> *havior as becometh holiness, not false accusers* [as gossip] *not*
> *given to much wine* [in the kitchen or anywhere else, not to use
> pot, any women, or anything else that causes them to go out of
> their minds] *teach them to love their own husbands* [and let
> all other husbands alone] *to love their children to be keepers of*
> *homes, looking for the blessed hope of the joyous and glorious*
> *appearing of God* [and His love for you] *and all these things that*
> *are in Christ's teachings. . . .*

That was certainly relevant. Could have been written for—tomorrow.

For while the woman of today may be, as my friend Bob Ardry was to conclude in *African Genesis,* the most unhappy primate in history, a deep inner *hope* was telling me she didn't need to be.

To myself I said the Modern Woman had seventy thousand years of true evolution up to the Woman who had the clear sense that God is the Father of Man and therefore all men are brothers. Only if and when she denies this shining heritage will she lose her place in the sun.

More than with every man, the story of every woman is nought but the resolving of her relationship to the Spirit.

My soul doth magnify the Lord, And my spirit doth rejoice in God my Savior, said the Blessed Mother.

If she chooses woman can use the wings of her spirit.

That was what I'd seen in the ambulance.

None of the other things made the slightest difference. The modern woman's failure had nothing to do with *mules.* A woman can drive three mules or three hundred. Or elect to drive one or whichever two it pleased her to harness together. Any or all of these in any order are possible *if* she finds within herself the spiritual life in some form, under some name, near or far, new or old, ancient or modern.

Without the winged spirit, the word *woman* is a mockery. Without her wings, she is as dangerous as a forest fire, always has been, look at Rome or France, she must consume everything in her way leaving scorched earth and disaster behind her.

Not what she has *done.* Some of that is beautiful.

What she has left *undone.* And plans and proposes to leave undone in the future.

These are alarms in the night, my sisters, and I would not drive them in if I didn't now know the Answer. I believed exactly that then—and it has stood the test of time. In fact, it has gotten gradually worse so that now I may quote St. Paul to the Corinthians with even more conviction. *Seeing that we have such hope, we use great plainness of speech,* Paul said in Corinth.

The Widow at Windsor, whose name was Victoria, said no good would come of giving women the vote. So far Her Majesty, a God-fearing woman who was able to drive three mules, one of them the British Empire, has proved right. Look at a list of what modern woman is using her franchise to lobby through the legislature—so I read in the papers:

> Criteria for Alimony.
> Nonfault Basis for Divorce.
> Better Day Care for Children of Mothers Who Work Whether They Have to or Not.
> Removing Restrictions on Night Work for Woman (at the same time making provision to give her adequate protection though even a modern woman in the market place must be aware that we need all the police to handle the riots and troubles kicked up by the children, God help them, who have been left to day care after nonfault divorces).

Never tell your illustration if you can show it, Howey said.

I can.

Norman Douglas, who wrote *Goodbye to Western Culture,* says you can tell the ideals of a nation by its advertising, especially the ideals of women, for they control the buying. A modern TV commercial begins with a shot of women in Merry Widow hats marching under signs VOTES FOR WOMEN. I was there, so I know what idealistic fervor waved those banners, with what high hopes we marched to get a better world to hand on to our children. Next on the small screen we see a young woman of today, singing:

> "You've come a long way Baby
> To get where you got to today.
> You've got your own cigarette now, Baby.
> You've come a long, long way."

This may seem to moderns a most dashing and fashionable achievement, but I don't believe it was quite the reward we had in mind. Better we had done something about one modern woman who brayed loudly enough to get the Bible and prayer out of our children's schools, although we are a nation founded Under God and the President of the United States takes his oath to protect and preserve us with his hand on that Bible.

The real and permanent grandeur of these States must be their religion, says the rebel people's poet Walt Whitman.

. . . add to godliness brotherly kindness and to brotherly kindness love . . . ?

Only way to keep that permanent grandeur. More than a hundred years ago De Tocqueville had said something like—the prosperity of America ought to be attributed to the superiority (not the equality) of her women. The best I could remember on the train left me a little rattled but it seemed to me the real need was to regain her spiritual superiority.

Times when the memories of my youth smash through barriers, they sweep in upon me and overwhelm my present thinking or my attempts to see into the future.

This was one of them.

My father's methods of preparing cases took over. He wanted evidence. Not just circumstantial testimony—though he believed in it. Computer statistics on juvenile delinquency, divorce rates, crowded insane asylums, increasing venereal disease, unwed mothers and fatherless sons, low moral standards and money madness, vulgar advertising and growing illiteracy in spite of more and more education—these he would have found as convincing as minnows in milk.

He preferred a few witnesses. Eye—qualified—persuasive.

I wanted witnesses who would affirm that One Woman Under God, by whatever name she called Him, can choose what she wants for herself and her children and her country—and that the time is now.

The Third Millennium.

The Aquarian Age.
Not one world any more—One Universe.

They were waiting to take the stand, my witnesses.

Harriet Beecher Stowe, Clara Barton, Pocahontas, Carrie Nation, Hetty Green, Emma Willard, Jane Addams (and Abigail Adams for that matter and then Abigail Holmes, wife of Justice Holmes) Mary Baker Eddy, Mother Cabrini, Grandma Moses, Marie Dressler, Willa Cather, Edna Ferber, Eleanor Roosevelt, Bess Truman, Helen Hayes, Dr. Rena Sabin, Anne Morrow Lindbergh, Katharine Hepburn, and Pope Rose Kennedy.

I can summon them all and sum them up quickly for myself.

Mrs. Eddy didn't start until she was fifty. In 1875, an advanced old age for a woman. She is still in my running for the greatest American woman. She founded a world Church with branches in London, Paris, Warsaw, Rome and a successful Publishing House, the first national newspaper called *The Christian Science Monitor,* and wrote an all-time best seller in the top ten. She was married three times, the second ended in divorce; she had a son.

In Exodus when God sent Moses to bring the children of Israel out of Egypt, Moses said to Him, *Behold when I say unto them The God of your fathers hath sent me unto you; and they shall say to me, What is his name? what shall I say to them?* And God said to Moses, *Thus shalt thou say—I AM hath sent me unto you.*

Personally I like that name very much, after all it is what we wanted to know—I AM—but many people call God or the Spirit by different names—In Roget's famed Thesaurus it gives Mrs. Eddy credit for calling Him Divine Mind, Divine Principle, Soul, Life, Truth, and Love.

Mother Cabrini was an Italian Catholic nun but she traveled more miles in America than a pony express rider—and often by the same means. She named herself, of course, the Bride of Christ and thus I suppose became the Mother of the schools and hospitals she founded in our nation when we *needed* them desperately. In those schools the pupils were taught Suffer the little children to come unto me and if one of you injures a child it were better for you if you had a millstone around your neck and were dumped into the sea. When I saw her once in her high school in the Bronx I did not know she was a saint, the first on North American soil, but I carry still the *joy* she radiated. Beyond any other woman I ever saw.

When they say to me What is his name—?

Clara Barton called it the Red Cross and Jane Addams called it Hull House, where my neighbors whom I love can find a refuge from poverty and pain and sin. Hetty Green called it In God We Trust, which is engraved on our *money,* and when she became the richest woman in America and was able to save the House of Morgan by lending J.P. nine millions in cash which she had in a safe deposit box, all Wall Street bore witness to her integrity and honesty. Harriet Beecher Stowe called it Uncle Tom—the black man must be freed from slavery And Carrie Nation called it Not in rioting and drunkenness and *add to knowledge temperance*—she said this with an ax in saloons to the theme song "Father dear Father Come Home with Me Now" before you spend all the money in your pay envelope. And Emma Willard, who led that suffrage parade the ad makes fun of, called it God created woman equal to man, give her the vote and she will uplift her country—

For myself, I had Amelia Earhart, who called Spirit A Hole in the Sky; Helen Hayes, the first lady of the theater, who in her books calls it the Comforter; Mary Pickford, America's Sweetheart, in a book she and I wrote together called *Why Not Try God?* Mother Meyer showed me the Kingdom of Heaven within and Edith Haggard, a Number 1 literary agent in the Fun City of New York, also active in the Episcopal Church, named it the Spirit of Woman with Wings of Honor—and things a Woman of Honor doesn't *do.*

That day on the train there was a blank where the future would fit in— and now I do see the tapestry as one piece so I will put it there for us.

Pope Rose.
In a truly remarkable issue of *Look* magazine dated November 26, 1968, Laura Bergquist quotes a fellow parishioner at St. Xavier as saying they call Mrs. Joseph P. Kennedy Pope Rose because they see her every morning at Mass find courage for what Rose herself calls the agony and the ecstasy of her life. I know that when she came down to Philadelphia to do the *Mike Douglas Show* she was both amused and touched by the title. And every man on that show remembers her as having a serenity which, they said, must be the flower of faith. Mrs. Rose Kennedy, another Hyannis Port neighbor testified, is the real power and glory and strength of that family.
Her sons, John F. Kennedy, the first Catholic President of the United States, and Bobby, who would have been the second, were active practicing Christians, she brought them up that way. Our mother, Eunice Shriver says, was a strict disciplinarian; she urged, prodded, cajoled, they must be *responsible.*
All her children rise up and call her blessed and always have and wherever they are I'm sure they still do and always will.
What does Pope Rose call the Power and the Glory?

Of course she calls Him the Blessed Trinity—but I think she also calls Him *All Is Well with the Child*.

All had been well with them here, they were faithful and they fought. All is well with them in the Kingdom of Heaven, where there are many mansions their Lord promised to prepare for them.

This makes *unbearable* sorrow bearable.

When we were working together at RKO, Katharine Hepburn, the only woman star of the Sixties, had already committed herself to a decision that if she meant to lead a professional life, was from there on to be the victim in time, energy, and desire of what she *did,* her career, her art, her talent, then she should never have any children. It would not be fair to them.

In Roy Newquist's book *A Special Kind of Magic,* and the book has that too, she confirms this as her way of life. He also quotes her answer to his question as to what people gave her inspiration. "I think," she told him, "Jesus Christ and Queen Elizabeth are the two people I admire enormously because I admire the principle of living for other people. It brings such definite results. It's the real answer instead of this Freudian business." From our early days just after she came to Hollywood, when she was honestly trying to influence Jack Barrymore to quit drinking, she told me that she admired her father and mother as *people* as well as loving them. Her mother's price, she said, was indeed beyond rubies. "And," she told Roy Newquist many years later, "the magics of life are the things that dominate us. Birth, love, death, and self-sacrifice. Those are the beautiful things, we can't describe them. Call it religion. The religious people explain all that in the name of God. I try to do it on the basis of love for man."

So her name for the Father is the Infinite Goodness of Man.

In the pinches, Louie Howe told me, Mrs. Roosevelt always prayed immediately and earnestly.

A very simple woman the name of I AM to her was God.

On the train, high up in the mountains, I put Anne Morrow Lindbergh as the central figure in this tapestry.

Perhaps this is because I saw her on the witness stand.

In her own books, her publishers' biographical material, any interviews with her or stories about her, the witness stand is not mentioned. I recall that long ago when Gabriel Heatter had asked me to be on his *We the People* show we were requested not to even speak of the kidnaping of the Lindbergh baby, much less Anne on the witness stand, but by whom I did not know.

I cannot accept this, whoever it was.

I believe the future of the world depends on the strength and spiritual superiority of the women of this country, their awakening from the wild frenzy of their first half century of freedom, so-called. They have a right to remember that the woman who wrote the most important book of our times, *Gift from the Sea,* was not just an ambassador's daughter, a Smith graduate, wife of a famous man, author of best sellers.

I cannot praise a fugitive and cloistered virtue that never sallies out to see its adversary, says Milton.

No woman knew more of pain, loss, danger, fame, fortune, sorrow joy and anguish than Anne Lindbergh. Those who accept her *Gift* with its heartfelt statements of faith, humor, hope, responsibility, drama, and again the agony and ecstasy must be given hope in their own lives by remembering that the giver of this gift is the same woman who, as the slim young wife of the nation's hero, found the empty crib, read the kidnap note, waited minutes that were eternities, saw the husband she loved walk into the Valley of Humiliation, was exiled for years from home, country, and family.

Once Rose Kennedy said her motto could well be the same as her son's. "I know not age nor weariness nor defeat." That comes to them from a book by John Buchan called *Pilgrim's Way* and was, President Kennedy said, his favorite. The motto could belong also to Mrs. Lindbergh. But any pilgrim's progress must show the desperate days. *I know not defeat* means nothing unless you know of the battle.

Under my central figure I stitch a line early in her book:

> *The shape of my life starts with a family. I have a husband, five children, a house. I have also a craft, writing, and therefore work I want to pursue. . . . I want to give and take from my children and husband to share with friends and community to carry out my obligations to man and to the world, as a woman, as an artist, as a citizen.*

All three mules. A very large order, she gives to herself. Anne Morrow Lindbergh was well aware of this for she has added:

> *I want . . . to live in grace as much of the time as possible. . . . By grace, I mean an inner harmony, essentially spiritual, which can be translated into outward harmony.*

Anne Morrow Lindbergh calls it Grace.

It was a star-filled night and I saw again what never ceases to move me, starlight bright enough so that the trees cast the loveliest shadows in the world. It seemed to me time to reread my letters. Nothing is any good, really, unless it is worth rereading, and going across the vast desert with the colors more modern than any in our newest art seemed a good place to put Paul's letters to the Californians to the test.

. . . *not given to much wine*—thank you for that, Father, you have no idea what a relief that is going to be to quite a number of my friends . . . *to the aged women that they be in behavior as becometh holiness . . .* anything over 27½ is aged for mini-skirts, and what Paul means is Behave yourselves with some dignity. And it is odd I know for I've seen it that if you start behaving some of it rubs off—the behavior pattern was what made England great for so many centuries . . . *teach them to love their husbands, to love their children, to be keepers of homes.* . . .

The wave of sadness that came over me then matched the shadows in the starlight. We were pulling into the Rockies now, the two big engines were beginning to *pull,* the curving line of silver cars behind was moving to the throb like a ballet. Words began to drop into the rhythm and pulse of that power. *Where my father lives, there is my home* . . . now what? Where did that come from? *For he and the woman who loves him is my home.*

The beat was like the story about the little engine that thinks it can— and then I thought I could I thought I could—pull the trainload of cars over the mountains to get the toys to the children on the other side in time for Christmas. I *think* I can, I *think* I can . . . I'd been reading it for generations.

Where *my father* lives there is *my home* . . .

Then I remembered. I could see Eleanor's face as she showed me the sheet of lined paper with the schoolboy typing.

The life of the wife of a newspaperman is not entirely a thing of beauty and nobody rated higher among old pros for the attempt to make it a joy forever than Seymour Berkson's wife, Eleanor Lambert. She drove three mules, Seymour, a dedicated editor who worked nights and disappeared for weeks on big stories, her career as top public relations expert in the madmadmadmadmad world of Fashion, and their son Bill, who'd written the poem now choo-chooing in my head as a Father's Day present.

> If success marry me some day
> It will be because
> I had a father who loved his son
> And kept him from adversity;
> It will be because
> I had a mother who loved her husband
> And her son so intensely
> So unselfishly, so unrewardedly.
> What small gift would repay
> Those years (now sixteen)
> Of work

In my behalf
And that one day (sixteen ago)
That gave me life?

Father, old-soldier, young father
We will do bigger things
In years to come—

You are my father and my home,
Wherever I may go
Whoever asks me
Where is my home
I will always answer;

The little engine inside my head supplied the rest in the tempo of the train itself:

Where my father lives there is my home,
For he and the woman who loves him
Is my home . . .

Where my father lives there is my home . . .

I'm never going to get any of these toys over this mountain in time for any old Christmas whatsoever. Not these toys, I'm not. I *thought* I could but my husband is what I left *undone* and sometime someplace on some sad starlight night no matter how you huff and you puff in the end you will have to admit it is too late.

You might notice that it isn't *the woman he loves* that his sixteen-year-old son wants to build their home with, it's *the woman who loves him.* He wants his father to have a wife who loves *him—*

Old John Henry Greenleaf Wadsworth Whittier Longfellow was only half right when he wrote, The saddest words of tongue or pen are those which say *It might have been.* The other half is equally sad . . . *No second chance.* In this life I cannot pass that way again.

You have to do something though.

The question is *what can I do now?*

Starting from where I am, halfway up this mountain?

What do I *do?*

3

In the reek and roar, the clang and shriek along El Camino Real, without, it seemed to me, a second's warning or any time lapse at all, came a change in my life.

Faithful said once to *Talkative,* a most unpleasant character, *I have*

*heard many cry out against sin who yet abide it well enough in the heart,
house and conversation.*

These words could be a big lead because I wanted to make this new life
as best I could, but after all I could not put on a robe and take a begging
bowl and go to stand in Times Square or Lafayette Park or the footprints
in Grauman's Chinese Theater in Hollywood. Nor retire to a nunnery as
ladies had been wont to do when they abandoned worldly ways in the
olden times.

I saw, too, that while that moment of knowing that God loves me had
seemed to come like a thunderbolt, there had been a pilgrimage of sorts
behind it. I'd mapped it with my grandfather so that whether I understood any of it then with my brain or intelligence, he had made the Bible,
and especially the New Testament, part of my blood stream, subconscious,
or soul. The very thinking of such things brought me face to face with
another difficulty.

Possibly I could be called what most people then meant by the word
sophisticate. I'd been part of that closed circle of elegance that in some
ways surpassed the round table at the Algonquin, that having been largely
restricted to writers, editors, and the theater. My center had been "21" and
yet even as I thought of it I realized that the most moving moment of the
New York holiday season was when the Salvation Army brought its band
into "21" and sang hymns and got tambourines full of folding money.
That Quentin Reynolds had always called his mother in Brooklyn at midnight. That the Krindlers, who owned and invented "21," ran it as the
tightest family affair since the Rothschilds. A good deal of sentiment
generated behind the famed Iron Gate. Nevertheless, wit there would
probably designate sin as a medieval concept dying out in our liberal
age. Freud had arrived, Karl Marx had shown a pattern of brotherhood,
we were very tolerant of Comparative Religions; it was our style to make
their language part of our really extensive vocabularies; to talk familiarly
of Christopher Isherwood's *Vedanta for the Western World;* to be familiar with the theory of *Satyagraha* as advocated by Mahatma Gandhi; to
know all about the wave of spiritualism sweeping into Europe as the result
of war; to read *The Little Way of the Little Flower,* Thérèse de Liseaux
along with lots of Tolstoy, especially his *Confessions.* All these were
permissible, provocative, and part of our personality presentation, private
and professional. Behind the sterility of the intellectual where lulled in
the sleep of reason we bring forth monsters, we did believe that the main
impulse of Art was Creative. I found I had gained a great deal from some
of these, especially Gandhi, who though he was a Hindu so loved Jesus
Christ.

But somewhere in the middle of Kansas I saw that it was to the simple
teaching of Christianity, teaching on which and under which the United

States had been founded, to a new fire in it, a new voice of it, that I was turning or returning. In other words I was going to try to be a Christian. *God who made thee mighty, make thee mightier still.*

"The Christian Ideal," it is said, "has not been tried and found wanting; it has been found difficult and left untried."

To come out in favor of this and possibly advocate trying it would sure startle a lot of people.

I found it necessary to fortify myself once again.

Einstein—old E=mc² himself—said, "In Christianity, stripped of its subsequent additions, subtractions and divisions, Christianity as Jesus taught it, is the cure for all the social ill of humanity."

Surely even Gandhi followed Jesus when he came right out and said that his theory of resistance without violence was founded on the Golden Rule of Christianity.

One I loved most especially. I'd been told of it while it was still off the record; later it was included in a very fine authorized biography of Billy Graham by John Pollock. In a forty-minute interview with Winston Churchill in the middle of the war that other greatest man of our century said, "I do not see much hope for the future unless it is the hope you are talking about, young man. We must return to God." Now as the "young man" referred to was Billy Graham what he was talking about to Sir Winston must have been the teaching of Jesus Christ and their return into our lives and hearts.

Then there was Herbert Hoover, not as a President or ex-President, but as one of the all-time foremost engineers, who said to me, "The greatest teacher who ever lived was Jesus. I wish we had any teacher in the engineering field as good. He proved what he taught."

So we were back at works works works.

As Christian said to Faithful *The Soul of Religion is the practick part. When Christ said Do you know all these things? and the disciples answered Yes, he addeth Blessed are ye if we do them.*

The quickest way would be to the Catholic Church and thus to the front page of the New York *Times,* as other ladies and writers had done quite sincerely and beautifully before me. I had been to a convent school, I spent more prayer time on my knees in the Lady Chapel at St. Pat's than anywhere else. It would—I believed—be dishonest. My grandfather's simple love of the Protestant Church held me. Besides my heart ached for the Protestant Church, it is almost impossible to found anything beautiful solely on a protest, they made it even harder for themselves than God had made it in the first place.

To me this was, I realized at long last, a search for the ultimate truth and I found it was my heart and not my head that guided me and *yet* I had a deep conviction that in our constantly growing age of science we would make spiritual advances that now seemed impossible dreams. In Paris there had come into my hands by what seemed chance, but I am sure now was not, some letters and lectures by a young French priest and paleontologist named Teilhard de Chardin. He had used the same juxta-position of words as Mary Baker Eddy a hundred years before. His was called Science and Christ. This was 1920, I think, and I quote one sentence I never forgot: "For my part I am convinced that there is no more substantial nourishment for the religious life than contact with properly understood scientific realities." So when De Chardin's *Phe-nomenon of Man* shook the Western, scientific, philosophical, and religious world, and Teilhard himself was the prototype of Morris West's priest-scientist in *The Shoes of the Fisherman* I was not surprised. I did not understand much of it but my reportorial instinct told me this was coming and that as we began to explore the Universe we would come to a new understanding of its Creator.

To me, this would be *a* second coming of the Christ teaching, given to us today, and I wanted to be part of it.

I may start out not knowing one team from the other but by the second quarter I am rooting for somebody. Mr. Hearst said, "I will always buy enthusiasm," and he had bought mine for many years. Now I had to root for all that had been and was being somehow revealed to me.

As we came through the rich farmlands of the Middle West, and the woods with their lovely streams, I was filled with gratitude. This, I said to myself, was what Handel meant when his organ played *He Is Risen*.

Now that I had been so blessed I wanted to share it, to shout, Praise the Lord.

How?

What should I do with this new life? This new woman?

Would I yield to the temptation to drag my reluctant sisters off bar stools to hear my good news? Would I seek a radio spot, a platform, a soapbox from which to do my shouting?

Two things restrained me . . . first a large question mark.

Would it be beyond me to grow in grace? Would I come forth like the lilies of the field, like Lazarus himself, or would I get out there if I made a big to-do with all my new-found enthusiasm about it and then fall flat on my face and let everybody down?

Somehow I had begun in the period of quiet thinking given me on the train to sense that there was still a steep hill ahead of me and that pos-sibly what the Teacher meant when he said, *Tell No Man*—what Billy Graham might mean when he sent the new converts back to their own churches—was that it was well to try the Practick Part first.

The fall of Lucifer hurt more people than any other.

At an early hour when we pulled into Fort Madison I put my coat on over my pajamas, got off, and walked through the crisp cold air of the little station park to the banks of the Father of Waters and it was so beautiful I wished, like Huck Finn, I could sit down in the sandy bottom where the water was about knee deep and watch the daylight come.

Obviously I couldn't, but as Huck said of that hour by the Mississippi, there wasn't a sound anywhere, just like the whole world (including all the passengers on the train) was asleep. Then there was a pale place in the sky and the river softened up away *off*—and then, with that quietude before the bull frogs or the birds could start, I was holding a rerun conversation with Mr. Hearst.

There he *was,* reading one of my stories in the Unemployed Women series. Its opening sentence said, *This is an inspiring story and you will be glad it took place in our city.* Kindly but firmly Mr. Hearst said, "I think it will be more satisfactory if you allow your reader to tell you whether it is an inspiring story or not. If it is, he will not fail to recognize it. If it is not, this opening line will have led him to expect something, he will be disappointed and therefore resentful and finally hostile. Let us allow the facts to speak for themselves. This I have found a sound rule in writing and in life. If the thing is there, let them tell you."

All right.

All right, I said to myself, as we ran along beside the Hudson and saw West Point on the other side, and finally came into the Grand Central Terminal and smelled *New York* once more.

I wanted to do something pretty spectacular. It would be more difficult to follow Brother Lawrence. He wrote *Is it not quicker and easier to do our common business for love of Him?* Well, to tell the truth I didn't think so. I thought a tambourine or becoming a Trappist would be easier. *With me,* wrote the good brother, *my time of labor is no different from the time of prayer. Amid the clatter and confusion of my kitchen* (and if you want to know, Brother Lawrence, clatter and confusion is a goodly description of a city room, too) *and with numerous people giving me orders* (like Howey and now, I hope I hope, some magazine editors or even movie producers, God forbid), *I hold God in as great tranquillity as on my knees.*

Tranquillity?

What good is that? Still—people do need to be tranquilized. As far as I know we did not then have pills for this, but if the need was there and it could be fulfilled Brother Lawrence's way?

He and Mr. Hearst seemed to agree.

In His service, I turn the cake that is on the pan before me. When that service is done . . . it is through his grace that I have work to do . . . so perhaps instead of turning the cake that is on the pan I should go quietly about my daily business, and hit the typewriter keys to make stories that mean through His grace I will have work to do.

If nobody noticed anything it would be better than to have them disappointed or resentful or filled with hostility.

If they *did*—if they saw that, as Brother Lawrence said, I was happier than a king—sooner or later they might say to themselves first, What has she got to meet life with that I haven't got?

In time, they might ask me.

CHAPTER 40

1 Park Avenue, Larchmont, New York
Clements' farm in Flemington, New Jersey
19 Beekman Place, New York City, New York
Mare Island Navy Yard, San Francisco Bay, California
RCAF Base, Brantford, Canada
Evalyn Walsh McLean's Friendship, Washington, D.C.

1 Park Avenue, Larchmont, I discovered the hard way was a summer palace and a man like its owner, Mr. Slepack, had never dreamed of anyone inhabiting it in the winter. Elaine and her three-year-old son Koko came home to live and so did her brother Mac. This was fortunate for the six of us plus dog and cats lived on Mac's salary as a reporter on the New York *Mirror*. As I recall this was $56.20 after taxes, tabs at the Pen and Pencil, and commutation ticket were taken out.

True, I had a feeling that the wind would be tempered to the newly shorn lamb and I was prepared for *intermittency*. At first my new-found confidence in answered prayer, the integration point really, and my desire to operate within the Practick Part of my journey seemed steady and secure. Would they stay planted on the rock when the rains came and the winds blew? Which there was every indication they were going to do both figuratively and literally.

1 Park Avenue, Larchmont, was the Laboratory as it were.

Here I'd make some tests as to whether the works *worked*.

While certainly our mansion was no woodshed, it leaked rain and snow like a sieve, the view windows rattled and jumped in the night, we had seven bedrooms but no heat in any of them. A long dark servants' wing was so remote that I worried about Ernest being lonesome. I have always found you are lonesome more easily when you are not getting any salary. I had a sixteen-cylinder Cadillac, but no gas card any more. A boathouse with no boat. My own elegant suite had a private icebox with nothing in it. Fortunately good Mr. Slepack, whom Elaine continued to persuade out of the rent, had left huge sacks of peanuts which she had promised to feed to the squirrels. Koko raided the peanuts and his Uncle Mac encouraged him saying, Who can tell the difference? An eccentric millionaire neighbor known to us as Sir Arthur had taken a patriotic fling at raising chickens in his back garden and showered us with eggs, since he didn't know where to sell them. Ernest was looking after a house designed to be run by at least four servants so I found myself frequently in the kitchen. Someday I am going to write a cook book and besides my early Spanish California and San Francisco Chinese dishes it will have a few recipes for *eggs* and a peanut soufflé I invented at that time.

Right then it seemed easier to turn the cake on the pan *in His service* than anything else I was doing. For my own work via the typewriter had prolonged a sinking spell into a good embalming job. With my whole heart I was trying now at my fiction and nothing sold. I got the stories on *paper,* but they stayed right there—nothing came *off* the paper.

One night I telephoned Mr. Hearst and begged him to let me go to England as a war correspondent but he said things would get a lot worse over there before they got better and because of my family I would have to keep the home fires burning. I didn't hint that I was burning last year's newspapers—too proud, I suppose. The next day Joe Connelly called and wanted me to go over to Brooklyn on a series about Murder Incorporated. You have to make *choices.* I decided that Little Augie had been great in his time. Lucky Luciano at this moment, No.

Both my careers at home and abroad were sitting on their tails and showing no signs of life whatever, either of them.

Dry prayer.

Here I learned about this chiefly from a book by St. Teresa of Avila I got out of the Larchmont Library. I was doing it already but St. Teresa identified it for me.

The honeymoon was definitely over. I had been prepared for intermittency, in the beginning it intermitted *out* and eventually intermitted back *in.* Now it was intermittent to the point of evanishment.

Oh how difficult it is to get an answer from You, Lord. When I heard Olivier as *Becket* say this, I went back eleven times, I was so glad to know someone else had been through it. I had felt I was insulting God when I prayed with nothing but words, words dry as old parchment, words without a pulse of hope, words as meaningless as a prayer rattle and as hypocritical as a whited sepulcher.

But St. Teresa said to keep right on, God would understand.

The high points at 1 Park Avenue were when Bill came home on leave. At such times Elaine promoted gas from some of her beaux and drove the Cadillac to the Peace Bridge to pick him up and whoever he brought with him, might be one or twenty-one. Jack Clements provided vegetables from his farm in New Jersey or said he did; I thought they came from a market on Tenth Avenue. Danny of the Pen and Pencil provided the roast. Ernest *outdid* himself on desserts and as for me I washed and ironed Bill's shirts, they were the size of tents and made of the same material.

His brother Bill insisted that young Dicky should go to Military School; bo a help if he knew his *Drill.* So by writing an Ad campaign and some brochures for the colonel in charge of New York Military Academy, next door to West Point, I got Dick enrolled there. On one leave Bill wanted to go and see Dick and when we got there the colonel asked him to take the Sunday Parade. His blue RCAF uniform had been made for someone with arms three inches shorter, and Bill St. Johns knew as much about Taking a Parade as our dog Michael, but the regiments of the New York Military Academy knew he was one of the Few to whom we owed so Much and they saw him through. Ah well, half of the senior class drilling that Sunday under the glorious trees of the N.Y.M.A. parade grounds were at Anzio or Kasserine Pass. Some of them died there.

Where were you the day of Pearl Harbor?
That day of Infamy lives in every memory.
We didn't have a radio but Mac had a girl whose brother owned a bowling alley where he got all the exercise he would *take.* He heard it there and came home to tell me the Japs had bombed Pearl Harbor. It was Sunday, as everyone alive then remembers, and Mac and I drove up to see Dicky at school. Dick was purple with pride because they'd been assigned to patrol the heights above the Point, Dick with a wooden gun bigger than he was. Mac and I had a time getting home. We'd spent all our money to feed Dick and his friends and we didn't have the fifty cents to pay the Nyack ferry or the George Washington Bridge toll. We had to go way down to the Battery, where it only cost ten cents. In a way I was glad, for we had a wonderful old-fashioned gab.

Monday Mac enlisted and left for Fort McClellan, Alabama.

On Tuesday Elaine went to Hartford, Connecticut, where she got a job on the assembly line at Pratt-Whitney making airplane engines.

Herbert R. Mayes, formerly of *The American Druggist,* now editor of *Good Housekeeping,* sent back another short story. At that moment it seemed to me almost like *sadism.*

And on Friday the long-haired one of my pair of yellow cats, *Fuzzy,* was run over.

Koko, Ernest, Michael, Wuzzy, and what was left of me remained. And what to do with us, I did not know.

I'd been hanging onto the rope of dry prayer as I tried to climb but it looked now as though I was going to have to eat it. Slipping and sliding, I prayed only that I could hold on till *spring* . . . but when I did and spring came Mr. Slepack called and said most kindly that he'd decided to move back to 1 Park Avenue a little early this year.

Now I not only had *no* cake or bread to turn in His Name, but Mr. Slepack had removed the pan.

2

During the Hauptmann trial John Aloysius Clements, the city slicker, had collected some farms in Hunterdon County, he lent me one for the summer with a rebuilt schoolhouse on it. The little Jersey farm was pastoral and green. A stream flowed through it and when it came to a wall of rock danced down and over making merry music all the way. The lilacs were about finished when I got there but the fragrance lingered on and at the front door there was a bed of tulips sending up straight green spears and showing tight buds of yellow and red.

With his left hand Papa Fix Clements was doing some public relations for the Florist Telegraph Delivery Association so he ordered me to compose a few bits of deathless prose to put in the boxes, for people who couldn't think of anything, and that gave us eatin' money.

Half an acre out back Koko and I decided to make into a victory garden. Corn, tomatoes, and artichokes. No string beans or broccoli. We dug, raked, pulverized, manured, and watered and when Uncle Papa Fix came down from the city we asked him how many tomato plants we ought to set out and he said, Oh, about eight dozen. Anybody but me would have known that eight dozen tomato plants will supply the Campbell Soup factory. No—Koko and I planted them, put little frilled collars around their scrawny necks, and watered them by hand from an enameled can. The farmers from as far south as Hagerstown came to hang over my rail fence and watch this. Clements had hysterics until one night Koko put a water snake in his bed. Koko learned quite a sizable Marine Corps vocabulary that way.

I read to him about the snake on the island where St. Paul was shipwrecked who came out and bit him and Paul called it a *viper.* Do you know what a viper is, Koko? I said. And Koko said, Yes, Grammy, it's what vipes the water off your windshield. I said actually it was a poisonous snake, and God didn't keep it from biting Paul—but it did not poison him. Everybody looked for him to swell up and drop down dead but God had rendered the viper harmless. The next morning Koko came into breakfast with a *good-sized* snake in each hand and a terrible scowl on his face and said, There's something the matter with these goddam snakes —they won't even bite me.

We also had a distant cousin who committed bigamy in our living room, but there was a war on and she'd had a hard time getting a husband so I didn't like to say anything.

On the whole for a bit things were reasonably quiet and I was working. Graeme Lorimer, an editor of the *Ladies' Home Journal* and son of George Horace Lorimer, the great editor of *The Saturday Evening Post,* had told Edith Haggard to see if I'd like to do a serial for him laid in wartime Washington to be called *Government Girl.* The price would render me solvent again. I said I'd love to. And—I was *working.* Not building brick walls with words—sometimes as much as a couple of pages came easily. The inner joy wasn't back but—I knew it once had been.

Thornwell, my second brother, enlisted in the Marine Corps and went to Quantico to get his commission. My baby brother Bryson enlisted in the Marine Corps. Bryson was born to be a Marine sergeant. That's what he'd been waiting for all his life. Having at last found an apartment in Hartford, Elaine came down and got Koko and took him back with her.

Dick and I went up to Brantford, in Canada, to see Bill get his wings. Then came his embarkation leave in New York and we said one of those swift, surface, hurried good-bys—*Are you sure you have everything?—* and he was gone. When it was safe, I suppose, he enclosed a clipping in one of his letters allowing me to figure they'd been torpedoed. They had to take to the lifeboats but their ship didn't sink, and they got back on board. Bill informed me that if you are cold enough and scared enough you can drink an entire quart of Canadian Club with no more effect than if it was root beer.

I'll hold the fort, madam, Ernest had been saying for twenty years.

Now we reversed the whole business.

First I heard him muttering about *our boys,* did they get *fed* properly at the front. An army, he said loftily, travels on its stomach, and then, having told a big fat lie about his age, off he went to the *Pacific* as a mess sergeant. *You'll* hold the fort, madam, till I get back. The next I knew he was kicking up a row with the colonel because they wouldn't give him anyplace to *put* things.

There I was alone on a New Jersey farm, eleven miles from a paved road, three miles from the Pennsylvania Railroad that ran one-hundred-car trains of tanks and guns and jeeps all night long. The only entertainment center in my life was a nine-party-line telephone. Mozart alone sometimes kept me serene enough to work—*Eine Kleine Nachtmusik* of all things human comes the nearest for me to saying that life was meant to be good and beautiful.

My chief company was lightning.

In a lightning storm, I am still happiest under the bed. I felt in my bones along with Publilius Syrus that it would be vain to look for a defense against it. All literature had conveyed to me that it was an enemy, or the weapon of an enemy hurled against me, bolt by bolt, accompanied by denunciations of thunder. In this my dog Michael and my cat Wuzzy heartily concurred. Their instincts were against lightning.

I was trying to work day *and* night. This serial was my big chance. Writers who don't *write* can just drift out of public favor and financial rewards. I'd seen it happen too often. I had in this one a big story that thrilled me, that I'd actually known about in Washington, where an overworked Secretary or head of some Commission relies more and more on a real classy secretary. This young lady can become a key figure in the world doings of our capital in wartime. I knew quite a lot of things from my work there which I wouldn't be allowed to write factually, but could use with tremendous effect in *fiction*—such as how the aviation industry got more than its share of steel cable. I also knew the Government Girl I was using as my title-heroine. So I was putting everything I had into it.

It sounds silly this far away from it, but to every woman her own fear, and, to be honest, the worst thing I had to cope with that summer was Jersey Lightning and if you've never seen it in *Jersey* you've never seen *lightning*. It goes *through* the house and forms little balls in the corners. In Jersey, also, there are three or four storms by day and two or three by night. They do not come and carry on for half an hour or so and then go away. They come and go away and circulate around and around in the Sourland hills and then come back again and again and you can hear trees splinter as they crack open and sometimes through the wind you can hear cows lowing in terror and horses screaming—or anyhow I thought I could.

On a night long to remember I set my typewriter table sort of against the stairwell where it wasn't on a line either with any windows *or* the fireplace—and I sat down hoping to finish—the fever of *IcanfinishIseetheend* was upon me and I wanted to race like a fire horse. But Wuzzy with a faintly *Oh dear not again* meow got into my lap and Michael, trembling all over, curled around my feet and over anent Lambertville or Colligan's Inn I heard what had disturbed them, the first faint distant rumbles. These came nearer ever nearer and I couldn't even hear my typewriter keys and the room filled with that ominous light like a dynamo and whether I began to pray or swear, wet or dry, I do not know.

Only as it moved away circling toward the trees and the hills once again thoughts that were not mine began to circulate in my head. This is the lions' den. Throw her in the lions' den. These storms . . . don't you see that they prowl round and round in circles in the cage of hills, lions and lightning are the same color, they are tawny yellow, a flash of lightning and the flash of a big lion's eyes—they are flashes of the same color—and that thunder that is now beginning to circulate back to me—that's the lions' growling, growling, a lion's growl is like the roar of thunder, isn't it? And the wind in the trees is the lions switching their tails—now they are coming closer and closer circling right around the house your house growling and roaring and flashing their eyes and switching their tails but *it shall not come nigh thee—*

As the sweat popped out on my forehead so my glasses were misted, Wuzzy began to give little cries, and I said, *Oh you shut up,* cats aren't afraid of lions, are they? and then I felt Michael's cold nose on my instep, I said, Oh Michael, servant of the living God is thy God whom thou servest continually in loyalty and love, and service to protect and preserve, able to deliver thee from the lions and the lightning so that they can do us no hurt? Oh Michael, it seems to me now I come to think of it that God didn't keep Daniel out of the lions' den, did he? No no—the others who were his enemies they had conspired to put him *in* the lions' den and God let them do it BUT, Oh Michael, he did not let the lions bite him! That's the point—so when the King came in the morning and cried out, Hast thy God protected you, Daniel said, Oh yes he has, he shut the lions' mouths and they didn't bite me and now people will have to believe in You—and now, Oh Michael, the lions have not bitten us and there is the sun coming up and we have finished our serial!

The morning, though I could hardly believe it, was bright and beautiful and the trees all fresh with showers and I could hear the waterfall playing *Eine Kleine Nachtmusik* and when I'd made coffee I said to Michael, "I wish you could have a cup of this with me—anyhow we've done it in the lions' den, but now comes the awful suspense as to whether it's any *good* or not. It ought to be lousy with all those lions growling at me and threatening to eat me all night."

And Michael said, or indicated, or I thought he would have said if he could, *If you could write it under those conditions maybe you didn't write it at all, maybe He gave you a hand and in that case it ought to be better than your best, how about that?*

Washington always changes and never changes.

It is full of strangers but thirty seconds later they are natives and the natives are now strangers.

I was doing a very odd job for J. Edgar Hoover and a few odds and ends in tracing German propaganda for the State Department and I had my old room at Evalyn McLean's back again.

I had come down to Washington partly to see Brother Thornwell at Quantico and he came over one night and after dinner we all went up into Evalyn's favorite tower room where her intimate social life took place.

Soon Ethel Barrymore, in satin and pearls, rose and said she must go to bed and Thorny got up too and said, "Miss Barrymore, I'm just a private in the Marine Corps but I'll be taking off soon and I'd sure go away proud if you'd kiss me good-by." With the sincerity of a patriot and the grace of the finest actress in the world, Ethel Barrymore turned in the doorway and held out her arms, she held him tightly for a moment and kissed him and made an exit that left us in tears. I wonder if we felt it *was* good-by, that as an observer for the Marine Air Force, his plane would vanish over Rabaul and we would never hear of him again.

At one of Evalyn's luncheons I sat next to Admiral Emory Scott Land, head of the War Shipping Administration. The admiral had been better known as Jerry when he'd captained the Navy football team in his day, but if anybody alive dared to call him that now I didn't know who it was. Certainly nobody connected with the press. I asked him why there was such a *gap* between the Navy and the press and he said if there was, it could be because until this war they'd almost literally never met. I tried to explain that the *people* wanted to know about their ships and their men and the press was the only way—and I must have persuaded him for later he called me in two or three times for suggestions on what to do about misunderstandings with the newspapermen.

This was important to me in a good many ways but chiefly because it was Admiral Land who sent me to San Francisco and Mare Island.

By the time I got back to the farm I was fairly frantic for news of *Government Girl.*

There was excitement in Edith Haggard's voice when she called and said, "The *Ladies' Home Journal* likes *Government Girl* very very much." She waited until my glee and gratitude had subsided and then said, "And RKO wants to buy the movie rights for Olivia de Havilland."

So I was able to take the house on Beekman Place as the summer came to an end.

For years it had belonged to a saintly bishop, who was the inspired landscape architect of gardens at Rhinebeck, and his wife. They had left it full of love and faith and joy. I felt particularly at home for it had a circular staircase like the one at Malibu, and below me I could see always the flow of the East River, to the left the lovely span of the bridge and downstream to the right the Brooklyn Navy Yard. Up on Fifty-seventh Street Miss Ethel Barrymore had an apartment and she'd call to say, Run run, there's a new *destroyer* or, The PT boats are coming back from patrol —or I'd call and say, Hurry hurry, a hospital ship is coming—

I had two colored boys to cook and do the housework again. Somehow I had a feeling that my spare bedrooms ought to go to the Travelers Aid.

It was very hard for servicemen to find a place to sleep in New York then, so this house was never empty.

With wives, families, men on leave, and the Travelers Aid the whole world seemed to me to be on the move and some of it stopped at my house. Wartime is different from all other time. You do not tell it by clock or calendar. I was amazed to find out some months had gone by when two things packed me up again and sent me West. Frances Whiting of *Cosmopolitan* had an idea I ought to do a serial for her about San Francisco with the Golden Gate open again—and Admiral Land decided this would be a fine cover for a couple of things *re* morale he wanted to know all about.

A man named Bechdolt gave me the idea for the serial—his firm had built Boulder Dam and then taken up shipbuilding and I asked him why. He said, Those were my men and my work on Midway that the Japs bombed—this he seemed to think made him want us to have more ships, after Pearl Harbor. So perhaps he was one of the very very few who knew what I was to see when I went to Mare Island Navy Yard at, I explained, the suggestion of Admiral Land for background for my new serial.

This is a *day* for me. I do not even know the date of it, but it was the day Bull Halsey was made commander of the Allied Naval Forces in the South Pacific and Mare Island celebrated as though it was the Fourth of July and New Year's Eve in one. They certainly thought Admiral Halsey their greatest man. This overflow of exuberance and confidence may have been one reason the admiral in charge, just called out of retirement for the job, told the P.R. lieutenant to show me the whole works.

I walked miles and miles and miles along roads full of holes and bumps, along boardwalks, on single planks and jerry-built bridges. Everywhere I looked in all directions I saw ships. The ships that had once been the United States Navy. All of it—*nearly* all of it. Tied up to repair docks. Shoved up to the open fronts of buildings. Battered, broken, bombed, wrecked, and ruined—a devastation beyond power to conceive or to take in. The young lieutenant, who was my escort, muttered and mumbled the whole way, partly his disagreement with the admiral for allowing me to make this tour of inspection and partly vows to get even with the power that had done this deed.

Finally he saw that I was literally out on my feet, staggering with the shock and fatigue of this ordeal, so we sat down on a bench and he let me cry on his shoulder. No woman could help crying at that sight. This must be what it meant when it said, The iron entered your soul, for my soul was full of a whole Navy destroyed by fire. Then it came to me that we were literally without a navy. Ever since Pearl Harbor—on the day of Pearl Harbor—why hadn't the Japs followed through and taken San

Francisco itself? The lieutenant said, In the end God always took care of the Navy, and then as an afterthought said, Probably they hadn't been able to stay to see how complete the damage was—and as he said it I forgave the Navy that had kept it a secret—been able to keep it a secret—even from the press.

In an attempt to console and reassure me, the lieutenant showed me a brand-new submarine, I was too *out* even to react to the astonishing fact that we had *submerged,* and then they sent me home in a PT boat so I crawled into bed with my backbone broken by that pile driver, my stomach heaving all night long as never before in my life, my heart filled with tears I hadn't shed—and all through the dark, sleepless hours I was glad Bill had been faithful and had gone to fight, for I knew now that the forces of all evil were turned loose in our world.

I tell you, it is something *else* when you *see* it.

That is why, probably, as my son Mac always said, the *combat* soldier is different from anyone on earth.

This time when I got on the Super Chief I was too exhausted even to want to think or pray. I didn't want to eat, speak, read, or do anything but sleep if I could.

I have quitted all forms of devotion and all set prayers, my only business now is to remain in the holy presence. Were I a preacher I would preach only that, were I a teacher I would teach only that. All very well for so advanced a Pilgrim as Brother Lawrence, but were I a woman whose sons and brothers and friends are scattered all over this war-torn globe, who had been submerged in a submarine without warning and seen the United States Navy looking like an old car junk yard, I would say, *You* will have to show me Your Holy Presence, if it's not Gennesaret but the Mississippi where You walk, You will have to do something about it, I cannot even cry out any more.

Bless the United States Navy and the Royal Canadian Air Force and the 126th Division and all the other divisions in the infantry, and the Marine Corps, which is undoubtedly now guarding Your heavenly scenes and all the streets thereof—but I must get some sleep.

I do not understand the man who will not sleep—so speaks God in some old French poem, I can't remember the author—I am quite able to look after My Universe while he catches a catnap.

So finally I slept.

I hadn't one single flicker of premonition, not one heartbeat of warning.

The only one who did apparently was Michael. When Elaine met me at the train she said Michael had been restless and night before last had howled a couple of times. I said that was probably because he had never before lived in a house in a city. No more had I. Maybe, as more time went by, we wouldn't like it.

Elaine was a superintendent now; she and Koko had come down from Hartford for a three-day leave. And I was glad to have her there. I felt Michael was wrong and we were going to love this house very much.

The telegram came the next morning.

We were sitting in front of the fire having our coffee. There were masses of gladiolas, coral and crimson and flame in a blue cloisonné jar in the corner. Outside, early fall sunshine showed that the vines were beginning to turn scarlet and gold.

Elaine reached for the telegram but I said I liked to open my own telegrams. The last thing I remember in that world where I had always lived up till then, a world where Bill was and was safe, was that it seemed odd this cable was addressed to Mrs. William Ivan St. Johns Sr.

We both knew what was in it before we read it.

His Majesty's Government regrets to inform you . . .

The dialogue was simple.

I just kept saying, No. No no no—No no no for quite a long time.

Bill?

Nothing bad could happen to Bill.

CHAPTER 41

The room had a fireplace on the south side; the north wall facing it was a big bookshelf chock full of books and underneath a big oak table with a copper lamp. To the east, and the river of that name, were three bow windows, seats cushioned in chintz, and these gave on the flower boxes and dwarf trees of a terrace. The west side had a wide door, through it I could see the parquet floor, a tiny conservatory, and the graceful staircases that led up to bedrooms and down to kitchen and dining room.

The telegram, suspended over every woman's heart in time of war, was delivered to me in that room. The days following, all more or less one, passed there without fully registering or separating.

Never bright beautiful morning again.

I knew now that in any split second something might change my whole world. When out of hours of numbness I knew this, I was grateful that the room was so old and wise and beautiful. It gave me *time*.

Characters old and new moved in this act, distantly to me.

My new houseman. He kept appearing in doorways bearing cups of tea and coffee and chocolate. That was his way.

Mrs. Roosevelt called.

Ethel Barrymore came. "I don't come to your house because those circular staircases are designed for middle-aged ladies to break their hips on," she'd said. Now she came. Knowing it was belittling and impossible to try to *talk about something else*. So we talked about Bill. The time at Sing Sing when Warden Lawes said, *Your son Bill hits best with men on bases.* That, Ethel said, will look well on his headstone. But in the end we decided to put simply *He Is Risen*.

The Red Cross sent Mac from war maneuvers in Tennessee.

My little brother Bryson was confined to barracks for growing a mustache, forbidden by Regulations. When he went up the sands of Iwo Jima with the Fifth Marines I doubt if anybody noticed whether he had a mustache or not. Just the same they planted that flag on Suribachi because somewhere they'd learned to obey.

Huge boxes of flowers came from Mr. Hearst with notes. The one I treasure says, *Do not let anyone tell you your pride in him is not some measure of comfort and always will be. Affectionately WRH.*

My most difficult call was to California, where Dicky was at Malibu and coaching tennis with Bill Tilden. My brother Bogart, who had flown with the RFC, said, "Just don't start shuffling the IF deck. Believe me, Bill was doing what he wanted to do more than anything else in the world. Man can ask no more than to reach that whether it's for six days or six hours or six years. No matter what the end."

Minutes later Big Bill Tilden called. He said Dick was scheduled in a tournament the next day at the Los Angeles Tennis Club and "I understand," he said, "his brother Bill would want him to play." I took a long breath and said, "Yes. Yes I'm sure he would." "And to win," Tilden said, and I said, "I—to play his best anyhow, without any alibi." "If he plays his best he will win," Bill said. I treasure the fact that Dick lost the first set and was three games down on the second before he won.

Figures came and went—and wires and letters.

A dripping silhouette under an umbrella was Janet Brundidge, wife of an old INS pal; weeping loudly, she shoved a half pound of butter at me—butter was rationed then.

Edith Haggard arrived leading a Danish masseur named Mr. Seedorf by the hand, took over my house, door, telephone, wires, reporters, and ordering food. In no time I was in quiet harmony outside.

I'm sorry, Red. Even a Nobel prize winner like Sinclair Lewis found those words all anybody could say.

He's just gone over a little ahead of us, Herb. Herb Howe. Who once wrote the piece that convinced me it was time to leave Hollywood.

There was I standing outside my tent crying and crying and the Colonel came along and said What's wrong, Sergeant and I said, "Oh sir, they have killed my boy, they have killed my boy." . . . *and I will be home as soon as I can madam to look out for things Ernest.*

Around then I felt there was a slight edge—or I imagined there was—because everybody kept telling me how brave I was. No fainting. No bitter weeping. No cries in the night.

They didn't understand.

That wasn't me, that was Bill.

"You think there's a chance he can see or hear me?" I said to my daughter and Elaine said, "Yes I do."

Any kind of chance.

He had trusted me. When he woke out of those fearful nightmares of childhood as he opened one eye his hands clutched me and he said, "Mama?" and I said, "Yes, Billy, I'm here." When he came up out of the anesthetic the time he had his knee operated on, he turned toward my voice before he opened his eyes and said, "Mama?" and I said, "Yes, Bill, I'm right here."

One chance out of four hundred and eighty-two million that he would open his eyes coming through the Valley and say, *Mama*—I wasn't going to let him find me a sodden wreck, and he not able to get back to comfort or help me. I'd be there saying, Okay Bill—I'm here—I'll hold the fort.

It took all the guts I had for by then I knew the rope wasn't going to hold. I said to myself, It just isn't going to hold, that's all. I never really thought it would.

Not if the worst happened.

His Majesty's Government regrets to inform you that your son Flying Officer William St. Johns has been killed in action.

Down underneath I kept on saying, No. No no no no.

Bill was the one everybody was so sure would come back safely. Don't worry about *Bill*. Even when he was flying missions over Berlin and Nuremberg on those terrible raids of 1943 I'd never been afraid for Bill. Not once. He'd flown over forty missions, he wore the ribbon that showed it, and in the snapshots he sent me now the crown of his cap was squashed and he wore it over one eye.

I knew the story quite soon. Coming back from a raid on Berlin, this was before they had fighter escorts, he was hit. Somehow he held the big bomber in the air until they were back over England and his crew could parachute to safety. The last thing they heard the Skipper say, his navigator wrote me, was, "Will you hurry up and *get out* of there?" and then he went down with his ship.

In those hours adding up to days and nights the IFs flew at me like hornets, like vultures—IF I'd said, NO of course not, I won't hold the fort for you you stay home and hold your own fort until your own country goes to war—then I could see him so plainly as he used to sit across from me in his old bathrobe and it seemed to me I must have been mad to let him go for any reason. If I could have stopped him. Perhaps I could not. I was glad I hadn't subtracted from the glory of his achievement.

But now I had to meet the plain fact.

Bill was dead.

He would not come home again and I did not know where he was or— if he was at all. It was an incredible feeling—my baby, my skinny little boy, my dear young son. Fury dried my tears. *Pray!* To what? Moloch, a god who demands the sacrifice of our children? I couldn't even ask Christ to wake in the boat of my storm-tossed soul and still this tempest of anger against heaven. There was nothing meek I could find anywhere.

Bill was dead.

And buried.

I hadn't been there in the sacred grounds of the RAF at Stratford-on-Avon near the church where Shakespeare lies. I hadn't seen his flag-draped casket nor heard the bugles bidding him farewell. This ought to make it easier to be sure there was a hole in the sky for all good pilots and he'd flown right up through it.

But in the density that surrounded me I was right back where I had been when my grandfather had been struck down in the night without warning and my father robbed at the crucial moment of his life of the guide who might have saved him. Reverend Rogers was a saint, people told me from Tombstone to San Diego, and I knew he'd ended nailed in a box and shoved into a dark dank hole in the *ground* not the sky. I'd seen that when I was only eight and so my imagination put Bill in the same place, and once again I was in the grip of anger and unbelief.

In spite of her own anguish—no one can be as close as brother and sister if they are close at all—my daughter Elaine had upheld and comforted me, but in this dark cloud of unknowing Mother Meyer's words came back over and over, *You will have to find the answer yourself or you will not believe it.*

All right.

I'm looking.

The rope is Faith, that much I know. I had a little crystal ball worn on a gold chain around my neck, and inside it was a grain of mustard seed. Superstition is a kind of prayer of course. Soon after the telegram came I slipped out and walked by the river and threw it as far as I could. A grain as big as that mustard seed might be all I needed but I didn't have it. Not even a grain.

If I tried going on up this Hill of Difficulty I would have no rope to hang on to and it was the steepest I'd ever seen.

The lions didn't bite Daniel.

Paul didn't swell up and drop dead when the asp fastened on his hand.

But my son was dead and buried, gone out like a lamp, nothing left, I had never before known such a sense of *nothing I can do.*

I sat by my bedroom window and saw the brown river flowing below me and I stared and stared at it and after a while I was quieter. The answer came quietly. Prayer is not you speaking to God. Prayer is God speaking to you. The answer—not the plea—listen, that is your part of prayer and you will not *listen.* If you pray in times of joy and abundance you will be able to pray in distress and need—

Be still!

I won't I won't I can't—the rope won't hold—I'd better curse God and die than always be expecting something—

I put out my hands.

Perhaps your hands asking for help are always praying hands.

For I found the rope.

A silence came upon the room, upon me. Do you hear silence? I did, I was in it, and then part of it became the words.

All is well with the child.

Beyond anything that can ever be, beyond even what my poor capacity to know, can know, deeper than my deepest breath and closer than the beat of my sore laboring heart, I knew my son lived.

We had been right. Nothing bad *had* happened to Bill.

Through the Valley, it said to me. Who was I to demand to know what he found when he came out? There came to my memory words said by a little dark man who lived in a basement apartment on East Forty-third Street—somewhere in there—his name was Gibran, Kahlil Gibran, and he said to us, *You are the bows from which your children as living arrows are sent forth.* I hadn't thought of Gibran in many years though he had written books now famous, but I remembered those words clearly and the flame of his dark eyes as he said it—I had sent forth a living arrow and how could I ask where and how my son was and what the Father's business for him might be? Can I insist that to live to the fullest he must inhabit this little piece of God's Universe where I have my address?

All is well with the child.

No mother has been given the right to ask more.

Missing my son, I have always. In the long nights I keep company with my memory of him as things used to be and sometimes I grow weary of my sorrow and wish him *here*. But of *grief* in its panic-fury I was healed in the moment when the promised Comforter told me all was well with him.

And a joy came. For I knew now why sometimes it is Faithful who must go first. Only Faithful can weave the rope with you, for you, so that it will *hold*. He has one thread of it over there and you have one here and between you—you weave a rope that *will* hold. Only Faithful could have written the letter that came to me.

On the outside it said simply:

The Enclosed to be mailed in case of my death.

P.O. St. Johns W.

Inside it said:

Somewhere in England

Dear Mama;

This won't be long for I hope you shall never read it. As a matter of fact I had decided not to write one of its kind but after reading a book called *These Our Children* a little piece struck me and as you read this, if you ever have to, it will convey more than I could ever write— Before I put the poem on paper I want you to know my life was full because of your teachings—to you and those I love I can say that through you all I have been always happy and shall remain always grateful.

TO MY MOTHER

Weep not, lady, though no more
He shall pass in by your door,
Though the garden gate is wide
And his footsteps scarce have dried
Where he trod his merry way
On his last leave's final day!

So he went as once he came,
Calling you by that dear name
As a school boy back from class
Buoyant as the clouds that pass
He was like a school boy. Then
Off to that harsh school of men.

Weep not lady! Did you teach
What the parsons try to preach
That a man's life only means
What the eager spirit gleans,
That at twenty he may see
What's still hid at 83.

This he knew; it was no end
Suddenly to meet his Friend!
Suddenly to meet those others
Those his comrades, those his brothers!
This is truth. This thing I know—
No such moment merits woe!

My blessings to you all, Ma dear— For I love you and always shall

Your son
Bill.

By the time he wrote that letter Bill was attached to the RAF and the life of an RAF pilot was no longer a matter of months, or even weeks, they counted it in days—perhaps only hours. So the letter *to be mailed in case of my death,* came to me from eternity.

Not only could Faithful and I weave the rope that would hold.

I ha' seen him eat o' the honey-comb sin' they nailed him to the tree.

CHAPTER 42

After this, I knew that as long as Mr. Hearst lived part of the old life would be active for me, but as a matter of fact my last assignment was a part of my new miracle.

In this new life, Mr. Mayer suggested I ought to come back to Hollywood and help him find some stories for a back-from-the-war Gable they didn't know what to do with. Very kindly, he said it would be a nice change for me. Dick wanted to go to Beverly Hills High School so until I could go back to Malibu permanently I found a place to live called The Hill that had belonged to Ernest and Hazel Holmes and was only a few blocks from the M-G-M studios.

One day in a drizzly gray February I was supposed to go to the races with Mr. Mayer to see one of his horses run, but I was overtaken with what reporters call *Stay-near-a-telephone*. I couldn't imagine why—but there it was. So I was out in the rose garden trying to save some old General MacArthur rose bushes when Ernest E. Adams, Jr., also back from the war, came to say, "Mr. Hearst is on the telephone, madam."

To be sure!

I ran as fast as I could but without too much surprise. Though of course he didn't call often any more.

The last time I'd seen him I knew he was an old man. He was in a wheel chair, so he must be, but he didn't seem to me much changed.

The call—the old call—the call I'd waited for through the years, breathless with impatience, caught me as it always did, right under the heart. "Yes, Mr. Hearst?" I said in my usual gasp.

The voice that spoke sounded just the same. "Adela," it said, "they have assassinated Gandhi."

"The Mahatma?" I said. "Oh—how dreadful. The world won't seem the same without him."

"The world will not *be* the same without him," Mr. Hearst said. "But I am sure he was prepared for martyrdom. I want you to do a series about him for us immediately. Mr. Mayer won't object?"

"Mr. Mayer?" I said. I'd forgotten he existed. "Oh no."

"Gandhi is the best known man in the world," Mr. Hearst said. "Do you have with you there the material we gathered when I was going to send you to India to write some interviews with him? We sent to England for books by and about him that were not available in this country."

The elephant memory was still working, I thought, and I said, "Oh yes—everything is right here,"

"We must present him as the greatest man of our time," Mr. Hearst said slowly and carefully. "It does not make any difference how long it takes his experiment in India to succeed or whether it ever does succeed. Gandhi's dream is the most colossal experiment in history. And human life is a series of noble experiments. This little dark man, born in total obscurity, never elected to anything, is better known than any emperor or war lord. Holding aloft the candle of God not a beacon of war, his stuck-out ears and big nose, his bald head and glasses, his little skeleton wrapped in shawls are more familiar than any majesty or magnificence and he brought the British lion to his bare feet."

My heart was prancing now to a rhythm I thought I'd lost—like a fire horse, like a combat soldier—*I* don't know—anyway, the magic of an assignment as only Mr. Hearst could give it filled me with emotion and imagination became real, as it had always done. News is history in the making—and all I'd researched about Gandhi to be familiar with the right questions came rushing from my head to my heart to my fingertips.

"How much do you want?" I said.

"Whatever it takes to tell it," Mr. Hearst said. "The first installment must be up here by eight o'clock."

"Eight o'clock?" I must have cried it aloud. "But *Mr. Hearst* it's after two now—"

"Do not forget that you are a newspaperwoman, Adela," Mr. Hearst said. "If we don't start this tomorrow morning the weeklies will beat us."

"I'll try," I said.

"I'm quite sure you will succeed," he said briefly, and hung up.

The first installment of 2500 words was in his hands by 7:49.
It began:

> Such a frail little old man, Mohandas Gandhi, to be mowed down by bullets on his well-worn path to pray for peace. Always there are two life stories. There are two life stories to be told of every man and to tell one without the other is useless and dishonest. One, his activities, the record of what he did, the stirring tale of his deeds. And the other, his inner life, what he was, to whom he prayed, how he thought. But in the life of Gandhi these two are one and indivisible, he refused ever to separate them.
>
> He was a saint.

He was a shrewd, efficient, political leader.

How can such a thing be? This is the true measure of greatness. That a man totally practices what he preaches.

Once while I was doing the series Mr. Hearst called to say that he hoped I would include that Gandhi was a greater showman than Barnum. "If," he said with the old chuckle, "he had gone to St. James' Palace on that London conference in a cutaway and striped trousers, it would have been more difficult for him. Going in a sheet leading a goat the eyes of the world focused upon him."

In one installment I had written a quote from one of Gandhi's books:

"When that fineness and rarity of spirit which I longed for have become perfectly natural to me; when I have become incapable of evil; when nothing harsh or haughty occupies, be it even momentarily, my thought world then and not till then will my non-resistance, my non-violence, my firmness in truth move the hearts of the world."

On the day he had read that article I said to Mr. Hearst, "Do you think anyone can do that? That is the—Practice Part, isn't it? Was he able to accomplish it?"

"He must have done so," Mr. Hearst said, "that must be where he got the power—that *is* the power. Gandhi understood it as the source of all real power. In no other way could he have ruled as he did."

So, I thought, this is that to which such men commit themselves. The Practice Part of their spiritual life comes from Within.

Then one day—and I remember that it was a first day of spring, the eucalyptus trees along the side of the hill were silvery and I could hear grandchildren and dogs and then quite suddenly I couldn't hear them at all. For I had written:

Gandhi offered us a blueprint for peace. Whether or not men accept that peace, we cannot tell. But if we do not, it will not be Gandhi who has failed. It will be humanity.

THE END

The End?

Never before in my life had I written those words. Why had I done it now? I sat staring at it. Then—I knew it was. I read the words above it. And I was filled with the wonder—another miracle—along my path. My last assignment from Mr. Hearst was *Gandhi*. Not a murder, not a kidnaping, not an abdication or a divorce or disaster. Maybe if it had been one of those Mr. Hearst wouldn't have been much interested, maybe he wouldn't have called me. So after thirty years around the world and back my last newspaper story for Mr. Hearst was the life of a saint and his blueprint for peace.

I cannot tell you what that meant to me then.

As though on a new road uphill I found a familiar signpost telling me it was the *right* road. I thought to myself, You are going to be a pretty forlorn fellow—and then it came up through that like a triumphant swell in music.

This was my farewell assignment. The last time the old team would be in there. I felt bereft and then I didn't because the timing was right and I knew it and I'd had the blessing to go out on something big and fine and uplifting like Gandhi's Practice Part.

I handed the sheets of gray copy paper—the same familiar sheets Winifred Black had handed me in the New case, and Damon had passed to me at the Democratic Convention—to the boy whose motorcycle was roaring outside my window.

Thirty years.

I called the number in Beverly Hills.

I said, "Mr. Hearst—" and could get no farther. He didn't speak. Finally I said, "Thank you—oh, thank you!" and he said, "I've always been glad I was able to persuade Mr. Campbell not to fire you when you were young—" I have no recollection of how that conversation ended or which of us hung up first.

He died not long after that.

Then I knew my newspaper life had ended and it had come about as a natural thing, and I would live it over and over again in memory—and I have in this book.

I had never written a book. I'd never had time nor money nor patience to wait for the returns. Maybe I didn't really have anything to say, either. Now I wanted to do the book about my father, Earl Rogers, that everyone had kept telling me *I must write* for so many years.

There are two small pictures that seem to me somehow to fit here and one is a real picture that sits on my desk. It is a snapshot of a young man in RAF uniform standing on a bridge that crosses the Avon. He is looking up at the Shakespeare Church and smiling broadly and on the picture is written, *You want to know why I'm smiling? I've just been to visit the Skipper's grave and he isn't there.* And the signature was that of one of the seven men who parachuted to life on that September day.

The other is about Bill, too. The RAF sent home his two suitcases and in them everything he owned, regardless. Pajamas that hadn't been washed and half-used tubes of toothpaste and his sunglasses and his diary, as well as his uniforms and topcoats and robes and sweaters.

They had come quite without notice in the morning and I was sitting on the floor beside them, the uniforms were too heavy for me to lift and the rest smelled of peanut butter and shaving lotion and sweat and I couldn't quite stand it. I didn't know what to do with them.

Vic Fleming came in. I was working on a Gable picture for him and I'd completely forgotten that he was coming to lunch to talk about it. He looked a lot like Jim Arness, and he stood staring down at me, not needing to ask a question. Then he knelt down and began to separate the things.

He put Bill's blue bathrobe in my lap and said, One of his kid brothers can wear that one—and then he put a uniform back in the suitcase and said, "The RAF can sure use those about now—" and when he had finished he said, "Never forget that cutting down Papa's pants for Junior was what made the United States great in the first place. The day we forget to use up everything, the Constitution and the Bill of Rights and the half-used cans of toothpaste we won't be the U.S.A. any more."

That seemed fair enough and I watched him walk away with the two suitcases without a tremor. The man who made *Gone with the Wind* had a right to ask you to be a good American.

At seventy-five I discovered one day that I do not come first with anybody in the world. For a moment, it shook me. Then I saw it as a priceless blessing. For with children, grandchildren, great-grandchildren, friends, neighbors I have a lot of seconds and thirds up on that board and you can win a lot of Olympic events with enough seconds and thirds.

More than that, you have a true freedom of communication. I can tell them the dramatic story of how I was healed of two and a quarter packs of cigarettes a day in the Hollywood Bowl on Easter morning, a blessing that purified me for if cleanliness is next to godliness cigarettes must go— a *filthy* not an immoral habit as I saw it. If they ask me I can tell them of this blessing, and sometimes even if they don't. They ought to and naturally at my age I know more about what is good for them than they do. It takes a good deal of tact and character not to mention this.

Also there is one final word. If you want peace, the first order is always Battle Stations. For it is one thing to see the land of peace from a wooded ridge and quite another to tread the road that leads to it.

Look. This is the Desired Country.

I have tried to tell something of a Pilgrim's Progress to get there, but Christian never says a word about what happens after you arrive, except *I have formerly lived by Hearsay and Faith but now I go where I shall live by sight and shall be with Delight.*

That, of course, is another story.